Communication
Yearbook / 17

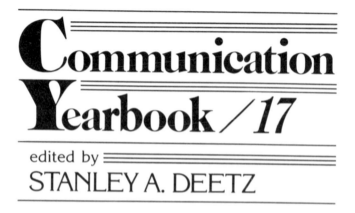

Communication Yearbook / 17

edited by
STANLEY A. DEETZ

Published Annually for the
International Communication
Association

SAGE Publications
International Educational and Professional Publisher
Thousand Oaks   London   New Delhi

P
87
.C5974
V 17
160565
Jan.
1994

For information address:

SAGE Publications, Inc.
2455 Teller Road
Thousand Oaks, California 91320

SAGE Publications Ltd.
6 Bonhill Street
London EC2A 4PU
United Kingdom

SAGE Publications India Pvt. Ltd.
M-32 Market
Greater Kailash I
New Delhi 110 048 India

Printed in the United States of America

Library of Congress: 76-45943

ISBN 0-8039-5433-6

ISSN 0147-4642

94 95 96 97 98 10 9 8 7 6 5 4 3 2 1

Sage Production Editor: Astrid Virding

CONTENTS

THE INTERNATIONAL COMMUNICATION ASSOCIATION

The International Communication Association was formed in 1950, bringing together academicians and other professionals whose interest focused on human communication. The Association maintains an active membership of more than 2,500 individuals, of which some two-thirds are teaching and conducting research in colleges, universities, and schools around the world. Other members are in government, the media, communication technology, business law, medicine, and other professions. The wide professional and geographical distribution of the membership provides the basic strength of the ICA. The Association is a meeting ground for sharing research and useful dialogue about communication interests.

Through its Divisions and Interest Groups, publications, annual conferences, and relations with other Associations around the world, ICA promotes the systematic study of communication theories, processes, and skills.

In addition to *Communication Yearbook,* the Association publishes the *Journal of Communication, Human Communication Research, Communication Theory, A Guide to Publishing in Scholarly Communication Journals, ICA Newsletter,* and the *ICA Membership Directory.*

For additional information about ICA and its activities, contact Robert L. Cox, Executive Director, International Communication Association, P.O. Box 9589, Austin, TX 78766; (512) 454-8299; fax (512) 454-4221; E-mail, Robert Cox@UTXVMS.CC.UTEXAS.EDU.

Previous Editors of the *Communication Yearbook* series:

Brent D. Ruben, Volumes 1 & 2
Dan Nimmo, Volumes 3 & 4
Michael Burgoon, Volumes 5 & 6
Robert N. Bostrom, Volumes 7 & 8
Margaret L. McLaughlin, Volumes 9 & 10
James A. Anderson, Volumes 11, 12, 13, & 14
Stanley A. Deetz, Volumes 15, 16, & 17

INTRODUCTION

In 1987 the *Communication Yearbook* series was redesigned to provide a more coherent, readable, and useful volume. These goals remained central as I worked with reviewers in selecting and shaping the essays for this the final volume of my editorship. While the scholarly contribution of each essay to specialized audiences is important, the volume is designed to be useful for those with a general interest in communication studies and for use in graduate and other classes to increase familiarity with the scope and directions of communication studies.

Communication Yearbook 17, like others in the series, is a compromise between the desires for diversity and breadth and the need for choice and focus. Like others, the volume favors North American and, to a lesser extent, European research concerns and methods, reflecting to a large extent the composition of the International Communication Association and the market for the series. Still, I have attempted to represent a somewhat broader set of international theoretical interests than are present in most North American scholarly journals in communication studies. As in volumes 15 and 16, I have tried to assure that theory and method differences connected to social group differences such as gender and ethnicity are treated explicitly in both major essays and the commentaries on them.

This volume is divided into four sections. The first three contain major essays and commentaries on them. The major essays were selected in an extended review process involving leading scholars in each of the institutional divisions of the field. Several of the reviewers aided the authors throughout the writing process and finally served as commentators on the essays. I selected the commentators based on their expertise in the subject area of consideration and their capacity to aid the reader in critically engaging the major essay. The final section is an editorial postscript, providing my own vision of the communication discipline and the contributions scholars and teachers might make in the future.

OVERVIEW OF THE ESSAYS

The first half of this volume focuses on interpersonal interaction, especially the constitutive processes within everyday communication. This is intended to complement the mass media focus of volume 15 and the organizational communication focus of volume 16. Accordingly, Section 1 contains six major essays that consider various issues in the relation of communication and identity construction. These include reconceptions and microanalyses of interaction processes examining knowledge construction, the "self," culture and ideology, emotions, narrative, and institutional life. Section 2 contains essays focusing on message characteristics and what messages do in interaction. Topics range from rather abstract concerns with message comprehension to detailed reconsideration of the relation of communication and health and the nature of emotional messages in the workplace. The three essays in Section 3 consider value and policy issues for communication studies in light of the ubiquitous nature of communication media and cultural pluralism.

Communication and Identity:
Constructions of the Personal and the Social

From the youth culture's preoccupation with finding the "self" in the 1960s to the embracing of multiple conflictual selves in the postmodern turn in the 1980s, the "person" has been a central issue of social thought during the last three decades. Issues regarding the status of the "individuality," "subjectivity," "agency," and "identity" have been at the forefront of intellectual and popular culture debate. In many respects, serious concern with the person came to the majority of interpersonal communication researchers somewhat later than the debates in many other disciplines. This was largely a result of research being dominated by a conception of the person as an existing, autonomous, psychological entity that leaves the "self" as theoretically and socially unproblematic. Not only is such a dominant position theoretically untenable, it becomes progressively more damaging in an increasingly culturally diverse pluralistic context. The need of the 1990s is to move out of these debates into more responsive and responsible research programs. The essays in the section reflect philosophical, social psychological, cultural studies, and communication attempts to accomplish such a move.

The first essay, by John Shotter and Kenneth J. Gergen, approaches the issue from the standpoint of social psychology. Using insights into language usage initiated by Wittgenstein and social processes initiated by the symbolic interactionists, social constructivists in psychology were among the first to propose a communication-based understanding of the interactional construction of personal experiences and social knowledge. Shotter and Gergen review the alternatives provided by social constructionism by focusing on three issues—the generation and sustenance of human knowledge, the conceptualization of the person, and the process of conversation. They argue that knowledge and personhood are relational and contextual problems that are undecidable in any lasting sense but are constantly decided in everyday conversational practices. The central research work is to understand these conversational practices.

In the second essay, Rom Harré approaches the question of the "self" from the standpoint of an analytic philosophy complemented by psychological research into the presentation and representations of social identities. In opposition to various feminist writers' conceptions of a pluralism of competing discourses producing multiple selves, Harré unpacks the "self" as a "double singularity." He argues that both self$_1$ as a personhood and self$_2$ as the unique set of beliefs each self$_1$ has of itself are discursively produced through the indexical properties of conversation.

Kristine L. Fitch, in the next essay, develops the social context as an underexplored aspect of interpersonal interaction. As most interpersonal communication researchers have studied relatively homogeneous populations that are much like the researchers themselves, they have taken for granted shared characteristics, cultural resources, and values that both shape findings and theories and leave invisible important interactional accomplishments. Fitch proposes an "ethnography of speaking" as a way to explore the systems of beliefs about personhood, relationships, and communication that constitute the common resources for a group of people through which they conduct their interpersonal lives (and interpersonal research). From such a stance, comparative analyses can illuminate the nature and impact of cultural influences and provide insight into how people transcend differences, coordinate their actions, and form relationships.

In his essay, Donal Carbaugh follows similar themes and provides a detailed account of how a particular conception of personhood is negotiated in the United States today. Carbaugh argues that personhood is an interactional accomplishment through creatively invoking cultural meaning systems. The prominent cultural model of personhood in America, coded as dignity, rests on a deeply structured system of values that are communicationally situated through "positioning."

Barbara Czarniawska-Joerges provides a different set of concerns through a consideration of institutional and narrative theory. She argues that individual identity is a modern institution. It constitutes a pattern of social action peculiar to modernity, evoking conflictual and integrated themes of essential nature, choice, and responsibility. The existence of such a conception and the manner of its narrative reproduction are of interest in their own right, but they become of even greater interest when we see how the conception is extended to organizations. In conceptualizing organizations as "superpersons," the conception of individual identity is reproduced and specific culturally produced properties are assigned to organizations. The implications of this view are shown in cases where the organizational "identity" has been challenged and reformulated.

In the final essay in this section, Teresa Harrison explores communication and interdependence in democratic organizations. The individual is constituted differently in democratic and bureaucratic organizations, especially in regard to the relation of independence and social collectivity. Interdependence is frequently conceptualized in a peculiar fashion only appropriate to the context of "autonomous" individuals placed in hierarchical authority relations. Understanding and facilitating productive democratic organizations requires different models of the individual and interdependence. The essay explores many of these models in specific firms using Giddens's structure/system distinction.

Taking Messages Seriously

The focus on "messages" has often been used as the defining characteristic of communication studies. While "what messages are" and "what messages do" have been conceptualized far too narrowly and superficially to focus a productive agenda for the field, messages and their conception must be taken seriously. No applied program and few theorists escape resting their work on assumptions about the relation of messages to individuals, collectivities, and the external world.

In the first essay in this section, Diane M. Badzinski and Mary M. Gill discuss the impact of discourse features on comprehension. They carefully argue that generally researchers have underestimated the relation between such features and message understanding. Through a review of comprehension models and discourse features, they show the need to study the relation between discourse features and comprehension within a theory associated with message understanding.

In the next essay, Eric G. Zook demonstrates how researchers, in failing to problematize the concept of health, have confined the study of health communication to an ancillary position with respect to health professionals and institutions. In contrast, communication could be seen as a central means whereby one can develop, maintain, and/or restore systemic integration. Through a phenomenological reconsideration of the nature of health, health is grounded within the experience of being-in-the-world rather than within the "object" (or physical) body. The implications for health care and communication are then explored.

Vincent R. Waldron, in the final essay, considers emotional expression. While individuals in work organizations are often treated in research and practice as rational beings, they often engage in emotional labor, and all work practices include an emotional side. Waldron argues that emotional states and expressions are constituted both strategically and through cultural processes within workplaces. Understanding the person as an emotive creature provides insight into organizations and opens important issues of investigation.

Media, Culture, and Diversity

New conceptions and research programs in communication are often driven by the development of ideas, reconsiderations, and critical examinations, but they are also led by material changes in the societies in which they take place. Rapid changes in communication and information technologies and the growth of multiculturalism represent material changes that are affecting all of life as well as research. Certainly, many of the issues in the first section of this volume arise from our "saturated" world as affected by shifts in social relations in pluralistic, mediated social contexts. This section explores three issues to show what communication studies might contribute to the international debates arising from these changes.

Paul Messaris examines the growing emphasis on visual media in primary and secondary education in relation to more general issues regarding the enhancement of cognitive skills. Messaris considers the potential visual "literacy," a TV-based education program, has for impact on the quality of thought in the areas of the formation of conceptual categories, analytic reasoning, spatial intelligence, and abstract/analogical thinking. While positive connections remain intriguing, there is good reason to be skeptical about them.

In the second essay, Sue Curry Jansen investigates how Western news configures transformations in global political formations through the use of key interpretive terms. The essay develops some of the structures, conditions, and theoretical issues in the "cultural wars" waged over the development and appropriation of a vocabulary of key terms. Evidence for the processes of elite domination in these ideological struggles is displayed in several domains. Finally, the implications for democracy and the "critical spirit" are explored.

Young Yun Kim initiates her discussion by demonstrating just how multiethnic we have become and are becoming. Issues of ethnicity and interethnic interaction are increasingly critical, and social science literatures have grown proportionally. The essay provides an overview of the concepts prominent in these literatures and proposes a framework for integrating the concepts from a communication perspective. Metatheoretical assumptions of pragmatism and systems theory are used to show the interdependence of context and behavior in interethnic interactions.

Editor's Postscript: Future of the Discipline

One of the few pleasures that arises from editing a series of volumes like the *Yearbook* is the intimate relation with the discipline. As you read more widely across literatures far from your areas of specialization, the discipline takes on an animated form with movements and tensions, hopes and fears, growth and decay. In talking with people while trying to conceptualize each volume and selecting the essays, you feel energies and passions that professional discourse often discourages. And, while the "animal" as a whole moves slowly and tentatively, you do get a sense that there are themes and directions that will matter and that cross normal divisions in the literatures. I have taken a bit of editorial liberty to include my reading of where this multiheaded beast might go.

I believe that we as part of a world community have an identifiable set of social problems for which communication studies can provide our best conception and chance for a meaningful response. These are significant social issues for us as members of the wider community and our responsibility as professionals. Essentially, I argue that if we are to have a social effect we must focus even more deeply on communication as an explanatory constitutive process rather than a phenomenon, work from an intent to foster codetermination rather than control, and embrace a pragmatist's understanding of the nature of theory and research in regard to social issues. Communication studies must be more completely severed from "informational" conceptions where meanings are assumed to be already existing, and must provide "communication" explanations of processes of meaning development and the social production of perceptions, identities, social structures, and affective responses. Critical and cultural studies, among other developments, have transformed theory and research in areas like mass and organizational communication, but if the field is to have a future these must be rethought as providing a way of perceiving and explaining the social world that can compete with modernist disciplines like psychology, sociology, and economics, and this new way of thinking must reform our applied conceptions and activities.

ACKNOWLEDGMENTS

I would like to thank my reviewers and the divisional officers of the International Communication Association for help in identifying appropriate essays and in improving the essays here. The following individuals are to be thanked for providing important and timely reviews in the selection process; Bill Owens, Michelle Dillon, Valerie Manusov, Bob Bell, Brent Ruben, Maria Cristina González, Mark Knapp, Lea Stewart, John Tiemans, Brant Burleson, Jenny Mandelbaum, Anita Pomenance, Ed Fink, Robert Kubey, Jim Applegate, Connie Bullis, Eric Eisenberg, Stuart Sigman, Peggy McLaughen, George Cheney, Fred Jablin, Kathy Krone, Harty Mokros, Art Bochner, Barnett Pearce, Dennis Mumby, Jim Anderson, Don Ellis, and Joe Cappela. Further, I have greatly appreciated the efforts of the commentators, initially for providing me and the authors with helpful comments for improving the major essays, and subsequently for their timely and thoughtful written commentaries.

The publication of this volume would not have been possible without the support of the International Communication Association, the editorial staff at Sage Publications, and the Department of Communication at Rutgers University. The editorial assistance of Mark Shifflet has also contributed greatly to the volume. Through the 4 years of working on the yearbook volumes, my family has accepted sacrifices with grace, displayed the patience of Job, and supported me at critical times. I add my public thanks to my many private joys with them. They join with me in being pleased to pass the editorship into the capable hands of Brant Burleson.

Stanley A. Deetz
Belle Mead, New Jersey

SECTION 1

COMMUNICATION AND IDENTITY: CONSTRUCTIONS OF THE PERSONAL AND THE SOCIAL

1 Social Construction: Knowledge, Self, Others, and Continuing the Conversation

JOHN SHOTTER
University of New Hampshire

KENNETH J. GERGEN
Swarthmore College

Social constructionism's relevance to communication studies is demonstrated through the development of three arguments. First, as theories of knowledge presume a theory of human functioning with others, traditional conceptions of the person are subject to transformation. Second, theories of communication are carefully intertwined with theories of the person and philosophies of knowledge. And, third, the conversational context of everyday life holds keys to understanding the entire edifice of constructed knowledge. From these central themes, seven "instructive statements" are proposed as rudimentary accounts of critical aspects of conventional exchange.

If we see knowing as not having an essence, to be described by scientists or philosophers, but rather as a right, by current standards to believe, then we are well on the way to seeing *conversation* as the ultimate context within which knowledge is to be understood.

—Rorty, 1980, p. 389

IN this essay, we shall attempt to set out the central lineaments of social constructionism as they are relevant to communication studies. As we see it, this challenge necessitates the close interweaving of three lines of argument in three disparate discursive domains that typically have been treated separately by relatively independent scholarly settlements. First, in their broadest sense, social constructionist deliberations concern the generation and sustenance of what we take to be human knowledge, where theories

Correspondence and requests for reprints: John Shotter, Department of Communication, University of New Hampshire, Durham, NH 03824-3586.

Communication Yearbook 17, pp. 3-33

of knowledge have typically been the provenance of philosophy. From Plato to positivism, epistemological inquiry has been pivotal to the philosophical project. Yet, to elaborate a theory of knowledge is also to presume a theory of human functioning—the character of the fully functioning individual. Thus, as it has wrestled with the perennial problem of relating mind to world, philosophy has necessarily fallen heir to particular assumptions concerning the nature of human mentalities, while, elsewhere, the problem of conceiving the person has been removed from epistemological debate and either bracketed for future inquiry or assigned for solution to the psychological sciences. In this analysis, we wish to recover this linkage between who and what we are and what it is that we can know in being who we are—that between ontology and epistemology. For, as we shall find, in recasting the problem of knowledge, traditional conceptions of the person are also subject to transformation.

At the same time, in its attempt to characterize the knowledge generating process, social constructionism is also committed to certain assumptions concerning human communication. In its attempt to articulate a peculiarly social epistemology, it also proposes certain assumptions regarding the process of conversation. Or to put it otherwise, theories of communication typically presuppose (or stand in an implicative relationship to) theories of the person and thus also to philosophies of knowledge. To play cards in any of these domains is simultaneously to constitute one's hand in the others. The current attempt is to keep these triplicate relationships in continuous interplay, for, in this sense, communication studies may prove pivotal to our understanding of the entire edifice of constructed knowledge.

In carrying out this analysis, the chief focus will be the conversational context of everyday life. For, as we see it, this is the context in which everything of intellectual importance both originates and is judged as worthy or not of further attention; such importance develops in the activities occurring *between* people. Thus, given our interest in such dialogically conducted processes, instead of studying existing bodies of words—linguistic forms that have already been judged (by someone?) as worthy of attention, that (someone?) takes to be a part of our supposedly "ordinary" language (e.g., Austin, 1962)—we shall focus upon the influences at work in the context of people's words as they are spoken, the influences determining their fate in the living moment of their use. Indeed, like literary deconstructionists, we attend to ambivalences and indeterminacies of meaning that arise, but, unlike literary critics, we shall not point toward the theoretical problems that emerge (Derrida, 1976, 1988).[1] The questions that we shall continually confront are these: "How, in practice, are these theoretically undecidable issues decided?" "What is at issue in such struggles?" "What, in practice, is involved in becoming and sustaining oneself as a person in a society in the midst of such contests?" As we shall see, these questions do not refer to a simple unitary domain giving rise to simple unitary answers, that is, to a coherent theory. Indeed, they require us to attend to a number of interrelated features of ongoing conversation: its *situated, developmental,* and *relational* nature.

Traditionally, epistemology has ignored such relational and contextually occasioned problems (Gergen, 1982, 1985). It has been concerned with the ways in which isolated, unsitituated, ideal[2] individuals gain orderly knowledge of passive objects, objects that react to their probings and manipulations but that do not "answer back," that is, that do not communicate with them. We shall call this I-it epistemological paradigm, the *passive-individualistic* paradigm. Central to it are the assumptions that (a) separate individuals understand the world external to themselves in terms of their own inner, mental representations of it; (b) these representations will all one day be unified into a single, systematic whole; and (c) the orderly whole will be arrived at as the result of a Darwinian process of elimination, in which the objectively superior system finally wins over all other candidates. Further, regarding a speaker's relation to his or her speech, it need only be adequate to its object; a listener is not required. Its communicative function is seen as secondary and derivative. Ideally, such a body of timeless, orderly knowledge is likened to a computational or calculational system. This paradigm is very likely the only epistemological paradigm we meet during our socialization into the disciplinary practices of the human sciences as professional academics. Thus it comes as no surprise that we feel a normative urge to assimilate problems of interpersonal understanding to this paradigm of individuals gaining an orderly knowledge of objects. We feel that that is how we *ought* to make sense of the issues in question. To propose otherwise, to outline another practice, another way of making sense through another paradigm,[3] "goes against the grain," so to speak, of our professional practices—it cannot be understood in terms of the traditional understandings they provide.

"FORE-STRUCTURES OF UNDERSTANDING" IN DISCIPLINARY TRADITIONS

In being socialized into a disciplinary practice, the training we receive is, of course, primarily in the realm of language use; we learn to intelligibly relate ourselves both to the subject matter of the discipline and to our disciplinary colleagues. Indeed, without us attempting to theorize why it is, or how it comes about, it is clear that a part of our training is being socialized into a whole body of what Bernstein (1983) has called "practical-moral knowledge"[4]: an orderly way of speaking, reading, writing, seeing, acting, reasoning, and evaluating, generally enabling those involved in the practice, pretheoretically, (a) to distinguish "units" constituting its subject matter, (b) to formulate intelligible questions about the possible relations between such units, and (c) to formulate criteria with which to judge the worth of claimed answers to these questions. As social scientists, we must develop a way of understanding that cannot simply be derived from observation; we must be able to formulate, in the terms of the discipline, what it is that we must account for in our observations. To put the matter in Wittgenstein's terms of "saying" and "showing": to learn what certain factual claims within a discipline "say," we must first learn in general what the discipline's way of talking "shows" us. We must learn how to judge and evaluate claims as those already within the discipline judge and evaluate such claims; that is, we must learn to function within the terms of the discipline.

The kind of knowledge involved here has, until recently, been ignored in accounts of scientific activity. We are not speaking here of a theoretical kind of knowledge, specifiable ahead of time in rules, maxims, or other such forms, but of a practical skill differentially realized in different, concrete contexts. But it is not simply a form of individual skill either—in the sense of a technical skill that an individual can master and apply alone—for its proper use depends upon the judgment of the others around one at the time of its application. Thus, although we may make use of our senses in our acquisition of it, it is not dependent upon them—indeed, it provides the background against which we sometimes question whether they are functioning well. This knowledge, embodied in our collective practices, is thus of a special "third kind" (Shotter, 1993), neither simply theoretical or practical-technical. It is a form of knowledge *from within* a relationship, in which, in its articulation, others around us continually exert a morally coercive force upon us *to be* persons of a particular kind, to assume a particular *identity*, and to exhibit a particular kind of *sensibility*: that is, to be persons who act and make sense of the events and activities studied through the "proper" use of the "proper" terms. If we do not develop the ability to act within the discipline in such a way as to sustain it as a professional tradition, then disciplinary practices are such that colleagues will justify rejecting our claims or will not take our claims seriously (Foucault, 1972). We fail to qualify as legitimate "knowers."

Thus coming to act from within such a *fore-structure of understanding*, as Gadamer (1975, pp. 235 ff.)[5] calls it, is clearly an important part of what it is to become a member of, and to participate in, a disciplinary practice. Without it, there is no way in which all the individuals involved in a scientific tradition could each investigate their own particular aspects of its subject matter and—no matter how much they might disagree about its details—all agree that in general they are investigating the same thing. How, then, might we characterize the nature of this, usually ignored, background knowledge? How are we to account for its genesis? How might we properly evaluate its nature? Is there any way in which we might judge it as inadequate to the problems we face? And what should our reaction be if we were to find it inadequate? We raise these questions because, as we see it, the problem of what is involved in people understanding and meaning something to each other, in different ways in the different practical contexts of their lives, has been framed within a particular epistemological tradition that has precluded genuinely viable solutions to them. The tools of that passive-individualistic tradition are ill-formed for solving the questions posed. Its uninvolved concern merely with the *form* of things in an external world leaves us puzzled as to how we appreciate the different meanings and significances they come to have for us once we become involved in some way with them within that world. But more than that, we cannot account for how such meanings and significances differ with the differing places people occupy in relation to each other; nor are we able to account for how it is, nonetheless, still possible for differing people to communicate with each other in ways that are mutually intelligible, in ways that, as time goes on, allow development toward what they take to be a greater adequacy. In short, it fails to provide not only the resources for understanding how human beings can construct and develop between themselves their disciplinary traditions but, even more important, those required for understanding the larger scale conversational traditions constituting a culture (Rorty, 1980).

The circumstances outlined above thus face us with a dilemma. While, on the one hand, our professional commitment to the passive-individualistic paradigm has been the source of the many insoluble puzzles we have faced in communication theory, on the other, we have to admit that the traditional paradigm has given rise to a venerable tradition of investigation and argumentation with many achievements to its name. But, so long as it remains the dominant tradition, tending, as it has, to eliminate all contenders, there are no other options available—no other means of conceptualizing human functioning, scientific knowledge, and the nature of communication. Indeed, to the extent that we remain committed to the terms of the perspective, there is no means by which this tradition can be proven wrong. At the same time, however, it is clear that such a paradigm lacks any absolute foundations; although it fails to advertise the fact, it has arisen (as we shall show) out of a particular cultural and historical context. In confronting this dilemma here, we shall not introduce our own approach by attempting to eliminate the tradition by showing it to be wrong. Rather, we shall simply proceed to develop, alongside it, a social constructionist alternative, one emphasizing a situated-developmental-relational view of knowledge and the self. Thus we make no claims to the inherent superiority—out of context, culture, and history—of constructionism. Its differences do, however, open for us an alternative array of practices and possibilities (see also Code, 1991).

In taking this more relaxed view of the classical paradigm—assigning to it the right to a voice in the conversational account of knowing we wish to discuss—we are already demonstrating something of the very different view of the development of understanding to which our social constructionist account of knowing and knowledge gives rise. Indeed, as we begin to develop our social constructionist view of knowledge, it will become clear that it gives rise also to a new view of what a disciplinary tradition, and dispute within it, might be like. Such a tradition need not consist of a hierarchically structured, monological, ahistorical *system* of knowledge, pitted against others of its kind in an eliminative struggle for supremacy. It can be seen as a dialogical, multivoiced, historically changing and developing *tradition of argumentation*, a tradition that affords an extended array of positions; each having its own situated fore-structure of understanding, with the different positions all giving rise to their own "situated knowledges" (Haraway, 1991), where those on the disorderly margins of the tradition would be very different than those at its orderly center—with the whole tradition consisting in a plurality of voices in conversation, each articulating its own different viewpoint.[6]

THE ENLIGHTENED SELF AND
THE MODERNIST WORLD

In introducing our current view, it is useful to make comparisons with its most immediate predecessor. Indeed, it will not just be useful to generate such comparisons, but we shall find that just such a procedure—the generation of a vocabulary in terms of which to articulate the differences, either with each other or with invented models—constitutes a methodology that itself offers a contrast to the traditional state establishment of theories or models [7] Instead of a monological rationality achieved-as-a-representation—which "sees" similarities and aims at discovering facts—we encourage a dialogically developing rationality, a rationality that generates perspicacious differences and makes connections between what we already know implicitly in practice but have not yet explicitly formulated in agreed terms—a rationality achieved-through-contrasts (Edwards, 1982; Taylor, 1990). By explicitly articulating aspects of our practices in this way, practices that formerly were just taken as implicitly correct, we can achieve a greater degree of freedom in relation to them: We can become aware of the other possibilities available to us within them. We are not thus constrained by what is "obviously correct" or how things "must be done."

In this case, we draw attention to a particular mode of conceptualizing the person and the resulting character of knowledge. We outline how in the recent past we have made use of the knowledge of ourselves implicit in our everyday practices in fashioning our more disciplined inquiries into our own nature. Without going into the detailed history of how or why we have developed this particular fore-structure of understanding in the conduct of our daily lives, and not some other (but see Taylor, 1989), we want to discuss briefly the philosophical climate determining what we have taken to be the general style of legitimate inquiry—that it ought to be an inquiry of a scientific kind in which one seeks a *theory* to truly represent an otherwise hidden, underlying reality.

Here we are speaking of the conception of the individual nurtured by Enlightenment philosophy and reemerging as the taken-for-granted being of twentieth-century modernism, a being that Geertz (1979) characterizes as "a bounded, unique, more or less integrated motivational and cognitive universe, a dynamic center of awareness, emotion, judgment, and action organized into a distinctive whole and set contrastively both against other such wholes and against a social and natural background" (p. 229). In this characterization, Geertz effectively articulates many of the features of the fore-structure of understanding implicit in both science and our everyday social practices. Although perhaps we need to add to it Flax's (1990) observation (in line with Foucault, 1970, 1972) that "the Enlightenment demand for the foundation of all legitimate authority in Reason and Truth ironically results in a system of ever more pervasive and decentralizing exercises of power by subjects over themselves under the anonymous and often unacknowledged 'tutelage' of the 'experts' and their 'expertise,' " if we are to capture more fully the kind of person we often feel we "ought" to be. And, currently, "we emerge as the possessors of many voices. Each self contains a multiplicity of others" (Gergen, 1991, p. 83), and we become more, rather than less, subject to laws not of our own making. And yet, in terms of history and culture, this particular conception proves to be highly particular. It grows from a certain discursive climate, marked by tensions, deviations, and suppressions.

For our purposes, it is useful to highlight five outcomes of Enlightenment deliberation: (a) rational analysis; (b) mental representations; (c) the formulation of such representations as systems; (d) the rebellion against the authority of traditional, religious systems of thought and the location of new forms of authority in ahistorical experience; and (e) the individual who possesses all the resources required to be psychologically autonomous. All these features, it seems to us, must not so much be replaced as displaced, so as to allow their contemporary "others" (their repressed other-side) a "voice" in current conversations. Let us explore them further.

First, the importance of analysis and representations: According to Cassirer (1951), what characterizes the style of Enlightenment philosophizing in the eighteenth century is the "recourse to Newton's 'Rules of Philosophizing' rather than to Descartes' *Discourse on Method*, with the result that philosophy takes an entirely new direction" (Cassirer, 1951, p. 7). Although Descartes's conception of reason was retained, his starting point in the individual's clear and distinct ideas—in "hypotheses" as Newton and his followers saw it—was rejected. A science must find its starting point, not in a theoretical abstraction, for such abstractions can be invented and modified as desired, but in observations, in individual experience. Thus, instead of proceeding by deduction from certain, indubitable axioms, Enlightenment philosophy aims at an *analysis* of experience into its basic facts. Thus the analytic method involves not merely untutored observation—that only describes mere appearances—but a special form of analytic observation: the grasping of an "underlying," hidden reality behind appearances. This involves the splitting of apparently simple events into certain basic elements in such a way that, by reconstructing them according to certain laws or principles, they can be *represented* as events within a rational system or framework—and thus explained. It is this emphasis upon analysis and upon its resulting in a systematic representation that still characterizes much of our thinking in the "human sciences" today (Foucault, 1970). The Enlightenment begins, then, with a loss of faith in the older form of philosophical knowledge, the (religious) metaphysical system. It is still concerned, however, with explanations. "But in renouncing, and even in directly opposing, the 'spirit of systems' (*esprit de système*), the philosophy of the Enlightenment by no means gives up the 'systematic spirit' (*esprit systématic*); it aims to further this spirit in another more effective manner" (Cassirer, 1951, p. vii). Thus, although the turn from the deductive to the analytic method in the eighteenth century marks a shift of focus, from reason to experience, from a starting point in axioms to one in observations, certain continuities remain. The overall urge to be systematic in one's explanatory activities is retained—and this is the third feature of Enlightenment thought we want to emphasize. For, without a system, it claims, without a rational framework within which to interlink contingent facts into a system of logically necessary entailments or dependencies, no soundly based, explanatory knowledge is possible in any field. We can only, seemingly, revert to the contingencies and likelihoods, the persuasions of rhetoric—the influences, once again, of mere opinion.

A fourth feature, first articulated by Descartes but retained by the Enlightenment, is that of methodical doubt of any authority derived from intellectual traditions of the past. Discussing this move in his *Meditations* of 1640, he said that, "although the usefulness of such extensive doubt is not apparent at first sight, its greatest benefit lies in freeing us from all our preconceived opinions, and providing the greatest route by which the mind may be led away from the senses" (Descartes, 1641/1986, p. 9)—for the senses, he thought, could so easily deceive us. In other words, he sought to establish "the method of properly conducting one's reason and of seeking the truth in the sciences"[8] by first setting aside the influences of previous traditions of thought. "I realized," as he put it in the "First Meditation," "that it was necessary, once in the course of my life, to demolish everything completely and start again from the right foundations if I wanted to establish anything at all in the sciences that was stable and likely to last" (Descartes, 1641/1986, p. 12). It is thus that he instituted the idea that, if one is prepared to undertake the hard analytic work involved, one can throw off the intellectual commitments entailed in one's previous, traditional involvements. And one can found a new intellectual system, not in a tradition, not in a way of life or in a way of being in the world, but in a set of theoretical principles, a set of foundational statements. As more recently described, this aspect of Enlightenment thinking forms the basis for the modernist *grand narrative of progress*: the mythic belief that through the application of reason we may forget history and progress our culture toward an ever more luminous future. As De Man (1983) expresses it, this ruthless forgetting was embodied "in the form of a desire to wipe out whatever came earlier, in the hope of reaching at last a point that could be called a true present, a point of departure that marks a new departure" (p. 148).

The fifth feature concerns the source of our own nature as human beings. Although Descartes's claim, that the seemingly diverse flux of our everyday ways of thinking could be analyzed into clear and distinct elementary ideas of an *innate* kind, Locke's 1690 *Essay Concerning Human Understanding* suggested different origins. He suggested that all our complex ideas could be seen as having their origins in a complex of simple sensations, in the simple impressions written on the "tabula rasa" of the mind of the individual by the "outside" world. And this was crucial to another aspect of Enlightenment thought. For Locke's views made it possible to argue that the supposed evil of ordinary people was not an innate, natural evil but an evil that had been generated externally and had been imposed upon "man"[9] by society, by his environment. Thus, if man was not naturally evil, there was no innate vicious-ness to be curbed. Thus, gradually, a sufficiently comprehensive intellectual system was formulated to contest the authority of the traditional medieval Catholic as well as the Protestant worldviews. If man's natural abilities to change the world were greater than had been imagined, then perhaps a more optimistic, brighter prospect for the future of man might be possible. The age of the Enlightenment thus came to express a buoyant optimism. Natural man (unburdened by any tradition) was the symbol leading the age out of medieval darkness. Indeed, as Kant expressed the dream of the age—in his famous essay of 1784, "What Is Enlightening"—the issue in question was (and still is) whether people themselves can be *self*-determining, or whether they must (in some sense) always be under the yoke of others?

It is within the intellectual climate created by Enlightenment thought, within its fore-structure of understanding, that we still to a large extent conduct our intellectual practices, our academic disciplines. In the current century—often earmarked as *modernist*—it still seems only "natural" to conduct our inquiries into ourselves in terms of analytically structured theo-ries, thought of as representing a hidden, underlying, ahistorical human essence, a human "reality" that could be discovered either by focusing upon self-contained individuals themselves (psychology) or upon the "systems" within which they live (sociology). With Geertz's characterization of Western personhood in mind, we will now turn briefly to the two major intellectual traditions within which the kind of systematic, analytic theories suggested by Enlightenment thought have been formulated (Gergen, 1991). Given our concern with personhood, we shall concentrate our attention upon formula-tions in psychology (and in linguistics) while leaving those in sociology upon one side—especially as, in line with Geertz's formulation, sociology has been concerned with the essentially, psychologically inert background against which, by contrast, the psychologically active person has been set. We will turn first to romanticism.

While reason and observation came to occupy a central role in our intellectual affairs in the seventeenth and eighteenth centuries, during the late eighteenth and nineteenth centuries, their supremacy was challenged and a new world was created—the world of the *deep interior*. Other human activities and tendencies came to be valued: the passions, feelings, the imagination, creativity, a moral sensibility, what is natural (or even biological) in people, a sense of important things hidden in the deep interior of the person that could only be brought out by them individually indulging in exceptional efforts of some kind. The artist became the hero of social life. As Gergen (1991) remarks: "Much of our contemporary vocabulary of the person, along with associated ways of life, finds its origins in the romantic period. It is a vocabulary of passion, purpose, depth, and personal significance: a vocabulary that generates awe of heroes, of genius, and inspired work" (p. 27). In such a view, it is the individual (as an artist) that is the source and center of all creativity.

Somewhere toward the end of the nineteenth century, romanticist energies began to wane and the natural sciences began to flourish. Although romanticism had furnished a rich resource for cultural innovation, little in its vision of things was of general use, it offered no solutions to people's practical problems, nor was it at all clear how its much talked of moral sentiments could be linked to justified moral action (MacIntyre, 1981). Tracing their lineage to the Enlightenment, through the powers of ahistorical, systematic reasoning and observation, the sciences began to offer a more attractive vision of things. They offered to lift people, all humankind, above the ignorance and superstition of the past. Indeed, modernism begins with a suspicion, ranging from disregard to antagonism, of everything to do with the past. The central metonymic emblem of such a new state of affairs, something that can be put together from scratch, and then switched on, started up, and set running upon a new course, is that of the machine. Not only, as Le Corbusier (1971) put it, could one think of a house as "a machine for living in" but one could think of a whole new world order in terms of machines within machines, of mechanisms within mechanisms, such that it became quite "natural" to speak of every functioning thing of importance as a mechanism of one kind or another.

SOCIAL CONSTRUCTION:
THE RESTORATION OF THE SUPPRESSED

By emphasizing features in the fore-structure of understanding in Enlightenment thought and the modernist conceptions to which it gives rise, our purpose has been to draw attention to that which has been suppressed: While in general the Enlightenment emphasized reason, closed systems (and mechanisms), the individual, inner mental representations, and what is timeless and beyond culture, it downplayed (denigrated even) a significant range of contradictory concepts. While reason was elevated, its "other side," rhetoric, was equated with the tawdry tricks of persuasion. The praise of closed systems, and their emphasis on the orderly and predictable, was set against the fear of chaos and confusion. The individual was championed, while the forces of the group were rendered intrusive and suspicious—equivalent to the loss of individual reason. The importance of accurate, internal representation was cast against the rowdy forces of instinct, passion, and desire. And the accolades for the timeless and acultural were contrasted with the superficial, the merely fashionable, or the culturally biased. In effect, the Enlightenment tradition made incomprehensible a responsive understanding of language and people's participation in the construction of their own subjectivities. A panoply of conceptual possibilities was discouraged in the name of unitary (one-sided, ahistorical) systems or frameworks of thought. The privileging of one side of these dualities over the other, while no doubt enabling in many powerful ways, has, however, been disabling in many others.

Thus, within the logic of the system or the bounded framework, it seems, we have arrived at an impasse: As individual academics faced with the task of producing coherent, theoretical monologues, we have outlined a large number of two-sided issues and produced no principle for deciding one way or the other, ahead of time, any of them. Indeed, as Taylor (1989) has put it, it seems in general that "frameworks today are problematic. . . . What is common to them all is the sense that no framework is shared by everyone, [or] can be taken for granted as *the* framework" (p. 17). And, in line with that conclusion, we have not in fact been seeking a framework, nor have we sought to resolve the dilemmas we have outlined above ahead of time, theoretically. Instead, we feel that what is required now, perhaps, is the relaxation of precisely that self-imposed constraint of the Enlightenment tradition; it is the attempt always to resolve all the dilemmas we face ahead of time that disables us. As we move into what some have called the *postmodern* condition (Lyotard, 1984), we are becoming more accepting of a pluralistic, only fragmentarily known, and only partially shared social world, a world in which the two sides of an apparent opposition *can* both be plausible, in which there are genuine dilemmas (Billig, 1991; Billig et al., 1988). Fragmentation and incoherence are present in both our world and our selves. Instead of a rich and stable community life, we are now entering into a series of mobile, changing, revocable associations, often designed merely for highly specific ends (Gergen, 1991; Taylor, 1989).

Let us then pick up the rejected shards of the Enlightenment tradition—the practical, everyday conversational activities, particularly those of a rhetorical and argumentative kind—and play with their possibilities. The point here is not to characterize the nature of these practical, conversational activities, ahead of time, theoretically, by resolving the many dilemmas to which such activities give rise. Rather, the attempt is to move dialogically—to initiate a constructive dialogue, a conversation to do with how knowledge or understanding is situated, developmental, and relational. This necessitates us accepting straightaway that the claims we shall make as to how such a paradigm is best articulated are both derivative and contestable. They are derivative in the sense that these conceptions gain whatever efficacy they possess from a host of preceding intelligibilities. The current views, to which we have given our names, would not be possible except for preceding "conversations" with George Herbert Mead, Mikhail Bakhtin, P. Berger and T. Luckmann, and Harold Garfinkel as primary protagonists. We are indebted as well to preceding "exchanges" with Rom Harré, Barnett Pearce, and Vernon Cronen. And various works of Stanley Deetz, Stuart Sigman, Bruno Latour, Steve Woolgar, and others have been vital aides-de-camp (see references for typical writings). No, the current account does not recapitulate any of these works, but their traces will and should be everywhere apparent. At the same time, all that we say is properly contestable. For we are speaking from a position within a certain horizon with its own particular fore-structure of understanding, with certain interests in mind. Others will approach these issues differently. But, as we see it, the challenge of articulation derives from our conversational involvements with each other.

In what follows, we shall attempt to develop a number of what might be called "instructive statements," which provide a rudimentary *account* of various crucial aspects of conversational exchanges. Such accounts are intended not to represent a state of affairs but to enhance a mode of comprehension, to "show" connections between things that otherwise would go unnoticed.[10] In our relational view, by working to coordinate our actions in different ways in different contexts, our different ways of speaking work practically to construct different forms of social relations, different forms of life. To that extent, we can expect accounts to be important at just those points in the flow of everyday interaction, when the people involved sense that a change in the character of that form of life is at issue; and that is how we intend our accounts to be read here—as suggesting a change in the disciplinary form of life currently oriented around the passive-individualistic epistemological paradigm.

(1) Accounts of "reality" originate in the contingent, indeterminate, and historical flow of continuous communicative activity between human beings. All reasoning—including that which is developed here—takes place within a tradition. At the same time, by virtue of the multiplicity of traditions making up a society, with their continuous "jostlings" and "juxtapositions" over sundry, unpredictable circumstances, any viable form of reasoning is forced to transcend the scope and the limits of its own tradition. As traditions develop and change, historically, it is the nature of these historically changing processes to which we must attend. Thus (for our purposes) the assumption of an already stable, well-formed, systematic reality "behind appearances," full of "things" identifiable independently of language, awaiting discovery by the

appropriate methods, must be replaced by another reality of a more social and more historical kind: that of a vague, still developing, still only partially specified, unstable, contestable reality, "furnished" and "furnishing" a two-sided fore-structure of understanding, open to further specification as a result of human, communicative activity. And what is important historically, in changing the cultural character of such a reality—and, with it, the kind of people we are—is not so much the actions of single individuals but the nature of the dialogical, discursive activity among them, within which values emerge and are shaped into usable forms while old ones are abandoned. Thus events occurring in such a reality, instead of making sense of them, monologically, from within a system, can be thought of as being made sense of, dialogically and argumentatively, from within a tradition.

As we have noted, our traditional urge to produce single, unified, monological, systems of knowledge gave rise to an ambition to locate a world beyond the social and historical[11] and to attempt to discover this world in the depths of either the psychic or the organic or in abstract principles or systems. It has been a part of who we are, of our identity as Western academic intellectuals, that we have felt these urges and ambitions and that these approaches were appropriate to the problems involved in our attempts to understand ourselves. But, in arguing for one or another of these systems, this third sphere of historically developing activity has usually been ignored. In foregrounding it here, we want to draw attention to the fact that the urges we have felt—to seek ahistorical systematic theories—have arisen out of the fore-structure of understanding furnished us by a particular tradition. In other words, we draw our identity from our "rooting" within a living, historical tradition, which is, as MacIntyre (1981) puts it, "a living tradition . . . an historically extended, socially embodied argument, and an argument precisely in part about the goods which constitute that tradition" (p. 207). We are arguing, then, for the value of recognizing the existence of this more historically situated form of argumentative reasoning, with its implications for our social and professional lives.

But more than this is required if we are to reinstate a historical dimension in our rethinking of the nature of human, communicative activities. For what does it mean to say that we must study communication historically? In the past, in linguistics and speech communication, we have tended to study impersonal bodies of already spoken words. But systems of words viewed at an instant in the past give us little insight into their part in making history, the struggles involved in their achieving acceptance. As we see it, to study something historically is to study it in terms of its function or use in making history, in making a difference in people's lives. Thus, instead of systems of "already spoken words," we shall take it that to study communication historically means to study the changes that words can make in the ongoing, practical, dialogical contexts of their contested use. This brings us to our next point.

(2) An utterance has no meaning in itself but only as a constituent of ongoing dialogue; its meaning is generated by its use within dialogue. In the classical passive-individualistic paradigm, meaning is to be understood in terms of the individual forming inner, mental representations. In accounting for the continuity of the flow of communicative activity between people, however, we can note that lone utterances begin to acquire meaning when others respond, or add some form of supplementary action (linguistic or otherwise), to what is said. As Bakhtin (1986) remarks: "[A speaker] does not expect passive understanding that, so to speak, only duplicates his own idea in someone else's mind. Rather, he expects response, agreement, sympathy, objection, execution, and so forth" (p. 69). In their responses to another person's utterance, listeners act out of their own particular repertoires; they actively appropriate the speaker's utterance to their own fore-structures of understanding: Hence their objections, questions, elaborations, and so on do not depend upon the preexistence of any common understandings between them and the speaker but are a part of the activity of constructing a shared understanding in, and appropriate to, the context of their conversation.

As an intrinsic unit of dialogue, an utterance is always produced in response to previous utterances and bounded by a change in speaking subjects. Further, to the extent that an utterance is not understood referentially but responsively, in terms of an answering response, common understandings emerge in the course of a process of testing and checking between speaker and listener. While, in the classical paradigm, the mind of the individual is an original source of meaning, in this view, there is no proper beginning or original source of meaning. From a practical point of view, we are always already situated in a relational context of meaning to which our utterance is a response, a supplement, an action that makes a difference, and that thus develops or specifies that already existing meaning further. But if the others around one fail to treat one's utterance as communication, if they fail to coordinate themselves in response to the opportunities it offers, then one's utterance is reduced to nonsense.

As Bakhtin (1986) puts it,

> A word (or in general any sign) is interindividual. Everything that is said . . . is located outside the "soul" of the speaker and does not belong only to him [*sic*]. The word cannot be assigned to a single speaker. The author (speaker) has his own inalienable right to the word, but the listener has his rights, and those whose voices are heard in the word before the author comes upon it also have their rights (after all, there are no words that belong to no one). (pp. 121-122)

In this view, divorced from their practical context of use, words as such lack any specific meanings in themselves; their meanings must be negotiated between speaker and listener.

But if this is the case, how should we study words in their use? Classically, we have thought it important to study linguistic *forms* and the systems or patterns they have constituted. In our concern with words in their speaking, however, what we value is not so much the normatively self-identical forms, irrespective of their context of use—that is, in terms of their place within the logic of an ahistorical system—but with the possibilities of using such words (forms) in a whole range of changeable and adaptable ways in an indefinite number of contexts. Clearly, their character as a relatively ordered, intercon- nected set of forms is important in speaking skillfully; but, rather than words themselves having a meaning, words are, we suggest, best thought of only as a *means* in the making of meanings. Jerzey Kosinski's *Being There* (1970) furnishes numerous puckish examples of how the words of an idiot may be turned into profundity by surrounding believers, while Garfinkel's (1967) "experiments" in questioning the routine grounds of everyday conversation demonstrate how even the most obvious candidates for meaning may be subverted or aborted.[12] Thus, as Volosinov (1973) puts it, "what is important for the speaker about the linguistic form is not that it is a stable and always self-equivalent signal, but that it is an always changeable and adaptable sign" (p. 68). To find their life, we must look into the living social circumstances of their use, not into the pattern of signs themselves.

(3) Responsive utterances work both to create meaning and to constrain further meaning in the continuously developing context of a conversation. What is involved in an active, responsive dialogue? And how might it be dialogically developed? As Vygotsky (1978) comments, in learning to coor- dinate his or her actions linguistically with the actions of others, "the child begins to perceive the world not only through his [*sic*] eyes but also through his speech" (p. 32). What Vygotsky is implying here is that a way of talking comes to possess an "instructive" or "directive" function. By "instructing" people in how to pay attention, and how to make socially intelligible sense of their surroundings, it can function as a *prosthetic device*, a device *through* which they can both perceive and act in ways not possible without it. For example, friends tell us about a couple, Sarah and Sam, who, they think, are breaking up: "Just notice how when they talk together, Sam keeps finding some insulting hidden significance in the way Sarah responds," they say. In terms of our prior acquaintance with marriages and their difficulties, our responsive understanding of our friend's injunction leads us to attend to Sam and Sarah's conversation as they suggest; and, sure enough, it seems to be just as they say. Positioned within the context of the injunction, what we now "see" we see in terms of the concept of "marital trouble."[13]

Of course, the directive function of language does not in itself completely determine our behavior. Others might make other discursive moves and respond to one's claims accordingly. In this sense, a responsive utterance operates to grant a *specific potential* to the meaning of a preceding utterance. The response will treat the utterance as meaning possibly *this* and not *that*, as possibly requiring one form of action as opposed to another, as having a particular rhetorical force as opposed to some other. In effect, the response serves to "develop" the initial utterance in some way, where "all real and integral understanding is actively responsive, and constitutes nothing other than the initial preparatory stage of a response [in whatever form it may be actualized]" (Bakhtin, 1986, p. 69).[14] Further, in offering only certain possibilities of response, the responsive utterance has the effect of shaping identity. One greets another and she returns one's greeting; the potential is opened up for further discourse, while silence would close it off. In treating her as a potential interlocutor, we offer her the possibility of *being* such. What anyone can be is thus, to an extent, up to the others around them. It is important "how the speaker [or writer] senses and imagines his [*sic*] addressee" (Bakhtin, 1986, p. 95). In this sense, while others can invite you into being, they can also negate your potential identity. From an enormous range of possibilities, others both influence the direction in which you can be someone and simultaneously narrow the possibilities of your being. Indeed, such relations as these—those between greetings, questions and answers, suggestions and acceptance, and so on—only come into existence between the rejoinders in a dialogue. Responsive relations of this kind are impossible simply among the sentences, the *forms*, of a language; they presuppose *other* participants in addition to the speaker in the speech process.

We can call this form of action -in which the formative influences shaping people's conduct are generated only within a conversational context—*joint action* (Shotter, 1980, 1984). Some of the major properties of joint action are as follows: (a) As people coordinate their activity with each other, the results may differ significantly from the predispositions (discursive traditions) of either interlocutor alone. (b) As each person responds to the other, they generate a "conversational organization" between them. As this organization cannot typically be traced to the predispositions of either individual, it is *as if* it has both a "natural" and an "externally caused" nature while, at the same time, those within it claim it as "their" conversation. (c) Although such conversational organization is unintended by any of the individuals within it, it does have what philosophers call an *intentional* quality; that is, it seems both to "imply" things, to "indicate," or to be "related to possibilities other than or beyond itself." Thus participants find themselves "in" a situation that has both an immediate structure as well as a *horizon* of possibilities to it and is thus "open" to their actions. Indeed, its current organization is such, as we have said, that it both invites and constrains the next possible actions of those within it. (d) Thus, not only are the meanings in such circumstances open to continuous reconstitution via an expanding sea of supplementation, but the speaking of any further words takes their effect against the background of a continuously updated but contentious understanding of what has been said so far. In other words, as Giddens (1984) describes it, the socially constructed but "unintended consequences [in such activities] may systematically (become) the unacknowledged conditions of further acts" (p. 8).

In light of all these considerations, we find that, not only is what is actually communicated undecidable, but it is also clear that who is responsible is also unlocatable. Thus all that is fixed and settled in one instance may be cast into ambiguity or undone in the next. The Sarah and Sam we mentioned above used to find themselves frequently generating laughter together until, one day, Sam announced that Sarah's laughter was "unnatural and forced," just her attempt to present herself as an "easygoing person" (thus to redefine the meaning of their laughter together). To which Sarah then replied, in an attempt to turn Sam's insult round upon him, "Oh, you're so hypocritical Sam that we really don't communicate at all." A move that Sam later tried to negate or alter by saying, "Oh, you're only saying that because you don't really want to see yourself as the difficult one." And so on. Indeed, as Sam and Sarah go on to talk about their relationship with others—friends, relatives, and the like—such instances of negation and alteration may become far removed from their original laughing interchanges and their meaning changed many times over.

Given this fundamentally open character of "what is meant" in and by an utterance or circumstance, the question arises as to the practical processes that people use in "managing," nonetheless, to produce an acceptable account of its nature. Here, Garfinkel's (1967) early work on the ad hoc considerations used by coders of records in a psychiatric clinic is apposite: Although ostensively operating according to certain explicit rules, coders clearly drew in an uncontrolled, ad hoc way upon background knowledge of how the clinic *was supposed* to work to decide how a particular case should be treated. Thus, as Garfinkel (1967) reports: "Characteristically, coded results would be treated as if they were disinterested descriptions of clinic events. . . . But if *ad hocing* is required to make such claims intelligible, it can always be argued that the coded results consist of a persuasive version of the socially organized character of the clinic's operations, regardless of what the actual order is" (p. 23). In other words, in claiming that their actions are guided by rules, people use their own judgment in relation to their background knowledge of a form of life to make it seem as if this were the case.

Studies of the ways in which communities of scientists work out (or up) mutually acceptable views of "the facts" (Latour & Woolgar, 1979); how psychologists collectively devise a vision of psychology's "subject matter" (Danziger, 1990); how families collectively "remember" their past (Middleton & Edwards, 1990); how political figures negotiate the spin to be put upon their public speeches (Edwards & Potter, 1992); and how those in relationships structure each others' identities (Shotter, 1987, 1992)—all serve to fill out the picture of the social organization of meaning in the daily practices of its making.

(4) It is in terms of "social languages" and "speech genres" that we can account for our ways of talking as working to hold social groups together as dynamic, relational wholes—they hold together as "behavioral or lived ideologies." Social groups tend to be sustained by those within them relating themselves to each other by their use of certain ways of talking to each other,

ways that they stabilize by holding each other to these particular modes of talk. Indeed, it was Mills (1940/1975) who long ago suggested that "we must approach linguistic behavior, not by referring it to private states within individuals, but by observing its social function in coordinating diverse actions" (p. 162), that is, its function in constituting social relations. Mills was particularly concerned with a group's "vocabulary of motives" and the function of this vocabulary on those occasions when one's actions are challenged and one must typify them in group terms. It is then that we draw upon it as a cultural resource (e.g., "I didn't *intend* to . . .", "I was only *trying* to help . . .") where, for us, intending and trying are taken-for-granted features of our ways of acting in the world. Here, reference to a stable motive works "as an ultimate in justificatory conversation" (p. 164) because it links puzzling or apparently unfitting acts back into the practices by which the social group sustains its identity. In other words, traditions are only held together by the efforts of those within them to sustain them.

Thus, as made clear in the work of Volosinov (1973, 1976) and Bakhtin (1981, 1986), it is a mistake to view the "ways of talking" of a group, or "vocabularies of motive" (as in Mills's case), as deriving from a unitary, rule-governed system. We are, however, clearly not free agents who can combine linguistic forms as we please. Rather, we speak only within certain *social languages* and *speech genres*—certain historically sustained speech traditions. Although all people within a culture may speak the same national language (e.g., English, German), many local meanings and patterns of related action may exist in striking contrast to others. The notion of a unitary national language is, Bakhtin and Volosinov claim, a myth. Only as an abstraction is it ever a unitary system. In the changing historical circumstances of our actual everyday lives, we live within a multitude of relatively circumscribed verbal-ideological and social forms of life with their own distinctive fore-structures, and fore-havings, of understanding. These forms of life, with their different existential horizons—Bakhtin mentions prayer, song, familial, and litigious types—are sustained by the forms of talk, the social languages, in terms of which activity within them is coordinated and made accountable (Bakhtin, 1981, pp. 295-296).

Interwoven with these social languages are also other stable ways of talking which Bakhtin (1986) calls "speech genres," that are "definite and relatively stable typical *forms of construction of the whole*." And he adds, "Our repertoire of oral (and written) speech genres is rich. We use them confidently and skillfully *in practice*, and it is quite possible for us not even to suspect their existence *in theory*" (p. 78). Indeed, as the work of Bakhtin and Volosinov emphasizes, various groups within a culture develop over time local languages—and genres within and across them—that coordinate their actions and give them a certain kind of unity over time. As a result of all these influences on our use of words, there are in practice no "neutral" words and forms—words and forms that can belong to "no one"; language has been completely taken over, shot through with implications and accents. For any individual living within it, language is not an abstract system of normative forms but rather a concrete heteroglot. All words have the "taste" of a profession, a region, an ethnicity, a generation, an age group, and so on. Each word tastes of the contexts in which it has lived its socially charged life. (Bakhtin, 1981, p. 293)

In other words, no matter how, as individuals, we might attempt to commandeer a word for our own use, we find its previous uses resisting—at least partially—the new responsive use to which we wish to put it. Thus, in new and different contexts, we attempt to "negotiate"—just as much in the sense of "navigate through" as "to bargain with"—these other "voices." But in speaking in this way, with a consciousness[15] of the limited possible meanings of our speech and the social relations they constitute, we are also speaking within an *ideological* horizon of some kind, a way of speaking that serves to coordinate social action in certain ways rather than in others—one that benefits some members in the group more than others. Thus, as Volosinov (1973) puts it, "it is a matter not so much of expression accommodating itself to our [so-called] inner world but rather of our inner world accommodating itself to the potentialities of our expression, its possible routes and directions" (p. 91). These limitations constitute what might be called a "behavioral or a lived ideology"—where such a behavioral or lived ideology is, again as Volosinov frames it, "that atmosphere of unsystematized and unfixed inner and outer speech which endows our every instance of behavior and action and our every conscious' state with meaning" (p. 91). Indeed, as we have seen above in our examination of the romanticist and modernist vocabularies, as well as in Volosinov's account of the traditions to which they gave rise in linguistics, more than happening simply to be unsystematized and unfixed, in Billig et al.'s (1988) terms, such lived ideologies contain irresolvable, dilemmatic themes[16] and thus, in principle, cannot be systematized and fixed. A living tradition, to repeat MacIntyre above, is a historically extended, socially embodied, two-sided, unsystematic argument.

(5) As linguistically coordinated social relationships acquire a history and become ordered or ranked, so we develop "official" ways of accounting for ourselves and our world, that is, local ontologies and social sanctions for their maintenance. In practice, however, there is much less argument and disorder than is suggested in principle. For, although there is no necessary relation between meaning and order, the relationship between them is nonetheless a close one. With no history at all between two interactants (if that were possible), any action on the part of one could serve as a prelude to any reaction of the other. One demonstrates understanding in a relationship not by grasping what is in the other's "mind" but in one's response to the other's

actions. If someone throws you a ball and you throw it back, and on each succeeding throw you do the same, then you have given her throw the meaning of an "invitation" for you to catch it as well as it functioning as a prelude for you to return the throw, and vice versa. The order imported into the sequence of events allows those involved to anticipate the consequences of their own actions—you come to "expect" the other to throw the ball back. Not to satisfy the other's expectations is to fail to "fit" one's actions into the "organized setting" developed between you and her—it is as if a "norm" or a "rule" has been transgressed.

In general, participants in any relationship will tend to develop a *positive ontology*, a set of mutually shared "callings" that enable interaction to proceed unproblematically; this way of talking seems to represent how things "are" for those involved in them. Thus, just as the ballplayers above establish routine patterns of anticipation, so do other social groups. Researchers in astrophysics, for instance, do not shift their theoretical vocabulary from moment to moment, for to do so would mean the destruction of the group's capacity to achieve what they term "productive" research results. The effective functioning of the group depends upon maintaining a relatively stable way of talking—and members of the group know that and, as we have mentioned before, hold one another to it. The positive ontology becomes the culture's array of sedimented or commonsense understandings. And it is precisely this sedimentation that enables scholars to treat such ways of talking as if regulated by an underlying, fixed structure, as if possessing a logical implicature governed by rules.

To the extent that they do embody an order and afford the anticipation of meanings, such practices tend to become self-sustaining. Their sustenance is also importantly dependent on various *sanctioning processes*, that is, emerging processes of rewarding those who remain within the traditions and punishing those who deviate. Such sanctioning may be intentional and systematic, as in the Inquisitionist attempt to eliminate all nonbelievers from the society or the Stalinist purge of dissidents. More typically, however, it operates through the subtle microprocesses of everyday interaction, in which slights, innuendoes, or silences are used to discredit those whose discourses threaten an established mode of life. Indeed, the founding moment of the women's movement originates in the "discovery that as women we had been living in an intellectual, cultural, and political world, from whose making we had been almost entirely excluded and which we had been recognized as no more than marginal voices" (Smith, 1988, p. 1). Indeed, these same processes are at work in the simultaneous construction of local realities, and their accompanying sanctioning processes, that have served as the focus for substantial exploration into the social basis for scientific knowledge (Barnes, 1974, 1986; Bloor, 1976; Collins, 1985; Foucault, 1970, 1972; Fuller, 1988; Knorr-Cetina, 1981; Mulkay, 1985; Woolgar, 1988). As such research suggests, scientific enclaves operate in much the same way as religions, committing themselves to given ontologies (linguistic fore-structures), coding the world in their terms (thus enhancing the seeming legitimacy of the fore-structure), and subtly reinforcing participants for remaining within a "framework" while persecuting those who deviate.[17]

(6) *Particularly in Western cultural settings, the local ontologies and moralities are individuating.* That is, they allocate to different individuals differing characteristics or properties, along with a range of "moral duties" required for sustaining the allocated position. As commonsense orders are developed and sanctioned, distinctions are commonly drawn among individual actors. Such distinctions may include individuating naming practices (Paul, Sandra), positional indicators (mother, father), and diectic shifters (he, she, I, you). As patterns of interdependence are developed, then, so are certain modes of action assigned to those occupying the individuated slots indexed by the language. Thus, for example, in the game of baseball, a ball must be "thrown" before it can properly be "struck." The individuating term *pitcher* is thus assigned to the individual who carries out the action at appropriate intervals. More subtly and pervasively, the name of an individual (e.g., Thomas Hodgkins) comes to designate not simply a physical body but an anticipated range of culturally defined actions in which this body participates (e.g., works at a specific job, gives affection to his spouse, nurtures his children, fishes on Sundays). If he suddenly ceased to engage in any of these activities, in an important sense he would cease to be the "real" Thomas Hodgkins. ("He's become strange." "He's lost it." "He just isn't himself," it might be said.) As we are proposing, then, relationships are not constituted by independent, self-contained individuals, but what we call the individual— along with all the attributes assigned to the individual (including psychological states of emotion, reason, and motivation)—is all derived from ongoing processes of relationship. The relationship precedes the individual, and not vice versa. As Gadamer (1975) puts it with regard to play: "All play is a being-played. The attraction of a game, the fascination it exerts, consists precisely in the fact that the game tends to master the players" (p. 95).

At the level of the individual, the sanctioning processes discussed above operate (at least in Western culture) as *moral imperatives*. The individual is singled out and treated as one who ought to, or must, carry out certain actions. Thomas Hodgkins may be the object of considerable objurgation if he fails to carry out the anticipated activities. He is not morally free to "decide" one day simply to quit work. So sedimented are the local moralities that most such possibilities lie outside the range of consideration. They remain in the spectrum of the invisible. At the same time, because those we designate as individuals are typically enmeshed in multiple relationships, the commonsense understandings of any given group in which one is a member may be inconsistent with other groups in which one participates. Thus, on various occasions, one may disobey the moral imperatives of a group in which he or she is otherwise a member in good standing. And such deviations will typically invite some form of the moral sanctioning process. Such conditions favor the development of a *grammar of accounts*, that is, modes of justifying, or defending, one's actions or mitigating possible retribution. The various modes by which persons in Western society "rationalize" or "explain away" their seeming faults have been the subject of broad and active research (see, for example, Antaki, 1988; Potter & Wetherell, 1987; Semin & Manstead, 1983; Shotter, 1984).

(7) Our psychological talk—supposed to be "about" our "perceptions," "memories," "motives," "judgments," and so on—does not refer to an already existing, inner reality of mental representations but consists in claims formulated upon the basis of one's position in a conversational context. As we propose, psychological talk—about emotion, motives, desires, and the like—does not represent or reflect a concrete, independent reality—in this case, an internal or "subjective" reality—but is itself a practical resource within relationships (Gergen, 1989). Typically, psychological talk is accompanied by an array of "proper" actions (to claim a state of "happiness" may be properly accompanied by a smile, but not a frown). Further, such composites of talk and action are favored within certain contexts and at particular junctures within a relationship, and not others. Thus, as explored in the case of *emotional scenarios* (Gergen & Gergen, 1988), to be accepted as legitimate, various emotional performances (e.g., words and actions that together perform "anger," "joy," "sadness," and the like) can take place only when subsequent to certain designated actions on the part of another. And, once the emotional performance takes place, the other is constrained to certain forms of reaction (e.g., apology, pleasure, remorse). Psychological discourse, then, is constrained by its position within a relational sequence. It operates pragmatically "to keep things going" along certain paths.

The pragmatic functions of psychological discourse are amply demonstrated in the process of self-justification. Psychological discourse, and vocabularies of motive in particular, may play a critical role in explaining seemingly errant or deviant activity. Explaining our conduct is not thus a general necessity but is often required when others have put our behavior in question, such as when there has been a breach of what was expected in a practical, everyday context. Without such breaches, there would be few such demands for an explanation. Hence Peters (1958) explains "the sense of outrage which the ordinary man has when the psychologist gets busy on his motives. For psychologists tend to use the term indiscriminately and to ignore the contextual usage of the word in ordinary language. Some of them, indeed, suggest that we have a motive for *everything* that we do. The effect of such a suggestion is to put all actions up for assessment" (p. 30). In the same way, we do not mind being asked why we are trying to break into a next-door neighbor's house by other neighbors (when he had asked us to get an important letter to redirect to him on holiday), for this is the sort of action that obviously requires some justification. But we do take it amiss when questioned about our motives for getting married or sending Christmas presents, for in such cases we are simply doing the done thing, and there should be no necessity of justification. Motive talk in this kind of everyday context is especially important as it demonstrates to others that one knows how to be a proper member of their society, that one comprehends when there appears to be a breakdown, to reinstate in their actions the appropriate social order.

But there are other points in everyday conversation when talk of mental states serves other functions. For instance, Middleton and Edwards (1990) studied the points at which students, when asked to talk among themselves about the feature film *E.T.* (which they had all previously seen), explicitly claimed to have remembered something; but they only explicitly talked of "memory" and "remembering," and gave what Middleton and Edwards called "metacognitive formulations," at specific points in the conversation: Talk of memory or remembering "generally occurred at points where the activity ran into trouble or difficulty, and especially, at moments when one person's account provoked sudden recognition, or disputation, from another person" (p. 28). In other words, such talk is used rhetorically, in justifying the "bridging of a gap" that has opened up in the otherwise routine flow of a conversation, in one particular way rather than another. Thus the reference to mental states allows the relationship to continue in one way rather than another. In talking of their relation to their own psychological capacities and liabilities, people are able to position themselves, for example, in a close or distant relationship to their own claims, thus later to receive the praise or mitigate the blame of others.

And, when viewed in this way, of course, people may make use of the resources provided by different vocabularies of psychological terms to formulate many different kinds of claims with many different kinds of practical, social effects: to claim responsibility (thus to receive praise and move to more influential social positions); to avoid responsibility (thus to avoid blame and being moved to less influential social positions); to support others (thus to support one's own group); to undermine others in favor of oneself; and so on, and so on. In this vein, Edwards and Potter (1992) have studied the rhetorical uses to which people put *factual reports* of "remembered" events at which they were present. They show how the *versions* people construct of "what really happened" not only served their own purposes but also worked to undermine those of others. For example, they discuss how John Dean and Oliver North in the United States, and Chancellor Lawson in Britain, when in political difficulties, publicly carefully formulated their testimonies so as to navigate a clever course between blamings, errors, mistakes, accidents, and responsibilities. At points of actual or potential dispute in a conversational exchange, they constructed versions of "the facts" that they could warrant by reference to agreed events but that nonetheless served what may be viewed as their own interests in very subtly constructed ways.[18] Sabini and Silver

(1986) also argue that our talk of emotion is used in the same way—again at those points in people's transactions with others at which they must justify or account for themselves in some way; other examples are displayed in Gergen and Davis (1985).

In all these cases, the precise character of our psychological talk is not caused by, nor does it refer to, any already existing, inner reality or mental representations. We use psychological terms to carry out social scenarios. Such terms serve to construct certain kinds of social relations in which we can be certain kinds of persons. Our talk "instructs" our listeners in how to respond to us. It is this "instructive" aspect of our talk, and the way in which it can shape our way of being as a person—as capable of interacting, talking, thinking, and evaluating in one particular way rather than another, according to its "fit" within a particular context—that constructionism brings into focus.

CONCLUSIONS

Our attempt has been to set out, in a general way, some of the important features of a social constructionist view of knowledge, one that emphasizes the situated, developmental, and relational character of knowledge claims and speaks importantly to issues of communication and personal identity. We have not attempted to set out a theory that can be judged true or false by universal criteria of objectivity. "Truth" can only be achieved from within an orderly and stable disciplinary practice. Rather, we are proposing an initial development of the fore-structure of understandings in terms of which such practices could function. To that extent, we have not attempted to offer a theory but a set of interrelated *accounts*. We have not attempted to offer models or representations that will enable the isolated, universal thinker to form an inner mental "picture" as an aid in grasping how things in general "hang together." Accounts are used at just those points in the flow of continuous communicative activity between people, when the "reality" constructed in that activity is at issue. They work in that context to direct people's attention to crucial features of the context, features that "show" connections between things that otherwise would go unnoticed.

The method we have employed involves doing self-consciously what is done by ordinary people in their everyday, nonrepresentational, responsive relations with each other, that is, creating a vocabulary in terms that make the nature of our background activities apparent in some way, that is, to account for them in *an* orderly fashion, in just *one* possibly useful way among others. "We want to establish an order in our knowledge of the use of language: an order with a particular end in view; one out of many possible orders; not *the* order. To this end we shall constantly be giving prominence to distinctions which our ordinary forms of language easily make us overlook" (Wittgenstein, 1953, no. 132). Thus, as Wittgenstein said about his invention of the notion of language games, they were not set up as ideal models or analogies, as a part of the usual preliminary to attempting to seek a final, theoretical *analysis* of our knowledge of language, in terms of a hidden, underlying *essence*, represented in a mentally surveyable "picture" or other "orderly scheme" of some kind. It is not beneath the surface that we should seek the phenomena of interest to us, for, to the extent that in practice we succeed in understanding one another without such an analysis, all the phenomena of interest must already be there, on the surface.

This is also to say that to "see" this practical order, this temporally developing order of possibilities or potentialities, only in terms of an already established, single, decontextualized, theoretical order is to falsify it. Indeed, the simple completeness of a spatial structure "forgets" the intrinsic incompleteness of a temporal or historical reality, of which there is always more to come and that contains, in some as yet unrealized form, this more.[19]

This practical use of invented models is, then, a new methodology to supplement that of attempting to represent states of affairs in terms of such theories or models. Instead of a monological rationality aimed at discovering a single underlying "reality," we propose a dialogically developing rationality aimed at making connections between what we already know implicitly in practice, but have not yet explicitly formulated in agreed terms, that works rhetorically in terms of "seeing connections" between potential differences— a practical rationality, or rationality-through-responsive-contrasts.

For our concerns, the dialogical character of rationality, and the nature of the situated, embodied, practical-moral knowledges it involves, is crucial. We say "knowledges" because (following Haraway, 1991) such knowledges are not general, but partial, associated with the different positions people occupy in different situations. In contrast to the traditional passive-individualistic paradigm, these knowledges are situated versus decontextualized, positioned versus universal, historical versus timeless, interested versus disinterested, embodied versus disembodied, pluralistic (two-sided even) versus unified, ethical versus instrumental, dialogical versus monological, and accountable to an audience versus provable within a formal system.

It is also this last characteristic—social accountability—that moves us beyond the accusation of an "anything goes" relativism, an accusation often leveled at social constructionist accounts of the nature of knowledge. It is in meeting this challenge that we can show the situated-developmental-relational paradigm at work: In terms of the passive-individualistic paradigm, there is presumed to be some basic, asocial, acultural, ahistorical system or framework of knowledge to which to appeal in determining the nature of true knowledge; traditionally, that is what proper objective knowledge is. In terms of that same paradigm, relativism is the claim that, when we turn to the examination of such systems or frameworks, none can be taken as basic in the way meant; all knowledge turns out to be relative to a specific theoretical framework, a form of life, a historical period, a culture, and so on. And, as there can be no overarching framework from within which to compare and to adjudicate claims to knowledge, there can be no escape from the predicament of being trapped within one's own self-contained rationality, which must just be judged as different than others—as there is no way in which it can be judged as better or worse. Rorty (1989), for instance, comes very close to making such claims when, in arguing for his insistence upon the contingent nature of "human nature" and against any claims in terms of ideas like "essence," "nature," and "foundation," he suggests that "what counts as being a decent human being is relative to historical circumstances, a matter of transient consensus about what attitudes are normal and what practices are just or unjust" (p. 189).

In terms of the new paradigm we have introduced, the problem of relativism takes on a quite different character. While it does not allow an instant, monological, computational-kind rationality, it does allow for a slow, back-and-forth development of a contested but negotiable practical understanding. Further, such contests and negotiations are not of an "anything goes" kind, but they are not grounded in any predetermined, outside, systematic standards either. They are "rooted" in the developed and developing conversational contexts within which the practical negotiations take place. As Haraway (1991) realizes, both traditional objectivism and relativism are ideal, God's-eye views from nowhere. "Relativism is a way of being nowhere while claiming to be everywhere equally. The 'equality' of positioning is a denial of responsibility and critical inquiry" (p. 191). Situated knowledges, by contrast, give rise to responsible knowledge claims, claims for which one can be accountable to the others around one, claims that can be sooner or later evaluated by others, in the still developing context one shares (or can come to share) with them.

This does not mean, however, that the current arguments—our own propositional standpoint—in any way disclose that final form of life that we all, as human beings, *should* live. There is no attempt here at a "God's-eye view." For our task in the future is just as much a task of making as of finding. Each time we encounter a limitation upon our forms of knowledge—as we did in revealing our entrapment in the traditional epistemological paradigm—we must try to identify it by contrasting our knowledge practices with alternatives and in the process distinguish that which is due to our relationships with each other and that which is other than, or beyond, them. Instead of, as individuals, working out from a firm foundation in "the real" to assess the soundness of various claims to knowledge, it is only from within contestable forms of social life, we claim, that we can reach out to that which is other than ourselves. For it is only in terms of the procedures and devices, the conceptual prosthetics such relations make available, that we are able to detect, fix, and establish, culturally and historically, such differences. But this is a process to which, of course, there is no foreseeable end, either in theory or in practice.

NOTES

1. We are aware that focusing upon the practical context of everyday conversational exchanges in this way opens up something of a gap between the version of social constructionism we explore here and poststructuralist accounts focused more upon the study of texts and text analogues. We feel that the bridging of this gap is an extremely interesting project—particularly that of exploring the part played by disciplinary texts in the constitution of a professional academic group—but do not have the space to attempt this here, however.

2. As both Nagel (1985) and Haraway (1991), for instance, point out, the construction of the ideal of a disinterested, disembodied, "objective" view of everything from nowhere entails the use of carefully devised procedures by which those at the center of things can seemingly detach themselves from their own particular makeup, from the social and political features of their everyday world, even from the human condition as such, to justify a claim to a God's-eye view of things. By contrast (in accord with Haraway), we shall argue only for a "situated objectivity," for the value of positioned, embodied, and accountable claims to knowledge, for the importance of views from somewhere, that is, for claims that can be justified by the giving of good reasons for them, in the context of their utterance.

3. A practice that can, of course, once it is established, just as the current passive-individualistic paradigm, give rise to a tradition of argumentation providing the context for a whole new tradition of empirical research.

4. Bernstein (1983, pp. 38-44) links his talk of practical-moral knowledge to Aristotle's concept of *phronesis*: the idea of wisdom in action, of a socially accountable moral intelligence.

5. Here Gadamer is following Heidegger. Heidegger was concerned to articulate an account of our being in the world, not from the position of an external observer merely contemplating it—the view from "nowhere"—but from a position of active involvement within it, where the different kinds of ways in which we might be involved in our surroundings—seeing entities as available for our use, or as entities with which to communicate, or as requiring destruction or salvation, and so on—influences how we see and act in those surroundings. Thus what surrounds us, what we see as immediately ready-to-hand within them, "is always understood in terms of a totality of involvements. This totality need not be grasped explicitly by a thematic interpretation. Even if it has undergone such an interpretation, it recedes into an understanding which does not stand out from the background. The essential foundation for everyday circumspective interpretation rests in this very mode. In every case this interpretation is grounded in *something we have in advance*—in a *fore-having*" (Heidegger, 1967, p. 191). Thus our ordinary, everyday understanding is always unique to, and "rooted in," its own concrete circumstances. In other words, the fore-having of Heidegger does not always give rise to the fore-structure of Gadamer; an (orderly) fore-structure arises when an (unordered) fore-having is interpreted thematically. For instance, in constructing the view from "nowhere" for ourselves, to take what we feel to be an "objective" position, we of course exclude our involvements and assume (though impossible) a complete disinterestedness—and fail to appreciate the countless different ways of seeing, thinking, speaking, acting, and evaluating associated with a practical way of being in the world. We must be careful to note the implicit themes or "pictures" in terms of which we—trained as we have been into certain disciplinary fore-structures of understanding—attempt to make sense of everyday phenomena in our reflections upon them.

6. Nancy Fraser (1989, p. 10) has also emphasized the need to insist upon "a plurality of agents and discourses" and for those who have put discourse at the center of their concerns "to develop an alternative to currently fashionable discourse theories that suppose a single, monolithic, 'symbolic order.' "

7. We bring out the nature of what *we* do, *our* practices, by comparison with what others (actual and invented) do, or don't do. While we will elaborate further upon this methodology below, two comments are worth making here: (a) As Taylor (1990) points out, the importance of contrasts is in their creation of a linguistic dimension in terms of which to articulate the character of things that were formerly left unnoticed in the background. For example, we shall articulate

the important, distinctive features of what is involved in knowing other people—until recently completely ignored as in any way a crucial issue—by contrasting it with what is involved in knowing objects. (b) It is also worth repeating what Wittgenstein said (1953, no. 130) about why he invented the metaphor of language games: "Our clear and simple language-games are not preparatory studies for a future regularization of language—as it were approximations, ignoring friction and air resistance. The language-games are rather set up as *objects of comparison* which are meant to throw light on the facts of our language by way not only of similarities, but also of dissimilarities" (no. 130). "The question is not one of explaining a language-game by means of our experiences, but of noting a language-game" (no. 655), that is, of (mentally) *seeing* what is being done with words in a particular context, as in our ordinary, practical affairs. If we always had to understand a person's reply to our questions, say, by use of logical analysis to *explain* them, the ordinary play of questions and answers in everyday life would be impossible. Some things we just do understand in practice without the need of any analysis or explanation.

8. To quote the full title of his *Discourse on Method* of 1637.

9. The term *man* here expresses both the humanism and the patriarchy implicit in Enlightenment thought. The degree to which this usage grates upon one's sensibilities is an indication of how far we have moved from these views. We will continue with this usage only to the end of the paragraph.

10. Some may want to call what we provide here "theory." We will not disagree. But we do wish to point out that in no way are we providing "representations" that could be judged as "corresponding with reality" in any way. What we are doing is providing a vocabulary of justificatory ultimates to which to appeal in accounting for otherwise puzzling conversational activities (see Mills, 1940/1975). In effect, we are saying "*attend to X* if you want to grasp the crucial features that give you insight into the issue in question here."

11. A "sui generis fear of history, an ambition to locate a world beyond the social and the historical" is, as Volosinov (1976, p. 14) sees it, a basic motif in "contemporary bourgeois philosophy." As Rorty (1989, p. 189) says, what "I have been urging in this book is that we try *not* to want something that stands beyond history and institutions."

12. For example, a student experimenter engages a "victim" subject as follows: "(Subject) 'I had a flat tire.' (Experimenter) 'What do you mean, you had a flat tire?' . . . (Subject) 'What do you mean, "What do you mean?" ' A flat tire is a flat tire. That is what I meant. Nothing special. What a crazy question!" (format modified, Garfinkel, 1967, p. 42).

13. What one has learned to do in thinking conceptually is not to compare the configuration of a supposed inner mental representation with the configuration of a state of affairs in one's surroundings but is something else much more complicated: One has grasped how to organize and assemble in a socially intelligible way—that is, a way that makes sense to the others around one—bits and pieces of information dispersed in space and time in accordance with "instructions" they (those others) provided and that now a supposed "concept" provides. It is "the functional use of the word, or any other sign, as means of focusing one's attention, selecting distinctive features and analyzing and synthesizing them, that plays a central role in concept formation" (Vygotsky, 1986, p. 106). Thus we know in practice what "marital trouble" is when we see it and, to other friends of Sarah and Sam, we will tell (no doubt) of other evidence of their misfortunes.

14. It is worth recalling here Mead's (1934) remark that "the mechanism of meaning is present in the social act before the emergence of consciousness or awareness of meaning occurs. The act or adjustive response of the second organism gives to the gesture of the first organism the meaning it has" (pp. 77-78).

15. "Etymologically, of course, the term 'consciousness' is a knowledge word. This is evidenced by the Latin form, *-sci-*, in the middle of the word. But what are we to make of the prefix *con-* that precedes it? Look at the usage of the term in Roman Law and the answer will be easy enough. Two or more agents who act jointly—having formed a common intention, framed a plan, and concerted their actions—are as a result *conscientes*. They act as they do knowing one another's plans: they act *jointly knowing*" (Toulmin, 1982, p. 64).

16. "In actual fact, each living sign has two faces, like Janus. Any current curse word can become a word of praise, any current truth must inevitably sound to many other people the greatest lie. This *inner dialectic quality* of the sign comes out fully into the open only in times of social crises or revolutionary changes" (Volosinov, 1973, p. 23).

17. "Within its own limits, every discipline recognizes true and false propositions, but it repulses a whole teratology of learning" (Foucault, 1972, p. 223).

18. They discuss, for instance, how Oliver North avoids a possibly incriminating position by beginning his testimony at one point by saying, "I'm working without refreshed recall, let me do the best I can to remember back to that period of time" (quoted in Edwards & Potter, 1992, p. 43).

19. In this sense, it is a mistake to use the notion of language games—representing ways of talking governed by rules—as a theoretical device in an attempt to *explain* linguistic phenomena. Their function is as linguistic "prosthetic" devices, through which to "see" linguistic phenomena in the light of the indefinite, but ordered vocabulary of terms they provide. Language games, like many of Wittgenstein's other metaphors—of language as a "tool-box," a "city," the "handles in a locomotive cab"—are, as he says, set up as "objects of comparison" with the purpose of producing that kind of understanding that consists in seeing connections. And this, of course, is precisely the kind of practical understanding being aimed at in rhetorical argumentation, where what is important is not the demonstration of connections in terms of logical proofs but the practical grasp by an audience of the connection that ties together two claims in an issue being debated.

REFERENCES

Antaki, C. (Ed.). (1988). *Analysing everyday explanation: A casebook of methods*. London: Sage.

Austin, J. L. (1962). *How to do things with words*. Oxford: Clarendon.

Bakhtin, M. M. (1981). *The dialogical imagination* (M. Holquist, Ed.; C. Emerson & M. Holquist, Trans.). Austin: University of Texas Press.

Bakhtin, M. M. (1986). *Speech genres and other late essays* (V. W. McGee, Trans.). Austin: University of Texas Press.

Barnes, B. (1974). *Sociological theory and scientific knowledge*. London: Routledge & Kegan Paul.

Barnes, B. (1986). *About science*. Oxford: Basil Blackwell.

Berger, P., & Luckmann, T. (1966). *The social construction of reality*. New York: Doubleday.

Bernstein, R. J. (1983). *Beyond objectivism and relativism*. Oxford: Basil Blackwell.

Billig, M. (1991). *Ideology and opinions: Studies in rhetorical psychology*. London: Sage.

Billig, M., Condor, S., Edwards, D., Gane, M., Middleton, D., & Radley, R. (1988). *Ideological dilemmas*. London: Sage.

Bloor, D. (1976). *Knowledge and social imagery*. London: Routledge & Kegan Paul.

Cassirer, E. (1951). *The philosophy of the Enlightenment*. Princeton, NJ: Princeton University Press.

Code, L. (1991). *What can she know? Feminist theory and the construction of knowledge*. Ithaca, NY: Cornell University Press.

Collins, H. (1985). *Changing order: Replication and induction in scientific practice*. Beverly Hills, CA: Sage.

Le Corbusier. (1971). *The city of tomorrow and its planning*. Cambridge: MIT Press.

Danziger, K. (1990). *Constructing the subject: Historical origins of psychological research*. Cambridge: Cambridge University Press.

Deetz, S. (1992). *Democracy in an age of corporate colonization: Developments in communication and the politics of everyday life*. Albany: State University of New York Press.

De Man, P. (1983). Literary history and literary modernity. In *Blindness and insight: Essays in the rhetoric of contemporary criticism*. London: Methuen.

Derrida, J. (1976). *Of grammatology* (G. Spivak, Trans.). Baltimore, MD: Johns Hopkins University Press.

Derrida, J. (1988). *Limited inc.* Evanston, IL: Northwestern University Press.

Descartes, R. (1986). *Meditations on first philosophy: With selections from objections and replies* (J. Cottingham, Trans.). Cambridge: Cambridge University Press. (Original work published 1641)

Edwards, D., & Potter, J. (1992). *Discursive psychology*. London: Sage.

Edwards, J. C. (1982). *Ethics without philosophy: Wittgenstein and the moral life*. Tampa: University of South Florida.

Flax, J. (1990). *Thinking fragments: Psychoanalysis, feminism, and postmodernism in the contemporary West*. Berkeley: University of California Press.

Foucault, M. (1970). *The order of things: An archaeology of the human sciences*. London: Tavistock.

Foucault, M. (1972). *The archaeology of knowledge*. New York: Harper Colophon.

Fraser, N. (1989). *Unruly practices: Power, discourse and gender in contemporary social theory*. Oxford: Polity.

Fuller, S. (1988). *Social epistemology*. Bloomington: Indiana University Press.

Gadamer, H. (1975). *Truth and method*. London: Sheed and Ward.

Garfinkel, H. (1967). *Studies in ethnomethodology*. Englewood Cliffs, NJ: Prentice-Hall.

Geertz, C. (1979). On the nature of anthropological understanding. In P. Rabinow & W. M. Sullivan (Eds.), *Interpretative social science: A reader*. Berkeley: University of California Press.

Gergen, K. J. (1982). *Toward transformation in social knowledge*. New York: Springer.

Gergen, K. J. (1985). The social constructionist movement in modern psychology. *American Psychologist, 40,* 266-275.

Gergen, K. J. (1989). Social psychology and the wrong revolution. *European Journal of Social Psychology, 19*, 463-484.

Gergen, K. J. (1991). *The saturated self: Dilemmas of identity in contemporary life*. New York: Basic Books.

Gergen, K. J., & Davis, K. E. (Eds.). (1985). *The social construction of the person*. New York: Springer-Verlag.

Gergen, K. J., & Gergen, M. M. (1988). Narrative and the self as relationship. In L. Berkowitz (Ed.), *Advances in experimental social psychology* (Vol. 21). New York: Academic Press.

Giddens, A. (1984). *The constitution of society*. Cambridge: Polity.

Haraway, D. J. (1991). Situated knowledges: The science question in feminism and the privilege of partial perspective. In *Simians, cyborgs, and women: The reinvention of nature*. London: Free Association Books.

Harré, R. (1983). *Personal being: A theory for individual psychology*. Oxford: Basil Blackwell.

Harré, R. (1986). The social construction of selves. K. Yardley & T. Honess (Eds.), *Self and identity*. Chichester, England: John Wiley.

Heidegger, M. (1967). *Being and time*. Oxford: Basil Blackwell.

Knorr-Cetina, K. (1981). *The manufacture of knowledge: An essay of the constructivist and contextual nature of science*. Oxford: Pergamon.

Kosinski, J. D. (1970). *Being there*. New York: Harcourt Brace Jovanovich.

Latour, B., & Woolgar, S. (1979). *Laboratory life: The construction of scientific facts*. London: Sage.

Lyotard, J. (1984). *The postmodern condition: A report on knowledge*. Minneapolis: University of Minnesota Press.

MacIntyre, A. (1981). *After virtue*. London: Duckworth.

Mead, G. H. (1934). *Mind, self and society*. Chicago: University of Chicago Press.

Middleton, D., & Edwards, D. (1990). Conversational remembering: A social psychological approach. In D. Middleton & D. Edwards (Eds.), *Collective remembering*. London: Sage.

Mills, C. W. (1975). Situated actions and vocabularies of motive. In D. Brisset & C. Edgley (Eds.), *Life as theater: A dramaturgical sourcebook*. Chicago: Aldine. (Original work published 1940)

Mulkay, M. (1985). *The Word and the world*. London: George Allen & Unwin.

Nagel, T. (1985). *The view from nowhere*. New York: Oxford University Press.

Pearce, W. R., & Cronen, V. (1980). *Communication, action and meaning*. New York: Praeger.

Peters, R. S. (1958). *The concept of motivation*. London: Routledge & Kegan Paul.

Potter, J., & Wetherell, M. (1987). *Discourse and social psychology: Beyond attitudes and behaviour*. London: Sage.

Rorty, R. (1980). *Philosophy and the mirror of nature*. Oxford: Basil Blackwell.

Rorty, R. (1989). *Contingency, irony and solidarity*. Cambridge: Cambridge University Press.

Sabini, J., & Silver, M. (1986). Envy. In R. Harré (Ed.), *The social construction of emotions*. Oxford: Basil Blackwell.

Semin, G. R., & Manstead, A. S. R. (1983). *The accountability of conduct: A social psychological analysis*. London: Academic Press.

Shotter, J. (1980). Action, joint action, and intentionality. In M. Brenner (Ed.), *The structure of action*. Oxford: Basil Blackwell.

Shotter, J. (1984). *Social accountability and selfhood*. Oxford: Basil Blackwell.

Shotter, J. (1987). The social construction of an "us": Problems of accountability and narratology. In R. Burnett, P. McGee, & D. Clarke (Eds.), *Accounting for personal relationships*. London: Methuen.

Shotter, J. (1992). What is a "personal" relationship? A rhetorical-responsive account of "unfinished business." In J. H. Harvey, T. L. Orbuch, & A. L. Weber (Eds.), *Attributions, accounts, and close relationships*. New York: Springer-Verlag.

Shotter, J. (1993). *Cultural politics of everyday life: Social constructionism, rhetoric, and knowing of the third kind*. Milton Keynes, UK: Open University Press/Toronto: Toronto University Press.

Sigman, S. (1987). *A perspective on social communication*. Lexington, MA: Lexington.

Smith, D. (1988). *The everyday world as problematic: A feminist sociology*. Milton Keynes, UK: Open University Press.

Taylor, C. (1989). *Sources of the self: The making of the modern identity*. Cambridge, MA: Harvard University Press.

Taylor, C. (1990). Comparison, history, truth. In F. E. Reynolds & D. Tracy (Eds.), *Myth and philosophy*. Albany: State University of New York Press.

Toulmin, S. (1982). The genealogy of "consciousness." In P. F. Secord (Ed.), *Explaining human behavior: Consciousness, human action, and social structure*. Beverly Hills, CA: Sage.

Volosinov, V. N. (1973). *Marxism and the philosophy of language* (L. Matejka & I. R. Titunik, Trans.). Cambridge, MA: Harvard University Press.

Volosinov, V. N. (1976). *Freudianism: A critical sketch*. Bloomington: Indiana University Press.

Vygotsky, L. S. (1978). *Mind in society: The development of higher psychological processes* (M. Cole, V. John-Steiner, S. Scribner, & E. Souberman, Eds.). Cambridge, MA: Harvard University Press.

Vygotsky, L. S. (1986). *Thought and language* (A. Kozulin, Trans.). Cambridge: MIT Press.

Wittgenstein, L. (1953). *Philosophical investigations*. Oxford: Basil Blackwell.

Woolgar, S. (1988). *Science: The very idea*. London: Tavistock.

Recovering Agency

W. BARNETT PEARCE
Loyola University of Chicago

SHOTTER and Gergen claim that they "set out the central lineaments of social constructionism as they are relevant to communication studies" (p. 3). If this is their purpose, they do not succeed. If you are looking for a social constructionist perspective on communication, you will not find it here. What you will find is a rather glib characterization of conversation ("situated, developmental, and relational") as a way of giving a social constructionist account of epistemology. While I have nothing against an essay on epistemology, even in *Communication Yearbook*, it is not quite the same thing as the social constructionist account of communication that the first sentence promises.

In my commentary, I try to differentiate what Shotter and Gergen actually accomplish (and it is far from trivial) from what a social constructionist account of communication might be. I focus on being sufficiently emancipated from the "old paradigm" so that its thematics are not thoughtlessly reproduced in the new and also on the thematic of "agency," which I believe is essential to a communication perspective on social constructionism. Without foregrounding communication and without a sufficient emancipation from the old paradigm, "agency" is likely to be given a much smaller place than the logic of social constructionism should afford it; and, without a sufficiently rich concept of agency, a social constructionist account of communication is necessarily impoverished.

WHAT HAVE SHOTTER AND GERGEN DONE?

The essay that Shotter and Gergen wrote and submitted for publication in this *Yearbook* is an "act," of course, and, like any other act, it is performed both *from* a context and *into* a context. The meaning of the essay (again, like any other act) depends on these contexts.

Correspondence and requests for reprints: W. Barnett Pearce, Communication Department, Loyola University of Chicago, Chicago, IL 60611.

Communication Yearbook 17, pp. 34-41

For example, Gergen recently lectured about social constructionism to a packed room at Loyola University of Chicago. In the following days, I found widely divergent reactions to his talk. Many of my friends from the psychology department were outraged at the radical position he took; but most of my friends from the sociology/anthropology department were unimpressed, saying that these ideas were familiar and not very sophisticated. Like beauty, outrageousness, it appears, is in the eye of the beholder. I believe that Gergen is capable of outraging *any* audience; in this instance, his remarks were skillfully tailored to the psychologists and psychophiles in the room.

Who did Shotter and Gergen have in mind as they wrote, revised, and edited this essay? There is ample reason to believe that psychologists and psychophiles working within the intellectual framework of the Enlightenment were the intended audience.

Note these four features. (a) The Enlightenment's preoccupation with epistemology is continued throughout the essay. The central question is this: "How can we *know*?" And *we* are professional knowers, academics in a discipline. (b) The issue of paradigm change is foregrounded. Unlike Kuhn's hypothesis of irrational "revolutionary" shifts, Shotter and Gergen offer a deceptively gentle description of all paradigms as being socially constructed.[1] In this view, paradigm change is a choice among alternatives. (c) The final section confronts the specter of relativity. No issue is so relevant to those who are deeply enmeshed in the Enlightenment's search for positive knowledge. Bernstein (1983) coined the phrase *Cartesian Anxiety* for the neurosis in which absolute certainty is taken as the minimal criterion for "knowing" and no meaningful distinctions are made among knowledge claims failing to attain this standard. (d) The essay contains a long summary of the most salient features of the Enlightenment's philosophy as it pertains to personhood and draws on Gergen's recent *The Saturated Self* to differentiate modern, romantic, and postmodern vocabularies of self.

These features suggest that Shotter and Gergen have "done" an apologia, a presentation of the social constructionist perspective to "outsiders" with a view toward either legitimating social constructionism as one among many viable perspectives or recruiting "old paradigmers" to social constructionism. Apologia are useful, perhaps necessary, and I will allow the essay to stand on its own merits for this purpose. In what follows, I focus on the essay as a contribution *to* social constructionist thought and practice, particularly its ability to enhance our understanding of communication.

SITING CONVERSATION

As part of the conversation among social constructionists, the primary contribution of this essay comes from its explicit focus on "the conversational context of everyday life." Shotter and Gergen cite conversation as the site "in which everything of intellectual importance both originates and is judged as worthy or not of further attention; such importance develops in the activities occurring *between* people" (p. 4).

This siting stands opposed to the analysis of whole texts or linguistic resources. That is, Shotter and Gergen are here declaring their independence from "literary deconstructionists" and refusing to privilege literary criticism as the model for social constructionist inquiry. This declaration should be heard as a part of extended conversations with Rorty's (1989) version of pragmatism and the "rhetoric of inquiry" movement (e.g., Simons, 1990). The implication of Shotter and Gergen's siting of conversation is to foreswear even the attempt to resolve "theoretical problems" in the ambivalences and indeterminacies of meaning that arise in texts in favor of focusing on the ways that speakers "in the living moment" continually confront and deal with these issues. The result is not a "coherent theory" applying to a "simple unitary domain" but a set of "instructive statements" that are part of a new paradigm.

The paradigm whose roots are in the Enlightenment is termed "passive-individualistic." In its place, Shotter and Gergen want (a) to call into being by means of this essay and their other work, (b) to invite others to join, and (c) to argue for the legitimacy of a paradigm characterized as "situated-developmental-relational."

"BAD ARGUMENT"

In a very precise sense, any effective apologia must employ "bad argument" (Rorty, 1979, p. 58). If paradigms are incommensurate, then what counts as a "good argument" in one paradigm will seem "bad" if heard in the context of another. "Bad argument," however, is necessary at the interface of two paradigms if one is to be comprehensible in the other. That is, if people working within the "passive-individualist" paradigm are to understand the "situated-developmental-relational" paradigm, the arguments for the latter must be expressed in the terms of the former, no matter how awkward or disingenuous those arguments seem from within the "situated-developmental-relational" paradigm.[2]

As an apologia, Shotter and Gergen's essay has two lines of bad argument. By calling them into the foreground, I hope to illuminate certain distinctive features of the social constructionist perspective.

Epistemology First!

Expressed most clearly by Descartes's search for something that he could not doubt, the Enlightenment foregrounded the question: "How can I know?" Actually, this only extended a longer tradition rooted in Plato's victory over the sophists.

Plato sharply criticized the sophists (personified by Gorgias) because they believed that reality was too slippery to be captured by thought and language. That is, Gorgias believed that "knowing," "reality," and "speech" were incommensurate, such that we cannot "know" reality and, if we could, we could not "communicate" it.[3] Persuasion, not epistemology, was thus primary. At the risk of committing an anachronism, one might say that Gorgias believed that knowledge was "situated, developmental, and relational" (see Engnell, 1973; Enos, 1976; Pearce & Foss, 1990).

If Gorgias had "won" the paradigm war with Plato, social constructionism might be the dominant paradigm today. Unfortunately, Plato carried the day by derogating the sophists as developing a "knack" rather than an "art" based on true knowledge and for offering their services to make the "worse" appear the "better." For whatever reason, Plato believed that reality consisted of immutable, eternal entities and that the only legitimate form of knowledge was of such things. From the sophists' perspective, Plato's was a crippling superstition; from Plato's perspective, the sophists substituted mere opinion for true knowledge. Ironically, despite Plato's fulminations against writing, he "won" the paradigm wars largely because his writings were better preserved than those of the sophists.

That great systemizer Aristotle, of course, tried to make space for both perspectives. "Rhetoric," he opined in the opening of *The Rhetoric*, "is the counterpart of dialectic." That means that you use rhetoric (like the sophists developed) in situations where dialectic (like Plato taught) would not work. In the *Nicomachean Ethics*, Aristotle differentiated three "domains" of human experience and described the "knowing" appropriate for each. *Episteme* is appropriate for *theoria*, but this kind of knowing is limited to "things that have to be what they are." That is, epistemology is a part of what Rorty (1979) called "spectator knowledge" in which the knower is over here and that which is known is over there. The epistemological question—or, more precisely, the conundrum—is how that which is over here can "know" that which is over there.

Communication clearly does not have to be what it is. Communication is, as Shotter and Gergen note, "situated, developmental, and relational." It is a part of what Aristotle called *praxis*, that is, those things that can be other than they are. Aristotle's examples of praxis included public speaking, statesmanship, and household management; in each, good judgment or *phronesis* is more appropriate than "knowledge." That is, the primary question for communicators is not so much "How *can* I know?" or even "What *do* I know?" as it is "What *should* I do?"

If the social constructionist perspective on communication shows it to be a form of praxis, then Shotter and Gergen's preoccupation with epistemology seems to me "bad argument." If I did not know better, I would infer that they were insufficiently emancipated from the old paradigm and hence insensitive to the thematics indigenous to the new paradigm that they are articulating.

Assuming that their essay is an apologia, however, I want to add to it the claim that, if we move into a social constructionist perspective, epistemology is not nearly so central an issue as it once was.

Conversation and Social Constructionism

In the social constructionist paradigm, Shotter and Gergen argue, epistemology is like conversation. That is, both are situated, developmental, and relational. While I agree with this statement, this is the place where I think their essay fails to accomplish the claim made for it in its opening sentence.

Specifically, Shotter and Gergen use a rather superficial characterization of conversation as a simile for epistemology; they do *not* use any of the social constructionist paradigm as a way of illuminating conversation.[4] To put it bluntly: If epistemology is like conversation, what is conversation like?

The problem lies in the literary figure of simile. I believe that, while human life *is* metaphorical, we only *use* similes to make rather crude comparisons. Similes reproduce the ocular metaphor of knowledge: The speaker says that, from here, two things look alike. The ocular metaphor reconstitutes the separation of knower from the known and thus continues some of the most venal parts of the old paradigm.

Understood as an apologia, Shotter and Gergen's essay may be understood as deliberately engaging in bad argument. Even so, however, as a contribution to *Communication Yearbook*, we might expect to find something more illuminating about communication. Let me plead guilty to selfish motives: While I'm pleased that an analysis of communication (even at such a superficial level as in this essay) contributes to social constructionism, we should also explore what social constructionism contributes to our understanding of communication.

"GOOD ARGUMENTS"

Let me develop two arguments within the social constructionist paradigm that cast light on communication. Facetiously, I call these "good arguments" in the same technical sense introduced above: They make sense *within* the social constructionist perspective but not within other traditions.

What Communication Does

If epistemology is the primary thematic in the "passive-individualist" paradigm, ontology (from *ontos*, the participle of the Greek verb *eimi*, "to be") has that place of pride in the social constructionist paradigm. That is, the primary question is this: "What exists?" The whole meaning of "being," however, undergoes a radical transformation in the social constructionist paradigm. Ontology is *not* an inventory of (as Plato would have it) immutable, eternal things that (as Aristotle would say) have to be what they are. Rather, ontology is a method for discerning local, temporary, contingent configurations of conversations. That is, it is not just that epistemology or reality has attributes *like* those of conversation. Rather, the events and objects of the human world comprise particular configurations of conversations.

The most immediate implication of this notion is that there is no "gap" between ontology and activity, no "distance" between the events/objects of the human world and the conversations in which we participate. The human world is in a condition of continual creation; our next act inevitably and unavoidably adds something to reality. As a result, the epistemological question of how our minds over here can "know" reality over there is nonsense, as is the notion that propositions suitable for being written on a chalkboard are the proper form of knowledge claims.

The work communication does is to make things, not talk about them. Conversations are the ontological "stuff" of the human world, not just a place where this stuff is shaped. At this point, we need some intense intramural debate about the same issues that Gorgias raised. What are the relationships among "reality," "experience," and "language"? Are these best understood as three things or are two or more the same thing? Imagine a set of Venn diagrams. Is "experience" (understood, as Dewey put it, as "forming coordinations" rather than "sensory stimulations") inside "language" or *vice versa*? Is "language" a *part* of reality or the *context* for it? Does our *use* of language distort reality or constitute it?

Recovering Agency

Some versions of social constructionism reproduce the "third person perspective" of the "passive-individualist" paradigm. A "first person perspective" is one of the distinctive features of the long history of the academic study of communication. In fact, the sharp contrast between the objective, sophisticated pretensions of the "third person perspective" and the more practical immediate utility of the "first person perspective" accounts for the low esteem in which we have been often held by more mainstream disciplines. Rhetoric began with the very practical question of how to win legal cases; the content of rhetoric was offered to the rhetor who had to argue the case. That is, it aspired to *phronesis*, not epistemology.

Social constructionism has affinities with Continental hermeneutics and the cluster of approaches that might be labeled "discourse theories." This is a dangerous intellectual alliance, however, because these approaches focus on whole texts, discursive formations, and speech communities rather than on the lived moments of social interaction. That is, they are part of an intellectual climate that favors macrotheories and dismisses particular cases.

Rhetoric's traditional preferential option for the perspective of the rhetor often gets lost when social constructionism gets too comfortable with discourse theories. At its best, traditional rhetoric focused on the agent who sought either to move effectively within a given situation or to reconstruct that situation; discourse theories focus on the epistemological consequences of being "in" language.

My own work in the coordinated management of meaning (Pearce, 1989; Pearce & Cronen, 1980) is a communication theory that attempts to retain this focus on the agent. The whole notion of "implicative forces" and "reflexivity" in CMM is *not* an attempt to reconcile micro- and macro-social theories but to understand how particular actions change or reproduce the contexts into which they are performed. Without this set of concepts (or some comparable ones), we are distanced from the analysis of any particular instance of communication and we have a little (but only a little) to say to individuals who must/want to take actions to change the circumstances in which they live.

I am not suggesting that a "return" to traditional rhetoric is the way to develop a social constructionist concept of agency, but at least its preferential option for the perspective of the rhetor is something that we can borrow from it—and this is an essential aspect of a social constructionist account of communication.

To their credit, Shotter and Gergen intend to "pick up the rejected shards of the Enlightenment tradition—the practical, everyday conversational activities, particularly those of a rhetorical and argumentative kind" (p. 13). My criticism is that they used these as a blunt object with which to batter an outmoded epistemology, not as jewels to be polished, placed into euphonious settings, and admired for what they are.

CONCLUSION

Shotter and Gergen have given us a powerful apologia for a social constructionist epistemology that sites conversation as the place where knowing and personhood develop. They conclude by affirming a dialectical, pluralistic epistemology grounded in mundane conversations and sharing their nature. In my comments, I have shown that this self-styled "postmodern" approach reaffirms the losing side of the Gorgias-Plato debates and consists of a social constructionist apologia addressed to psychophiles in the Enlightenment tradition. Using the "bad arguments" in the essay as information about specific points of incommensurability between the "passive-individualistic" paradigm and social constructionism, I argued that ontology rather than epistemology is the primary concern for social constructionists and that the meaning of what "exists" shifts from truth claims about immutable, eternal things to moral claims about local, temporary, mutable things. Finally, I cautioned against importing too much of the "linguistic turn" into social constructionism so as to maintain the historic and distinctive communication emphasis on the agent. While I agree with Shotter and Gergen about the need to differentiate ourselves from the model of literary criticism, they valorize conversations in principle without providing a set of concepts for actually engaging with specific conversations.

NOTES

1. The "deceptive" part of this gentleness lies in the subtle way Shotter and Gergen nominate the language game *of* their paradigm as the language game in which to talk *about* paradigms. This is a classic Russellian paradox that privileges their paradigm in any metaparadigmatic discussion.

2. Wittgenstein (1922, 6.54) concluded the *Tractatus* with a self-reflexive acknowledgment that he had been using "bad argument" in this sense. "My propositions are elucidatory in this way: he who understands me finally recognizes them as senseless, when he has climbed out through them, on them, over them. (He must so to speak throw away the ladder, after he has climbed up on it.)" This concept will be instantly recognizable in the contexts of Toulmin's "field dependent logic" or MacIntyre's notion of "argumentative traditions."

3. A certain kind of mind has little patience for these questions. Remember that the sophists were inveterate tricksters. The question of whether we can "know" or "communicate" anything of "reality" is not an existential question. Rather, it serves to call into question what we mean by "knowing" and "communication," to say nothing of "reality." As such, it is a powerful deconstructive move, exposing language games that can trap us.

4. I'm exaggerating, but only somewhat. The essay alludes to Shotter's concept of "joint action," which he has developed in other places in ways that are a very useful social constructionist perspective on communication. In the current essay, however, this work is backgrounded.

REFERENCES

Bernstein, R. J. (1983). *Beyond objectivism and relativism: Science, hermeneutics, and praxis.* Philadelphia: University of Pennsylvania Press.

Engnell, R. A. (1973). Implications for communication of the rhetorical epistemology of Gorgias of Leontini. *Western Speech, 37,* 175-184.

Enos, R. L. (1976). The epistemology of Gorgias' Rhetoric: A re-examination. *Southern Speech Communication Journal, 42,* 35-51.

Pearce, W. B. (1989). *Communication and the human condition.* Carbondale: Southern Illinois University Press.

Pearce, W. B., & Cronen, V. E. (1980). *Communication, action and meaning: The creation of social realities.* New York: Praeger.

Pearce, W. B., & Foss, K. A. (1990). The historical context of communication as a science. In G. L. Dahnke & G. W. Clatterbuck (Eds.), *Human communication: Theory and research* (pp. 1-20). Belmont, CA: Wadsworth.

Rorty, R. (1979). *Philosophy and the mirror of nature.* Princeton, NJ: Princeton University Press.

Rorty, R. (1989). *Contingency, irony, and solidarity.* New York: Cambridge University Press.

Simons, H. W. (1990). *The rhetorical turn: Invention and persuasion in the conduct of inquiry.* Chicago: University of Chicago Press.

Wittgenstein, L. (1922). *Tractatus logico-philosophicus.* London: Routledge & Kegan Paul.

Social Constructionism and Communication Studies: Hearing the Conversation But Losing the Dialogue

HUGH WILLMOTT

University of Manchester, England

AT the heart of Shotter and Gergen's wide-ranging and provocative account of social constructionism (hereafter "constructionism") there is a contradiction. Constructionism,[1] Shotter and Gergen argue, does not "in any way disclose that final form of life that we all, as human beings, *should* live. *There is no attempt here at a 'God's-eye view'* " (p. 28, second italics added). We are told that constructionism seeks to promote a "dialogical, multivoiced" tradition that "affords an extended array of positions . . . with the different positions all giving rise to their own 'situated knowledges' " (p. 8). At the same time, we are asked to take constructionism seriously—or, at least, seriously enough to accept the constructionist claim that to represent the practical, communicative order of everyday life in the manner of traditional epistemology *"is to falsify it"* (p. 27, italics added). What is to become of the position of traditional epistemology in the multivoiced tradition favored by constructionism? Is it to be treated as a voice of equal power and authority to that of constructionism; or is it to be treated as a voice that is irredeemably false?[2]

One way of developing this commentary would be to explore how Shotter and Gergen contrive to manage and efface the tensions of this contradiction. This response would have the merit of showing how our efforts to sustain an argument invariably harbor and suppress elements that threaten to derail it. Alternatively, this commentary could focus exclusively upon the most visible target of Shotter and Gergen's essay: traditional epistemology. In which case,

Correspondence and requests for reprints: Hugh Willmott, School of Management, University of Manchester, P.O. Box 88, Manchester M60 1QD, United Kingdom.

Communication Yearbook 17, pp. 42-54

questions could be raised about the unity and influence that Shotter and Gergen ascribe to this epistemology as well as about the coherence of their attack upon it. For me, however, the chief interest of their essay lies less in its contradictions or ascriptions than in its moral-practical commitment to develop an alternative conception and practice of "knowledge, self, and others."

What motivates Shotter and Gergen's constructionism, this commentary will emphasize, is not simply a (scholastic) concern to challenge, supplement, and/or replace traditional epistemology. It is also driven, more or less explicitly, by a moral-practical concern to remember, and thereby transform, the relationship between knowing (epistemology) and being (ontology).[3] Less philosophically, constructionism seeks to challenge the authority and value of modern traditions and practices in which the nature and significance of the connection between being and knowing has become distorted and suppressed. In the first section of the commentary, I elaborate this reading to indicate why Shotter and Gergen's constructionism is interesting and instructive: a voice worthy of engaging in close and critical conversation.

But I also want to argue that constructionism is tantalizing and ultimately unsatisfying. This is not because it harbors unresolved contradictions or is disinterested in recognizing their presence![4] No, my sense of disquiet with constructionism stems from doubts about the capacity of constructionism to facilitate the fulfillment of what I take to be its emancipatory intent: "to achieve a greater degree of freedom in relation to [our practices]" (p. 5). Despite holding out the possibility of a radical transformation of social practices, constructionism offers little insight, beyond its attentiveness to knowledge as "situated-developmental-relational" (p. 5), into how obstacles to the process of transformation may be addressed and overcome.

WHY CONSTRUCTIONISM IS INTERESTING: DEBUNKING MONOLOGICAL RATIONALITY

Constructionism is based upon the understanding that all knowledge, including scientific knowledge, is socially organized and lacks absolute foundations. In common with other phenomenological and hermeneutic traditions of social theory, all social practice is understood to rely upon particular, historically contingent sets of taken-for-granted assumptions in order to support and sustain their "good sense."[5] Each set of background assumptions is described as a "fore-structure of understanding" (hereafter FSU), a phrase drawn from Gadamer (1975; see Shotter & Gergen, this volume, p. 6).

Constructionism contends that when knowledge appears to rest upon a solid bedrock, this impression is indicative of an absence of reflexivity about the understandings that are shared and sustained (through processes of conversation) by those who believe in the sound authority of such authoritative knowledge. Although the presence and operation of the FSU is routinely unacknowledged, its presence is signaled whenever taken-for-granted "background expectancies" are breached (see Garfinkel, 1967). On such occasions, Shotter and Gergen (p. 6) observe, it becomes apparent how "others around us continually exert a morally coercive force *to be* persons of a particular kind, to assume a particular *identity*, and to exhibit a particular kind of *sensibility*." As I shall argue, however, not only is this compulsion routinely internalized so that our consciousness becomes identified with a particular sense of self-identity, and such that the scope of our actions become disciplined through our self-knowledge (Foucault, 1982). In addition, the routine exertion of moral pressure arises from an egotistical concern to ensure that others continue to reproduce the reality of the social media through which our taken-for-granted sense of self is routinely secured and expressed (Willmott, 1986). By problematizing the foundations of knowledge, constructionism shows that truths that seem to be well founded, if not self-evident, are actually achieved, precarious, and therefore vulnerable to challenge. But, as I shall argue later, constructionism continues to take for granted the presence and necessity of the self-expressive compulsion to exert a morally coercive force upon self and others.

The Constructionist Critique of Traditional Epistemology

Shotter and Gergen apply the constructionist critique of foundationalism to the claims of "traditional epistemology." This epistemology, they argue, is distinguished by its application of a single, seemingly authoritative standard of rationality to all research questions. Its *monological rationality* generates what appear to be definitive interpretations and assessments of the reality of diverse forms of knowledge and modes of being. Characterizing this mode of knowledge generation as the "I-it epistemological paradigm, the *passive-individualistic* paradigm" (p. 5), Shotter and Gergen (p. 5) contend that it "has been concerned with the ways in which isolated, unsituated, ideal individuals gain orderly knowledge of passive objects, objects that react to their probings and manipulations but that do not 'answer back.' "

A characteristic feature of the FSU of traditional epistemology, constructionism argues, is that its very operation dims awareness of how it acts to constitute and limit the range of questions that are addressed as well as the means of addressing them. It is only with a shift of paradigm that the presence and operation of FSUs become a topic of investigation rather than an unexplicated resource for reaffirming the authority of monological rationality. With this shift, it becomes apparent, or at least plausible to believe, that there is something problematic about the claims *and effects* of the I-it paradigm, including its normative urge (induced by everyday and scientific training in the disciplines of the I-it paradigm) to assimilate problems of interpersonal understanding to that of individuals gaining an orderly knowledge of objects (p. 5). For example, with a shift to the constructionist paradigm, it becomes possible to address such questions as " 'What, in practice, is involved in becoming and sustaining oneself as a person in a society in the midst of such contests [over theoretically undecidable issues]?' " (p. 4).

Constructionism and Critical Social Theory

It is relevant to note that constructionism's objection to the dominance of the monological rationality is shared by the wider tradition of critical social philosophy. For example, in his critique of Popper's (1963) philosophy of (social) science, which closely parallels Shotter and Gergen's appraisal of the I-it paradigm, Habermas (1976, pp. 203-204) argues that the facticity of statements is contingent upon how "testing conditions" are defined within the particular FSU, to use Shotter and Gergen's terminology, that underpins the production of (scientific) knowledge. The fetish of believing in the immaculate propagation of seemingly objective facts can be dispelled only through an appreciation of how this process rests upon a particular FSU and not upon a foundational bedrock.

Of course, from within the bubble of monological rationality, constructionist arguments are nonsensical.[6] It is deemed ludicrous to suggest that traditional epistemology lacks an adequate understanding of human communication or, more specifically, that it makes "incomprehensible" an appreciation of "language and people's participation in the construction of their own subjectivities" (p. 13). For the "I-it paradigm" understands itself to be *the* means of enlightening human beings by providing them with objectively valid knowledge—knowledge that dispels the illusions associated with erroneous, nescient forms of knowledge. As its knowledge is understood to be value-free, it is considered to have no morally coercive force. It simply provides the facts; it does not, and cannot, compel people to accept the facts. From this perspective, facts only acquire compulsive force by value commitments.

Against what may be characterized as the technocratic self-understanding of the I-it paradigm, the argument of critical social philosophy is that, in practice, monological rationality becomes morally compulsive in the absence of more reflexive traditions (e.g., constructionism, critical theory) that cast doubt upon the authority and value of its knowledge claims. Its effects, which Shotter and Gergen deem to be morally noxious, are exerted more by default (out of self-deluded ignorance) than by design. As I noted earlier, just as Habermas's critique of Popper's critical rationalism goes beyond a scholastic objection to its lack of reflexivity by seeking to expose its moral-political effects,[7] the intent of constructionism is to achieve "a greater degree of freedom" (Shotter & Gergen, p. 8) from (modern) social practices that are dominated by the I-it paradigm. In the absence of tradition(s) that contest(s) the disciplinary weltanschauungen of this paradigm, modern civilization unintentionally but ineluctably suffocates and decomposes under the hegemony of monological rationality.

The Dominance of the I-it Paradigm and the
Suppression of Dialogue

At the heart of the constructionist objection to the I-it paradigm is the latter's noxious effect upon communication. Its mode of operation translates and reduces everything to what is graspable within an FSU that takes for granted its mastery of the generation of objective knowledge. In effect, its own FSU renders the I-it paradigm impervious to, and dismissive of, what is other than itself. Its self-understanding is that its method is empowered to eliminate all bias and partiality. It knows best. The "truth-effect" of its operation, to borrow a bit of Foucauldian jargon, is the subordination of all interpretations of reality to one superordinate, systematic, decontextualized, and universal rationality. Communication is obliged to conform to this monological, universalistic rationality, or it is devalued, suppressed, or excluded as "irrational." As Horkheimer (1976) ironically observes, "If a theoretical procedure does not take the form of determining objective facts with the help of the simplest and most differentiated conceptual schemes available, what can it be but an aimless intellectual game, half conceptual poetry, half impotent expression of states of mind" (p. 219).

Within the bubble of monological rationality, learning *about* the other is confined within its self-referential, self-assured bounds, and learning *from* the other is out of the question. Whether in the process of scientific inquiry or the course of everyday life, the I-it paradigm of knowledge production converts the meaning of the other to confirm its own, monological "good sense". The reality of the other's nature or character—as contrasted with the other's (nescientific) self-understanding—is decided by the authority of monological rationality. Its moral-practical consequence is to inhibit and distort communication. For what is the point of seeking to understand the other's knowledge if it is already certain that the other's knowledge and self-understanding are inferior to one's own? Unrecognized and unacknowledged is the achieved, accomplished, socially constructed organization of "factual" knowledge—an achievement that depends upon the openness of social reality *and* effects a (temporary and precarious) social closure. The closure is always temporary because a correspondence with the other is unattainable.

In criticizing the I-it paradigm, Shotter and Gergen argue that an awareness of the accomplished character of "factual" knowledge entitles constructionism to falsify the claims of traditional epistemology and, to argue, on this basis, that knowledge generated within the I-it paradigm is unsound. Against this understanding, it is possible to suggest that the knowledge produced by the I-it paradigm is not false but limited, and that its moral-practical implications are detrimental only so long as its limitations are not fully appreciated by those who are exposed to its influence. It is when people lack the capacity to reflect critically upon claims made by the I-it paradigm that it exerts its hegemonic power. As Deetz (1992) has observed, "The problem is not I-it relationships, but . . . the closing of communication. The recognition of 'the otherness of the other' breaks a discursive stoppage by posing questions to any 'it' conception. The 'other' exceeds every possible conception of it" (p. 342).

The practical-moral commitment of constructionism resides in its intention to break such stoppages. By developing "a situated-developmental-relational view of knowledge and the self" (Shotter & Gergen, p. 7), its promise is to "work practically to construct different forms of social relations, different forms of life" (p. 14). The question to be addressed in the next section is how far constructionism can take us in guiding this "work."

WHY SOCIAL CONSTRUCTIONISM IS UNSATISFYING: MISSING DIALOGICAL RATIONALITY

We have noted how constructionism goes beyond a scholastic concern to correct the self-understanding of traditional epistemology. Shotter and Gergen's belief in the emancipatory relevance and value of constructionism is forcefully stated as follows:

> By explicitly articulating aspects of our practices in this way, practices that formerly were just taken as implicitly correct, *we can achieve a greater degree of freedom in relation to them*: We can become aware of the other possibilities available to us within them. We are not thus constrained by what is "obviously correct" or how things "must be done." (Shotter & Gergen, p. 5, italics added)

If constructionism is motivated and justified by a (practical-moral) concern to "achieve a greater degree of freedom" and thereby to facilitate "a change in the disciplinary form of life currently oriented around the passive-individualistic [I-it] epistemological paradigm" (Shotter & Gergen, p. 14), then it is relevant to consider whether it is capable of promoting a qualitatively different relationship between knowledge, communication, and self-identity. How relevant and helpful is constructionism in its effort "[to speak] importantly to issues of communication and personal identity" (p. 26)?

Some Limits of Constructionism

In the opening paragraph of their essay, Shotter and Gergen declare that a theory of knowledge presumes upon a theory of human functioning and an idea of the fully functioning individual. Assuming that constructionism amounts to a theory of knowledge,[8] it too must presume an idea of "the fully functioning individual" (p. 4) and contrive to realize this idea. We may then ask: What idea of the fully functioning individual is presumed by constructionism? Unfortunately, beyond a critique of the (dualistic) conception of the person developed within the I-it epistemological paradigm, there is little indication of what kind of "fully functioning individual" constructionism envisages, or how constructionism contributes to the realization of this ideal.

Very broadly, it is possible to identify two intertwined aspects of social transformation. First, there are the historical and contextual conditions that either support and/or impede transformation. Shotter and Gergen's constructionism has virtually nothing to say about these conditions. Indeed, it would seem to be incapable of analyzing these conditions, focused as it is upon interpersonal processes of communication rather than the historical structures that, arguably, are a medium and outcome of this communication. For example, constructionism would seem ill-equipped to address such questions as this one: What are the social and historical conditions that weaken the authority of monological rationality and/or strengthen the development of dialogical rationality? To do so demands a social theory capable of situating the critical intent of constructionism in a wider cultural and historical context where, it could be argued, established metanarratives, dominated by monological rationality, are becoming unsettled and complemented by the material and ideological conditions of postmodernity (Harvey, 1989) and by post-dualistic modes of knowing and being, such as those nurtured and promoted inter alia by feminist and ecological movements (Smart, 1993).

If, as postmodernists claim, monological rationality is breaking up, will this facilitate a dialogical revitalization of the Enlightenment tradition in a way that remembers the connection between knowledge and emancipation? Or is the more likely scenario one of hypermodern fragmentation in which any impulse to generate a dialogue between traditions is frustrated by an assumption of incommensurability between diverse (monological) traditions that renders dialogical effort irrational (Willmott, in press-a, in press-b)? Restrictions of space make it impossible to pursue the question of whether the (post)modern condition makes it more or less likely that dialogical rationality will flourish. I will therefore confine my comments to the *(inter)personal processes* of "changing the cultural character" (Shotter & Gergen, p. 14) of a (post)modern world that continues to be dominated by monological rationality.[9] Even more narrowly, I will limit my reflections to constructionism's capacity to reveal and resist the social psychological appeal of monological rationality. In this, I am guided by the belief that, in addition to criticizing the self-understanding of this rationality and exposing its moral-practical consequences, it is necessary to appreciate and analyze the perverse psychological appeal of monological rationality. If the dominance of monological rationality is to be effectively challenged and neutralized, we must not only understand what sustains its development interpersonally (and, of course, historically) but also identify means of dissolving this power.

The Seduction of Monological Rationality

To illustrate the operation of monological rationality, and the extent to which we can become fetishistically ensnared by it, we can refer briefly to Deetz's (1992, pp. 293-294) observations on the willingness of modern individuals, occupying comparatively privileged and "powerful" positions in society, to comply with corporate "dress for success" clothing. In the desire for success—which I interpret principally as a means of overcoming insecurities about self-identity that are inflamed by the individualizing effects of modernity (Willmott, 1992, in press-c)—corporate employees routinely manage a physical image of self that is "known" to be a precondition of success. As Deetz (1992) argues, when this desire is fulfilled, it is not the complex, heterogeneous person that receives confirmation but the monological, corporate image.

To this observation can be added the suggestion that, even when the employees strive to preserve a sense of self-identity by contriving to play their corporate roles at a distance (Goffman, 1959), a primary truth-effect of their actions is to strengthen the corporate code and thereby to suppress aspects of the person that cannot be recognized or accommodated within it (see Kunda, 1992; Willmott, in press-b). Commenting upon the "dress for success" example, which can be taken as emblematic of many other contemporary social practices, Deetz (1992) notes how communication

> is systematically distorted on both the personal and the social level. The individual self-manipulation prohibits self-differentiation and the pursuit of common understanding with co-workers. Rather it functions to create a false-consensus with others and a normalization of self. At the social level, it suppresses the individual as filled with competing needs and interests and subject in many discourses, positions other individuals in prescribed relations to the person, and creates an arbitrary relationship to the environment. (p. 294)

The appeal of monological rationality, as exemplified in the example of dressing for success, resides in its power to construct a sense of certainty and control—albeit that the mastery it offers may be shown, on reflection, to be precarious and perverse (see Heller, 1976; Wolfe, 1988). The reasons for this are not difficult to grasp and are alluded to, but not explored, by constructionism. A sense of individual control is conveyed by constituting human beings as "separate individuals" who are empowered to "understand the world external to themselves in terms of their own, inner mental representations of it" (Shotter & Gergen, p. 16). In Shotter and Gergen's terminology, this is the "individualistic" element of the "passive-individualistic," I-it paradigm. A feeling of remoteness and passivity, and associated lack of responsibility, arises from the sense of separation. In Deetz's example, nobody feels personal responsibility either for the corporate code or for complying with it. Perversely, the construction of the modern person as an autonomous individual makes it difficult for any person, even, and perhaps especially, the more "powerful," to perceive him- or herself as more than a languid consumer of social worlds that seem to exist and develop independently of their actions. In sum, the paradoxical appeal of monological rationality resides in its capacity to produce our sense of individual power while absolving the individual of responsibility for the world that he or she routinely reproduces.

Resisting the Seduction

We have noted how constructionism challenges and debunks the authority of monological rationality. But constructionism offers little insight into, or guidance on, how to reduce the distortions of communication resulting from its domination. Constructionism suggests that the revelations induced by the constructionist paradigm will, of themselves, be sufficient to move (or convert) individuals to participate in the "back-and-forth development of a contested but negotiable practical understanding" (p. 28). In contrast, Deetz argues that the movement from reflection to praxis is conditional upon combining utopian vision (e.g., the idea of dialogue), entryism (e.g., extending acceptable codes of conduct), and resistance (e.g., acting in ways that are guided by alternative, dialogical values; Burrell, 1990). The catalyst for bringing these elements together, Deetz (1992, pp. 337 et seq.) suggests, is the development of *a mode of being*, involving the microemancipatory praxis as "*responsiveness*," that nurtures and develops a more playful and balanced orientation to human interaction and social advancement.

"Responsiveness" involves seizing each moment of indeterminacy, conferred by the irremediable openness of human being, "with care and moral direction, rather than with instrumentality and decision rules" (Deetz, 1992, p. 338). Fundamental to such praxis, Deetz argues, is *the development of forms of communication that are self-destructive*. As Deetz (1992) puts it, in provocative opposition to the commonsense view, "Communication is not for self-expression but for self-destruction. The point of communication as a social act is to overcome one's fixed subjectivity, one's conceptions, one's strategies, to be opened up to the indeterminacy of people and the external environment" (p. 341).

It is precisely the "self-destructive" potential and value of (dialogical) communication that is overlooked and unexplored in Shotter and Gergen's constructionism. As it stands, their advocacy of an alternative, "situated, developmental, and relational" paradigm takes for granted the understanding that communication is for purposes of self-expression; and that this paradigm operates to disclose how self-expression is either facilitated or frustrated through processes of social interaction. Certainly, constructionism serves to raise questions that are unasked or inadequately answered within "the passive-individualistic [I-it epistemological] paradigm" (p. 5). But this alone is insufficient. For a condition and consequence of developing this "new paradigm" is a commitment to the total "destruction" of self.

Of course, this does not mean the destruction of the mind and/or body. Rather, the "object" of destruction is the power/knowledge relation between the individual's self-knowledge as a separate, autonomous entity and the domination of the I-it paradigm that acts to sustain a dualistic mode of being (see Sampson, 1983). This destruction is necessary if communication is not to be constrained and distorted by a compulsion to reproduce power/ knowledge relations (e.g., corporate codes of conduct) that secure and reproduce a continuous and solid sense of self-identity as a "successful" and "fulfilled" person. In Deetz's (1992) words, the process of becoming fully open to the other demands an "overcom(ing of) one's fixed subjectivity, one's conceptions, one's strategies, etc." (p. 341). Otherwise, communication continues to be distorted by the compulsive effort to sustain and defend the sense of self as a separate entity.

CONCLUSION

Constructionism is interesting, yet also tantalizing and ultimately unsatisfactory, I conclude, because it champions the possibility of dialogical rationality, yet offers so little purchase on questions of how, practically, a move in this direction is to be made or of how difficulties encountered in making this move are to be surmounted. It leaves me feeling frustrated because it is limited in its exploration and illumination of the historical context and interpersonal processes of struggle toward more dialogical forms of communication. It raises expectations that it is impotent to fulfill.

To return to the contradiction that was identified in the introduction to this commentary: There would seem to be two ways of eliminating the inconsistency between a forceful dismissing of traditional epistemology and a concern to accommodate diverse traditions within a "contested but negotiable" process of "practical understanding" (p. 28). One way would be to accept that any attempt to engage in a negotiated process of practical understanding is doomed to failure because the advocates of traditional epistemology are congenitally resistant to dialogue. The problem with this "resolution" is that it ignores the presence of those who have migrated from the FSU of traditional epistemology to a position that more closely resembles constructionism. Although still uncommon, the presence of such "migrants" would seem to suggest that dialogue may be possible, and that resistance to such dialogue is socially organized rather than congenitally given.

The other way of resolving the contradiction would be to concede that constructionism cannot falsify the claims of traditional epistemology any more than its own claims can be falsified by traditional epistemology. This concession would seem to be more consistent with constructionism's emphasis upon the situated quality of conversation and knowledge production. This resolution demands a degree of modesty about the capacity of constructionism to know, or interpret, the other, however. The development of such modesty, I have suggested, is conditional upon understanding communication as a medium for dissolving, rather than expressing, self.

If constructionism is to fulfil its ambition to transform everyday communication, it is relevant to engage more directly with traditions of critical social theory that have wrestled with the project of developing a radical alternative to traditional epistemology, and to explore how constructionism may add to, and be rounded out by, their insights. If the dialogue between traditions is to foster a process of mutual enrichment and enlightenment, rather than degenerating into diverse monologues, it is necessary to be open to the other rather than engaging in conversation principally as a means of confirming one's self. In turn, this move invites and demands a conscious shift in our understanding of communication: from one where communication is routinely regarded as a means of self-expression to one where it becomes the medium of self-destruction.

NOTES

1. I am aware that issue could be taken with Shotter and Gergen's characterization of social constructionism. No doubt, many pages could be filled by comparing their version of constructionism with diverse other formulations, to some of which they make passing reference (p. 14). It is not difficult to resist this temptation. I shall strive to concentrate on (what I understand to be) the substance of what they have to say and will not bother with the question of whether the labeling of their intellectual position as social constructionism infringes someone's Trades Descriptions Act.

2. One possibility, perhaps, is to argue that traditional epistemology has some legitimate claim upon spheres of knowledge, such as science, that lie beyond the "practical, everyday context" (Shotter & Gergen, p. 7). But this seems unlikely given that, as far as I can judge, Shotter and Gergen's constructionism regards as equally spurious the division that is routinely made between the communicative order of everyday life and the communicative order of scientific research: "The conversational context of everyday life . . . is the context in which *everything of intellectual importance* . . . is judged as worthy or not of further attention" (Shotter & Gergen, p. 4, italics added).

3. Which is why, I take it, that "knowledge, self, others, and continuing the conversation" are untidily, yet quite deliberately, strung together in the subtitle of the essay.

4. As deconstructionism has taught us, communication is constituted through paradox: Rhetorically, communication makes an implicit claim to correspond to what it signifies yet is incapable of fusing this connection. The enlightening potential of deconstructionism resides in revealing this paradox as it exemplifies it. Points of contact between constructionism and deconstructionism are noted but unexplored by Shotter and Gergen (p. 4 and note 1). See Norris (1990) for an informed discussion of the emancipatory significance of deconstruction.

5. The constructionist concern to break out of the I-it paradigm is shared with a number of other phenomenologically or hermeneutically inspired methodologies. For instance, ethnomethodology differentiates its interests from those of "folk sociology" (Zimmerman & Pollner, 1971, p. 82) in which the commonsense reasoning that informs "folk" analysis does not itself become a topic of investigation. Indeed, Shotter and Gergen (pp. 17, 19) usefully draw upon ethnomethodological studies to illustrate their constructionist arguments. The version of constructionism developed by Shotter and Gergen, however, pursues a different agenda than that of ethnomethodology. In particular, their constructionism goes well beyond the "indifference" of ethnomethodologists to other forms of analysis. Orthodox ethnomethodologists are interested only in researching how (all) forms of communication depend upon members' methods of accomplishing their sense of an objective reality of social facts (Garfinkel, 1967; but see also Pollner, 1991). In

contrast, Shotter and Gergen's constructionism is concerned with differentiating and evaluating alternative and competing traditions of accomplishing a sense of knowing and being.

6. See, for example, Popper's (1976) response to Habermas's critique of critical rationalism.

7. Whether this critique is amenable to rational grounding or not—and much ink has been spilled in debating this question—it rests upon the belief that human knowledge/communication is indissolubly linked to processes of emancipation in which human beings mobilize their critical faculties to reduce a (fetishized) dependence upon hypostatized powers (McCarthy, 1978).

8. In response to this question, Shotter and Gergen might say that they explicitly disavow any claim to have set out a theory of knowledge, that they offer no more than "a set of interrelated accounts" (p. 26, italics omitted). I would accept that they do not provide a theory of knowledge in the (traditional) sense of an epistemology that differentiates truth from falsehood, although, as I noted in the introduction to this commentary, they do occasionally slip into this mode. More often, their position is that " 'truth' can only be achieved from within an orderly and stable disciplinary practice" (p. 26) and therefore that the idea of a theory of knowledge, as conceived within the disciplinary practice of traditional epistemology, is misconceived. So, although Shotter and Gergen do not have a theory of knowledge as conventionally understood (because they reject the idea of such a theory), they do have a theory about how knowledge develops and changes: through a "back-and-forth development of a contested but negotiable practical understanding" (p. 28). Their theory, in essence, is that what counts as objective knowledge is contextually produced and is conditional upon the contests and negotiations that emerge in the course of human conversation. Their objection to traditional epistemology, as I understand it, is that the idea and the practice of traditional epistemology operates to constrain and obstruct this "back-and-forth" process.

9. Saying this, I strongly endorse the view that any radical change in interpersonal relations is conditional upon inter alia changes in the organization and control of human labor processes (Knights & Willmott, 1990). I also believe the reverse to be the case, however. It is necessary to work simultaneously to change both "spheres" because, in reality, the interpersonal and the politico-economic are not different worlds but dimensions of the reproduction of the same world (Knights & Willmott, 1985, 1989). Enlightened transformations of the organization of labor processes will not occur without enlightened transformations of people who must struggle, individually and collectively, to make such changes.

REFERENCES

Burrell, G. (1990). *Response to Deetz.* Paper presented at the Critical Theory and Management Studies Colloquium, Shrewsbury, England.

Deetz, S. (1992). *Democracy in the age of corporate colonization.* Albany: State University of New York Press.

Foucault, M. (1982). The subject and power. *Critical Inquiry, 8,* 777-795.

Gadamer, H. (1975). *Truth and method.* London: Sheed and Ward.

Garfinkel, H. (1967). *Studies in ethnomethodology.* Englewood Cliffs, NJ: Prentice-Hall.

Goffman, E. (1959). *The presentation of self in everyday life.* Harmondsworth, England: Penguin.

Habermas, J. (1976). A positivistically bisected rationalism. In T. W. Adorno, H. Albert, R. Dahrendorf, J. Habermas, H. Pilot, & K. R. Popper, *The positivist dispute in German sociology.* London: Heinemann.

Harvey, D. (1989). *The condition of postmodernity.* Oxford: Basil Blackwell.

Heller, J. (1976). *Something happened.* London: Cape.

Horkheimer, M. (1976). Traditional and critical theory. In P. Connerton (Ed.), *Critical sociology.* Harmondsworth, England: Penguin.

Knights, D., & Willmott, H. C. (1985). Power and identity in theory and practice. *Sociological Review, 33*(1), 22-46.

Knights, D., & Willmott, H. C. (1989). Power and subjectivity at work: From degradation to subjugation in social relations. *Sociology, 23*(4), 1-24.

Knights, D., & Willmott, H. C. (Eds.). (1990). *Labour process theory*. London: Macmillan.

Kunda, G. (1992). *Engineering culture: Control and commitment in a high-tech corporation.* Philadelphia: Templeton University Press.

McCarthy, T. (1978). *The critical theory of Jurgen Habermas*. London: Hutchinson.

Norris, C. (1990). Deconstruction, postmodernism and philosophy: Habermas on Derrida. In C. Norris, *What's wrong with postmodernism: Critical theory and the ends of philosophy.* London: Harvester Wheatsheaf.

Pollner, M. (1991). Left of ethnomethodology: The rise and decline of radical reflexivity. *American Sociological Review, 56,* 370-380.

Popper, K. (1963). *Conjectures and refutations: The growth of scientific knowledge*. London: Routledge & Kegan Paul.

Popper, K. (1976). Reason or revolution. In T. W. Adorno, H. Albert, R. Dahrendorf, J. Habermas, H. Pilot, & K. R. Popper, *The positivist dispute in German sociology*. London: Heinemann.

Sampson, E. (1983). Deconstructing psychology's subject. *The Journal of Mind and Behaviour, 4*(2), 135-164.

Smart, B. (1993). *Postmodernity*. London: Routledge.

Willmott, H. C. (1986). Unconscious sources of motivation in the theory of the subject: An exploration and critique of Giddens' dualistic models of action and personality. *Journal for the Theory of Social Behaviour, 16*(1), 105-122.

Willmott, H. C. (1992). Postmodernism and excellence: The de-differentiation of economy and culture. *Journal of Organizational Change Management, 5*(3), 58-68.

Willmott, H. C. (in press-a). Breaking the paradigm mentality. *Organization Studies.*

Willmott, H. C. (in press-b). Strength is ignorance; slavery is freedom: Managing culture in modern organizations. *Journal of Management Studies.*

Willmott, H. C. (in press-c). Theorising human agency: Responding to the crisis of (post)modernity. In M. Parker & J. Hassard (Eds.), *Towards a new theory of organizations.* London: Routledge.

Wolfe, T. (1988). *The bonfire of the vanities*. London: Cape.

Zimmerman, D. H., & Pollner, M. (1971). The everyday world as a phenomenon. In J. D. Douglas (Ed.), *Understanding everyday life*. London: Routledge & Kegan Paul.

2   Is There Still a
Problem About the Self?

ROM HARRÉ
Oxford University and Georgetown University

The puzzling concept of self is analyzed as a double singularity. Self₁ is the self as the bare numerical identity of personhood and self₂ is the unique set of beliefs each self₁ has about itself. These *selves* are shown to be discursively produced through the indexical properties of conversation. The dichotomy has been challenged by certain feminist writers. At one level, the challenge can be resolved by treating it as an observation about the multiple selves₂ any self₁ must handle. A deeper level of challenge suggests that the ways the problems of handling multiple selves₂ are dealt with affect the sense of personal identity expressed as self₁. The deeper challenge is met by showing first that the only tenable theory of selfhood is grammatical. The first person pronouns index speech acts with spatial location of speaker and speaker's position in a moral order. In the light of that demonstration, it is shown how the problems of selves₂ can affect the way that pronouns index speech acts with positions in a local moral order but cannot affect the indexing of the content of the same speech acts with the spatial location of the embodied speaker.

The rest of his life would be spent watching her slip away from him, not knowing who he was, not knowing who she was.

—Tony Hillerman, 1989, p. 170

It is in and through language that man constitutes himself as a *subject,* because language alone establishes the concept of "ego" in reality, in *its* reality which is that of being. The "subjectivity" we are discussing here is the capacity of the speaker to posit him [her] as "subject." It is defined not by the feeling which everyone experiences of being him [her] self . . . but as the psychic unity that transcends the totality of the actual experiences it assembles and that makes the permanence of the consciousness. Now we hold that that "subjectivity," whether it is placed in phenomenology or in psychology, as one may wish, is only the emergence in the being of a fundamental property of language. "Ego" is he [she] who *says* "ego." That is where we see the foundation of "subjectivity," which is determined by the linguistic status of "person."

—Emile Benveniste, 1983

Correspondence and requests for reprints: Rom Harré, Department of Psychology, Georgetown University, Washington, DC, 20057.

Communication Yearbook 17, pp. 55-73

A MONG the conceptual problems that never seem to be laid to rest are the cluster surrounding personhood. What is it to be a person? What is it to be just this person? These questions have prompted various kinds of inquiries: psychological, interactional, sociological, historical, political, and philosophical. I do not think that the more empirically oriented inquiries can flourish unless some prior philosophical work has been done. But is not that work long since completed? How could there still be anything for a philosopher to say on the subject after 2,000 years of reflection on the topic? Surprisingly, I think there is. Thanks to the example of Wittgenstein, a new discipline can be imposed on our reflections—the discipline of attention to language in the uses of which concepts are created, reproduced, and maintained. Language is the source both of metaphysical illusions and of philosophical insights. I shall be conducting my inquiry into the status and nature of the self in pursuit of a Wittgensteinian *ubersicht,* tangential to traditional philosophical investigations into the criteria of personal identity and the well-established forms of psychological research into the presentations and representations of social identities.

The concept of personhood appears in our accounts of both the public and the private domain. We will recognize other beings as individual persons possessed with a sense of their own individual personhood. I shall refer to these as the "fact" of identity and the "sense" of identity, respectively. There is yet another distinction to be drawn: "identity" may be qualitative—personal identity in that sense is what kind of being someone is. It may, however, be numerical—personal identity in that sense is which individual being someone is.

The problem to which this essay is addressed concerns the nature of one's sense of individuality as a person and the relation of that aspect of personhood to one's beliefs about what kind of person one is. I shall introduce the otherwise redundant concept of "self" to construct a simple terminology for expressing these distinctions. The Cartesian explanation for both the fact and the sense of personal identity is that each human being is a doublet—one body with one substantial mind or "ego." It is the numerical identity of the Cartesian ego that is supposed to account for human individuality. *Ego* is sometimes translated as *self.* I shall call my sense of personal identity, my sense of "self$_1$," and my belief about what kind of person I am, my beliefs about my "self$_2$." Now this is a convenient nomenclature, but it does run the risk of suggesting that these "selves" are substances, which is emphatically not an implication of my usage. As a rule, "self$_2$" is what is meant by social identity. For the purposes of this essay, I shall define a person as a human being with a sense of self$_1$ and beliefs about his or her self$_2$.

First I would like connect these distinctions to some everyday contexts in which the concepts of self, identity, and so on are bandied about. Consider the use of such a sentence as "I am not myself today." This declaration does not rest on my discovering that after all I am someone else. It means something like the following: "I, the speaker, have become aware that I am not the same kind of being today that I took for granted yesterday. I am grudging where I was generous, irritable where I was amiable, forgetful where I was attentive" and so on. This is the self$_2$, the presentation of which Erving Goffman (1959) studied so perceptively. But what are we to say of the one who was cheerful yesterday and grumpy today? This in some deep sense is even more myself. Doris Lessing has described "the self that burns behind the diversity" of Goffmanesque presentations. This is the self to which the pronoun *I* is sometimes said to refer. In the terminology proposed above, the Lessing self is the self$_1$ and the Goffman self, the self$_2$. In general, for each human being, the self$_1$ is assumed to be a singularity while self$_2$ admits of multiplicity. Self$_1$ taken in the Cartesian manner as an inner entity is that which Hume sought but could not find. I shall begin with a sketch of an analysis of the use of the pronoun *I* to show that its use can be explained without any assumptions about Cartesian egos. This sketch is drawn from some earlier and more detailed studies (Harré, 1991; Muhlhausler & Harré, 1990).

The pronoun *I* is an indexical. As I shall use that term, it refers to the way "I" serves to index the content of the statements to which it is prefixed with certain aspects or facts about the speaker and the act of speaking. What is thus indexed can be worked out by asking what is added to the content of a statement when the identity of the speaker is disclosed. I shall discuss only three of the possible personal indices:

a. the content is indexed with the spatial location of the speaker while speaking, a necessary condition of which is his or her embodiment;

b. the pronoun together with the tense of the main verb indexes an utterance with the temporal moment of the act of speaking;

c. the illocutionary force of the utterance is indexed with the moral standing or "position" of the speaker.

Psychologically, the three indices are related to perception (consciousness), memory, and agency (responsibility). The sense of self$_1$, one's sense of personal identity, would be taken as a sense of being located at a singularity in the spatial manifold, in the temporal manifold, and in a manifold of persons. Most philosophical discussions of personal identity since Locke (1670) have focused on the temporal index, because to have a sense of being located as a successive singularity in a manifold of events seems to require memory and perhaps the imaginative faculty of foresight. In the traditional scheme, self$_1$ is a substance, perhaps the ego; themselves$_2$ too are among its occasional attributes. In the new scheme, persons are human beings who have a mastery of certain discursive practices. They have the ability to present themselves as cognitive, emotional, and temporal singularities with just one point of view on the world.

To investigate how $self_1$ and $self_2$ could be related to one another, in some way other than the merely formal, I shall consider some arguments from a literature rarely drawn upon by analytic philosophers, namely, poststructuralist, feminist writings about "women's ways of being." Writings from this corpus are often very puzzling, because they are frequently in an unfamiliar style. I shall try to show, however, that they have some interesting contributions to make to the analytic philosophy of personhood.

THE DOUBLE SINGULARITY PRINCIPLE

Using my simple $self_1$ and $self_2$ terminology for the Lessing self and the Goffman self, respectively, and assuming that personhood is somehow engendered in the interplay between them, it is possible to spell out a pair of locally powerful normative constraints on how a person should be. Only those human beings who display a singular, continuous $self_1$ are to be counted as psychologically normal, that is, as persons properly so called. Disruptions of the Lessing singularity, such as fugue, amnesia, Alzheimer's condition, and so on, are to be counted as disorders. Only those human beings who display or present a singular, harmonious, and coherent $self_2$ are to be counted as morally acceptable. Thus dissimulation, Machiavellianism, vacillation, insincerity, and hypocrisy are to be counted as vices. I shall call this the "double singularity principle." I particularly wish to draw attention to the normative character of the principle. It is not an inductive generalization of the observable behavior of human beings. It is a normative principle serving to delineate the boundaries of what is to count as a proper person; deviations from either singularity are to be taken as failings. They do not count as empirical refutations of principle. I shall illustrate this important point later with the case of "multiple personality."

Normative constraints can be challenged. It might be argued that life ought not to be ordered in accordance with the double singularity principle. I propose to explore the force of that principle through an analysis of an important set of challenges to its authority and hegemony. The challenges I have in mind come from feminist authors of a poststructuralist bent, to whom I have already referred.

THE FEMINIST CHALLENGE TO
THE DOUBLE SINGULARITY THESIS

I believe I can detect two levels of resistance to this thesis among feminist authors. The first level of challenge comes from Dorothy Smith (1987) and Julia Kristeva (1981). In her most recent work, Smith describes a woman's experience as typified by a "bifurcated consciousness." A woman's mind consists of "two modes of consciousness that could not coexist with one another." At a first reading, this observation seems to make no sense. Smith's state of mind could not literally be that of bifurcated consciousness, otherwise she would not be able to realize that she remembered, planned, or feared different things in different circumstances.

Smith, however, provides a helpful gloss in which the two modes are explained as being "different organization[s] of memory, attention, relevances and objectives, and even different presences." If we take "presence" to mean something like a Goffmanesque presentation of self, it is clear that what I have called the self$_1$ is conserved for Smith throughout her life. Her memory is unimpaired, for instance. But from time to time she entertains thoughts and undertakes patterns of action that either could not be performed together or that, though thought together, were mutually contradictory. It is easy to see that self$_1$ is robust and conserved as a singularity given that Smith's account of her "contradictory" life depends on all the thoughts, episodes, and so on being indexed with the unique and singular spatiotemporal trajectory and moral standing of their author as an embodied being. There is no doubt that her sense of personal identity in the philosopher's sense is unimpaired and persists through sequences of the presentation of very different selves.

Kristeva is well known for her proposal that traditional feminist programs ought to be transcended. Demands for a right of entry to an alleged "man's world" confirm its moral quality and social structure while radical feminism confirms the masculine/feminine dichotomy in the very act of celebrating one of its poles. "In the third attitude," she says, "which I strongly advocate . . . the very dichotomy man/woman as an opposition between two rival entities may be understood as belonging to *metaphysics*. What can identity, even sexual identity mean in a new theoretical and scientific space where the very notion of identity is challenged?" Though there are some opacities in the passage, for instance, what might be meant by "metaphysics" or "space," Kristeva's intent is quite clear. The notion of identity, which is brought into question, is that of self$_2$. Kristeva writes from the standpoint of a self$_1$ singularity. Dichotomies that depend on the "self$_1$/self$_2$ distinction, like "knower/known," are preserved in her "third attitude," in which lower order dichotomies are transcended.

Commentary on the Challenge at Level 1

In Strawson's (1956) account of persons as basic particulars, the practices of identifying and individuating persons as singularities are rooted in the singular material bodies in which persons are usually one to one embodied. Only as a persisting material being can a person be identified and reidentified by others. Later in this essay, I shall have cause to revise this thesis in light of the existence of human beings like Miss Beauchamp, in whose discursive practices Morton Prince (1905/1968) found three persons displayed. Miss Beauchamp presented herself as three selves$_1$. The principle of noncontradiction applies strictly, that is, grammatically, to material beings and their material attributes so the "contradictory self" cannot be a Strawsonian person. It is noteworthy that, in Strawson's treatment, it is the spatiotemporal singularity of each person's unique perceptual point of view that fixes limits to the resolution of "contradictory experience." It cannot, it seems, undercut the material singularity of the embodied person.

A conservative resolution of the first level of attack on the double singularity thesis might take the following form:

a. Adopt the self$_1$/self$_2$ distinction. Self$_1$ is to be mapped on to the old polar concepts "knower," "manager," and so on and self$_2$ on to the old polar complements "known," "managed," and so on.

b. Require there to be a self$_1$ to provide discursive continuity as a singular logical subject and multiple selves$_2$ to provide for the (perhaps) contradictory, that is, presentationally incompatible, pairs of attributes a person displays from time to time and context to context.

Multiplicity of selves$_2$ can be made tolerable ad hoc. They could be temporarily successive as in the lives of those to whom the concept of "working mother" applies. They could form a hierarchy as in the lives of those to whom the concept "successful candidate for sex-reassignment surgery" can be applied. One person's multiple selves$_2$ make their appearance and perhaps exist only in the contextually and historically various discursive practices that a skilled human being can produce.

I am inclined to conclude that the Smith-Kristeva line is not philosophically radical, because it leaves the duality of a person and his or her attributes in place; indeed, these authors depend upon it in presenting their position.

A Second Level of Feminist Challenge to the Self$_1$/Self$_2$ Distinction

Commenting on a draft of a recent paper of mine (Harré, 1991), Bronwyn Davies (personal communication, 1990) remarks—apropos of the claim that the surface grammar of many discursive practices seems to demand a distinction between self$_1$ as substance and selves$_2$ as its attributes—that the dichotomy can be brought into question.

Davies proposes two main psychological/philosophical theses concerning the personal identity of women. One is that women not only live contradictory lives but also are (or possess) contradictory *selves*. At first glance, one is inclined to interpret this claim in the sense of selves$_2$. It would be roughly equivalent to the suggestion that women (like other people, I would add) are often called upon to act according to the prescriptions for two or more kinds of persons at one and the same time and in the same situation. A pathological form of this psychological phenomenon is the double bind of Gregory Bateson's account of the etiology of schizophrenia. This claim seems to be innocuous as a criticism of the double singularity thesis, though it would be implausible to attribute it exclusively to women. But Davies also claims that the self that knows, my self$_1$, and the self or selves that are known, my self or selves$_2$, are not as firmly demarcated in women as in men. Taken together with the first thesis, this entails that the self$_1$, the female knower, can be contradictory and so must be, in some sense, multiple.

> The split between self$_1$ and self$_2$ is not a meaningful ([or] comfortable) one for women and for feminists. It does not accurately describe their experience. You have a male formula here for male managed selves that doesn't apply to female selves . . . you readily accept a boundary between your two categories, presumably because you experience such a boundary. I suspect that for most women when there is such a boundary they feel false/unreal/taken over by the male forms of discourse they have learned to use. The multiple public selves are separated not by a clear category boundary, as for men, but by something more like a semipermeable membrane—with considerable permeability from selves$_2$ to self$_1$. (Davies, personal communication, 1990)

I confess to having had great difficulty at first in understanding Davies's point. It was not easy for me to see how a necessary condition for the possibility of some form of discourse is demarcated from that which it makes possible by an *experiential* boundary. Since the eighteenth century, it has surely been clear that my self as knower must be transcendental to whatever I know, including myself. I do not have an empirical glimpse of myself empirically glimpsing myself.

I shall try to show in the course of this essay that Davies's remarks, which are hard to interpret in an empirical or ontological sense, can be understood if, in the manner of Wittgenstein, they are taken to be grammatical. This interpretation might go as follows: The "selves," through the display of which one presents oneself as a proper person in various situations, influence the way one uses first person expressions in managing one's part in a complex discourse. If, as I have argued (Harré, 1991), the self is not a thing but a way of organizing the cognitions, perceptions, and so on of a human being as a unified person, then influences on the grammar of first person talk are influences on self$_1$. Whether, in the end, the idea of a radically disjointed women's grammar of reflexive discourse can be sustained is a serious question. The claim that there is or should be such a grammar is certainly intelligible. It might be like the claim that Inuit, the language of the Eskimos, lacks a grammatical form for self-commentary or self-exhortation. If, as I shall argue, the self$_1$/self$_2$ distinction is real only in discourse and so a shadow cast by grammar on persons in action, then, if there is an autonomous women's grammar, it might cast a different shadow than that cast by the grammar of speech characteristic of men. Looked at in this way, Davies's remarks can be seen to take us beyond the simple Goffmanesque challenge of Smith and Kristeva.

Among contemporary French feminist writers who have had something to say about the dichotomy I am discussing, Heléne Cixous is perhaps the best known. In interpreting her writings, I have benefited from a recent exegetical work by Moi (1985). With the help of her paraphrases, it is possible to see one of Cixous's more sweeping claims as a "grammatical proposal," in the sense in which I am using that term in this essay. As a thesis about the grammatical conventions of reflexive discourse, it can be put to the test. Drawing mostly from *La jeune née* by Cixous and Clement (1975), Moi shows Cixous's attempts to map (or perhaps better declares the propriety of so mapping) all binary oppositions onto the opposition male/female. One can see how this claim is antistructuralist. Lévi-Strauss, for example, bases his structural analyses of all cultural artifacts, both discursive and material, on the *axiom* that all structures are binary oppositions or constructed out of binary oppositions. Cixous's thesis would make all structuralist analyses sexist at a stroke.

In her exposition of Cixous's position, Moi uses the terms for the biological sexes, namely, *male/female*. But she must surely mean the social dichotomy of gender for which the English expressions would be *masculine/feminine*. So far as I can make out, there is no historical, anthropological, or grammatical argument to justify the placing of the masculine/feminine distinction at the meaning-giving base of all binary oppositions. Perhaps Cixous's grounds for holding such a strong structural thesis are political. Using a term from Saussurean linguistics, namely, "paradigm," Moi (1985) goes on to say: "These examples show that it doesn't matter which 'couple' one chooses to highlight: the hidden male/female opposition with its inevitable positive/negative evaluation can always be traced as the underlying paradigm" (p. 105). Among the oppositions will be some in which, as students of the self, we might be interested, such as "knower/known." There are others the sexism of which is very hard to discern such as "*maintenant/autrefois*." All must be traced to "where logocentrism colludes with phallocentrism" (p. 105). One should notice how much this view (and that of Davies) is at odds with the feminist science movement. Smith, for instance, is insistent on the need to incorporate the deliverances of women's subjectivity in social science. This is as much as to give a privileged place to personal knowledge, knowledge indexed with its producer and its moment of production. The Davies-Cixous program of melding the singularities of selves$_1$ into the multiplicity of selves$_2$ by dissolving the opposition effectively rules out the Smith strategy. Of course, this is an unintended consequence. To resolve the apparent incoherence in the accounts of "self" offered by Davies and Cixous, we must develop the analysis of self$_1$ rather more deeply.

THE HISTORICAL PROGRESSION OF
TREATMENTS OF THE CONCEPT OF "SELF"

I am not doing too much violence to the history of philosophy to identify a progression from the introspective to the transcendental to the grammatical in accounts of the *nature* of the self, the singularity of which is constitutive or taken to be constitutive of one's personal identity as a self$_1$. I shall discuss these accounts in what I believe to be their order of development.

The Self$_1$ as Empirical

First, then, what of the self as revealed to the inner eye of self-reflection? A common starting point for discussion of personal identity is Locke's proposal to base the sense of self$_1$ on the "reach of (memorial) awareness." Locke distinguishes what it is for a being to be a "man," that is, a human being, from that "wherein *personal identity* consists." A "man" (as a member of the human species) is an embodied rational being. The identity of a "man" consists not only in the identity of the "immaterial spirit" but also requires that there be the "same successive body" (Locke, 1670/1974, Book II, chap. XXVII, sec. 8). A person, according to Locke, is such a being as has through reason and reflection a conception of itself. "Everyone is to himself what he calls a self." It is by the consciousness that always accompanies thinking that "makes everyone to be what he calls *self . . .* and as far as consciousness can be extended backwards to any past action or thought, so far reaches the identity of that person."

Butler's devastating demonstration of the paradoxical character of this suggestion was based on the simple observation that, to assemble a set of ideas as mine, I must already have the concept of personal identity. So personal identity cannot consist in my awareness of an ensemble of such ideas.

Confined to the empiricism of "ideas," psychologists from Hume to Husserl abandoned the project of a psychology of self-as-object in favor of a sketch of a concept of self-as-structure. If the concept of "self" is empirical, what is its denotation? Parfit's recent study (Parfit, 1984) is framed in the Lockean way and so inevitably culminates in the Humean answer: There is nothing to which the concept of self refers. But the empiricist position is "unstable." For example, Husserl remarks: "The pure Ego appears to be necessary in principle, and as that which remains absolutely self-identical in all real and possible changes of experience, it can in no sense be reckoned as a real part or phase *of the experiences themselves*" (Husserl, 1913/1970, sec. 57, p. 172). This transcendental account contrasts with his position in an earlier work (Husserl, 1900/1967) in which he follows much the same line as Hume. The phenomenology-reduced ego is "simply identical with . . . [the] interconnected unity" of many experiences. I owe to Tim O'Hagan the observation that, if Husserl was a Humean in 1900, he was a Kantian by 1913.

The Self₁ as Transcendental

Kant's elaborate, threefold hierarchy attributes the singularity of the point of view of a conscious being to a transcendental unity of apperception, but the agentive powers of such a being are assigned to a noumenal ego. The psychological question is one of function rather than denotation. From whence comes the experience of personal unity, the self₁? The Kantian answer is that it comes from an awareness of a structure in experience imposed by "synthesis." The self-created order in subjective experience matches the synthetic order "found" in the world as experienced. So far, we are traversing familiar territory. One could sum it up by saying that from a psychologist's point of view philosophers have managed to create a road map in which all routes end in one of two cul-de-sacs. Either the self is just a structural property of experience, in which case there is no "self" to study, or it is a transcendental condition for such a structure and so not given in experience, and hence not available for empirical investigation. And yet the duality of selves is a familiar image in much contemporary thought. Is the very idea of a guiding, managing, and experiencing self just a trope? Or worse, a mistake?

But the overview is so far incomplete. A queer sort of homespun transcendentalism is to be found in the writings of G. H. Mead. Often deferred to but never developed is Mead's hypothesis of a social origin for both the selves I have labeled as self₁ and self₂. There is still a problem about the self. Is there a third way out of the maze? I want to show first of all that it is not to be found in the surviving writings of G. H. Mead.

Reflexivity is introduced by Mead in the following words: "The self has the characteristic that it is an object to itself" (Mead, 1934, p. 136). The self is at once, for Mead, both transcendental and empirical. Some ambiguity attends his account of what this self might be. He says that we must distinguish between "the experience that immediately takes place and our organization of it into the experience of a self" (p. 135). I shall read the last phrase of this remark as "the experience belonging to a self." It is this self that is aware and that is the referent of the "I" from Mead's famous "I"/"me" dichotomy. As he says, it is "the 'I' which is aware of the social 'me' " (p. 173). Mead's solution to the problem of how the selves can be both transcendental and empirical is to claim that there can be a retrospective grasp of the perceiving acting self of a moment ago (Mead, 1934, p. 196). So the "I" is aware contemporaneously of the managing self, the "me," but this "me" is retrospectively only itself as it once was. It seems abundantly clear that, however Mead thought these "I's" and "me's" were developmentally constituted, only the "me" was capable of being attended to.

The Self₁ as Grammatical Form

The problem that troubled our seventeenth-century predecessors about the self was the difficulty of giving an account of how the sense we have of ourselves (and share with them) of a psychological singularity is to be accounted for. Can we observe a unified and singular self? Is that the source of the experience of ourselves as individuals? Evidently not. Is it then a sense of a certain order or structure in experience? This late eighteenth-century alternative is still with us. But, though I have no quarrel with it as phenomenology, the nature and origins of whatever it is that is sensed as "structure" is not accounted for. For constructionists, the structure of self is discursively manifested. Selfhood appears as a feature of certain kinds of human practice, including such activities as telling a story, taking the blame, and reporting on the state of the attic. In all of these, a singularity of presented personhood is involved. So far as I know, the first intimations of an account that does not invoke an ego, empirical or transcendental, supposedly lying behind and so explaining the presented singularities of self, is that suggested by William James. I shall quote his comments on this problem in full, because they make fascinating reading from our perspective. From James (1977) we have the following:

> The individualized self, which I believe to be the only thing properly called self, is a part of the content of the world experienced. The word experienced (otherwise called the "field of consciousness") comes at all times with our body as its center, center of vision, center of action, center of interest. Where the body is, is "here"; when the body acts is "now"; what the body touches is "this"; all other things are "there" and "then" and "that." These words of emphasized position imply a systematization of things with reference to the focus of action and interest which lies in the body. . . . The body is the storm center, the origin of coordinates, the constant place of stress in all that experience-strain. Everything circles round it, and is felt from its point of view. The word "I", then, is primarily a noun of position, just like "this" and "here" . . . the word "my" designates the kind of emphasis. I see no inconsistency whatever in defending, on the one hand, "my" activities as unique and opposed to those of outer natures and, on the other hand, in affirming, after introspection, that they consist of movements in the head. The "my" of them is the emphasis, the feeling of perspective-interest in which they are dyed.

If only one could write like that.

Taking this paragraph apart yields three main theses:

1. Self-referring expressions do not denote anything. They are indexicals, locating the content of our discourses relative to the place and moment of bodily existence.
2. Experiences of selfhood are a class of bodily located feelings. In this sense, the self is part of the world experience.
3. The structure of experience derives from the grammar of characteristic ways of speaking and not from the "bodily" experiences of goings-on "in the head."

> Those who think that James thought that the meaning of self was a funny feeling in the glottis have not read him.

The "I" as subject of predication is not the body. "I" does not denote the material entity that anchors the whole reference system. "I" is like the zero meridian, not like the town of Greenwich. Let us now look in more detail at what it is to talk as a person, and thus to be one!

TALKING AS A PERSON

To say that we display our personhood in the ways we talk is true but liable to serious misunderstanding. To display something is usually to bring to public gaze that which has been hidden, something that is already there, some hidden singularity, the real person. I believe that personhood is not revealed, however, but constituted in the course of making use of certain discursive practices.

1. There are speech acts in which a speaker takes responsibility for an action (it may be a linguistically as well as a manually performed action). Such actions include reports on how the world (and one's own body) seem/appear to be/are from the speaker's point of view. In a literal sense, "point of view" is a speaker's location in space and time, among material beings some of which are also speakers. And, in a metaphorical sense, "point of view" includes one's "location" in networks of empirical beliefs and moral principles. Let's call such instances of speaking "declarations."

2. Much of our work as speakers is taken up with the telling of stories, sustained narrations, in which there is a story line or lines. In our culture, stories are, more often than not, held together by reference to the people about whom the story is told. (In other cultures, the episode may be the dominant organizing element in narration.)

Every narration is also a declaration. "Take my word for it . . ." and so on and every declaration is also a narration. For instance, to report what one is hearing is to narrate a part of one's autobiography. The distinction between told and lived narratives is an abstraction from real speaking because every episode of storytelling is itself a bit of living and every stretch or strip of life is discursively produced.

Grammatical Conditions for Autobiography as a
Discursive Practice

Let's look at the person/self distinction, necessary to telling a story of one's own life, in light of the feminist, poststructuralist critique of language reported in an earlier section. One notes that, like any instantiation of the knower/known, the distinction between person as speaker and self as spoken about is a binary opposition. According to Cixous, for example, all such oppositions are mappings of descendants of the male/female opposition as has been conceived by men and ultimately obtain their meaning from it. If one is taken by this kind of analysis, fanciful though it may seem, confirmation seems to be ready to hand in the fact that the person/self distinction opposes something active to something passive, just the very leading feature of the patriarchal oppositional understanding imposed on the male/female distinction according to some feminists.

The grammatical form typical of that kind of knower/known discourse (that is, discourse in which the knower is explicitly referred to) that is reflexively addressed to the topic of the speaker "themself" (the preferred neutral reflexive singular personal pronoun) is the iterated first person of which ordinary English conversation provides innumerable and diverse examples. I will begin with a brief analysis of examples in which the iteration of the first person indicator is explicit. One common pattern is the grammar of self-commentary:

"I (epistemic verb: *think, know, feel, believe,* and so on) that I (perception verb: *see, feel, hear,* and so on) something."

Simple perception statements can be used for all sorts of purposes, including reporting, complaining, warning, declaring, and so on. The first person pronoun indexes the content of the statement with the point of view of the speaker. The statement tells of how things appear from the speaker's bodily location. The first person also indexes the statement with the moral authority of the speaker. Here we have the familiar double indexical force of the use of the first person described in the first section of this essay. Contrast "A buffalo is sitting in a pond" with "I can see a buffalo sitting in the pond." We should notice also that the latter not only reports how things are in the pond but is also a contribution to the autobiography of the speaker.

The effect of embedding the simple perceptual claim in the iterated frame is twofold. The illocutionary force of the original claim is changed. For instance, with "I think I can see a buffalo in the pond," declarative commitment is weakened. And in the iterated frame, the indexical force of the embedded "I" is suspended in another way, in that the statement expresses a reflexive comment on the embedded claim as if that claim were indexed to someone else. But spatiotemporal indices attaching to the empirical content of the utterance are unchanged.

A rather similar referential structure occurs in statements couched in the "narrative" voice, the voice of the storyteller. Urban (1989) has called this grammatical phenomenon the "anaphoric 'I.' " For instance, the storyteller may say ". . . and then Doris said, 'I can't abide your smoking in the car!' " The embedded "I" is coreferential with the proper name "Doris" and so an anaphor for that name thus preserving its denotational power. It has no indexical force whatever. According to Urban, one should assume an implicit indexical preceding the whole declaration, because the storyteller lends his or her authority to the telling of the episode in which Doris made this protest. Thus it runs:

"I, the narrator, say 'Doris said, "I can't abide your smoking in the car." ' "

The outermost "I" is a genuine indexical.

Now let us examine a report of the same episode as narrated by Doris. It might run: "And I said to Bill I can't abide your smoking in the car."

Explicated in full in the manner of Urban, we have the following: "I, the narrator, say, 'I, Doris, said to Bill, "I can't abide your smoking in the car." ' " This has the form of explicit autobiography. In that statement, Doris treats her past acts as matters on which to report. She becomes the subject of commentary to herself in her current role as narrator.

In each of the cases I have analyzed, it is only too easy to allow the grammar to cast an ontological shadow on the world, to slip into thinking that the assumption of a duality of self is called for as a material condition for the use of the grammar of autobiography. The indexical and denotative "I" are reified to produce the illusion of an ontological distinction between person and self.

So poststructuralist feminists, such as Cixous, rejecting that dichotomy as (a) a binary opposition that serves covertly to maintain the male/female distinction that they take to be the source of all dichotomies, and (b) as an overtly active/passive one, must eschew the iterated first person form. Strictly speaking, they should avoid the use of any version of the distinction between indexicality and anaphora in their discourses. For instance, Cixous ought not to say, "Je m'appelle Heléne" when asked her name. Any autobiographical discourse of either of the forms exemplified above is ruled out for the same reason. The grammatical conditions for telling an autobiographical story always include indexicality and anaphora. "I (as speaker) say (Heléne Cixous) did, thought, proposed this and not-this." Smith's predicament, in the form she first presented it, namely, as the dilemma of one who is forced to present a contradictory self, cannot be stated without assuming the binary opposition between knower and known and putting herself on both sides of it.

The grammatical conditions for Cixous (or Smith) to present her case publicly include acceptance of the complex rules for the use of indexical expressions, particularly for the iterated first person. But this is the very grammar that poststructuralist, feminist linguists must declare off limits. Smith can only state her claim by subverting it, in that the grammatical forms that she must choose are those from the reification of which the person/self dichotomy arises and in which the necessary singularity of the narrator's voice is constituted. But this is the very singularity her discourse is directed at denying. If she is to declare her *self* contradictory as the many who are known, she must adopt the voice of the noncontradictory narrator as the one who knows.

FURTHER ANALYSIS OF THE FEMINIST CHALLENGE
TO THE DOUBLE SINGULARITY THESIS

What were the material conditions for the intelligibility of her claim that she suffered from multiple, because mutually incompatible, selves? It is not the least bit like the material conditions under which Morton Prince surmised that Miss Beauchamp was a multiplicity of selves. Dorothy Smith, the singular person, remembers very well both taking her children to the park and discussing sociology with her (male) colleagues. The material conditions include that she be aware that she is simultaneously or successively engaged in the presentation of herself according to diverse criteria for a proper display of personhood. The material conditions include self-perception and memory. These seem to entail that Smith exists and functions both as a singularity, the one who observes and remembers, and as a multiplicity, the ones who are observed and whose diverse activities are remembered. In short, Smith is and must be the one $self_1$ and several $selves_2$. The $self_1$ is surely the Strawsonian person, and the material conditions for that concept to have application can be summed up as "singular embodiment." The phrase *is a self* must be read with respect to the general thesis of this essay that selves are constituted discursively.

My thesis is that the reflexivity that appears in this analysis is neither paradoxical nor particularly the preserve of persecuted Woman. The selves that Dorothy Smith conjures up are grammatical fictions. There is just one Dorothy Smith and the many things she does. Dorothy Smith, the "knower," is not another entity, an ego, or something of the sort, nor are the "knowns," as clusters of incompatible actions, entities either. There are just people, including female people, among whom is Dorothy Smith. There is what they have done and their reports of what they have done. It is another potentially pernicious metaphor to report all this reporting as Dorothy Smith "describing her experiences." She is describing what she did and among the things she did was to feel or think this or that.

The Importance of Miss Beauchamp

Exploring personhood can take another way. Under what conditions do we take a being to count as a person? If the root ideas in the concept of personhood are singularity and continuity, how will these reveal themselves in the criteria one might fall back on in difficult cases? If material conditions alone sufficed, then the singularity and continuity of Dorothy Smith's embodiment would be enough for a brusque dismissal of her claim to multiplicity of selfhood as either confused or naive. Morton Prince's famous patient suffered no amoebalike multiplication of her body. She was always materially self-identical, and yet we are inclined to accept Prince's account as at least opening up a logically or conceptually possible case for declaring that there were contemporaneously three persons who were, from time to time, embodied as the one materially recognizable Miss Beauchamp.

Let us try putting the "How do you know?" question in this context. As it is clear that Miss Beauchamp does not remember "being" Sally or the third anonymous self while she is awake as the psychological being continuous with her original self, one might be tempted to revive Locke's reach of conscious recollection idea to develop a criterial account of cases such as hers. Should we say that Morton Prince knows there are many Miss Beauchamps because she discloses three universes of recollections, each internally coherent but distinct from the other two? Consulting the text reveals a different criterial procedure. It is built around the discursive practices made possible by indexical devices such as personal pronouns. Three coherent life stories are being told and three coherent sets of plans and intentions are being avowed. In reading the protocols, no doubt somewhat tidied up, one is struck by the way that the memories displayed in the talk are not neatly closed off in universes that would match the pronominal distribution of reported events. Miss Beauchamp's multiple selves are constituted in public discourse. But which of our two kinds of selves are so constituted in her case? It is because these are selves, that is, tellers of independent autobiographies, that we are inclined to interpret her case as one of many persons in one body. In this respect, Miss Beauchamp stands in the sharpest possible contrast to Dorothy Smith. For the latter's case is dependent on there being only one autobiography being told. The multiplicity on which Smith's political case against the sociology profession hangs is a multiplicity of selves$_2$.

But this tack seems to recoil on the strong embodiment thesis of James's treatment of the psychology of personal identity. Or, to take up the arguments of a more recent author, it seems to recoil on Strawson's case for the human body as the material root of both the singularity and the continuity of personhood. Though people do not fix their identity day by day by pausing to check from which body they are viewing the material world, nevertheless, singularity and continuity of material point of view is a root idea in the concept of person, according to Strawson. Can this point be made to fit with the emphasis that I have placed on autobiography?

Autobiographical discourse is talk in which the contents of historical claims are indexed with the speaker. Autobiography is in the first person. It does not use the reflexive subject's proper name. The grammar of indexicals looks like a good bet for clues to the conditions for personal identity as constituted in discursive practices.

First person singular indexicals in languages like English serve to tie the content of reports, declarations, and so on to speaker-relative locations in two "universes," so to speak. The material content is interpreted with respect to the spatiotemporal location of the speaker and the act of speaking, while the performative or illocutionary force is interpreted with respect to the location of the speaker in various moral universes of roles, rights, duties, and so on. A declaration like "I'll pick you up at your place tomorrow" indexes the meeting point with a place and time relative to the physical being of speaker and addressee and is marked with that degree of commitment that is usual in these two person's moral universe. If personhood is engendered in discursive practices, the local concept of "person" must have a material and a moral aspect. Is memory quite irrelevant to the concept of "personhood"? Is it just that with these first person practices in place we can, among other things, tell autobiographical stories of how we remember our lives to have been? Would the concept of "person" be any different if that practice had not taken root on the footing of grammar but was not necessitated by it? What is the significance of the temporality of self? It appears, I suggest, as a condition for the moral force of indexical talk. Commitments and promises and declarations of all sorts are future directed. The idea of a commitment is internally related to the idea of its fulfillment. Intentions and the consequent actions are, as Wittgenstein remarked, connected in language. Systematically forgetting one's promises lays one open to accusations of moral unreliability. Having an intact memory then is part of the concept of personhood, not because it is constitutive of one's self$_1$ or personal identity, as Locke thought, but because it is a necessary condition for the fulfillment of moral commitments. It is part of the fact that persons are moral agents. It is not a phenomenological condition for personhood but a social one.

Let us test out this idea with an example. Michael Faraday, after his midlife crisis, suffered a serious loss of memory power. He found he needed to write down what he was doing at the beginning of an experiment so that he could return to his plan after about 20 minutes to find out what experiment he had begun. His brain-located memorial devices did not provide him with that information any more so he had to devise an external memory store. Would it make any difference to my standing as a person in the eyes of the others if I had to have recourse to a short-term diary for keeping track of my commitments? I think not. I think I could dispense with psychological memory in favor of a surrogate, a prosthetic memory, without ceasing to meet the criteria for personhood. What this argument shows, I think, is that it is the indexical properties of first person discursive practices that count for personhood rather than the specific psychological conditions for their fulfillment.

A Resolution of the Second Level of the Feminist Challenge

We are now in a position to attempt a resolution of the apparently self-defeating claims made by Davies and Cixous, in their explicit and implicit rejections of the double singularity thesis. Both authors are writing in the first person. What of indexicality? As I have argued in dealing with the challenges of the first level, women's speaking practices are identical to those of men with respect to the use of the first person to index the empirical content of their remarks with their spatial locations as embodied speakers. Women's grammar exhibits the same double indexicality that is characteristic of the speech of men. So far as I know, Cixous never challenges the binary oppositions between *now* and *then* or *here* and *there* as sexist, though that challenge would seem to be implicit in Moi's gloss on Cixous's position. The oppositions inherent in spatial (and we could add temporal indexicality too) are intact. But there is plenty of evidence for the claim that the first person indexing of the illocutionary force of utterances by which speakers commit themselves to the course of action adumbrated in their speech acts is weaker, or better, more diffuse, among women speakers than among men. Gilligan (1982), and many other sociolinguists since, have emphasized the importance women attach to the discursive achievement of moral consensus.

For me, the really interesting thing about this analysis is that the provisional and tentative character of women's commitment to (moral) positions taken up in speaking is a self$_2$ phenomenon. It is Goffmanesque selves that are thereby produced, but through the second locative element, namely, position in a local moral order. In the indexical grammar of the first and second person, the form of the Lessing self is affected. Consensual morality implies group indexicality for locating the human source of the illocutionary force of a moral judgment, for instance. Davies cannot be right about spatiotemporal indexicality. Even Cixous never claims to be able to perceive the material world from places and times other than those where and when she is materially embodied. But Davies is surely right about the second locative aspect of indexical first person talk. With respect to that function of the use of indexical expressions, the discursive practices of women's talk do not engender the sharp boundaries between self$_1$ and selves$_2$, between Lessing singularities and Goffmanesque multiplicities, that are found in the talk of men.

REFERENCES

Benveniste, E. (1983). In K. Silverman (Ed.), *The subject of semiotics.* New York: Oxford University Press.
Cixous, H., with Clement, C. (1975). *La jeune née.* Paris: UGE.
Gilligan, C. (1982). *In a different voice.* Cambridge, MA: Harvard University Press.
Goffman, E. (1959). *The presentation of self in everyday life.* Garden City, NY: Doubleday.
Harré, R. (1991). The discursive production of selves. *Theory and Psychology, 1,* 51-63.
Hillerman, T. (1989). *Talking god.* New York: HarperCollins.
Husserl, E. (1967). *Ideas.* New York: Collier. (Original work published 1900)
Husserl, E. (1970). *Logical investigations* (J. N. Findley, Trans.). London: Routledge & Kegan Paul. (Original work published 1913)

James, W. (1977). *The writings of William James.* Chicago: Chicago University Press.

Kristeva, J. (1981). Women's time. *Signs, 7,* 13-35.

Locke, J. (1974). *An essay concerning human understanding* (J. Yolten, Ed.). London: Dent. (Original work published 1670)

Mead, G. H. (1934). *Mind, self, and society.* Chicago: Chicago University Press.

Moi, T. (1985). *Sexual/textual politics.* London: Methuen.

Muhlhausler, P., & Harré, R. (1990). *Pronouns and people.* Oxford: Basil Blackwell.

Parfit, D. (1984). *Reasons and persons.* Oxford: Oxford University Press.

Prince, M. (1968). *The dissociation of personality.* New York: Johnson Reprint Co. (Original work published 1905)

Smith, D. E. (1987). *The everyday world as problematic.* Boston: Northeastern University Press.

Strawson, P. F. (1956). *Individuals.* London: Methuen.

Urban G. (1989). The "I" of discourse. In B. Lee & G. Urban (Eds.), *Semiotics, self and society* (pp. 27-51). Berlin: Mouton de Gruyter.

Williams, B. A. O. (1973). *Problems of the self: Philosophical papers, 1956-72.* Cambridge: Cambridge University Press.

Relationally Engendered Selves

HARTMUT B. MOKROS
Rutgers University

MARGARET A. CARR
Psychological Group of Princeton

For as soon as we exist, we are born into language and language speaks (to) us, dictates its law, a law of death: it lays down its familial model, lays down its conjugal model, and even at the moment of uttering a sentence, admitting a notion of "being," a question of being, an ontology, we are already seized by a certain kind of masculine desire, the desire that mobilizes philosophical discourse.

—Heléne Cixous, 1981a, p. 45

We are selves only in that certain issues matter for us. What I am as a self, my identity, is essentially defined by the way things have significance for me. And as has been widely discussed, these things have significance for me, and the issue of my identity is worked out, only through a language of interpretation which I have come to accept as a valid articulation of these issues. To ask what a person is, in abstraction from his or her self-interpretations, is to ask a fundamentally misguided question, one to which there couldn't in principle be an answer.

—Charles Taylor, 1989, p. 34

DISCUSSIONS of the self and personal identity are notably prominent in contemporary discourse. Contested therein has been the implicitly held, taken-for-granted assumption in Western thought of the self as a unique, autonomous, self-contained psychological entity. Challenges to this assumption, offering alternative conceptualizations of self, have, as Sampson (1989) notes, come from a variety of perspectives including cultural psychology (e.g., Shweder, 1991), feminism, social constructionism, systems theory,

Correspondence and requests for reprints: Hartmut B. Mokros, Department of Communication, Rutgers University, New Brunswick, NJ 08903.

Communication Yearbook 17, pp. 74-91

critical theory, and deconstructionism. If the philosopher Charles Taylor (1989) is correct, that our assumptions about identity and the self have shaped "our philosophical thought, our epistemology and our language largely without our awareness" (p. ix), then the articulation of alternative conceptualizations of self will no doubt prove difficult and will likely meet with resistance (see Duncan, Kanki, Mokros, & Fiske, 1984).

Apparent in the variety of approaches from which the Western conceptualization of the self has been challenged has been a breaking away from traditional disciplinary orientations and boundaries. This is particularly notable in recent empirical attendings to the nature and accomplishment of routine practices of everyday life as *meaningful* activity wherein selves and identities are realized. Everyday routines are interactive and communicative processes. Thus it is within interaction and communication, within discursive practices, that meanings, selves, and social order are constituted, reproduced, and transformed—socially constructed, as it were (e.g., Gergen & Davis, 1985; Hecht, 1993; Shotter & Gergen, 1989).

Rom Harré, whose essay provides the basis of our discussion, has been a notable voice within this social constructionist tradition. His work is well known to students of social interaction, social relationships, and the self (e.g., Harré, 1980, 1983, 1986; Harré & Secord, 1972). Influenced by Wittgenstein (1953), Harré has been at the forefront in urging a "turn to discourse" for the study of social behavior, a turn that he has recently termed "the second cognitive revolution" (Harré, 1992). It is in the spirit of this "turn to discourse" that we have approached our reading and discussion of Harré's text—as a series of interactive engagements.

If we take seriously the notion of self as interactively constituted, then what does Harré's textual engagement with the work of feminist scholars and the range of interactive perspectives on the self convey about his conceptualization of self? How does he engage/recognize these personal and theoretical selves? And, insofar as he fails to engage fully/misrecognizes these selves, what consequence does this hold for the particulars of his model of the discursively constituted self? How may we explain the problematic in this engagement and his proposal?

We approach these questions by first laying out the key points made by Harré, as we see them. Next, we explore his engagement with "poststructuralist feminists" (and they with him) and conclude that he fails to engage them. We see this as reflecting the fundamental difference that exists between an account of self, from a discursive perspective, that nevertheless focuses on individual agency and its experience as such (Harré), as opposed to one that emphasizes situated interaction and focuses on the relational nature of self. Finally, we briefly consider three additional literatures, not engaged by Harré, that "speak" to a relational sense of identity and self from an interactive rather than a restricted discursive perspective.

THE DOUBLE SINGULARITY PRINCIPLE

"The problem to which this essay is addressed," according to Harré, "concerns the nature of one's sense of individuality as a person and the relation of that aspect of personhood to one's beliefs about what kind of person one is" (p. 56). This, for Harré, is an examination of the relationship between what he calls $self_1$ and $self_2$, namely, the relationship between an enduring, singular, or unitary sense of self and the multiplicity of selves as social presentations (e.g., Goffman, 1959) that arise from one's "unique set of beliefs each $self_1$ has about itself" (p. 55). A sense of personhood is said to be the product of the interplay between $self_1$ and $self_2$.

Harré claims two normative constraints on the enduring ($self_1$) and social ($self_2$) qualities of persons. Psychological normality (as opposed to disorder) is achieved through the maintenance (and social display) of a singular and continuous $self_1$. Social normality (i.e., moral acceptability) is achieved through the display of a singular, harmonious, and coherent $self_2$ (within any given social situation). He refers to these two normative constraints as the "double singularity principle." It is his goal in this essay "to explore the force of that principle through an analysis of an important set of challenges to its authority and hegemony . . . [that] come from feminist authors of the post-structuralist bent" (p. 58).

From the outset, and throughout this exploration, Harré argues against any essentialist singularity claims—$self_1$ or $self_2$—as substantive. This move, as is apparent from the discussion above, is neither new nor controversial. The motivation for this line of argument is apparently to invite the reader to consider how it is that we implicitly, and unproblematically, claim in everyday experience a $self_1$ as substantive. Thus he argues for a take on personhood as discursively constituted with "the $self_1$/$self_2$ distinction . . . real only in discourse . . . [as] a shadow cast by grammar on persons in action" (p. 61), a shadow that is the product of first person discursive practices. The double singularity principle, and the $self_1$ and $self_2$ distinction that underlies it, are thereby the unintended consequences (e.g., Giddens, 1984) of grammatical activity wherein "the indexical and denotative 'I' are reified to produce the illusion of an ontological distinction between person and self" (p. 68). Yet he concludes that "the discursive practices of women's talk do not engender the sharp boundaries between $self_1$ and $selves_2$ . . . that are found in the talk of men" (p. 72).

Through these moves, Harré both undermines and co-opts feminist challenges to the authority of the double singularity principle. He asserts that feminist writers, "of the poststructuralist bent," challenge the "authority and hegemony" of the double singularity principle. But, it may be asked, in what sense is this a concern of "feminism [a]s a *politics*" (Weedon, 1987, p. 1)? If the sense of concern for feminists with issues of self differs from that of Harré, as we believe it does, then what does this say about the qualities of his discursive engagement with the feminists he encounters?

HARRÉ AND THE FEMINISTS: ADDING CONTEXT

Harré must be acknowledged for his willingness to approach feminist theorists for answers to the question of whether there is still a "problem" with the self. Women theorists in general and feminist theorists in particular are rarely invited to participate in addressing such issues.

Usually, "gender or sexual division is either not visible, in the manner of a blind spot, or taken for granted, in the manner of an a priori" (de Lauretis, 1990, p. 130). Harré is willing to struggle (although his struggle is obvious and revealing) to enjoin what selected feminists might be saying. He understands that these feminist sayings have something to do with the knower/known, active/passive, subject/object polarities. And it seems that he admits the possibility that feminists may have something to say that is relevant to his conception of the self. But his engagement with these feminists seems undertaken more to teach them philosophical manners than to read what they say. If, as he says, he has argued for a discursively constituted self, why engage the feminists this way? These feminists offer more. It is fair to say that they begin where Harré's essay ends, with a discursively constituted self—but not in the restricted sense of a grammatical shadow.

Surely the most obviously problematic move, from a discursive perspective, that Harré makes is to decontextualize "feminists." It is unclear why he selects "these" feminists, these quotes, and, stripped from their contexts, it is unclear whether these quotes function as he claims. To whom, of what, at what time, and for what purpose do these various feminists write? Only by addressing these questions, which requires that these feminist writings be situated in their own contexts, can we see how their work "talks back" (D. E. Smith, 1987, p. 8) to Harré. We present this, admittedly incomplete, recontexualization of the feminists in the order in which they are encountered in Harré's text.

Dorothy Smith

Harré first considers the work of the sociologist Dorothy Smith (1987). Although he claims to cite her "most recent work," the passage he quotes concerning "bifurcated consciousness" is situated in the introduction (p. 7) of a book that pulls together papers dating to the early 1970s. Smith's reference to "bifurcated consciousness" introduces her experiential recognition of gender as an everyday problematic. Smith describes here her personal experience of incompatibility. This incompatibility results from the juxtaposition of the everyday world of mother with that of the, initially experienced, "genderless" world of the academic sociologist. She came to see this "genderless" world as "structured by a gender subtext . . . within [which] . . . women were the Other" (p. 7). Within this experience of incompatibility, she comes to recognize "our exclusion as women from the textually mediated organization of power which has come to predominate in our kind of society" (p. 4) and conceives of the project of a women's sociology. This project is to open a place for work "in which we are subjects and speak for ourselves" (p. 16) not as a science but as "a part of society and situated in institutional contexts" (p. 9). She sees sociology as constituent of patriarchal relations of ruling, with women taken as objects. Furthermore, she seeks "to do more than opening the social science discourse to women's voices and concerns . . . [namely to] be specifically subversive . . . [of] knowledge . . . vested in relations of ruling" (p. 212).

It should be noted that her earlier work has been critiqued by some feminists as essentialist (e.g., Lorraine, 1990), that is, as overlooking differences among women and their contexts and of privileging the experience of women. Smith acknowledges in her book that "taking a standpoint outside the textually mediated discourses of social science has meant renouncing theoretical projects that seek full development and coherence prior to an encounter with the world" (p. 11). This is a necessary consequence if one, as she does, starts with a women's "standpoint" and then proposes to explore how it is shaped in the extended relations of larger social political relations.

The politics of gender and how they relate to self are absent in any meaningful sense from the engagement with Smith that Harré offers. When the issue of gender is introduced, his engagement positions Smith as "persecuted Woman" (paranoid female?), who "conjures up" problematic selves that unbeknownst to her are but "grammatical fictions," and as surely not alone (with her gender mates) in a reflexive sense of incompatible selves.

Julia Kristeva

The second feminist engagement Harré entertains is with the work of the French psychoanalyst-linguist Julia Kristeva. He first presents an oft-quoted passage frequently encountered in feminist debate in which Kristeva (1981) presents the "third attitude . . . [in which] the very dichotomy man/woman as an opposition between two rival entities may be understood as belonging to *metaphysics*" (p. 33). He groups this "well known . . . proposal that traditional feminist programs ought to be transcended" with Smith's project as a "line," reducible to concerns with self$_2$ (i.e., Goffman selves), which thereby fails to challenge the double singularity principle and is ultimately seen as "not philosophically radical" (p. 60).

This conclusion is interesting given the frequent debate about the *radicalism* of Kristeva's work in feminist discussions. She herself introduces the issue of her *radicalism* in a passage shortly following the passage cited by Harré. On the "*radicalness of the process*" (italics added) she says: "This process could be summarized as an *interiorization of the founding separation of the sociosymbolic contract*, as an introduction of its cutting edge into the very interior of every identity whether subjective, sexual, ideological, or so forth" (p. 34). This founding separation is the entry of each individual into the symbolic from the preoedipal unity with the mother. She challenges the "myth of the archaic mother" as a way of undercutting the denial of separation of the "hysteric" (female) and the enhancement of it by the obsessional (male). She is explicitly antiessentialist as there is "no essential womanhood, not even a repressed one" (Weedon, 1987, p. 69).

Kristeva (1981) situates her essay by noting the differences in the French feminist context from that in the United States because of different psychoanalytic and sociopolitical milieus. Her paper is political, analyzing feminism in a specifically French psychoanalytic context. In contrast to the rejection by feminists of the "normatizing form" (Kristeva, 1981) of psychoanalysis in England and the United States that represses the unconscious (Gallup, 1982), in France feminism has gravitated to Freudianism for the *radical* "challenge it offers to discourses which assume the unified, self-present subject of rationality" (Weedon, 1987, p. 71). This is made possible by the Lacanian reading of Freud, in which psychoanalysis is situated linguistically, with the self thereby constituted in the symbolic realm.

In Lacanian theory, however, "the very existence of language is predicated upon separation from the presumed state of nature and so from the mother" (Editorial, 1981, p. 2). Language represses " 'woman,' in the sense of the feminine, [who] has no access to language" (Weedon, 1987, p. 69). Kristeva goes beyond Lacan. Thus, as Weedon (1987) notes, while agreeing that "the division between subject and object is the precondition for rational language and is realized in the syntactic structure of the language system itself with its distinct subject and predicate," Kristeva emphasizes that "language exceeds the boundaries of rationality and the symbolic order" (pp. 88-89). The unified subject, referred to as the *thetic* subject, is viewed by Kristeva as "an inherently unstable effect of language" (Weedon, 1987, p. 88). Given that this is Harré's thesis, albeit sans a "subject in process" extension, it is quite curious that he dismisses Kristeva as philosophically nonradical.

The failing is one of sampling. It is this theory of the "subject in process" that is of most interest to feminist poststructuralism for its radical possibilities. Yet, the claim made in the paper Harré quotes may be seen as a political stepping back. Weedon (1987) writes of the passage: "To make femininity and masculinity ever-present aspects of language which exceed rationality and are rational respectively is to propose an ahistorical model of language, gender and the unconscious in which actual historically specific power relations between women and men become irrelevant" (p. 90). Kristeva thus moves away from the more radical claims of the "subject in process" theory that "posited . . . a series of shifting identities, held in check and in cohesion only by the arbitrary imposition of paternal law" (P. Smith, 1989, p. 87).

After dismissing Smith and Kristeva with a "conservative resolution of the first level of attack on the double singularity thesis," Harré moves on to "a second level of feminist challenge to the self$_1$/self$_2$ distinction" (p. 60). Here he engages Davies and Cixous, in that order.

Bronwyn Davies

To this point, it is debatable whether Harré has truly engaged the feminists so as to allow their voice to address the question, "Is there still a problem about the self?" This is not the case with respect to his engagement with Davies. He presents Davies's personal comments "on a draft of a recent paper" of his, which would seem to give us some assurance that Davies is addressing the same subject matter as Harré. Moreover, he seems to take seriously Davies's remarks of a "less firmly demarcated" self$_1$ and self$_2$ "in women" than in men, as suggesting some feedback from the attributional qualities of self$_2$ to the substantial referent of self$_1$. Despite some avowed difficulties, he is able to "interpret" Davies's remarks as grammatical and supportive of his argument (Harré, 1991) that "the self is not a thing but a way of organizing the cognitions, perceptions, and so on of a human being as a unified person" (p. 61).

We do not have the benefit of reference to Davies's published work to construct a context for her remarks or to imagine how she might "talk back" (see D. E. Smith, 1987, p. 83) to Harré's reduction of her experience to grammatical concerns. Thus, lacking full representation of her comments, we cannot really evaluate Harré's claim in his conclusion that she is wrong "about spatiotemporal indexicality" (p. 72). Her remarks evoke themes of U.S. and British feminist discourse, which Harré himself references in his conclusion. One response to his argument is that the "experienced" self of women (as currently historically and culturally constituted) is organized according to criteria emphasizing responsiveness to context, an issue not addressed by Harré, rather than emphasizing unity. This would account for the proposals of multiplicity as well as for less distinction between internalized and behavioral selves.

This is indeed the stated thesis of Carol Gilligan's (1982) well-known proposal that the moral concerns of women are oriented toward responsibility to interpersonal context rather than to individual rights and adherence to abstract principles. Although Harré refers to this work in his conclusion, he misrepresents and trivializes its claims. He represents Gilligan's thesis as showing that the illocutionary force of women's utterances, that is, commitment to action promised in speech acts, is "weaker" or "more diffuse" than in men's. It seems here as if he intends to account for the discursive constitution of the self through speech act theory. Herein is revealed a shortcoming of his argument throughout, namely, the failure to consider the (macro)situatedness of micropractices of self-constitution and expression.

Instead, Gilligan (1982) proposes a difference in voice based in a principled and fundamentally different moral framework, with a female adherence to an "ethic of care" as opposed to a male adherence to an ethic of individual rights. Jean Baker Miller (1976) previously took a similar stance, arguing that women's relational sense of self is the consequence of their subordinate social position.

Within the psychoanalytic tradition, the sociologist Nancy Chodorow (1978) has proposed a theory for the origins of the less individuated nature of women and their diffuse ego boundaries (which Freud noted pejoratively). Chodorow sees these characteristics as positive in light of the masculine disavowal of affective ties. Her theory, based in object relational theories of psychoanalysis, focuses its attention on the fact of mothering. Early infant care by females is thereby seen as the source of differently "engendered" selves (a theme we shall return to). These engendered selves reproduce the pattern of female child care and male avoidance of these roles. It is this site, child care, which is contested and marked for social change.

Theories of women's relational emphasis have been criticized as merely reversing the hierarchicization of polarities (Benjamin, 1988). Chodorow's (1978) work is criticized as "overoptimistic," as emphasizing early primary structuring rather than later processes of change or maintenance, and as "losing sight of Freud's radical deconstruction of the ego" (Weedon, 1987, p. 62). But the incorporation of historical and cultural contexts into the theoretical constitution of the unconscious is a move welcomed by feminist poststructuralists. And Chodorow's concepts have been picked up and elaborated in an approach to the constitution and maintenance of a gendered subjectivity that applies to persons and to (philosophical) texts (Lorraine, 1990).

Heléne Cixous

After professing interest in the possibility of an "autonomous women's grammar" reflecting a different self$_1$/self$_2$ distinction in women as suggested by Davies, Harré engages with Torril Moi's (1985) treatment of the work of Heléne Cixous. He begins by seeing "one of Cixous's more sweeping claims as a 'grammatical proposal.' " Without actually quoting Cixous, Harré engages with her discussions of the relationship between binary oppositions in meaning and the male/female opposition. He concludes that her thesis is antistructural, antisexist, and "political" rather than based on any "historical, anthropological, or grammatical argument" (p. 62). He goes on to note the contradictions between her approach and that of other feminists (e.g., D. E. Smith, 1987), which is "insistent on the need to incorporate the deliverances of women's subjectivity in social science" (p. 62).

Cixous would presumably retort, "Let's not look at syntax but at fantasy" (Cixous, 1981a, p. 54). Her psychoanalytic thesis: Binary oppositions in the realm of meaning (the symbolic) are based on the original binary opposition, male/female, and the hierarchy male over female is based on the difference: penis/lack of penis. She addresses much of her work to the Lacanian theory, the theory that marks women as "other" (Kuhn, 1981, p. 37). It is, indeed, antistructuralist, that is to say, antisexist. And it is, indeed, the opposition male/female, not the social dichotomy of gender as Harré concludes, that is relevant (although there is greater ambiguity in the use of these concepts in French feminism than in Anglo feminism).

The Cixous proposal is originally situated in *La jeune née* (Cixous & Clement, 1975). Therein, she and Catherine Clement *conversationally engage* the question of whether the place of the hysteric (specifically Freud's Dora) is heroic or victimized, active or passive, radical or conservative. The two feminists take and retain different, although not purely polarized, perspectives.[1] The subject is taken up again in "Castration or Decapitation," wherein Cixous (1981a) writes:

> In fact, every theory of culture, every theory of society, the whole conglomeration of symbolic systems —everything, that is, that's spoken, everything that's organized as discourse, art, religion, the family, language, everything that seizes us, everything that acts on us—it is all ordered around hierarchical oppositions that come back to the man/woman opposition, an opposition that can only be sustained by means of a difference posed by cultural discourse as "natural," the difference between activity and passivity. (p. 44)

Cixous's concern is with hierarchy, power, and oppression, which in overvaluing the symbolic, specifically the Symbolic of Lacan, supports the valuation of men over women. In fact, she explicitly focuses on encouraging the speaking and writing of women: "But first she would have to speak, start speaking, stop saying that she has nothing to say!" (Cixous, 1981a, p. 50) and "Write your self. Your body must be heard" (Cixous, 1981b, p. 250).

Some of Cixous's ideas, particularly the linking of the feminine with women's sexual organs, is seen as essentialist although her "gestures towards a historical perspective" in the constitution of masculine and feminine are more agreeable to poststructuralist feminism (Weedon, 1987, p. 68). Cixous seems to try to avoid the problems of decentering subjectivity by focusing on feminine writing that "will always surpass the discourse that regulates the phallocentric system; it does and will take place in areas other than those subordinated to philosophico-theoretical domination" (Cixous, 1981b, p. 253), areas Harré systematically avoids.

Failing to Engage

Harré tells the reader that he will "try to show . . . that they [poststructuralist feminists] have some interesting contributions to make to the analytical philosophy of personhood" (p. 58). He does not demonstrate this, at least in part because he does not fully engage their contributions. His repeated emphasis on the texts' difficulty is reminiscent of Freud's puzzlement in regard to what women want, which Cixous (1981a) relates to keeping women in "a place of mystery" (p. 49).

The failure to engage the feminists on their own terms (and contexts) leaves open what question he wishes to put to these feminists. Is he asking whether feminist claims about selfhood speak to all selves? Although he seems to in the end acknowledge that women's selves may be constituted differently than men's, he does not engage with the implications. Given that this is the point from which feminists begin to speak, one wonders why he engages them to begin with.

Harré says he is looking to see if something is being said about the self$_1$/self$_2$ relationship. Occasionally he seems to deal with this relationship but more often he seems to be saying that gender is a self$_2$ issue and therefore relatively peripheral to discussion about self and identity ("in the philosopher's sense"). Does he recognize that even the limited feminist sample portrayed is saying that gender is both a self$_1$ and self$_2$ issue and neither, because the distinction doesn't hold? In acknowledging the distinction as a grammatical one, does he recognize its imposition on selves in our current politically gendered culture? Does his dismissal of Dorothy Smith as just a "person" dismiss the issue? Another way of saying this is to ask whether Harré does really enter into a dialogue with feminist discourses or whether he attempts to classify and define them away—analytically. We assert the latter and will now consider possible sources of Harré's "difficulty."

First, feminists consistently point to a feminine characteristic of greater comfort with diffuse boundaries and responsiveness to immediate bodily experience than are characteristic of the masculine self. This sense of female selfhood is seen to be embodied in early preverbal interaction with mother that is never disavowed as it is in the constitution of a masculine sense of self (Chodorow, 1978).

Second, feminists maintain that there is nothing sacred or ahistorical about the self as experienced or described. Rather, the sense of self, feminine or otherwise, is historically and culturally constituted within social institutions and power relations through language and other symbolic practices.

Third, the contemporary constitution of selves has everything to do with a basic division of human experience into male and female categories such that the self and theories of self as currently formulated are based on this division and the valorization of one side of this polarization, namely, the male.

This has the effect of saying that our institutionalized way of knowing represents only one side of a gendered polarization with knower elevated and separated from known; that women are represented as "other" or "object"; and that embodied, relational, contextual knowing is devalued and unrepresented in systems and procedures of knowing.

From this perspective, Harré's essay can be seen as (a) making a move toward giving women voice, yet at the same time (b) demonstrating the futility of attempting to fit feminists into an analytic philosophical discourse. To thus attempt to "fit them in" is to co-opt them, disappear them as feminists disappear in Harré's discourse. As Gallup (1988) suggests, "Rather than treat the body as a site of knowledge, a medium for thought, the more classic philosophical project has tried to render it transparent and get beyond it, to dominate it by reducing it to the mind's idealizing categories" (p. 4). If Harré had been able to fully engage feminist theories, he might have heard what they have to offer the analytic philosophical enterprise. The tensions within feminism between revaluing an essential feminine and undoing the feminine/masculine opposition by critiquing relations of power might have served to illuminate the tensions between the experience of the self as a center of agency and the self as discursively constituted.

RELATIONALLY SITUATED SELVES

Harré's engagement with the feminists reveals a notable omission in how he frames his problem—an absence of concern with context and situation. When situation is explicitly included in discussion of the $self_1$/$self_2$ relationship, the moral constraint of the double singularity principle appears much less certain and exclusive than Harré claims.

For example, everyday experience suggests that persons are expected, that is to say, morally obligated, to adapt themselves to the contingencies of the social situation. Yet, persons are also expected, or morally obligated, not to be so adaptive to situations as to give social others the sense that there exists only a multiplicity of selves. This would imply that identity is to be seen as a "dialectic" between $self_1$, $self_2$, and the social situation—with identity revealed through the individual's entry into and maintenance of relationships with others. It is through the other that the self becomes apparent, not, as Harré seems to suggest, through a person's agency.

We began this commentary by noting that the articulation of alternative conceptualizations of self encounter difficulties because the conceptualization of a singular, autonomous self is incorporated into our epistemology and language (see Mokros, 1993). Indeed, this would seem to be true for at least some philosophical enterprises that aim to offer foundations for empirically oriented inquiries. There are, however, several lines of inquiry that have made important strides toward offering an alternative perspective on self, one that sees self as interactionally constituted, as sensible only with reference to the other. We will briefly examine three of these lines of inquiry as potential sources for the development of a relation- and communication-based theory of the self.

The Preverbal Self

Microanalytic studies of mother-infant interaction suggest that preverbal senses of self are "dyadic phenomena" embedded in the structures of interaction (e.g., Beebe & Lachman, 1988). During the preverbal life of the infant, particularly the first 6 to 9 months of life, noninstrumental social activities between mother and baby are commonly characterized as coactivity that is dancelike in its qualities. The structuring of this coactivity, of moments that are "purely social interaction" or "free play" (Stern, 1977), is clearly a joint accomplishment. The path to this accomplishment may be said to pose a coordination problem (Duncan & Fiske, 1977; Lewis, 1969) for mother and baby. Each must be able to communicate about initiation, maintenance, termination, and avoidance of social interaction if their coordination problem is to be solved. This of course implies the ability to signal these structuring moves and to recognize the signals of the other. Additionally, these moments of coordinated activity, of coactivity, are clearly a source of stimulation, arousal, and pleasure for both participants.

Although efforts at making, managing, or avoiding social interaction aim at coordinated attunement, they are also and sometimes prominently characterized by interactive mismatch (see Stern, 1977, pp. 3-5). Stimulation may be left wanting (e.g., baby signals engagement readiness but mother does not even though seemingly available to do so); stimulation may prove over- or not sufficiently arousing to maintain interactional involvement. Thus it is the coordination and missteps in these early social interactions that provide the foundations of the tension between autonomy and relatedness, what we regard as the most fundamental ongoing experience of personhood.

It is through interactional involvement, through experiences of attunement and mismatch, that qualities of a "core sense of self" develop in the preverbal period of life, according to Stern (1985). These qualities include a sense of self-agency, self-coherence, self-affectivity, and self-history, not as "cognitive construct" but as "an experiential integration" (Stern, 1985, p. 71). Self as organization is here not seen as entity based but as a systemic organization, based in patterns of interaction between the baby and "self-regulating others." That is, the mother (or other caregiver) serves as regulator—interpreter and modulator—of the infant's states of activation and arousal within interaction (Stern, 1977).

While it is typical to think that the process of development is a progression from egocentrism to sociocentrism, from an internal self to a social self, these earliest periods of life may be thought of as quite the opposite, as first and foremost experiences of social being (Vygotsky, 1962). From this perspective, the foundations of an awareness of affectivity and agency are anchored in, and observed through, the activity and agency of others. According to Stern, all subsequent development of self builds on these foundations. Characteristically, with but few exceptions, the context within which these foundations of self are established is in interaction with female others. The implications of this structural asymmetry in the social constitution of selves have only begun to be addressed (e.g., Chodorow, 1978). This of course comes as no surprise to feminist scholars.

Self as Situated

Studies of early mother-infant interaction, according to Stern (1977, 1985), identify the earliest foundations of self as defined in relationship to the other, in and through communication. This suggests that an emergent sense of self is best seen as situated (Benhabib, 1992). The longitudinal research of Judy Dunn (1982) provides a powerful example.

Dunn studied the development of sibling relationships between firstborn children who were between the ages of roughly 2 to 4 years at the time of the birth of a second child. She notes that to understand the developmental qualities of these sibling relationships requires knowledge about the mother's interaction with the first born in the period prior to and immediately following the birth of the second child. She reports the following:

> In families where there had been a relatively high frequency of joint play and attention between mother and daughter before and immediately after the birth of the baby, the firstborn daughter was more likely to behave in a hostile and unfriendly way to the sibling 14 months later. . . . In these families, moreover, the younger sibling was much less friendly to the elder than in other families. . . . In [contrast] families where there had been frequent incidents of prohibition and much confrontation between mother and daughter in the first month after the baby was born, the firstborn girls were particularly friendly to their siblings. For firstborn boys there was no such clear pattern linking the sibling interaction with the earlier relationship between mother and son. (Dunn, 1982, pp. 172-173)

Dunn interprets this finding using Chodorow's (1978) theory. She provides many additional observations that underscore the general point we wish to make here, namely, that an understanding of early sibling relationships requires knowledge of the broader familial context. The quality of self in relationship is itself relationally situated.

A view of the self as situated is also clearly revealed in Csikszentmihalyi's (1982) studies of everyday experience in naturally occurring contexts using the experience sampling method. Based on numerous studies, Csikszentmihalyi has proposed a theory that posits four general states of experience that result from the interaction between individuals and the immediate environment in which they find themselves situated. He refers to these as anxiety, boredom, apathy, and flow. Flow, a state of perceived optimal enjoyment and involvement, results when situational challenges are relatively high and individual talents complement or mesh with these challenges (Csikszentmihalyi & Csikszentmihalyi, 1988).

Using Csikszentmihalyi's method and model, Wells (1988) studied mothers' experiences across a variety of everyday contexts. She reports that mothers with younger preschool children were significantly less likely to be in states of flow than mothers of older children. In addition, if alone or alone with children, mothers were more likely to be in states of boredom and apathy than when with other adults. At these times, they were more likely to be in states of anxiety and flow. Wells also reports that time spent in flow was positively related to perceptions of parental competence but unrelated to generalized self-esteem evaluations completed prior to study. She speculates that "mothers may have clearer ideas about what they expect of themselves as mothers, and receive clearer feedback about themselves as parents, than they are clear about what to expect of themselves as persons" (Wells, 1988, p. 336). Thus, even though optimal experience for these women was most likely to occur in nonmothering contexts, their sense of self-worth in these contexts was associated with stereotypical maternal role expectations rather than specific qualities about themselves.

These lines of research expand the vocabulary that may be brought to bear in the development of a theory of the self as socially constructed, as interactionally constituted. The work of Dunn (1982) and Wells (1988) suggests some of the types of outcomes, for child (Dunn) and mother (Wells), that result from the gender-based context within which the foundations of selves are constituted.

The Ongoing Relational Constitution of Self

Conceptualization of self as an ongoing relational achievement requires, as the feminists have noted, attention to bodily and affective bases of experience—to feelings of attunement and failures to socially bond. Indeed, an alternative to the discursive framework presented by Harré is to see an enduring sense of $self_1$ as constituted in the tracing of affective experience in social encounters. $Self_1$ is then to be seen as a baseline record of "relational or social worth" that is reproduced or transformed, and thereby updated, in any given social encounter.[2]

The work of Erving Goffman suggests the viability of such an alternative framework.[3] Social encounter, according to Goffman (1955, 1956a), always indexes qualities of its participants (demeanor) and establishes the participants' "make" of the situation and therein regard or respect for each other (deference). It is the social regard extended to a person's expression of demeanor and deference and that person's awareness of such social regard that defines "face"—a sense of self in relationship. The notion of face is a relational notion of self that is, although not well developed by Goffman, affectively valenced (e.g., Goffman, 1956b) along a continuum from pride to shame. Thus, to be "in face" is to experience pride in social (through other or generalized other) acceptance, while to be "out of face" or to "lose face" is an experience of embarrassment or shame. From his perspective, $selves_2$ may be viewed as methods or strategies to present, protect, save, regain, and restore face.

It is the recent work of Thomas Scheff (1990; see also Retzinger, 1991) that most profoundly shows how moral responsibilities (deference) and affective or emotional experiences within the micromoments of everyday life motivate persons and account for an ongoing sense of self. Human motivation, Scheff argues, is based in the need for mental and emotional connectedness, to social others, to the "social bond." The success of maintaining connectedness in everyday interaction depends upon relative attunement or jointly focused attention within which participants experience "a mutual understanding that is not only mental but also emotional . . . not agreement but rather empathic intersubjectivity: mind reading" (p. 7).

Emotional experiences arise continuously within the social bond, providing an ongoing read of the quality of attunement. In particular, the experience of shame and social efforts to rework or repress shame experiences are seen as central to the regulation of participation in the social bond and to the constitution of the individual.

Although he does not make this claim, Scheff offers method and theory that serve to undo the impact that traditional ways of viewing self have had on our ways of thinking about the human condition and thereby to radicalize privileged and everyday discursive practices. As Scheff (1990) puts it: "The language of laypersons and experts in modern societies systematically denies the social bond and the emotions: repression of the idea of the bond and the emotions of pride and shame is institutionalized. My book proposes the need for a new language, based on models of bond-relevant behavior, with emphasis on the complexity of behavior and on the key role of sequences of emotion" (p. 19).

CONCLUSION

We have suggested that feminist writers take as a given, as a starting point, a discursive conceptualization of the self but not in the restricted and acontextual sense proposed by Harré. They, however, demand more than this, namely, an expansion of the discursive so as to include the discourse of the body in relationship—of the material self as a relational symbolic experience. This is a perspective that escapes the logical, rational, cognitive (phallocentric) restrictions that are implicit in grammatically based discursive accounts unknowingly anchored to the traditional Western conceptualization of self. It is a perspective that views selves as relationally engendered—within social interaction, engendered through the otherness of the other and engendered within an always-present polity.

Our major point of difference, then, with Harré is with his claim that "there are just people, including female people . . . . There is what they have done and their reports of what they have done" (p. 69). While this conclusion may seem enlightened, there is something very amiss in how it has been achieved. Indeed, we view this claim as antithetical to a social constructionist perspective, wherein communication is seen to constitute reality, including people. It makes no sense to speak of people without speaking of others. This requires a new way of thinking that is only accomplished with much difficulty. It is a way of thinking that is at the core of feminist discourse and it is a way of thinking that is emerging in a small but growing number of empirical lines of inquiry. In contrast, to say, as Harré does, that all there is is what persons have done and reports of what persons have done, is to claim ontological primacy to self-agency. The analysis Harré offers generates a discursive self in the absence of the other.

Harré's claim that the distinction between person and self is a grammatically produced illusion is certainly of interest. To stop there and ignore differences in the strength with which this illusion is experienced and reified interactionally and historically, however, also cuts short analysis of the appeal that a unified, singular self offers for everyday thought and social practice.

Social interaction involves "choosing" from among multiple possibilities of $self_2$ presentation (Goffman, 1959) in a socially (morally) responsible fashion. The missituating of social presentations, from the vantage point of the generalized or social other (Mead, 1934), is *socially* problematic, threatening the immediate social order and its received conceptual foundations.

In response, social members routinely employ highly ritualized accounting practices to repair the social situation (Goffman, 1967, 1971). These accounting practices typically appeal to failings of $self_1$, deviations from a unitary self, as the source of social troubles. Appeals to $self_1$ as a source of troubles forefront a singular, received reality. Problems arising in relationship may thereby be treated as products not of relationships (of social interactions and institutions) but of individuals, observable in "their" behavior and validated in their accounts.

Such a perspective is of course not incompatible with a view of $self_1$ as by-product (of the indexical properties) of grammar in use. What this perspective adds is how $self_1$, as by-product, functions both creatively and reproductively as a *pragmatic* solution in social encounters (see Silverstein, 1975).

NOTES

1. As Kristeva's translator has noted, it is as dangerous to speak of feminism as a unity as to speak thus of the feminine (Jardine, 1981, p. 10).

2. It is of course no accident and of considerable significance that what we refer to here as social or relational worth is called "self-worth" or "self-esteem" in both everyday and privileged contexts.

3. The power of Goffman's insights has been grossly trivialized and dismissed, placed as they were into the pigeonhole of the "dramaturgical model." Lost thereby is the subtlety and power of the analytic vocabulary he introduced.

REFERENCES

Beebe, B., & Lachman, F. (1988). The contribution of mother-infant mutual influence to the origins of self- and object representations. *Psychoanalytic Psychology, 5*, 305-337.

Benhabib, S. (1992). *Situating the self: Gender, community and postmodernism in contemporary ethics*. New York: Routledge.

Benjamin, J. (1988). *The bonds of love: Psychoanalysis, feminism, and the problem of domination*. New York: Pantheon.

Chodorow, N. (1978). *The reproduction of mothering: Psychoanalysis and the sociology of gender*. Berkeley: University of California.

Cixous, H. (1981a). Castration or decapitation. *Signs: Journal of Women in Culture and Society, 7*, 41-55.

Cixous, H. (1981b). The laugh of the Medusa. In E. Marks & I. de Courtivron (Eds.), *New French feminism* (pp. 245-264). Brighton: Harvester.

Cixous, H., with Clement, C. (1975). *La jeune née*. Paris: UGE.

Csikszentmihalyi, M. (1982). Towards a psychology of optimal experience. In L. Wheeler (Ed.), *Review of personality and social psychology* (Vol. 2). Beverly Hills, CA: Sage.

Csikszentmihalyi, M., & Csikszentmihalyi, I. S. (Eds.). (1988). *Optimal experience: Psychological studies of flow in consciousness*. Cambridge: Cambridge University Press.

de Lauretis, T. (1990). Eccentric subjects: Feminist theory and historical consciousness. *Feminist Studies, 1*, 115-150.

Duncan, S. D., & Fiske, D. W. (1977). *Face-to-face interaction: Research, methods and theory*. Hillsdale, NJ: Lawrence Erlbaum.

Duncan, S. D., Kanki, B., Mokros, H., & Fiske, D. W. (1984). Pseudounilaterality, simple-rate variables and other ills to which interaction research is heir. *Journal of Personality and Social Psychology, 46*, 1335-1348.

Dunn, J. (1982). *Siblings*. Cambridge, MA: Harvard University Press.

Editorial. (1981). *Signs, 7*, 1-3.

Gallup, J. (1982). *The daughter's seduction: Feminism and psychoanalysis*. Ithaca, NY: Cornell University Press.

Gallup, J. (1988). *Thinking through the body*. New York: Columbia University Press.

Gergen, K. J., & Davis, K. (Eds.). (1985). *The social construction of the person*. New York: Springer.

Giddens, A. (1984). *The constitution of society*. Berkeley: University of California Press.

Gilligan, C. (1982). *In a different voice: Psychological theory and women's development*. Cambridge, MA: Harvard University Press.

Goffman, E. (1955). On face-work: An analysis of ritual elements in social interaction. *Psychiatry, 18*, 213-231.

Goffman, E. (1956a). The nature of deference and demeanor. *American Anthropologist, 58*, 473-502.

Goffman, E. (1956b). Embarrassment and social organization. *The American Journal of Sociology, 62*, 264-274.

Goffman, E. (1959). *The presentation of self in everyday life*. Garden City, NY: Doubleday.

Goffman, E. (1967). *Interaction ritual*. Garden City, NY: Doubleday.

Goffman, E. (1971). *Relations in public*. New York: Harper.

Harré, R. (1980). *Social being: A theory for social psychology*. Totowa, NJ: Littlefield, Adams.

Harré, R. (1983). *Personal being: A theory for individual psychology*. Oxford: Basil Blackwell.

Harré, R. (Ed.). (1986). *The social construction of emotions*. Oxford: Basil Blackwell.

Harré, R. (1991). The discursive production of the selves. *Theory and Psychology, 1*, 51-63.

Harré, R. (Ed.). (1992). New methodologies: The turn to discourse. *American Behavioral Scientist, 36*.

Harré, R., & Secord, P. F. (1972). *The explanation of social behavior*. Oxford: Basil Blackwell.

Hecht, M. L. (1993). 2002—A research odyssey: Toward the development of a communication theory of identity. *Communication Monographs, 60*, 76-82.

Jardine, A. (1981). Introduction to Julia Kristeva's "Women's time." *Signs, 7*, 5-12.

Kristeva, J. (1981). Women's time. *Signs: Journal of Women in Culture and Society, 7*, 13-35.

Kuhn, A. (1981). Introduction to Helene Cixous's "Castration or decapitation." *Signs, 7,* 36-40.

Lewis, D. K. (1969). *Conventions.* Cambridge, MA: Harvard University Press.

Lorraine, T. E. (1990). *Gender, identity, and the production of meaning.* Boulder, CO: Westview.

Mead, G. H. (1934). *Mind, self and society.* Chicago: University of Chicago.

Miller, J. B. (1976). *Toward a new psychology of women.* Boston: Beacon.

Moi, T. (1985). *Sexual/textual politics.* London: Methuen.

Mokros, H. B. (1993). The impact of a native theory of information on two privileged accounts of personhood. In J. R. Schement & B. D. Ruben (Eds.), *Information and behavior: Vol. 4. Between communication and information* (pp. 57-79). New Brunswick, NJ: Transaction.

Retzinger, S. M. (1991). *Violent emotions: Shame and rage in marital quarrels.* Newbury Park, CA: Sage.

Sampson, E. E. (1989). The deconstruction of the self. In J. Shotter & K. J. Gergen (Eds.), *Texts of identity* (pp. 1-19). London: Sage.

Scheff, T. J. (1990). *Microsociology: Discourse, emotion, and social structure.* Chicago: University of Chicago.

Shotter, J., & Gergen, K. J. (Eds.). (1989). *Texts of identity.* London: Sage.

Shweder, R. A. (1991). *Thinking through cultures: Expeditions in cultural psychology.* Cambridge, MA: Harvard University Press.

Silverstein, M. (1975). Shifters, linguistic categories and cultural description. In K. H Basso & H. A. Selby (Eds.), *Meaning in anthropology* (pp. 11-56). Albuquerque: University of New Mexico.

Smith, D. E. (1987). *The everyday world as problematic: A feminist sociology.* Boston: Northeastern University Press.

Smith, P. (1989). Julia Kristeva et al.: Or, take three or more. In R. Feldstein & J. Roof (Eds.), *Feminism and psychoanalysis* (pp. 84-104). Ithaca, NY: Cornell University Press.

Stern, D. N. (1977). *The first relationship: Infant and mother.* Cambridge, MA: Harvard University Press.

Stern, D. N. (1985). *The interpersonal world of the infant: A view from psychoanalysis and developmental psychology.* New York: Basic Books.

Taylor, C. (1989). *Sources of the self: The making of modern identity.* Cambridge, MA: Harvard University Press.

Vygotsky, L. (1962). *Thought and language.* Cambridge: MIT Press.

Weedon, C. (1987). *Feminist practice and poststructuralist theory.* Oxford: Basil Blackwell.

Wells, A. J. (1988). Self-esteem and optimal experience. In M. Csikszentmihalyi & I. S. Csikszentmihalyi (Eds.), *Optimal experience: Psychological studies of flow in consciousness* (pp. 327-341). Cambridge: Cambridge University Press.

Wittgenstein, L. (1953). *Philosophical investigations.* New York: Macmillan.

Discursive Practice and Legitimation of the Polymorphous Self

MARTHA COOPER
Northern Illinois University

ANNE GRAVEL
Pennsylvania State University

ERHAPS, like Nietzsche's will to power and Foucault's will to truth, there is a will to self, to know the self, to exert power over the self, to find the self, to have a self. So, we search for our selves. Eventually, we may find that we have only to create ourselves. The resources that we use to fashion ourselves are our discursive practices. Harré presents one version of how this is done. Other versions exist. Two other versions, in particular, remind us of the influence our discursive resources exert on the construction of the self while reminding us of the space for creative energy on the part of that being that constructs itself.

Harré's essay attends to how the self—both as a sense of enduring personal identity (self$_1$) and as a potentially changing socially enacted identity (self$_2$)—is created, reproduced, and maintained through language use. In the course of his essay, he develops two ideas about personhood achieved through language use. First, he posits a "double singularity principle" that calls for continuity and coherence in both self$_1$ and self$_2$.

Later, he elaborates a "thesis of double indexicality" that claims the existence of both a material and a moral function for indexical statements, self-referential statements such as those found within autobiography. His essay thus provides a frame for discussion of two issues germane to any contemporary investigation of the nature of the self. First is the question of

Correspondence and requests for reprints: Martha Cooper, Communication Studies Department, Northern Illinois University, DeKalb, IL 60115.

Communication Yearbook 17, pp. 92-103

unity or coherence of self ($_1$ and $_2$). Second is the question of the functions of discursive practices that call the self into being.

This essay addresses each of those questions by situating Harré's work alongside that of other constructionist views of the self, in particular those that emerge from Continental philosophy following the work of Michel Foucault and contemporary feminist theory and criticism, especially as it relates to autobiography as a discursive practice.[1] In doing so, we intend to raise some questions about the utility of Harré's distinction between self$_1$ and self$_2$, but, more important, we intend to elaborate on the position that an understanding of self as constructed through discursive practices can lead to liberation from inhibiting, repressive, and marginalizing concepts of the self. We begin with a discussion of a postmodern constructionist view of self that emphasizes the work of Foucault and then turn to a discussion of feminist concerns about the discursive creation of self.

SOCIAL CONSTRUCTION OF SELF
THROUGH DISCURSIVE PRACTICE

The notion that the self is constructed rather than received enjoys currency for a number of theorists (Levine, 1992). Among them, existentialist thinkers such as Sartre and postmodern writers such as Foucault argue that what distinguishes humans from other animals is that humans create themselves. As Harré observes, among constructionists, the self is manifested discursively. Consequently, the resources of symbolic systems and the realities of discursive practices provide the ground in which to investigate the nature of the self. Because Harré's position is that the self is not just manifested in discursive practices but is actually constituted in the course of making discursive practices, the nature of discursive practices themselves becomes the key to understanding the nature of the self.

Harré's position echoes that of Foucault (1984), who argued that "it is not enough to say that the subject is constituted in a symbolic system. It is not just in the play of symbols that the subject is constituted. It is constituted in real practices—historically analyzable practices. There is a technology of the self which cuts across symbolic systems while using them" (p. 369). The distinction between symbolic systems and the discursive practices that use those systems to which Foucault points is an important one. For it is within that distinction that Harré's thesis of double indexicality becomes problematic.

Harré's thesis of double indexicality explains how self-referential statements, the declaratives and narratives common to autobiography, function grammatically to construct self$_1$. For Harré, the grammatical function of the "I" of self-referentiality is to position the source in regard to what is said or written. Self$_1$ is constructed in relation to perception (spatial location of the source), memory (temporal moment of speaking or writing), and responsibility (moral position of the source). By linking the function of discursive practice to the psychological constructs of perception, memory, and responsibility, Harré contributes to an understanding of the personal consequences of constructing the self through discourse but fails to grapple with the social consequences of doing so.

The problem with Harré's position is stated succinctly by Levine in his introduction to constructionist views of the self, including Foucault's: "No discussion of the self can any longer confine itself to psychology, or the 'internal' conditions of 'mind.' (The very concepts of 'internal' and 'mind' are, after all, also in question.) Language and history and social context in fact become psychology, as psychology and anthropology and sociology become language and history" (Levine, 1992, p. 2). Levine's position rests on his and others' recognition that discursive practices function in a social construction of reality that moves beyond the purview of a single person. That position is particularly clear within Foucault's studies of the self as discursively constructed.

Foucault consistently viewed discourse as situated in history, hence his suggestion that the discursive practices through which the self was constructed were *historically analyzable practices*. The functions of these practices take on a social rather than merely personal or psychological character because discursive practices generally function to create systems of knowledge, power, and ethics that imply the appropriate relation one ought to have with oneself (Foucault, 1984, p. 352). As such, Foucault's view of the function of discursive practices substitutes social constructs of knowledge, power, and ethics for Harré's psychological constructs of perception, memory, and responsibility. Illustrations drawn from Foucault's work in regard to the self highlight the difference.

When describing the nature of his last project, the series of volumes on sexuality, Foucault explained that three types of study were possible. He claimed: "First, a historical ontology of ourselves in relation to truth through which we constitute ourselves as subjects of knowledge; second, a historical ontology of ourselves in relation to a field of power through which we constitute ourselves as subjects acting on others; third, a historical ontology in relation to ethics through which we constitute ourselves as moral agents" (Foucault, 1984, p. 351). Perhaps more interesting than his comment about his work, however, is the substance of the work itself. In *The History of Sexuality* (1980), Foucault reviewed how sexuality has been used as a way of discovering the truth about ourselves, how various technologies have developed to constrain and control our sexual behavior, and how we monitor our adherence to these rules and obligations of our own making as a way of assessing our own morality. Hence Foucault argued that we create ourselves in regard to sexuality insofar as we constitute knowledge of, power over, and ethics for ourselves in this area.

If the functions of discursive practice are outlined from a social, historical perspective, rather than from an individualizing, psychological perspective, then the mutability of the self across time and culture becomes apparent. Foucault remarked that "techniques of self . . . can be found in all cultures in different forms" (1984, p. 369). Foucault's studies, *The Use of Pleasure* (1985) and *The Care of the Self* (1986), provide rich descriptions of practices of the self in classical Greece, during the first and second centuries in Imperial Rome, and afterward during the rise of Christianity, while his essay "Technologies of the Self" (1988) provides a brief overview of comparative practices. He pointed out that in ancient Greece during the fifth century B.C., for example, the self was an object of concern and care. He noted that the oral culture fostered two communication practices—rhetoric and dialectic—that assisted the Greek citizen in taking care of himself. Moreover, he observed that diverse views regarding care of the self—Plato's suggestion of dialectic as a procedure, the Epicureans' suggestion of philosophizing about the soul, and Philo of Alexandria's collective prayer meetings and spiritual banquets— were all tied to concern for the community, the polis, the city-state. And he observed that these procedures, these practices, were taught to the young as they prepared for leadership roles, thereby suggesting that the self was constituted in a context of pedagogy, whose aim was to prepare the citizen for public life (Foucault, 1988, pp. 19-21, 23-27).

In contrast, Foucault's description of the self as constituted in Imperial Rome emphasized the amount and role of writing. He argued that the Romans saw a relationship "between writing and vigilance" that encouraged more introspection, and he noted the importance of letter writing for people like Cicero and Seneca. The practice of letter writing, according to Foucault, encouraged concern for recalling the everyday details of life and, through those recollections, reactivated the rules of appropriate conduct. Those rules were obtained through yet another communication practice. Foucault pointed out the switch from the Greek pedagogical model of dialogue to the Roman approach to education in which the Master talked and students listened. Thus "the art of listening" developed as a way to retreat into the self and take stock of one's conduct. These practices in Rome were not so much tied to preparation of the young for public life as to a construction of ethos by the old who were facing death (Foucault, 1988, pp. 27-34).

The early Christian period provided other, different technologies of the self, according to Foucault. He pointed out the use of diary writing and Christian confession as practices that encouraged constant reflection on faults, temptations, desires, and so forth. In addition, practices such as witnessing, penance, and even martyrdom encouraged renunciation of the self and life to grow closer to God and purify the spirit. These practices were designed for all at all stages of life and were not the exclusive domain of any age group (Foucault, 1988, pp. 35-44).

The importance of Foucault's comparative analysis is that it radically undermines any inclination to adopt a naturalized view of self that can be used to inhibit, repress, or otherwise marginalize individuals or groups whose discursive practices differ from the dominant social order. Levine (1992) summarizes the point nicely:

> The concept of the "self," fully naturalized into a coherent, stable, and normative essence, is precisely what is invoked to dismiss deviations from the norm as symptoms of illness or criminality. In a world society in which difference becomes a condition of everyday life for almost everybody, the self has frequently become a historically constructed ideal for rejection of resistance to authority. . . . The impetus for the theoretical constructions of writers like Lacan and Foucault, for example, must certainly derive from a deeply felt need to affirm polymorphousness, to break down naturalized structures of gender, racial, and even individual differences. (pp. 8-9)

By focusing on how the self is constituted differently through different discursive practices, the alternatives available for constructing the self come alive. The vitality of a postmodern and constructionist position stems from its recognition that the self need not be received but may always be constructed, thus giving power to the individuals and groups whose selves are at stake. As Foucault put it, "From the idea that the self is not given to us, I think that there is only one practical consequence: we have to create ourselves as a work of art" (Foucault, 1984, p. 351).

DISRUPTION OF SELF$_1$ THROUGH DISCURSIVE PRACTICE

From the perspective of writers like Foucault, the challenge for those attempting to create themselves rather than merely to receive themselves through the available symbolic order is to create new discursive practices that subvert the ideologizing tendencies of the prevailing symbolic order. Levine (1992) summarizes the problem as one of agency: "The 'self' of contemporary social debate . . . remains an agitator for individual action and agency" (p. 10). The program of many contemporary feminist writers, especially those concerned with women's autobiography, takes up this challenge. Their work provides particularly fertile ground in which to investigate the issue for two reasons. First, they provide a direct challenge to the notion of a unitary and consistent self, such as that proposed by Harré's notion of self$_1$. Second, their focus on women's writing offers a case in point of discursive practices used by a group that has frequently been marginalized. We begin by contrasting their views with those of Harré's as related to the principle of double singularity and then move to a fuller discussion of the liberating potential of women's writing for construction of self. Our discussion presents a number of ideas articulated by feminist theorists and critics that suggest some problems with Harré's concept of self. By doing so, we mean to emphasize the utility of approaching the idea of a constructed self from a variety of perspectives.

Harré argues that, for any given statement or speech act, particularly those that employ the self-referential "I," the source assumes a singular position in time and space, thus giving a certain constancy to one's being that is perceived as self$_1$. Over time and through space, a given individual might assume various positions, thus giving rise to a perception of multiple selves$_2$, but the principle of double singularity simply calls for a consistency among each of these selves$_2$ and for self$_1$. According to Harré, autobiography appears to provide a case in point of such consistency as it seems to require assuming a position of singularity from which the writer may look back over his or her experience and through which he or she may develop coherence for multiple episodes in which self$_2$ is enacted. A fundamental problem for such an explanation is that, in the context of women's writing, autobiography may aim toward precisely the opposite outcome. The project of many feminist writers is to use the writing process, particularly autobiography, as a means of challenging the concept of a unitary and consistent self.

Fragmenting the Self

From a Lacanian perspective, to which some of the work of Kristeva, Irigaray, and others is linked, the self is not a unified being—it experiences conflicts and inconsistencies throughout its existence. Human beings lose the comfort of complete identification with the image of their body once they move out of infancy, through the mirror stage, and into the realm of the symbolic order, where language mediates their experience (Lacan, 1977). It is the symbolic that allows people to organize their experience into a coherent, whole "self," but the illusory nature of that "self" (Harré's self$_1$) arises again and again as its order is threatened by the unconscious, which may not conform to the rules and norms of the socially sanctioned symbol system. As people become aware of the inadequacies of one set of interpretations and object identifications, they move on to adopt new ones. Thus discursive practices, from therapy sessions to telling one's story to everyday interactions, emerge as attempts to provide a unified and coherent interpretation of self and action. As people shift their objects of identification, they catch glimpses of their fragmented selves.

While Lacan's writings emphasize the deterministic nature of the symbolic on all human discourse and behavior, many feminists have chosen to examine the potentially freeing qualities of this psychoanalytic perspective on the self. For many French feminists, the assumption that the self is necessarily coherent embodies all that is wrong with theory itself: The values of patriarchy, with all its binarisms, are embedded in the symbolic order, which is rigid and unresponsive to efforts to broaden its nature. Psychoanalytic feminist Juliet

Mitchell explains Lacan's contribution to the dialogue on sexuality and its relationship to the self by noting that the unconscious reveals a fragmented subject with a shifting and uncertain sexual identity. According to Mitchell (1982): "To be human is to be subjected to a law which decentres and divides: sexuality is created in a division, the subject is split; but an ideological world conceals this from the conscious subject who is supposed to feel whole and certain of a sexual identity." For Mitchell, "psychoanalysis should aim at a destruction of this concealment and at a reconstruction of the subject's construction in all its splits" (p. 26).

Celebrating the Self

Within the framework of discursive practice that Harré uses to define the self, he neglects to acknowledge that the project of some feminist writers is to celebrate as liberating the paradox of representation he perceives as confining. While Harré points to the dilemma feminist writers like Cixous face when attempting to inscribe the "feminine" using the ideologically laden grammatical tools of language, his focus presents an overly deterministic and necessarily limiting view on the potential of women's writing to redefine the self. It is precisely the deterministic order of language that feminists like Cixous are trying to escape even while acknowledging its compelling influence on discourse. The symbolic system, laden with the values and dominated by the practices of patriarchy, orders, unifies, and makes coherent the experiences of all born into it. To subvert the coherence of the symbolic system means to highlight through radical discursive practice the internal conflicts and contradictions of that order. What appears to Harré as a challenge to the normative constraints of $self_2$ is an attempt to challenge the silent order that shapes $self_1$, particularly the assumption that the self is singular and unified. While the expression of self ($_1$ and $_2$) cannot completely escape the unifying force of the symbolic, some discursive practices can harness the reflexive power of language to foreground the tensions and contradictions inherent within the self ($self_1$).

Cixous calls upon women to create such discursive practices in her treatise on writing, "Laugh of the Medusa" (1976), even while decrying the tools of writing as belonging to the patriarchal symbolic order. She explains:

Women must write through their bodies, they must invent the impregnable language that will wreck partitions, classes, and rhetorics, regulations and codes, they must submerge, cut through, get beyond the ultimate reserve-discourse, including the one that laughs at the very idea of pronouncing the word "silence," the one that, aiming for the impossible, stops short before the word "impossible" and writes it as "the end." (Cixous, 1989, p. 741)

In dismissing Cixous's position, Harré raises questions about her focus on the masculine-feminine binarism and explains that her position undermines the very difference between men's and women's writing. Rather than advocating a feminine essentialism, however, as some Anglo-American critics have, Cixous pictures a trajectory of the "bisexual" that accounts for all selves (Cixous, 1989, p. 740). One of Cixous's principal concerns is that women's writing not become essentialist, as men's has. The fragmentation that initially liberates woman from man's pen stays with her to embody the heterogeneous, individualized "feminine" perspective on writing. Woman's inscription in the symbolic doesn't have contours, Cixous maintains, but allows a multiplicity of manifestations, a multiplicity of selves. This discourse is sustainable because it arises from within, from woman's empathic multiple identifications with others: "To life she refuses nothing. Her Language does not contain, it carries; it does not hold back, it makes possible" (Cixous, 1989, p. 744). Though the presentation of a singular, unified voice is nearly inevitable, even as one tries to call attention to its illusory nature, this doesn't mean some form of subversion is not possible or desirable. Cixous's play of double meanings and metonymic signifiers can easily challenge conventional meanings arising from the dominant use of the singular "I." A plurality of $self_1$ is made visible in the act of subverting the "grammatical," conventional $self_1$ known as "I."

No doubt Harré would argue that no matter what Cixous's practice looked like it would still manifest itself as a singularity in $self_1$. But it is precisely that language of the singular that Cixous's work challenges and with it the notion that experience is so ordered—spatially, temporally, historically. Indeed, Cixous's discourse does as much to refract the experience of the reader in the text as it does to subvert the dominance of the symbolic order.

Recontextualizing the Self

Cixous's prescription for reinventing the self, particularly as it relates to Harré's explanation of the singular $self_1$, finds support in contemporary discussions of women's autobiography as related to the so-called fragmented feminine self. Some theorists have differentiated women's autobiographical practice from men's according to focus and style: Women's selfhood, it is argued, is portrayed as "fragmented" and their selves are usually defined relationally to others. Whether or not women's experience can be characterized as "fragmented" as opposed to men's remains to be seen. Problems with referentiality may be left to biologically oriented scholars like Gilligan and Chodorow or psychoanalytic scholars like Kristeva and Rose to explore. It is rather the paradox of representation that Harré perceives as problematic that has become the focus of attention among rhetorical and literary critics and other scholars of language. Reading women's autobiography begins to appear like an exercise in deconstruction under the theoretical lens of some scholars as the fragmented female voice is observed in a variety of texts, those produced by both men and women. The same tendency among such theorists to characterize women's voices merely as symptoms of the postmodern self (something Bella Brodski and Marianne Gooze warn reifies women's marginal status) underlies Harré's attempts to understand the self that is discursively created by women's autobiography. "Feminists can make only limited use of poststructuralist theories without sacrificing their firm conviction that there is an inextricable and undeniable connection in autobiography between the bios and the graphe—between a woman's life and her personal written expression" (Goozé, 1992, p. 425). Without a closer examination of the behavioral, historical, and psychosocial foundations of the gendered self, philosophers of the self can little afford to relegate women's writing to a secondary function, continuing to arouse concerns over the hegemonic force of their own theoretical enterprise.

By not explicitly acknowledging the constraints of the symbolic order on the construction of self and the dangers posed by an ideology of the unitary self, Harré's account of self-construction inhibits understanding of how the autobiographical self interacts with the symbolic order. It is important not to lose sight of the goal of the many theorists and critics of women's autobiography who see the writing process as an act that constitutes the self and the practice of autobiography as an attempt to inscribe the self within the larger discursive systems that dominate personhood. Domna Stanton (1987) maintains that for these feminist theorists: "The female 'I' was thus not simply a texture woven of various selves; its threads, its life-lines, came from and extended to others. By that token, this 'I' represented a denial of a notion essential to the phallogocentric order: the totalized self-contained subject present-to-itself" (p. 15). These writers spread the warp from the woof beneath their fingers, exposing the gaps between the supposedly "unified" weave of the fabric of the textual self.

Within women's autobiography, the importance of reconstructing the self lies not just in disrupting the unity of self$_1$ but in providing a construction of self that can be used by others for the invention of their own stories. The process of empowerment encouraged by women's autobiography is neglected by Harré's psychological explanation of autobiography as he occludes the sociopolitical functions of that discursive practice. Anglo-American feminists have emphasized the process of writing as a self-constituting activity, focusing not on the obstacles posed by the patriarchal power of language but on the liberating potential of autobiographical practice. According to Carolyn Heilbrun, the importance of telling one's life, of narrating one's stories, lies in providing women with new plots with which to empower themselves *both* at a personal level and at the level of community:

> If I had to emphasize the lack either of narrative or of language to the formation of new women's lives, I would unquestionably emphasize narrative. Much, of a profound and perceptive nature, has been written about the problem of women coping with male language that will not say what they wish. . . . But what we

speak of here . . . is not so much women's lack of a language as their failure to speak profoundly to one another. . . . The problem . . . is one not of language but of power. And power consists to a large extent in deciding what stories will be told. (Heilbrun, 1988, p. 43)

Issues of power lie at the heart of the process of autobiographical writing, maintains Mauritian critic Françoise Lionnet, who believes telling one's story is the only way out of the political and economically fashioned identity that has created the self. The extent to which that identity has been internalized by the individual shows in the autobiographies of such women as Maya Angelou and Maryse Condé in which the narrative depicts a struggle to understand, refashion, and reclaim new identity. For Lionnet, autobiographical writing is to be valued as a socially as well as a personally therapeutic process, for it appropriates the occluded "histories" of the oppressed and reinterprets and revalues them in terms of their writers' understanding of their lives. The autobiographical process presents these creatively reconstructed women as exemplars of adaptation and survival.

Lionnet advocates *métissage* as a practice that can overcome the constraints of the dominant modes of discourse, for it is the process by which the individual negotiates his or her life based on his or her unique cultural and personal experience—every outcome is unique, contributing to an understanding of both culture and person. Resistance and self-empowerment arise equally out of writing, according to Lionnet, both part of a process that involves celebrating the pluralities of experience, interpretation, and the self:

It is by positing a Nietzschean perspectivism on reality that we can perhaps focus on a positive—if somewhat utopian—view of writing as an enabling force in the creation of a plural self, one that thrives on ambiguity and multiplicity, on affirmation of differences, not on polarized and polarizing notions of identity, culture, race, or gender. . . . it is this plurality of potentialities which eventually helps bring the personal in line with the political. (Lionnet, 1989, p. 16)

Indeed, it is this very plurality of potentialities that allows for the possibility of change in the sociopolitical world and for growth in the personal.

CONCLUSION

As we suggest in this commentary, conceptualizing the self as a discursive construct without careful attention to the historicity of discursive practices generally can lead to overemphasizing unity and deemphasizing diversity as found in gender. In addition, we have argued that shifting our attention from the historicity of discursive practices can obscure the usefulness of such practices as women's autobiography, practices that serve very concrete functions in their cultural contexts. The notion of self as embodied in the text might be read as a symptom of the poststructuralists' decentered self—or it might be reified as the only enduring author of narrative discourse. At the very least, the assumption of a relationship between the textual and referential self and the nature of that relationship might need revising. For the moment, it is in the slippage between unity and ambiguity that women are placing themselves and their autobiographical practice. The ambiguity that has marginalized women's voice for so long has now become a source of strength and allowed movement into the mainstream, more public eye. But to rest there is to become complacent, in danger of developing a new essentialism with little consciousness of its power—and the feminist project will not allow such a state to exist for long. Clearly, examinations of the relationship between the textual, experiential, and referential self cannot exist without a corresponding examination of the historical bases for discursive practices. Sacrificing either would lessen visibility of both the boundaries imposed by ideology and its institutions and the opportunities afforded by women's creative practices for those who seek to understand and grow from their experience. If, as Harré's project suggests, the problematics of self are to be reduced to a dialectic between "unified" discourses, then surely a most valued, if disruptive, part of our polyphonic potential has been lost, along with an opportunity for social and intellectual growth.

NOTE

1. Although the joining of the work of Foucault, who neither wrote extensively about women's experience nor privileged gender as a fundamental construct within discursive practice, with feminist theory and criticism may seem unusual, there is a body of work that suggests compatibilities among these theoretical positions. See Diamond and Quinby (1988).

REFERENCES

Cixous, H. (1976). Laugh of the Medusa. In R. Davis & L. Finke (Eds.), *Literary criticism and theory: The Greeks to the present* (pp. 733-748). White Plains, NY: Longman.

Diamond, I., & Quinby, L. (Eds.). (1988). *Feminism and Foucault.* Boston: Northeastern University Press.

Foucault, M. (1980). *The history of sexuality: Vol. 1. An introduction* (R. Hurley, Trans.). New York: Vintage.

Foucault, M. (1984). On the genealogy of ethics: An overview of work in progress. In P. Rabinow (Ed.), *The Foucault reader* (pp. 340-372). New York: Pantheon.

Foucault, M. (1985). *The use of pleasure* (R. Hurley, Trans.). New York: Pantheon.

Foucault, M. (1986). *The care of the self* (R. Hurley, Trans.). New York: Pantheon.

Foucault, M. (1988). Technologies of the self. In L. H. Martin, J. Gutman, & P. H. Hutton (Eds.), *Technologies of the self* (pp. 16-49). Amherst: University of Massachusetts Press.

Goozé, M. E. (1992). The definitions of self and form in feminist autobiography theory. *Women's Studies, 21,* 411-429.

Heilbrun, C. (1988). *Writing a woman's life.* New York: Ballantine.

Lacan, J. (1977). The mirror stage as formative of the function of the I. In J. Lacan, *Ecrits: A selection* (pp. 1-7). New York: Norton.

Levine, G. (1992). Constructivism and the reemergent self. In G. Levine (Ed.), *Constructions of the self* (pp. 1-13). New Brunswick, NJ: Rutgers University Press.

Lionnet, F. (1989). *Autobiographical voices: Race, gender, self portraiture.* Ithaca, NY: Cornell University Press.

Mitchell, J. (1982). Introduction I. In J. Lacan, *Feminine sexuality* (pp. 1-26). New York: Norton.

Stanton, D. C. (1987). Autogynography: Is the subject different? In D. C. Stanton (Ed.), *The female autograph: Theory and practice of autobiography from the tenth to the twentieth century* (pp. 3-20). Chicago: University of Chicago Press.

3 Culture, Ideology, and Interpersonal Communication Research

KRISTINE L. FITCH
University of Colorado, Boulder

Traditional interpersonal communication research and theory are limited, first, by a culture-specific system of understandings of the nature of persons, relationships, and communication itself that creates scope conditions for theory that generally go unrecognized, and, second, by focusing on practices and processes of communication without detailed consideration of the culturally shared understandings that make them sensible. In overcoming these limitations, ethnography of speaking is used to describe a notion of interpersonal ideology as a system of beliefs within which people live out their interactional lives. Interpersonal ideology, from this view, is a set of premises about personhood, relationships, and communication that structure negotiation of meaning through language use within a speech community. This conceptualization of ideology is distinguished from a critical approach and illustrated by way of description of three broad categories of interpersonal communication/relationships in which such premises are revealed: choices between linguistic alternatives, speech act performance, and communicative style.

U NTIL recently, the world beyond interacting individuals has received little explicit attention in interpersonal communication research and theory. The "culture," "society," or "system of competing groups" (as that world is variably described), within which persons coordinate meanings, form and dissolve relationships, and construct identities, has generally been viewed as secondary in importance to the goals, plans, competence, and personal attributes of the persons who interact (or are available for interaction).[1] Traditionally, interpersonal communication theories explain the processes and practices people engage in, with little attention to the system of

AUTHOR'S NOTE: I wish to thank Art Bochner, Sally Planalp, and Karen Tracy for helpful comments on earlier versions of this essay. The errors and omissions are, of course, my own.

Correspondence and requests for reprints: Kristine L. Fitch, Campus Box 270, University of Colorado, Boulder, CO 80309-0270.

Communication Yearbook 17, pp. 104-135

common resources from which they draw as they choose whether to self-disclose (or not), reduce uncertainty (or nurture it), talk (or remain silent). Further, most interpersonal communication research is conducted among white middle-class North Americans, and most theories are constructed by people who approximate that profile. Yet, little notice is taken of those shared characteristics or the impact they might have on the shape of findings and theories that are implicitly presented as describing universal aspects of communication.

In this essay, I will propose that this approach to interpersonal communication has two significant limitations. First, it is driven by a culture-specific system of understandings of the nature of persons, relationships, and communication itself that creates scope limitations for theory that generally go unrecognized. Second, focusing on practices and processes of communication without detailed consideration of the culturally shared understandings that make them sensible provides unsatisfying answers to fundamental questions about the nature of interpersonal communication: How do people create meaning? How do they transcend differences in schemas, unknowable intentions, variable interpretations, conflicting goals, and other individual complexities to a degree that allows actions to be coordinated and relationships to form?

In addressing these questions, I propose to join in a conversation already begun by Lannamann (1991) and Montgomery (1988, 1992) and specifically to amplify the voice of the ethnography of speaking as one that may be particularly instructive. I will describe an ethnographic perspective on the notion of "interpersonal ideology"—the system of beliefs about personhood, relationships, and communication that constitute the common resources for a group of people, within which they live out their interpersonal lives. My aim is to characterize, rather than create, that perspective. The contribution that the ethnography of speaking can make to this discussion is an intellectual tradition committed to empirical, systematic inquiry grounded in comparative analysis that illuminates the nature and impact of cultural influence on communicative practice.

THE ABSENCE OF CULTURE AND HISTORY IN INTERPERSONAL COMMUNICATION RESEARCH

Lannamann (1991) presents an extremely useful discussion of some ideological biases in the current practice of interpersonal communication research and theory. Montgomery's (1988, 1992) elaboration of the impact of socially constructed relational ideals on intimate relationships provides a relevant, though significantly different, view of the world beyond interacting individuals and its impact on interpersonal communication. I will briefly summarize and expand upon each of these views, then propose an interpretive ethnographic view of interpersonal ideology that incorporates elements of both of the previous ones into a perspective that attempts to allow for both critical and empirical voices to be heard. This perspective will then be illustrated in terms of three aspects of interpersonal communication in which interpersonal ideology may be observed, and the implications of incorporating such a conception of ideology into interpersonal research and theory will be discussed.

Lannamann (1991) provides evidence for the existence of several culture-specific assumptions underlying interpersonal communication research and theory that remain obscured by ideological commitments to logical positivism. First, he notes a focus on individuals and dyads to the exclusion of social collectivities such as social class, the law, educational systems, and so forth. This focus gives rise to implicit assumptions that individuals control their own destinies to a great extent, that power is exerted by individuals upon individuals, and that the category of the self as a skin-bound, unitary individual is a natural, biologically determined entity rather than a cultural construction. Second, he proposes that most mainstream interpersonal research proceeds from an assumption that communication is based on rational, instrumental thought: It is goal oriented, with the primary goals being mastery, efficiency, and control. Third, he notes the frequency with which inquiry focuses on subjective experience—the perceptions of knowing actors and/or their hypothetical responses to experimental manipulations—as opposed to the communicative practices that shape perception, interpretation, and responses to interactional contingencies. Finally, Lannamann describes the traditional approach to interpersonal communication as an ahistorical one that ignores the social and historical forces that shape thought, perceptions, evaluations, and the experiences of the individual: "The social origins of the person are effaced or pushed back behind the research process and discussed as potentially interesting independent variables in the measurement of cognitive states" (Lannamann, 1991, p. 188).

Lannamann's concern is that ideological commitments such as these are associated with particular interests, though he stops short of specifying in any detail what those interests are. He also notes that they are pervasive and predominant in the discipline, such that they generate the validity claims against which knowledge is judged, thus enabling certain distinctions and denying others. The danger is that "the discipline is at risk of reifying what are essentially cultural forms of thought and treating them as if they represent natural facts" (Lannamann, 1991, p. 190). By studying interpersonal communication from this unexamined framework of biases and describing that framework as "empirical fact," power relationships are ratified and, at the same time, rendered invisible to analysis and criticism.

The response Lannamann proposes to this problem is to recognize that the material practices of people, including interpersonal communication practices, reflect the hegemony of one class's ideas over another. Social ideologies, from this view, are the basis for power struggle between groups. As such, ideology is essentially political (i.e., concerned with or relevant to the struggle for domination between genders, classes, races, or other social groups). Contradictions between material processes and consciousness are thus central to inquiry. This is consistent with Fiske's (1991) discussion of conflictual social theories more generally. A central claim of such theories is that white, patriarchal, capitalist societies are structured around conflicting social interests. Their stability and coherence are achieved by the ability of the power bloc to promote and hold its interests against those of subordinated social groups. Of particular relevance to communication theory is the claim that such struggle is most powerfully played out in discourse processes: the symbolic meanings of key terms, the strategic options for exerting control over interaction and relationships, and so forth.

Lannamann's discussion of the ideological biases present in interpersonal communication research is insightful and well documented. Some elements of critical theory limit its potential as a comprehensive basis for interpersonal theory, however. First, the unique contribution of critical theory is the illumination it offers on the conditions in which power is exercised. That is, it goes beyond the experiences and relationships of individuals to show how group membership(s), and the unequal power of groups, shape those experiences. Yet, in focusing insistently on the dimension of power imbalance between groups, critical theory creates a cloud of its own. It runs the risk of re-creating the limitations of American logical positivism in reverse, offering little insight, for example, into relationships among people who consider themselves peers and interact as such. It would be forced to reject as unfriendly data the creative solutions of people who, well aware of the power imbalances that structure their experiences, reject the premises in which such power imbalances are based and yet find ways to forge a productive existence within the system. Implicitly, it creates the temptation to generalize from the power struggles of one society (or many, in the case of gender roles or economic class structures) to the automatic assumption of parallel power struggles in another.

Second, there is certainly a strong case to be made that power imbalances are often masked by unquestioned acceptance of the dominant ideology. Nonetheless, the rich variety of human organization revealed in culturally situated communication research suggests that power is only one of many interactional arrangements that may be so masked. Consider, for example, the emphasis on interpersonal harmony described as characteristic of many Asian cultures (see, e.g., DeVos, 1985; Lebra, 1976; Smith, 1983; Song, 1992; Suzuki, 1976; Tu, 1985). The pervasiveness of that value across dimensions of intimacy, liking, and similarity of individuals distinguishes it sharply from a U.S. middle-class view in which harmony would be viewed as important (and/or attainable) in some situations but not in others.

It might also be the case that one unintended consequence of the value placed on interpersonal harmony emerges from a class struggle in which the interests of one group win out over the interests of another and that subordination of the less powerful group is achieved through the hegemony of that pervasive, pleasant-sounding value. To reduce investigation of interpersonal harmony as a relational ideology to a matter of power imbalance, however, is to enact another version of the "hammer methodology": Struggle between groups is the "hammer," and the unique contours of any social system can probably be pounded into something of a coherent shape with it (just as many research questions have been, and can be, shaped into something addressable through LISREL). Limiting description of the widely diverse possibilities of human interaction patterns to discovery of power imbalances creates a certainty of investigator bias and virtually requires dismissing participants' own perceptions as uninformed. That is, even as he rejects the Marxist notion of false consciousness, Lannamann proposes that the observer's position is one that is more conscious of larger social and historical patterns and thus constitutes a privileged view of the personal choices and relational goals of the participant: "Power . . . is an *observer's distinction* of the recursive constraints structuring a *participant's distinction* of recursive choices" (italics added, 1991, p. 198). However noble the aims of such research, and however able and well informed the researcher, automatically granting privilege to the observer's view over the participant's smacks uncomfortably of a hegemony that is all too similar to that which is being challenged.

Despite these limitations of critical theory as a comprehensive framework for interpersonal investigation, Lannamann's article uncovers significant biases in North American middle-class-dominated interpersonal research. Montgomery's (1988, 1992) development of ideas about communication as an interface between couples and society approaches the world beyond interacting individuals in a different, and potentially complementary, way.

TOWARD A "SOCIAL IDEOLOGY" OF INTIMATE RELATIONSHIPS

In her development of ideas about communication as an interface between couples and society, Montgomery (1988, 1992) includes a notion of a society-wide set of ideals about what constitutes "good" communication within intimate relationships. From this view, social groups pressure members to conform to their norms for relationships while allowing for change to occur by way of interaction among members. Couples are faced with the dual challenge of maintaining a balance between autonomy and dependence within the relationship and developing a unique identity for themselves as a couple, represented to the community. This social ideology of relationships thus "brings together the society's beliefs, values, and attitudes about what is good and what is not [in communication and in relationships] . . . [it is] a value-laden public standard for communication that is based partly on facts and partly on myths" (Montgomery, 1988, p. 345).

This move to include the world beyond interacting individuals in accounts of interpersonal communication practice complements Lannamann's in the sense that persons are viewed as formulating strategies and choosing among alternatives within a context that extends beyond their own cognition, experience, and free will. Montgomery elaborates certain specific social assertions about the nature of personal relationships drawn from institutional influences, cultural artifacts, and social networks to make the point that such assertions carry a certain "logical force" for interaction and relationships among members of the society. Among the questions that may be pursued from this view, she proposes, are how standards for "good" communication may vary from social ideals due to relationally negotiated criteria and/or the idiosyncratic criteria of each partner in a relationship, how different collectivities' ideologies about personal relationships interrelate within a culture, and how the negotiation of autonomy/connection is related to relational stages of dyads, cultural eras, and strategies for resolution of that central tension.

Montgomery's view is a useful one in that it sketches in some detail the white middle-class American view of relational choices and tensions facing dyadic partners and presents a plausible theoretical link between the interactions of couples and the social context within which those interactions take place. At least implicitly, it meshes with the critical perspective in that it allows for exposing power imbalance as "the natural order of things" when that imbalance is part of the social ideology within which relationships are constructed and evaluated. As a perspective that incorporates cultural context into the study of interpersonal communication, however, Montgomery's model has three limitations: It is itself based on culture-specific theoretical assumptions about relationships, personhood, and communication; it misplaces "culture" as something that exists primarily within cognitive structures; and it lacks a clear definition for what constitutes membership in a "culture," "society," and "social collectivity."

First, Montgomery illustrates the idea of culture and its influence on personal relationships by way of examples that are recognizably drawn from U.S. media, institutions, and patterns of social networks. Curiously, they are never labeled as such or contrasted with other examples from other cultures, leaving unclear what "cultural" values are propagated by those sources as opposed to (once again) describing communication as a universal phenomenon. More problematic is the possibility that the theoretical terms of this position are themselves laden with white middle-class American values and beliefs about interpersonal communication and relationships. The idea that autonomy versus dependence is the "*the* fundamental challenge facing members of close relationships" (Montgomery, 1992, p. 475) seems to characterize only those social systems in which individual autonomy is crucial to identity, such that excessive dependence represents a loss of "self." Similarly, the idea that couples must develop a distinctive identity for themselves *as a couple* so as to maintain intimacy and "contribute to their sense of worth and specialness" (Montgomery, 1992, p. 481) seems quite appropriate to an individualistic culture. Its applicability to systems in which, for example, marriage is viewed primarily in terms of presenting an escape from repressive home life and only secondarily as an arena for establishing personal or couple identity (e.g., Komarovsky, 1962; Rubin, 1976) seems more questionable. In such a system, autonomy and dependence of the couple within a social system may be far less crucial questions than adherence to prescribed roles. "Worth and special-ness" may not be meaningful objectives viewed as pursuable within, or by way of, intimate relationships (see also Howell, 1973; Weis, 1990).

Finally, the placement of "communication" at the center of all interpersonal processes should be examined carefully for the beliefs and values that such a position carries with it. It may certainly be argued that putting communica-tion at the center rather than at the periphery of inquiry is what distinguishes us as a discipline, and I am not attempting to displace it. The danger here is the failure to recognize a tendency, within this (white middle-class American-dominated) field to view the communication process in ways that are specific to the culture. That is, communication is consistently, though often implicitly, represented as a process through which unique, autonomous individuals bridge the differences between themselves to form discussable entities called "relationships" (for more detail on the term *communication* as a culturally laden symbol, see Katriel & Philipsen, 1981). This unspoken (so to speak) understanding of the nature of communication may account for why studies of communication behavior consistently focus on a relatively narrow band of possibilities. Goal-oriented, consciously formulated talk is more than merely central to the equation. It is often insinuated that all communication behavior, or at least all that is worth studying, is of that nature. Studies of ritualized sequences, of phatic communion (e.g., Ray, 1987), and the rich communicative possibilities of silence (Braithwaite, 1990, reviews 28 studies of silence) are marginalized or left out of theory building altogether.

A second difficulty presented by Montgomery's position, in terms of understanding the impact of culture on personal relationships, is the vague-ness with which "culture" and "social ideology" are defined. Within the theoretical framework constructed for elaborating the argument proposed, there is no specific consideration of the concept of "culture" or "society," even though "social ideology" is a central term in the equation being worked out. "Society" is presented as a set of loosely connected "practices" or "messages" emanating from "multiple collectives representing special inter-ests in social, political, and economic events" (Montgomery, 1992, p. 490). Her purpose, in all fairness, was not to develop that idea in detail but to illustrate the way in which certain social groupings acted as communication agencies concerned with the conduct of personal relationships. In the absence of a clear understanding of what culture is, in contrast with a social collective, and where and how culture may be observed to influence interpersonal communication, the explanatory power of the concept comes into serious question. It seems worthwhile to clarify this point before proceeding.

The set of communicative resources from which symbolic meaning is constructed is usefully viewed as a common code that links the messages and practices of social collectivities into a more or less coherent whole. It is that common code that should be viewed as culture in its most profound and influential sense; and the value messages that emerge from the (sometimes contradictory) voices of social collectivities constitute interpersonal ideology. An illustration may add coherence to this seeming contradiction. A relative of mine is, by his own definition, critically identifiable by his involvement in two social collectivities for which some shared meaning seems to exist in white middle-class American society. One is the Southern Baptist church, which defines itself as fundamentalist in its Christian principles. Another is a friendship/professional network that may fairly be described as "yuppie." From the first collectivity emanate messages of connection with humanity that include charitable works such as helping the homeless, involvement in prayer groups, and so forth. From the second, the messages seem on the surface to be quite contradictory. There is an emphasis on personal material gain, potentially at the expense of others; competition; "busyness" as a reflection of personal worth and importance (e.g., "I'm so busy that a cellular phone is a necessity, not a luxury.")

Underlying these supposed contradictions, there are meaningful similarities. Both systems exalt the self-sufficient individual: the Baptists by extending a helping hand so that the needy may achieve that status; the Yuppies by way of a competitive system in which status is gained on the basis of material objects possessed by an individual. Each system tempers this emphasis on individualism with a recognition of the need for community or connection to other individuals: the Baptists by encouraging involvement in church groups, the Yuppies by emphasizing "networking." In each system, the benefit of community involvement is ultimately an individual gain: enhanced spirituality for the Baptist, enhanced personal opportunity by way of "contacts" for the Yuppie.

This relative has little difficulty hearing the different voices of his social collectivities as harmonious, and it is thus unproblematic to conclude that a common culture unites them. Certainly there will be other social collectivities whose messages are not so easily reconciled within a single worldview (it is probably impossible to be simultaneously a Hare Krishna and a Yuppie or a Skinhead and a Jew). At some point, the question would become whether divergent, coexisting collectivities are part of the same culture or constitute different cultures.

A further definitional problem in this perspective on social ideology is that it seems to be limited to cognitive structures: "Ideologies rest more on faith (e.g., 'gut feelings,' 'good hunches,' 'intuitive hypotheses') than fact" (Montgomery, 1988, p. 352). This seems odd, given the later observation that "partners' standards *for* communication are embodied *in* their communication" (Montgomery, 1988, p. 356). If such standards are observable on the level of couples' interaction, where and how may cultural ideals be identified?

When social ideology is relegated to "intuition" (i.e., cognitive processes), it becomes a value-laden version of social knowledge, a construct that has informed interpersonal research for some time (see, e.g., Cantor, Mischel, & Schwartz, 1982; Cody & McLaughlin, 1985). Locating shared understandings and values about interpersonal communication in long-term memory creates an unnecessary difficulty in that it removes a socially constructed system of meaning from the realm of observable communication phenomena. This makes the connection between the shared resources that are assumed to exist, and the interaction that such shared resources are supposed to inform, one that is indirect and potentially more deterministic than anyone has yet been prepared to argue.

Again, a specific example may help to show the difference between a cognitive concept of social knowledge/social ideology and a cultural perspective on language use. Consider, for example, the assumption of shared understandings of the nature of "professors" as opposed to "students" that inform interaction between professors and students (Planalp, 1985). Examination of this type of communication resource begins from a concept of relational schemata as conceptual frameworks used to derive relational implications of a message, which may in turn be modified in accord with ongoing experience with relationships. Such schemata provide the cognitive equivalent of definitions of relationship that guide message interpretation and production. Evidence for the existence of such schemata and their influence on communication behavior is drawn from data that measure cognitive processes such as memory, because "social knowledge is presumed *not* to be directly observable, because it is implicit knowledge that is not accessible to awareness. . . . Even if it were accessible, the reporting would be intrusive during interaction and direct reports would not be trustworthy due to experimental demand" (Planalp, 1985, p. 9). By contrast, consider the identification of symbolic aspects of the term *communication* as used by many North Americans (Katriel & Philipsen, 1981). Each may be considered an investigation of social knowledge, yet the differences are significant. In this approach, a term that is heard in everyday interaction, *communication,* is explored for its symbolic connotations among the members of a speech community. It proceeds from direct observation of language use, that is, noting instances of use of the term. The symbolic dimensions of the term are probed by way of analytic induction that focuses on comparison and contrast of interactional events described as "really communicating" as opposed to "mere talk" or "chitchat." Data are drawn from naturally occurring interaction or from reflection on specific instances soon after they occur.

There is an inferential step in this analytic process that, because it is the inference of the researcher, calls the entire enterprise into question for many empiricists. It should be emphasized, however, that the grounds for such inferences are explicated as publicly and completely as possible. The assumption is that, although infusing a commonplace term with symbolic meaning clearly does involve cognitive processing, the knowledgeable use of the term in interaction constitutes explicit evidence of its meaningfulness in the community. Certainly, reflections of the members of the community on their understanding of cultural terms play a key role in the discovery and elucidation of those terms. The pursuit of cultural knowledge that makes such terms available as resources for interaction takes place through examination of the talk itself. There is less emphasis on predicting which resources will be used when than on describing what the resources are that account for why things mean what they do in interaction.

One advantage of a cultural approach is a closer connection between the phenomenon under study (language use within and about interpersonal relationships) and the explanatory concept (culture). This is not to say that social cognition approaches to the study of relationships are without value. To discount the cognitive elements of cultural resources would be to reduce culture to an unworkably behavioristic concept. Clear ideas of the nature and function of culture in shaping inferences drawn from behavior, selection, storage and retrieval of information in memory, and so forth, can greatly enrich current investigations of mutual knowledge and its impact on relationships. That contribution is providing a social/historical context within which such processes are inevitably played out. Lacking such a conceptual base leaves established bits and pieces of mutual knowledge isolated in individual, atemporal minds.

A final, related difficulty in Montgomery's explication of social ideology is the lack of definition of what constitutes membership in a culture or society. There are frequent references in this work to "we as a society" with no specification of who "we" are, and are not: "Our social world is a contrast of positively and negatively signed entities. And, as far as communication is concerned, the positives are valued over the negatives. . . . People in good relationships are to be supportive, cheerful, and agreeable in word and deed" (Montgomery, 1988, p. 345). "Society considers [verbally and nonverbally sharing, disclosing, and revealing oneself] to be 'real communication' as opposed to 'mere talk' " (p. 347). "While the social-level ideology specifies 'Be open,' a dating couple within that society might find that they do better by modifying that standard: 'Be open only when it will not hurt the other's feelings' " (p. 353).[2] More specific allusions such as "in this country" and "in contemporary America" (Montgomery, 1992, p. 495) are limited to examples of the influence exerted by social networks on couples' interaction rather than identifying *all* of the illustrations of social practices and messages about autonomy and connection as recognizably middle-class American. Equating nationality with culture is a theoretical move that places the analytic vigor of the concept of culture in significant danger, given the homogeneity of theorists and the subject pool predominantly represented in research (i.e., college students at research universities) and the oft-discussed diversity of the U.S. population. In the absence of evidence that the tenets of "culture" given by

Montgomery as illustrations of the concept extend to other social classes and ethnic groups, it seems wise to specify with more precision who is, and is not, part of the speech community under discussion.

This is not to insist that encounters among people from different socioeconomic or ethnic backgrounds necessarily constitute intercultural communication or to make the obvious point that intercultural communication encounters are often more problematic than those that take place within the (increasingly narrow and decreasingly important) band of homogeneity described by most current interpersonal research. Rather, I mean to point to a gap in the general condition of interpersonal communication theory that cannot be addressed without more detailed ideas about culture, cultural membership, and the influence of culture on communication practice. Currently lacking is a detailed understanding of the scope conditions of theories developed within a particular cultural group that reflect the beliefs of that group about communication and interpersonal relationships. There is also much room to explore the limitations of that worldview in its definitions of what may be hypothesized, what are accepted as data, and what conclusions may be drawn from data. Both Lannamann and Montgomery have taken important steps toward addressing those issues by their distinctive, yet complementary, views of how to take account of the social ideological framework of interpersonal communication as part of both the process and the study of the process. The insights provided by their work make it possible to extend this discussion into a construct of interpersonal ideology that is

grounded in material practices, that is, language use;

well informed, though not dominated, by the possibilities of human interpersonal structures, including power imbalances that may be invisible to participants and contrary to the welfare of certain groups;[3]

inclusive of the beliefs and values about persons, relationships, and communication that are so basic that they are rarely stated, much less challenged; and

grounded in a firm notion of what is and is not cultural (as opposed to that which is specific to individual or circumstantial groupings of persons).

A CULTURAL VIEW OF
INTERPERSONAL IDEOLOGY

So far, two formulations of the concept of interpersonal ideology have been discussed. The critical view proposes that any ideology springs from a politically charged arrangement of competing groups, in which the ideology is that view of truth that is granted legitimacy because of its maintenance of the existing power structure. The social collectivity view of ideology, by contrast, is that it is a value-laden public standard for communication. As a set of beliefs, values, and attitudes, it does pertain to a particular social group, but it does not necessarily give one group power over another.

A cultural view of the concept of interpersonal ideology is somewhat different than either of these. There are many directions from which such a view might be offered, and ethnography of speaking that proceeds from an anthropological linguistic stance as it applies to interpersonal communication research and theory will be articulated here.[4] This perspective starts from a presumption that each cultural system should be studied on its own terms to discover the ways of speaking that are meaningful within the speech community. Fundamental to this approach is the notion that language as such is not everywhere equivalent in role and value; "communication" may have a different scope and meaning in different social groups (Hymes, 1972).[5] From this view, comparative study across culturally situated cases provides one kind of basis for claims to universal properties, functions, or aspects of communication. A further implication of this view is that research conducted within a single speech community is necessarily suspected to reflect a culture-specific set of processes and ideals that may be grossly inaccurate for explaining and predicting communication behavior in a different community. Claims that amount to "here's how communication process X works" can thus more accurately be put forth as "here's how communication process X works among largely white largely middle-class American college students in the Midwest."

INTERPERSONAL IDEOLOGY AS A PART OF CULTURE

Interpersonal ideology may thus be viewed as *a set of premises about personhood, relationships, and communication that structure negotiation of meaning through language use within a speech community.* Assuming that such an ideology exerts influence on interaction presumes that a shared worldview is created by participation in a system of linguistic resources, with their uses and meanings. This perspective further presumes that, beyond the microlevel of identities and relationships negotiated through communication processes, those processes also create, and reveal the existence of, a speech community.[6]

Interpersonal ideology, from this view, is a subset of culture more broadly defined. It is that aspect of culture in which personhood and communication are related most specifically to interpersonal relationships, as opposed to (for example) beliefs about wellness and illness, pedagogical concerns, economic and religious practice, and so forth. In some ways, this is of course an impossible distinction, because all of these arenas of social life have interpersonal and relational elements. Much as the area of interpersonal communication has found it useful to develop a focus on relationships distinct from organizational communication and rhetoric, it can be analytically useful, however, to specifically examine those values and beliefs that pertain to interpersonal relationships, in whatever relational units are culturally valid. That may be couples, friends/ acquaintances, networks, and families, or there may be other cultural units of analysis that are more meaningful within a given system.

With that delineation in mind, the definition just offered may be expanded upon by listing some defining characteristics of interpersonal ideology.

(1) Interpersonal ideology is a set of premises. Although "values," "beliefs," and "attitudes" are often grouped together as constitutive aspects of culture, *premises* seems a far more accurate cover term for those common understandings of personhood, relationships, and communication that I mean to describe as "ideology." *Premise* captures more fully the taken-for-granted, usually invisible sense in which culture is generally experienced as an influence on everyday interaction. A social group may have *beliefs* that, they are well aware, other social groups dismiss as fantasy or error ("Skinheads" seem a clear example of such a group). A *premise,* by contrast, is a belief that is so basic and fundamental to one's understanding of the world that people generally cannot, in the absence of a convincing contrast case, conceive of how anyone could disagree with them. The belief that, regardless of how closely connected they may be to others, or how profoundly their behavior is influenced by group membership, persons think and act as individuals is one such premise. It is one that might be purposefully contrasted with others: that persons are fundamentally sets of bonds to others, such that individual characteristics are secondary in identity (see Fitch, 1989); that persons are role occupants in an ongoing "road show" of social life, in which the particular actor performing the role is of far less importance than the smooth flow of the drama (see Geertz, 1983, pp. 62-64); and so forth. The premises that constitute interpersonal ideology, then, are those that, when stated, seem the most patently obvious—how could they be otherwise?—but that may be shown to differ from premises about personhood, relationships, and communication in another speech community.

From this view, interpersonal ideology is quite distinct from "attitudes." Attitudes, while they may stem from beliefs and values, are not directly expressive of the core premises that constitute the ideology of a group. LeVine (1984) notes that

> members of a community can vary greatly in thoughts, feelings, and behavior, yet hold in common understandings of the symbols and representations through which they communicate . . . [E]very human community functions with a group consensus about the meanings of the symbols used in the communications that constitute their social life, however variable their behaviors and attitudes in other respects, because such a consensus is as necessary for encoding and decoding messages in social communication in general as agreement about speech rules is to encoding and decoding in the linguistic mode. (pp. 68-69)

Although attitudes toward self-disclosure and its appropriateness in a given situation may vary, for example, the understanding of a self as a bounded, autonomous entity that may (or must) be revealed so as to increase intimacy is rarely questioned as a premise underlying interpersonal relationships (although Bochner, 1982, Brown & Rogers, 1991, and Parks, 1982, offer lucid challenges to this view).

(2) Interpersonal ideology structures negotiation of meaning through language use. Although the premises that constitute interpersonal ideology are so deeply held that they are ordinarily invisible, as noted above, they should not be viewed as static or monolithic entities. Culture, as some anthropologists have noted, is as much a set of oppositional ideals as it is guidelines for understanding. Bilmes (1976), for example, proposes that cultural ideals often take the form of continua, in which a maximal amount and a minimal amount of the same attribute are each viewed as desirable. (Desires for "autonomy" and "connection" as competing desires of partners in an intimate relationship, or a couple within a society, are examples of such oppositional pairs.) Bilmes suggests that positive aspects of cultural ideals are invoked for purposes of negotiation of identity and interpersonal relationships. In this sense, ideology is not a single voice that drowns out all others but a conversation between voices that sometimes harmonize and other times clash.

The idea of culture as a conversation is akin to Kenneth Burke's parable used to illustrate his dramatistic mode of analysis:

> Imagine that you enter a parlor. You come late. When you arrive, others have long preceded you, and they are engaged in a heated discussion, a discussion too heated for them to pause and tell you exactly what it is about. In fact, the discussion had already begun before any of them got there, so that no one present is qualified to retrace for you all the steps that had gone on before. You listen for awhile, until you decide that you have caught the tenor of the argument; then you put in your oar. Someone answers; you answer him [*sic*]; another comes to your defence; another aligns himself against you, to either the embarrassment or gratification of your opponent, depending upon the quality of your ally's assistance. However, the discussion is interminable. The hour grows late, you must depart. And you do depart, with the conversation still in progress. (Burke, 1957, pp. 95-96)

Renato Rosaldo (1989), drawing this connection to Burke, thus describes cultural analysis as a process of capturing the thread of the ongoing conversation rather than discovery of "the" social system. This contrasts with a view of "the social system" as a static arrangement, whether it is one group subordinate to another, two social collectivities habitually emitting contradictory messages, and so forth. Rosaldo notes that struggle and contradiction are inherent in social life but implies that such struggle is a general condition of human existence rather than one created by power imbalance between social groups: "More an argument than a cozy chat, the conversation embodies conflict and change. Taking the form of challenge and response, this eternal debate outlives the structures that shape any of its particular phases" (Rosaldo, 1989, p. 104). This view of interpersonal ideology as a conversation does not negate the possibility—even probability—of power differences, in which some voices are heard too softly or are illegitimately interrupted or ridiculed. It does imply that conflicting ideals are the natural condition of human groups, that no social group is completely without power, and that interaction is "a flow of tugs and pulls, requests and counterrequests, where tempo and grace are of the essence" (Rosaldo, 1989, p. 125). Thus, even in a system where one group is generally dominant, there is room for creative circumvention, or outright rejection, of dominance by appealing to an opposing ideal. Allowing for such a possibility enables criticism of a system as generally oppressive without resorting to the simplistic (and inevitably inaccurate) suggestion that such oppression operates uniformly across relationships and circumstances. It captures an aspect of personal identity and relationships that is often noted in theory but, curiously, frequently overlooked in research practice: Identities such as "age," "gender," "ethnicity," and relationships such as "friend," "superior/subordinate," "lover" are not static. Rather, they are accomplished through talk (for specific illustrations of this claim, see Staiano, 1980; Wieder & Pratt, 1990).

(3) Meaning is negotiated through language use within a speech community. A central aspect of this cultural view of interpersonal ideology is that such ideologies pertain to groupings of people that, whatever their individual differences, share valued ways of speaking. Who is, and is not, a member of the group is a matter of speaking in ways that show an understanding of the ideology:

> To know, and to use appropriately, the meanings, rules, and speech habits of a local group signals and affirms that one is a member of it. . . . Knowledge of, and ability to participate in, a particular community's spoken life are not only resources for information transmission but are resources for communal identification, and communal being, as well. Speech is both an act of and a resource for "membering." (Philipsen, 1992, p. 14)

Two aspects of this definition of membership should be emphasized. First, as noted earlier, ideology is presumed to have a cognitive component but, more significantly, to be observable in talk. There may be a cognitive category (or several) that indexes "individuality" as a defining feature of persons. That is far less important than use of language that can only be sensible within a system of premises in which individuality or uniqueness figures prominently, as in these examples:

> When you realize what self image you are projecting and how you're interpreting and responding to your image of other persons, you will be more able to determine whether you are promoting impersonal-quality or interpersonal-quality communication. (Stewart & D'Angelo, 1980, p. 126)

Of course, since an individual's interpretations of the behavior of others will also have implications for how that individual responds to that behavior, an individual who is relatively non-complex in relational cognition should also manifest relatively limited patterns of responses to the behavior of others. (Martin, 1992, p. 151)

Second, the relationship of persons to a speech community is a matter that may be empirically established by familiarity with, as well as use of, the ways of speaking that define the group:

To know the local parlance, but be unwilling to use it, or feel not permitted to use it, or to feel that using it would insinuate oneself somewhere that one does not belong, reveals a relationship, perceived or real, that places one at some distance from the group. To have once used the local parlance and then to eschew it because one is "beyond all that" places one in relation to a group, as a former member or as one temporarily distanced from the group. These patterns of use and nonuse have expressive import for the individual and the audiences to which they are revealed and addressed, because they are intricately woven into the texture of lives and societies. (Philipsen, 1992, p. 14)

From this view, any speech community may be systematically studied and discussed in ways similar to Taylor's (1991) description of "the scientific community." Taylor argues that demarcation of the scientific community, especially separation of scientists from less exalted beings, is a matter of employing a rhetorical style that embraces the *topoi,* appropriate arguments, and unique ethos of the community. Use of those interactional elements in discourse is the basis on which claims to participation in activities that count as science and replication of findings are grounded and refuted. In much the same way that controversy over cold fusion research findings revealed the rhetorical construction of persons and arguments as "inside" or "outside" the speech community of scientists, Carbaugh's identification of a cultural code used among some "mainstream North Americans" defines a speech community in relation to which people may be positioned differently. When a claim is made, for example, that "[this study] deals with American [generally mainstream North American] patterns of communication" (Carbaugh, 1988, p. 2), that claim should be understood to mean that

a. "mainstream North Americans" are those who recognize and use the code therein described;
b. there will unquestionably be Americans who recognize, but do not use, the code as a result of being distanced from "the mainstream," whether because of their own decision, isolation due to historical or geographical factors, or discrimination; and
c. there will be persons living in North America who are sufficiently distanced from the mainstream that they neither recognize the code nor use it.

The certainty that there will be persons who fit categories (b) and (c) who consider themselves, and are considered by others to be, Americans does not in itself call into question the analytic vigor of the concept of speech communities. Rather, it testifies to the inevitable contact between, and overlap among, speech communities while suggesting a conceptual focus for the examination of group identity: that of shared, valued ways of speaking. This definition of speech community may still sound far too imprecise to fit anywhere into empirical study, but arguably that need not be the case. Although identification and elaboration of cultural codes seems a question most suited to interpretive methods, quantitative methods might certainly be used to measure the frequency and distribution of the use of the code—and in that sense serve as a check on the validity of the researcher's formulation as well.

The final step needed to elaborate on this definition is to specify fundamental elements of interpersonal ideology: some central premises on which interpersonal communication and relationships within a speech community are based. At the same time, I will suggest modifications in current research and theorizing in interpersonal communication needed to understand and account for the constitutive force of culture on communication practice.

CENTRAL PREMISES IN
INTERPERSONAL IDEOLOGY

A useful starting point is the realization that conceptions of the self—what a person is, as opposed to a tree, a flower, or a fish—are themselves cultural constructions:

> The Western conception of the person as a bounded, unique, more or less integrated motivational and cognitive universe, a dynamic center of awareness, emotion, judgement, and action organized into a distinctive whole and set contrastively both against other such wholes and against its social and natural background is, however incorrigible it may seem to us, a rather peculiar idea within the context of the world's cultures. (Geertz, 1976, p. 225)

When the self is assumed to be primordially an autonomous individual, it is not surprising that much research and theory centers on or presumes that selves are essentially "skin-bound individuals." Taking seriously the point that unique selfhood is a cultural belief requires a realization that individuals—their plans, their perceptions, their speech acts—are not a universally valid starting point or unit of analysis for communication inquiry. Communicative practices that involve presentation and maintenance of that uniqueness must be viewed as the result of a cultural imperative, not the inevitable extension of a natural fact of human existence everywhere. In the spirit of such recognition, it should be possible to make explicit the specific cultural background of the subjects among whom research is conducted. Such specification can and should go well beyond demographic characteristics: If subjects are 90% white middle-class North American college students, a number of well-substantiated points might be made about the cultural premises about personhood, relationships, and communication that they are likely to bring with them as a result of their social/historical background.

Closely related to a speech community's beliefs about the nature of personhood are evaluations of certain kinds of relationships as more desirable than other kinds. Interpersonal ideologies thus define particular kinds of relationships as consistent with other cultural values, and those collective definitions exert a discursive force on the relational choices of persons in the community. Fitzpatrick (1988) makes the useful point that dominant models of "good" marriages in the United States do not necessarily match the lived experience of a significant proportion of the population. Professional prescriptions for communication that reflect only the traditional ideals of happy marriages may thus be grossly inappropriate for other types. Societies will have traditional ideals about "good" as opposed to "bad" relationships that reflect, on a deeper level, community-specific beliefs about personhood, relationships, and communication. The fact that the marital types outlined in Fitzpatrick's work do not seem to be related to social class, age, religion, and so forth (as she claims they do not) does not contradict the notion that a shared ideal exists, that the ideal is specific to a particular speech community, and that this ideal drives much conceptualization of couples' interaction, intimacy, and so forth. Identification of three (or more) distinctive types of marriage supports the idea that within every ideal there is room for creative arrangement of resources, but the resources themselves are common ones. "Independents," "Separates," and "Traditionals" all orient to self-disclosure, expression of affection, interdependence, and gender roles in some way, even if that orientation amounts to rejection of generally accepted patterns of belief and behavior.

Finally, beliefs about ways of speaking generally, and how communication is related to relationships—indeed, the idea *that* communication is related to the quality of relationships—are notions that must be understood as related to community-specific values and beliefs about persons and relationships. Communication that involves openness, sharing one's uniqueness, and acceptance of the other as a unique individual may be values that are associated with a narrowly definable social group.[7] That those ways of speaking are seen by, for example, blue-collar workers in the United States as less functional and less appropriate than other styles of speaking is suggested by substantial research evidence (e.g., Foley, 1989; Komarovsky, 1962; Philipsen, 1975, 1976; Rubin, 1976; Weis, 1990). It is certainly possible that many existing interpersonal theories might capture aspects of communication that are universal. Nonetheless, by formulating them within a single cultural context, and by conceptualizing culture (when it is addressed at all) as something that influences communication behavior only in particular contexts, or only on certain "levels" (e.g., cognitive processing), predominant theoretical positions have centered on metaphors that are, under closer scrutiny, culturally loaded. "Open" as opposed to "closed" communication is one such metaphor. It represents the self as an autonomous unit, for which the communication options are limited—like an oyster—to "open" or "closed." Once that specific metaphor is understood *as* a metaphor that is part of a broader culturally situated belief system, it is possible to examine other speech communities for beliefs about communication that complement, contrast with, or in some way may reasonably be compared with the openness/closedness distinction. From such comparisons, then, theories may be developed that more accurately capture universal aspects of interpersonal communication and relationships as well as the ways in which culture shapes those processes.[8]

The formulation of interpersonal ideology that I have summarized here centers on valued ways of speaking. Like the critical perspective described by Lannamann, this entails a research focus on material practices in which the opposing ideals of a social system serve as the background for constructing shared meaning out of the inevitable contradictions of interactive life. Unlike the critical perspective, there is no a priori conviction that social groups are engaged in eternal struggle and that the means of resolving life's contradictions in productive ways are necessarily unevenly distributed. If and when evidence emerges from the systematic examination of data that inequities exist, no absolute relativism is assumed. There is no presumption, that is, that a repugnant system will be defended: only a commitment to understanding the social system on its own terms before a critique is mounted.

Similar to Montgomery's position that persons enter into, maintain, and dissolve relationships against a backdrop of assumptions about what constitutes "good" as opposed to "bad" communication and relationships, the perspective I have outlined here holds the examination of those fundamental premises to be a necessary step in research and theory. In contrast to the autonomy/dependence model she puts forth as basic to couples' establishment of a unique social identity, however, this perspective proposes that *some* set of opposing ideals underlie relationships and personhood. Those oppositions must be discovered through examination of the ways of speaking of particular speech communities rather than assumed to be universal.

ASPECTS OF COMMUNICATION THAT
REVEAL IDEOLOGY

I have claimed that culture is neither a "level" nor a "context" of communication behavior but a constitutive force that pervades the construction of shared meaning to some degree on every level and in every context. Having made that claim, it is nonetheless fair to admit that culture is more readily observable in some kinds of communication behavior than others. Thus I conclude with a brief description of three broad categories of interpersonal communication/relationships in which premises about personhood, relationships, and communication are revealed. The purpose of these illustrations is twofold. First, I hope to demonstrate the pervasiveness of the influence of such premises by showing their relevance to a wide range of speech activities. Second, by giving a sense of the diversity of interpersonal ideologies that regulate communication conduct in different speech communities, I hope to illustrate some of the rich variety of alternative belief systems on which communication theorists may draw to advance understanding of interpersonal interaction.

(1) Choices between linguistic alternatives. Every human language incorporates within its structure linguistic features that Michael Silverstein (1976) describes as "shifters": systems of resources whose meaning shifts according to factors of the speech situation. One such linguistic feature is personal address: terms used to address and refer to the self and others, such as pronouns, kin terms, names and nicknames, titles, and so forth. In every known language, speakers have alternative means of addressing and referring to others. By selecting among those alternatives in the act of addressing others, speakers evoke personal identities and define the nature of the relationship between themselves and those addressed. Such social expressions are both contingent upon, as well as expressive of, interlocutors' understandings about the nature of humans as beings, as selves, constructed within each speech community. Despite theoretical attempts to posit universal principles of personal address behavior (e.g., P. Brown & Levinson, 1987; R. Brown & Gilman, 1960), cultural conceptions of persons and desirable relationships between them necessarily vary across time and place, and personal address is a category of communication behavior that reveals those conceptualizations in powerful ways.

There are currently close to 100 personal address studies that focus on the communicative link to cultural meaning that they provide (for an extensive bibliography, see Philipsen & Huspek, 1985). At a very basic level, personal address indexes those features of identity and relationship that are most obvious and enduring, such as age, sex, and kinship relation. Even those presumably biological facts are imbued with complex cultural significance. For example, I describe elsewhere (Fitch, 1991) a range of terms related to mothers used in Colombian Spanish. The richness of cultural meaning revealed through the literal and figurative uses of *madre* terms suggests that the figure of the mother is a central one in interpersonal life and that the attributes and characteristics of mothers extend well beyond family interaction. *Madre* terms invoke premises of nurturance, respect, affection, and legitimate status among Colombians. At the same time, the role of "mother"—both literal and symbolic—encapsulates a central conflict in Colombian interpersonal life: the need to exert strong authority, balanced against an equally powerful need to forge profound ties of affection, trust, and interdependence with others.

Beyond the symbolic aspects of biological characteristics and relationships, personal address behavior is often a lucid indicator of social change and the adjustments of the premises of interpersonal ideology that are necessary to accomplish those changes. The uses and meanings of the term *tóngzhi* (comrade) in the People's Republic of China, as described by Scotton and Zhu (1983), are a rich example. When the Communist party assumed power in 1949, a policy was instituted to promote use of *tóngzhi* in place of honorific titles such as *mister, miss,* and terms for employers, owners, and proprietors. The symbolic meaning the party wished to promote was one of equal footing among all people, as workers having a common goal of building the country into a strong and prosperous nation. Scotton and Zhu's field study of the actual uses of the term after the Cultural Revolution showed that, although widespread agreement existed among Chinese about what *tóngzhi should* mean and how it should be used, it was frequently used to manipulate social distance. An employee, for example, would ordinarily address a supervisor by title at the time this study was conducted (language planning efforts to the contrary). When making requests for favors or special dispensation from the superior, however, use of *tóngzhi* served to emphasize to the superior an idealized equal status, thus suggesting a reduced social distance and a greater personal right of the employee to ask the favor. Scotton and Zhu conclude that manipulation of variation in meaning of linguistic forms such as *tóngzhi* in Chinese (and use of first name or an affectionate nickname could function in similar ways in English and other languages) may be exploited by speakers to negotiate rights and obligations attendant upon a relationship. By making salient a particular characteristic of a relationship, that is (in this case, the symbolic unity of all workers striving toward a common goal), the speaker negotiates a particular relationship by drawing upon common ideological premises that are presumed to be shared within the speech community.

At the heart of personal address behavior is selection between alternative forms to realize interpersonal objectives and to reconcile conflicting ideals within an interpersonal ideology. A theme that cuts across numerous personal address studies is the resolution of competing ideals by way of norms that distinguish public from private identities and acceptable relationships. Jonz's (1975) study of the U.S. Marine Corps describes a fundamental tension in an overtly hierarchical system existing within a broader North American social context in which egalitarianism and personal freedom are valued. Jonz describes as problematic the contradiction between a need for overt, unquestioned authority structure, in the interest of efficiency and discipline on the battlefield, and the need for close personal relationships between people who must live together for extended periods of time and literally trust their lives to one another. The authority structure is established through clearly specified selection procedures and enforced through separation of living quarters and dining and recreation facilities. It is further reinforced through severe penalties for boundary crossing in either direction: Both fraternization and insubordination are punishable offenses. The tension between authority and intimacy is resolved, Jonz claims, through establishing different rules for personal address in public as opposed to private settings. When no other hearers are present, more informal and intimate address terms may be used, among peers and (to some extent) between superiors and subordinates. There is also acknowledgment of dispensation from established regulations on the basis of personal relationship, although the option to extend dispensation is reserved for superiors.

Beyond the extensively studied phenomenon of personal address, other linguistic items that act as shifters may reveal cultural beliefs. The range of stylistic features that have been described as "women's language" (Lakoff, 1975) or, alternatively, as "powerless language" (O'Barr, 1982) are an example. There is evidence to suggest that presence of such features as hedges, tag questions, "empty" adjectives, and so forth denote powerlessness in U.S. English-speaking society.[9] There has been no attempt to test that proposition, however, in other speech communities or to examine whether there are some speech acts for which the very style viewed as powerless in some circumstances is prized in others. Without examination of the cultural meaning of linguistic features such as these (i.e., What are the culturally valued ways of speaking that make a particular set of features sound "powerless"?), it will be difficult to distinguish gender-linked differences in communication behavior from the value loadings that particular features have apart from gendered usage.

(2) Performance of speech acts. One of the strongest influences from outside of communication theory, apart from the ubiquitous presence of social psychology, has been the contribution of linguistic and pragmatic literature to understanding of speech as action. Parallel to examination of the things people do with words has been a current of inquiry into the cultural nature of how they do those things. Some have started from a universal perspective and had little, if any, concern about cultural influence (e.g., Searle, 1969, 1979). Others have proceeded from a cultural view of speech action that has a comparative element or purpose (e.g., Ahern, 1979; M. Rosaldo, 1982; Rushforth, 1981; Verschueren, 1985). Still others have approached the question of culture and speech acts through development of a semantic metalanguage to describe and compare them across languages and cultures (Wierzbicka, 1985) or through cross-national linguistic examination of particular acts such as requesting, apologizing, thanking, or giving compliments (e.g., Blum-Kulka, House, & Kasper, 1989; Hollos & Beeman, 1974; Manes, 1983; Manes & Wolfson, 1981; Valdes & Pino, 1981). Work of this kind can provide a body of theory and research that broadens and enriches current investigation of interpersonal processes such as compliance gaining, self-disclosure, relational escalation/deescalation, and so forth in that it offers rich cultural detail of performance of particular speech acts that are clearly related to those processes.

An example of one such line of research is that which pursues formulation of directives. In directing the behavior of others, and in responding to alternative forms of directives (requests, commands, suggestions, and so on), interactants act upon shared understandings of the nature of interpersonal power and the desirability of making power differences salient when directing the behavior of others. Clearly evident in such studies is that cultural preferences for direct or indirect formulations of directives make any simple equation of politeness with indirectness untenable. Rather, there are logical connections between the belief system of the speech community and the preferred form of directives—and those connections take richly textured forms. Among the Ilongot of the Philippines, for example, described by Rosaldo (1973; M. Rosaldo, 1982) as one of the most egalitarian societies she had ever seen, interaction among intimates in private is characterized by brief, direct directives. Such directives are not construed as overly brusque because of the cultural belief that humans' behavior is formless and erratic unless given shape through direct commands. Directing behavior in public presents an opposite imperative: There is an expectation that directive intentions will be hidden within witty, artistic speech to acknowledge the equality and autonomy of all persons. Summarizing the interpersonal ideology through which this apparent contradiction is made to seem coherent is beyond the scope of the point being made here. In essence, though, directives seem to function along a public/private dimension similar to personal address.

By contrast, Rushforth (1981) describes Bear Lake Athabaskans as a speech community in which respect for individual autonomy is shown through indirect directives or an avoidance, when remotely possible, of directives of any kind (other research suggests similar avoidance among other Native American communities, e.g., Basso, 1979; Scollon & Scollon, 1981). Because of a belief that every individual should be his or her "own boss," attempts are made to avoid imposing one's will on others. Telling others what to do is viewed as a failure of the speaker to be "controlled": gentle, polite, humble, careful. This seems, as an ideology, to be significantly similar to the Ilongot belief system. In both, persons are viewed as autonomous individuals who, ideally, engage in egalitarian relationships. Among the Athabaskans, that ideal is realized through indirect directives. Among the Ilongot, that ideal is realized, except in very public, formal settings, through direct formulations.

A very different sort of social purpose is served through direct imperatives in a community of migrant workers described by Weigel and Weigel (1985). They describe directive use in this agricultural community in the southeastern United States as characterized by an overwhelming use of direct imperatives, regardless of social rank, familiarity, presence of outsiders, and task expectations. This pattern, they claim, is attributable to a social organization of clearly unequal power between crew leaders and the farmworkers under their supervision. Ensuring compliance with directives on the part of the farmworkers is the goal of such utterances. Convivial social relations are viewed as unimportant and even undesirable. Directives in this community thus serve the social purpose of keeping a rigidly controlled social hierarchy intact.

A final contrast of a system of interpersonal relationships revealed through direct imperatives is described by Blum-Kulka (1990). In comparing directive use during family dinner conversations between North Americans and Israelis, she notes that the Israelis tended to be more direct, especially to children, than were the Americans. The value reflected in this pattern is one of minimizing social distance through directness, in the manner described at length as *dugri* speech by Katriel (1986). For Israeli parents, the desire to minimize distance is combined with a more explicit acknowledgment of power difference between adults and children than seems to be the case among American parents, who display more attentiveness to children's independence.

The particulars of diverse systems such as those described here are not the point of these brief illustrations. The specifics of how the Ilongot, migrant workers, or Israeli parents perform directives are of less theoretical interest than the fact that, taken together, these studies show that the ways in which people attempt to gain compliance through directive use are traceable to the interpersonal ideology of their speech community. That directive use varies across speech communities because ideologies are different is obvious but is not the most significant contribution of this body of research. Far more important is the fact that they demonstrate ways of focusing on the material process of directive performance as a way of examining an interpersonal process of pervasive interest in the field.

(3) Communicator or interaction style. The communication aspects of self-presentation, and the communicative and relational consequences of self-presentations that are perceived to be inadequate or deviant from social norms, are far-reaching issues in interpersonal communication research. Investigations of communication competence, reticence/communication apprehension, conflict resolution, management practice, and so forth all incorporate stylistic dimensions. Although Norton's (1978, 1983) work has been the most directly focused on description and measurement of "communicator style," the concept of interpersonal style is pervasive and influential in the field. A similar notion of conversational style has developed in sociolinguistics (see Gumperz, 1982; Tannen, 1984) in which style is defined as all of the linguistic means by which speakers encode meaning in language and convey how they intend their talk to be understood: pitch, volume, intonation, rate of speech and turn taking, cohesion devices, and so forth.

In the same way that culturally situated pragmatic research can shed light on interpersonal processes by way of description of speech act performance, ethnographies of speaking can reveal accomplishment of personal identities and relational configurations congruent with the interpersonal ideology of a speech community. Such work can thus illuminate how self-presentation as a universal process is enacted in culturally specific ways. Rather than confirming that self-disclosure is generally evaluated positively under many circumstances, for example, or seen as a necessary step in the development of intimacy between persons, ethnographic evidence suggests that quite different communication styles may be more highly valued in other speech communities.

In one of the best-known studies in this tradition, Tamar Katriel (1986) describes an open, confrontational style of disagreement that is prized in modern Israeli culture. *Dugri* speech, as it is described by natives, is characterized as sincere, assertive, natural, solidary, and matter-of-fact speech. This interactional style serves the communal function (Philipsen, 1989) in two ways. It rejects the genteel European heritage from which many native-born Israelis of Jewish descent wish to free themselves: the European Jews' stance of defensiveness, passivity, and restrictedness as a protective mechanism to avoid persecution. At the same time, it contributes to building a new Jewish identity in Israel that resists externally imposed standards of evaluation and conduct. The society toward which *dugri* speakers strive is one that is egalitarian and accepting of persons and conditions just as they are, without artifice or pretense. In talking *dugri*, and being willing to be spoken to in that fashion, Israelis show themselves as strong enough to put aside concerns for selves (their own and that of coparticipants) to accomplish the greater good of a society that can withstand any external force or criticism. Although speaking *dugri* does involve honest expression of opinions and feelings, it is different than self-disclosure as that is generally conceptualized in U.S. interpersonal literature. The purpose of speaking *dugri* is not primarily to ventilate personal points of view or to increase intimacy in a relationship but to correct a situation that the speaker views as detrimental, even at the expense of the hearer's feelings.

An interactional style that creates and sustains interpersonal involvement by way of disagreement, criticism, and complaint has been described by several authors (Heilman, 1976, 1982; Myerhoff, 1978; Schiffrin, 1984; Tannen, 1981, 1984) as characteristic of American Jewry, particularly those of European descent. In this speech community, disagreement is a valued resource for sociability and the display of relational stability. Evident from the consistency of the findings across such studies is that, within this speech community, meaning is systematically attached to that particular style of communication, beyond the content expressed. Analysis of positive evaluations of this argumentative style reveal shared premises. Fighting is a partnership, requiring shared rules, values, and vocabulary, such that it constitutes a profoundly sociable activity. Overlap and interruption may be cooperative, helpful, and supportive rather than competitive. Finally, argument may be valued both for its outcomes and as an ongoing activity. The significance of this coherent, community-specific evaluation of argument, interruption, and disagreement is to suggest that communication behaviors may be usefully viewed, at least in part, as stylistic options that are exercised both in response to individual motivations and perceptions *and* as responses to cultural imperatives to present oneself as a type of communicator that is valued (or at least understood) by the community. Traditional interpersonal communication research has focused almost entirely on individual choices and behaviors, viewing the cultural imperatives as irrelevant or of secondary importance (except, perhaps, in intercultural communication encounters).

A final example of conversational style that has been associated, across a number of studies, with an identifiable speech community is African American speech characterized by confrontation and ridicule of others within close and important relationships (see, e.g., Abrahams, 1976; Kochman, 1981, 1990; McCollough, 1992; Smitherman, 1977; Stanback, 1985, 1989). Integral to verbal artistry that is valued and cultivated within that community is an assertive self-expression that often happens at the expense of others' dignity and self-esteem. It is a style with clear historical roots, both in the oral traditions of African languages that retain their linguistic impact on speech patterns and in the forceful rejection of passivity that characterized Blacks' traditional position of oppression within U.S. society. Examination of the communication style of African Americans at the level of speech communities shows the variability of meaning attached to particular ways of speaking as those relate to the shared experiences and resulting premises of different groups of people. Additionally, such study can address the difficulty of describing "African American speech" (or "white American speech," for that matter) as a simple correlation between ethnicity and communication. By describing ways of speaking that reveal speaking as situated practice within speech communities, the multiplex influences of gender, social class, geographic origin, and so forth may all be addressed (if not always neatly separated). Systematic comparison across such case studies can both capture the common threads of responses to a common heritage across time and changing circumstances, and illuminate the differentiating effects of those other factors that in turn account for distinctive forms of response.

CONCLUSION

The objective of this essay was to join in a conversation about the need to examine the world beyond interacting individuals in the course of interpersonal communication research and theory. I have followed the lead of recent work that has proposed examination of interpersonal/social ideology as a productive focus for such consideration by describing, on the basis of considerable previous ethnographic work by others, a cultural view of interpersonal ideology. That view is distinct from a critical perspective in that it does not presume power imbalance as a starting point. At the same time, a commitment to describing the lifeworld of participants allows for exposition of competing definitions of reality that are accorded different degrees of legitimacy, as those are played out in interaction and relational development.

The cultural view of interpersonal ideology is also distinctive from a social approach to interpersonal communication, in that far greater emphasis is placed on specific definition of members and boundaries of the social group(s) whose messages influence the perceptions and experiences of persons. There is also greater emphasis on examination of material practice (i.e., discourse) rather than conceptualizing social ideology as a primarily cognitive phenomenon.

I have urged throughout this essay a more thorough understanding of culture, such that interpersonal communication research might be more deeply informed by the pervasive influence of cultural premises on communication practice. It is also necessary to note that ethnographers, for their part, have not always directly addressed the central concerns of interpersonal theory and research. The theories discussed here as potentially limited in their applicability outside the cultural context in which they were formulated nonetheless offer rich possibilities for testing and elaboration in other speech communities.

LeVine (1984) points out both the difficulty, and the promise, of culturally informed research:

> As the other social sciences take increasing account of the world at large, they will have to take the concept of culture more seriously. This will require methodological readjustment, because cultural analysis runs counter to the preference for simplification that is prevalent in social science research. A greater tolerance for complexity, however, will reward investigators with a deeper understanding of the phenomena they are studying and a firmer basis for interpreting the data they collect. (p. 84)

It is predictably the case that communication models that take culture as a constitutive element of communicative practice will be less elegant than ones that describe interaction in terms of small numbers of discrete variables that occur in mutually exclusive categories of observable variation. The predictive strength and generalizability of cultural models may not, in a traditionally empirical sense, equal their explanatory depth. Culture is, after all, an overwhelmingly complex phenomenon, and its relation to interpersonal life is only beginning to be understood. In its search for parsimonious theory and replicable results, however, the field of interpersonal communication might do well to be aware of a Javanese folktale figure described by Clifford Geertz (1976): " 'Stupid Boy,' . . . having been counseled by his mother to seek a quiet wife, returned with a corpse" (p. 239). Elegance aside, communication theory without well-developed notions of culture risks producing intellectual corpses of a most stultifying kind.

NOTES

1. Coordinated management of meaning theory, and the work stemming from it, are notable exceptions (see, e.g., Pearce & Cronen, 1980).

2. Montgomery's point in that article was not to suggest that such values and beliefs about communication are true in any universal sense. To the contrary, she meant to hold those beliefs up to question in light of empirical evidence, some of which supported, some of which contradicted, those beliefs. My argument here is that, by not defining which "society" holds those beliefs and which "society" produced the research findings she discusses, there remains no clear suggestion of what social ideology is or whose behavior it influences.

3. I am not proposing absolute relativism, such that any cultural pattern is legitimate and any status quo worthy of preservation as long as it is captured in its full and living authenticity. I *do* mean to suggest that cultures should be understood on their own terms before the researcher engages in critique. Philosophies from beyond the culture's boundaries must be proposed in ways that recognize and extend the logic and rationality internal to the culture. See Huspek (1989/1990) and Neilsen (1974) for expansion (though in Huspek's case, not support) of this point.

4. Debate rages between ethnography that examines cultural ways of speaking from an anthropological, comparative tradition and "cultural studies" that examine the ways in which ideologies are upheld or suppressed through the symbols, themes, and practices of popular culture (see, e.g., Carbaugh, 1988; Fiske, 1991). Although choosing the term *ideology* to denote a central aspect of the concept under discussion might seem to incur an obligation to take up that debate, it is not the discussion I see as most relevant. Cultural studies clearly has much to offer the field of communication (Grossberg, Nelson, & Treichler, 1992, offer a taste of the richness and promise of this approach). A commitment I share with cultural studies is to expose the premises of culture operating in places where they currently go unexamined and largely unnoticed. The view of culture that drives each enterprise seems to be the basis for most of the differences in the practice of them. Cultural studies, as I understand it, approaches culture as a creation of the power structure, such that to reveal culture at work is to expose power at work maintaining its position. The view of culture from which I proceed is an apolitical one—that is, an organic product of a people's history and experiences—such that revealing culture at work is centered on making it explicit, not questioning, challenging, or unseating it. This difference leads to differences in agenda: cultural studies' is to expose the machinations of the power structure; mine is to pull interpersonal communication research back from overgeneralization from what is currently an acultural and thus narrow scope of methods and theory. Another difference lies in the distinct arenas in which these projects are most often (though not always) carried out: cultural studies in popular (usually mediated) communication, Hymesian ethnography in the interpersonal dealings people have with each other. That closer fit seems some grounds for suggesting the applicability of the latter without, again, negating the potential contribution of cultural studies.

5. A question that often dominates critique of ethnography as practiced from the anthropological linguistic perspective is the problem of "writing the other": How can an outsider adequately represent the worldview of members of a community to which they do not belong? The methodological/analytic issues of how much distance a researcher can ever achieve from the hidden premises of his or her own culture are legitimate ones that careful ethnographers take pains to address within the context of the specific cases they pursue. Lest there be doubt about the possibility that an outsider can produce an account of a culture that the natives and the scholarly/philosophical world find accurate enough to be useful, however, attention might be directed to Alexis de Tocqueville's (1835/1945) incisive description of U.S. society or his compatriot's more recent ones (Varenne, 1977, 1986). All are often cited as definitive insights on U.S. culture, despite the nonnative status of their creators.

6. It should be noted that this definition of interpersonal ideology draws most heavily on Philipsen's (1992) definition of a cultural code: ways of speaking that reveal answers to the questions: (a) What is a person? (b) What is society? (c) How are persons and societies linked through communication? The difference is that I am not focused on links between persons and societies but on culturally situated interpersonal relationships.

7. Equating open, complete, "honest" communication with "good" communication is a view that is usefully challenged, in various ways, by several authors in Coupland, Giles, and Wiemann's (1991) collection of essays exploring "miscommunication."

8. Brown and Levinson's (1987) politeness theory, though not without its weaknesses, is an account of direct versus indirect speech that is precisely what I am suggesting as most valuable. It draws on data from three quite distinctive cultures to provide an account of face threat, and attention to face threat, as universal aspects of interaction. It then specifies the ways in which cultural values may be expected to enter into the broader equation.

9. Enormous controversy surrounds the question of whether stylistic differences between male and female ways of speaking are more accurately viewed as manifestations of cultural difference between men and women or as evidence of pervasive power imbalance between males and females, such that women's ways of speaking are consistently devalued. A cultural view of *linguistic phenomena* such as hedges and tag questions as shifters does not imply accepting the "two cultures" view of gender and communication. Rather, it opens the way to establishing whether the powerless attribution is traceable to the gender of the speaker rather than to the linguistic feature itself.

REFERENCES

Abrahams, R. (1976). *Talking black.* Rowley, MA: Newbury House.
Ahern, E. (1979). The problem of efficacy: Strong and weak illocutionary acts. *Man, 14,* 1-17.
Basso, K. (1979). *Portraits of "the whiteman": Linguistic play and cultural symbols among the Western Apache.* New York: Cambridge University Press.
Bilmes, J. (1976). Rules and rhetoric: Negotiating the social order in a Thai village. *Journal of Anthropological Research, 32,* 44-57.
Blum-Kulka, S. (1990). You don't eat lettuce with your fingers: Parental politeness in family discourse. *Journal of Pragmatics, 14,* 259-288.
Blum-Kulka, S., House, J., & Kasper, G. (1989). *Cross-cultural pragmatics: Requests and apologies.* Norwood, NJ: Ablex.
Bochner, A. P. (1982). On the efficacy of openness in close relationships. In M. Burgoon (Ed.), *Communication yearbook 5* (pp. 109-124). New Brunswick, NJ: Transaction.
Braithwaite, C. (1990). Communicative silence: A cross cultural study of Basso's hypothesis. In D. Carbaugh (Ed.), *Cultural communication and intercultural contact* (pp. 321-328). Hillsdale, NJ: Lawrence Erlbaum.
Brown, J., & Rogers, E. (1991). Openness, uncertainty, and intimacy: An epistemological reformulation. In N. Coupland, H. Giles, & J. Wiemann (Eds.), *"Miscommunication" and problematic talk* (pp. 146-165). Newbury Park, CA: Sage.
Brown, P., & Levinson, S. (1987). *Politeness: Some universals in language use.* New York: Cambridge University Press.
Brown, R., & Gilman, A. (1960). The pronouns of power and solidarity. In T. A. Sebeok (Ed.), *Style in language* (pp. 253-276). Cambridge: MIT Press.
Burke, K. (1957). *The philosophy of literary form.* New York: Vintage.
Cantor, N., Mischel, W., & Schwartz, J. (1982). Social knowledge: Structure, content, use and abuse. In A. H. Hastorf & A. M. Isen (Eds.), *Cognitive social psychology* (pp. 33-72). New York: Elsevier/North-Holland.
Carbaugh, D. (1988). *Talking American: Cultural discourses on* Donahue. Norwood, NJ: Ablex.
Cody, M., & McLaughlin, M. (1985). The situation as a construct in interpersonal communication research. In M. Knapp & G. Miller (Eds.), *Handbook of interpersonal communication* (pp. 263-312). Beverly Hills, CA: Sage.
Coupland, N., Giles, H., & Wiemann, J. (Eds.). (1991). *"Miscommunication" and problematic talk.* Newbury Park, CA: Sage.

DeVos, G. (1985). Dimensions of the self in Japanese culture. In A. J. Marsella, G. DeVos, & F. L. K. Hsu (Eds.), *Culture and self: Asian and Western perspectives* (pp. 141-184). London: Tavistock.

Fiske, J. (1991). Writing ethnographies: Contribution to a dialogue. *Quarterly Journal of Speech, 77*, 330-335.

Fitch, K. L. (1989). *Communicative enactment of interpersonal ideology: Personal address in urban Colombian society.* Unpublished doctoral dissertation, University of Washington, Seattle.

Fitch, K. L. (1991). The interplay of linguistic universals and cultural knowledge in personal address: Colombian madre terms. *Communication Monographs, 58*(3), 254-272.

Fitzpatrick, M. A. (1988). *Between husbands and wives: Communication in marriage.* Newbury Park, CA: Sage.

Foley, D. (1989). Does the working class have a culture in the anthropological sense? *Cultural Anthropology, 4*(2), 137-162.

Geertz, C. (1976). "From the native's point of view": On the nature of anthropological understanding. In K. H. Basso & H. Selby (Eds.), *Meaning in anthropology* (pp. 221-239). Albuquerque: University of New Mexico Press.

Geertz, C. (1983). *Local knowledge.* New York: Basic Books.

Grossberg, L., Nelson, C., & Treichler, P. (Eds.). (1992). *Cultural studies.* New York: Routledge.

Gumperz, J. (1982). *Discourse strategies.* New York: Cambridge University Press.

Heilman, S. (1976). *Synagogue life.* Chicago: University of Chicago Press.

Heilman, S. (1982). Prayer in the Orthodox synagogue: An analysis of ritual display. *Contemporary Jewry, 6*, 1.

Hollos, M., & Beeman, W. (1974). The development of directives among Norwegian and Hungarian children: An example of communicative style in culture. *Language in Society, 7*, 345-355.

Howell, J. (1973). *Hard living on Clay Street.* Garden City, NY: Anchor.

Huspek, M. (1989-1990). The idea of ethnography and its relation to cultural critique. *Research on Language and Social Interaction, 23*, 293-312.

Hymes, D. (1972). Models of the interaction of language and social life. In J. Gumperz & D. Hymes (Eds.), *Directions in sociolinguistics: The ethnography of communication* (pp. 35-71). New York: Holt, Rinehart & Winston.

Jonz, J. G. (1975). Situated address in the United States Marine Corps. *Anthropological Linguistics, 17*(2), 68-77.

Katriel, T. (1986). *Talking straight: Dugri speech in Israeli sabra culture.* Cambridge: Cambridge University Press.

Katriel, T., & Philipsen, G. (1981). "What we need is communication": Communication as a cultural category in some American speech. *Communication Monographs, 48*, 301-317.

Kochman, T. (1981). *Black and white styles in conflict.* Chicago: University of Chicago Press.

Kochman, T. (1990). Cultural pluralism. In D. Carbaugh (Ed.), *Cultural communication and intercultural contact* (pp. 219-224). Hillsdale, NJ: Lawrence Erlbaum.

Komarovsky, M. (1962). *Blue-collar marriage.* New Haven, CT: Yale University Press.

Lakoff, R. (1975). *Language and women's place.* New York: Harper & Row.

Lannamann, J. W. (1991). Interpersonal communication research as ideological practice. *Communication Theory, 1*(3), 179-203.

Lebra, T. (1976). *Japanese patterns of behavior.* Honolulu: University of Hawaii Press.

LeVine, R. A. (1984). Properties of culture: An ethnographic view. In R. A. Shweder & R. A. LeVine (Eds.), *Culture theory: Essays on mind, self, and emotion* (pp. 67-87). New York: Cambridge University Press.

Manes, J. (1983). Compliments: A mirror of cultural values. In N. Wolfson & E. Judd (Eds.), *Sociolinguistics and language acquisition.* Rowley, MA: Newbury House.

Manes, J., & Wolfson, N. (1981). The compliment formula. In F. Coulmas (Ed.), *Conversational routine: Explorations in standardized communication situations and prepatterned speech* (pp. 11-132). The Hague: Mouton.

Martin, R. (1992). Relational cognition complexity and relational communication in personal relationships. *Communication Monographs, 59*(2), 150-163.

McCollough, M. (1992). *Black and white women's friendships: Claiming the margins.* Unpublished doctoral dissertation, Temple University, Philadelphia.

Montgomery, B. (1988). Quality communication in personal relationships. In S. W. Duck (Ed.), *Handbook of personal relationships* (pp. 343-359). New York: John Wiley.

Montgomery, B. (1992). Communication as the interface between couples and culture. In S. A. Deetz (Ed.), *Communication yearbook 15* (pp. 475-507). Newbury Park, CA: Sage.

Myerhoff, B. (1978). *Number our days.* New York: Simon & Schuster.

Neilsen, K. (1974). Rationality and relativism. *Philosophy and Social Science, 4,* 313-331.

Norton, R. (1978). Foundation of a communicator style construct. *Human Communication Research, 4,* 99-112.

Norton, R. (1983). *Communicator style: Theory, application, and measures.* Beverly Hills, CA: Sage.

O'Barr, W. M. (1982). *Linguistic evidence: Language, power, and strategy in the courtroom.* New York: Academic Press.

Parks, M. R. (1982). Ideology in interpersonal communication: Off the couch and into the world. In M. Burgoon (Ed.), *Communication yearbook 5* (pp. 79-107). New Brunswick, NJ: Transaction.

Pearce, W. B., & Cronen, V. (1980). *Communication, action and meaning: The creation of social realities.* New York: Praeger.

Philipsen, G. (1975). Speaking "like a man" in Teamsterville: Culture patterns of role enactment in an urban neighborhood. *Quarterly Journal of Speech, 61,* 13-22.

Philipsen, G. (1976). Places for speaking in Teamsterville. *Quarterly Journal of Speech, 62,* 15-25.

Philipsen, G. (1989). Speech and the communal function in four cultures. *International and Intercultural Communication Annual, 13,* 79-92.

Philipsen, G. (1992). *Speaking culturally: Explorations in social communication.* Albany: State University of New York Press.

Philipsen, G., & Huspek, M. (1985). A bibliography of sociolinguistic studies of personal address. *Anthropological Linguistics, 27,* 94-101.

Planalp, S. (1985). Relational schemata: A test of alternative forms of relational knowledge as guides to communication. *Human Communication Research, 12,* 3-29.

Ray, G. (1987). An ethnography of nonverbal communication in an Appalachian community. *Research on Language and Social Interaction, 21,* 171-188.

Rosaldo, M. (1982). The things we do with words: Ilongot speech acts and speech act theory in philosophy. *Language in Society, 11,* 203-237.

Rosaldo, R. (1973). I have nothing to hide: The language of Ilongot oratory. *Language and Society, 2,* 193-223.

Rosaldo, R. (1989). *Culture and truth: The remaking of social analysis.* Boston: Beacon.

Rubin, L. (1976). *Worlds of pain: Life in the working-class family.* New York: Basic Books.

Rushforth, S. (1981). Speaking to "relatives-through-marriage": Aspects of communication among Bear Lake Athapaskan. *Journal of Anthropological Research, 37,* 28-45.

Schiffrin, D. (1984). Jewish argument as sociability. *Language in Society, 13,* 311-334.

Scollon, R., & Scollon, S. (1981). *Narrative, literacy and face in interethnic communication.* Norwood, NJ: Ablex.

Scotton, C., & Zhu, W. (1983). *Tongzhi* in China: Language change and its conversational consequences. *Language in Society, 12,* 477-494.

Searle, J. (1969). *Speech acts.* New York: Cambridge University Press.

Searle, J. (1979). *Expression and meaning.* New York: Cambridge University Press.

Silverstein, M. (1976). Shifters, linguistic categories, and cultural descriptions. In K. Basso & H. Selby (Eds.), *Meaning and cultural anthropology* (pp. 11-55). Albuquerque: University of New Mexico Press.

Smith, R. J. (1983). *Japanese society: Tradition, self, and the social order.* Cambridge: Cambridge University Press.

Smitherman, G. (1977). *Talkin' and testifyin': The language of black America.* Boston: Houghton Mifflin.

Song, J. S. (1992, May). *Constructing many selves in oneself: Other-oriented selfhood encoded in Korean language and communication praxis.* Paper presented at the meeting of the International Communication Association, Miami.

Staiano, K. V. (1980). Ethnicity as process: The creation of an Afro-American identity. *Ethnicity, 7,* 27-33.

Stanback, M. H. (1985). Language and black women's place: Evidence from the black middle class. In P. Treichler, C. Kramarae, & B. Stafford (Eds.), *For alma mater: Theory and practice in feminist scholarship* (pp. 177-191). Urbana: University of Illinois Press.

Stanback, M. H. (1989). Feminist theory and black women's talk. *The Howard Journal of Communication, 1,* 187-194.

Stewart, J., & D'Angelo, G. (1980). *Together: Communicating interpersonally.* Reading, MA: Addison-Wesley.

Suzuki, T. (1976). Language and behavior in Japan: The conceptualization of personal relations. In T. Lebra (Ed.), *Japanese patterns of behavior* (pp. 142-157). Honolulu: University of Hawaii Press.

Tannen, D. (1981). New York Jewish conversational style. *International Journal of the Sociology of Language, 30,* 133-149.

Tannen, D. (1984). *Conversational style: Analyzing talk among friends.* Norwood, NJ: Ablex.

Taylor, C. A. (1991). Defining the scientific community: A rhetorical perspective on demarcation. *Communication Monographs, 58*(4), 402-420.

Tocqueville, A. de. (1945). *Democracy in America.* New York: Vintage. (Original work published 1835)

Tu, W. (1985). *Confucian thought: Selfhood as creative transformation.* Albany: State University of New York Press.

Valdes, G., & Pino, C. (1981). Muy a tus órdenes: Compliment responses among Mexican-American bilinguals. *Language in Society, 10,* 53-72.

Varenne, H. (1977). *Americans together.* New York: Columbia University Press.

Varenne, H. (1986). *Symbolizing America.* Lincoln: University of Nebraska Press.

Verschueren, J. (1985). *What people say they do with words.* Norwood, NJ: Ablex.

Weigel, M., & Weigel, R. (1985). Directive use in a migrant agricultural community: A test of Ervin-Tripp's hypotheses. *Language in Society, 14,* 63-79.

Weis, L. (1990). *Working class without work.* New York: Routledge.

Wieder, L., & Pratt, S. (1990). On being a recognizable Indian among Indians. In D. Carbaugh (Ed.), *Cultural communication and intercultural contact* (pp. 45-64). Hillsdale, NJ: Lawrence Erlbaum.

Wierzbicka, A. (1985). A semantic metalanguage for a crosscultural comparison of speech acts and speech genres. *Language in Society, 14*(4), 491-514.

The Problem With Disempowering Ideology

JOHN W. LANNAMANN
University of New Hampshire

> Is it surprising that prisons resemble factories, schools, barracks, hospitals, which all resemble prisons?
>
> —Foucault, 1979, p. 228

IS power, either sovereign or disciplinary, at stake in all cultural contexts at all times? If there is a common currency among the wide variety of contemporary writers identified with interpretive studies, postmodernism, critical cultural studies, and poststructuralism, it is the tendency to deconstruct all metanarratives of unity, including the narrative of liberation implicit in most accounts of cultural power. Lyotard (1979/1984) wants to "wage war" on totalizing discourses and Geertz (1973) dismisses the idea of cultural universals, pointing out that

> there is a logical conflict between asserting that, say, "religion," "marriage," or "property" are empirical universals and giving them very much in the way of specific content, for to say that they are empirical universals is to say that they have the same content, and to say they have the same content is to fly in the face of the undeniable fact that they do not. (pp. 39-30)

As soon as the blanks of a proposed empirical universal are filled in, the universality disappears. The solution that Geertz (1983) advocates is a tacking back and forth between the most local of detail and the more general apprehension of the relational web constituted by the parts. Proponents of interpretive ethnography, as well as those whose ethnographic approach is informed by critical social theory, are deeply suspicious of empirical univer-

Correspondence and requests for reprints: John W. Lannamann, Department of Communication, University of New Hampshire, Durham, NH 03824-3586.

Communication Yearbook 17, pp. 136-147

sals. Fitch (this volume) provides a compelling argument against treating power as a universally relevant tool for cultural analysis.

Yet, in spite of the strong arguments against empirical universals, issues of power and opposition surface regularly in the work of a number of ethnographers writing in widely divergent contexts (Conquergood, 1991, 1992; Huspek & Kendall, 1991; Rosaldo, 1989; Willis, 1977). While this is hardly evidence of a universal, the diversity does suggest the utility of approaching the investigation of cultural practices ready to listen for the discourses of power. These writers do not treat power as separate from culture but as a constitutive part of cultural activity. By foregrounding the operation of power in cultural contexts, politically engaged ethnography traverses a route that differs from the ethnographic tradition inspired by Hymes (1972) where a commitment to grounded observations deflects questions of power unless the category is unambiguously displayed in cultural practices (Carbaugh, 1988; Philipsen, 1975). The distinction between the two ethnographic traditions is based on differing views of society; politically engaged ethnography is appropriate when society is understood to be fundamentally based in conflict; apolitical ethnography follows from theorizing society as based on consensus (Fiske, 1991).

For those who choose the consensus model, the term *critical studies* brings with it the baggage of a normative, monolithic narrative of liberation. Fitch associates critical theory with the claim that "stability and coherence are achieved by the ability of the power bloc to promote and hold its interests against those of subordinated social groups" (p. 107). She implies that the search for power in all cultural contexts, regardless of differing cultural meanings concerning the relevance of the category, is a conceit of critical theorists who maintain a simplistic notion that ideology is a veil hiding the oppressive structures of the powerful.

The discursive closure that results from the application of the label "critical theory" suppresses the seething diversity of an ongoing tradition of ideological critique.[1] It is unnecessary to dismiss ideological criticism as heavy-handed liberation dogma simply because some of the tools, forged by Horkheimer, Adorno, and Marcuse in response to the ascendent fascism in Germany, still carry a trace of the Frankfort school's urgency.

The false consciousness approach to ideology that Fitch criticizes has already given way to the arguments coming from a long line of critical scholars ranging from Gramsci (1968) through to Hall (1980) and Grossberg (1993). These writers shift the emphasis from what is "false" about consciousness to the ways in which the fragments of everyday practice produce the often contradictory contexts in which we continue to struggle over the meaning of our lives.

THE DIALOGICAL NATURE OF IDEOLOGY

Hall rejects the notion that there is a simple already orderly connection or, as Althusser terms it, an "expressive" link between the ideology of a group and its relation to the economic means of production (Hall, 1985, p. 94). Instead, Hall extends Gramsci's criticism of class reductionism in classical Marxist theory and provides a way to think of ideology as discursively realized. This move locates ideology in the material practices of cultural members rather than in the consciousness of individuals or classes of individuals.

Commenting on the materiality of ideology, Volosinov (1973) writes: "Despite the deep methodological differences between them, the idealistic philosophy of culture and psychologistic cultural studies both commit the same fundamental error. By localizing ideology in the consciousness, they transform the study of ideologies into a study of consciousness" (p. 12). There is a parallel between the idealist position criticized by Volosinov and the interpretive orientation to ideology offered by Fitch. She characterizes interpersonal ideology as "a set of premises about personhood, relationships, and communication that structure negotiation of meaning through language use within a speech community" (p. 115). The premises, Fitch argues, are the cognitive component of ideology and become observable in talk. Language use is steered by a certain already determined structure of consciousness, an "interpersonal" ideology. Choices between linguistic alternatives, the performance of speech acts, and aspects of communicator style are taken to be empirical evidence of the sense-giving premises.

The "interpersonal" status of this version of ideology, however, is unclear because the abstract premises that guide communicator choices are offstage. The premises are not treated as a shaping influence in the emerging interactive process. Rather, the interaction is thought to simply "reveal" the ideology of the culture. Ideological analysis from this perspective is directed toward examining the ways of speaking that "show an understanding of the ideology" (Fitch, p. 118). Instead of an *inter*personal ideology, this approach implies a "personal" ideology, a form of abstract objectivism in which ideology appears as a culturally normative system of cognitions determining personal action. In short, the definition privileges an abstract structure of premises over the generative potential of interactive practices.

By defining ideology as a set of premises, a collection of "basic and fundamental" beliefs, Fitch neglects both the materiality and the contingency of ideology. Removed from practice and reconstituted as an abstract system, interpersonal ideologies seem to be a kind of historical residue. This theoretical distillation of material practice strips ideology of its temporality and hides its socially constructed and maintained character. Like a stereophonic recording played through a monophonic system, the dynamic contours of ideology and the spatially located sources of ideology are flattened or conflated. This results in what members of the Bakhtin circle refer to as a "persistent deafness and blindness to concrete ideological reality." Bakhtin and Medvedev (1985) criticize the inclination to "imagine ideological creation as some inner process of understanding, comprehension, and perception" within individuals because such an orientation hides the fact that ideology "unfolds externally, for the eye, the ear, the hand." Bakhtin and Medvedev (1985) conclude that ideology "is not within us, but between us" (p. 8). Returning ideology to the concrete material conditions of conversation means reintroducing what Toulmin (1988), in his argument for the recovery of practical philosophy, termed "the 'oral', the 'particular', the 'local', and the 'timely' " (p. 338).

The Oral

Located between individuals, ideology is behavioral and dialogical (Bakhtin, 1981). It emerges between positioned subjects as they work to construct meaning. Ideologies are not simply read off from class positions (Hall, 1988). They are produced *in* interactions that are filled with contradictions and uncertainty. As Billig et al. (1988) put it, "Ideology does not imprint single images but produces dilemmatic quandaries" (p. 46). Ideological practices, then, are more like arguments between people than instruction sets held in the heads of cultural members.

This line of reasoning parallels Toulmin's criticism of modern philosophers for judging the validity of arguments by examining only the formal relations among the supporting propositions. Lost in such an examination are the issues of *who* is being addressed, the *forum* of the discussion, and the particular *examples* used to support the argument (Toulmin, 1988, p. 339). The process of argumentation, a concrete and conversational process between particular people, is hidden from view. Only the formal propositions abstracted from their concrete conversational origins gain attention. The formalist approach in philosophy is similar to the propositional approach to ideology where abstract premises about personhood, relationships, and communication appear as frozen nuggets of cognition. When applied to ideological inquiry, a focus on the oral leads to the study of those forums in which perpetually incomplete, fragmented, and contradictory lines of action are discussed, negotiated, and argued. Ideology is constructed and realized in practical speech behavior, a fundamentally social activity (Stewart, 1983).

The Particular and Local

Toulmin (1988) notes that, during the seventeenth century, Western philosophy began to privilege general principles over particular cases. As he puts it, "Abstract axioms were in, concrete diversity was out" (p. 340). Understanding produced under the constraints of specific circumstances was suspect. A similar Enlightenment bias informs the cultural premises approach to ideological analysis. A premise, Fitch argues, is a belief that is "basic and fundamental to understanding the world" (p. 116). As a general principle, it provides a way of interpreting the specific and local experiences of everyday life. From this perspective, ideological practice involves the application of culturally shared cognitive categories to subdue the flux of daily life.[2] Specific social actions appear to be entailed not by the unique interactional setting but by the abstract premises that constitute the interpersonal ideology. During their talk, cultural members simply instantiate the general ideological beliefs of the culture.

Where abstract ideology is vague and its relation to politics mystified, concrete ideological practice is specific and productive of the politics of everyday life. Volosinov (1973) writes that the specificity of ideology consists "precisely in its being located between organized individuals, in its being the medium of their communication" (p. 12). The medium of ideological practice, Volosinov argues, is sign activity and this sign activity is always an enactment in the specific and local setting.

The Timely

A particular position is always a position in time as well as space. This is particularly true in the case of ideological practice. Ideological practice is not the result of a synchronic set of premises. Rather, it emerges in the continuous flow of social interaction. The "ideological phenomenon par excellence" according to Volosinov (1973) is the word, because it is malleable and sensitive to the specific contingencies of use (p. 13). This is not to claim that ideology is fixed in the word or that the word somehow embodies an existing ideology. Rather, it is in the concrete social use of the word that an ideology emerges.

The conversational evolution of ideology is the result of interactional responsiveness, the form-giving characteristic of utterances in situated speech. Bakhtin (1986) discusses the utterance as "a link in the chain of speech communication of a particular sphere" in which each utterance is "primarily a *'response'* to preceding utterances of the given sphere" (p. 91). The utterance is particular and local. It is bounded by speaking turns and it is situated by its responsiveness in the flow of conversation (Shotter, in press). The meaning of the utterance does not preexist interaction but is realized "in the process of active, responsive understanding" (Volosinov, 1973, p. 102). It is in this interactive moment (McNamee, 1992) that the politics of position are worked out, for, in the call and response of speaking and listening, rights and responsibilities are at stake. Utterances are the medium of ideological practices because they provide practical answers to the question: "Who should live in whose reality?" (Shotter, 1992, p. 7). The answers to this question position people in a constantly shifting mosaic of power relations.

POWER

One of the consequences of neglecting the dialogical dimension of ideology is that the concept of power becomes disposable; it can be reduced to a complex of other, more elementary forms. Without an interactive component, ideology is reduced to a shorthand for the beliefs and values of a culture, essentially a set of abstract cognitive forms. Power simply becomes one possible construct competing among many for the interpretation of cultural practices. In this apolitical perspective, all cultures are assumed to have an ideology, but there is little reason to place an emphasis on power because, as Fitch puts it, "power is only one of many interactional arrangements" (p. 107) potentially defined by the cultural premises that constitute ideology.

When power does surface as an analytic category in a monological version of ideology, it is trivialized as unilateral power. In such a guise, power is recognizable as something an individual person or separate group has, a possession to be exercised at the expense of another. This perspective characterizes many of the approaches to power in the interpersonal communication literature (for an extensive review, see Berger, 1985). These unilateral conceptions of power rely on an individualist ontology and a lineal epistemology of cause and effect. The unilateral power concept encounters grave problems when it is applied as an analytic tool in the limited context of a single culture (Bateson, 1972; Lannamann, 1991). When it is applied cross-culturally, the problems are amplified and the modernist bias of the concept becomes readily apparent. Power loses its warrant for universality when it is separated from the material conditions of conversation and studied as if it were an individual possession legitimated by a shared cultural premise. Fitch is correct in her criticism of privileging this conception of power in the analysis of culture. Power cannot be convincingly argued to be found in one person or group in any cultural context.

Dialogical Power

From a dialogical perspective on ideology, power cannot be comprehended as unilateral. When ideological practice is seen as interactive, power must also be understood as emerging dialogically between people. One of the benefits of a dialogical understanding of ideology is that it provides a means to understand the ways in which conversational choices become constraints. A dialogical understanding of power accounts for the ways in which power is productive. Power is not a structural system lurking *behind* ideological practice. It is emergent *in* the practice of communicating as people invite others to respond from various positions. This practice involves the recursion of interactional choice and interactional constraint. Power develops as utterances specify ways of responding.

Foucault (1979) elaborates the role of choice and constraint in his discussion of sovereign and disciplinary forms of power. Sovereign power involves the direct imposition of will upon another. This form of power is primarily coercive and does not rely on individual consent. It is exercised in a direct, physical way and involves domination by force. As a unilateral play of power, it is the form of power most visible in a monological version of ideology. This version of power is, however, a blunt instrument for understanding the subtle politics of communicative interaction because it obscures the ways in which cultural members jointly produce various forms of interactional constraints. Hall (1988) comments on the limitations of emphasizing the coercive side of power: "As soon as you say 'hegemony' people see marching boots, rolling tanks, censorship, people being locked away. What they cannot understand is the one thing we need to understand in societies like ours, which is how people can be constrained while walking free" (p. 61).[3] To understand how we can be constrained while walking free, it is necessary to supplement the examination of the coercive side of power with an understanding of consent, the "hidden side of power" (Deetz, 1992, p. 49).

Foucault's discussion of the pantopticon illustrates how interactive settings produce a form of relational power in which subjects become participants in their own disciplinary control.[4] He argues that disciplinary power operates through a process of consent, a central component in the mechanism of surveillance. Foucault (1979) emphasizes that the relational quality of disciplinary power "automatizes and disindividualizes power" (p. 202). He elaborates: "Power has its principle not so much in a person as in a certain concerted distribution of bodies, surfaces, lights, gazes; in an arrangement whose internal mechanisms produce the relation in which individuals are caught up" (p. 202). In short, disciplinary power is *inter*individual.

Disciplinary power is generated in the dialogue of ideological practice. In this sense, it dwells in the gap between interpersonal interaction and the dialogism of what Bakhtin (1981) refers to as "inner speech." The nature of this inner speech is social in that it is always a response to previous chains of ideological practice. As Holquist (1983) puts it, "The body answers the world by authoring it" (p. 317). Disciplinary power is exercised when the answers authored by the person, even in his or her "inner speech," are specified by the tendencies and feel of the emerging social interaction. Thus, although effective action may appear to be unfettered by external sources of unilateral power, it is always conditioned by how we are " 'positioned' in relation to the others" around us (Shotter, in press).

Dialogical power as a form of joint action. Foucault's discussion of disciplinary power also provides a way to think about power without recourse to abstract formulations of individual intentions or ideological premises. Disciplinary power is not tied to the intentions of individuals because it is in the constructing of relations between the interactants that ideological constraints upon discourse exert their influence. When disciplinary power is successful, authority becomes invisible. The power relation is maintained by the dialogical practices of the subjects in relation to each other.

Interactive possibilities and constraints are constructed as interactants respond to each other and to the unfolding situation. This dialogical practice is not governed by the private intentions of the individual, nor is it determined by abstract ideological premises. Yet, the interactive moment is not a free-for-all. As Hall (1983) indicates, the symbols we use "do not swing about from side to side in language or ideological representation alone" (p. 40). Utterances are both responses to previous action and invitations to respond in particular ways.

The constraints arising during interaction cannot adequately be described as either products or processes, nouns or verbs. Considered from a dialogical standpoint, power is material but not objective—living but not autonomous—and has intentionality but is not intended. Interactive constraints are material in the sense that they intervene in the social world, but, because they are authored by positioned speakers, they are not objective. The constraints are living, in the sense that they have their existence only when enacted, but this life is not self-sustaining. The constraints have the quality of intentionality in the sense that they are a by-product of outwardly directed action, but as a transpersonal outcome of interaction they cannot be traced to individual intent. These characteristics belong to a form of social action that Shotter (in press) suggests occupies a "zone of uncertainty" lying between the spheres of human actions and natural events. He refers to this zone as a form of joint action in which "not only unintended joint outcomes are produced (rather than outcomes intended by the individuals involved), but as a part of that outcome, a 'situation' is created that the participants experience themselves as being 'in' " (Shotter, 1987, p. 227).

In joint action, the iteration of individual choices can produce a set of unintended consequences that, on the surface, appear similar to traditional conceptions of unilateral power. The unintended consequences of joint action may stabilize certain political arrangements, repress resistance, and limit debate about access to cultural resources. Unlike the conception of unilateral power, however, an understanding of power focused on joint action provides a way to understand how, in Hall's (1988) terms, "we can be constrained while walking free" (p. 61).

The differences between a monological and a dialogical understanding of power can be illustrated by examining the North American ideological commitment to individualism (Bellah, Madsen, Sullivan, Swidler, & Tipton, 1985; Lannamann, 1991; Sampson, 1977, 1981). In a monological version of ideology, individualism is considered to be a central cultural premise about personhood. When the premise of individualism is linked to questions of power, there is often an implied absence; the agent responsible for oppression is behind the scenes. This absence lurks in the background of Jacoby's (1975) discussion of individualism: "Even as society announced it, the idea of the individual as an autonomous being was ideological. The unemployed, like the employed, were to think that their lack of luck, or their luck, was due to private abilities and was not determined by the social whole" (p. 104).

The trace of the absent agent can be seen in the mysterious image of a society making announcements to influence the thinking of the unemployed. When ideology is apprehended monologically as a set of cultural premises, the abstract concept of power is used to account for the missing agent. But the actual operation of power is mystified. Power "structures" and "relations of power" must stand in for concrete details because, given the joint nature of interaction, it is impossible to show a direct connection between the abstract cognitions of individuals and the outcomes of social interaction.

A dialogical approach to the interplay between power and the ideology of individualism begins with an examination of the unintended consequences of joint action. The concrete ideological practice of talk can create an oppressive regime of power between the participants that is quite separate from the individual beliefs or intentions of the participants.

For example, Tomm and Lannamann (1988) describe a family therapy case in which a husband acted as if his depression were genetic while his wife tended to be less patient with that diagnosis, acting instead to encourage him to get up and do something about his depression. The resulting interaction had a powerful unintended consequence. The more the husband acted like his depression was an unavoidable part of his life, the more the wife encouraged him to overcome the depression by fighting back with a combination of willpower and optimism. These invitations to act as if his depression were controllable positioned him in interactively created situations that seemed hopeless, thereby confirming his belief in the genetic basis of the depression. His response to these situations confirmed her suspicion that the depression was an intentional response to stressful situations requiring further encouragement. In this manner, the ideological practices of the couple produced a set of unintended consequences that constrained them. The power that oppressed this couple was emergent in their dialogue; it was not *in* the abstract ideological premise of individualism or the derivative claim that depression was a problem possessed by self-contained individuals, not a shared problem of a social community. Their joint actions continually reaffirmed the cultural ideal of individualism, but the power of this ideological formulation was in its dialogical realization.

This example is somewhat distant from the public arena, which has been the traditional target of ideological critique. Yet, the powerful unintended consequence of the joint process described here is very similar to the working of power and domination explored in Willis's (1977) discussion of how working-class kids end up with working-class jobs in spite of the best intentions of their schoolteachers. Dialogical power is always situated locally and reproduced interactively.

CONCLUSIONS

The answer to the question, "Is power at stake in all cultural contexts at all times?" depends on which version of ideology is adopted. When ideology is emptied of practice, it becomes a set of abstract premises that are related to power only coincidentally. Ideology, then, becomes a synonym for world-view, and power is reduced to the status of a culturally contingent variable.

When ideology is examined from a dialogical perspective, questions of power are always salient. In the process of interaction, it is impossible to escape being positioned and responding to the positions invoked by others. Even when these positions are mutually accepted, unintended consequences of social interaction may produce a powerful set of constraints that shape identities, relationships, and lines of action. To imagine a culture without power would be to imagine a society in which dialogue did not produce social accountability.

There is another reason for continuing to ask questions about power in cultural studies. One of the lasting effects of the poststructuralist upheaval during the last decade was the radical destabilization of the relation between signifiers and signifieds. Narratives that claim empirical observations as their warrant have lost the luster of certainty and now must be judged by their rhetorical value. As Fiske (1991) puts it, "Discursivity is not descriptive but generative" (p. 330). When an ethnographer puts an observation into the discourse that finds its way into our journals, documentaries, or news accounts, the discourse is not an innocent or a passive telling. As a text, the report intervenes in the social world it describes (Gergen, 1973; McNamee, 1988). Thus, in addition to (or perhaps instead of) the traditional question of validity, we must begin to ponder the ways in which our professional discourse reconstructs and then reenters the social worlds we set out to describe. The identification of power, whether described as a cultural finding or as a construction of the author, has the potential to begin a dialogue about positioned subjects and their access to cultural resources. Without the rhetorical crutch of empirical "description" to justify cultural analysis, this seems as good a starting place as any.

NOTES

1. Fitch's selection of the label "critical theory" to characterize my work provides an example of how discursive closure prematurely seals off the possibility of entertaining contradictory discursive themes. Instead of noting my struggle to balance the themes of social constructionism, the multivocality of power, second order cybernetics, and the criticism of modernist narratives of unity, she frames the thesis in terms of an "automatic assumption of parallel power structures" in differing societies (p. 107). The rush to capture the "critical" moment in my work may explain why my definition of power as an observer's distinction was so effortlessly transformed into evidence that my approach maintained a commitment to a false consciousness model of ideology. In fact, my phrasing was meant to capture the sentiment of Maturana's aphorism that "observers ultimately observe themselves" (Maturana & Varella, 1987). Those who describe power are inextricably bound up in it.

2. Fitch does allow for the possibility of opposing premises in a single ideology, but these oppositions remain at the level of "cultural ideals," which, in turn, drive the conversations where differences are displayed and oppression is realized. What is missing from her account is a way

to reconcile the cultural idealism with the materiality of social interaction. This would require a more reflexive analysis in which consciousness is seen not as a product of individual cognitions but as a dynamic process jointly produced in interaction with others.

3. My use of Hall and Foucault should not imply that the work of each is necessarily compatible. Hall (1988) criticizes Foucault's orientation to power for dispersing power (the microphysics of power) everywhere and thereby failing to account for the influence of such concentrated power centers as the state or the media. In short, Hall (1988) criticizes Foucault for a conception of "difference without a conception of articulation," a conception of "power without a conception of hegemony" (p. 53).

4. The pantopticon refers to an architectural design for prisons that involved the eighteenth-century equivalent of the modern one-way mirror. In the proposed plan, prison guards in their surveillance towers can see prisoners but, because of the careful use of backlighting, the prisoners are unable to see their observers. This arrangement leads to a form of self-discipline because subjects who cannot be certain if they are under surveillance become their own observers. If the system is successful, the guard becomes unnecessary because the subject has constructed a reality that requires compliance.

REFERENCES

Bakhtin, M. M. (1981). *The dialogic imagination* (M. Holquist, Ed.; C. Emerson & M. Holquist, Trans.). Austin: University of Texas Press.

Bakhtin, M. M. (1986). *Speech genres and other late essays* (V. W. McGee, Trans.). Austin: University of Texas Press.

Bakhtin, M. M., & Medvedev, P. N. (1985). *The formal method in literary scholarship* (A. J. Wehrle, Trans.). Cambridge, MA: Harvard University Press.

Bateson, G. (1972). *Steps to an ecology of mind*. New York: Ballantine.

Bellah, R. N., Madsen, R., Sullivan, W. M., Swidler, A., & Tipton, S. M. (1985). *Habits of the heart: Individualism and commitment in American life*. New York: Harper & Row.

Berger, C. H. (1985). Social power and interpersonal communication. In M. L. Knapp & G. R. Miller (Eds.), *Handbook of interpersonal communication* (pp. 439-499). Beverly Hills, CA: Sage.

Billig, M., Condor, S., Edwards, D., Gane, M., Middleton, D., & Radley, A. (1988). *Ideological dilemmas: A social psychology of everyday thinking*. London: Sage.

Carbaugh, D. (1988). *Talking American: Cultural discourses on Donahue*. Norwood, NJ: Ablex.

Conquergood, D. (1991). Rethinking ethnography: Towards a critical cultural politics. *Communication Monographs, 58*, 179-194.

Conquergood, D. (1992). Ethnography, rhetoric, and performance. *Quarterly Journal of Speech, 78*(1), 80-123.

Deetz, S. (1992). *Democracy in an age of corporate colonization*. Albany: State University of New York Press.

Fiske, J. (1991). Writing ethnographies: Contribution to a dialogue. *Quarterly Journal of Speech, 77*, 330-335.

Foucault, M. (1979). *Discipline and punish: The birth of the prison*. New York: Vintage.

Geertz, C. (1973). *The interpretation of cultures*. New York: Basic Books.

Geertz, C. (1983). *Local knowledge: Further essays in interpretive anthropology*. New York: Basic Books.

Gergen, K. J. (1973). Social science as history. *Journal of Personality and Social Psychology, 26*, 309-320.

Gramsci, A. (1968). *Prison notebooks*. London: Lawrence and Wishart.

Grossberg, L. (1993). Cultural studies and/in new worlds. *Critical Studies in Mass Communication, 10*, 1-22.

Hall, S. (1980). Cultural studies: Two paradigms. *Media, Culture and Society, 2*, 57-72.

Hall, S. (1983). The problem of Ideology: Marxism without guarantees. In B. Matthews (Ed.), *Marx 100 years on* (pp. 57-86). London: Wishart.

Hall, S. (1985). Signification, representation, ideology: Althusser and the post-structuralist debates. *Critical Studies in Mass Communication, 2,* 91-114.

Hall, S. (1988). The toad in the garden: Thatcherism among the theorists. In C. Nelson & L. Grossberg (Eds.), *Marxism and interpretation of culture* (pp. 35-73). Urbana: University of Illinois.

Holquist, M. (1983). Answering as authoring: Mikhail Bakhtin's translinguistics. *Critical Inquiry, 10*, 307-319.

Huspek, M., & Kendall, K. (1991). On withholding political voice: An analysis of the political vocabulary of a "non-political" speech community. *Quarterly Journal of Speech, 77*, 1-19.

Hymes, D. (1972). Models of the interaction of language and social life. In J. Gumperz & D. Hymes (Eds.), *Directions in sociolinguistics: The ethnography of communication* (pp. 35-71). New York: Holt, Rinehart & Winston.

Jacoby, R. (1975). *Social amnesia: A critique of contemporary psychology from Adler to Laing.* Boston: Beacon.

Lannamann, J. W. (1991). Interpersonal communication research as ideological practice. *Communication Theory, 1*, 179-203.

Lyotard, J. F. (1984). *The postmodern condition: A report on knowledge* (G. Bennington & B. Massumi, Trans.). Minneapolis: University of Minnesota Press. (Original work published in 1979)

Maturana, H. R., & Varela, F. J. (1987). *The tree of knowledge: The biological roots of human understanding.* Boston: Shambhala.

McNamee, S. (1988). Accepting research as social intervention: Implications of a systemic epistemology. *Communication Quarterly, 36*, 50-68.

McNamee, S. (1992). *Pathologizing discourse.* Paper presented at the annual meeting of the Eastern Communication Association, Portland, ME.

Philipsen, G. (1975). Speaking "like a man" in Teamsterville: Culture patterns of role enactment in an urban neighborhood. *Quarterly Journal of Speech, 61*, 13-22.

Rosaldo, R. (1989). *Culture and truth: The remaking of social analysis.* Boston: Beacon.

Sampson, E. E. (1977). Psychology and the American ideal. *Journal of Personality and Social Psychology, 35*, 767-782.

Sampson, E. E. (1981). Cognitive psychology as ideology. *American Psychologist, 36*, 730-343.

Shotter, J. (1987). The social construction of an "us": Problems of accountability and narratology. In R. Burnett, P. McGhee, & D. Clarke (Eds.), *Accounting for relationships: Explanation, representation, and knowledge* (pp. 225-247). London: Methuen.

Shotter, J. (1992). *Notes on Bakhtin's theory of the utterance.* Unpublished manuscript, University of New Hampshire, Department of Communication.

Shotter, J. (in press). *Cultural politics of everyday life: Social constructionism, rhetoric and knowing of the third kind.* Buckingham, England: Open University Press.

Stewart, S. (1983). Shouts on the street: Bakhtin's Anti-Linguistics. *Critical Inquiry, 10*, 265-281.

Tomm, K., & Lannamann, J. W. (1988). Questions as interventions. *The Family Therapy Networker, 12*(5), 38-41.

Toulmin, S. (1988). The recovery of practical philosophy. *American Scholar, 57*, 337-352.

Volosinov, V. N. (1973). *Marxism and the philosophy of language* (L. Matejka & I. R. Titunik, Trans.). Cambridge, MA: Harvard University Press.

Willis, P. (1977). *Learning to labor: How working class kids get working class jobs.* New York: Columbia University Press.

The Contested Spaces
of Cultural Dialogue

MARK NEUMANN
University of South Florida

IN her essay, Kristine Fitch proposes to address a series of issues that characterize the relations among culture, ideology, and speech communities that are often absent in interpersonal communication research. Her concerns point to broader ideological and epistemological issues that challenge the traditional generalizing frameworks that organize empirical research in the social sciences. Recent debates in a number of disciplines have questioned the legitimacy of totalizing narratives and "neutral" theories that warrant scientific investigations into various arenas of social life. "The authority of 'grand theory,' " observes George Marcus and Michael Fischer (1986), "seems suspended for the moment in favor of a close consideration of such issues as contextuality [and] the meaning of social life to those who enact it" (p. 8).

Fitch gravitates toward similar concerns as she explores the ideological, epistemological, and cultural biases of traditional interpersonal communication theory and research, and she affirms an ethnographic approach to the study of speech communities. With some reservations, she embraces John Lannamann's (1991) ideological critique of interpersonal communication literature and Barbara Montgomery's (1992) characterization of "social ideology" as steps toward developing a "cultural view of interpersonal ideology"—an ethnographic approach toward understanding the distinctive material practices of language and meaning in speech communities.

I appreciate Fitch's view that interpersonal communication research and theory could benefit from a cultural and historical contextualization of communication practices, but I am troubled with her larger, somewhat unclear, objectives of an "ethnography of speaking," which seems to replace one universalizing paradigm with another. Although she argues that language and

Correspondence and requests for reprints: Mark Neumann, Department of Communication, University of South Florida, Tampa, FL 33620.

Communication Yearbook 17, pp. 148-158

communication hold different meanings among different social groups, and that "each cultural system should be studied on its own terms to discover the ways of speaking that are meaningful within a speech community" (p. 115), her larger objective is a comparative study that seeks to make "claims to universal properties, functions, or aspects of communication" (p. 115). Her attraction to diverse and culturally situated cases of communication practices seems to be somewhat at odds with her broader desire to "accurately capture universal aspects of interpersonal communication and relationships as well as the ways in which culture shapes those processes" (p. 122). This goal of generalized theorizations of communication through ethnography is, in some ways, reminiscent of an early anthropological project that sought to systematically describe cultural diversity in an attempt to achieve generalizations about humankind. Such a comprehensive vision was, of course, steeped in an ideology of social progress that unraveled in the twentieth century as the emergence of interpretive anthropology critiqued the idea of a value-free understanding and representation of cultural life (Marcus & Fischer, 1986, pp. 17-44).

While Fitch wants to engage in a conversation that centers on culture, ethnography, and ideology, she chooses not to address a range of questions that characterize the problems and critical potential that those concepts suggest. Despite her references to a number of scholars (Geertz, 1976; Myerhoff, 1978; Rosaldo, 1989) who describe the contingencies and politics of interpreting culture, she offers an apolitical conception of culture, ethnography, and ideology that ignores current problems and questions at the center of cultural interpretation and critique.

My commentary attempts to critically examine the concept of speech communities and the problems associated with representing them through ethnography. In the first section, I draw upon Mikhail Bakhtin's (1981, 1984) dialogical perspective as a way of challenging the concept of speech communities as a metaphor for understanding interpersonal communication. This is followed by a discussion that considers the problems associated with representation of communities and cultures through ethnography. In the second section, I discuss Fitch's notion of "interpersonal ideology" and argue for an explicitly critical approach for examining the relationship of language to social organization and interaction.

THE MULTIPLE VOICES OF CULTURE AND ETHNOGRAPHIC REPRESENTATION

Fitch takes an apolitical view of culture, which she defines as "an organic product of a people's history and experiences" (p. 116) that may be clearly revealed and reflected through ethnographic description. She locates "the cultural" in a body of communicative practices and resources that produce a "common code that links the messages and practices of social collectivities into a more or less coherent whole" (p. 111). This idea of individuated cultural coherence and commonality is accessible, she suggests, as one becomes familiar with the language and speaking practices of a speech community. Understanding and using particular ways of speaking define the boundaries of various groups as well as constitute who is a member of the community being studied (Philipsen, 1992). While this perspective attempts to locate the boundaries of community membership in a common production of meaning, it raises larger questions about the nature of speech communities and our ability to represent them through ethnography. I argue that the representation of culture, or in this case the speech community, is much more problematic. For example, Bakhtin's (1981, 1984) persuasive characterization of the dialogical processes that make up everyday life pose a challenge to Fitch's notion of unified speaking practices that organize a speech community or culture as a coherent whole.

Bakhtin characterizes language as a multiplicity of voices. We come into consciousness in multilingual environments, he argues, as we learn to speak a language that is inhabited with many voices. From birth, we are in a ceaseless process of mastering a variety of social dialects derived from parents, class, past generations, religion, region, country (Booth, 1984). Each of us is always speaking a variety languages that are continually positioning and locating us as subjects in the social world. "Speaking dialogically is speaking *with* a multiplicity of other voices," suggests Leonard Hawes (1989, p. 64). "Dialogical discourse is speech that opens onto the threshold of crisis and possibility at every moment. Its speaker is not a finalized subject, but a subject in process, a subject always coming to consciousness by means of speaking the truth of his or her experience" (Hawes, 1989, p. 64).

For Bakhtin, a multitude of languages coexist within any culture or speaking community. "These stratifications of language," observes Caryl Emerson (1984), "do not exclude one another; they intersect and overlap, pulling words into various gravitational fields and casting specific light and shadow. Living discourse, unlike a dictionary, is always in flux and in rebellion against its own rules" (p. xxxi). This overlapping of languages proliferates the potential and possibility for making meanings. Rather than understanding communication as involving shared meaning, Bakhtin emphasizes how language is a site of opposition and struggle over diverging discourses that become energized through difference and dialogue. "This means that every speaking subject speaks something of a foreign language to everyone else," suggests Emerson (1984, p. xxxii). "To understand another person at any given moment, therefore, is to come to terms with meaning on the boundary between one's own and another's language: to translate." Yet, it is never a perfect translation because we cannot ever fully understand another's language or erase the differences between the voices that speak them.

Bakhtin's dialogical perspective encourages a rethinking of the nature of speech communities. Because language is permeated with a multiplicity of voices, he argues, "there is no single plane on which all these 'languages' might be juxtaposed to one another" (Bakhtin, 1981, p. 291). As the terrain of language is multiplied and the possibilities of meaning are proliferated through speaking, the dimensions of communication are continually moving, changing, conjuring possibilities for subjectivity and reorganizing social life. The idea of distinguishing any single or unified speech community becomes an increasingly complex enterprise. Bakhtin's ideas call attention to the ways that ethnographic descriptions of speech communities are not mirrorlike reflections of a culture or community that constitutes itself through speaking. Instead, speech communities are the constructions of the researcher who attempts to identify their boundaries in the process of writing ethnography.

Understanding and representing contemporary cultural life raises a series of questions that are centered in the politics of interpretation. There is "no politically innocent methodology for intercultural interpretation," observes James Clifford (1992, p. 97): "Who determines where (and when) a community draws its lines, names its insiders and outsiders?" Such questions emphasize that cultural representation is an interpretive activity that creates textualized visions of identity, community, and society. Cultures are not merely observed and reflected through a descriptive research report. Instead, our views of cultures are historically situated, interpretive, constructions of an ethnographer's experience with others. The ethnographic author, in a sense, *writes* the culture and, in doing so, constructs a representation of other and self. Clifford (1986) argues that "if 'culture' is not an object to be described, neither is it a unified corpus of symbols and meanings that can be definitively interpreted. Culture is contested, temporal, and emergent" (p. 19). From this perspective, culture is no longer a matter of the relationship between the observer and the observed; nor is it a relationship between a "reader" and a "text" (as in the case of Geertz, 1973). Cultural representation is always a partial understanding of a culture, one that reformulates its terms in an ongoing process of interpreting the experiences and relations between self and other, and self and world.

While the dialogical perspective reformulates the possibilities for conceptualizing a speech community, it also has been central in orienting issues of ethnographic representation toward a field of discursive practices. Traditional models of ethnographic reportage tended to privilege the singular voice of the researcher as one who restrained and managed the multiple voices of culture through his or her description. Ethnographic accounts were taken to be authoritative representations of *the* culture. Bakhtin's dialogical model, however, questions this practice. If language is understood as a scattered and contested dialogue of multiple voices that no person ever completely masters, then it seems clear that an ethnographer can only hope to be a speaking voice among others in a community. The dialogical model suggests that one speaks "*with* a multiplicity of other voices, rather than speaking *for* others and their experiences" (Hawes, 1989, p. 64). For ethnography, this means that textual production becomes, to some extent, democratized, an arena that evokes a historically situated and intersubjective encounter of voices that struggle for expression and meaning. For Clifford (1986), the dialogical perspective "locates cultural interpretation in many sorts of reciprocal contexts, and it obliges writers to find diverse ways of rendering negotiated realities as multisubjective, power-laden, and incongruent. In this view, 'culture' is always relational, an inscription of communicative processes that exist, historically, *between* subjects in relations of power" (p. 15).

This critique of writing ethnography underscores the role of the researcher as a participant as well as an observer of culture life. It is a view that emphasizes the researcher's interactive relationship with the people he or she chooses to study and complicates the claims one may make about the world that becomes constituted in ethnographic writing. As Michael Jackson (1989) suggests, attempts to systematically study a group of others often say a great deal about the estranged posture of the observer.

> The orderly systems and determinate structures we describe are not mirror images of social reality so much as defenses we build against the unsystematic, unstructured nature of our *experiences* within that reality. Theoretical schemes and the neutral, impersonal idioms we use in talking about them give us respite from the unmanageable flux of lived experience, helping us create illusory word-worlds which we can more easily manage because they are cut off from the stream of life. (pp. 3-4)

Jackson draws upon William James's (1904/1976) notion of "radical empiricism" in an attempt to redeem the experience of the researcher engaged in fieldwork. The experience of the researcher is a valid contribution to understanding social life in a realm of interaction and intersubjectivity. He suggests that researchers explore the dimensions of experience that connect them with others. "In this process we put ourselves on the line," urges Jackson (1989, p. 4); "we run the risk of having our sense of ourselves as different and distanced from the people we study dissolve, and with it all our pretensions to a supraempirical position, a knowledge that gets us above and beyond the temporality of human existence."

The representation of cultures and speech communities described by Fitch is, in many ways, an attempt to render a unified and coherent image of social interaction that will provide a basis for comparative analysis of communication and lead toward a more culturally informed body of generalizing communication theory. Although her approach emphasizes social interaction, most of the studies she discusses portray social life in ways that exclude the experience of the researcher and suggest a representation of communicative practices that become stabilized, frozen, in an ethnographic account. The difficulty with this approach is that it discounts the ways that representations of culture are partial and temporally bound understandings of how people communicate and live, and it diminishes the lived experience of the re-searcher who produced the ethnographic account. From Jackson's (1989) perspective, cultural comparison is "less a matter of finding 'objective' similarities and differences between other cultures than of exploring similarities and differences between our own experience and the experience of others" (p. 4). The meaning of culture does not lie waiting to be discovered by the researcher but exists in the relations between people (particularly between ethnographers and the people they write about) and the differences that separate their lives. Clearly, the differences within and between cultures and speech communities are central to questions of comparative analysis. It is important, however, to consider how such differences add to the difficulties of ethnographic representation. Bakhtin's dialogical perspective and the critiques of ethnographic writing provide a context for reintroducing issues of ideological conflict and struggle in interpersonal communication research and theory because they insist that all forms of speaking and writing are politicized activities that occur in a contested discursive space.

STRUGGLING THROUGH LANGUAGE

For Fitch, the concept of ideology is significant on two levels. First, ideological analysis is at the center of her critique of traditional approaches to studying interpersonal communication. Drawing from Lannamann's discussion of ideological and epistemological assumptions inherent in interpersonal communication research and theory, Fitch questions the extent that literature (a) reflects a bias toward individuals over social collectivities and social classes; (b) reflects an orientation toward rational, goal-oriented, instrumental thought; (c) reflects an approach to understanding that rests on hypothetical responses to experimental procedures; and (d) generally excludes questions of cultural, social, and historical forces that influence people's lives. On another level, Fitch views ideology as a framework that constitutes communication practices in social life. Here, she proposes a construct of "interpersonal ideology," which she describes as "a set of premises about personhood, relationships, and communication that structure negotiation of meaning through language use within a speech community" (p. 115). These two differing uses of ideology serve as both a basis for critiquing traditional interpersonal research and an orientation for future research and theorizing. Although I disagree with some of the criticisms she makes of Lannamann's work, I will focus my comments here on how she employs the concept of ideology to create a construct for understanding communicative practice.

To some extent, Fitch's notion of "interpersonal ideology" expresses an interest in how ideology functions in the maintenance of social organization. Although she confines her arguments to the description of speech communities, her discussion could usefully be extended with a broader and more precise definition that describes how ideology is a fundamental means of managing social contradictions, reproducing class relations as well as the orders of power and control that organize everyday life (Althusser, 1971; Hall, 1991; Hawes, 1989). James Kavanagh's (1990) useful summary of Althusser provides a clear description of the relevance of ideology to the production and reproduction of social relations.

> Ideology designates a rich "system of representations," worked up in specific material practices, which helps form individuals into social subjects who "freely" internalize an appropriate "picture" of their social world and their place in it. Ideology offers the social subject not a set of narrowly "political" ideas but a fundamental framework of assumptions that defines the parameters of the real and the self; it constitutes what Althusser calls the social subject's " 'lived' relation to the real." (p. 310)

Fitch is correct to understand ideology as a set of material practices that constitute people as social subjects in various social relationships. Yet, her formulation of interpersonal ideology does not seem to move her analysis toward any claims or arguments that make "ideological" analysis matter. This is due, in part, to her reluctance to embrace the issues of struggle and power that are central to critical theory. While her essay suggests the ways that communication may serve to bind people together in different ways, there is an absence of how different communication practices function on ideological terms, that is, to manage social and class differences and to reproduce the relations that ensure social order. Ironically, her examination of forms of personal address, speech acts, and communicator styles implicitly carries examples of unequal relations of status, class, and power that are maintained through communicative practices. For example, the Chinese use of *tóngzhi* to suggest equal rights between superiors and subordinates, crew leaders' use of direct imperatives to maintain a hierarchy between themselves and migrant workers, or the Israeli use of *dugri* speech as way of rejecting European heritage are all instances where the potential conflict and struggle over social and cultural identity and power are managed by communication practices for the purpose of maintaining order. For Fitch, these examples tend to lead to conclusions about commonality, the prospect of universal aspects of communication, and representations of unified speech communities, yet avoid critical questions about cultural politics, power, and class, questions that allow ideological analysis to maintain its "edge" (Kavanagh, 1990, p. 312).

Given that ideology functions to classify people in and through categories such as race, class, gender, and ethnicity, these categories often become the site of ideological struggle. According to Stuart Hall (1991), "Ideological struggle actually consists of attempting to win some new set of meanings for an existing term or category, of dis-articulating it from its place in a signifying structure" (p. 110). In this sense, people sometimes resist, and shift, the meanings of an ideological system of representations that reinforce and reproduce familiar relations of self and society. For example, in a description of life on the island of Antigua in the British West Indies, Jamaica Kincaid (1988) provides a narrative that suggests how ideological struggle is made real through language. In this passage, she laments how a life lived in the shadow of British colonialism has stripped her of any firm sense of cultural tradition and a native tongue, painfully leaving her with only the English language to express her experience of life on the island.

> Isn't it odd that the only language I have in which to speak of this crime is the language of the criminal who committed the crime? And what can that really mean? For the language of the criminal can contain only the goodness of the criminal's deed. The language of the criminal can explain and express the deed only from the criminal's point of view. It cannot contain the horror of the deed, the injustice of the deed, the humiliation inflicted on me. (Kincaid, 1988, pp. 31-32)

On one hand, her narrative suggests how the English language closes off the possibilities for expression because it is a language that expresses the worldview of a British colonialism that has left her culturally "homeless." In this sense, "language" refers to a whole history of British occupation and oppression that imposed laws, language, books, and schools on the island that served to glorify the English and erase or distort the history of the West Indians. On the other hand, Kincaid's use of the language does exactly what she says it cannot accomplish—give voice to the humiliation and anger she experiences in having to use that language. Her example illustrates how the material practices of language function dually to maintain a dominant representation of cultural life yet hold the seeds for undoing that system of representation. According to Hall (1991, p. 112), even though ideology is always inscribed in culture, the multivoiced nature of language accounts for a constant and unending possibility of "shifts of accentuation in language and ideology," always locating language as the site of struggles over questions of meaning and identity in social life.

The brief excerpt from Kincaid's narrative of life on Antigua recalls Bakhtin's notion that language is a diverging set of discourses where multiple possibilities for meaning may come alive. But Kincaid also reminds us of the ways that people live between a number of worlds, that the possibilities for producing meaning come not only from an attempt to share a language but from the tension and difference between people who struggle for expression and a sense of identity.

Although Fitch may conceive of culture and history as "the world beyond interacting individuals," Bakhtin's dialogical perspective suggests that multiple and contradictory voices of history and culture flow through each moment of interaction. But it is also important to remember that cultures travel, and the deep ethnographic predicament of the current time involves confronting a world of scattered traditions, perpetual rootlessness, and mobility (Clifford, 1988, 1992). Expansive global transformation and mobilization have loosened any firm ideas we may hold of distinctive cultures. Kincaid's story of life under British colonialism is but one small instance that reminds us that the modern age has continually disconnected people from geographic regions, traditional spheres of home, place, and identity, casting them into new human environments of diverse social organization. "As the modern public expands," argues Marshall Berman (1982, p. 17), "it shatters into a multitude of fragments, speaking incommensurable private languages." David Rieff's (1987, 1991) recent accounts of Miami and Los Angeles, for instance, convey this sense of how contemporary cities have become locations that both bind and divide a wide range of immigrants, exiles, and refugees from Latin America and Asia, creating a postmodern urban landscape of multiple, fragmented voices struggling with each other for expression and recognition. Such displacements and juxtapositions of individual lives magnify the dimensions of intercultural dialogues in ways that are simultaneously full of possibility and conflict.

This merging of worlds, cultures, and lifestyles requires that we reimagine the conditions and objectives of ethnographic writing. Clifford (1988) suggests that a "modern 'ethnography' of conjunctures, constantly moving between cultures, does not, like its Western alter ego 'anthropology,' aspire to survey the full range of human diversity or development. It is perpetually displaced, both regionally focused and broadly comparative, a form both of dwelling and of travel in a world where the two experiences are less and less distinct" (p. 9). Such an approach reconciles us to understand that cultural studies can never claim to encompass the whole truth or even attempt to know it. Ethnography cannot avoid cultural comparison, but it should not be conceived of as a sense of comparison that leads toward general or universal theorizations of human life and communication. Instead, contemporary ethnography embraces its own voice as one that not only speaks among other voices but *takes a stance* in a convergence of diverse worlds. In seeking to describe the ways that communication moves people toward a common life, calling forth dimensions of identity and positions of subjectivity, ethnographic writing may also express the sources of conflict, difference, systems of representation that keep them apart. Ethnography is not only a matter of writing between cultures but existing between them as well. Clearly, we all belong to many speech communities, but marking their boundaries or cataloging their practices does not make living in them any easier.

Rather than conceiving of singular speech communities or cultures, it is, perhaps, more reasonable to consider how contemporary life, as Mary Louise Pratt (1991, p. 34) suggests, comprises numerous "contact zones," a variety of "social spaces where cultures meet, clash, and grapple with each other, often in contexts of highly asymmetrical relations of power." They are places where questions of speaking and communication become entwined with issues of power, order, and difference that register in the lived relations of social and cultural life. Such contexts invite us to consider not only how social organization becomes possible through practices of communication but how social life is a contested enterprise rife with conflict. The ethnographic representation of those worlds is not merely to describe them. It is unavoidably a pursuit that recognizes the situated, subjective, and political position of the researcher. It is a posture that can evoke an understanding and appreciation for modern problems of identity, community, and meaning while reinvesting ethnography in a practice of cultural critique.

REFERENCES

Althusser, L. (1971). Ideology and ideological state apparatuses. In L. Althusser, *Lenin and philosophy and other essays*. London: New Left.

Bakhtin, M. (1981). *The dialogic imagination: Four essays*. Austin: University of Texas Press.

Bakhtin, M. (1984). *Problems of Dostoevsky's poetics*. Minneapolis: University of Minnesota Press.

Berman, M. (1982). *All that is solid melts into air: The experience of modernity*. New York: Simon & Schuster.

Booth, W. C. (1984). Introduction. In M. Bakhtin, *Problems of Dostoevsky's poetics* (pp. xiii-xxvii). Minneapolis: University of Minnesota Press.

Clifford, J. (1986). Introduction: Partial truths. In J. Clifford & G. E. Marcus (Eds.), *Writing culture: The poetics and politics of ethnography* (pp. 1-26). Berkeley: University of California Press.

Clifford, J. (1988). *The predicament of culture: Twentieth-century ethnography, literature, and art*. Cambridge, MA: Harvard University Press.

Clifford, J. (1992). Traveling cultures. In L. Grossberg, C. Nelson, & P. Treichler (Eds.), *Cultural studies* (pp. 96-116). New York: Routledge.

Emerson, C. (1984). Editor's preface. In M. Bakhtin, *Problems of Dostoevsky's poetics* (pp. xxix-xliii). Minneapolis: University of Minnesota Press.

Geertz, C. (1973). Deep play: Notes on the Balinese cockfight. In C. Geertz, *The interpretation of cultures*. New York: Basic Books.

Geertz, C. (1976). From the native's point of view: On the nature of anthropological understanding. In K. H. Basso & H. Selby (Eds.), *Meaning in anthropology* (pp. 221-239). Albuquerque: University of New Mexico Press.

Hall, S. (1991). Signification, representation, ideology: Althusser and the post-structuralist debates. In R. K. Avery & D. Eason (Eds.), *Critical perspectives on media and society* (pp. 88-113). New York: Guilford.

Hawes, L. C. (1989). Power, discourse, and ideology: The micropractices of common sense. In J. A. Anderson (Ed.), *Communication yearbook 12* (pp. 60-75). Newbury Park, CA: Sage.

Jackson, M. (1989). *Paths toward a clearing: Radical empiricism and ethnographic inquiry*. Bloomington: Indiana University Press.

James, W. (1976). *Essays in radical empiricism*. Cambridge, MA: Harvard University Press. (Original work published 1904)

Kavanagh, J. H. (1990). Ideology. In F. Lentricchia & T. McLaughlin (Eds.), *Critical terms for literary study* (pp. 306-320). Chicago: University of Chicago Press.

Kincaid, J. (1988). *A small place*. New York: Penguin.

Lannamann, J. W. (1991). Interpersonal communication research as ideological practice. *Communication Theory, 1*(3), 179-203.

Marcus, G. E., & Fischer, M. J. (1986). *Anthropology as cultural critique: An experimental moment in the human sciences.* Chicago: University of Chicago Press.

Montgomery, B. (1992). Communication as the interface between couples and culture. In S. A. Deetz (Ed.), *Communication yearbook 15* (pp. 475-507). Newbury Park, CA: Sage.

Myerhoff, B. (1978). *Number our days.* New York: Simon & Schuster.

Philipsen, G. (1992). *Speaking culturally: Explorations in social communication.* Albany: State University of New York Press.

Pratt, M. L. (1991). Arts of the contact zone. *Profession, 91,* 33-40.

Rieff, D. (1987). *Going to Miami: Exiles, tourists, and refugees in the new America.* New York: Penguin.

Rieff, D. (1991). *Los Angeles: Capital of the Third World.* New York: Simon & Schuster.

Rosaldo, R. (1989). *Culture and truth: The remaking of social analysis.* Boston: Beacon.

4 Personhood, Positioning, and Cultural Pragmatics: American Dignity in Cross-Cultural Perspective

DONAL CARBAUGH
University of Massachusetts, Amherst

This essay contends that the communication of personhood is a transitory, sometimes durable interactional accomplishment that creatively invokes cultural meaning systems. A cultural pragmatic perspective that integrates communicational and cultural dynamics is discussed, developed through the concept of positioning, and demonstrated with several instances of interactive talk. The demonstration yields some of the interactional workings of one cultural model of personhood that is prominent in America today, a deeply structured system of values referred to here as a code of dignity. This coding of communication is comparatively analyzed, thus drawing attention to its tendency to supplant others. Implications of the approach and findings are discussed.

E VERY social interaction presupposes and creatively invokes culture, intelligible forms of action, and identity, with these further implicating social relations, institutions, and attendant feelings. Interacting through symbolic forms carries with it claims, tacitly or consciously, about the kind(s)

AUTHOR'S NOTE: An early version of this essay was written while in residence as a Visiting Senior Member of Linacre College, Oxford. Parts of the essay were presented to members of the seminar on discursive psychology at Oxford, as a keynote address at the Annual Symposium of the Finland Association for Applied Linguistics, and to a public forum at Nuffield College, Oxford, all in fall 1992. I am particularly grateful to Rom Harré, who arranged for my visits to Linacre College, to Liisa Lofman for the invitation to speak in Finland, to Margaret M. Yee for the invitation to speak at Nuffield, and to several participants in the seminar, symposium, and forum for their discussion and comments. In particular, I thank Jens Brockmeier and David Zeitlyn for consistently lively discussions related to the essay.

Correspondence and requests for reprints: Donal Carbaugh, Department of Communication, University of Massachusetts, Amherst, MA 01003.

Communication Yearbook 17, pp. 159-186

of person one (and other) is, how one is (currently being) related to others, and what feelings are to be associated with this social arrangement. Whether one immediately understands, or agrees with, the persons, relations, and feelings being shaped through the symbolic action, once caught up in it, one will find oneself a subject in it, variously (often institutionally) related through it, and feeling from "good" to "bad" to neutral about it. In spite of one's intentions to convey such messages, one will find that in effect he or she will have done so (Carbaugh, in press-a, in press-b; Goffman, 1967).

In this essay, I want to explore just how the above process works. Through discussing the communication of personhood, I want to develop the idea that, through primarily linguistic interaction, participants publicly constitute social standings (not necessarily "statuses") as moral agents in society. I build on the assumptions that various forms and meanings of personhood are discursively constructed and that these discursive constructions are historically grounded, culturally distinct, socially negotiated, and individually applied (Carbaugh, 1990b, 1990c). The general argument is that personhood is a transitory, sometimes durable interactional accomplishment that creatively implicates cultural meaning systems.

Several recent studies suggest, I think, more general problems to which the essay responds. One involves the difficulty of hearing "macronotions"—such as society, class, ethnicity, institutions, culture—within "microprocesses." The essay attempts to show that the micro-macro distinction or concentric, or hierarchical, models are less helpful than another, one that unveils in interactional processes the radiants of, for example, culture. From this view, it is not, then, that culture, or society, or class is merely "environmental" to, or a logical context for, interaction, although each may be that to some degree, but, moreover, that such things are immanent in the actual patterning of the actual interactions themselves (Sapir, 1931). As much has been demonstrated in studies of racial discrimination in South Africa (Chick, 1990), gender (West & Zimmerman, 1991) and cultural identity generally (Wieder & Pratt, 1990). Race, gender, culture, and so on are not just abstract concepts but feature in the actual patterning of interactive processes, with the study of this process being of the utmost importance. The approach taken here is indebted to authors such as Goffman (1967) and Geertz (1973; see also Shweder, 1992). Yet it seeks, moreover, as others have, to integrate the interactionist focus of the former with the more heavily cultural focus of the latter. Specifically, it proposes an integrative view of macro- and microprocesses, to hear in situated interactions, culture at work (e.g., Basso, 1990; Katriel, 1991; Varenne, 1977).

Similar lines of work address a second related problem: Can one hear in interaction, notions previously deemed "psychological" or "mental"? Several authors have proposed relocating mental notions, moving them from behind, in the brain or head, or somehow underlying human action, into concrete discursive practices. Rather than moving notions (e.g., culture) from the outside into discourse, as above, the problem here is moving notions from the inside (e.g., personality) out. Of special concern here has been the refiguring of concepts such as "self" and "person," along with notions like personality and attitude and so on beyond exclusively mindful matters, to discursive practices. Philosophical (Harré, 1983, 1991a, 1991b), anthropological (Lutz, 1988), discursive psychological (Billig, 1987, 1991; Edwards & Potter, 1992; Potter & Wetherell, 1987), and social constructionist (Gergen, 1985) works have advanced discourse-based theories of these various, previously held to be mental, concerns. Such studies enrich communication theory as they suggest, similar to ethnomethodology, how concepts about mentation do not just refer to mindful matters but also consist in socially based, objectively identifiable, interactional dynamics. In these studies, however, one sometimes finds more by way of abstract statements about discourse, or persons as discoursed, and less by way of attention to actual moments of mutually intelligible, everyday social interaction. While usefully advanced is a view of the rhetoric of psychology, or the communication of sociology, often missing is the interactional meaningfulness of such accomplishments to participants, the so-called native view. Further, and related to the above, if interaction is used as data (this being rather rare for some), it is treated more as a messenger about particular persons, consciousness, or intimate relations, or more as an objective "technology of talk," and less as a resource within a sociocultural system. My contention is that an allied yet distinct approach is warranted, an approach that renders the cultural features of concrete interaction audible and that helps us hear in communicative practices not just selves but the forming of communal persons, and not just interactive dynamics, but the expression of systems of cultural meanings (see Moerman, 1988, and the special symposium on ethnography and conversation analysis in *Research on Language and Social Interaction*, 1991).

CULTURAL PRAGMATICS

Some scholars and lines of research have been searching for ways to hear communal processes in dialogical action. Many such efforts are erected around one central premise: Ways of speaking are inextricably tied to ways of being. The accent on "speaking" draws attention to intelligible forms of acting, including means nonverbal and linguistic, while the accent on "identity" highlights ways of being (kinds of personas, or beliefs about identities with one's unique self being one such kind), including social relations, institutions, and feelings. One of the earliest modern writings on the topic is Bakhtin's demonstration of ways speech genres are caught up in systems of joint action. These enable some actions and persons while constraining others, amplify some ideas while muting others, thus invoking in joint actions ideological systems. Bakhtin refers to this process as "cultural communication" (Bakhtin, 1986). Although not drawing explicitly on Bakhtin, Philipsen (1987) has noted similar dynamics and made a plea for explorations of "cultural communication" especially through forms such as rituals, myths, and social dramas that create and realize models for "membering" and "remembering." Similarly, Eriksen (1991) has shown how ethnic identities are contextually managed through forms of interaction in cultural contexts. Fitch (1991) has interpreted how the symbol of "mother" gets culturally coded into everyday communicative forms in Colombia, a coding that helps extricate the cultural shaping of the identity from other patterns that are more general. A closely related and well-established body of work in the coordinated management of meaning seeks to integrate cultural dimensions, interactive episodes, and identity (Cronen & Pearce, 1991-1992).

The current study adopts a similar approach as it seeks to integrate both pragmatics, socially situated symbolic interaction, and its cultural dimensions, the systems of meanings that are presupposed for and implicated by that very interaction. The approach draws attention to the linguistic and momentary character of meaning-making in any society (thus pragmatic) and the conceptual and actional forms for persons, relations, and feelings that are both immanent in and a necessary condition for that symbolic interaction to be, indeed, richly meaningful (thus cultural).

The cultural dimension suggests focusing upon the twin interactional accomplishments of coherence and community: What are the boundaries of indigenous coherence being created with this pragmatic action, and for what community is this conceptual and actional form intelligible? Note that the questions are mute on the criterion of approval or agreeableness. Agreement of opinion is not a requisite condition for coherence. Communities differently position members, as do families, and are sometimes subsequently laden with disapproval and conflict (e.g., Carbaugh, 1992). Questions of (de)legitimacy thus are central, as are the processes in which such questions are raised and addressed. In such times, the discourse being used creates for the involved participants some common ideas about their (and "others'") places within these essentially contestable social interactions. A cultural study thus attempts to explicate the larger discursive system of coherence in which interactional positions for social persons and their relations, even if contested, are more deeply meaningful. One method of analysis, and explanation, involves attending carefully to the cultural structuring of personhood in interactional processes. Attending to cultural features and meanings of person(s) enables one eventually to posit the common premises, symbolic categories, dimensions, and domains of meanings that are getting coded (about, e.g., identity) in those particular forms of action (Carbaugh, 1988a, 1988b, 1990a; Carbaugh & Hastings, 1992).

COMMUNICATING PERSON, SELF,
INDIVIDUAL: A DESCRIPTIVE THEORY

Claims about personhood need to be distinguished, analytically, from related concerns about self and individual. Where "person" highlights culturally located agents-in-society, "self" highlights a more phenomenological locus of experience (awareness or consciousness) and "individual" a more biologically based member of humankind (Harris, 1989). These distinctions roughly parallel Harré's treatments of social being, personal being, and physical being, with Harré's concept of self$_2$ drawing attention to the former, and his self$_1$ deliberately straddling all three (see Harré, 1979, 1983, 1991a, 1991b). While explorations of each are necessary and productive, the former is the main focus in what follows (and, arguably, provides the socioculturally efficacious, discursive sense of all three).

Following upon earlier work (Carbaugh, 1988a, 1988b, 1988c; Harris, 1989), I use the concept "personhood" to summarize how agents-in-society are constituted in the cultural practices of social interaction. Based on ethnographic evidence, I presume that every communication system, through its situated symbolic practices, constructs two reciprocally related kinds of participant role: (a) cultural notion(s) of person, for example, an ethnically, nationally, gendered, or class identity (Geertz, 1976, p. 225; Hymes, 1961, p. 335), and (b) a system of social kinds that elaborates the basic cultural notion(s). When using language, individuals creatively invoke (or are heard to invoke) some features of their social and cultural roles, with each being possibly positioned relative to the other (this is demonstrated below). This suggests the following: For the construction of cultural models of person and the various social kinds, there are various means and meanings of communication available, with each being distinctive in its rituals of entry, performance, evaluation, and departure. In the United States, for example, if one performs "being a mother," or "a wife," one symbolizes a distinctive social position, but, moreover, one has symbolically invoked a system of social practices, relations, and properties. Doing "mother," in other words, does not just invoke a social standing but invokes many (e.g., father, husband, daughter, son). In so acting, or being identified as so acting, a terminological or symbol system (of persons, relations, actions) is implicated that radiates cultural dimensions of sex, gender, and age status as well as domains of meanings including domestic and possibly others (e.g., political, economic, and religious). Attending to the interactional accomplishment of social identities, one "can show how members of various social kinds are reckoned to have differing agentive capacities and hence to be unlike each other as authors of actions" (Harris, 1989, p. 604).

Through analyses of social interaction, the social kinds (if one starts there) may be eventually linked to cultural models, with the latter identifying the larger symbolic boundaries of coherence in being such a person. Possibly highlighted then are social positions of the person (e.g., as mother), cultural notions of what person is, can, and should be (e.g., as an African or American). For example, whether it is intelligible to be a disembodied spirit, as some Native Americans believe, depends both upon the cultural notions that render such a being commonly meaningful and upon the social kinds for whom such a being is accessible and performable. The communication of personhood, then, invites questions about a system of discursive practices, tacking among social kinds and cultural notions, with elements of each being played with or against the other(s). Exploring the cultural pragmatics of agents-in-society may help unveil how social kinds and cultural notions of being get interactively expressed and related. And, further, through comparative study, cultural distinctiveness and cross-cultural generalities for conceiving, evaluating, and acting personhood may be suggested (see Fitch, 1991).

Person as a Discursive Activity: Positioning

The primary site in which common sense is made of persons-in-society is *discursive activity*, expressive practices that make available particular positions for participants to take up and address (and with which to hear others taking up and addressing; see Davies & Harré, 1990; Harré & Van Langenhove, 1991; Hollway, 1984; Tannen, 1990). Such activity demonstrates the various interactional ways in which cultural agents, and social kinds, are interactionally (de)legitimated. Through such activities, there is an intricate and ever-present social playing of positions, each with its moral messages of rights and duties from unquestioned cultural beliefs of "person" generally, to the interactional accomplishment of the more specific social kinds and their interrelations. In short, each discursive utterance simultaneously positions, within sociocultural discourses, its producer as well as the recipients of the messages. This focus on discursive activities of positioning helps draw attention to the interactive dynamics of identities within utterances and events, and the ways these vary systematically by contexts, among specific participants, on particular occasions, with each such utterance event locating and relating persons through particular speech sequences and genres (Bahktin, 1986; Hymes, 1972; Levinson, 1989).

Persons as Variously Located With Various Qualities

What is the nature of the positions being interactionally foregrounded, muted, or elided? The primary site, or place, of person positions varies by the culturally shaped, discursive context. Various loci of such agentive activity, however, can be usefully identified, with each at different times becoming the primary site of positioning activity. A fundamental, and most general, locus is whether persons are present or not and addressed as (if) present within the interaction or not. If focusing on those present, interaction can fluctuate variously among a speaker, addressee, or audience focus. If focusing on the not-present, persons can be addressed *as if* present, or not. Regarding qualities, person positions can be deemed material to immaterial, passive to active, resource endowed to deprived, and so on. For example, one may discuss a mutual friend, "Steve is a superb rock climber," attributing qualities to a nonpresent material other (thus attempting to identify the nonpresent other) and in so doing say something about oneself as present speaker (one who would evaluate, compliment), while also positioning the present recipient of one's message (one allegedly interested in Steve and/or rock climbing and/or speaker's evaluation). As a second example, consider the witches (men and women) of Salem, Massachusetts, who sometimes address "fairies" and other nonmaterial yet "present" persons. In such discourse, an agent-in-society is addressed, in the immediate present, although this agent is not a material presence (Mahoney, 1993).

Such examples make apparent the need for distinctions between persons as agents-in-society whether present or not, the focus of interaction or not, material or not, and so on. Further distinctions are required among agents, whether a site of self (or a site of consciousness) and/or an individual (a material member of a kind), a point to which I return in concluding. Similarly, various forms of ancestor worship and voices, as well as the treatment of sacred animals (e.g., cows in India, alligators in Tallensi), demonstrate how the status of person as an agentive discourse in society need not necessarily coincide with a material presence or even a site of *human* consciousness (e.g., an unconscious person, the "brain dead"). While more could be retrieved from the examples (speakers' claims to moral positions and so on), these serve to illustrate various locations and qualities of persons through discursive activities (see also Levinson, 1989, esp. pp. 168-174).

Conversational Moves and Further Dimensions of Agentive Action

Personhood is interactionally managed through various moves and dimensions of discourse, each of which may occur simultaneously. Sometimes a position or social standing is explicitly claimed, "I'm your teacher," a basic first order action that could be called an *explication*. Such involves an explicit *avowal* of a speaker to being a particular kind of person or an *attribution* about another (present or nonpresent); for example, "Keith is brilliant." Each such explication of a position, moreover, implicates others. To avow one position (e.g., as teacher) is to implicate another for one's recipients (e.g., as students). To attribute a position to another (e.g., as excellent teacher) is to implicate others for self as utterer of that message (e.g., as gracious supplicant). Thus much positioning work is done more subtly, through intonation and other means of inviting inferences about the positions of one or an other (see Gumperz, 1982). For this dimension of action, one could discuss *implications* of personhood. If one explicitly takes up one position, one thus implies things about it as well as addresses an other, or one set of positions, rather than others. An example captures some of the complexities in this dynamic. Upon returning home one evening, I found my spouse attempting to open the door to the house. I asked, "Did you try the key?" and was met with "looks that could kill." The example shows the extent to which social positions are so implicated. Through questioning the obvious, I was trying to implicate one position for myself (e.g., as good-natured problem solver, joker) but had another nonverbally implicated for me by my spouse (e.g., an unwanted critic of her intellectual capacities), mainly because I had implicated her as a particular kind of person (e.g., mentally challenged, problem creator). In a sense, there are "shadows" of identities, or implicated agent positions, in all discursive practices, to borrow Goodwin's (1990) descriptive term. Each such configuration draws participants into particular social positions and relates them accordingly. The implications are often very richly textured as they convey messages through various forms of talk, about persons, social relations, institutions, and the domains and dimensions of the social activity itself (Carbaugh, 1989).

Further moves or dimensions of agentive interaction take the form of extensive explications or implications of social positions. I refer to these as *elaborations* simply as a way to describe the degree to which a particular bid for agentive standing is developed over time and is perhaps being negotiated (explicitly or implicitly).

As further claims are being made about the nature of persons, and how they are related, the moral grounding for each is established or shaken. For example, a particular social standing may be explicitly avowed by one, or attributed to another, with further interaction negotiating the validity of this standing, "My, yes, he is a solid scholar." As a result, we can eventually hear, if subsequently validated, the *social ratification* of a person as such an agent. If, on the other hand, a particular standing is avowed, or attributed, and subsequent talk (and symbolic action) ignores that standing or explicitly denies it (e.g., "that's not the way a professor acts"), we can claim the momentary *rejection* of that person as such an agent and perhaps infer another for him or her.

Some Derivations and Uses of the Dimensions:
Issues of Voice

The above conversational moves and dimensions of agentive action help ground certain kinds of claims. For one, the dimensions can help identify some agentive positions as explicated, immaterial, and socially ratified, such as in some seances, while others are implicated, present, and denied, such as the blue-collar women below when they discuss unemployment. On occasions, when a speaker explicates, or implicates, and elaborates him- or herself as a kind of person, and if further interaction ratifies that speaker as such, we could claim the speaker indeed had a socially efficacious *voice*; that is, the speaker was able to speak, spoke, was heard, and socially validated as such. All conditions would be necessary for the constitution of *voice*. On the other side, as one attempts to explicate, or implicate, and elaborate a social standing (for one and/or others), and if there is no subsequent uptake or ratification by others of one so positioned, or if one is explicitly rejected, then one's voice, as such, has been refused, or denied, or another devalued voice has been attributed (if implicitly)—and so on.

Contested positions are also usefully disentangled as one traces the discursive processes through which each such position is explicated, implicated, and/or elaborated as well as the processes by which each becomes or is partly ratified or rejected by others. Current environmental debates provide a rich location for such studies. "Developers" and "environmentalists" often elaborate one position while rejecting another, with the motives and meanings of each grounding the discursive contest (Carbaugh, 1992).

The dimensions also help unravel contradictory conversational messages, for example, as a speaker explicates one social position while implicating another. During a recent gathering of academics at Oxford, where status games run deep, one participant said, with somewhat of a delightful irony: "I like to be modest about all of the things I've done. When I go places to speak, it annoys me when they introduce me by referring to . . ." and then listed several prominent accomplishments. The dimensions help unravel some of the complexity by pointing to an asynchrony between the speaker explicitly avowed (e.g., a self-professed preference for modesty, a propensity for understatement) and the one being implicated through the avowal (e.g., one somewhat vain, filled with pride by listing accomplishments). An ironic position is created that explicates modesty while implicating arrogance. Similar dynamics occur in communication systems generally, as in some prominent scenes of U.S. culture where individuality is explicated while collectivity is implicated (Carbaugh, 1988c) or in one organizational setting where workers explicate themes of "equality" yet elaborately implicate dramatic inequities among social positions (Carbaugh, 1988b).

Dimensions of Social Relations

As agents are discursively located and interactionally negotiated, fundamental dimensions of meaning about social life are being activated. These often involve assessments regarding the design and distribution of material (e.g., economic) and symbolic (e.g., knowledge) resources. Whether and how these are discursively designed leads to various conceptions and evaluations of social relations from *equal* (i.e., the equitable distribution of resources) to *unequal* (i.e., the resource endowed and the resource deprived). Such assessments are invoked through social interaction as various positions and their differences in rights and duties are morally conceived and socially arranged. A second general dimension of assessment, sometimes coterminous with the first, involves the degree to which discursive positions are construed as *close*, psychologically intimate, or more *distant*. When the former dimension is highlighted in discourse, issues turn on equal and unequal distribution of resources, relations of power, and issues of control surface. When the latter dimension is highlighted in discourse, issues turn on the closeness or distance of participants, and their relations of intimacy (high degree of closeness) or solidarity (relatively high distance, yet equal). Taken together, all combinations are interactionally possible, though not always salient, such as relations of equality and closeness (e.g., some forms of spousal discourse), equality and distance (e.g., solidarity), inequality and closeness (e.g., parent-child), and inequality and distance (e.g., CEO-assembly line worker). Through discursive activities, not only are social positions, capacities, and qualities constituted but social relations and institutions as well. As Goffman (1967) put it: "The line maintained by and for a person during contact with others tends to be of a legitimate institutionalized kind" (p. 7).

The loci and qualities of agents, as well as the dimensions of agentive interaction and social relations, are especially useful in contexts where social standings are being contested (Carbaugh, 1988b, 1992). Further, conflicts and confusion between diverse cultural agents, such as Russians and Americans, show how deeply discourse runs into cultural meaning systems (Carbaugh, in press-a, in press-b; Chick, 1990; Philipsen, in press; Wieder & Pratt, 1990). To demonstrate some of the cultural foundations of these processes, and the ways in which these interact, I take a descriptive turn first to a popular, cultural discourse in which the person, as "American," is established (the term in quotation marks being a popularly used geographic and national designator). This makes it easier to identify and compare its cultural shape relative to Others. I conclude, then, by discussing some of the implications of the general approach and analysis.

AN AMERICAN CODING OF DIGNITY

As people in America speak and listen in public, at times they create a common position for themselves as Americans. This cultural discourse is partly constructed through these key cultural symbols (in quotes) and their associated premises: The person is "an individual," with "a self," that vilifies "social roles, institutions, and society." Drawing on previous analyses of an American televised "talk show," I will describe and interpret instances of public talk that makes creative uses of each of these cultural features of personhood (Carbaugh, 1988c).

The Person as "an Individual":
Translating Social Differences Into Human Commonality

Consider the following social interactions. The first involves responses to a question about whether women should be permitted, or required, to engage in combat duty while performing military service. Speakers A and B are audience members. Speaker C is a feminist author. D is the president of the National Organization of Women.

Extract 1 (Carbaugh, 1988c, p. 22)

    1) A: Nobody wants to do it [combat duty] but by the same
    2)   token I think that a woman ain't made to do some of
    3)   the things a man can do.
    4) Audience: I agree . . .
    5) B: Some women are actually
    6) C: some women are stronger than
    7)   men.
    8) B: That's true.
    9) Audience: (Applause)
    10) D: Some individuals are stronger than some individuals.

A second example arose after a discussion in which a few women with working-class, unemployed spouses implicitly blamed "the feminists" for crowding others, especially unemployed men, out of the job market. E is an audience member who described her situation to F, a panelist and female director of the Democratic National Committee. G is the host of the program, Phil Donahue.

Extract 2 (Carbaugh, 1988c, p. 23)

    11) E: Three years unemployed. No compensation, no nothin'.
    12) F: That's what's happening throughout this country.
    13)   Especially in the industrial heartland. And it's
    14)   what's happening to families like yours. It is
    15)   happening to men and women. You and I are not opposed
    16)   to each other, we are not on different sides. We are
    17)   on the same side of individuals who are trying to
    18)   make it.
          . . .
    19) G: If a man and a woman are both out of work and there
    20)   is one job opening and they are both equally
    21)   qualified, who should get it [the job]?
    22) Audience: The man. (Applause)

These interactions pose and respond to a fundamental question: How shall participants be characterized with regard to present issues? More specifically, through what terms shall agents be described as the topics of military duty and unemployment are discussed?

Note first the two positionings of persons being proposed here. One involves the explication of social difference through gendered positions, making "men" and "women" the principal agents in the action. In both extracts, this motivates a second position, an explication of common humanity through an inclusive symbol whereby the principal agent becomes an "individual." Note further that, by characterizing the issues through a gendered discourse, speakers position themselves as ones who orient to the difference (with regard to the present issue). This often is heard as if one proposes, acknowledges, promotes, and so on, the difference, and overlooks the commonality. Likewise, by characterizing the issues with "individuals," speakers position themselves as ones who orient to commonality, thereby promoting it, and thus overlooking the gendered differences. Therefore positions are being explicated as the gendered terms of difference ("men" and "women") are played against another term of commonality ("the individual"). At the same time, other positions are being implicated for the utterer as one who would orient to (uphold, or criticize, or negotiate) the explicated position(s). Thus the dynamics of positioning occur in two directions. One involves the playing of each explicated position (of difference and commonality) against the other. The second dynamic involves what each such position immediately implicates for the person who is speaking it. Is she or he at this moment ratifying, rejecting, negotiating the—gendered or common humanity—position? In short, the dynamic involves a play between the familiar cultural positions being discussed and the immediate interactional position being implicated for one who would so position persons.

Note how the play between the explicated and implicated positions occurs within a general vacillating cultural form. That is, the interactional process moves in a "back-and-forth," spiraling sequence, tacking between the positions of difference and commonality, with each position motivating the other, as speakers with each in turn become positioned by the one, then the other. Through this form, social positions of difference and common identification are being expressed.

If we listen a bit more closely to the content of the gendered positions being mentioned here, we find each is being built on specific premises of difference. For example, in lines 1-3 about combat duty, explicated is a gender-based, biological difference in physical capacity that is used to justify differences in moral rights (as men and women) and institutional duties (as soldiers in the military). Similarly, in extract 2, regarding unemployment, some characterized the "unemployed" as "husbands," leading in line 22 to applause for the familial difference (between men-husbands and women-wives) as a justification for awarding "the man" a job (presumably as primary wage earner in the family). This positioning of gender difference (re-)creates a sense of "man" as physically stronger and the primary wage earner and thus implicates for "woman" a position that is physically weaker and less than, or other than, the primary wage earner. Further, this positioning process brings rather close to the interactional surface a domain of family life with "man's" moral place being measured economically and "woman's" being measured relationally (as wife and emotional supporter of the unemployed husband).

This gendered discourse about the military, employment, and family life is also about nonpresent and/or hypothetical persons. In so being, it casts characters with regard to these issues along gender lines. Yet, as it does, it implicates for the present speakers an identity as one who would so position, that is, as one who would publicly acknowledge, address, and perhaps promote differences of gender. Thus, as speakers invoke a gendered position in their talk, they position themselves (and talk about the issue) within a culturally based and historically grounded system of personas, social relations, and institutions. As the discourse is being spoken, others are being invited to speak and hear the issues in this way, each gender being distinctive (e.g., men are men and women are women), based upon differing capacities (e.g., physically), and with differing responsibilities (e.g., militarily and familially). Structuring discourse this way thus implicates one's self (and others) as ones who in some way come into contact with, "live" (or should live, or should contest living) at least on some occasions this difference, as a basic condition of social life. Spoken as such, distinctive positions for "man" and "woman" are being created and are thus made basic determinants of social positions, relations (e.g., soldier, wife, husband), and institutions (e.g., armed services, family).

Yet, this discourse of difference, like many others concerning race, class, and so on, amplifies the sounds of social stratification (along gender lines) and divisiveness (e.g., disagreements over the nature, value, and application of the gendered difference). Through the vacillating form, this precipitates challenges to this kind of discourse itself, and its speakers, and generates counterproposals that explicate yet another type of position. For example, through the comment on lines 5-7, one belief of difference was challenged as the audience member and the feminist author co-constructed the premise: "Some women are actually . . . stronger than men." This saying invites a characterization of persons in terms other than social difference. Similarly, the gendered answer (line 22) to Donahue's question (lines 19-21) while applauded or ratified by many was not unanimously endorsed. The discourse of difference thus stratified participants not only through the vision of social life it created (i.e., by drawing distinctions between men and women) but also because the immediate social reaction to this discourse was itself somewhat divisive (see, e.g., lines 4, 8). Thus, as discourse explicates gender difference, it implicates differences of opinion about that difference and thus precipitates a site of contest, not necessarily between men and women but between the different evaluations, from ratifications to rejections, of the value and use of gendered discourse. Created in the face(s) of this difference is a felt need for, and expression of, a position of commonality.

After the challenge on lines 5-8, the president of the National Organization of Women (NOW) said: "Some individuals are stronger than some individuals." Similarly, on lines 16-18, the female director of the Democratic National Committee (DNC) said: "We are on the same side of individuals who are trying to make it." In both of these examples, the language shifts from a gendered positioning to another that does not deny, nor does it elaborate, gender but repositions the debate onto a different agentive plane, to a more inclusive cultural space, a common denominator of persons, where all are deemed "individuals." The language the director of the DNC uses is particularly interesting in this regard, because it artfully builds such a space (see lines 12-18). She prepares the position carefully through inclusive and centralizing geographic terms ("this country" and "the industrial heartland"), familial images ("families like yours"), conjunctive phrasing ("men and women"), explicit negations of difference ("not opposed to each other," "not on different sides"), pronominal shifting (from "you and I" to "we"), with the eventual "we" as "individuals" (line 16) functioning as a potently inclusive anaphoric reference that entitles all of the above, previously quoted phrases.

The explicating of persons as "we-individuals" thus carries a possible arbitral tone through the assertion of an alleged (and perhaps unquestionable here?) universalizing cultural premise of common humanity: Each person and every people (men and women, blacks and whites, rich and poor, and so on) are all at base individuals. Elsewhere I have referred to this potent symbol and premise as part of a political code because it derives prominently from the U.S. Constitution. Part of its cultural force is as an "equivocal affirmative" in that its common use at once affirms, or asserts, what is both radically distinctive to each person (as a uniquely particular self) and what is universal to all persons (as an organismic embodiment of humankind). In an "individual" breath, dual beliefs in a distinctive humanness of each and a common humanity for all are affirmed (Carbaugh, 1988c, pp. 21-39 ff.). These beliefs are elaborated through statements such as (with the words in quotations being explicated cultural terms): "We-individuals" as citizens in "this country" are "not opposed to each other" but "on the same side." Such statements implicate cultural beliefs about the person and its associated political institutions (e.g., the U.S. Constitution and the Bill of Rights) and thus potently foreground, if equivocally, commonalities in person capacities and duties (as "individual" citizens). The movement between positions is thus not a mere shift of phrase but the marking of a cultural transition from social identities and institutions of difference to another, a cultural persona of a common humanity, a potent political agent.

I hasten to add that, in the extracts presented here, some tensions are possibly discussable but significantly not taken up. We cannot claim to know exactly of what the phrase "the same side" or those "trying to make it" consists (because this was not explicated). While the cultural and political beliefs just cited provide one possible account of "the same side" (i.e., we-individuals), there are possible others, for example, of women against the patriarchy. In fact, using the principle of the vacillating form, we can expect the sequence to turn yet again back upon itself, as the mentioning of "the same side" precipitates yet an "other side." That such a position is not taken up attests, I believe, both to the robustness of the cultural position described above and to the difficulty of formulating a position "other" than "individuals who are trying to make it." But, if we were to speculate about possible "other (third?) sides" on this occasion, those brought close to the interactional surface by these speakers are perhaps "Republicans" (for the director of the DNC) or "men" (for the president of NOW), neither being pursued here. Perhaps such a form, so positioned, occasionally plays itself out.

Note a related consequence of the above vacillating cultural form. Because of its solidified positioning of an "only one" (self) or an "everyone" (we-individuals), discourse of social group difference is difficult to elaborate and sustain. Explications of identities that build images of difference based upon gender or ethnicity or class or social groupings, rather than those based upon commonality (or an everyone-or-only-one kind of talk), seem eventually to succumb to "inclusive" language. In this case, especially domestic discourses of difference from unemployed family members, get quickly talked over and supplanted by another that is more inclusive and politically based. U.S. public discourse, political language, consumerism, and some parts of television, being, in a sense, numbers driven—here's a little something for everyone—easily assumes an inclusive political position as a common denominator and mutes, or quickly refracts, some of the more particular group-based and serious discourses of difference. Such a vacillating tendency between positions of commonality and difference seems somewhat general and almost inevitable, although its nature and use needs to be understood, so that voices worthy of being elaborated, whether of difference or commonality, are indeed heard (see Scollon & Scollon, 1981).

The "Individual" Has a "Self":
From Relational Constraints to Independence

The one cultural premise stated above, that each person is unique, is elaborated with cultural terms of "self" and its closely associated terms, as one who has "rights" and makes "choices." Use of these terms and their meanings positions participants as uniquely independent sites of personal reflectiveness. What is deemed worthy of elaborate expression, from the vantage point of this system, is the highly particular, idiosyncratically distinct world of the one (Carbaugh, 1988c, pp. 41-86 ff.).

Consider the following story told by a nun about the effects of an "anger clinic" that she attended.

Extract 3 (Carbaugh, 1988c, pp. 69-70)

23) Nun: Before that [the clinic] I was a people pleaser. I
24) grew up being a people pleaser. I'm fourth in the family
25) and that made a lot of difference. The only way I could

26) get along is really by pleasing my parents all the time.
27) I learned I don't have to please anybody else, I can
28) please my self. And once I became really convinced I can
29) please my self, I don't have to do what you're telling
30) me, then I became free and I was able to tell them,
31) "hey, I don't want to do that!"

    . . .

32) Donahue: Thanks a lot sister . . .
33) Audience: (Applause)

In lines 23-26, the nun is narrating a phase of life in which she is positioned solely within a relationship in which her primary task was to work for others, as both a "people pleaser" and "fourth in the family." So positioned, duties to others overshadowed senses of her self. In lines 27-29, she repositions her story through "self," relocating her as one who now is not solely a constrained relation ("people pleaser") but a "self" who is "free" from such constraint and, further, she is able to say so (line 31).

Stories such as this one again show a vacillating form of positioning, yet here the movement is not from positions of difference to commonality, as above (although there are similarities), but from an explicit, constraining relatedness to an extricable, uniquely independent site of reflectiveness and expressiveness. Her story tells us why she went to an anger clinic: to learn to extricate her being from obligatory constraints and thus to discover her self. Forms such as this one, not without a deep structural link to the *Odyssey,* demonstrate a voyage in which there is positional movement from one caught up in a historical system of constraining relations to the charting of new territory in which one's uniqueness and independence are discovered.

Of what does this renewed position consist? Consider the following metaphorical utterances (each in fact was made but not within the following sequence).

Extract 4 (Carbaugh, 1988c, p. 79)

34) I filled myself up with drugs.
35) To be angry with a stranger or someone who only knows
36)   you a little bit is to reveal a piece of your self
37)   that you don't want that other person to see.
38) Now that I have a part-time job, I feel much more secure
39)   within myself.
40) The problem is that we never really learn who we are
41)   before we give ourselves away to somebody in marriage.

As is demonstrated here, the resources of "self" are material (the body, its parts, and what they contain, e.g., "drugs"), symbolic (e.g., information "revealed," feelings of "security"), or both material and symbolic (e.g., something "given" to another "in marriage"). From this position, all such resources (including one's physical capacities, thoughts, feelings, consciousness) are conceived as within a contained body, with a necessary and deeper awareness of these resources becoming a motive for the journey of "self" (Carbaugh, 1988c, pp. 77-84).

Given a discursive form like this one, in which the relationally constrained person (social deixis) and the independent self (personal deixis) are played against one another, the task of "self" becomes the shaping of a position, a site of extricable oneness, in which personal uniqueness of resources and freedom from past constraints can become realized and expressed.

The "Self" Vilifies "Social Roles" (Institutions, History): The Renunciation of Sites of Restraint

As "self" becomes positioned in discourse, it runs rather uneasily into other positions that are institutionally constrained and/or historically grounded. These positions are identified variously as "social roles," the "society," "history," or "this country." Specific examples include "husband" or "wife," or any such term that implicates duties to another, or "worker" and "soldier," or any such term that implicates institutional ("stereotypical") constraints on one's actions. The nun's comments above are partly constructed in this way with the roles of "child" and "people pleaser" explicating the constraints on action that hampered "self" (not to mention being a "nun"). Extracts 1 and 2 likewise show how the duties or expectations of constraining positions, as "man"/"woman," are played against another, the freer "individual." Positioning in this way consists in an agonistic form of discourse in which a site of enslavement is identified, such as "social role," or "society," and is subsequently vilified and renounced, because such positions constrain "self." This motivates a repositioning of person onto the preferred, freer plane of self. The form thus again plays the culturally solidified positions of constraint and difference against its more liberating senses of "self" (Carbaugh, 1988b, pp. 87-107 ff., 1988-1989).

Consider the following utterance, made by a woman during a discussion of gender roles:

Extract 5 (Carbaugh, 1988c, p. 100)

42) While we're talking about men and women, if people would
43) just concentrate on themselves, and their goals, and
44) being individuals. Society says that you have to earn
45) money to be of any value. I feel that that's very
46) ingrained in men right now. That is what women are
47) fighting. I feel that I am fighting that right now
48) myself.

The form of this utterance is agonistic, or polemical; it plays two positions for persons, one against the other, while preferring the one over the other. In particular, the playing of the position goes this way: the terms, "men" and "women" (42, 46), and "society" (44), identify historically grounded, socially differentiated, institutionally bounded notions of being; so positioned, one's place is said to be duty-ridden, predicating actions here as a "have to" (44); it is deemed a cultural rut, enslaving, or "ingrained" (46); and, because such positions are duty-ridden and enslaving, they must be fought (47). The preferred position from which, and for which, the fighting is done requires and prefers "concentration" on "self" (43, 48) and "being individuals" (44).

In folk terms of the preferred position of the person, "If we could just be ourselves, and stop trying to be something else, we all would be better off." Put in terms of folk forms for action that are associated with the position, "If we could just sit down and talk it out, we all [each of us] would be better off." Such positions and forms of action seek to shed one restraining position, the common sense of which includes institutional and historically based identities (e.g., men, women, the unemployed, blacks), in favor of a freer other, the "self." Or so they say in some American scenes.[1]

Coding Dignity Over Honor

The above symbols, forms, and premises of positioning can be summarized as a coding of personhood, a symbolizing of the person through particular symbols, forms, and their meanings. Treating this discursive position as a deeply coded one is an effort to cast more generally the beliefs and values immanent in this kind of discursive action. Following prior work about similar discursive activities, I call the code a code of dignity (Berger, Berger, & Kellner, 1974; Carbaugh, 1985; see especially Philipsen, in press).

When a coding of dignity is occurring through terms like *individual* and *self,* a model for the person is being presupposed and implicated, preferred and promoted. One cluster of values relates to indigenous conceptions of the person and thus I refer to them as an ontological dimension of the code. These values support the cultural notion of personhood described above and thus figure prominently in the coding of the person as such: the *intrinsic worth* of each person, the ability to recognize and support individuals as holding some socially redeemable value, even if this is difficult at first to notice; *self-consciousness*, or self-awareness, or personal reflectiveness, the ability to ascertain who one is and is not, what one can and cannot do, to know one's necessities, abilities, capacities, and limits, independent of, as well as within, one's typical roles; *uniqueness*, to know how one's necessities, abilities, and capacities differ from others'; *sincerity*, or authenticity, or honesty, to be forthcoming and expressive about oneself, to coalesce one's outer actions with one's inner thoughts and feelings.

The above clustering of values of person are associated with and overlap another. This other clustering of values adds a pragmatic dimension to the code and thus refers to valued means of sociation, or preferred ways of relating person, so conceived, with others. The basic social principle is *equality*—to ensure persons have inalienable rights to being and acting and (equal) opportunities to make choices, and to conduct evaluations, if necessary, on the basis of standardized criteria (applied to each equally). Favored actions include *cooperative negotiation*—saying who one is and what one strives toward, to ably hear who another is and what he or she strives toward, and to conduct action with both in view; *validation of personal differences*, acknowledging through cooperative conduct the unique qualities of each person; *flexibility*, being willing to change one's sense of oneself, others, one's relationship with others, one's habits of action, and so on (e.g., "to grow") as a result of cooperative conduct.

In the above extracts, all of these values for persons, sociation, and pragmatic action are appealed to. Note, however, the exigencies for this coding of the person. What precipitates the coding of dignity are discourses in which different, often stratified positions and domains are being explicated or implicated (e.g., gender and family or the military, race, and education). These alternate social positions bring into discourse a coding based not upon personal uniqueness but upon institutional and historical precedence, a positioning of honor. Philipsen (in press) has elaborated the code of honor, with its attendant emphasis on political connections, historical precedence, magnanimity, loyalty, piety. From the vantage point of a code of dignity, the positions of honor are often heard as relationally constrained or stereotypically obliged. Such a hearing presses the code of dignity into service. This is nicely exemplified above as women discussed, through a version of the honor code, "unemployed" men and the "man's" need of a job to support the family, but were responded to in another code that emphasized equal standings while muting the gendered and familial divisions of labor. Thus the vacillating forms in use here suggest deeply different systems of values about what person, relations, and pragmatic action is (and should be). Displayed therefore is not just differences in the positioning of the immediate persons but deeper differences between ways of culturally coding social interaction, persons, and life itself.

How the Code of Dignity Hides
Its Cultural Features and Forms

There is an irony built into the above discourse of dignity. It consists of a general dynamic: the common meanings made when coding conversation this way are highly individualized and liberating, while the forms and moral status of those very meanings are largely collectivized and constraining. Put differently, discursively coding the person in terms of dignity amplifies meanings of individual and self while muting the common cultural premises and forms that make those very meanings possible (Carbaugh, 1988c, pp. 28-33, 57-59, 84-86, 109-112 ff., 1988-1989).

For each feature—each symbol, form, and premise—of the code of dignity discussed above, we can formulate a statement that must be practically necessary for the discursive action to take the shape it does. For each, the meaning the form promotes (i.e., individualized persons and actions) silences the form of those meanings (i.e., collectivized persons and actions). Consider the following summary of the ways the coding of dignity works:

a. the cultural construction of individuality,
b. the collective celebration of the unique self,
c. the communal rejection of group-based roles and identities.

For the first two, the common meanings of, for example, individual boundedness and uniqueness hide the connecting forms of action (the cultural and collective) that are required for their promotion and realization. Similarly, in the third, the overt meanings, such as obligation or conformity to a group, or audience, are renounced, just as the group conforms in being ones who so obediently renounce. In this way, each feature of the code both grants through its cultural contents, yet takes away through its cultural forms, the conditions of its making. Bateson, of course, reminded us that being agents-in-society is inherently double binding, and here we have demonstrated in discursive practices just how this is so.

One possible danger of this coding to which I now turn—there are others— is its unreflective application, especially in intercultural contexts. It is sometimes naively used to assert or to replicate its own presumably universalizing sense: that is, that all people are at base individuals, or constructable as such. This is especially troublesome in multicultural contexts such as some courtrooms and classrooms, where the coding of dignity confronts deeply different others, whose codes for being operate quite differently.

Coding Dignity in Cross-Cultural Perspective: Personhood and Politeness

Larry Wieder and Steven Pratt (1990) have discussed a psychology classroom in America's heartland that was convened on the topic of race and ethnic relations. The professor of the class had asked the students to get together in groups to discuss their own cultural heritages. For students tutored in the code of dignity, this presented no problem. One's unique background could be put into a disclosive form of action, thus positioning that person as an able discussant. For others, especially for some native (Osage) people, this was not permissible. To position as an Osage first of all required a relational assessment of the situation, leading to the culturally salient condition of being with tribal members previously unknown to them. If Osage wanted to display the native identity under this condition, they must orient to the cultural rule of modesty: Do not sound more knowledgeable than other group members, especially when discussing matters of the tribe's heritage. Under this condition, the most knowledgable Osage produced appropriately vacuous comments, ostensibly about their cultural heritage, saying, for example, "I don't know, what do you think?" Ironically, such statements explicated (but implicated much more deeply) to present natives true membership as a native, while those natives voluble on the topic explicated, in effect, nonmembership as a native (although at the same time aligning them with the position being presupposed and valued by their professor). The complexity in the situation runs deep, as those Osage highly disclosive on the topic displayed, in the special sense introduced above, some position of dignity, while simultaneously dishonoring another, of their tribe.

Many other cultural positions and their other-than-dignity workings could be described, ranging from the positioning of persons as sites of transindividual consciousness as is the case in the Russian *dusa* or soul (Carbaugh, in press-a, in press-b; Wierzbicka, 1989), as dispersable particles and substances as is the case among some Hindi speakers (Marriott, 1976), as well as other positions that are astrally projectable, among many others (see the reviews in Carbaugh, 1988c, pp. 15-19, 112-119; Shweder & Bourne, 1984). Each such cultural agent, so acted and conceived, provides a radically alternate conception of persons, social relations, emotions, and actions. Such dynamics run deeply into many discourses and cultural worlds, even into aspects of Western worlds where parasocial positions are at work (Caughey, 1984). Further, there no doubt are other general ways of culturally coding positions than the ones of dignity and honor discussed above.

Of special interest with regard to intercultural dynamics are differences in what is preferred as "positive face" among various peoples, especially the nature and value of likeness or difference among persons. Ronald and Suzanne Scollon (1981), building on politeness theory (Brown & Levinson, 1978), have described how Athapaskans prefer positioning with cultural others on the basis of deference (thus asserting and assuming difference), while Anglos position with cultural others on the basis of solidarity (thus asserting and assuming similarity). They note how assertions of solidarity hold a kind of logical and often cultural power over others, as when the code of dignity presumes a common humanity for all (e.g., basically as individuals who can and should speak their mind). Coding persons and actions this way can lead easily to supplanting others' faces, those for whom real differences are presumed and preferred (see also Chick, 1990). The extent to which oral and literate discourse positions persons with culturally distinctive faces and the extent to which the coding of dignity supplants others—perhaps even in academic theories (see Barnlund, 1979), face-to-face interaction (Liberman, 1990), and upon mediated occasions (Carbaugh, in press-b)—needs to be understood. Each such discursive activity activates cultural positions, and how this is so warrants our serious attention (see Brown & Levinson, 1987, pp. 13-15). We can and must better understand the cultural pragmatics that are at play, for such dynamics, especially in the New Europe, increasingly animate the stages of our multicultural world.

CONCLUDING REMARKS

Throughout the above discussion, I have used the concepts of personhood and cultural agent rather interchangeably. I have attempted not to become too committed to either one. My purpose has been to begin by granting equal status to a diverse range of cultural positions, from those humanly embodied (a more familiar sense of personhood) to others that are not necessarily embodied in human organisms (other cultural agents). Examples of the latter include sacred crocodiles among the Tallensi that are considered to be persons because they "combine the human spiritual aspects with a living body" (La Fontaine, 1985, p. 127), the witch's "fairies" mentioned earlier that are not necessarily embodied at all, or still others for whom a human body is insufficient for granting the status of "person," although still presumably holding some social position (La Fontaine, 1985, p. 131). Some of these notions risk sounding rather fanciful or farcical because they challenge deeply held positionings of "person" in which the human body contains the site of conscious activity. This is a strong and pervasive belief about persons and cultural agents, but it is no less cultural in its form and meaning because of that.

For purposes of reflecting upon one's own cultural ways, and for better theorizing, it would behoove us to distinguish the qualities of claims we are attributing to a discursive position and whether these consist (a) in a socially explicated, implicated, and ratified being (a person, or agent-in-society); (b) in a phenomenal site of consciousness, awareness, or reflectiveness (a self); and/or (c) in an organismic entity (an individual member of humankind or some other species). The distinctions are important because they help disentangle the array of cross-cultural data being accumulated about personhood and discursive practices, such as those mentioned above. The questions here, of course, are not whether, for example, a disembodied consciousness is "real" but whether and to what degree this kind of agent is coded, explicated, elaborated, and ratified (or renounced) in a discursive scene or system.

Furthermore, the distinctions help cut into the sources of some public disputes that are very lively, at least in some corners. For example, many environmental discourses revolve precisely around the cultural status granted certain agents such as owls, plants, valleys, animals, and so on. Current U.S. vice-president Albert Gore has been criticized for granting "butterflies" the same status as "people." The issue, so presented, draws attention to the "butterfly" as a cultural agent-in-society and suggests asking whether, and to what degree, this agent resembles other agents (especially "people") in terms of its social standing. If a "California valley" is a "legal person," as a famous court case declared, then what about "owls," "butterflies," and so on. Environmental debates are notable sites for alternate positionings of agents, places, animals, plants, and so on and warrant our careful study.

With regard to other court cases, the abortion debate rests heavily upon the question of what a "constitutional person" is. What status, if any, does (and should) a "result of pregnancy" have as a cultural agent? From the vantage point of legal discourse? Moral, domestic, political, and religious discourses? What various positions of agents and persons are being created in this debate? Of what does each consist? Similarly, what of surrogate parenting? What standing does a woman donor of an egg have regarding the result of the egg's use? Is she more like a "man" who donates sperm or a "woman" who gives birth? Or is there another position needed? If a "child" is a fully fledged constitutional "person," able to exercise a legal proceeding (e.g., divorce from his or her parents), what effect does this have on other institutions of social interaction such as the family, school, or law enforcement agencies? On another front, some feminist discourse rests firmly on the explication, and assertion, that female consciousness, or feminine consciousness, is inherently transindividual, thus positioning a kind of cultural agent (but not necessarily a biological type?) as distinct from a traditional male or masculine one (Gilligan, 1982; Tannen, 1990; but see Goodwin, 1990; West & Zimmerman, 1991). These practical issues and cultural matters would repay careful scrutiny through cultural pragmatic studies of personhood and positioning.

Like the concept of personhood, the concept of positioning adopted here needs further development (see especially Levinson, 1989). From the vantage point of cultural pragmatics, I attempted to draw attention to these aspects of the positioning of persons: (a) to the cultural premises, symbols, forms, and meanings of positioning, and their sometimes unreflective use, especially in intercultural encounters that involve an American coding of dignity; (b) to discursive activity, especially to situated social interactions as the site of person—social and cultural—positions, treating discourse as if prior to positions, and not the other way around (I shall return to this shortly); and (c) to the forms of interaction through which positioning gets done. Particularly noteworthy was the way one positioning of the person occurs as a response to another. This suggests a perhaps general cyclical or spiraling form of positioning that inheres within a relationally based, vacillating process. Some resulting questions are these: What is the nature and function of this position, so discursively produced? Yet further, to what prior position, or role, or social or cultural agent, is this one responding? Is this one knowingly responding to another at all? What does the play between or among these positions produce? (d) Positioning thus consists in a *system* of terms (pronouns, nouns, conjunctions, and so on), forms, and their meanings, including a consideration of oppositional positions (and their terms, forms, and meanings). Considering one term (e.g., a pronoun or a noun) therefore is deemed insufficient for locating the cultural positioning of persons in conversation. (e) Some positions suggest a code, or a deep structuring of beliefs and values that is immanent in various forms, terms, and meanings of persons and actions.

Different types of analyses are suggested with the vocabulary introduced earlier, specifically a move-by-move account of explications, implications (avowed and addressed), elaborations, ratifications, rejections, and so on. Thus what I present here is only one working-through of the general possibilities, with a special focus on agentive qualities, codes, and vacillating forms. Others are, of course, invited to develop these and other features of the framework as well as the discursive activities that amplify (or mute) them. Of particular interest is a system for interpreting implications, with messages about persons, relations, institutions, emotions, and discourse itself (Carbaugh, 1989, 1990b) being already of some value in, for example, discursive studies of self (Harré, 1991a, 1991b), with other such studies being recommended (Varenne, 1990). Other investigators have used the system to describe students' statements about their forms of communicative action (Baxter & Goldsmith, 1990), to explore relations between oral and literate forms in a classroom (Gnatek, 1992), to examine various forms of actions in a new age community (Mahoney, 1993), to comparatively assess discourses of two cultural communities (Philipsen, in press), and to further explore the discursive bases some Americans use to build a renunciative voice (Scollon, 1992).

I mentioned that cultural pragmatic studies of positioning take discourse as primary, then ask of it what positioning of persons is getting done here? Or, put differently, cultural pragmatic studies hypothesize that social and cultural kinds of positioning are occurring in discourse, then collect a corpus to discover if this is indeed the case and, if so, how so, with what consequences? One begins, then, not by assuming a typology of persons, relations, or actions as something prior to discursive action but by assuming that activities of positioning indeed take place in discourse and then investigating the nature of that activity in that discourse through a conceptual framework. What positions are getting discoursed here? What are their social locations, qualities, processes of ratification (or refusal)? What social relations are being constructed in these activities? The framework suggests ways to pose such problems and a vocabulary with which to address them. Beginning with discourse, and questions about it, helps construct a communication theory as well as a communicative explanation of positioning. One therefore does not begin with blank grids of content to fill but with parameters of positioning along which to look and listen (see Zeitlyn, in press). Investigating this way enables one to describe a particular shaping of discursive activity and eventually to posit a system of culturally potent terms and forms of expression that accounts for persons being conceived, and conducted, as such. The resulting argument is that the discursive activity, as a culturally shaped form of communication, provides one account for persons and agents, on some occasion, being what they are.

It is only appropriate that an essay on positioning conclude with a bit of authorial self-explication. I cannot escape the position I address. I cannot either, nor could anyone, address all of its implications. Yet there are two features of my authored position I want to mention in ending, feeling they are not yet elaborated quite enough. Each is a voice of criticism that I have discussed in detail elsewhere (Carbaugh, 1990a). One has to do with my discourse as a user and critic of academic theory. In particular, I have attempted to adapt and develop a communication theory that explores sociocultural notions of the person. My main objective has been to integrate a cultural dimension into interactional studies, believing as I do that meanings of identity, positioning, personality, and the like, as well as concerns more macro (e.g., culture, race, ethnicity), are at base at least partly the result of everyday communicative practices. By exploring such concerns this way, we can better grasp how the moment-to-moment living through of everyday practices constructs positions for ourselves, others, and relations among us. Yet, also, I adopt and advocate the approach and its related others not only for the study of personhood and positioning but indeed for the study of all social and even physical matters, such as studies of time (e.g., Brockmeier, 1992) and space (e.g., Carbaugh, 1992). Part of my effort has been constructed, then, from an academic position with the development of academic concerns, theories, and methods in mind. Further, I draw attention to my discourse as an exercise in cultural criticism. I deem it essential that popular American discourse includes a reflective ability, an ability to see itself as a cultural artifact, an ability that I have tried here and elsewhere to develop. My tactic has been to select typical everyday discursive practices and describe some of what they interactively produce. I also have tried to loosen their grip on *US* by discussing some implicit ironies and paradoxes in their use. Thus this essay is caught in the vacillating movement described above including reactions to prominent theoretical *and* cultural concerns. My main proposal in these academic and cultural matters is then to conceive of persons more as transitory interactional accomplishments that creatively implicate, produce, and develop cultural meaning systems (which are themselves thus cross-culturally variable). My main reaction has been to treatments of identity that rely exclusively on immutable psychological or biological endowments (with these being, from the vantage point of my proposal, the result of a potent discursive heritage). People are not everywhere positioned the same, nor are they anywhere positioned the same in all social contexts. Needless to say, I believe our cultural practices, and our theories too, should recognize as much and move themselves along as well.

NOTE

1. That "self" is no less a historical and institutional practice tends to escape the common cultural sense. Further, that each individual's self-concept is in its way subject to constant explication, elaboration, and ratification/rejection also escapes the common cultural sense. This

is the result of cultural conceptions of persons based more upon biology and psychology and less upon social and cultural communicative processes. Some of the ironies and dynamics of this belief are taken up below and elsewhere (Carbaugh, 1988c).

REFERENCES

Bakhtin, M. (1986). *Speech genres and other late essays* (V. W. McGee, Trans.). Austin: University of Texas Press.
Barnlund, D. (1979). Communication: The context of change. In D. Mortensen (Ed.), *Basic readings in communication theory*. New York: Harper & Row.
Basso, K. (1990). *Western Apache language and culture*. Tucson: University of Arizona Press.
Baxter, L., & Goldsmith, D. (1990). Cultural terms for communication events among some American high school adolescents. *Western Journal of Speech Communication, 54*, 377-394.
Berger, P., Berger, B., & Kellner, H. (1974). *The homeless mind*. New York: Vintage.
Billig, M. (1987). *Arguing and thinking: A rhetorical approach to social psychology*. Cambridge: Cambridge University Press.
Billig, M. (1991). *Ideology and opinions: Studies in rhetorical psychology*. London: Sage.
Brockmeier, J. (1992). *Anthropomorphic operators of time: Chronology, activity, language and space*. Paper presented at the 8th Triennial Conference of the International Society for the Study of Time, Cerisy-la-Salle, France.
Brown, P., & Levinson, S. (1978). Universals of language usage: Politeness phenomena. In E. Goody (Ed.), *Questions and politeness* (pp. 56-289). London: Cambridge University Press.
Brown, P., & Levinson, S. (1987). *Politeness*. London: Cambridge University Press.
Carbaugh, D. (1985). *Some sensitizing concepts for (inter)cultural communication theory*. Paper presented at the International Communication Association, Honolulu, HI.
Carbaugh, D. (1988a). Comments on culture in communication inquiry. *Communication Reports, 1*, 38-41.
Carbaugh, D. (1988b). Cultural terms and tensions in the speech of a television station. *Western Journal of Speech Communication, 52*, 216-237.
Carbaugh, D. (1988c). *Talking American: Cultural discourses on Donahue*. Norwood, NJ: Ablex.
Carbaugh, D. (1988-1989). Deep agony: "Self" vs. "society" in Donahue discourse. *Research on Language and Social Interaction, 22*, 179-212.
Carbaugh, D. (1989). Fifty terms for talk: A cross-cultural study. *International and Intercultural Communication Annual, 13*, 93-120.
Carbaugh, D. (1990a). The critical voice in ethnography of communication research. *Research on Language and Social Interaction, 23*, 262-282.
Carbaugh, D. (Ed.). (1990b). *Cultural communication and intercultural contact*. Hillsdale, NJ: Lawrence Erlbaum.
Carbaugh, D. (1990c). Toward a perspective on cultural communication and intercultural contact. *Semiotica, 80*, 15-35.
Carbaugh, D. (1992). "The mountain" and "the project": Dueling depictions of a natural environment. In J. Cantrill & C. Oravec (Eds.), *Conference on the discourse of environmental advocacy*. Salt Lake City: University of Utah.
Carbaugh, D. (in press-a). "Soul" and "self": Soviet and American cultures in conversation. *Quarterly Journal of Speech, 79*.
Carbaugh, D. (in press-b). Competence as cultural pragmatics: Reflections on some Soviet and American encounters. *International and Intercultural Communication Annual, 17*.
Carbaugh, D., & Hastings, S. O. (1992). A role for communication theory in ethnography and cultural analysis. *Communication Theory, 2*, 156-165.
Caughey, J. (1984). *Imaginary social worlds*. Lincoln: University of Nebraska Press.

Chick, J. K. (1990). The interactional accomplishment of discrimination in South Africa. In D. Carbaugh (Ed.), *Cultural communication and intercultural contact*. Hillsdale, NJ: Lawrence Erlbaum.

Cronen, V., & Pearce, W. B. (1991-1992). Grammars of identity and their implications for discursive practices in and out of academe: A comparison of Davies and Harre's views to coordinated management of meaning theory. *Research on Language and Social Interaction, 25*, 37-66.

Davies, B., & Harré, R. (1990). Positioning: The discursive production of selves. *Journal for the Theory of Social Behaviour, 20*, 43-63.

Edwards, R., & Potter, J. (1992). *Discursive psychology*. London: Sage.

Eriksen, T. (1991). The cultural contexts of ethnic differences. *Man, 26*, 127-144.

Fitch, K. (1991). The interplay of linguistic universals and cultural knowledge in personal address: Colombian madre terms. *Communication Monographs, 58*, 254-272.

Geertz, C. (1973). *The interpretation of cultures*. New York: Basic Books.

Geertz, C. (1976). From the native's point-of-view: On the nature of anthropological understanding. In K. Basso & H. Selby (Eds.), *Meaning in anthropology*. Albuquerque: University of New Mexico Press.

Gergen, K. (1985). The social constructionist movement in modern psychology. *American Psychologist, 40*, 266-275.

Gilligan, C. (1982). *In a different voice*. Cambridge, MA: Harvard University Press.

Gnatek, T. (1992). *Terms for talk in peer-group teaching of literacy*. Unpublished doctoral dissertation, University of Massachusetts, Amherst.

Goffman, E. (1967). *Interaction ritual*. New York: Anchor.

Goodwin, M. (1990). *He-said, she-said: Talk as social organization among black children*. Bloomington: Indiana University Press.

Gumperz, J. (1982). *Discourse strategies*. Cambridge: Cambridge University Press.

Harré, R. (1979). *Social being*. Oxford: Basil Blackwell.

Harré, R. (1983). *Personal being*. Oxford: Basil Blackwell.

Harré, R. (1991a). The discursive production of selves. *Theory & Psychology, 1*, 51-63.

Harré, R. (1991b). *Physical being*. Oxford: Basil Blackwell.

Harré, R., & Van Langenhove, L. (1991). Varieties of positioning. *Journal for the Theory of Social Behaviour, 21*, 383-407.

Harris, G. (1989). Concepts of individual, self, and person in description and analysis. *American Anthropologist, 91*, 599-612.

Hollway, W. (1984). Gender difference and the production of subjectivity. In J. Henriques, W. Hollway, C. Urwin, L. Venn, & V. Walkerdine (Eds.), *Changing the subject: Psychology, social regulation and subjectivity*. London: Methuen.

Hymes, D. (1961). Linguistic aspects of cross-cultural personality study. In B. Kaplan (Ed.), *Studying personality cross-culturally*. Evanston, IL: Row, Peterson.

Hymes, D. (1972). Models of the interaction of language and social life. In J. Gumperz & D. Hymes (Eds.), *Directions in sociolinguistics: The ethnography of communication*. New York: Holt, Rinehart & Winston.

Katriel, T. (1991). *Communal webs: Communication and culture in contemporary Israel*. New York: State University Press.

La Fontaine, J. (1985). Person and individual: Some anthropological reflections. In M. Carrithers, S. Collins, & S. Lukes (Eds.), *The category of the person*. New York: Columbia University Press.

Levinson, S. (1989). Putting linguistics on a proper footing: Explorations in Goffman's concepts of participation. In P. Drew & A. Wootton (Eds.), *Goffman* (pp. 161-293). Cambridge: Polity.

Liberman, K. (1990). Intercultural communication in Central Australia. In D. Carbaugh (Ed.), *Cultural communication and intercultural contact*. Hillsdale, NJ: Lawrence Erlbaum.

Lutz, C. (1988). *Unnatural emotions*. Chicago: University of Chicago Press.

Mahoney, J. (1993). *Which is witch? Identity construction in a Salem, Massachusetts' community*. Unpublished master's thesis, University of Massachusetts, Amherst.

Marriott, M. (1976). Hindu transactions: Diversity without dualism. In B. Kapferer (Ed.), *Transaction and meaning*. Philadelphia: Institute for the Study of Human Issues.

Moerman, M. (1988). *Talking culture*. Philadelphia: University of Pennsylvania Press.

Philipsen, G. (1987). The prosect for cultural communication. In L. Kincaid (Ed.), *Communication theory: Eastern and Western perspectives*. New York: Academic Press.

Philipsen, G. (in press). *Speaking culturally*. New York: State University of New York Press.

Potter, J., & Wetherell, M. (1987). *Discourse and social psychology*. London: Sage.

Sapir, E. (1931). Communication. *Encyclopedia of the Social Sciences, 4*, 78-81.

Scollon, R. (1992). *The shifting discourse of American individualism from the authoritarian to the infochild*. Unpublished manuscript, Haines, AK.

Scollon, R., & Scollon, S. (1981). *Narrative, literacy, and face in interethnic communication*. Norwood, NJ: Ablex.

Shweder, R. (1992). *Thinking through cultures*. Chicago: University of Chicago Press.

Shweder, R., & Bourne, E. (1984). Does the concept of the person vary cross-culturally? In R. Shweder & R. LeVine (Eds.), *Culture theory*. Cambridge: Cambridge University Press.

Tannen, D. (1990). *You just don't understand*. New York: Morrow.

Varenne, H. (1977). *Americans together*. New York: Teachers College Press.

Varenne, H. (1990). Review of D. Carbaugh, *Talking American. Language in Society, 19*, 434-436.

West, C., & Zimmerman, D. (1991). Doing gender. In J. Lorber & S. Farrell (Eds.), *The social construction of gender*. London: Sage.

Wieder, L., & Pratt, S. (1990). On being a recognizable Indian among Indians. In D. Carbaugh (Ed.), *Cultural communication and intercultural contact*. Hillsdale, NJ: Lawrence Erlbaum.

Wierzbicka, A. (1989). Soul and mind: Linguistic evidence for ethnopsychology and cultural history. *American Anthropologist, 91*, 41-58.

Zeitlyn, D. (in press). Reconstructing kinship or the pragmatics of kin talk. *Man, 28*.

Recovering History and Conflict

GORDON NAKAGAWA
California State University, Northridge

HE preparation of this commentary on Donal Carbaugh's essay coincides with a series of noteworthy events in Los Angeles, where I have lived for the past 10 years. Most salient, of course, is the trial involving four police officers accused of using excessive force under the color of authority in violating the civil rights of Rodney King, which has been in full swing for several weeks. High-profile coverage in both national and local media has been insistent (some say, irresponsibly unrelenting and inflammatory). Not surprisingly, here in LA, one predictable communication effect has been a definitive circumscribing of the conversational/interactional agenda: Not a day passes among family, friends, acquaintances, and strangers without some mention of the progress of the trial or the impending verdict or the projected aftermath.

This second of two trials of these officers comes 2 years after the beating of Rodney King, an event that was videotaped, commodified, distributed, circulated for mass consumption, and inscribed on the national consciousness (if not its conscience). And this second trial comes 1 year after the acquittal of these same officers in the trial whose verdict sparked the worst civil unrest and violence in modern U.S. history. The material losses and the palpable fear, cynicism, and anger among people of color and whites alike make up only part of the unhappy legacy. It is not merely coincidental, many have claimed, that hate crimes, most especially those targeting people of color, skyrocketed during 1992 in Los Angeles County, reaching an all-time high. Add to this complex of forces an unyielding recession in California and the 1990 census report on income differentials (issued in early 1993) that demonstrably confirms the ever-widening gap between the haves and have-nots (with the most conspicuous discrepancy between whites and African Americans and Latinos). While it is neither sensible nor warranted to claim any sort of simple determination between and among these phenomena, they are, still,

Correspondence and requests for reprints: Gordon Nakagawa, Department of Speech Communication, California State University, Northridge, CA 91330.

Communication Yearbook 17, pp. 187-192

very much part of a specific conjuncture of history, race, class, and locale that structure our everyday cultural sense-making and interaction.

I open my commentary with these observations as a way of situating and contextualizing my remarks about Carbaugh's lucid and insightful treatment of the interactional construction of cultural personhood and the attendant coding of (U.S.) American dignity. In this commentary, I wish to offer, in Carbaugh's terms, my own brief explication, elaboration, ratification (and, occasionally, a refusal) of the predicating assumptions and larger implications of his perspective. In constructing a position (so to speak), I will provide a synopsis of his essay, followed by a series of questions that I hope will usefully enter into and continue what I regard as a dialogue with Carbaugh (or, more properly, with the discursively constructed position and cultural meanings articulated in his essay).

AN EXPLICATION OF
CARBAUGH'S CULTURAL PRAGMATICS

In his careful, systematic inquiry into the discursive construction of personhood, Donal Carbaugh usefully continues and elaborates a theoretical position and attendant line of research initiated a decade ago. Creatively synthesizing the contributions of Harré, Hymes, Goffman, Geertz, and others, Carbaugh develops an ethnolinguistic perspective on the cultural pragmatics by which symbolic interaction gives rise to different kinds of persons, relations, and feelings, all constructed by and within a coherent system of meanings.

Operating out of a triadic structure of "person" (conceived as the active agent-in-society), "self" (consciousness, the locus of experience), and "individual" (the material or physical being), Carbaugh focuses attention on the constitution of personhood in the activities and forms of cultural communication. Two intersecting but analytically separable roles constitute personhood: the "cultural" (specifying features such as nationality, gender, or class) and the "social" (elaborating the cultural role through various relational positions). Implicative of a web of social relations, and reciprocally invested, these roles converge in the interactive accomplishment of particular kinds of agents-in-society.

Constitutive of the "positions" that persons can occupy are discursive activities that make possible assessments of legitimacy, which varies "systematically by contexts, among specific participants, on particular occasions" (p. 164). Conversational moves and dimensions that negotiate positioning include actions involving explication, elaboration, implication, ratification, and rejection. Each move or dimension positions the personhood of self and others in culturally specific ways.

Significant uses of these dimensions include the potential for an explanatory accounting of "voice" (or its absence), whenever "a speaker explicates, or implicates, and elaborates him- or herself as a kind of person, and if further interaction ratifies that speaker as such, we could claim the speaker indeed had a socially efficacious *voice*; that is, the speaker was able to speak, spoke, was heard, and socially validated as such" (pp. 166-167). Similarly, these dimensions may be employed to tease out the bases for contested positions (as in a debate or controversy) or to make sense of contradictory conversational messages.

Finally, in addition to conversational dimensions, Carbaugh identifies two fundamental social dimensions. The first centers on power/control instantiated in equal/unequal access to resources; the second addresses intimacy/solidarity issues manifest in close/distant relations. Any and all combinations are possible, with consequent changes in positions, social relations, and institutions. These dimensions prove to be particularly useful in "contexts where social standings are being contested" (p. 168).

The bulk of the essay comprises an extended examination of (U.S.) American personhood through a meticulous analysis of excerpted discourse from the *Donahue* talk show. Carbaugh convincingly demonstrates the viability of his theoretical scheme while simultaneously generating considerable insight into (a) the complex positioning of the person as "an individual," (b) a presupposed normative orientation away from "relational constraints" in the direction of "independence" of and for the individual's "self," and (c) a refusal to allow one's identity to be arbitrarily constrained by "social roles," institutional boundaries, or historical determinants.

Carbaugh summarizes his analysis by identifying a "code of dignity," which he generalizes from the symbols, forms, and meanings consistent with the positioning of (U.S.) American personhood. Counterposed to a "code of honor" are social positions that stress not personal uniqueness but "institutional and historical precedence." The consequence is the construction and implication of deep structural differences in the cultural coding of "social interaction, persons, and life itself."

Toward the conclusion of the essay, Carbaugh highlights the potential and real ramifications of cross-cultural comparative analyses of the (U.S.) American code of dignity when differential coding and positionings are constructed. This discussion broaches significant cross-cultural and intercultural issues.

INTERROGATIONS AND IMPLICATIONS

In this section, I pose questions and explore some implications of Carbaugh's theoretical commitments. My concerns are twofold: (a) the significance of historical specificity in cultural analysis and (b) the predicating assumption of consensus as grounding cultural communication and thus implicitly serving particular privileged (normative) interests.

(1) What is the significance of historical specificity in analyzing discursive practices, subject positions, and cultural meaning systems? While Carbaugh

acknowledges that "discursive constructions are historically grounded" (p. 160), he appears to view history as largely unproblematic, that is, as simply a received backdrop for the contingent, transitory, improvisational construction of cultural positions and meanings. Far from recommending a pursuit of cultural origins, my appeal here is for what Foucault (1979) has termed a "history of the present" (p. 31). Critical historicizing in this sense does not aim at identifying origins of cultural phenomena; nor does it seek to establish a simple determinism or even a correlation between the current interests and politics and diachronic events in specific communities. Rather, the goal is to explicate the configuration of power, knowledge, and discourse that gathers past events, present actions, and future possibilities into a condensation of sociocultural tradition as it makes itself felt concretely in our current projects.

San Juan (1992), following Gramsci's lead, notes: "Historical specification requires that any conjuncture or cross section of life be analyzed as concretely as possible, concreteness being a function of the multiple determinations that reciprocally interact and so overdetermine each other, marking what Gramsci calls an ethico-political catharsis" (p. 60). The concern here, with Gramsci (cited in Said, 1979), is to begin the process of accounting for the "inventory of traces" that structures our current social and cultural order.

(2) To what extent does consensus as a predicating assumption in cultural communication implicitly serve privileged (normative) social interests? Carbaugh maintains that an overarching system of coherence makes intelligible a community's utterances and actions. This system, Carbaugh continues, legitimates particular social positions and relations "even if contested." While this formulation offers a useful way of investigating the commonsense, consensual meanings, activities, and interactional forms operating in a given community, it overlooks (and thus privileges) the hegemony of a sociocultural formation that is "structured in dominance" (see Hall, 1980).

My concern here is not to reduce the totality of a sociocultural formation to a "dominant ideology" but to reopen the question of how multiple, contradictory ideological discourses articulate with each other in complex societies. In particular, I suggest that processes of (de)legitimation and contestation are central, not peripheral, to the positioning of cultural subjects in discursive activities. Accounting for these intersecting ideologies, as they are actualized in discursive practices, requires consideration of what Hall (1985) identifies as

> an interdiscursive field generated by at least three different contradictions (class, race, gender), each of which has a different history, a different mode of operation; each divides and classifies the world in different ways. Then it would be necessary, in any specific formation, to analyze the way in which class, race and gender are articulated with one another to establish particular condensed social positions. (p. 111)

Discourse, as Carbaugh consistently observes, is always socially and culturally situated; but it is also politically inscribed, privileging particular meanings, relations, and forms of interactions, while silencing others. Hence the "agonistic" accomplishment of subjugated or oppositional subject positions in our discursive practices warrants careful attention. Racialized, gendered, class-based subjects are positioned not in a neutral discourse but in a complex discursive formation that privileges certain interests, forms, meanings, and practices over others. For instance, a politically invested explication of cultural practices of racial domination, according to Cornel West (1990, cited in San Juan, 1992), would entail "a microinstitutional or localized analysis of the mechanisms that sustain white supremacist discourse in the everyday life of non-Europeans (including the ideological production of certain kinds of selves, the means by which alien and degrading normative styles, aesthetic ideals, psychosexual identities, and group perceptions are constituted) and ways in which resistance occurs" (p. 12). What is needed, then, is an analysis of the social differences (e.g., race, gender, class, or sexual orientation) as they articulate with the structural conditions and forces that sustain relations of domination. A critical (and not merely descriptive) examination of this continuous deployment of power in the interactional accomplishment of sociocultural positions would go a long way in recovering the dissensus and conflict that keep a single discourse from becoming self-evident and dominant.

CONCLUSION

In continuing a thoughtfully developed perspective on the relation between culture and communication, Donal Carbaugh usefully and productively explores the discursive construction of personhood and the concomitant American code of dignity. Convincingly demonstrating the improvisational constitution of positioned subjects and of cultural meaning systems, Carbaugh's strength lies in his unwavering attention to discursive activities that give rise to coherence, community, and consensus.

The questions that I have raised about Carbaugh's perspective may be more a matter of his commitment to develop a descriptive theory than of any singularly intrinsic shortcomings. Nevertheless, the seemingly ahistorical treatment of the site and event of interaction and the consensus model that effectively elides structures of dominance that circumscribe discursive and interactional practices strike me as unresolved, problematic issues.

I began this commentary with an inventory of fragments that compose part of the historical context in which I have found myself positioned. Instantiated by these social divisions and structural inequities is a particular historical conjuncture, which elevates particular interests over others. Our attempts to erase, forget, or ignore this sociocultural formation that is structured in dominance only serves to fix and essentialize various subject positions. In the absence of a critical self-examination of this formation, persons/identities continue to be constituted in ways that invite reproduction of a hegemonic order. Our task, it seems to me, is to recover the suppressed conflict and to restore the voice, the face, and the dignity of the historically and socially marginalized—without then privileging difference and dissensus.

REFERENCES

Foucault, M. (1979). *Discipline and punish* (A. M. Sheridan, Trans.). New York: Vintage.
Hall, S. (1980). Race, articulation and societies structured in dominance. In UNESCO (Ed.), *Sociological theories: Race and colonialism* (pp. 305-345). Paris: UNESCO.
Hall, S. (1985). Signification, representation, ideology: Althusser and the post-structuralist debates. *Critical Studies in Mass Communication, 2,* 91-114.
Said, E. W. (1979). *Orientalism.* New York: Random House.
San Juan, E., Jr. (1992). *Racial formations/critical transformations: Articulations of power in ethnic and racial studies in the United States.* Atlantic Highlands, NJ: Humanities.
West, C. (1990). Toward a socialist theory of racism. In C. West, *Socialist perspectives on race.* New York: Democratic Socialists of America.

5 Narratives of Individual and Organizational Identities

BARBARA CZARNIAWSKA-JOERGES
Lund University, Sweden

This essay reports on a series of empirical studies conducted in public sector organizations in Sweden between 1985 and 1990. The analysis for these studies employs a framework that combines institutional theory with a narrative approach. "Identity" is considered, along with the "market" and the "state," as a modern institution. The analysis of the ways in which a modern identity is constructed supports the claim that identity has a narrative character. This perspective is then applied to interpretation of developments in public sector organizations, whose identity has been challenged and is currently reformulated.

IN spite of the claim that machines and organisms are the most popular images of organization (Morgan, 1986), the conception of organizations as *superpersons* is another metaphor that is as popular and taken for granted. This superperson is seen as a decision maker, understood sometimes as the leader, sometimes the management group or the organization as a collective (Czarniawska-Joerges, 1993).

ORGANIZATIONS AS SUPERPERSONS

Conceptualizing organizations as superpersons is probably most typical for apologetic theories that present organizations as consensus based. Accordingly, they tell us how organizations learn, unlearn, produce strategies, and all the things that individuals usually do. The following quotation illustrates this image. "As an organization gets older, it learns more and more about coping with its environment and with its internal problems of communication and coordination. At least this is the normal pattern, and the normal organization tries to perpetuate the fruits of its learning by formalizing them" (Starbuck, 1983, p. 480).

Correspondence and requests for reprints: Barbara Czarniawska-Joerges, P.O. Box 7080, Lund University, S-220 07 Lund, Sweden.

Communication Yearbook 17, pp. 193-221

The constructionist view espoused in this essay attempts to problematize this image of organizations. Organizations are not people at all (whether aggregates, collectives, or superpersons) but *sets of collective action* undertaken in an effort to shape the world and human lives (Czarniawska-Joerges, 1992a). This definition, like all others, is related to a certain understanding of human nature, namely, that "there is nothing to people except what has been socialized into them—their ability to use language, and thereby to exchange beliefs and desires with other people" (Rorty, 1989, p. 177).

By using language, people endow their action (and inaction) with meaning. Consequently, understanding organizations calls for an understanding of meanings ascribed to and produced by a given set of collective actions. Both actions and their meanings are socially constructed in exchanges taking place between people. Human beings are social *constructors* and organizations are social *constructions.*

While my definition and assumptions are arbitrary, they serve as a useful point of departure to examine the "organization-as-superperson" metaphor. If the everyday and theoretical languages insist on certain usages, it is meaningless to claim that they "miss the point" or "use a wrong definition." One has to scrutinize the context of such usages to understand their emergence. A promising route is that of conceiving of individuality as a modern institution.

INDIVIDUALITY AS AN INSTITUTION

Individual identity is a modern institution, claims Meyer (1986). But what is an institution? For current purposes, the definition adopted by Meyer, Boli, and Thomas ("institutions as cultural rules giving collective meaning and value to particular entities and activities"; 1987, p. 13) is not adequate because it begs an explanation of what the "cultural rules" are. Another kind of problem is created by Mary Douglas's definition ("institution [as] legitimized social grouping"; 1986, p. 46), whereby both institutions and organizations are groups of people, and it is hard to say how they differ. Berger and Luckmann's definition is more appropriate. They argue that "institution posits that actions of type X will be performed by actors of type X" (1966/1971, p. 72). In their work, a constructive reciprocity is assumed; that is, performing an X-type of action leads to the perception that a given actor belongs (or aspires to) type X and vice versa.

For the purposes here, *institution* can be simply considered a pattern of social action. In our case, *actors* are, in fact, "legitimized social groupings." Actors include work units, profit centers, departments, corporations and public organizations, associations of organizations, and all those whose interactions "constitute a recognized area of institutional life," anything that can be called an "organization field" (DiMaggio & Powell, 1983, p. 148).

Actors leave or are being pushed out of the field whereas new actors arrive (witness the powerful entry of environmentalists into political, industrial, and academic fields). Action patterns, in spite of their stability and repetitiveness, which earn them the name "institution," change both in their form and in their meaning. Finally, the process itself is recursive. Actors perform actions; actions create actors or, rather, their identities.

One conventional school of thought claims that an identity is to be found in the individuals themselves, whether in their genotype or a "soul." To acquire an identity means therefore to find one's true "I" and exhibit it. The argument is of course much more complex than this (see Bruner's, 1990, discussion of "essential" and "conceptual" self). This perspective has been severely criticized by the social environment school, who claim that the society creates individuals as persons. This "nature or nurture" debate is bypassed in the constructivist thinking where a creation of identity is a two-way process, an idea that begins, most likely, with George H. Mead's "transactional self" (Bruner, 1990; Mead, 1934). Identity is created by individuals' interactions with the social environment where the individual comes, indeed, with his or her genotype, and the society, with all its rules, institutions, values, and, above all, language. In this process of construction, not only individual identities are created but the society is reproduced or changed.

May this reasoning be used in relation to organizations? Using it, we come to a possible answer as to why the image of organization as a superperson persists. In the first place, the notion of an individual as an institutional myth developed within rational theories of choice is core to organization theory (Meyer et al., 1987). Second, and as a result of it, organizations are personified to embody the critical notion of accountability (Douglas, 1990). This is required because individuality as an institution fits together with other modern institutions—the state and the market. The invention of a "legal person," which makes organizations accountable both as citizens and as consumers and producers is a necessary link between the three and is then reflected in the everyday language. Thus, in organizational literature, there is an equivalent of the "essential self" definition, where an organization's identity is seen as that which its members believe to be its distinctive, central, and enduring characteristics (Albert & Whetten, 1985; Alvesson & Björkman, 1992; Dutton & Dukerich, 1991).

Both in everyday language and in organization theory, this operation is mostly seen as unproblematic; organizations "make decisions," "learn," "unlearn," and "behave ethically" (or not, as the case may be). In this essay, we shall problematize the notion of organization as superperson by setting it in the context of *modernity* and, in this light, examine the fruitfulness of the analogy between the organizational and personal identities. Its promise lies in the fact that the notion of individuality as modern institution both depsychologizes the concept of "identity" (Bruner, 1990; Gergen & Davis, 1985) and frees it from a sociological determinism. It also decouples, and this may be the most difficult aspect to accept, the notion of identity from subjectivity and consciousness (which are, for example, still closely connected in Berger, Berger, & Kellner, 1974). It socializes the notion through and through by eschewing the duality of the "agency" and "structure," in the way radical constructivists do (Fuller, in press; Latour, 1992).

To understand organizational life, for example, one must grasp its social character, the way it is produced by human and nonhuman actors. Identities are one product of such a construction, being produced in interactions, where people account for their actions by placing them in a relevant narrative (MacIntyre, 1981/1990). The individual identity, a typical institution of "high modernity" (Giddens, 1991), persists through an ability to narrate one's life, formulate it into a narrative composed of terms that will be accepted by the relevant audience (on the importance of rhetoric in this process, see Cheney, 1992). But questions remain. Which terms are accepted and what audience is relevant? These will change with time and place so that we have to limit our analysis to the *modern identity narrative.*

THE MODERN IDENTITY NARRATIVE

Traditionally, one speaks about a "form" and a "content" or "substance" of a narrative. This dichotomy unavoidably brings to mind an image of the form as being external, holding the contents inside ("a container"). Thus it seems perfectly possible to analyze the form irrelevant of the content, the contents irrelevant of the form. From such a point of view, surely any narrative, any text, has a content, a core, an inside? Surely any form, any shell, any vessel can be holding many different contents? To those who believe in such a separation, no other position makes much sense.

This misapprehension causes many troubles in criticism but even more when transferred to the analysis of identity as a narrative. Thus we shall replace it with a terminology borrowed from Russian formalists (Bakhtin & Medvedev, 1928/1985) and speak about *material* and *device* in the place of form and content. With *material* and *device,* this outer-inner dichotomy vanishes and thus it is easier to see why the one cannot be considered without the other. In addition, their metaphorical character attracts more attention to their analytical possibilities, whereas form and content are truly dead metaphors (Lakoff & Johnson, 1980). Note that discussing any material presumes a device—a formless material does not exist.

In analyzing a text, we may choose a device other than its author—indeed, we often do so, but we are simply constructing a new text with the original material for the next analysis. By the same token, whenever we set out to analyze a "device," it simply becomes material to be elaborated with the use of a metadevice, as it were. These metaphors coming from the vocabulary of culture (work) rather than nature (force) make the essence of the operation more clear. Materials are usually denoted by uncountable nouns (*wood, wool, concrete*), which even grammatically call for a device to make them into analyzable units. Devices are, obviously, always made of some kind of material. This makes the distinction arbitrary and spurious, its usefulness judged only by the purpose at hand. In fact, the following discussion of identity's material and devices begins with a typical "device material," which combines the traits of the two.

Modern Identity: The Material

What is "an identity" in this conception? According to Vytautas Kavolis (as quoted by R. H. Brown, 1989), the concept of identity encompasses three elements:

an overall coherence between the individual's experience and the way this experience is expressed,

a memory—on the part of the individual and others—of a continuity in the course of the individual's life, and

a conscious but not excessive (artificial or manipulative) commitment to the manner in which the individual understands and deals with his or her "self."

Kavolis evokes the concepts of opinion, memory, and self-awareness, thus emphasizing that it is not a matter of identity as "essence" but an impression of identity that a self-narrative achieves or fails to achieve. Hence the peculiarity of modern identity: based on interaction, it aims to achieve an impression of individuality, that is, independence from other people's reactions. If we contrast modern identity with, for example, the one typical of so-called heroic societies, we notice that the latter was composed on the basis of *particularity* (roughly put, a social stance) and *accountability* (of an individual toward the community, not toward the abstract societal institutions; MacIntyre, 1981/1990), both related to the community and not, as with modern identity, the individual's own life history.

There are further specifications of a modern identity that distinguish it from any other historical form of identity: *self-respect, efficiency, autonomy* (internal locus of control in psychological terms) and *flexibility,* that is, the absence of a long-term commitment to one and the same object (Meyer, 1986). These can again be contrasted with, for example, traditional Roman virtues (Pitkin, 1984): *pietas* (reverence for the past), *gravitas* (bearing the sacred weight of the past), *dignitas* (a manner worthy of one's task and station), and *constantia* (faithfulness to tradition).

It is modern identity's individual and not community-based character that makes *autobiography* the most appropriate device analogy. As one of the leading specialists in the field, Philippe Lejeune (1989), put it:

Through autobiographical literature appears the conception of the person and the individualism characteristic of our societies; we would find nothing similar in ancient societies, or in so-called primitive societies, or even in other societies contemporaneous with our own, like the Chinese communist society where the individual is . . . prevented from looking at his personal life like private property that is capable of having exchange value. (pp. 161-162)

Of interest (but not surprising), modern identity as described by Berger et al. (1974) tallies more with what nowadays is described as a postmodern identity and thus it is treated together with the latter topic in the final section of this essay.

Modern Identity: The Device

Treating identity as a narrative—or, more properly, identity construction as a continuous process of narration where both the narrator and the audience formulate, edit, applaud, and refuse various elements of the ever-produced narrative—leads us to the literary genre of autobiography. In fact, this is an analogy that works both ways: Elizabeth W. Bruss (1976) presents autobiographies as an institutional way of creating personal identities, thus proposing to see text as action, much as I propose to see action as text:

All reading (or writing) involves us in choice: we choose to pursue a style or a subject matter, to struggle with or against a design. We also choose, as passive as it all may seem, to take part in an interaction, and it is here that generic labels have their use. The genre does not tell us the style or the construction of a text as much as how we should expect to "take" that style or mode of construction— what force it should have for us. And this force is derived from a kind of action that text is taken to be. Surrounding any text are implicit contextual conditions, participants involved in transmitting and receiving it, and the nature of these implicit conditions and the roles of the participants affects the status of the information contained in the text. (Bruss, 1976, p. 4)

Genre is a system of action that became institutionalized, and it is recognizable by repetition. Its meaning stems from its place within symbolic systems making up literature and culture (and therefore is diacritical, like that of the other signs). In the same sense that we can characterize the modern identity only by contrasting it with nonmodern identities, we may see autobiography as a genre acquiring specificity by difference from other genres. This permanence and autonomy (Lejeune, 1989), constitutive of a genre, become with time forces impeding its change and transformation. And yet, genres are never homogeneous and clearly separate. To begin with, several textual strategies are possible within one and the same genre (Harari, 1979). These can be characterized by a role that is given in the text to three personages typical of the genre: an Author, a Narrator, a Character (Eco, 1990; Lejeune, 1989). I shall illustrate these in the examples relating to construction of organizational identity.

One typical strategy is that of an omnipresent Author, who claims responsibility both for the acts reported in the text (and supposed to be taking place in "reality") and for the text itself. This strategy is often taken by the founders and the leaders of big corporations. When there is a ghostwriter involved, like in the "Iaccoca story," it is truly ghostly in that the writer is not allowed to appear in the text (Lejeune, 1989). The text and the world in the text have the same creator and, by the same token, create the author's identity. One could claim that this is the most pure form of autobiography as identity creation, where a person, an organization, and a text all become one.

An introduction of a Narrator is a common device. There is a person who tells the story, but the story could have been written by somebody else, although it might be the narrator acting within the text in the role of the author. The distance created gives more room for manipulation: The narrator can praise the author in a way the author could not do herself but also can distance herself if necessary. In terms of organizational identity, this strategy opens up many possibilities. A narrator can be, for example, a PR officer who is telling a story of a mighty author—a founder, a CEO. Or the narrator might be only a sample of a collective author—an organization.

The strategy that is most complex and therefore gives most room to a skillful writer is one that introduces a Character. Here the possibilities of distancing, identification, and self-reflection are limitless. The three can be one but they can also be separate if needed. In *A Portrait of the Artist as a Young Man,* the mature James Joyce is the narrator, the young James Joyce is the character, whereas James Joyce the writer authors both of them. These actorial shifting operations (Latour, 1988) are actually easier to perform in relation to an organizational identity because of its assumed collective character. Additionally, while the shifting of personal identity might sin against the coherence or continuity requirement or else put into doubt the reality claim, narrating organizational identities sails clear from all these dangers. There can be several and different authors (for example, top executives); the narrators can distance themselves at their will; and there are a variety of characters accessible without the danger of producing a schizophrenic impression. Here is, then, the point when organizational identity and personal identity are at their closest and at their furthest: An organization cannot be legitimately claiming autism or boast of defective "other perception" ("nobody understands us"; Bruss, 1976). Organizational identity makes sense in relation to institutions of market and state, and one of them must "understand it." The process of identity formulation is always an interactive one and there are rules to this interaction as there are rules to the material and device with which to form a modern identity.

To sum up, I am proposing a concept of organizational identity, which is based on four elements:

a. a definition of individual identity as *modern institution* (i.e., temporal and local),

b. an (institutionalized) metaphor of *organization as person,*

c. a description of an individual identity as *emerging from interactions* between actors rather than existing as a form of an essence that is consequently exhibited, and

d. an analogy between organizational narratives and autobiographies as *narratives constituting identity* ("autobiographical acts").

Let us now move from the concepts to three exemplifications in organizational practice. The first case relates a refusal of a group of organizational actors to accept an established identity of the other; the second examines the particulars of identity formulation and change; and the third illustrates a massive effort on the part of the relevant organization field. The three cases come from separate studies conducted within the Swedish public sector in the years 1985 to 1992.

THE BEAUTY CONTEST

In 1976, after a long period of Social-Democratic rule in Sweden, a bourgeois government came to power inheriting a budget deficit that since then has continued to grow. It has been repeatedly stated that the prime responsibility for the poor shape of the public sector rests with the public administration (it was not until the 1990s that the politicians were added to the list of the accused). The so-called bureaucrats, control greedy and inefficient, spent taxpayers' money in an effort to control them with an ever-increasing strength. The private sector became the positive hero of the Swedish nation as the one who survived world crisis thanks to its thrift and in spite of the obnoxious state interventionism (which, to an observer, looks more like a repeated bailing out of the companies in crisis). The public sector must then follow the example and become economical and service oriented, decentralize power, and strive for efficiency. It was in this context that I conducted a study of the general directors of Swedish state agencies upon which the following description is based (Czarniawska, 1985).

When the Social Democrats came back into power in 1982, they found a budget deficit of 68 million Skr and the guilty in place: state administration (Siven, 1984). Domestic programs were searched for cutback budgets, savings, rationalization, and so on. The private sector, previously a profit-greedy villain, became a hero, a model, and a source of inspiration. In the eyes of the audience, the public administration went from being the Public Benefactor to the Public Devil.

Traditional Identity Challenged

The identity of the public sector organizations, taken for granted for more than 50 years (if the 1938 agreement between labor and industry is taken as the turning point), suddenly became problematic as it became clear to both politicians and administrators that the government can change and that no economic growth can continue forever. The context changed, and the narrative of success began to show at the seams.

The state agencies were told that even production of values, the only domain of some of them, can be seen as a process that shares many similarities with other production processes. And the most common trait of all production processes is that they can be analyzed in terms of their effectiveness (assessment of output) and in terms of efficiency (costs versus benefits). This kind of analysis, even if not completely alien to the public administration, is best developed within the private sector. Thus the private sector became the most obvious source of inspiration for the new identity formation, but not, however, without problems.

The outcome should be measured, but how? Is money a good output measure for most agencies? Furthermore, the measures are meaningful only when they can be compared with a standard. In the private sector, competitors are such a standard, but that can be applied only to some agencies like the State Rail and the like. The others were looking for such standards—could, for example, the public agencies in other Nordic countries be used?

In the terms used in this essay, the material of one type of identity (economic categories) became a metaphorical device for another. But "efficiency," "cost-benefit analysis," "profit-orientation," and such are not free-floating devices. Separated from a coherent narrative where they belonged, they lead to awkward linguistic inventions and sometimes even more awkward reality (see, e.g., Rombach, 1991).

The split between the material (public services) and the device (economic categories) was only one of the problems in construction of the new identity. Another was the problem of double identity, expressed in the uncertainty as to who the narrator is and who the audience is. It has been discovered, to the surprise of many, that public administration is a producer and, consequently, also employer, a utilizer of human labor. The state agencies considered themselves immune to problems related to this exploitation, the need for workers' protection. A challenge to traditional identity brought to light not only a realization of a new role, of a new material to be taken into account, but also the awareness that there were not many devices to elaborate it in a satisfactory way. The private sector became again the model of consistency, continuation, and self-awareness, even if the accompanying ethical judgment is somewhat ambiguous. It is expedient to be able to hire, fire, and restaff the personnel according to organizational needs, but is it moral? Or, in terms of double identity, are state organizations the master of the public or a public servant?

The ambiguity is not new; it is the arrangement that has been reversed. Within the previously legitimate identity, the administration had to become a Public Master to better fulfill its role as a Public Servant: a paradoxical sweep but with a great rhetorical value. According to the current demands, public sector organizations are to become Organization Masters to remain Public Servants. The inconsistency was moved inside: To serve citizens, the public employer must tightly control them as employees. As a result of the requirement of coherence, the narrative became fragmented.

How to Tell the Control Story

In the study conducted in 43 state agencies (Czarniawska, 1985), my interlocutors—the general directors of the agencies—were well aware of the demand for change put on the identity of their agencies and the internal and external communication problems it created. The central issue was that of control. Is the agencies' identity basically that of the controlled or of the controllers?

Many of my interviews began by a spontaneous rendering of what the interlocutors perceived as a specificity of the Swedish system: the formal independence of agencies that, unlike those in other Western countries, were not the internal organizational units of ministries but separate bodies whose autonomy was guaranteed by the constitution. Legally, however, nothing prevents the ministries from steering and controlling the agencies (Tarchys, 1983). Are the agencies then autonomous are not?

Paraphrasing one of my interlocutors, I introduced a notion of the myth of independence, which is a very successful narrative strategy. In reality, the ministries have at their disposal three basic instruments of formal control: budget, appointment of executives, and special commissions (task forces). Applied fully and directly, they do indeed provide an ample opportunity for control. A shared myth of agencies' independence, however, allows for creating, within the same legal framework, a range of relations varying from a strong dependence to a strong independence. Relative to a constellation of factors such as the personalities of the main actors, the historical precedents, the political weight of the agency, the political weight of the ministry—a ministry can fully use existing instruments and actually if not formally make an agency into an internal unit of a ministry. In an opposite situation, general directors use the same instruments as their means of control. Budget becomes a tool for obtaining a minister's commitment, to be called upon during the final battle with the Ministry of Finance. Some general directors propose their candidates for top executive positions within the agency while the ministry only confirms the choice. Some even choose their own positions. Between these two extremes, there are a wide range of situations in which the formal instruments of control become the bargaining fields. Needless to say, the informal contacts decide on the actual contents of the formal processes, whereas the "myth of independence" puts a nice historical gloss on the narrative.

The challenge that came from the private sector can be compared to a challenge to a person to prove the consistency of words and deeds. But a narrative of identity is expected to produce an impression of coherence, continuation, and self-awareness, and not to stand a "reality test." If we look at actual actions, they often appear incoherent, disjointed, and with few signs of awareness. This is because

> the individual is an institutional myth evolving out of the rationalized theories of economic, political and cultural action. This myth leads people to posture as individuals, in a loosely coupled way, and they can be fairly convincing about it. . . . This enactment of the institutionalized theory of rational behavior is rarely troubled by the internal inconsistencies and self-contradictions that are so typical of human action. (Meyer et al., 1987, p. 26)

The private sector seems not to be playing fair, claiming that public administration has a double face. Actually, there is no reason to expect fair play from a reader or a spectator. A typical reader of an autobiography, like a spectator of an autobiographical act, "has a tendency to reduce the ambiguity instead of analyzing it; he [or she] wants to know clearly 'which of the two is speaking' " (Lejeune, 1989, p. 56). Also, as usual, there is more to the story than meets the eye.

Whose Story Is This?

One can say that the private sector usurps the role of the narrator and even the author, relegating the public administration to a side character in its own autobiography. No wonder that the public sector organizations have trouble formulating a new identity on the competitor's terms.

This is, however, but a mirror reflection of a manoeuvre successfully accomplished by the public administration in the 1960s. As the social problems were to be solved once and for all due to the efforts coming from the public sector, the private sector seemed of no importance. Those were the times when the public sector was the narrator and the author, with the private sector lurking backstage as a shady character.

Is this seesaw between the narratives the only possibility? Do both sectors need to define their identities at the expense of each other? A possible alternative is a diacritical definition of both sectors as complementing each other and giving meaning to each other's activities. Heilbroner (1988) imagines a future historian (a narrator) who thus perceives the authorship of our times:

> A single socioeconomic whole where the task of authority maintenance and of production are divided into two spheres of responsibility and competence. The economic responsibility of the private sphere can be defined as production of those services and goods which can be produced with profit, whereas its political responsibility lies in maintaining the societal discipline in the matter of work habits. . . . In this light, the political task of the public sphere lies in acting in accordance with the ancient privilege—that of maintaining the state's authority—

whereas its economic function consists in producing all those goods and services which are needed by the socioeconomic whole but impossible to produce within the private sphere as they cannot be produced with profit. (pp. 41-42)

This is a coauthorship of the socioeconomic sphere, as it were, maintained even by changing narrators. This is a matter of a future possibility rather than today's reality. As to the latter, I ended my exploration of state agencies by writing the following allegorical tale of two sisters, making use of narrative knowledge.

*   *   *

Once upon a time there were two sisters who, like all siblings, sometimes fought and sometimes were nice to each other. They lived together in a big country. One was called Patricia while the other's name was Ophelia (the name an allusion to *offentlig sektor,* or "public sector," in Swedish).

Ophelia was the pretty, the lively, the interesting one of the two. She had many friends and admirers. Neighbors came by just to say hello to her. Everybody loved Ophelia.

One day somebody knocked at the door. Two dark knights stood there, one's name was Oil Crisis and the other's Budget Deficit. "Welcome," said Ophelia, who opened the door. But they went past her and started talking to Patricia in confidence.

"What's wrong with me?" Ophelia asked a sympathetic neighbor. "Haven't the faintest, but recently Patricia has gone out to meet a consultant very often indeed. Maybe you should go and talk to him too." And this is what Ophelia did.

"To begin with," the consultant said, "your clothes are in bad taste." Ophelia was surprised. "What do you mean? I have comfortable clogs, well-fitting jeans, and my favorite college sweatshirt on!" "Nobody wears those anymore," said the consultant. "Worse still, you are too fat for elegant clothes."

"How can you say that! People used to say that I look healthy and relaxed!"

"This was when you were young and fresh. Besides, you look awful without any makeup!"

"I thought that water and soap were the best friends of a girl!"

"No," said consultants. "Apart from diamonds, the best is Lancôme. Soap contains alkalines and God knows what water contains nowadays."

And this is how it went. While Patricia met interesting strangers from all over the world, Ophelia went more and more often to the consultant.

*   *   *

Let us follow her there.

IDENTITY AS DO-IT-YOURSELF KIT

In the 1980s, Swedish public sector organizations became clients of major consulting companies and then began to form consulting companies for their own purposes. Although much of it concerned technical matters, especially EDP, the major part of it, and the focus of this section, was management consulting. The following analysis is supported by a study I conducted of management consulting in public sector organizations (Czarniawska-Joerges, 1990).

In the late 1970s, the Swedish Ministry of Industry employed the Boston Consulting Group to help them plan industrial policies. County governments, state agencies, and local authorities began to pay high fees to well-known consultants to restructure their organizations, to prepare cutback programs, or, more generally, to instill "economic thinking" in organizations (Brunsson & Olsen, 1992). Typically, for public sector operations, central permission was given:

> At the end of August, 1984, the Ministry of Civil Affairs, represented by the Minister . . . and the State Secretary . . . organized a meeting with about 20 consulting companies, the majority of which were privately owned, but some of them were subsidiaries of multibranched Statskonsult AB [a state-owned consulting company]. Other participants were representatives of other Ministries and some central agencies. The aim was to propose an inventory of consulting competence which can be used in works of the Ministry of Civil Affairs on what was expected to be a large government bill concerning the public sector. (Premfors, Eklund, & Larsson, 1985, p. 6)

And large it became: At the conference organized by the National Audit Bureau in 1989, "Good Advice or Only Expensive?" a sum of 6 billion Skr (about $1 billion U.S.) was mentioned as an annual consulting cost in the public sector (Czarniawska-Joerges, Gustafsson, & Björkegren, 1990).

What was the main attraction of management consulting for the public sector organizations? To understand this, one must know more about what is called "an investigation culture," for many years a trademark of the public sector. Said one consultant:

> What the public sector is good at, and what they devote a great deal of their time to, is to investigate things, establishing a basis for a decision. The report is then distributed for formal comments and there is then a long process where people sit around and change and correct the text of the document until finally it goes up for decision. This drawn-out process reduces the propensity-for-change that is implicit in the whole thing, so that finally they are left with some sort of diluted document which some board has to decide upon and then do something about it.

What do consultants offer instead? Let us take a closer look to see how management consulting can help in establishing a new identity.

Name-Giving and Labels

It is popular knowledge that the first, and perhaps the most important, phase of consulting is that of making a diagnosis. This is either a cause or a result of two common similes: the work of consultants as compared to that of physicians ("company doctors") or that of car mechanics ("fixing the system").

An alternative understanding can be reached via other similes. In my study, I compared consultants to traveling merchants who sell tools that produce control in the form of shared meaning, which is necessary for any collective action. During the first contact with an organization, merchants have to establish what is needed or what can be sold (these might or might not be the same things). To do that, a merchant/consultant must give names to the most important matters, must introduce a preliminary order in the existing system of meaning, must establish a *starting point identity,* as it were, for the client. And so, for instance, a consultant might say: "You used to be an 'appropriation authority' but now you are to become an 'assignment authority.' Your problem is the misfit of goals and functions. Your internal organization did not follow the change in your identity. Our main target will be the accounting system" (from an interview with a consultant).

How does one arrive at a set of successful labels? There appear to exist two schools of thought. The "doctor/mechanic" school claims that labels must be authoritatively attributed by consultants, the rationale being that the "patients" do not like to face unpleasant truths given a choice (alternatively, that it does not make much sense to talk to a car to establish the defect). Also, there are usually some labels already in place and in conflict with each other. Another school, more of the merchant type, claims that labeling must be done by the clients themselves. Labeling gives understanding, and this is what the whole process is all about.

Which labels are effective? Those that produce an "aha!" experience, a feeling that important but somehow hidden knowledge and understanding have been released with the production of the label. But labels still refer to what is or what has been. Often enough, labeling serves to establish what has to be changed, the identity that has to be rejected. The future and the hope of change lie in metaphors.

Metaphors and Change

Metaphors serve a very important function in the construction of new identities (see Czarniawska-Joerges & Joerges, 1988, for a detailed discussion of the role of linguistic artifacts—like metaphors, labels, and platitudes—in organizational control). They convene new meanings by fitting them into imagination-stimulating messages. Their role consists partly in reducing the uncertainty produced by an encounter with what is new; they refer to something that is better known than the object of the metaphor. They can be seen as shortcuts in explanation as they are used to evoke a single image that encompasses the entire range of meanings of the object. They are also easily acceptable because their "decorative" characteristics answer the need for color and a touch of life in otherwise gray organizational reality. It is the metaphor's evocative, and not reflective, power that is the most important (Geertz, 1973). Metaphors are the material of which future identities are made.

Metaphors are rarely sold per unit. They usually come in systems or kits of metaphors. I encountered at least three types of kits: (a) analytic kits, (b) personal and organizational identity kits, and (c) construction kits. The kits are more or less ready-made. Again, the "doctor/mechanics" have usually complete kits, whereas the "merchants of meaning" have Lego-like elements that can be assembled for a specific purpose. A consultant so explained a presentation of the identity kits: "We give them four or five metaphors to choose from, a whole range of different roles; teacher, broker, free-lancer."

Where do metaphors come from? They come from reading the work of other consultants and from researchers, from public lectures, seminars, and fiction. In large consulting companies, the metaphors are tried on and polished or ornamented in internal seminars before being offered for sale.

How do metaphors work? If a label introduces order, certainty, by giving names to things, a metaphor has almost an opposite effect. It breaks through old labels, creating a hope for change, for something new. Labels say what things are; metaphors say what they are like and what they could be like. The positive effect of metaphorical thinking is especially visible when there is a feeling of a trap, exhaustion, and a cul-de-sac as a result of prolonged difficulties.

But the strength of the metaphor does not lie only in its aesthetic appeal. A powerful metaphor initiates and guides social processes. An organizational identity formulation is a collective process, which must be coordinated and organized like any other organizational process. Consultants take care of this too.

Translation as the Mechanism of Change

At the time of my study, consultants and clients alike agreed that the public administration was hungry for identity kits. Central questions were these: Who are we? What do we do? Who are we like? The labels from the private sector became metaphors in this specific context. This created a need for translation. Public opinion formulated a powerful demand that the public administration should become market and service oriented, profitable, and self-supporting. But what does this mean in a public sector organization?

The head of a leading consulting agency remembered the case of announcing the era of "adaptation to the market" to his public sector client:

> They really do not understand any of it. "Are we really supposed to sell? Shall we do it? Are we not going to follow the budget?" and so on. There is a widespread

confusion. And then I came in here and defined the assignment, which involved helping them to create an organization which we called [the delegated responsibility for results].

The "delegated responsibility for results" reads "profit centers" in the language of the private sector. One can look for equivalents of all the crucial concepts in a similar manner. An internal consultant who wanted to use the idea of "service management" had to do a thorough translating job first.

I've got it in my blood and I have remade it so that it fits into our world. We don't talk about market segments, we talk about target groups. We don't speak about service concept, we deal in service-ideas. We have to go down to the language level and adapt it so that we can align with our world. It makes sense in our world and it's exciting.

The language problem does not exist on one side only. People from business companies do not understand the public sector language either, but, fortunately, they do not have to understand it very often. Imagine, then, formulating your identity in a language alien to yours and one in which your competitor is fluent!

While all this might sound like a very specific, locally limited case, I would like to suggest that, in fact, it grasps the mechanism of change much better than traditional models of it. Innovation, because this is the type of change we are speaking about here, is traditionally connected to the idea of "diffusion" (for a recent review, see Levitt & March, 1988).

Diffusion assumes that objectlike ideas move through space in accordance with the law of inertia (Latour, 1986). The movement starts with the "initial energy" ("initiative," "order," "command," "instruction"). The initial energy is usually connected to power and leadership and seen as coming from an individual source. According to the law of inertia, the objects will move uninhibited unless met with "resistance." This resistance takes the form of "resistance to change," "political resistance," and so on. Resistance produces "friction," which diminishes the initial energy. Friction, in the social world as well as in the technical world, is a negative phenomenon when movement is desired. That is, so long as the model of diffusion is accepted.

[The] model of diffusion may be contrasted with another, that of the model of translation. According to the latter, the spread in time and space of anything—claims, orders, artefacts, goods—is in the hands of people; each of these people may act in many different ways, letting the token drop, or modifying it, or deflecting it, or betraying it, or adding to it, or appropriating it. (Latour, 1986, p. 267)

Ideas do not "diffuse." It is people who pass them from one to another, each of them translating it according to his or her own frames of reference. Such meeting of *traveling ideas* with a frame of reference, that is, *ideas in residence,* can be called "friction," but now it acquires a positive tone. There is no initial energy (all ideas exist all the time; Merton, 1985). Energy comes precisely from friction, that is, from the meeting of ideas and their "translators." Insofar as one can speak about inertia of social life, that is, habits, routines, and institutional behavior, it is this inertia that stops the movement of ideas. Without friction, there is no translation; at best, it is the case of *received ideas.* Friction can be seen as the energizing clash between ideas in residence and traveling ideas, which leads to transformation of both.

Thus we have the role of consultants as merchants of ideas and the initial translators. However significant their role, however ready-made their kits, they cannot provide their clients with a ready-made identity. If identity is an autobiographical narration, sooner or later the clients must try their voices themselves, and the patience of the audience. Thus we come to the final stage of identity formation. The first described the initial shock that challenges the old identity; the second showed how professional help can be used; the third demonstrates the actual attempt.

IN SEARCH OF A NEW IDENTITY

By the 1990s, the Swedish public sector was put into a pillory. In the political arena, there was talk of a crisis of legitimacy. At the organizational level, it would be more appropriate to speak of an identity crisis. The "Swedish Model," a child of Social Democracy, was announced dead and buried, among other places, in the report *Study of Power and Democracy in Sweden* (1990), which attempted to describe current trends that as yet lack a clear status or distinct identity.

What was demanded next was the creation of new identities that clearly demonstrate the break with the past (public authorities with a supervisory function) but that, nonetheless, avoid the mechanical imitation of models in the private sector. In the following, I shall exemplify this process with observations coming from an ethnographic study of municipalities and social insurance offices in Sweden (Czarniawska-Joerges, 1992b). Units at the local level (municipalities), county level (social insurance offices), and central level (the government and its agencies on the one hand the federative bodies on the other) will be explored.

The "municipality" is managing rather well, at least in external presentation. Local government offices are turned into limited companies, speculating in the financial markets, speaking the same language as the inhabitants, using visual presentations, and trying to depict themselves as "producers in the service sector." But things are not working so smoothly internally: The municipality's traditional identity as a miserly employer that expects sacrifices on the part of its personnel continues to be a burdensome image. The "Association of Local Authorities," on the other hand, is having considerable success, both internally and externally. The association's internal identity is easily established because it is a highly professional organization. In the outside world, gales are blowing, both from government quarters and in the major municipalities, but the association is nonetheless fighting for a new role as a "molder of public opinion" and a "guide." This also applies to the "Federation of Social Insurance Offices,"[1] but, in this case, it is more a question of tornadoes blowing in all directions. The federation itself is more political than professional, and this is a disadvantage when building up a consistent organizational identity.

The "social insurance offices" are facing considerable problems in their search for an identity because there are many external mandatory restrictions and very little autonomy. The "parent body," that is, the National Social Insurance Board, has even more serious problems of identity because it is perhaps the state agency that has been the most bitterly attacked and most heavily criticized.

It is the modern identity that organizations in the public sector are once again trying to construct because the one they acquired with the emergence of the welfare state has lost its legitimacy. Self-respect was felt to be self-righteousness; efficiency was regarded as nonexistent; autonomy was seen as arrogance; and flexibility, as political opportunism. What they try to do, then, is to find a narrative expressing a new identity through changes in legitimate rhetorics (McCloskey, 1986).

Public sector employees are well aware that their rhetoric must change—particularly when they present themselves to the outside world. But there still exists the traditional rhetoric that holds back every attempt to achieve change. Perhaps it would be appropriate to speak of several traditional rhetorics that used to be accepted as legitimate in discussion within and about the public sector.

Traditional Rhetorics

There were at least three legitimate rhetorics within the public sector—political rhetoric, "officialese," and the language of experts.

Political statements are usually poor at *logos*—that is, the logical argument—but this is counterbalanced by rich *pathos,* appealing to the audience's emotions. Hyperbole is favored. Threats are described as black and sinister, while promising developments are depicted in all the colors of the rainbow. This rhetoric is also often employed by the mass media (journalists report what politicians say and politicians learn to formulate their ideas in media terms).

Officialese—the language of bureaucracy—has three main characteristics. It is full of *congeries* (the obvious is reiterated) and its logos is unnecessarily complicated (it can take time and require some expenditure of energy to perceive the repetition). The third characteristic is the low aesthetic level, which is partly due to lack of skill but more often is the product of commitment to bad (clumsy) rhetoric.[2] Figures of speech such as metaphors and irony are avoided in favor of empty parallelism—that is, phrases that are built identically, therefore achieving the effect of monotony. In terms of narrative strategies, suspense is avoided, and both *ethos* and *pathos* kinds of appeals—that is, references to the speaker or to the listener—are sacrificed to logos.

It is true that officials who can write well have existed throughout the ages, but officialese has always been under constant fire. Of course, "writing well" means different things in different eras. In recent years, the language of experts has become the ideal. *Expert* rhetoric is based on the "objective truth." It is designed to give the impression that the expert in question has direct contact with reality, while the readers suffer from distortions resulting from their subjectivity. Ethos, that is, a claim to credibility based on the authority of the speaker, actually forms the basis of the argument, in spite of the claim that it is logos only, that is, the force of argument as such—that persuades. In addition, the expert would hotly deny that any rhetoric was being employed. The aim is to imitate science, thus the argumentation consisting of "proofs" and "confirmation" is achieved by employing statistics. A great many metaphors are employed (derived from the world of science and describing objects and their characteristics), resulting literally in an impression of "objectivity," that is, that the argumentation involves material objects and not symbols and ideas.

All three have problems now. Political rhetoric is attacked for its "emptiness," and this is no news. The main ally of the politician, the journalist, however, is at the same time their foe. On the other hand, the mass media shape what is accessible and popular in mass communication, therefore encouraging politicians to follow their example. On the other hand, one of their favorite pastimes is turning against the politicians and attacking them for exactly this kind of "journalistic" rhetoric without "proper weight" to it. As the aesthetic claims gain in legitimacy, officialese is perceived as litter in our literary ecology. Expert rhetoric, the most legitimate of the three in the earlier periods, suffers most under the postmodern winds that unmask the hidden authority claim and refuse to give anybody the status of the metanarrative. The utterances coming from the public sector organizations try to adjust.

Trying to Change

I chose, for scrutiny, an article in *Dagens Nyheter* (a Swedish daily) that was something of an event during the time of my study, was widely discussed by my interlocutors, and represents attempts to change the traditional rhetorics, albeit with mixed success. I should also add that the daily press has an enormous role in the formation of public opinion in Sweden—every household subscribes to at least one of the two main dailies, which are much alike. In addition, the identity discussed here is that of a state agency among the most criticized and at the same time very central.

In the article, titled "Scrap the National Insurance Board" (April 13, 1989), a principal administrative officer employed by the board wrote:

> Several articles have appeared in these pages which have dealt with activities in the public sector. Amongst other things, views have been presented regarding methods for restricting the development of costs, thus benefiting the tax-payer.

Thus the article establishes its legitimacy by linking into an ongoing discussion. It is claimed, however, that something is missing in this public debate:

> Evaluation of the Insurance Board's operations is not undertaken in a manner which gives the state information as to whether the resources invested in the Board have provided the yield which was intended. What specific services does the Board produce? Who demands these services? Are they necessary and, if so, do they give value for money?

The first sentence quoted above implies that the government receives "information as to whether the resources invested have provided the yield which was intended" from all other government bodies, with the exception of the National Insurance Board. The reader is confronted with a conspiratorial hypothesis, and this impression is reinforced by the rhetorical technique characteristically employed in this context: *interrogation.* Rhetorical questions, of course, mean asking questions that have an apparently given answer. In the above case, the answers will be a triple "no." This total state of negation means that argumentation once more has to start from the beginning:

> There are 26 insurance offices in Sweden and each office is a separate legal entity managed by a board. . . . As a result of the board representation on these boards and committees, the general public has a good insight into the operations of the insurance offices. In addition, the offices have jointly formed an organization to promote their interests—the Federation of Social Insurance Offices—which provides the county offices with administrative services. . . . There is an established contact network with the general public, providers of social care, employers, other organizations, etc.

These are just a few sentences extracted from a full column of descriptions of the status of the county insurance offices. Unfortunately, the effect created by use of the rhetorical question technique drowns in the volume of information provided. The conspiratorial introduction is allowed to fade away and, when the author returns to his original point ("This is the perspective in which the need for the Board's supervisory function should be discussed"), the reader has forgotten the introduction and the original drama has dissipated.

Now, however, comes the dark side of the picture:

> The central control of data-procession operations and the day-to-day workload of the county offices means that the offices rely on up-to-date instructions from the Board on services required with regard to the general public. If there are delays in making payments due to the malfunctioning of the computer system or because personnel are waiting for new instructions before they can explain the position to the public, county office staff have to deal with the complaints.

The description is unclear and this effect is reinforced by the complex language employed ("services required with regard to"). The reader is distracted by several hidden implications. Why doesn't the computer system work? Do the county offices always have to wait for the board's instructions? What is the connection between the two? In addition, the argumentation is weakened by the conditional use of "if," which implies that the problems described have not (yet) happened. "Central control by the Board also inhibits the creativity of the county offices, hindering initiatives to achieve more effective routines and improved service to the general public."

This arouses the reader's suspicions because "creativity"—something that is desirable per se—is not exactly what is expected of a county insurance office. The reader is pacified, however, by mention of "improved service," which is a familiar, albeit empty, concept.

The article examines at length the various departments at the National Social Insurance Board and finally presents a proposal:

> There are major opportunities to achieve more efficient administration in the social insurance sphere and thus to reduce costs significantly. It is no longer justified to continue the Board's supervisory activities. County offices should be entrusted with the task of administering social insurance and the benefits system on their own responsibility. . . . This would provide greater scope for creative initiatives to reduce the risks of injuries, improve the health environment and undertake rehabilitation measures, in conjunction with employers, worker protection organizations, employment offices and local care services. . . . A review of the Board's role in the social insurance field is therefore required from an economic point of view. It is important that this review adopts an unbiased approach and has access to a broad range of expert resources, including people with experience of structural change and business know-how.

Here we have a mixture of political and bureaucratic rhetoric. On the one hand, a solution to several societal problems is promised, while, on the other, the article employs all the expressions commonly found in bureaucratic documents that are devoid of content. On the one hand, a proposal is made that is totally at variance with conventional practice (When have there ever been "unbiased" official reports?), while, on the other, a coupling is made with trendy ideas (expert resources from the business world) that the reader may find unpalatable.

The above example is, in my perception, very typical of the attempted change. The provocation achieved was extremely weak. The inconsistent logos, in combination with the officialese language, diluted the message to such an extent that I wonder if the readers from outside the board could understand how revolutionary the ideas expressed actually were. What was meant to be revolutionary ended up as a cryptic message to the insiders that to those outside looks exactly like what they know and do not like about the public administration. But is it at all possible to change a dominant rhetoric? Will not the old identity always reappear from behind the attempts to appear different?

Long Live Officialese

Most of the people I talked to were extremely dissatisfied with language like that employed in official documents. This dissatisfaction could be summarized by saying that officialese was regarded as both incomprehensible and aesthetically unsatisfying. The incomprehensibility is partly because the language of bureaucracy does not keep pace with developments in everyday Swedish.

Old-fashioned language is often linked to legal rhetoric. The local offices claimed, however, that "officialese is not the result of the fine distinctions required in a legal context, but because the written text is supposed to look as if it emanates from a public authority." As Michel Foucault might have put it: Language creates power, and incomprehensibility is one of the most significant ways of expressing the fact that the speaker is an important person.

It would be an exaggeration, however, to say that my interlocutors were the only people to perceive officialese as a problem. On the contrary, there is a campaign going on in the media ridiculing the language of the bureaucracy. And at the insurance offices, there are special brochures about how to write and speak good Swedish. The question is why officialese continues to survive.

Part of the answer is routines, but another part is power. Officialese belongs to the narrative of Authoritative Administration, not to the new one—Humble Administration. There are, in fact, many factors that impede changes in the language used. It is very difficult to deal with certain hidden linguistic habits, for example, and there are not so many positive models to turn to either. Media language contains platitudes and fashionable trendy phrases, which seem attractive at first but become increasingly repulsive, rather like a cake that one has eaten too much of.

Even the most heavily committed protagonists in the struggle for better official language think in terms of "correct," or possibly "simple," language. Hardly anyone refers to language as "interesting" or as something that can "involve the reader." Is anyone brave enough to imagine "a beautiful bureaucratic language"?

Everyone in the organizations I studied agreed that traditional communication modes fail to meet contemporary requirements. But, at the same time, both the diagnosis and the cure seemed to be trapped in the same perspective that had originally caused the disease. There is continued faith in the modernist, naive-realist perspective in which words refer directly to phenomena in the real world. There is a firm belief that, if you find the "right" word, everyone will understand. This is reinforced by a fear of rhetoric, as such. It is condemned in advance as "empty" or merely a matter of "verbal initiatives." Such views are the result of bitter experience (especially of politicians), but they are also partly due to failure to distinguish between the symbolic and the practical. Accusations that politicians "don't do what they say" are peculiar in that politicians never do anything, in a physical sense. They always talk. Sometimes there is a connection between what they say and what happens, and sometimes there is no such link. This may be due to hypocrisy, but it is at least as likely to be the result of their lack of skill (in transforming their words into someone else's deeds) or of random factors. Understanding this requires a grasp of the complex role played by rhetoric in the actions of organizations, and this attempt has hardly begun (for interesting examples, see Cheney & McMillan, 1990).

As it is now, rhetoric is an instrument of power for veterans but seems "blackboxed" to newcomers. The result is a kind of fatalism, where people consider it "normal" for official documents to be both incomprehensible and deadly boring. Attempts to improve the situation are based on a mechanical or, rather, a cybernetic view of "communication" in which a "sender" transmits a "message" to a "receiver" in the hope that the "channels are set free." Within the social constructivist perspective, the discourse and its conditions, including the participants and their identity, are created and re-created in the interaction itself. A rhetoric is never "right" or "wrong" per se. Rhetorics and identities must be tried out and accepted within the relevant organizational field.

TENTATIVE IDENTITIES WITHIN
BLURRED ORGANIZATIONAL FIELDS

The search for a new identity can be seen as an attempt to change the public sector organization field (DiMaggio & Powell, 1983). Following Giddens (1984), an organizational field can be analyzed in terms of actors and structures, where structures are patterns of interactions between the actors.

A Search or a Quest?

The interesting point about the creation of a new field is that the actors are uncertain of their identity and also that the structures are not given. *Identities* and *structures* are the result of structuration processes. Actors' identity can be created with the help of models, but in practice their relevance is confirmed or rejected in concrete interactions. It is not sufficient to select an attractive model and then present it. The new identity must be accepted by the other actors involved, both those who are operating on an established stage with a clear identity (e.g., the private sector) and also by others who find themselves in a similar situation. The same applies to structures. The government's actions have created a new space, a certain amount of freedom, a vacuum, but new rules have not been established. These new rules must be created through action. You can only know what is right or wrong after you have acted (or someone else has). The difference between this process and the trial and error method is that there are no rules to be "discovered" and no "referees" who know the answers (even if the local authorities, for example, would be happy to see the government take on the referee role and while the Association of Local Authorities is trying to grab the role for itself).

The problem is exacerbated by the fact that it is not just individual identities that are disintegrating but also other institutions. In the case of persons, building up an identity is described as an interaction between an individual (who is developing) and relatively stable institutions. But, in this case, we have the reverse situation—there are "individuals" who used to have strong identities and there is an organizational environment of institutions that are in a state of radical change.

Processes of this kind obviously involve great risks. On the one hand, the risks are concrete (e.g., municipal currency speculation scandals) while, on the other hand, there is considerable risk of public ridicule. The transformation is taking place on stage. The citizens, who want good entertainment without paying too much, are sitting expectantly in the audience along with competitors who would prefer to see a real fiasco and press critics who will be writing their review of what "actually" happens.

Is there any help coming from a narrative approach as presented here? At least two insights emerge. One is that public sector organizations, like everybody else, are only partly authors of their autonarrative. This insight is twofold. First, the acknowledgment of this fact can widen the understanding of the situation without pushing toward fatalism. Second, self-conscious attempts may be made to limit the role of others as authors and increase one's own role.

Within this second task, another insight is at hand encompassed in the difference between a "search" and a "quest." *Search* has been, until now, a legitimate term in organization theory, and this might be part of the problem rather than the solution. The notion of *quest,* as used in medieval ballads, was not the meaning of a search for something already adequately defined like oil or gold.

> It is in the course of the quest and only through encountering and coping with the
> various particular harms, dangers, temptations and distractions which provide

any quest with its episodes and incidents that the goal of the quest is finally to be understood. A quest is always an education both as to the character of that which is thought and in self-knowledge. (MacIntyre, 1981/1990, p. 219)

A search for excellence, or only for a new identity, assumes that such an identity already exists and waits to be discovered. This can be correct only if this new identity is to be authored by somebody else, for example, the private sector. If the public sector wants to remain its own author, then it must embark on a quest where identity will be formed as an autobiography but in accordance with what are legitimate autobiographies of our times. This, however, must be discovered in the process of formulation itself.

A Postmodern Identity: An Oxymoron or a New Quest?

It has been claimed here that one of the major problems in searching or questing for a new organizational identity is the general turbulence in organization fields: Institutions are undergoing transformations. It has also been postulated that individual identity is a modern institution. Should it not follow that the institution of individual identity is undergoing a transformation as well?

The defenders of modernity will come up with a negative answer (e.g., the untiring defender of modernity, Marshall Berman, 1992). Another negative answer can be grounded not in the faith that modernism will "win" but in a claim that all phenomena described as "postmodern" belong, in fact, to modernity. Indeed, Berger et al.'s (1974) description of modern identity is very close to what has been considered an emergent postmodern identity, to which I shall turn later. They point out four peculiar aspects of modern identity: its *openness* (life as a project), *differentiation* (due to the individual's immersion in plural and unstable lifeworlds, reality loses substance and acquires complexity), *reflectivity* (necessarily resulting from the other two), and *individuality* (the individual as the final test of existence and reality). For Berger et al. (1974), identity is still related to subjectivity and, although strongly influenced by institutions, not an institution itself.

What are the claims of those who see institutional transformations taking place? The most radical claim problematizes the notion of identity, calling it a myth, an illusion, and claiming that "in postmodern culture, the subject has disintegrated into a flux of euphoric intensities, fragmented and disconnected" (Kellner, 1992, p. 144), thus "postmodern selves . . . are allegedly devoid of the expressive energies and individualities characteristic of modernism" (p. 146). Kellner himself presents a less radical version of the claim that can be of great relevance for organizations in quest for an identity.

First and foremost, Kellner emphasizes the central role played by the mass media in structuring contemporary identity. Television everywhere and newspapers specifically in Scandinavian countries (where every household subscribes to at least one daily) assume some of the traditional socializing functions of myth and ritual—integrating individuals into the social order, celebrating prevalent values, offering role models (Kellner, 1992). In the times of mourning a lack of public participation, it is important to point out that television is not only a competitor for politics in offering sports or entertainment, it also offers central politics as played before the cameras rather than a local meeting with little drama to it.

The main characters of TV genres, considered typical for postmodernity, have multiple identities and multiple pasts that might or might not have influence on the present, with the character of influence being changable as well. "In each case, their identity is fragmented and unstable, different and distinctive in each character, yet always subject to dramatic change" (Kellner, 1992, p. 151). Looking for analogies in organizational worlds, one immediately thinks about large corporations who humbly give up their established role to engage in a quest for the good of the community, where the "ecological conversion" is the most popular type of dramatic change. In both personal and organizational identities, speed and mobility are values that replaced resistance to change and stability.

The changes and adaptations in identity also set the public's role differently. The social environment is not any more ready to accept the "adult personality" as formed once and for all; it is supposed to appreciate chameleonic changes. This is based on a shared assumption that identity is constructed and not given, that it is a matter of choice and style rather than of genotype or soul. Redefined as matter of choice and style, individual identity moves from a "serious" arena of life to "leisure." It becomes a game, a play, celebrated by organizations with even more fanfare than by individuals (even if, as in the case of Benneton, the playfulness signals, at the same time, a very serious involvement in the matters of the world).

Thus both societal arenas and organization fields are filled with players rather than *actors* in the literal sense of the world. Postmodern identities are "constituted theatrically through role-playing and image construction." There are no referees in this game, Rorty (1992) reminds us, because nobody knows the rules in advance. It is the admiration and applause from another player that demonstrates the "winners." Language and pictures are of utmost importance in the play.

In this context, it will come of no surprise to say that fashion is very important for the ways identities are constructed and changed. Fashion promotes both conformity and freedom, creativity and reification (Simmel, 1904/1973)—all these are needed for a modern identity. It is the device that changed more than the materials; multiplicity and constant change, which for the moderns was both the main discovery and the main source of anxiety (Berger et al., 1974), acquire a taken-for-granted place in the postmodern identity formation. There is, both Kellner (1992) and Rorty (1992) point out, a continuity between modernism and postmodernism that some radical postmodernists negate. For organizations, then, there is no need to despair of plunging into unknown, frightening relativism. It is a quest where their active role gives them a possibility of influencing the rules as much as the other players. What they cannot count upon, though, is an arrival of an arbiter who will tell everybody what the new rules are (although, no doubt, many will try).

NOTES

1. Social insurance covers medical care, rehabilitation in case of work accidents, and so on for all citizens. Although the resources are administered centrally by a National Social Insurance Board, the activity is carried out by county social insurance offices. The local origins of social insurance are still sedimented in its former federative organ, the Federation of Social Insurance Offices.

2. This is connected with the belief that skillful rhetoric is a sign of dishonesty. Roger Brown (1969, p. 340) speaks ironically of "tweed rhetoric," observing that "one can be quiet, modest, tweedy, and yet a villain."

REFERENCES

Albert, S., & Whetten, D. (1985). Organizational identity. In L. L. Cummings & B. M. Staw (Eds.), *Research in organizational behavior* (Vol. 7, pp. 263-295). Greenwich, CT: JAI.

Alvesson, M., & Björkman, I. (1992). *Organisatorisk idenitet.* Lund, Sweden: Studentlitteratur.

Bakhtin, M. M., & Medvedev, P. N. (1985). *The formal method in literary scholarship.* Cambridge, MA: Harvard University Press. (Original work published 1928)

Berger, P. L., Berger, B., & Kellner, H. (1974). *The homeless mind.* London: Penguin.

Berger, P. L., & Luckmann, T. (1971). *The social construction of reality.* New York: Doubleday. (Original work published 1966)

Berman, M. (1992). Why modernism still matters. In S. Lash & J. Friedman (Eds.), *Modernity and identity* (pp. 33-58). Oxford: Basil Blackwell.

Brown, R. H. (1989). *Social science as civic discourse.* Chicago: University of Chicago Press.

Brown, R. W. (1969). *Words and things.* New York: Free Press.

Bruner, J. (1990). *Acts of meaning.* Cambridge, MA: Harvard University Press.

Brunsson, N., & Olsen, J. (Eds.). (1993). *The reforming organization.* London: Routledge.

Bruss, E. W. (1976). *Autobiographical acts.* Baltimore: John Hopkins University Press.

Cheney, G. (1992). The corporate person (re)presents itself. In E. Toth & R. Heath (Eds.), *Rhetorical and critical approaches to public relations* (pp. 165-183). Hillsdale, NJ: Lawrence Erlbaum.

Cheney, G., & McMillan, J. J. (1990). Organizational rhetoric and the practice of criticism. *Journal of Applied Communication Research, 18*(2), 93-114.

Czarniawska, B. (1985). The ugly sister: On relationship between the private and the public sectors in Sweden. *Scandinavian Journal of Management Studies, 2*(2), 83-103.

Czarniawska-Joerges, B. (1990). Merchants of meaning. In B. Turner (Ed.), *Organizational symbolism.* Berlin: de Gruyter.

Czarniawska-Joerges, B. (1992a). *Exploring complex organizations.* Newbury Park, CA: Sage.

Czarniawska-Joerges, B. (1992b). *Styrningens paradoxer.* Stockholm: Norstedts.

Czarniawska-Joerges, B. (1993). *The three-dimensional organization.* London: Chartwell-Bratt.

Czarniawska-Joerges, B., Gustafsson, C., & Björkegren, D. (1990). Purists vs. pragmatists: On Protagoras, economists and management consultants. *Consultation, 9*(3), 241-256.

Czarniawska-Joerges, B., & Joerges, B. (1988). How to control things with words: Organizational talk and control. *Management Communication Quarterly, 2*(2), 170-193.

DiMaggio, P. J., & Powell, W. W. (1983). The iron cage revisited. *American Sociological Review, 48,* 147-160.

Douglas, M. (1986). *How institutions think.* Syracuse, NY: Syracuse University Press.

Douglas, M. (1990). *Thought style exemplified: The idea of the self.* Unpublished manuscript.

Dutton, J. E., & Dukerich, J. M. (1991). Keeping an eye on the mirror: Image and identity in organizational adaption. *Academy of Management Journal, 34*(3), 517-554.

Eco, U. (1990). *The limits of interpretation.* Bloomington: Indiana University Press.

Fuller, S. (in press). Talking metaphysical turkey about epistemological chicken and the poop on pidgins. In D. Stump & P. Galison (Eds.), *Disunity and context: Philosophies of science studies.*

Geertz, C. (1973). *The interpretation of cultures.* New York: Basic Books.

Gergen, K. J., & Davis, K. E. (Eds.). (1985). *The social construction of the person.* New York: Springer-Verlag.

Giddens, A. (1984). *New rules of sociological method.* London: Hutchinson.

Giddens, A. (1991). *Modernity and self-identity.* Oxford: Polity.

Harari, J. V. (1979). *Textual strategies.* Ithaca, NY: Cornell University Press.

Heilbroner, R. L. (1988). Rhetoric and ideology. In A. Klamer, D. McCloskey, & R. Solow (Eds.), *The consequences of economic rhetoric.* Cambridge: Cambridge University Press.

Kellner, D. (1992). Popular culture and the construction of postmodern identities. In S. Lash & J. Friedman (Eds.), *Modernity and identity* (pp. 141-177). Oxford: Basil Blackwell.

Lakoff, G., & Johnson, M. (1980). *Metaphors we live by.* Chicago: University of Chicago Press.

Latour, B. (1986). The powers of association. In J. Law (Ed.), *Power, action and belief.* London: Routledge & Kegan Paul.

Latour, B. (1988). A relativistic account of Einstein's relativity. *Social Studies of Science, 18,* 3-44.

Latour, B. (1992). The next turn after the social turn. In E. McMullin (Ed.), *The social dimensions of science.* Paris: Notre Dame Press.

Lejeune, P. (1989). *On autobiography.* Minneapolis: University of Minnesota Press.

Levitt, G., & March, J. (1988). Organizational learning. *Annual Review of Sociology, 14,* 319-340.

MacIntyre, A. (1990). *After virtue.* London: Duckworth. (Original work published 1981)

McCloskey, D. N. (1986). *The rhetorics of economics.* Brighton, Sussex: Harvester.

Mead, G. H. (1934). *Mind, self and society from the standpoint of a social behaviorist.* Chicago: University of Chicago Press.

Merton, R. (1985). *On the shoulders of giants: A Shandean postscript.* San Diego: Harcourt Brace Jovanovich.

Meyer, J. W. (1986). Myths of socialization and of personality. In T. C. Hellner, M. Sosna, & D. E. Wellbery (Eds.), *Reconstructing individualism* (pp. 208-221). Stanford, CA: Stanford University Press.

Meyer, J. W., Boli, J., & Thomas, G. M. (1987). Ontology and rationalization in the Western cultural account. In G. M. Thomas, J. W. Meyer, F. O. Ramirez, & J. Boli (Eds.), *Institutional structure.* Newbury Park, CA: Sage.

Morgan, G. (1986). *Images of organization.* Beverly Hills, CA: Sage.

Pitkin, H. (1984). *Fortune is a woman.* Berkeley: University of California Press.

Premfors, R., Eklund, A., & Larsson, T. (1985). *Privata konsulter i offentlig förvalting* (Wp No. 9). Stockholm, Sweden: Department of Political Science.

Rombach, B. (1991). *Det går inte att styra med mål.* Lund, Sweden: Studentlitteratur.

Rorty, R. (1989). *Contingency, irony and solidarity.* Cambridge: Cambridge University Press.

Rorty, R. (1992). Cosmopolitanism without emancipation: A response to Lyotard. In S. Lash & J. Friedman (Eds.), *Modernity and identity* (pp. 59-72). Oxford: Basil Blackwell.

Simmel, G. (1973). Fashion. In G. Wills & D. Midgley (Eds.), *Fashion marketing*. London: Allen & Unwin. (Original work published 1904)

Siven, C. (1984). Politik och ekonomi i Sverige under 1970-talet. *Ekonomisk debatt, 2,* 83-95.

Demokrati och makt i Sverige. Maktutredningens huvudrapport [The study of power and democracy in Sweden]. (1990). SOU.

Starbuck, W. H. (1983). Organizations as action generators. *American Sociological Review, 48,* 91-102.

Tarchys, D. (1983, September 1). Regeringskansliet behöver förstärkning. *Dagens Nyheter.*

Articulating Identity in an Organizational Age

LARS THØGER CHRISTENSEN
Odense University, Denmark

GEORGE CHENEY
University of Colorado at Boulder

Properly speaking, *a man has as many social selves as there are individuals who recognize him* and carry an image of him in their mind. To wound any of these images is to wound him. But as the individuals who carry the images fall naturally into classes, we may practically say that he has as many different social selves as there are distinct *groups* of persons about whose opinion he cares.

—James, 1890/1950, Vol. 1, p. 291

What distinguishes modern organisations is not so much their size, or their bureaucratic character, as the concentrated reflexive monitoring they both permit and entail. Who says modernity says not just organisations, but organisation—the regularized control of social relations across indefinite time-space distances.

—Giddens, 1991, p. 16

In a very general sense, systems avoid tautological or paradoxical obstacles to meaningful self-descriptions by "unfolding" self-reference. That is, the (positive or negative) circularity of self-reference is interrupted and interpreted in a way that cannot—in the last analysis—be accounted for. . . . Only an observer is able to realize what systems themselves are unable to realize.

—Luhmann, 1990, p. 127

Every society up to now has attempted to give an answer to a few fundamental questions: Who are we as a collectivity? What are we for one another? Where and in what are we? What do we want; what do we desire; what are we lacking?

Correspondence and requests for reprints: Lars Thøger Christensen, Department of Marketing, Odense University, 55 Campusvej, DK-5230 Odense M, Denmark.

Communication Yearbook 17, pp. 222-235

Society must define its "identity," its articulation, the world, its relations to the world and to the objects it contains, its needs and desires. Without the "answer" to these "questions," without these "definitions," there can be no human world, no society, no culture—for everything would be undifferentiated chaos. . . . Society constitutes itself by producing a *de facto* answer to these questions in its life, in its activity. It is in the *doing* of each collectivity that the answer to these questions appears as embodied meaning; this social doing allows itself to be understood only as a reply to the question that it implicitly poses itself.

—Castoriadis, 1987, pp. 146 ff.

IN her interesting essay, Barbara Czarniawska-Joerges (hereafter abbreviated C-J) explores the important case of the transformation of the Swedish welfare state to consider issues in organizational identity and, by implication, institutional self-definition in the contemporary world. C-J highlights and interprets *narratives* of organizational identity, not only to tell her story of how such institutional changes have occurred and manifested themselves but also to stress the importance of the institution's own narratives in the development of its identity. C-J reminds us of the important parallels between individuals' struggles for identity, as revealed in their discourses, and the struggles of collectivities. Indeed, "identity" is an issue for social units of all size in the modern world because identity is no longer given (i.e., the very notion of an "identity crisis" presumes multiple options rather than solid tradition), because of the maze of messages and styles that constitute postmodern consumption (e.g., "Be an individual by joining those who use this product") and because of the various "fault lines" for unity or fragmentation today (contemporary Europe reveals both tendencies and the resulting tensions). While we had considered the possibility of constructing our own counternarrative or metanarrative to develop our commentary on C-J's provocative study, we choose instead to organize our discussion around four important themes in the study of organizational identity. Under each theme, we make some comments about C-J's essay and then elaborate on the role of the theme (if you will) in the larger "narrative" of the identity of the modern organization.

WHAT DO WE MEAN IN APPLYING "IDENTITY" TO ORGANIZATIONS?

It is now commonplace for scholars and laypersons to discuss the *identities* of organizations, thus taking a term that in Western thought was typically associated with the individual person and applying it to collectivities (see, e.g., Albert & Whetten, 1985; Cheney, 1991, 1992; Cheney & Tompkins, 1987; Cheney & Vibbert, 1987; Christensen, 1991; Deetz, 1992; Tompkins & Cheney, 1985). And the term includes under its head both the strict sense of an organization's name or identifying emblems (e.g., logos) and the much broader sense of a system's representations by/to itself and by/to others. As Ramanantsoa and Battaglia (1991) observe with respect to the organizational world today: "At first invisible and silent . . . companies have now become the subject of their own discourse in an effort to win coherent identities, legitimacy and institutionalization" (p. 2). To invoke the term *identity* in any context is to entail surprise, irony, and sometimes paradox. For example, the English word *identity* derives from the Latin *identitas*, referring to sameness rather than difference. Still, at least since the Enlightenment, one's identity has been taken to mean that which distinguishes him or her and that which makes that "self" unique (e.g., Mackenzie, 1978). In the domain of organizations, especially that of legal corporations, firms have gradually attained the status of juristic, artificial, or legal persons (see, e.g., Coleman, 1974). Thus that which was originally thought to be explicitly *collective* in nature—the development of corporate bodies such as craft guilds in the late Middle Ages—has come to be treated as individual: In the language of advanced capitalism, the corporation *is* a person with attendant rights and to a lesser extent ascribed responsibilities (see, e.g., Nader & Mayer, 1990). In this way, individuals can "incorporate," enhancing their power, transcending themselves in time and space, limiting liability, and joining what is called in French and in Spanish "S.A.," the anonymous society. Yet, even though our world is populated with such persons as well as with "natural" ones (i.e., each of us, a living body recognized as an individual person), we as citizens have great difficulty in conceptualizing and acting upon identities when they are posited at the organizational or institutional level.

Perhaps it is in large part because of the modern emphasis on the individual as "the building block" of society that we are so perplexed by the phenomenon of organizational or institutional identity. But, as Weber argued early in this century (1978), such phenomena ought to be treated as real to the extent that they are seen as such by persons and to the extent that they make a difference in daily life. Put another way, consistent with Weber's brand of interpretive sociology, organizational and institutional identities frequently become meaningful in the interactions between and among individuals and groups.

Today we witness all sorts of organizations struggling to articulate their identities in the marketplace of discourse and images. Some corporations, for example, work to personalize their identities in various ways, including the use of visible representatives (such as Hollywood celebrities or CEOs) or characters (such as Xerox's monk-scribe of some years ago). Other organizations prefer, or even feel compelled, to "center" or "ground" themselves in key values or concerns (e.g., customer service; see, e.g., Christensen, 1991; Gay & Salaman, 1992). Of course, the effort to establish a clearly identifiable tradition is constantly in tension with the impulse to change and with the need to adapt to changing times and circumstances.

C-J's case examination of public sector organizations in Sweden during the years 1985 to 1990 reveals the dilemmas for organizations and individuals in a larger system in flux. These organizations are trying to find new articulations of identity and new patterns of communication that fit changing circumstances. The comfortable patterns of tradition have been shaken both directly by the realization of economic stress and indirectly by a growing ambiguity with respect to some of the most significant institutions, or "markers of certainty," in modern society: "the economy" and "the political" (Lefort, 1988).

The importance of "finding" new identities for the organizations in question is evident from the participants in C-J's ethnographic investigations. At the same time, however, these people realize that they are only partially in control of the process; as C-J puts it, that actors (individual and collective) "are only partly authors of their autonarrative" (p. 216). This of course is true of all identities, individual and organizational, but the modern stress on individuality and choice has obscured the fact, leaving many persons (natural and legal) with the impression that they can singly author themselves. Existing symbolic resources, market forces, and the range of multiple interpretations (expressed well in Jacques Derrida's, 1976, notion of "undecidability") have challenged the certainties long associated with identity as essence and identity as willful choice. Thus C-J is quite right, following Alasdair MacIntyre (1981), to offer the metaphor of the "quest" as a substitute for the metaphor of the "search" for an identity: The quest suggests that what is sought will be defined in large part through *the process of formulation* itself; it is not "prepackaged." The startling turbulence of politics and economics in the world of late underscores the importance of this kind of openness to evolving definitions of what organizations are and do.

Identity as a Social Construction: The Relative
Autonomy of Identity as a Human Symbolic Creation

To take a social constructionist perspective on the identity of an individual or an organization is to say that what we call "identity" is in large part a product of interaction and an expression that makes use of the symbolic resources at the disposal of the actor (see, e.g., Burke, 1950/1969; Tompkins & Cheney, 1990). To take a radical social constructionist perspective, as C-J seems to promote in her essay—although she sometimes contradicts herself on this point—is to so minimize the importance of such things as a system's physicality, phenomenological experience, and drive toward self-distinction and maintenance as to make them almost meaningless. While we are generally sympathetic with C-J's stress on the social dimension of identity, we believe that she moves into dangerous argumentative territory when she suggests that individual and organizational identity are nothing but the products of socialization.

Generally speaking, C-J assumes a perspective on identity similar to that of John Meyer (e.g., 1986). In his essay "Myths of Socialization and of Personality," Meyer notes the irony that, in a society that so asserts the value of individuality as does the contemporary society of the United States, there is a strong emphasis on conformity. The very term *socialization,* as it has figured in academic and nonacademic discourses, is biased toward the larger social unit. The individual person is expected to "fit into" the larger social unit and derive his or her sense of self from participation in that organization or institution. At the same time, we don't hear much said about "individuali-zation," the process by which the individual, "unique" person affects the social order, perhaps even modifying or transforming it in accord with that individual's values or desires.

Indeed, most contemporary academic treatments of identity argue "for" the minimization of the individual in this sense. Michel Foucault (1984), for instance, believed that the "Age of the Individual" would undermine its own celebration of the person by indulging the search for identity so extremely as to surrender the self to social forces quite beyond the control of individual persons. And "postmodernist" thinking has regularly declared the "death of the self" as it has brought about—at least for a time—the "death of the author" in literature (see, e.g., Valdes & Miller, 1985). Put another way, in terms consistent with François Lyotard's (1984) brand of postmodernism, the "Grand Narrative" of the Individual has evaporated, leaving society's inhabitants entirely without "drives," "missions," and well-formed interiors. And, work-ing from a basically postmodernist perspective, one would say much the same thing about organizations in their own pursuit of "selfhood."

None of these trends in contemporary social theory or in commentary on (post)modern society should be carried too far, however. To oversocialize and thereby overdetermine the individual person is to suggest a trajectory for society that is far more predictable and far less creative than the actual world we inhabit (Castoriadis, 1987). In this way, "the return of the actor" to social theorizing is not only a healthy counterbalance to the excesses of the "social-ized" image of the person but is truly essential to capturing key aspects of what the individual person "is." Cornelius Castoriadis's notion of the "social-historical" (1987) and Anthony Giddens's recent book *Modernity and Self-Identity* (1991) achieve just the type of theoretical balance we seek.

C-J cites Richard Rorty approvingly to the effect that "there is nothing to people except what has been socialized into them" (Rorty, 1989, p. 177). While there is a certain sense in which this proclamation is absolutely correct—that is, in its emphasis on the inviolable linkage of individual identity to the society of which one is a part—the statement steers the user and the hearer toward utter disregard for such matters as the brain, the body, consciousness, and the larger physical world in which we live.

The "traditional" conception of identity as essence, as what a thing really *is,* runs the risk of either unreconstructed Realism or unrefined Idealism, depending on where the observer "locates" the essence of something. C-J does well to avoid these theoretical problems. On the other hand, there is a conception of identity, based in perception and interpretation, that allows the observer to say what a thing really is. This perspective centers on the phenomenological experience of the observer (or the society) and gives it great power to determine the "nature" of an individual person or an organization. While any identity is highly dependent on social accreditation—which has been well established since William James (1890/1950) and has been recently reinforced with specific application to organizational life by Berg and Gagliardi (1985)—to embrace fully the perceptual-representation version of identity is in effect to make actors rather like empty channels through which society expresses itself. Thus, with regard to C-J's case, the organizations and their members should not be seen as mere victims of roles prescribed for them by larger social forces. Such theoretical excesses must be tempered with a recognition of the elements we will now discuss.

Identity as a System's Drive: Being, Coherence, and a Sense of Self as Distinct From the Environment

Writings that complement and to some extent counter a one-sided emphasis on identity *as a* social construction have recently appeared in a number of disciplines: for example, the biological notion of "autopoeisis" described by Maturana and Varela (1980), the anthropology of knowledge developed by Edgar Morin (1986), the new systems theory of Niklas Luhmann (e.g., 1990), and the second-order cybernetics of von Foerster (e.g., 1974, 1984), Krippendorff (1984), and others. These distinct but parallel sets of ideas together explain what systems do—in fact, must do—to function and to maintain themselves. For example, in contrast to the usual emphasis of systems theory on the openness of an organization to its environment (market, competitors, other institutions, audiences, and so on), Luhmann observes just how much of an organization's communication is really part of a *closed*, self-referential, and circular system, especially when an organization's ways of constructing its messages are taken into consideration (see Karl Weick's, 1979, use of the term *enactment*). We introduce this set of ideas to make the argument that identity/individuality is not just an external or social construct but is also an internal drive necessary for living systems to persist. We mean to curb the excesses of a purely social constructionist perspective on identity by insisting that some of the dynamics of identity—whether the identity of an individual person or of a corporate person—are in fact "internally" organized. At the same time, we acknowledge that the dynamics of identity are both shaped and informed by transindividual factors—that is, "socialization." We elaborate our point below, drawing especially from the work of Morin (1986).

Identity is, as Morin (1986) has demonstrated, closely linked to the way living systems make sense of themselves vis-à-vis the encompassing "environment." So, identity is a center of knowledge about the self. Knowledge, more specifically, has its source in what Morin calls the continuous "computational" activities of the living. Rather than being a simple assessment of an external world, computation is a self-referential act of calculation through which the living system gets to know itself as distinct and at the same time connected to other things. (In a way, Morin's discussion of the simultaneous needs for separation and connectedness parallels Burke's, 1950/1969, consideration of the grounds for rhetoric as being in "congregation" and "segregation." Segregation is a fact of life at parturition; congregation can never be achieved totally but is sought at times through physical and symbolic connection with others.)

By specifying a world of its own, implying a delineation of boundaries between the self and others, the living system creates a phenomenological domain in which it is able to interact and produce the information necessary to maintain itself. This relatively "contained" conception of identity does not necessarily imply either narcissism on the practical level or solipsism on the theoretical level. As Morin insists, organizational closedness is a precondition for openness, and vice versa (see Luhmann, 1990). Being on the one hand open and indissolubly connected with the environment, the living system on the other hand articulates ontological separations between the self and the nonself, between sense and nonsense.

This distinction, which is maintained and confirmed through communication, is necessary for the system to persist as a relatively autonomous entity. The breakdown in the ability to make such delineations is one of the prime characteristics of schizophrenia in individual humans. In addition to considering the powerful social force of identity in contemporary public discourse, we need to conceptualize identity as an essential "drive" of living systems, whether individual or collective. An understanding of the interplay between this drive and the institutional forces of late modernity ought to be an important goal of organizational scholars.

For example, in C-J's case, the key participants are in fact coauthors of their own narratives of identity. They are subject to larger social forces, such as the transformation of the welfare state and the substitution of "private" symbols for "public" ones in the discourse of the day and the pressures of economic competition. But they and their institutions must still identify, define, and delineate themselves in particular ways. (Of interest, the same pressures and the same imperative face higher education in the United States today.) Organizations simply cannot function otherwise; and this is the point of introducing the theory of Morin (1986) and related ideas. The fact that their old patterns of communication—such as a familiar reliance on "officialese"—does not work in the case of the Swedish public sector organizations does not mean that these institutions are doomed to be without institutional identities or characteristic modes of communication. The identity of an organization can be only so fragmented before the organization ceases to function as an organization. This is an important extension of Chester Barnard's (1938/1968) theory of organizational systems: to ensure survival and success, an organization must (in Barnard's view) communicate a common purpose, maintain a system of communication, and secure essential contributions from its members. An effective organization has a reasonably clear sense of its own boundaries, its own purpose, and what makes it different than other (perhaps similar) organizations. And an effective organization has bodies of knowledge associated with each of those aspects of the sense of "self."

Here we are reminded of the crisis in higher education in the United States today. Far from being solely budgetary in nature, this crisis entails challenges to the basic identities of educational institutions and their constituent groups: professors, students, administrators, and staff. This problem will require creative responses whereby academic leaders do not simply fall back upon characteristic modes of communication. To reestablish a solid sense of "self," the academy in the United States must develop greater internal consensus around goals and values *and* express its identities in a compelling way to skeptical outside publics.

IDENTITY, NARRATIVE, AND SYSTEMS OF DISCOURSE: THE TELLING OF ONE'S STORY

The linkage of individual identity to narrative was made explicit by Nietzsche in several works (see, e.g., 1954). "The self, according to Nietzsche, is not a constant, stable entity. On the contrary, it is something one becomes, something, he would even say, one constructs" (Nehamas, 1985, p. 7). Without circling back into the argument we have just made about the limits of the social constructionist perspective on identity, we bring Nietzsche and those who have followed him (e.g., Heidegger, Derrida, and Foucault) into this discussion so as to stress the important, recursive nature of the telling of one's own story. The telling of one's own story, particularly at points when an identity is challenged from the "outside," becomes an important contributor to identity itself. Many organizations are intuitively aware of this; that is why they present detailed and dramatic tales of their founders and their triumphs over adversity (e.g., Ramanantsoa & Battaglia, 1991). Consider, for example, Procter & Gamble's *The House That Ivory Built: 150 Years of Successful Marketing* (1989). By establishing a self-referential "universe of discourse," such sagas or autobiographies can become part of what the ongoing organization is for new recruits and for old hands. Other examples of self-referential communication include advertising and public relations material designed to influence both employees and external audiences (e.g., Christensen, 1991; Hébert, 1986), annual reports as celebrations of collective visions (e.g., Cheney & Frenette, 1993; Olins, 1989), corporate design and architecture constructed to foster "the right corporate spirit" (e.g., Berg & Kreiner, 1991), and art collections as indications of organizational pride (e.g., Joy & Baba, 1991). Less direct, but equally important, is the telling of one's own story through acts of socially expected or even required behaviors, such as the conducting of opinion polls and market analyses. Such acts "see" and therefore define as relevant certain aspects of the "environment"; these communication projects "tell" both internal and external audiences that the organization is functioning in accordance with the needs and wants of its customers or clients (see Christensen, 1991). All this is to suggest a strongly process-oriented conception of identity: identity as an ongoing process of articulating sameness and difference, permanence versus change, and foreground in contrast with background (see Holland, 1978).

C-J is keen to the importance of narrative in the construction of identity, for both individuals and institutions: She refers, for instance, to "the narrative character" of identity as she describes the experiences of several public sector organizations in Sweden in the late 1980s. In this regard, C-J turns to literature for indications of the authorial resources for organizations in the ongoing (re)construction of their identities. Some of these resources are quite similar if not identical to those available to individual persons: that is, the dominant modes of defining the self within the context of the larger society. Other resources, such as what she terms "actorial shifting operations" (referring to the embodiment of the narrator in various persons or characters), are much easier to accomplish for organizations than they are for individuals. Because of their collective nature and the possibility for diffused responsibility, authorship, and actorhood, organizations have many options for constructing their narratives—even the option of "the divine passive" (e.g., "It has been decided that . . .") in which the organization appears only in the background of the discourse as a kind of deus ex machina (see Sennett, 1980). On the other hand, the very public nature of many organizations and their own active roles in creating their environments create physical and rhetorical constraints on what can be effectively said about the "self," the organization. The U.S. National Aeronautics and Space Administration (NASA) was severely constrained during the months immediately following the explosion of the *Challenger* space shuttle in January 1986 because of the almost mythic proportions taken on by the mission (with the first teacher aboard) in the agency's own discourse.

In her consideration of the identities of the public sector in Sweden, C-J moves to a level of analysis beyond the narrative per se to consider systems of discourse about the market, the state, and the relationship between those two modern institutions. While such a perspective may be relevant, C-J doesn't seem to take the implications of it all that seriously. This is most apparent as C-J reveals her point of view on the situation—or, more precisely, her villainology. C-J poses the important question, "*Whose* story is this?" Answer: "The private sector usurps the role of the narrator and even the author, relegating the public administration to a side character in its own autobiography" (p. 203). While there is a certain sense in which we can agree with this claim, we hasten to emphasize that in this case it is not the private sector as such that is taking control of the story but an ideal *image* of the private as a specific way of organizing, in contrast with that of the public sector. Being only one aspect of a more encompassing institution of modernity, the economy, the ideal of the market comes together with the celebrated notion of "public opinion." These ideas together form an ambiguous but powerful theme that might be called "consumer democracy," a means of interpreting society that is shared by many citizens and that infuses various practices and institutions (e.g., consider how frequently today students in higher education are understood through appeal to the metaphor of "consumers"). For these reasons, the roles of narrators and authors do not belong exclusively to the private sector, as C-J seems to suggest. The discourse that privileges "private" over "public" is part of a larger social process that is continually redefining the "markers of certainty," often by promoting simple dichotomies (e.g., private versus public, capitalism versus socialism, free enterprise versus centralized economic control, or corporate efficiency versus governmental waste). Beginning with the unexplained economic turbulence of the mid- to late 1970s and perhaps culminating in the recent decline of the images of the long-heralded welfare states of western and northern Europe, the merits of the market have become increasingly idealized, not the least by public decision makers. This trend in itself is fraught with irony because the image of an unfettered "free market" being exalted has only a loose connection to the practices of contemporary capitalism, which involve strong public-private "partnerships" and cooperation. In fact, some of the prominent business leaders who promote this image are the same ones who decry the bitter fruits of competition and demand governmental financial support in hard times. Nevertheless, *the images* of *"free* enterprise" and Adam Smith's "invisible hand" of market forces are resilient players in the dramas of decision making over the future of social services, education, utilities, and other institutions.

In responding this way to C-J, we are in part drawing upon Foucault's (e.g., 1984) conception of discourses as historically situated sets of thoughts, expressions, and practices that provide parameters for what will be considered important problems and reasonable solutions. *Discourse* in this sense refers to a prevailing way of thinking about and acting within the world: in a sense, paradigm plus practice. By making distinctions, setting boundaries, and highlighting certain aspects of experience, discourses provide "subtle and covert prior structuring" (Cooper & Burrell, 1988, p. 102). Conceptualized this way, discourses do not determine individual meanings, but they do suggest a range of possibilities within which individual meanings will be constructed. While the discourse of identity certainly affects current management practice and thinking, almost to the point of prescribing constant engagement in self-referential storytelling, the enactment of this discourse in the organizational setting is not determined in any simple way by developments in the environment. Organizations are in a very real sense authors of their own identities, though such identities can always be challenged by other social actors. Similarly, the post-Enlightenment emphasis on identity-as-uniqueness generated a host of concerns, meanings, and practices that are still defining elements of life in the Western world. At the same time, the limits of that discourse are tested through extreme formulations of identity-as-uniqueness (e.g., the construction of novel identity in "cyber-space"), the emergence of paradoxes (e.g., being oneself by being a member of some group), and the development of resistance on the margins of society (e.g., alienation from accepted means of constructing the self and proposals of "alternative" forms, such as communal and nonconsumer ones).

Key organizing terms that relate to capitalism today—*free market, open trade, competition, consumer choice, efficiency,* and so on—are neither univocal nor stable with respect to meaning. *Efficiency,* for example, has numerous meanings, including "getting the biggest bang for the buck," reducing waste, speedy work, low cost, individual standards of production, and standards of production for organizations. And, while the value of efficiency is often victorious in decision-making struggles, it can be demonstrated in certain situations to be in opposition to notions of quality. When efficiency is conceived simply as the production of as many units as possible for a given amount of resources and then is applied to an institution such as education, efficiency actually can undermine quality. (Does any student really want a thoroughly *efficient* university?) Such a realization in concrete organizational situations can undermine the celebration of efficiency that seems to be all around us at the current time. This is simply to suggest that, while a market or private enterprise-oriented discourse certainly is dominant today (as C-J suggests), it should not be expected to remain in its current form. And the larger set of symbols associated with it, viewed as a "toolbox" for the creation of identity, certainly allows for greater individual and organizational creativity than the "end" of C-J's story posits.

EPILOGUE

What then should be the rest of our story? What can we expect for the future of the public sector in Sweden or for similar institutions around the world? If the "public sphere" (as Habermas, 1989, frequently calls it) has been so thoroughly co-opted and privatized and undermined, how can it effectively create or author a new identity for itself? Part of this answer lies in the flexibility of symbolic resources, as described above. Another part of the answer can be found in the fact that the current stage of advanced corporate capitalism will continue to produce problems of its own, particularly in its search for new "needs," new images, and new markets. Another part of the answer is the inherently creative process of constructing narratives of identity. All of these partial answers may offer little comfort to those struggling within the public sector to maintain a sense of autonomy and efficacy. But, if they and others are to revive the public sphere, they must do so with symbols and images that reflect in a creative way the institutional and discursive world of today. If notions of "the public" can be appropriated by private interests, so it is that symbols of private success can be used and adapted cleverly by those who would reinvigorate the public domain. Under social conditions where discourses and narratives are no longer stable, univocal, or grand, the *process* of telling one's own story probably becomes more important than are the conditions for producing that story. The quest for identity remains a significant challenge to individuals and institutions.

And what of organizational identity, as a fact of life and as a topic of research? Clearly, organizations today are pursuing their own identities. They believe that identities are things they must have. Identity in this sense has become a common point of reference for organizational leaders and spokespersons in all sectors of society. The fact that all this talk about identity floods both academic and lay discourses on organizations doesn't necessarily mean, however, that there *are* such identities. Perhaps all of the talk indicates the opposite: the loss of a referent, an anchor, a sense of self with respect to participation in and interaction between organizations. One of the most important things to notice is that, in many cases when identity is discussed and managed in contemporary organizations, most often it becomes reduced to names, logos, insignia, and other concrete but superficial and volatile aspects of the organization. Of interest, these aspects are treated by some organizations not as mere indications of a larger identity but *as* identity per se. When that happens, it might seem to outsiders that identity has become localized, controlled, and divorced from the sense of something more complete or more basic. The separation of identities in such cases from their supposed referents, offering support for postmodernist notions of "autonomized" signs referring only or mainly to themselves (see, e.g., Baudrillard, 1988), reflects a fundamental change in modern society, however—a change that requires new understandings of what identity is, can, and should be.

Still, while we and C-J eschew a return to a pure identity-as-essence ideal, we all recognize the importance for every living system to "find" something more fundamental and more important than a name or a logo. Such a quest will continue to characterize the endeavors of human beings, whether social workers, public relations officers, members of Parliament, or plumbers.

REFERENCES

Albert, S., & Whetten, D. (1985). Organizational identity. In L. L. Cummings & B. M. Staw (Eds.), *Research in organizational behavior* (Vol. 7, pp. 263-295). Greenwich, CT: JAI.

Barnard, C. I. (1968). *The functions of the executive* (30th anniversary ed.). Cambridge, MA: Harvard University Press. (Original work published 1938)

Baudrillard, J. (1988). *Selected writings* (M. Poster, Ed.). Stanford, CA: Stanford University Press.

Berg, P., & Gagliardi, P. (1985, June). *Corporate images: A symbolic perspective on the organization-environment interface.* Paper presented at the Conference on Corporate Images, Antibes.

Berg, P., & Kreiner, K. (1991). Corporate architecture: Turning physical settings into symbolic resources. In P. Gagliardi (Ed.), *Symbols and artifacts: View of the corporate landscape* (pp. 41-67). Berlin: de Gruyter.

Burke, K. (1969). *A rhetoric of motives.* Berkeley: University of California Press. (Original work published 1950)

Castoriadis, C. (1987). *The imaginary institution of society.* Cambridge, MA: Harvard University Press.

Cheney, G. (1991). *Rhetoric in an organizational society: Managing multiple identities.* Columbia: University of South Carolina Press.

Cheney, G. (1992). The corporate person represents itself. In E. L. Toth & R. L. Heath (Eds.), *Rhetorical and critical approaches to public relations* (pp. 165-183). Hillsdale, NJ: Lawrence Erlbaum.

Cheney, G., & Frenette, G. (1993). Persuasion and organization: Values, logics and accounts in contemporary corporate public discourse. In C. Conrad (Ed.), *The ethical nexus* (pp. 49-76). Norwood, NJ: Ablex.

Cheney, G., & Tompkins, P. (1987). Coming to terms with organizational identification and commitment. *Central States Speech Journal, 38,* 1-15.

Cheney, G., & Vibbert, S. L. (1987). Corporate discourse: Public relations and issue management. In F. M. Jablin, L. L. Putnam, K. H. Roberts, & L. W. Porter (Eds.), *Handbook of organizational communication* (pp. 165-194). Newbury Park, CA: Sage

Christensen, L. (1991, June). *The marketing culture: The communication of organizational identity in a culture without foundation.* Paper presented at the 8th International Conference of the Standing Conference on Organizational Symbolism, Copenhagen.

Coleman, J. (1974). *Power and the structure of society.* New York: Norton.

Cooper, R., & Burrell, G. (1988). Modernism, postmodernism and organizational analysis: An introduction. *Organization Studies, 9,* 91-112.

Deetz, S. (1992). *Democracy in an age of corporate colonization.* Albany: State University of New York Press.

Derrida, J. (1976). *Of grammatology.* Baltimore: Johns Hopkins University Press.

Foucault, M. (1984). *The Foucault reader* (P. Rabinow, Ed.). New York: Pantheon.

Gay, P. D., & Salaman, G. (1992). The culture of the customer. *Journal of Management Studies, 29*(5), 615-633.

Giddens, A. (1991). *Modernity and self-identity: Self and society in the late modern age.* Stanford, CA: Stanford University Press.

Habermas, J. (1989). The public sphere: An encyclopedia article. In S. E. Bronner & D. M. Kellner (Eds.), *Critical theory and society: A reader* (pp. 136-142). New York: Routledge.

Hébert, N. (1986). *L'enterprise et son image.* Paris: Bordas.

Holland, N. N. (1978). Human identity. *Critical Inquiry, 4,* 451-469.

James, W. (1950). *The principles of psychology* (Vols. 1, 2). New York: Dover. (Original work published 1890)

Joy, A., & Baba, V. C. (1991, June). *Corporate art collections and organizational culture: An ethnographic inquiry.* Paper presented at the 8th International Conference of the Standing Conference on Organizational Symbolism, Copenhagen.

Krippendorff, K. (1984). An epistemological foundation for communication. *Journal of Communication, 34,* 21-36.

Lefort, C. (1988). *Democracy and political theory.* Cambridge: Polity.

Luhmann, N. (1990). *Essays on self-reference.* New York: Columbia University Press.

Lyotard, F. (1984). *The postmodern condition: A report on knowledge* (G. Bennington & B. Massouri, Eds.). Minneapolis: University of Minnesota Press.

MacIntyre, A. (1981). *After virtue*. London: Duckworth.

Mackenzie, W. J. M. (1978). *Political identity*. New York: St. Martin.

Maturana, H. R., & Varela, F. (1980). *Autopoeisis and cognition: The realization of the living*. Dordrecht, the Netherlands: D. Reidel.

Meyer, J. W. (1986). Myths of socialization and of personality. In T. C. Heller, M. Sosna, & D. E. Wellbery (Eds.), *Reconstructing individualism* (pp. 208-221). Stanford, CA: Stanford University Press.

Morin, E. (1986). *La methode III: La connaisance de la connaisance. Livre premier: Antropologie de la connaisance*. Paris: Editions du Seuil.

Nader, R., & Mayer, C. J. (1990). Corporations are not persons. In B. Ollman & J. Birnbaum (Eds.), *The United States Constitution: 200 years of anti-federalist, abolitionist, feminist, muckracking, progressive, and especially socialist criticism* (pp. 214-216). New York: New York University Press.

Nehamas, A. (1985). *Nietzsche: Life as literature*. Cambridge, MA: Harvard University Press.

Nietzsche, F. (1954). *The portable Nietzsche* (W. Kaufmann, Ed.). Harmondsworth, England: Penguin.

Olins, W. (1989). *Corporate identity: Making business strategy visible through design*. London: Thames and Hudson.

Procter & Gamble. (1989). *The house that Ivory built: 150 years of successful marketing*. Lincolnwood, IL: NTC Business Books.

Ramanantsoa, B., & Battaglia, V. (1991, June). *The autobiography of the firm: A means of deconstruction of the traditional images*. Paper presented at the 8th International Meeting of the Standing Conference on Organizational Symbolism, Copenhagen.

Rorty, R. (1989). *Contingency, irony and solidarity*. Cambridge: Cambridge University Press.

Sennett, R. (1980). *Authority*. New York: Random House.

Tompkins, P. K., & Cheney, G. (1985). Communication and unobtrusive control in contemporary organizations. In R. D. McPhee & P. K. Tompkins (Eds.), *Organizational communication: Traditional themes and new directions* (pp. 179-210). Beverly Hills, CA: Sage.

Tompkins, P. K., & Cheney, G. (1990, October). *Some propositions about identification, communication, and organizational control*. Paper presented at the Helsinki Institute of Technology, Finland.

Valdes, M. J., & Miller, O. (Eds.). (1985). *Identity of the literary text*. Toronto: University of Toronto Press.

von Foerster, H. (1984). *Observing systems*. Seaside, CA: Inter-Systems.

von Foerster, H. (1974). *Cybernetics of cybernetics*. Urbana: University of Illinois, Biomedical Computer Laboratory.

Weber, M. (1978). *Economy and society* (Vols. 1, 2; G. Roth & C. Wittich, Trans.). Berkeley: University of California Press.

Weick, K. (1979). *The social psychology of organizing* (2nd ed.). Reading, MA: Addison-Wesley.

Organizational Narratives and the Person/Identity Distinction

BARBARA LEVITT
Santa Clara University

CLIFFORD NASS
Stanford University

P ERSON" is the most valuable label that an entity can possess. Once labeled a "person" or a "self," an entity acquires an enormous range of rights and privileges. In every society, a "person" is protected by a rich and varied set of rules and regulations not available to "nonpersons" or things. "Persons" are assumed to have consciousness, understanding, emotions, and a host of other unique capabilities.

In postmodern societies, as suggested by Czarniawska-Joerges, "identity" is even more important. The fundamental attribute of identity is a societally accepted claim of a connection to the society. One can think of identity as the counterpoint of anomie: Anomie involves an endogenously generated sense of disconnection with a society, while identity is an exogenously (societally) provided declaration of a particular social position. The possession of an identity provides an entity with a toolbox for action that guides its behavior and, perhaps even more important, provides the ability to claim legitimacy for actions. This legitimacy increases the ability of the entity to make claims on societal resources. Thus identity, like the label of "person," is a useful characteristic.

There are four key contentions in Czarniawska-Joerges's essay. First, in postindustrial society, the label "person" and the possession of an identity are distinct and problematic. Second, the assignment of "person" and "identity" is guided by narrative, particularly the choice of metaphor. Third, the sources of identity narratives are a critical consideration. Finally, the narratives of identity of an organization affect the performance of the organization.

Correspondence and requests for reprints: Clifford Nass, Department of Communication, Stanford University, Stanford, CA 94305-2050.

Communication Yearbook 17, pp. 236-246

This commentary will discuss and elaborate these four contentions. One of the themes running through this commentary is the similarity in ontological problems, in postindustrial society, of individuals and organizations.

THE PERSON/IDENTITY DISTINCTION

In small, traditional societies, bound by mechanical solidarity, the distinction between person and identity is irrelevant. Each individual born into the society is a "person." Because there is a very limited division of labor, there is no need to assemble to meet shared goals, and thus there are no organizations. As long as the societies are isolated from "foreigners" or "strangers," there are no problematic living beings. Because societies tend to have few advanced information-processing technologies, there are no artificial objects, such as computers, that may warrant the status "person." Hence the assignment of the term *person* is a relatively simple and noncontroversial matter. Thus there is no need to erect symbolic boundaries around personhood in the form of identity.

Similarly, identity is so straightforward in traditional societies that even the concept of identity is unimportant. Because all individuals in traditional societies agree on the criteria by which social position is determined (whether the position is determined at birth or based on achievement or other characteristics), and because all individuals have complete knowledge of the relevant attributes of each other individual, identity is a given. Furthermore, each "person" has one and only one identity, and each identity is assigned to one and only one "person." Thus the self/identity distinction has no practical implications.

Czarniawska-Joerges correctly notes that, in modern and especially postmodern societies, the acknowledgment of and the linkages between personhood and identity are highly problematic. With a rich and complex division of labor, individuals coordinate through organizations that seem to operate as autonomous and unitary social actors. Postmodern language permits organizations to make announcements, arrive at decisions, cheat consumers, and have individual and social responsibilities. U.S. law permits organizations to make contracts, to sue for libel, and to be "essentially people" for the purposes of the 14th Amendment to the Constitution. The research literature discusses organizations as being born and dying as members of particular species within particular ecologies (Hannan & Freeman, 1977), as participating in social networks that provide resources (Stinchcombe, 1965), and as possessing legitimacy (Meyer & Rowan, 1977). Indeed, the word *organization* comes from the same root as the word *organism,* the Arabic word *worg* (Beniger, 1986). Of course, modern societies also confront individuals from outside the society and technologies that seem to capture most of what is defined as reflecting "personhood." This leads to a need to create boundaries around personhood by creating the concept of the "other." The notion of "others" opens the way for the emergence of the dichotomy between personhood and identity.

Identity also becomes problematic in postindustrial societies. Because society is fragmented, there is not a single set of characteristics that are agreed upon as relevant to identity. That is, identity is context specific. Because individuals and other social actors are atomized, knowledge of the relevant characteristics of an individual entity is very limited; thus an individual does not automatically receive a social position, even within a given context. Because any social actor can have a social position, it becomes possible for organizations to possess identities, even if one is reluctant to assign organizations the label of "person."

Because the label "person" is relatively complex and ambiguous, and because identity is context specific and there is disagreement over, and ignorance of, relevant characteristics, there is no necessary match between "person" and "identity" in postmodern societies. An entity (e.g., human or organization) can be a "person" and have multiple identities, based on context and societal beliefs about the entity. Conversely, a human or organization can be a "person" with *no* identity, when the ambiguity of the characteristics makes placement in the social structure difficult or impossible.

All entities that can do so strive for the label "person" or for an identity. There are a large number of examples of entities attempting to become "persons." Marginal groups, such as slaves in the antebellum South, Jews in Nazi Germany, and aboriginal groups throughout the world have struggled, or struggle, against "dehumanization." Concerned with harsh treatment, combatants during wartime fear demonization. Corporations sued for and won the right to be viewed as people with respect to the 14th Amendment to the U.S. Constitution. Early researchers in artificial intelligence tried to argue that computers can be "essentially human."

Similarly, a great deal of individual and organizational energy is devoted to the establishment of an identity. Identity is the source of legitimacy, which is, in turn, the most stable basis for the exertion of power. Organizations are able to address or conceal most technical problems, and they are often able to recover from strategic errors and financial losses. Organizations must be perceived as having a role in society, however, even if that role is of dubious value, or they cannot obtain a societal response.

NARRATIVES OF PERSON AND
NARRATIVES OF IDENTITY

How can an entity demonstrate that it warrants the label "person" or the assignment of an identity? A critical insight of the Czarniawska-Joerges essay is to realize that the demonstration must emerge from narrative. There is no unfiltered, external reality, at least in postmodern society, that provides a measure of either "person" or "identity." Instead, these are social constructions that emerge from the use of stories and metaphors to place an entity. The nature of narratives that establish person and narratives that establish identity are very different, however.

Narratives of "Person"

In general, societies are very conservative in the assignment of "personhood" to entities that have previously not been labeled persons. This conservative tendency becomes clear in the battles over abortion rights, animal rights, and euthanasia, among others. It is perhaps even more striking in the case of the backlash from both the computer science and the philosophical communities (e.g., Dennett, 1991; Searle, 1981; Weizenbaum, 1976) against the idea that computers can be people.

In the case of establishing "personhood," an entity, whether human or organization, cannot create an account or provide metaphors to demonstrate its status as a person because nonpersons do not have the legitimacy to make the necessary claims. Any attempt to "prove" personhood involves the *assumption* of personhood, because all of the words that justify the label "person" may only be used by, and applied to, "persons" (Ayer, 1952). The traditional characteristics with which one may justify the label "person," such as "consciousness," "emotions," or "soul," cannot be empirically verified. If an entity claims to have unmeasurable characteristics, such as a "soul" or "consciousness," the society can rule the claim false. If an entity makes claims to verifiable characteristics, such as biological functions, the society can rule the trait irrelevant. Literature provides clear examples: Shakespeare's Shylock fails to prove his humanness with a list of characteristics (e.g., "If you cut me, do I not bleed?"); Shelley's Frankenstein cannot convince the townspeople that, although flawed, he is a conscious person rather than a monster or machine; and robots in science fiction (see Nass, Lombard, Henriksen, & Steuer, 1992) have adopted a variety of unsuccessful ploys to make claims to humanity, claims that are dismissed by refusal to recognize the rights of the claimant. The assignment of "person" in a postmodern society is an essentially arbitrary process over which the referent has little control.

Once society declares (as Czarniawska-Joerges declares) that organizations cannot be "persons," no linguistic or behavioral tricks can overcome that decision. Behaviors that seem usefully linked to an aggregated actor are declared "mere reifications"; organizational descriptions that seem to imply a "self" are viewed as "conveniences" that at best disguise the underlying reality. To aggregate these interactions, even if patterned, into a unified entity is to ignore the ways in which interpersonal communication deludes outside viewers into thinking of the organization as a single entity. The individuals who compose the organization may create narratives that imply a unified whole, but this can be seen as individuals making sense of their own behaviors and the behaviors of others. Under this view, organizations that refer to themselves as entities with the same ontological status or characteristics as "persons" are a priori employing non sequiturs.

On the other hand, if a society accepts the idea of organizations as "persons," the *society*, not the organization, adopts language and metaphors that support the claim. That is, there is an *externally generated* narrative that grants organizations the status of persons. Having accepted this view of organizations, the society gains an enormous vocabulary to describe organizations, rich paradigms to view organizations, and powerful theories to predict the behavior of organizations, because there are far more rich and complex metaphors and far deeper understandings of "persons" than of any other entity. In fact, one can create very rich theories of organizations that make no mention of the fact that organizations usually comprise people (e.g., Inbar, 1979; Levitt & March, 1988; Nass & Lee, 1993). Under this view, the fact that organizations are aggregates of persons is a secondary concern; the key issue is that it is coherent and reasonable to associate the language of "personhood" with organizations. Despite these differences, both those who reject the idea of organizations as persons and those who accept it agree that organizations (and humans) cannot narrate their way into existence; at best, they can reenact, through narrative, that which has been assigned by the external society. In sum, no entity, regardless of the perceptions of the society, can narrate itself into "personhood."

Narratives of Identity

In contrast to assignments of "person," postmodern societies are generally anxious to assign an identity or identities to the entities they confront. When societies assign an identity to an individual or organization, the entity is assigned a social category that enables one to predict behavior of the entity and to define and legitimately address appropriate and inappropriate conduct. Because of the fragmentation of entities and the extensive contingencies associated with virtually all norms, failure to assign an identity cripples a highly differentiated society in its ability either to make sense of the entity's behavior or to justify a societal response. Thus the lists of the nature of postmodern identity that Czarniawska-Joerges provides—coherence, continuity, and commitment or self-respect, efficiency, autonomy, and flexibility—are precisely those characteristics that make behavior predictable and comprehensible. It is interesting to note that the components of heroic identity, such as particularity and accountability, highlight that which is unique: Predictability and legitimacy derive from a rich and shared understanding of the nature of each individual and society as a whole.

Individuals and organizations in postmodern societies receive an identity and then establish a historical and anticipated continuity of behavior that is consistent with an identity already existing in the given context (note the similarity of the idea of identity to the idea of roles). That is, to have an identity, one must construct a coherent past, an ironic recourse to a basis for legitimacy characteristic of traditional rather than formal-legal, postmodern societies (Weber, 1913/1977).

How can one create a history and hence acquire an identity? As Czarniawska-Joerges argues quite compellingly, neither individuals, organizations, nor the society as a whole can *undo* the past by creating fictitious events. What entities can do is create or have created a *narrative* that *reenacts* the past by adopting a new set of metaphors in particular, and language in general, to make past behavior seem to be consistent with what is required in a given context. Because metaphors, like all tropes, have an inherent imprecision, metaphors and narratives can describe almost any behavior in such a way that the old behaviors are seen as consistent with the current context.

Narratives also can be used to provide historical accounts for shifts in identity. Although Czarniawska-Joerges underemphasizes the point, the extent to which the public administration organizations she studies do *not* claim to be "radically new," "following a new vision," or "thoroughly influenced by private sector and societal norms and demands" is remarkable. Instead, the new metaphors that the organizations adopt tend to imply that the organizations have always obeyed the new norms of the society. Thus, for example, although it was a "surprise" to "many [in the organizations] that public administration is a producer and, consequently, also employer" (p. 201), the organizations never referred to themselves as *having become* employers. Instead, they made claims that they always were employers and that they therefore had a full understanding of what was required.

The critical point about the organizational consultants is that they do not simply tell organizations how to change their future behavior, they also tell the organization how to narrate its past. This can be made clear by continuing the allegory of the two sisters presented by Czarniawska-Joerges. In her allegory, Ophelia, the once-popular sister, has become disliked because changes in societal norms have made her "old-fashioned" behaviors suspect.

As the story continues, Ophelia actively works with consultants to remedy her delegitimated identity. A large-scale campaign reconstructs Ophelia's past. A great deal of attention is paid to the few now-fashionable outfits that she had worn. The society is told that Ophelia has been steadily losing weight for years and the soap she uses on her face is a special formulation designed for glamorizing.

The campaign, like most attempts at identity reconstruction in postindustrial society, is dramatically successful. One of the reasons for the success of the reconstruction of Ophelia's identity, and of organizations' identity in postmodern society, is that her power and privilege derive from prior high status. The exchange and power networks that Ophelia established over the years can be called on to legitimate the new claims, in a manner similar to the way that privilege reproduces itself when transplanted in a thoroughly new environment (Veblen, 1927). That is, the value of history is not just a matter of legitimating social position, there are concrete liabilities of newness (Stinchcombe, 1965).

Other reasons for Ophelia's success result from the real and perceived origins of the narrative and the effects of identity narratives on behavior, as noted by Czarniawska-Joerges. The following sections explore these reasons.

WHO NARRATES IDENTITY?

Although entities cannot make claims to personhood, individuals and organizations *can*, to a large extent, construct their own identities. In a fragmented and atomized society, an entity has unique claims to knowledge of its previous behavior and the meanings of those behaviors (in contrast to small, traditional societies exhibiting mechanical solidarity, in which a great deal of information is known about each entity); society does not have a detailed knowledge, memory, or understanding of the behaviors of each individual and organization. Thus an entity has a variety of identities from which to choose and can readily pick and refer to those prior behaviors that are consistent with the chosen identity. Furthermore, an entity's presumed superior knowledge of its own behaviors gives a priori authoritativeness to its own constructions of its history. Although the society must eventually accept the claim to identity—identity is always externally granted—the entity can have a great deal of involvement, in contrast to the case of "personhood." Thus it is not necessarily the case, contrary to Czarniawska-Joerges, that it is undesirable for an entity to be associated with the construction of the identity. What an individual or organization in postmodern society loses in claims to objectivity, it gains in claims to unique knowledge and insights. That is why authorized biographies are such a valuable commodity.

How does this play out in the organizations that Czarniawska-Joerges describes? In the study of 43 state agencies in 1985, the agencies switched from using the description of "Public Master to better fulfill its role as a Public Servant" to the description of "Organization Masters to remain Public Servants" (pp. 201-202). Although this description was seemingly imposed by the outside environment, the agencies clearly adopted the new definition. There was no real problem in making the new identity consistent with the past, as there had always been internal control mechanisms in the state agencies, regardless of their ideology, just as the activities of the state agencies had always been to some extent directed to the public. All that was necessary was a changed emphasis on the particular characteristics of the organization. Note that the agencies did not say, "Whereas before we were Public Masters, now we are Organization Masters"; instead, they simply indicated that they always were "Organizational

Masters." There was little evidence of serious attempts to dismantle the agencies: Although there were harsh commentaries, the agencies retained their primary functions. Indeed, the state agencies' claims to continuous activity in the relevant domain ensured their continued viability.

Was there a crisis of identity in the state agencies, as suggested by Czarniawska-Joerges? The answer, for the most part, seems to be "no." For such a crisis to occur because of past behaviors, three things would have to be true. First, the organization would have to have a history inconsistent with its new identity; that is, there must be questions of consistency. There is, however, a great deal of homogeneity in all large organizations, whether public or private (Scott, 1981). Thus the organization already acted, for the most part, in ways that were consistent with the private sphere. A second requirement for crisis would be that the previous identity of the organization would conflict with the newly imposed/desired definition. Multiplicity and fragmentation of identity are characteristic of all entities in postmodern society, however; it is almost impossible for identities to come into conflict. At most, entities must locate their identities within particular contexts. A final requirement for an identity crisis is that the agencies did not want to adopt a new identity. The behavior of the agencies belie this notion. The agencies aggressively used consultants, and although there may have been statements of righteous indignation, there seemed to be little actual resistance. Indeed, the choice of a new identity was still in the hands of the organization; although the consultants (as a reflection of the society) may have provided a limited set of options from which to choose, it was the organizations, not the consultants or the society as a whole, that made choices within those options. Thus the agencies, as do all postmodern entities, had a much greater control of their identity than implied by Czarniawska-Joerges. The choice of a new identity was not a crisis but a problem and an opportunity.

This is not to say that the agencies did not have a serious problem, or even a crisis, of legitimacy. The way to solve the problem, however, was not to deny the past and radically re-create themselves. This strategy is necessarily ineffective because, if one denies the past, then one has no special claim to persisting in the future. The key to retaining and enhancing legitimacy is to present a narrative that the social system was misguided in challenging legitimacy in the first place.

The agencies were, then, to a much larger extent than suggested by Czarniawska-Joerges, the "authors" of their identities, which explains their ability to survive. It may have been a very clever ploy to give the impression that the consultants actually created the identities, but one cannot forget who paid for the consultants and who had control over their supposedly independent decisions. It would seem that, rather than being forced into a crisis, the state agencies cleverly co-opted the consultants into being the "narrators" of a story written by the agencies.

DO NARRATIVES GUIDE BEHAVIOR?

A final reason for the success of Ophelia's campaign, as for all attempts to adopt a new identity, is that, just as it was not necessary for Ophelia to change her past, it was not necessary for her to change her *self* identity or her *future* behavior. An assault on one's identity *can* lead to a change in how one defines oneself or how one behaves in the future. Individuals and organizations with previous identities, however, tend to respond by establishing a buffer between themselves and the society. That is, the identity that gets applied to an entity need have little to do with the ways in which the entity perceives itself or the entity's current and future behavior. The point here is that an entity can accept or create defining metaphors to be used by the society without "internalizing" those metaphors or allowing those metaphors to affect the organization's actual behavior.

Both individuals and organizations tend to desire and achieve very high levels of inertia—the goal of an individual or organization is to protect what it perceives to be its "core" activities while seemingly conforming with the identity to which it has been assigned (Levitt & Nass, 1989; Thompson, 1967). For example, if Ophelia presents herself as "big-boned" and describes her soap as possessing "healthful" characteristics, there is no reason she cannot have actual independence from societal demands. Although she may have to non-self-consciously wear her nicest dress for key occasions, providing "evidence" of her conformance with the desired identity, she can, for the most part, continue her activities without concern for conformance, at least in action. In postmodern societies, individuals and organizations do not have to be concerned with "presentation of self in everyday life" (Goffman, 1959); situations and relationships are so fragmented that everyday life is simply a set of disjointed episodes. If there is a myth in this situation, as suggested by Czarniawska-Joerges, it is a myth of *dependence*, a myth that Ophelia's behaviors are directed by the society.

One can extend Ophelia's story to what is known about organizations. Organizations often construct structural solutions to buffer their core activities from the external environment (e.g., Thompson, 1967). In one of the most important discussions on this issue, Meyer and Rowan (1977) describe the ways in which formal structures are created for purposes of "myth and ceremony" so that the organization can protect the status quo. For example, organizations can be identified as "caring about affirmative action" or "being involved in public affairs" simply by creating positions associated with that function, even if the positions have no effect on the actual practices of the organization. Organizations may not have been the authors of the narrative, but they can respond to the narrative by creating externally oriented symbols. Thus the organization can seem to respond to societal demands while failing to alter its fundamental practices; that is, organizations can "comply but not obey."

Consultants, as in the case of the agencies described by Czarniawska-Joerges, are often used to administer "rituals of abasement" in which the organization admits limited failure and demonstrates its willingness to come into conformance with the "objective" determinations of the consultants. The comments of the consultant are then "taken seriously" and are usually termed to have had led to "important changes." As in the case of the most concrete data, however, the recommendations of the consultants are virtually never made public. Thus consultants can provide metaphors for the organization even when the metaphors provided by the consultants are ignored. In sum, there can be a "loose coupling" between some of the structures of the organization and the work that goes on within.

Although organizational structures may serve as symbols or metaphors for the society, these same structures need not be symbols or metaphors for the members of the organization. Thus an affirmative action office may be discussed at great length by company officials when speaking to individuals outside the organization, serving important legitimating functions, but may be given short shrift in internal communications. That is, organizations can change the narrative depending on the audience. The fragmentation of societal institutions and the atomization of individuals makes this dual narrative possible without causing the schizophrenia alluded to by Czarniawska-Joerges. Thus the societally imposed identity may have little to do with the perceptions or behaviors of the organization and its member.

Organizations that do not have the resources to produce new behaviors or new structures can protect themselves simply by creating new narratives. The story is told of a proud parent sitting at a university graduation who says, "This must be an excellent school. Look how many students received honors from their departments." This proliferation of awards need not have anything to do with how teachers teach or students learn or how either defines the university. In sum, contrary to Czarniawska-Joerges, entities are quite capable of maintaining multiple narratives of identity, narratives that have a great deal to do with how the organization is treated but very little to do with how the organization actually behaves.

DISCUSSION

Czarniawska-Joerges paints a compelling picture of the importance of narrative for understanding organizations in postmodern society. Essentially, the content and real and perceived source of narrative distinguish "person" and "identity" for both individuals and organizations. Because of the contextualization, fragmentation, and atomization of postmodern society, we have shown that narratives of identity need not be tightly coupled to past, present, or future organizational performance. That is, although unmanaged identities can delegitimate and constrain organizations, a managed identity can be a superb tool for obtaining autonomy as well as legitimacy. If the organization lacks its own storyteller/narrator, or needs the legitimacy of an external account, consultants can be brought in to invent a narrative that maintains social legitimacy without disrupting day-to-day operations. This strategy can work even with products: The disastrous introduction of a product with the identity "New Coke" was brilliantly reconstructed to create the valuable identity of "old" or "Classic Coke." While advertising and market research are children of the Industrial Revolution (Beniger, 1986), it is public relations specialists and corporate spokespersons who gain prominence in postmodern society.

Thus postmodern organizations are confronted with multiple narratives generated by multiple constituencies. Becoming both subject and object of these narratives may create the appearance of organizational instability and inconsistency in the face of environmental change. Thus it seems that the optimal strategy is to hire consultants and media specialists to author seemingly unauthorized autobiographies.

REFERENCES

Ayer, A. J. (1952). *Language, truth, and logic.* New York: Dover.

Beniger, J. R. (1986). *The control revolution.* Cambridge, MA: Harvard University Press.

Dennett, D. C. (1991). *Consciousness explained.* Boston: Little, Brown.

Goffman, E. (1959). *The presentation of self in everyday life.* New York: Doubleday.

Hannan, M. T., & Freeman, J. (1977). The population ecology of organizations. *American Journal of Sociology, 82,* 929-964.

Inbar, M. (1979). *Routine decision-making.* Beverly Hills, CA: Sage.

Levitt, B., & March, J. G. (1988). Organizational learning. *Annual Review of Sociology, 14,* 319-340.

Levitt, B., & Nass, C. I. (1989). The lid on the garbage can: Institutional constraints on decision making in the textbook publishing industry. *Administrative Science Quarterly, 34*(2), 190-207.

Meyer, J. W., & Rowan, B. (1977). Institutionalized organizations: Formal structure as myth and ceremony. *American Journal of Sociology, 83,* 340-363.

Nass, C. I., & Lee, P. (1993). *A materialist approach to the distribution and skill level of work: The case of information work in the United States, 1900-1980.* Unpublished manuscript, Stanford University.

Nass, C. I., Lombard, M., Henriksen, L., & Steuer, J. (1992, May). *Anthropocentrism and computers.* Paper presented at the annual meeting of the International Communication Association, Miami, FL.

Scott, W. R. (1981). *Organizations: Rational, natural and open systems.* Englewood Cliffs, NJ: Prentice-Hall.

Searle, J. R. (1981). Minds, brains, and programs. In D. R. Hofstadter & D. C. Dennett (Eds.), *The mind's I* (pp. 353-372). Bantam: Toronto.

Stinchcombe, A. L. (1965). Social structure and organizations. In J. G. March (Ed.), *Handbook of organizations* (pp. 142-193). Chicago: Rand McNally.

Thompson, J. (1967). *Organizations in action.* New York: McGraw-Hill.

Veblen, T. (1927). *Theory of the leisure class: An economic study of institutions.* New York: Vanguard.

Weber, M. (1977). *Economy and society* (G. Roth & C. Wittich, Eds.). Berkeley: University of California Press. (Original work published 1913)

Weizenbaum, J. (1976). *Computer power and human reason: From judgment to calculation.* San Francisco: Freeman.

6 Communication and Interdependence in Democratic Organizations

TERESA M. HARRISON
Rensselaer Polytechnic Institute

Until recently, research in organizational studies has tended to assume that interdependent relationships are patterned on the model of bureaucratic hierarchy. This essay explores two alternative models of interdependence found in democratic employee-owned organizations. Structuration theory is used as a framework for understanding differences between bureaucratic and democratic organizational systems and the principles through which they are structured. The analysis suggests that the types of systems differ in the nature of interaction occurring within them, in their methods of information processing, and in the amount of overt conflict they engender. Furthermore, new discourses may be required to reconceptualize the administrative, managerial, and technical practices required for democratic organizations to compete effectively with traditional bureaucracy.

OVER the past decade, research in organizational communication has experienced a period of intense growth, fueled by the exploration of a diverse array of methodological perspectives. Given the range of new topics that have appeared in the field and the varied perspectives for studying them, it is reassuring to note that there is a remarkable degree of consensus over the issue of how to conceive the general focus of inquiry. Most researchers would agree that the study of organizational communication focuses upon communicative behaviors that transform previously independent individuals into social collectivities.

Hawes (1974) introduced the term *social collectivity* to avoid certain problems that plague the use of the noun *organization*. Organizations are too easily conceived as static entities, structures that are already developed and

AUTHOR'S NOTE: I would like to express my appreciation to Timothy Stephen, Michael Huspek, and two anonymous reviewers for their helpful comments in preparing this manuscript.

Correspondence and requests for reprints: Teresa M. Harrison, Department of Language, Literature, and Communication, Rensselaer Polytechnic Institute, Troy, NY 12180-3590.

Communication Yearbook 17, pp. 247-274

that exist as contexts in which various activities, such as communication, take place. Hawes wished to focus attention instead on the interactional processes that give rise to organized relationships. In so doing, he relied upon Weick (1969/1979), who recognized that social collectivity is the outcome of interdependence, which is created when two or more individuals participate in cycles of patterned, interlocked behavior to meet their individual goals. What is fundamental to interlocked behavior cycles is that each individual needs the "instrumental" act of the other to perform his or her own "consummatory" act (Weick, 1969/1979). Thus interdependence is created because each individual needs the behavior of the other to achieve his or her own goals.

Hawes converted these insights into an approach to organizational communication that most have found compelling. But he also laid out an agenda for research in the field that has been largely ignored. By designating "social collectivities" as the phenomena of interest for organizational communication, Hawes (1974) challenged us to examine " 'how' organizations come into existence in the first place, 'how' such patterned behavior evolves, 'how' the collectivities maintain themselves, and 'how' they disengage" (p. 500). Furthermore, his use of the term *social collectivity* was intended to acknowledge that this phenomenon takes many different forms, including "negotiations, interviews, families, communes, social movements, volunteer organizations, business/industrial organizations, and White House administrations" (p. 502). Hawes argued that part of the challenge of organizational communication was to explore the similarities and differences between these forms and inquire into the conditions under which collectivities are established as discrete entities and how they enact environments, make decisions, establish values, and change.

Although most would agree in principle with this focus on communication as constitutive of organizations (Bantz, 1989), a far more limited approach to the study of social collectivities and interdependence has been taken. Research in the field is typically restricted to business, industrial, and other profit making organizations and, to a lesser extent, governmental institutions. Consistent with the emphasis on profit making and governmental organizations, research also tends to assume that interdependent relationships are patterned on the model of bureaucratic hierarchy.

When issues related to organizational structure are addressed by research in the field, it is usually not with the intention of exploring the underlying nature of interdependence but within the context of examining a particular kind of interdependence, the structural form that has become known as bureaucratic hierarchy. "Bureaucratic hierarchy" is the form of organizational design articulated under the rubric of "classical organization theory." Weber, Fayol, and Taylor were its prime architects. Weber's (1946) bureaucracy is a model for traditional top-down hierarchy, a scheme for legitimizing the distribution of decision-making authority among positions within a hierarchy. Fayol's (1949) "principles of management" offer more extensive advice about how to design and differentiate positions on a hierarchy; there are suggestions to centralize decision making, ensure unity of command, and enforce a scalar chain of communication, for example, to help the administrator to produce an orderly and predictable flow of behavior. Finally, Taylor (1967) showed how science could be used to identify the "one best way" to organize tasks and work processes, providing a rational basis for division of labor.

Most researchers would acknowledge that bureaucratic hierarchy is not the only form that organizational structure can assume; however, most research nevertheless appears to take the model for granted. For example, three of the four dimensions appearing in Jablin's (1987) review of the research on organizational structure (configuration, complexity, and centralization) are defined in ways that explicitly presuppose a top-down hierarchical model. In much other research, bureaucracy lurks in the background, implicitly framing concepts central to organized life. The very idea of management, for example, is difficult to separate from hierarchical connotations; some individuals, because they occupy positions closer to the top of a hierarchy, are designated within the class known as management. Given an alternative model of interdependence, it may be possible, and make more sense, to distinguish between tasks that are managerial and those that are not. In other words, how one conceives of management depends upon the model of interdependence that is brought to bear.

It is easy to understand why organizational communication researchers have focused upon bureaucratic hierarchy; hierarchies have been the characteristic form of organizational structure throughout most of the world for the last century. While theorists have repeatedly "discovered" new forms of "organic" bureaucracy (Lammers, 1988), until recently there have been relatively few attempts, in theory or in practice, to move beyond the fundamentals of the bureaucratic model.[1] Research focusing on bureaucratic hierarchy has taught us much about the communication practices that constitute and reproduce hierarchies, but it has done little to illuminate the fundamental nature of interdependence or to explore the utility of models that represent potential alternatives to hierarchy.

It is worth considering alternatives to bureaucracy for two reasons. First, as noted above, the central concern of organizational communication research is with the nature of interdependence instead of the utility of any particular form of interdependence. We learn more about communication by focusing upon the variety of ways in which interdependence is accomplished through communication practices. Second, any critique of organizational communication within bureaucratic hierarchies presupposes the ability to envision an alternative. Critical theorists appear to have such visions in mind when they suggest, for example, that corporations be evaluated in terms of whether different interests have an opportunity for equal impact on decision making (see, e.g., Deetz & Mumby, 1990). It is worth addressing questions about what forms of interdependence might more effectively realize normative standards for communication practice that we bring to bear in evaluating organizations. It is also worth pursuing questions about how such alternative forms might be realized in practice.

The purpose of this essay is to explore the foundations of two forms of interdependence that constitute distinct alternatives to bureaucratic hierarchy. I begin by tracing a brief history of social theorists' attempts to understand the nature of interdependence and structure in organizations. This analysis argues that, although Weick's (1969/1979) model provides a basis for appreciating the communicative foundations of interdependence, it does not adequately explain how particular forms of organizational interdependence are created and maintained. Giddens's (1979, 1981, 1984) theory of structuration provides an alternative metatheoretical framework that can be used to compare bureaucratic with democratic organizational systems. More specifically, I argue that concepts central to the analysis of a "reproduction circuit" can be useful in making such a comparison; these concepts are explained using the familiar practices and structures of bureaucratic hierarchy.

In the second major section, the concepts involved in the reproduction circuit metaphor are used to describe two types of democratic organizations. Specific attention is directed at the patterned communication practices within such organizations. The analysis suggests that democratic systems differ from hierarchies in the nature and amount of the face-to-face interaction they sustain, in their methods of information processing, and in the amount of overt conflict they engender. Furthermore, it appears likely that new "democratic" discourses will be required to reconceptualize the administrative, managerial, and technical practices required for democratic organizations to offer viable competition with traditional bureaucracy.

MODELS OF INTERDEPENDENCE

To inquire into the nature of interdependence is to ask how a social entity composed of diverse elements comes to be seen as coalescing as a whole; that is, how are the parts of a social entity connected and in what way do they hang together? The issue of interdependence has concerned organizational researchers as well as scholars across the social sciences who investigate a broad range of social phenomena, including families, communities, and nation-states. Interdependence is regarded as the outcome or product of structure, the cyclical patterned interchanges that transpire between and hence bind the constituent elements of a given social entity. Any effort to understand how interdependence develops and the various forms it may take must begin by understanding the way that the concept of "structure" has been conceptualized in social theory.

Historically, researchers have failed to be faithful to the processual, action-oriented nature of structure articulated by its earliest theorists. Burrell and

Morgan (1979) tell the tale of functionalist approaches to structure in this way: Two of the earliest functionalist theorists, Radcliffe-Brown and Malinowski, conceived of structure as a network of relations that exist between the parts of a social entity; they understood that the continuity of structure is manifested in recurrent activities or behaviors taking place between those parts. As Burrell and Morgan (1979) note, this particular perspective is echoed clearly in the open systems theory developed by Katz and Kahn (1966/1978). Heavily influenced by Floyd Allport (1962), Katz and Kahn (1966/1978) wrote that "structure is to be found in an interrelated set of events that return upon themselves to complete and renew a cycle of activities. It is events rather than things which are structured, so that social structure is a dynamic rather than a static concept." Further, they claimed that a "simple linear stimulus-response exchange between two people would not constitute social structure. To create structure, the responses of A would have to elicit B's reactions in such a manner that the responses of the latter would stimulate A to further responses" (p. 24).

With time and empirical research, this processual, action-oriented view of structure gradually lost focus in favor of a static, reified view; structure came to be seen as the way that parts or dimensions of a social entity were arranged with respect to each other. Burrell and Morgan (1979) suggest that this was a case of an analytic metaphor overshadowing the concept it was intended to illuminate. Social systems were depicted in terms of a biological or organismic analogy; structure was one of a system's constituent elements. Such a view focused attention on how parts of a social entity functioned to maintain a whole rather than on the interrelationships between those parts, with the result that structure was likened to the morphology of an organism or the girders of a building (Giddens, 1984). The tendency to reify structure was abetted further by functionalist researchers' commitment to a positivist epistemology, which favored attempts to implement structure in terms of static dimensions such as centralization, formalization, and flexibility.

Weick's Model of Interdependence

Weick's (1969/1979) model of interdependence has been of considerable importance because it reclaimed the processual nature of structure for organizational studies. The model itself is an abstraction, a framework aimed at illuminating how the basic units of collective structure are formed and become more complex as additional "interlocked behavior cycles" are aggregated into "stable subassemblies" or complex patterns of behavior that become organizational processes. This view is particularly useful in stressing that interdependence between human beings does not arise naturally, it must be created purposefully—designed—by individuals who are trying to accomplish something. The model also supplies a compelling rationale for understanding why interdependence is a processual accomplishment: The behavior cycles performed by interdependent individuals are undertaken to reduce equivocality. That is, they are performed so as to decrease uncertainty and increase the likelihood that actors will be able to achieve their respective goals.

In its depictions of organizational behavior as "enactments" of equivocal stimuli that organizational members come to "see" in particular ways, the Weickian model has contributed to the development of a view of organizing as sense-making. The evolutionary sequence summarized in cyclical patterns of enactment, selection, and retention emphasizes that organizational actors are responsible for both creating and processing the raw data that constitute inputs to organizational sense-making. Organizational members "enact" their environments by bracketing portions of a stream of experience for closer inspection or by behaving in ways that call for responses from others. Such enactments take the form of equivocal displays, that is, displays that are not simply ambiguous but can be interpreted plausibly in two or more ways.

Equivocal stimuli are rendered sensible in cycles of interlocked behavior that constitute a selection process. Here, actors make sense of a given enactment through the imposition of cause maps or other schemes of interpretation. What is selected is both a particular enactment (given that there are many equivocal displays that potentially can be chosen) as well as a particular interpretation of it. Selections are made retrospectively on the basis of whether a given enactment and its interpretation is familiar because it fits well with previously enacted environments or is otherwise helpful in terms of enabling rapid adaptation to changing conditions. The products of selection are stored as enacted environments retained in the memories of organizational actors and in other organizational storage devices; they are available for application to future cycles of equivocality reduction.

All of this is familiar ground. But, valuable as this perspective may be, it is important to recognize that interdependence is never manifested or experienced in quite such abstracted terms. Weick's model is an important conceptual tool for understanding how coherent patterns of organization emerge from ongoing sequences of interlocked behaviors, but it retains an unreal, skeletal quality because most of the cultural, situational, and historical contexts associated with these processes have been stripped away. The model does not address, for example, the social, cultural, or historical conditions under which interdependence is initially created or induced and subsequently maintained. To the extent that such conditions are recognized at all, they are seen as the outcomes of previously enacted environments produced within the life cycle of the organization.

Furthermore, there is little comment on the symmetry or asymmetry that may characterize relations of interdependence, what we would otherwise understand as power or authority differences between interdependent individuals. Although "people in different positions have differential access to power, which means they have differential success in imposing their enactments on other people both inside and outside the organization" (Weick, 1969/1979, p. 168), there is no effort to trace the implications of power discrepancies for particular kinds of enactments by particular kinds of people or, more crucially, for selection processes. The hallmark of equivocality is that such stimuli are amenable to more than a single interpretation. How then are choices made among the variety of competing enactments? To say that enactments are selected on the basis of their adaptive utility to changing conditions is to beg the question: "Adaptive to whom?" The Weickian model tells us very little about *which* enactments and *which* interpretations are likely to be selected and retained.

Thus Weick's model is essentially a framework without specific content. It persuasively depicts the generic cyclical and evolutionary processes by which interdependence is created. But the model never explicitly comments on the character of interdependence or on how or why particular enactments arise and particular interpretations are incorporated into the routine practices of a collectivity. Thus, although "Weick's conception of organizing provides the direct frame for a definition of organizational communication that empha- sizes collective action and meaning" (Bantz, 1989, p. 238), it should be clear that the organizing processes articulated by this frame are necessary but not sufficient for understanding how particular forms of interdependence de- velop. How can we account for the overwhelming prevalence of bureaucratic forms of interdependence in organizations? How can we explain the appear- ance of alternatives to bureaucracy when they arise? We must turn to other conceptions of interdependence for additional detail.

Distinguishing Between System and Structure

The idea that social collectivities are created when individuals engage in interlocked behavior cycles has also been advanced by symbolic interaction- ist theorists to explain the general development of social structure. Berger and Luckmann (1966), whose overarching project was to understand the formation of society, portray social life as comprising institutions, the out- comes of face-to-face interaction that has become patterned and habitualized over time. More specifically, nascent institutions are created when individu- als "typify" each others' actions by subsuming them under particular catego- ries of role performance (for example, "a man," "a European," "a buyer"; Berger & Luckmann, 1966, p. 31). Typifications provide a basis for expecta- tions for behavior ("actions of type X will be performed by actors of type X"; p. 54), which are used by actors to guide their choice of appropriate social conduct.

Blumer's (1969) conception of "joint action" portrays social life in fami- lies, organizations, and nations as consisting of the "fitting of lines of action to each other," thus constructing an "organization of conduct of different acts of diverse participants" (pp. 16-17). Joint action is possible because most situations are "structured" (Blumer, 1969, p. 86); that is, individuals share common meanings for situations and common expectations for appropriate behaviors within given situations and it is to these meanings that social scientists are referred in understanding the basis for particular kinds of action.

Each of these approaches to the development of interdependence distinguishes between the specific actions that bind participants and the meanings informing those actions, which shape the ongoing course of interaction. Giddens (1979, 1984) draws this distinction more sharply in his differentiation between system and structure.

The patterns of interlocked behaviors, institutions, and joint actions described by Weick, Berger and Luckmann, and Blumer are essentially equivalent to what Giddens (1979, 1984) calls "systems" or "reproduced relations between actors or collectivities, organized as regular social practices" (p. 66). Social systems are patterned relations of interdependence manifested as recurrent social practices. Understanding Giddens's unique perspective requires that one realize that social systems are not themselves structures; instead, social systems *have* structures, which serve as the basis for the production and reproduction of particular practices in particular sequences under particular circumstances of occurrence.

More specifically, structure consists of rules and resources that actors draw upon in the course of interaction and that serve as the basis for an actor's selection of subsequent behavior. Rules define what behaviors mean, which behaviors are appropriate, and which are liable to sanction within given situations. Thus rules consist of what an actor needs to know to accomplish something, as Giddens (1979) puts it, "to know how to go on" (p. 67). Resources, on the other hand, are "vehicles" of power, capabilities over materials and persons, through which actors' intentions and interactional programs are actualized. Actors "sustain the meaning of what they say and do through routinely incorporating 'what went before' and anticipations of 'what will come next' into the present of an encounter" (Giddens, 1979, p. 84). In so doing, actors draw upon structure for knowledge about how to act and for the power that enables action. Thus structure may be conceived as the stocks of knowledge and abilities that actors draw upon to shape conduct, making interaction possible, meaningful, and legitimate.

Unlike social systems, which consist of actions that take place in real time and space, structure does not have an ongoing material existence. Instead, at any single point in time, structure has a "virtual" existence. As actors draw upon rules and resources in the routine mobilization and performance of conduct, these structures are reconstituted and can be said to exist materially only in those moments of reconstitution. When not specifically reconstituted in practices, structure exists as "memory traces"; those structures that fail to be reconstituted on a routine basis gradually fade from memory.

What Giddens refers to as the "duality of structure" is the process whereby actors draw upon structure to constitute their social practices, and, in so doing, structure is itself reconstituted in the knowledgable production of social practice. Structure is thus both the medium and the outcome of social practice. Through the routine reproduction of social practices, structure also may be said to bind space and time, "mak[ing] it possible for discernibly similar social practices to exist across varying spans of time and space" (Giddens, 1984, p. 17). Structures that are "deeply layered," producing practices that endure across history and across geography, are called *institutions*.

As Cohen (1989) points out, structure adds political and cultural content to the skeletal framework of social systems. That is, structure explains why particular kinds of practices and patterns appear in interlocked sequences of organizational behaviors. Furthermore, it is through structure that the positions of actors within a social system and relations of autonomy and dependence between these positions are defined.

Reproduction Circuits and Bureaucratic Systems

Although there has been considerable interest among social theorists in developing generic models of interdependence, there have been relatively few attempts to apply these models to explaining the development of any particular kind of organizational structure, much less to explaining how different organizational designs might emerge within a given society.[2] Historically, bureaucratic hierarchy has been seen as a natural and necessary feature of organizational life, so fundamental that many can scarcely imagine how interdependent relationships in organizations might be organized in any other way. Questions like those posed by Hawes, which ask how organizations come into existence and how their patterned behaviors evolve, simply never come up in most studies of organizational communication.

But such questions are central to a theoretical perspective in which organizational systems are seen as the accomplishment of individuals who draw upon structure to routinely reproduce patterned communication practices. Differences between bureaucratic and democratic organizational systems may be illuminated by understanding how particular structures give rise to and are instantiated by particular practices. It will not be necessary to bring all of Giddens's structurational apparatus to bear in this kind of comparison. The following will describe the specific methodological path we shall take and the concepts and themes that will be relevant.

Giddens (1979, 1984) describes two methodologies for employing structurational theory in empirical research. The *analysis of strategic conduct* centers on practices and attempts to portray how actors draw upon rules and resources in the constitution of their social actions. Such analyses generally emphasize the cultural and hermeneutic aspects of social practices, focusing on what actors know in engaging in specific practices, what they are able to articulate about their conduct, what they are trying to accomplish, and their reflexive monitoring of the ongoing development of action. *Institutional analysis*, on the other hand, places methodological brackets around strategic conduct and centers on structures, seeking to demonstrate how rules and resources become institutionalized historically and geographically as features of social and societal systems (Giddens, 1979).

Cohen (1989) suggests a third methodological focus, which he calls *systems analysis* and argues is implied by Giddens's (1984) recent focus on the time-space patterning of social systems. In systems analysis, the investigator first brackets off the contingencies of day-to-day interaction to focus on the patterning of practices as they occur across time and space and, second, brackets off the chronic reproduction of structure to focus on institutionalized structures as if they existed in virtual space. This dual bracketing allows us to examine, in a kind of snapshot fashion, what lies in between: the patterning of a given set of practices and the institutionalized structures that serve as their media and their outcomes.

The key word in the development of both bureaucratic and democratic organizational systems is *reproduction*. Although isolated or random actions are not without interest, we focus upon sequences of practices that recur repeatedly because reproduced sequences are those responsible for the creation of a system. It will be useful to conceive of an organizational system as a *reproduction circuit*, which Cohen (1989), following Giddens (1984), defines as "a cycle of routinised activities and consequences which are reproduced across time-space within and between institutionalised locales" (p. 124). Two sets of concepts, *social integration, social position, system integration* and *structures of signification, legitimation, and domination* are central to a systems analysis of organizations as reproduction circuits.

The first set of concepts is used to characterize social systems. *Social integration, social position*, and *system integration* describe the patterns of reciprocated practices taking place between actors that make up the configuration of a particular social system. The second set of concepts concerns the structures that are drawn upon in producing a social system. *Structures of signification* and *structures of legitimation* refer to modes of discourse, symbolic orders, and interpretive schemes and to a legitimized order of rights and obligations, all of which constitute actors' mutual knowledge about the meaning and appropriateness of particular practices performed under given circumstances. *Structures of domination* refer to the material and authoritative resources that allow actors to generate command over materials or other actors (Giddens, 1979).[3]

Consistent with the relationship between system and structure discussed earlier, the two sets of concepts are implicated in the duality of structure. Structures of signification, legitimation, and domination are drawn upon in producing patterns of interaction and are reconstituted in the reproduction of those patterns. A social system (defined by a particular configuration of social integration, social positions, and system integration) is created when cycles of patterned modes of interaction are reproduced in social settings over time.

Social systems comprise patterned face-to-face or mediated interactions; that is, interactions take place in a given order and are regularly distributed over time and space. *Social integration* refers to the degree to which a system is "tied" together or connected through reciprocal practices extending over sequences of interaction in which various actors are present or absent (Giddens, 1984). A sequence of interactions is bound by the presence of particular human bodies, which provide connections or linkages between encounters. Such encounters are ordered serially; that is, some must take place before others can occur. Further, encounters typically take place in locales (settings) that are "regionalized" or zoned for particular kinds of interactions between particular actors, a condition that shapes the potential for copresence between specific actors. Social systems are thus more or less integrated depending upon the extent to which actors regularly traverse time-space paths that enable them to be together in the same place at the same time.

Participants are positioned within the time-space coordinates of the system; they are also positioned relationally with respect to each other. This means that particular *social positions* are situated within a system such that actors who occupy given positions regularly encounter other actors positioned reciprocally. Furthermore, each social position specifies a particular identity (Giddens, 1984) to which is attached a given range of prerogatives, obligations, and corresponding practices (Cohen, 1989) constituted by a specific intersection of signification (meaning), legitimation (normative sanctions), and domination (power). The positions within any social system are characterized by asymmetrical distributions of rights and resources and hence by political inequality.

This rather arcane vocabulary can be demystified when illustrated by the familiar and distinctive distribution of interaction across time and space characteristic of bureaucratic systems. Bolle de Bal (1989) points out that bureaucracy can be viewed as a social system aimed at minimizing face-to-face relations. As we know, organizational interactions are sorted into specified hours of the day and are generally confined to work locales, as opposed to home or other social settings. Workspace locales for a given organizational system are markedly regionalized; that is, the presence or absence of particular organizational actors pattern the interactions that take place on factory shop floors as opposed to company headquarters, in mail rooms as opposed to penthouse suites, and in employee cafeterias as opposed to executive dining rooms.

Individuals positioned distinctively within bureaucratic systems—workers, first line supervisors, middle management, executives—are distributed in regular and predictable ways across such regionalized spaces and possess particular interactional capabilities and obligations. Thus certain kinds of interactions (e.g., order giving/information giving between first line supervisors and shop floor employees, mutual decision making between executives at headquarters) take place between individuals positioned in particular regions. Deviations from these patterns, such as the plant manager who shows up to chat with workers on the shop floor, are either atypical events or efforts aimed directly at modifying the bureaucratic character of the system (e.g., executives who manage by "walking around").

System integration occurs when a pattern of interaction established in relations of copresence is extended across time or space. For small systems, social integration *is* system integration. For systems in which participants are geographically or temporally separated, however, specific mechanisms of system integration—in the service of both coordination and control—must be employed. The seriality of sequences of encounters can be maintained to some degree by the movement of agents to sites where specific interactions need to occur. McPhee's (1988, 1989) analysis of the sequencing of encounters between dyads of superordinates and subordinates in transporting information, directives, stories, and resources down through the vertical chain illustrates how the movement of bodies in reciprocated interaction accomplishes social and system integration. Electronic media, literacy, and writing can be used to overcome temporal and spatial distance by distributing codified rules that coordinate and control actors' practices.

System integration is further facilitated by surveillance, the documentation of information, and the development of analytic expertise (e.g., statistical inference), all of which allows agents, for example, managers, to coordinate the spatiotemporal sequencing of work activities. Conceived in this way, as Oliver (1987) points out, one of the functions of bureaucratic hierarchy is "as an information system, designed to move information from where a problem exists to where a decision is made" (p. 451).

The pattern of interactions that compose a bureaucratic organizational system is founded upon the complex interplay of institutionalized *structures of signification, legitimation, and domination* known more familiarly to us as bureaucracy, hierarchy, and division of labor. These structures may be conceived as interpretive and legitimating schemes that reflect mutual agreements over the rights assigned to and claims that can be made upon actors occupying particular positions. Differential power sustains the entire complex, although we may rarely be conscious of it, for "the fundamental asymmetry of power between employers and workers lies in two factors above all others"—employers' possession of capital and workers' difficulties in organizing effectively (Rueschemeyer, 1986, p. 76).

In allocating authority and materials to some positions over others, the agreements reflected in bureaucracy, hierarchy, and the division of labor legitimize certain interests—and the technologies they represent—over others. These technologies (e.g., bookkeeping, accounting, and finance; industrial engineering; management information systems) have their own "technical vocabulary, perspective and standard modes for interpreting and attacking problems" (McPhee, 1985, p. 163). In legitimizing these interests and vocabularies over others that could be represented by organizational actors (employee rights, safety, craftsmanship, for example), bureaucratic hierarchy sets the conditions for discourse and debate by selecting actors who will enter into decision-making interactions, by defining what counts as a valid issue, what counts as a legitimate line of argument, and the values that will be invoked in the disposition of decisions. The resulting "managerialism" is portrayed by Deetz (1992) as a "discursive genre" that "entails a set of routine practices, real structures of rewards, and a code of representation. It is a way of doing and being in corporations that partially structures all groups and conflicts with, and, at times, suppresses, each group's other modes of thinking" (p. 222). Attempts to regulate or suppress conflict may be viewed as a characteristic feature of bureaucratic systems.

While system integration extends a pattern of interaction out into time and space, the reproduction of a system extends an entire cycle of routinized activities across time and space. The consequences of activities—objects, events, and circumstances transformed in interaction—are transmitted to other agents who perform their transformative or mediating activities, which are then transmitted to other agents and so on and eventually "feed back to their sources whether or not such feedback is reflexively monitored by agents in specific social positions" (Giddens, 1984, p. 192). A classic example of generalized bureaucratic reproduction cycles is provided by Cohen's (1989) description of committee meetings that produce policies, which are subsequently implemented, the results of which are stored in files, eventually to be retrieved and employed in the production of future policies by the committee producing the original policy.

System reproduction may be accomplished through homeostatic causal loops producing a "loose" rather than causal determinism, through which unintended consequences of social action may also be incorporated into system reproduction (Giddens, 1984, p. 27). But system reproduction requires some degree of reflexivity in the sense of actors who possess the relevant forms of mutual knowledge and requisite capabilities (information, expertise, or other authoritative and material resources). The defining feature of administered systems, or organizations, is system reproduction via reflexive self-regulation, in which agents monitor system activities and incorporate knowledge about system functioning into reproduction processes. Each cycle of reproduction introduces the possibility of change into the system, in which case a reproduction circuit may become a circuit of change.

In the context of reproduction, it is also worth noting that the mutual knowledge reflected in structures of bureaucracy, hierarchy, division of labor, and managerialism has been codified by generations of educators (social scientists, textbook writers, and teachers) following their original expositions by Weber (1946), Fayol (1949), and Taylor (1967). These institutions have structured most of the organizational systems that comprise our social, cultural, religious, and educational lives. Thus it seems scarcely surprising that actors are able to knowledgably reproduce the practices characteristic of bureaucratic systems.

DEMOCRATIC SYSTEMS IN
EMPLOYEE-OWNED ORGANIZATIONS

Given a world populated by bureaucratic organizations, how do democratic organizations come into being? The logic of structuration explains the reproduction of a deeply layered institution like bureaucracy; the real challenge is accounting for the isolated but persistent appearances of democratic organizations. But democratic systems are not invented out of thin air. As Giddens (1984) states, "It is not the case that actors create social systems: they reproduce or transform them, remaking what is already made in the continuity of *praxis*" (p. 171). Structure, as Benson (1977) and Huspek (in press) point out, is not monolithic, unfolding in an orderly fashion, but comprises contradictory tendencies generated in ongoing processes of social construction that take place in partially nested, partially autonomous subsystems. Rival or competing structures "can be said to generate colliding world views, competing ideologies, that are vying for . . . allegiance" (Huspek, in press). Knowledgable actors, aware of the grounds for their behavior and the institutions that legitimize action, can come to "penetrate" or understand the limits and licenses afforded by competing social structures and use "practical consciousness" to create novel social systems (Giddens, 1979).

One of the enduring structural contradictions in Western society is formed by the antithetical conceptions of authority that underlie our democratic public institutions and our private economic institutions. Out of this contradiction or "macro-system fault" and through the reproduction of selectively appropriated societal practices (Stryjan, 1989), democratic "employee-owned organizations" are formed. I focus on two different types of employee-owned organizations, which, following the work of Gherardi and Masiero (1987), will be differentiated on the basis of their origins and the kind of social pact that unites organizational actors.[4] The two models may be initially compared in terms of the motives giving rise to their creation and the way that ownership is defined. Later I will examine relationships between structures of membership/ownership and the interactional practices that constitute their organizational systems. Because the models contrast so greatly, they offer two different sources of insight regarding how democratic organizational systems may evolve.

Democratic Organizational Systems Defined

In the category called "Type 1," organizations are "alternative" or "collectivist-democratic" cooperatives (Mellor, Hannah, & Stirling, 1988; Rothschild & Whitt, 1986), "worker" cooperatives (Clarke, 1984; Jackall & Levin, 1984), "foundation" cooperatives (Gherardi & Masiero, 1987), and other forms of employee-owned organizations that conform to the following description.[5] Type 1 organizations are created by individuals who seek specifically to construct economic and political alternatives to traditional bureaucratic organizations, even at the expense of profitability. Ideologically opposed to inequalities in power, labor, and rewards, members of these organizations have experimented with decision-making methods, work designs, and methods for distributing surplus that create and maintain egalitarian work relationships.

Type 1 organizations tend to be employee owned in a collective sense. In contrast to conventionally owned companies where stockholders share in net profits and are entitled to exercise control in accordance with the amount of stock they own, members of Type 1 organizations typically equalize share ownership (or membership) and voting rights between individuals, usually through a one person-one vote formulation (Rosen, Klein, & Young, 1986). In many situations, members may not sell their shares to an outsider but must surrender them upon leaving the organization. Although these organizations are employee owned, the concept of "ownership" plays very little role in the identity of its members. The right to participate in organizational governance is based upon labor performed for the company rather than share ownership (Ellerman, 1982; Tannenbaum, 1983).

"Type 2" organizations include "phoenix" cooperatives (Cornforth, Thomas, Lewis, & Spear, 1988; Mellor et al., 1988), Gherardi and Masiero's (1987) "federative" cooperatives (created to save jobs potentially lost from the closing or sale of an enterprise), the celebrated plywood cooperatives of the Pacific Northwest and other "producer" cooperatives (Clarke, 1984), and certain organizations with employee stock ownership plans (ESOPs). ESOPs have become increasingly visible in the United States over the last decade; but it is important to realize that such plans are actually company benefit programs that allocate company stock to employees, usually without direct employee payment. ESOP plans are highly flexible. Some companies use them for profit sharing with employees, others for raising capital, and some have used ESOPs to fend off hostile takeovers. I will be specifically concerned with those companies where a majority of stock has been bought by its employees through the use of an ESOP to prevent a factory, plant, or business closing—a situation that became increasingly familiar in the 1980s—or because the owner(s) of a company want to transfer ownership to their employees (e.g., Zwerdling, 1982). In each of these situations, a radical transformation of the company is undertaken that has the potential to develop a democratic system.

Unlike members of Type 1 organizations, the individuals involved in Type 2 organizations are not motivated by democratic principles. These employee ownerships tend to occur under conditions of impending unemployment; the central motive driving the formation of these organizations frequently is to create or retain jobs. Additionally, employee-owners are likely to be more interested in the traditional capitalistic values of efficiency and profitability (Woodworth, 1981), if only because their organizations face the challenges of economic survival.

Not all worker buyouts have sought to create democratic forms of decision making; however, in practice, buyouts are more likely to lead to attempts to create democratic systems of governance than other types of employee ownership (Hochner, Granrose, Goode, Simon, & Appelbaum, 1988). When democratic forms are created, it is at least partially out of distrust of decision makers who may have been responsible for the conditions leading up to the buyout and partially out of a newly found desire to exercise more control over the work environment. In democratic ESOP companies, ownership is defined in terms of owning shares of the firm, which may be distributed on the basis of seniority, pay scale, some combination of the two, or some other formula. The basis for participation in decision making is derived from one's status as a shareholder; however, organizations differ in their schemes for allocating voting power. In some organizations, owners may possess votes equal to the number of shares owned; other organizations may follow a one person-one vote rule; and other organizations may vary the formulas depending on the issue (Blasi, 1987).

Reproduction Circuits in Democratic Organizations

Membership in bureaucratic organizations is taken for granted in Western society; individuals are not normally called upon to account for their decisions to initiate or belong to such organizations. Such is not the case, however, for members of democratic organizations who must justify relatively unique organization designs and operations to themselves as well as to other individuals and organizations in the environment. Gherardi and Masiero (1987) have coined the term "co-op idea" to refer to the social pact created between organizational members or the "logic of action with which an organization defines its relationships with its environment and, as a result, its own internal structure" (p. 324; see also Gherardi, Strati, & Turner, 1989). They argue that strategic choices and developmental patterns will not be uniform across democratic organizations; instead, choices and patterns will be legitimated and guided by the meanings and understandings that members attribute to their organization as conceptualized by the social pact.

Structures. Type 1 organizations are initiated by those who seek explicitly to reproduce the character of participatory or representative democracy in their organizations. Thus members generally share beliefs in the rationality of democratic or equal control (Mellor et al., 1988). Cooperatives informed by a "community pact" (Gherardi & Masiero, 1987) are guided by members' reactions against capitalism and desires to create egalitarian conditions in wages, work, face-to-face relationships, and control. Other Type 1 organizations are grounded in principles that are more or less ideological. For example, members of cooperatives resembling Rothschild and Whitt's (1986) collectivist-democratic ideal type are committed to realizing a form of organizational democracy that is antithetical to bureaucracy on eight dimensions (e.g., authority, rules, status). On the other hand, the Cheeseboard cooperative (a store that sells cheese, bread, and other foods) described by Jackall (1984) draws upon images of family and family relations rather than any particular ideological position. Although the particular kind of democratic principle structuring Type 1 organizations may differ, organizations within this category are similar in that each legitimizes the allocation of authority to the collective membership of the organization.

If Type 1 organizations are attempts to reproduce some version of democracy within organizations, then Type 2 organizations (especially those formed through ESOPs) may be best regarded as attempts to reproduce capitalist structures of ownership among individuals of middle and working classes. ESOPs were conceived originally as a mechanism to redistribute wealth. Louis Kelso, the originator of the ESOP idea, and Senator Russell Long, ESOPs' chief legislator, both believed that high concentrations of wealth in the hands of a few was a condition greatly at odds with democratic assumptions of equality and a broad distribution of property (Blasi, 1987). Employee stock ownership plans were viewed as a way to shift capital to the middle and working classes.

The concept of "ownership" is a powerful structure of signification and legitimation, an interpretive scheme shared by both management and workers that can be drawn upon to justify new behavioral routines and that leads to higher expectations for control among employees. Ownership confers a status on employees that legitimizes their participation in a new range of rights and responsibilities within the organization. As Quarry, Blasi, and Rosen (1986) commented, "It is fair to say that in this country employee ownership has been the only legitimate method for democratizing the firm at the management level." This is because "employees as owners are perceived to be much less threatening than employees as nonowners. In a number of cases, this process has been gradual, with companies first sharing ownership and later sharing control as well" (pp. 23-24). The employee-organization relationship is thus redefined as an owner-property relationship. As Ivancic and Logue (1991) have pointed out, participants in these organizations typically experiment with democratizing existing ownership structures, but not because democracy itself is viewed as a value. Instead, democracy serves a pragmatic function: It is a way to protect investments by distributing control among multiple employee-owners. Put differently, democracy is used as a means for managing joint ownership.

Interaction patterns in democratic systems. If bureaucratic systems can be characterized as minimizing face-to-face interaction, then democratic systems may be characterized as rich in face-to-face interaction and thus relatively high by comparison in their degree of social integration. Most Type 1 organizations reject distinctions between work and other social settings. Interpersonal relationships are holistic rather than segmented into personal and professional spheres; in fact, friendship networks are a major source of new recruits (Rothschild & Whitt, 1986). While settings for interaction may be regionalized to some degree, efforts are made to destroy the inequalities that support the bureaucratic distribution of actors across such regions. The relevant dimension for distinguishing between organizational members seems to be the amount of time that each devotes to organizational activity. Group meetings, which can be attended by all organizational members, constitute a nearly universal pattern of interaction among members of both Type 1 and Type 2 democratic organizations.

In the smallest and simplest of Type 1 organizations, group meetings are the only routinized venue for interaction; all other interaction between members takes place when and as it is needed. Translated into practice, the authority of the collective in Type 1 organizations is represented almost universally in a one person-one vote decision-making formula. Most of these organizations, however, are committed to achieving consensus and strive to make decisions that are satisfactory for all (see, for example, cooperatives described by Jackall, 1984; Rothschild & Whitt, 1986; Sandkull, 1984; Zwerdling, 1984). Interaction in group meetings can be long, arduous, and sometimes fraught with conflict.

Significant effort is devoted to ensuring that the relative status of individuals is equalized; thus members of Type 1 organizations typically attempt to minimize divisions of labor and avoid conferring special responsibilities on individuals or any other practices that could create differentiated social positions within the system. Members rotate jobs to equalize expertise derived from task familiarity. Further, members teach each other what they need to know to develop expertise parity. And, assuming that information about the operations of the organizations has been collected and collated, it is typically available to all members of these organizations.

In larger Type 1 organizations, it is neither possible nor desirable for each member of the organization to participate directly in all organizational decision making. In these organizations, opportunities for participatory and representative decision making are woven together in an effort to maximize individual autonomy within a large group. Hoedads, for example (Gunn, 1984a), is a reforestation cooperative, composed of roughly 300 members, whose work (tree planting, forest thinning, forest trail construction, and fire fighting) is carried out by teams or crews in locations distant from the central office for weeks at a time. Decisions are distributed into three tiers of responsibility: individual crews act as autonomous work groups in the conduct of day-to-day activities; a council, composed of members elected from each of the crews, considers issues that affect the cooperative as a whole; and task forces, whose membership may be open to the crews or elected, are created to research problems that require specific information or particular expertise. General meetings, which can last for several days, take place a couple of times a year to consider task force issues as well as any other issues that are known by the council as likely to be controversial.

Interaction patterns vary considerably among Type 2 organizations. Pacanowsky (1988), for example, describes a "lattice" patterning of communication contacts at W. L. Gore Associates, which amounts essentially to an unrestricted flow of communication among individuals based purely on need. Because Type 2 organizations are frequently rebirths of bureaucracies or are otherwise not ideologically antibureaucracy, however, interaction patterns can be considerably more similar to those within traditional bureaucracies. For example, Type 2 organizations generally do not differ from traditional bureaucracies in expectations for daily member attendance. Furthermore, many of these organizations, such as the plywood cooperatives, may use assembly-line operations and work units staffed by supervisors (Gunn, 1984b). At most Type 2 organizations, including the plywood cooperatives, however, enterprise-level decision making takes place among a board of directors elected from the general membership as well as in general meetings where members vote on policy matters affecting the organization as a whole.

The hierarchical work unit structure in the plywood cooperatives has been criticized by some analysts as less than fully democratic (Gunn, 1984b). On the other hand, Greenberg (1986) has argued that members' work group practices redefine the nature of the relationship between supervisor and subordinates: "Work is organized to allow for considerable space for individual initiative, informal work cooperation, and self-management, with supervision generally in the background as a nonthreatening and assistance-giving institution" (p. 50).

At Fastener Industries, another Type 2 organization, employees practice ownership by voting their stock (Rosen et al., 1986). In 1980 the retiring founders of Fastener Industries, a company that makes nuts, bolts, and other fasteners, used an ESOP to transfer ownership to approximately 125 employees. The ESOP plan in this company passed through full voting rights to employees on their stock, which is vested within 1 month of employment and allocated according to relative level of pay. Votes are allocated according to the number of shares held; however, because salary differentials between employees are not great, power is relatively equal. Like most other Type 2 organizations, employees elect members of the board of directors, which is reformed every 2 years (Ivancic & Logue, 1991; Meek, Woodworth, & Dyer, 1988).

While the ability to vote shares is important in reproducing ownership at Fastener, there are other informal practices through which the structure of ownership is reproduced on a daily basis. Information is shared through financial reports to employees and employee input is elicited in several ways: through regular roundtable meetings between small groups of employees and the president (a process that cycles through all employees every 6 months), meetings between plant managers and employees at the shop floor level (that take place at the request of employees), and general shareholders' meetings.

Despite efforts to equalize wages and other resource allocations among members, some individuals inevitably wield more influence than others over decisions. In the case of Type 1 organizations, influence is allocated to individuals informally on the basis of their contributions to the organization, in terms of work hours, expertise, and displays of commitment. At the Cheeseboard (Jackall, 1984), for example, status (as represented in one's ability to claim choice jobs) and influence over decisions was allocated informally on the basis of the number of hours worked and expressions of commitment. Similarly, in the food cooperatives described by Brown (1989), members' influence depended on the hours donated to store operations as well as the expertise and commitment that was seen as a consequence of such involvement. Although some cooperatives are guided by charismatic leaders (see Gherardi & Masiero's, 1987, description of "foundation" cooperatives), decision-making influence does not necessarily translate into decision-making authority. Food co-op members, for example, had a particular understanding of leadership, which translated into spending time developing future plans, "working with the membership to help them understand and decide among these alternatives," and "never stepping far beyond what the membership had already agreed to" (Brown, 1989, p. 495).

In Type 2 organizations, members are more willing to allocate influence to those possessing technical expertise and are far less committed to equalizing expertise among organizational members. In Gherardi and Masiero's (1987) "federative" co-ops, decision-making authority regarding management, productivity, or company strategy is delegated to technical groups, despite the existence of worker assemblies legally mandated for cooperatives in Italy, which have nominal decision-making authority. The social pacts of such federative cooperatives, which were created to preserve employment, legitimate such delegations of authority as long as employment levels are maintained.

System integration in democratic systems. Like bureaucracies, democratic organizations also need to ensure system integration by coordinating and controlling members' activities. In bureaucracies, coordination and control are accomplished largely through the promulgation of rules and standardized procedures that mandate action and the movement of information to appropriate decision makers. Nonroutine decisions are routed further up the hierarchy. In Type 1 and Type 2 organizations, by contrast, coordination and control are accomplished through a combination of member homogeneity, trust, and cultural control.

Significant regularities in behavior can be established simply by recruiting homogeneous memberships. Successful democratic organizations in the past have been aided by the presence of common ethnic ties (such as among the Basque members of the Mondragon cooperatives of Spain), shared ideologies, and shared professional interests that result in fewer variations in individual behavior. Further coordination and control is derived by members' participation in the shared understandings that make up the organization's "social pact" (Gherardi & Masiero, 1987). These pacts create relations of trust that allow firms to be administered on the basis of reciprocity and tacit negotiation of acceptable behaviors. Relations of trust are based on reciprocal expectations that members will behave in ways that are viewed as appropriate and in the common interest (Gherardi & Masiero, 1990). Oliver (1987) describes such voluntary and implicit regulation of behavior as "cultural control." In the process of interaction, particularly in group meetings, members tacitly negotiate understandings about decisions that can be made by individuals or groups and those reserved for ratification by the entire membership. Members receive overt and covert messages about actions that are regarded as transgressions of authority, while "groans of protest" greet items perceived as too trivial to be raised at meetings (Oliver, 1987, p. 459).

Homogeneity, trust, and cultural control cannot completely eliminate conflict, however, which is one of the most dramatic and pervasive characteristics of democratic interactional systems. Even the simplest of cooperatives, those small enough to make decisions in group meetings aimed at producing consensus, are not immune to conflict. Democratic structures of authority legitimate and create a norm for the expression of personal opinions and the exercise of personal choice. If bureaucratic structures minimize or suppress conflict, then democratic structures may be conceived as inviting, authorizing, almost mandating the existence of conflict. Thus one paradox of democratic organizations is that, if individuals feel free to participate in decision making and to engage in full and open expression, then such practices manifest and even emphasize the presence of conflict (Rothschild & Whitt, 1986). As Mansbridge (1982) has noted, the experience of protracted conflict can become painful to participants and encourage the development of strategies that mask or avoid it.

Attempts to minimize involvement and dissent, however, may lead to the departure of the organizational members most committed to democratic processes, which can in turn lead to the gradual elimination of contributions to decision making, further departures, corresponding increases in authority on the part of remaining organizational members, and ultimately failure to reproduce democratic practices (Stryjan, 1989). Thus one challenge in reproducing democratic organizational systems is to construct routine practices that preserve equalized power relations among participants and allow conflict to occur while at the same time providing a way to allow decisions to be made with some degree of efficiency.

Democratic system reproduction. When system reproduction occurs, the organization's "assumptions guide decisions, decisions shape rules and institutions, and they, in turn, shape daily routine" (Stryjan, 1989, p. 50). This process must be accomplished on a continuous basis through experimenting and adapting rather than by discovering the perfect organizational design (Stryjan, 1989). The reproduction of democratic systems presumes some minimal conditions, however. A routine set of specific organizational practices first must be established. As Kanter (1972) notes, abstract ideals must be translated into concrete social practices. Unfortunately, many of those involved in the most recent phase of cooperative activity came together on the basis of their common rejection of bureaucracy rather than because of agreement about what a democratic organization should look like (Gamson & Levin, 1984; Jackall & Crain, 1984). Gamson and Levin (1984) recommend the explicit development of a framework of social statutes defining the purpose of the organization and the rights and responsibilities of members, if only to provide a context for the interaction required to translate abstract principles of democracy into a code for acceptable behavior.

The reproduction of democratic systems also requires the ability to get things done to sustain the organization's business without eviscerating democratic processes, striking a delicate balance between substantive and instrumental rationality. Members frequently lack basic communication competencies needed for making decisions in democratic groups. Such a situation was illustrated by Zwerdling (1982), who described a large Type 2 organization with a committee decision-making system comprising elected representatives that was undermined consistently when stalemates were resolved by decisions imposed by a strong leader. Some expertise in self-management and democratic decision making would seem to be important to the reproduction of democratic systems.

Members of Type 1 organizations that experience growth and financial success discover that they cannot do without certain practices traditionally associated with running a business, such as establishing financial controls, some basic divisions in labor, procedures for organizing the production of goods or services, as well as the need to attract individuals with specialized technical expertise. Size seems to be the critical factor here, in terms of both the number of members and the volume of business. The frequently referenced "iron law of oligopoly" (Michels, 1949) predicts that members of large democratic associations will succumb to the need for elite leadership, due to requirements for more efficient communication and decision making than that which can be accomplished in meetings, and for technical expertise, which is inevitably possessed by a few who consequently acquire inordinate power.

Type 1 organizations have been hampered economically because of their tendency to avoid the use of accounting, management systems, and divisions of labor under the assumption that none of these traditionally bureaucratic practices could be tolerated by a genuine democracy (Gamson & Levin, 1984; Schuller, 1981). And researchers have historically tended to see the adoption of such practices as indicative of democratic "degeneration." The concepts of responsibility, authority, and leadership are not rendered obsolete in democratic organizations, but they do need to be redefined. More recently, it has been recognized that concepts such as "leadership" and "supervision" can be renegotiated in democratic contexts. Even the notion of "hierarchy" can take on new meaning, as Brown (1989) suggests when she notes that, in the food cooperatives of St. Paul, hierarchical levels denoted sites for decision making of increasing organizational generality rather than sites for authority exercised over others.

Further, there is increasing recognition of the need for technical practices such as "administration," "accounting," and "management information systems" to be renegotiated in democratic contexts. As Schuller (1981) argues, the practices of bureaucratic hierarchy have been supported by a language of bureaucratic hierarchy. New forms of democratic organization will require the creation of an alternative discourse that can support democratic practices. Such alternatives must be used to express the selective appropriation of meanings for concepts borrowed from bureaucratic hierarchy. The development of alternative codes must borrow from existing ones rather than develop in isolation from them, because, as Schuller (1981) also argues, "To abstain completely would mean abandoning any challenge to the dominant group's control of existing terminology" (p. 278).

CONCLUSION

This brief review of the literature of democratic organizations illustrates the utility of the structure-system distinction in understanding alternative—in this case, democratic—forms of interdependence. Although few definitive conclusions can be drawn, it appears that structures of democracy and ownership give rise to democratic systems that differ greatly from traditional bureaucracies. In contrast to bureaucratic systems, the broad configuration of interaction in democratic organizations appears to be patterned as less restricted and regionalized and less likely to be regulated by status considerations other than by those related to knowledge and technical expertise. Democratic systems are integrated by mechanisms of control and coordination that center on unhindered access to organizational information as well as homogeneity and trust, derived from the similarity of members recruited to the organization or based upon social pacts that create norms for appropriate behavior. In contrast to bureaucracy, members of democratic systems strive to eradicate differential access to resources and materials that create inequalities between positions created within the system. Individuals elected within schemes of representation, those with specialized knowledge or technical expertise, and those who have acquired interpersonal influence, however, are positioned to play special roles within these systems. And, finally, democratic systems are characterized by conflict, the "central feature of democratic decision making," according to Gamson and Levin (1984, p. 235). This constitutes only the most superficial of comparisons, but little more can be said with confidence about the nature of the interaction that constitutes democratic systems because there have been no studies that have sought specifically to describe communication within democratic organizations.

Even on the basis of such sketchy information, however, it is apparent that new programs for research are suggested in the examination of democratic interdependence. Chief among them are questions about how democracy is constituted in interactional practices. Current research is dominated by the existence of hierarchical differentiations among organizational members; in consequence, surprisingly little is known about communication practices among organizational equals, presumably the primary relationship of interest in studies of democratic systems. Expertise and hierarchical authority are thoroughly confounded in traditional organizational studies; however, studies of democratic systems would highlight the impact of knowledge and expertise claims and the role they play in organizational decision making, which might well become recast as the study of organizational argumentation. In place of traditional studies of managerial communication, one imagines the study of a discourse of accountability, in which elected representatives or others employed in managerial tasks and their organizational constituents confer under the auspices of democratic authority. Clearly, not every decision needs to be made by every organizational actor in a democratic system. So how are decisions explained and justified to organizational constituents and how is the right to participate discursively redeemed? Furthermore, because power is never absent from interactional relations, what types of resources other than expertise (e.g., conversational, presentational, coalitional) are implicated in relations of autonomy and dependence among actors in democratic systems?

Not to be ignored are questions about the kinds of practices and strategies that can facilitate the development of democratic interdependence. Social scientists have historically devoted their efforts to fine-tuning the operations of bureaucracy, typically by attempting to make such operations somewhat more "organic." Democratic praxis will be promoted by analogous efforts by researchers, perhaps devoted to the "rationalization" of processes of industrial democracy, assuming that "rationalization" is reconceived in a language of industrial democracy. Among the most pressing are needs for conflict strategies that provide opportunities for free expression and dissent while minimizing deleterious psychological impacts on organizational members. Equally important will be the reconceptualization of traditional bureaucratic tools, such as information and accounting systems, in forms that can be responsive to organizational performance defined in terms of the twin goals of profit and democratic accountability.

Why study democratic forms of organizational interdependence? First, communication in democratic organizations appears to be more consistent with the normative standards for communication of many researchers in our field. Research devoted to understanding and promoting the development of such organizations is more consistent with the values and the kind of world such researchers may be trying to realize. Second, it is apparent that managers of traditional bureaucracies in Western industrialized countries are appropriating democratic practices in the service of their objectives. Rejections of bureaucratic authority on the part of demographically diverse organizational members, the introduction of flexible manufacturing methods that rely on greater levels of employee discretion in decision making and teamwork, and

requirements for speed and discretion presented by new information technologies are all fueling a new era of experimentation with autonomous work
groups, flattened hierarchies, and cultural methods of building commitment
(Lawler, 1986; Passmore, 1988; Reich, 1983; Whyte, 1991). Efforts to de-
mocratize bureaucracies can no doubt benefit from research that examines
how such practices work in genuinely democratic contexts. But, finally, it
seems most likely that organizations in the future will come increasingly to
defy the application of bureaucratic and democratic categories and occupy an
intermediate position on this continuum. Communication researchers who
understand the nature of bureaucratic and democratic interdependence are
best positioned to provide guidance to such organizations in negotiating
democratically responsible and economically competitive syntheses.

NOTES

1. This is not to ignore past research that has sought to incorporate participative decision making,
employee involvement, and other democratic processes into traditional organizational contexts. But
it is important to note that, unlike the Scandinavian countries and Germany, where participation in
the form of labor-management "codetermination" is legally mandated, such efforts in the United
States and Britain have rarely attempted to alter bureaucratic organizational forms (Harrison, 1992).
More recently, Heydebrand (1989) has argued that a wide array of financial, regulatory/legal,
technological, and social conditions have begun to undermine the efficacy of bureaucratic features,
thus stimulating the evolution of new organizational forms. It will be increasingly important to focus
our attention on studies of communication and interdependence within such new organizational
arrangements. This essay proposes and illustrates a communication perspective that may be useful
for such studies by exploring the nature of interdependence in bureaucracy's polar opposite, the
"ideal" type known as democratic organization.

2. The few researchers who have focused on the nature of interdependence and its relationship
to organizational or societal forms have also been interested in equalizing power relationships
between members. Herbst (1976), who has worked on democratization projects in Scandinavian
countries, argued that interdependence based on task relationships between members differentiates between hierarchy and its alternatives. More recently, Whyte (1991) has analyzed a variety
of "transactional" dyadic relationships (e.g., exchange, authority, joint payoff relationships) and
related them to the type of organizational form in which they are most likely to be found
(bureaucratic versus cooperative). See also Eisler (1987), who contrasts "dominator" versus
"partnership" models of interdependence between men and women and traces their origins and
confrontations in ancient history.

3. Distinctions between structures of signification, legitimation, and domination are made for
analytic purposes only; interpretive schemes, normative orders, and relations of autonomy and
dependence are bound together in relations of mutual support.

4. The differentiation between these two models is ad hoc, based upon case studies, descriptions, and typologies provided in the literature. This distinction is well represented in typologies
that appear in the literature of democratic organizations; I make no independent claims regarding
its validity.

5. The legal form of the organization is not necessarily related to organizational objectives,
especially because legal forms may vary across national boundaries. Thus, for example, organizations formed under statutes defining "cooperatives" may fall into both Type 1 and Type 2
categories, especially in Great Britain and in Italy. Similarly, democratic organizations formed

through the statutes that create employee stock ownership plans (ESOPs) may also fall into both Type 1 and Type 2 categories.

REFERENCES

Allport, F. (1962). A structuronomic conception of behavior: Individual and collective. *Journal of Abnormal and Social Psychology, 64* 3-30.

Bantz, C. (1989). Organizing and *The social psychology of organizing. Communication Studies, 40*(4), 231-240.

Benson, J. (1977). Organizations: A dialectical view. *Administrative Science Quarterly, 22*, 1-21.

Berger, P., & Luckmann, T. (1966). *The social construction of reality.* New York: Anchor.

Blasi, J. R. (1987). *Employee ownership through ESOPs: Implications for the public corporation.* New York: Pergamon.

Blumer, H. (1969). *Symbolic interactionism: Perspective and method.* Berkeley: University of California Press.

Bolle de Bal, M. (1989). Participation: Its contradictions, paradoxes, and promises. In C. J. Lammers & G. Szell (Eds.), *International handbook of participation in organizations* (pp. 11-25). Oxford: Oxford University Press.

Brown, L. H. (1989). Locus of control and degree of organizational democracy. *Economic and Industrial Democracy, 10*, 467-498.

Burrell, G., & Morgan, G. (1979). *Sociological paradigms and organisational analysis.* Portsmouth, NH: Heinemann.

Clarke, T. (1984). Alternative modes of co-operative production. *Economic and Industrial Democracy, 5*, 97-129.

Cohen, I. (1989). *Structuration theory: Anthony Giddens and the constitution of social life.* New York: St. Martin.

Cornforth, C., Thomas, A., Lewis, J., & Spear, R. (1988). *Developing successful worker co-operatives.* London: Sage.

Deetz, S. (1992). *Democracy in an age of corporate colonization.* Albany: State University of New York Press.

Deetz, S., & Mumby, D. K. (1990). Power, discourse, and the workplace: Reclaiming the critical tradition. In J. A. Anderson (Ed.), *Communication yearbook 13* (pp. 18-47). Newbury Park, CA: Sage.

Eisler, R. (1987). *The chalice and the blade.* Cambridge, MA: Harper & Row.

Ellerman, D. (1982). On the legal structure of workers' cooperatives. In F. Lindenfeld & J. Rothschild-Whitt (Eds.), *Workplace democracy and social change* (pp. 299-313). Boston: Porter Sargent.

Fayol, H. (1949). *General and industrial management* (C. Storrs, Trans.). London: Pitman.

Gamson, Z., & Levin, H. (1984). Obstacles to the survival of democratic workplaces. In R. Jackall & H. Levin (Eds.), *Worker cooperatives in America* (pp. 219-244). Berkeley: University of California Press.

Gherardi, S., & Masiero, A. (1987). The impact of organizational culture in life-cycle and decision-making processes in newborn cooperatives. *Economic and Industrial Democracy, 8*, 323-347.

Gherardi, S., & Masiero, A. (1990). Solidarity as a networking skill and a trust relation: Its implications for cooperative development. *Economic and Industrial Democracy, 11*, 553-574.

Gherardi, S., Strati, A., & Turner, B. A. (1989). Industrial democracy and organizational symbolism. In C. J. Lammers & G. Szell (Eds.), *International handbook of participation in organizations* (pp. 155-166). Oxford: Oxford University Press.

Giddens, A. (1979). *Central problems in social theory.* Berkeley: University of California Press.

Giddens, A. (1981). *A contemporary critique of historical materialism*. Berkeley: University of California Press.

Giddens, A. (1984). *The constitution of society*. Berkeley: University of California Press.

Greenberg, E. (1986). *Workplace democracy: The political effects of participation*. Ithaca, NY: Cornell University Press.

Gunn, C. (1984a). Hoedads co-op: Democracy and cooperation at work. In R. Jackall & H. Levin (Eds.), *Worker cooperatives in America* (pp. 141-170). Berkeley: University of California Press.

Gunn, C. (1984b). *Workers' self-management in the United States*. Ithaca, NY: Cornell University Press.

Harrison, T. (1992). Designing the post-bureaucratic organisation: Toward egalitarian organisational structure. *Australian Journal of Communication, 19*(2), 14-29.

Hawes, L. (1974). Social collectivities as organizations. *Quarterly Journal of Speech, 60,* 497-502.

Herbst, P. G. (1976). *Alternatives to hierarchies*. Leiden: Martinus Nijhoff.

Heydebrand, W. V. (1989). New organizational forms. *Work and Occupations, 16,* 323-357.

Hochner, A., Granrose, C. S., Goode, J., Simon, E., & Appelbaum, E. (1988). *Job-saving strategies: Worker buyouts and QWL*. Kalamazoo, MI: W. E. Upjohn Institution for Employment Research.

Huspek, M. (in press). Dueling structures: The theory of resistance in discourse. *Communication Theory.*

Ivancic, C., & Logue, J. (1991). Democratizing the American economy: Illusions and realities of employee participation and ownership. In M. D. Hancock, J. Logue, & B. Schiller (Eds.), *Managing modern capitalism: Comparative strategies of industrial renewal and workplace reform* (pp. 215-247). Westport, CT: Greenwood.

Jablin, F. M. (1987). Formal organizational structure. In F. M. Jablin, L. L. Putnam, K. H. Roberts, & L. W. Porter (Eds.), *Handbook of organizational communication* (pp. 389-419). Newbury Park, CA: Sage.

Jackall, R. (1984). Paradoxes of collective work: A study of the Cheeseboard, Berkeley, California. In R. Jackall & H. Levin (Eds.), *Worker cooperatives in America* (pp. 109-135). Berkeley: University of California Press.

Jackall, R., & Crain, J. (1984). The shape of the small worker cooperative movement. In R. Jackall & H. Levin (Eds.), *Worker cooperatives in America* (pp. 88-108). Berkeley: University of California Press.

Jackall, R., & Levin, H. (1984). Work in America and the cooperative movement. In R. Jackall & H. Levin (Eds.), *Worker cooperatives in America* (pp. 3-15). Berkeley: University of California Press.

Kanter, R. (1972). *Commitment and community: Communes and utopias in sociological perspective*. Cambridge, MA: Harvard University Press.

Katz, D., & Kahn, R. L. (1978). *The social psychology of organizations*. New York: John Wiley. (Original work published 1966)

Lammers, C. J. (1988). Transience and persistence of ideal types in organization theory. In *Research in the sociology of organizations* (Vol. 6, pp. 203-224). Greenwich, CT: JAI.

Lawler, E., III. (1986). *High involvement management*. San Francisco: Jossey-Bass.

Mansbridge, J. (1982). Fears of conflict in face-to-face democracies. In F. Lindenfeld & J. Rothschild-Whitt (Eds.), *Workplace democracy and social change* (pp. 125-137). Boston: Porter Sargent.

McPhee, R. D. (1985). Formal structure and organizational communication. In R. D. McPhee & P. K. Tompkins (Eds.), *Organizational communication: Traditional themes and new directions* (pp. 149-177). Beverly Hills, CA: Sage.

McPhee, R. (1988). Vertical communication chains: Toward an integrated approach. *Management Communication Quarterly, 1,* 455-493.

McPhee, R. (1989). Organizational communication: A structurational exemplar. In B. Dervin, L. Grossberg, B. J. O'Keefe, & E. Wartella (Eds.), *Rethinking communication: Vol 2. Paradigm exemplars* (pp. 199-212). Newbury Park, CA: Sage.

Meek, C., Woodworth, W., & Dyer, W. G., Jr. (1988). *Managing by the numbers.* Reading, MA: Addison-Wesley.

Mellor, M., Hannah, J., & Stirling, J. (1988). *Worker cooperatives in theory and practice.* Milton Keynes, England: Open University Press.

Michels, R. (1949). *Political parties: A sociological study of oligarchical tendencies of modern democracy.* New York: Free Press.

Oliver, N. (1987). Coordination and control in a small producer cooperative: Dynamics and dilemmas. *Economic and Industrial Democracy, 10,* 447-465.

Pacanowsky, M. (1988). Communication in empowering organizations. In J. A. Anderson (Ed.), *Communication yearbook 11* (pp. 356-379). Newbury Park, CA: Sage.

Passmore, W. (1988). *Designing effective organizations.* New York: John Wiley.

Quarry, M., Blasi, J., & Rosen, C. (1986). *Taking stock: Employee ownership at work.* Cambridge, MA: Ballinger.

Reich, R. B. (1983). *The next American frontier.* New York: Times Books.

Rosen, C., Klein, K., & Young, K. (1986). *Employee ownership in America.* Lexington, MA: Lexington.

Rothschild, J., & Whitt, A. (1986). *The cooperative workplace.* Cambridge: Cambridge University Press.

Rueschemeyer, D. (1986). *Power and the division of labor.* Stanford, CA: Stanford University Press.

Sandkull, B. (1984). Managing the democratization process in work cooperatives. *Economic and Industrial Democracy, 5,* 359-389.

Schuller, T. (1981). Common discourse? The language of industrial democracy. *Economic and Industrial Democracy, 2,* 261-291.

Stryjan, Y. (1989). *Impossible organizations: Self-management and organizational reproduction.* New York: Greenwood.

Tannenbaum, A. (1983). Employee-owned companies. In L. Cummings & B. Staw (Eds.), *Research in organizational behavior* (Vol. 5, pp. 235-268). Greenwich, CT: JAI.

Taylor, F. W. (1967). *The principles of scientific management.* New York: Norton.

Weber, M. (1946). *From Max Weber* (H. H. Gerth & C. W. Mills, Eds.). New York: Oxford University Press.

Weick, K. (1979). *The social psychology of organizing.* Reading, MA: Addison-Wesley. (Original work published 1969)

Whyte, W. F. (1991). *Social theory for action: How individuals and organizations learn to change.* Newbury Park, CA: Sage.

Woodworth, W. (1981). Forms of employee ownership and workers' control. *Sociology of Work and Occupations, 8,* 195-200.

Zwerdling, D. (1982). At IGP, it's not business as usual. In F. Lindenfeld & J. Rothschild-Whitt (Eds.), *Workplace democracy and social change* (pp. 221-240). Boston: Porter Sargent.

Zwerdling, D. (1984). *Workplace democracy.* New York: Harper & Row.

Dialogue as Democratic Discourse: Affirming Harrison

ERIC M. EISENBERG
University of South Florida

THE unequal distribution of power in most organizations presents an enduring ideological problem for the United States. Describing the early twentieth century, Charles Perrow (1986) identifies the issue succinctly: "On the one hand, democracy stressed liberty and equality for all. On the other hand, large masses of workers and nonsalaried personnel had to submit to apparently arbitrary authority, backed up by local and national police forces and legal powers, for ten to twelve hours a day, six days a week" (p. 53). While working conditions have improved for most Americans over the years, this fundamental contradiction persists. In a society that is committed in the abstract to democratic values, it is at the very least ironic that most U.S. workers have both few liberties at work and little power to influence the decisions that most affect their work lives.

It is clear that Teresa Harrison would like to see this situation change. In her superb essay, she offers three arguments:

a. that academics have focused disproportionately on the kinds of communication that create and maintain hierarchies and not enough on alternative forms of interdependence,

b. that Giddens's metatheory of structuration is especially useful in analyzing both bureaucratic and democratic organizational systems, and

c. that two types of democratic organizational systems may be identified and the role of communication in fostering these alternatives to traditional hierarchy can be effectively demonstrated.

Correspondence and requests for reprints: Eric M. Eisenberg, Communication, University of South Florida, Tampa, FL 33620-7800.

Communication Yearbook 17, pp. 275-284

THE ACADEMIC BIAS TOWARD HIERARCHY

According to Harrison, academics are complicit in the maintenance of hierarchical, bureaucratic organizations in which power is closely held at the top. She argues that while there are many alternative ways to organize, academic theorists have focused almost exclusively on one kind of interdependence, bureaucratic hierarchy. In so doing, we have systematically decreased the likelihood of discovering communication practices that might produce workable alternatives. Harrison sees a need for new "democratic" discourses that will enable us to envision alternatives to hierarchy.

I agree with Harrison and can offer something of an explanation. It is useful to remember that early organizations were fashioned after armies (Morgan, 1986) and that the field of organizational communication was to a large extent launched by the "Triple Alliance" of academics, managers, and the military (Redding, 1985). Even today, the military plays a significant role as both a customer and an overseer of work processes. Hence it is not all that surprising that we have inherited a bias toward classical, hierarchical models of organizing.

Alternatives to classical models are not as unexplored, however, as Harrison makes them out to be. Outside of the academy, the search for new structures is well under way. Following a decade of downsizing and flattening of hierarchies, most contemporary organizations are experimenting with some form of increased employee participation and involvement. These changes are well reflected in the popular press, but Harrison is indeed correct that academic theory and research have lagged behind practice.

Further consideration of these practical initiatives reveals Harrison's review of different types of democratic organizations to be somewhat limited in scope. Contemporary attempts to create alternatives to hierarchy take many forms other than employee-owned organizations. Initiatives of this sort are occurring with increasing regularity and at many levels. For example, at the *interorganizational* level, strategic alliances and joint ventures are increasingly common. High levels of vertical integration, through which companies strive to be relatively self-sufficient by bringing component parts and processes in-house, are giving way to a more flexible, "modular" style of organizing that seeks alliances on an as-needed basis. The result is that organizations that formerly had many hierarchical levels and functions assume flatter, simpler structures by vending out aspects of their operations to strategic partners.

At the *organizational* level, some of our best known companies (e.g., Dana, 3M, Hughes Aircraft) are restructuring to minimize centralized control through the creation of autonomous business units that are allowed to operate independently so long as they meet financial goals. Power is delegated to strategic business units in the hopes of avoiding the "giantism" (Peters, 1987) that leaves big organizations inflexible and unresponsive to customers and changing market conditions. Within these business units, management often attempts to create "high-involvement organizations" in which decision-making author-ity is pushed down to the lowest possible level (Lawler, 1986).

Finally, at the *work group* level, there is a widespread desire to replace individual work with high-performance work teams. This may have some-thing to do with the decline of individualism and the rise of community as a guiding philosophy for the United States (Bellah, Madsen, Sullivan, Swidler, & Tipton, 1991). Although not without their problems, these "self-directed" work teams are expected over a period of time to take control of their schedules, budgets, and in some cases the hiring and firing of team members (Eisenberg & Goodall, 1993; Wellins, Byham, & Wilson, 1991).

The most radical alternatives to hierarchy in formal organizations may not originate in the United States. In Scandinavian countries, for example, par-ticipative action research (PAR) has for some time explored forms of organ-izing that involve greater power sharing and the overturning of hierarchies (e.g., Elden & Levin, 1991). One notable example is a Swedish company called Skaltek AB. Skaltek AB has 90 employees and revenues of $17 million annually; it also has no hierarchy or titles. All staff members are called "responsible persons," not employees, and everyone is personally responsible for the quality of their work. When a customer has a complaint, he or she contacts the "responsible person" who did the work (Osterberg, 1992).

There are still other places to look for novel ideas of this sort. The World Business Academy publishes a journal (*Perspectives*) and a newsletter (*At Work: Stories of Tomorrow's Workplace*) devoted exclusively to providing proven examples of these new organizational forms. Finally, ecofeminists (e.g., Eisler, 1987) have taken a leadership role in promoting a "partnership" model of interdependence. For these writers, hierarchy is the common enemy of both women and nature. The ecofeminists' program is based on a critique of hierarchy, which they believe exists mainly to support the dominator societies of today and those who run them (Eisler, 1987).

In summary, while Harrison's concern about the lack of research on alternative forms of interdependence is accurate, it is also true that the problem is receiving significant attention from others outside of the academic community.

ANALYZING COMMUNICATION IN HIERARCHICAL AND DEMOCRATIC SYSTEMS

Harrison begins her discussion of "models of interdependence" with the claim that, over time, perspectives on organizational structure that were fundamentally processual became corrupted and steadily more static. In response to this unfortunate trend, Karl Weick's (1979) model of equivocality reduction stands as an important corrective; it "reclaimed the processual nature of structure for organizational studies" (Harrison, p. 251). Harrison is frustrated with Weick's model, however, in that it constitutes "a framework without specific content" (p. 253). In an attempt to locate more specific content implications, she invokes Giddens's metatheory of structuration.

Harrison's explication of Giddens's work is excellent. She both places the work in a compelling intellectual context and provides definitions and examples that make the otherwise daunting vocabulary comprehensible. She also explains in detail the balancing act in which all social actors are continually engaged, both invoking social rules and resources and modifying and constructing new ones. Central to her ideas (and Giddens's) about how this process occurs is the notion of a "reproduction circuit."

According to Giddens (1984), a reproduction circuit is "a cycle of routinised activities and consequences which are reproduced across time-space within and between institutionalised locales" (p. 124). Harrison gives a good example of how a particular kind of circuit—that which reproduces bureaucratic hierarchy—works in an organization. She observes further that the work of generations of educators has echoed these ideas about the nature and necessity of hierarchy, which in turn produces college graduates ready and eager to draw on precisely these rules and resources in the further reproduction of bureaucracies.

From my perspective, two things are missing from Harrison's otherwise compelling account of the reproduction of bureaucratic hierarchies: a sense of struggle, and an expanded role for the environment. First, with the exception of one brief caveat ("each cycle of reproduction introduces the possibility of change into the system"; p. 259), I found the discussion of *how* certain organizational forms come to be reproduced rather bloodless. My own experience "inside" these reproduction circuits is that there is much conflict, shifting coalitions, confusion, and just plain banging around.

Along these lines, I find work by Patricia Riley (1983) and Stephen Barley (1986) to be especially resonant. Both revel in the marked differences between subgroups as the negotiated order unfolds. I am *not* saying that Giddens's framework is incapable of handling the decidedly ungraceful way in which reproduction proceeds, only that the vocabulary of structuration, at least as Harrison applies it, feels to me overly sanitized. Put differently, I would like to see more about the circuits of *resistance* alongside the circuits of dominance.

My second point has to do with a lack of emphasis on the external environment, including legal, political, and social forces. For example, significant obstacles to the implementation of democratic organizations are federal and state laws concerning the hiring, firing, and overall treatment of employees. In addition, union contracts may discourage the significant work redesign that often accompanies decentralization of power. Both kinds of hurdles exist at a level that transcends individual organizations but are at the same time two of the most serious obstacles in altering traditional hierarchical structures.

Writers such as Stanley Deetz (1992) and Stewart Clegg (1989) offer a more sweeping consideration of the relationship between an organization's form and its social environment. Deetz, for example, argues that the suppression of democracy by bureaucratic forms is not limited to any individual organization but is instead symptomatic of the larger corporate "colonization of the lifeworld." According to Deetz, this broader kind of control pervades the organization of contemporary Western society and applies to families and the media as well as to businesses.

Also worth mention is Clegg's application of Giddens's notion of circuits of power and resistance. While similar to Harrison's in many respects, one important difference is Clegg's emphasis on the impact of changes and events in the broader consumer culture on the reproduction of power within organizations. As such, he sees the pull of the marketplace and the dominant values of a consumer society as in large part responsible for the organizational forms that appear. In the "postmodern postscript" to his book on power, Clegg (1989) writes:

> In the post-modern world, power consists less in the control of the relational field of force in each circuit and more in the way in which the obligatory passage point of the market has become a "black hole," sucking in ever more agency and spewing out an ever more diffuse power as the pursuit of things becomes an all encompassing passion. . . . The conceptual execution of sovereign power heralded only superficially a new realm of freedom; the easing of surveillance seems sure to offer even less freedom if these old concepts are reborn in the unity of the self-regarding and ceaselessly restless consumer sovereign reflexively monitoring the appearance of things through one's self and one's self through things. (p. 275)

While the application of structuration theory to organizational reproduction is no doubt valuable, we must not when doing so forget the more straightforward lessons of open systems theory. Specifically, the rules and resources one draws upon in constituting organizational reality come from far and wide and may at times be better seen as features of society than of any single organization or industry.

TYPES OF DEMOCRATIC ORGANIZATIONAL SYSTEMS

I have little to say about what is perhaps the most significant contribution of Harrison's essay, the typology of democratic systems in employee-owned organizations. She draws important distinctions between two types of organizations that are often grouped together—those committed to equal power and alternatives to hierarchy (Type 1) and those more accurately seen as modifications of traditional organizations wherein the primary commitment is to improved productivity and survival of the organization, not to democratic principles per se (Type 2). Not only does this distinction make a lot of sense,

Harrison does a fine job of using Giddens's work to fully explore all relevant implications.

Beginning with the section on system integration, however, Harrison raises some deeper issues that ought perhaps to be the basis of another paper, as they are not sufficiently developed here. First, she discusses the key role played by homogeneity, trust, and cultural control as instruments of coordination in democratic systems. Each of these processes is problematic, however, with costs and benefits to both employees and other stakeholders. Her argument is reminiscent of Meyer and Rowan's (1977) groundbreaking work on institutional organizations. From their perspective, institutions (e.g., hospitals, schools) operate from a "logic of confidence" and a presumption of "good faith" among professionals (e.g., physicians, teachers) who work for the most part on their own. Institutions use trust as an organizing strategy to buffer the technical core of the organization from public scrutiny, because opening up a public discussion of the actual quality of teaching or health care risks their social legitimacy.

Meyer and Rowan did their initial work in the 1970s, however, and the ability of any organization to resist public scrutiny has steadily eroded since. Institutions of all kinds are increasingly being asked, and in many cases forced, to be more accountable for the quality of their outcomes. Certainly this is true in hospitals and universities. Consequently, we may have cause to wonder whether it is socially and politically possible to endorse things like homogeneity and trust as practical mechanisms of organizational self-regulation. While these strategies can indeed work internally in an organization, they raise suspicions externally. And, while we may find familiar the scenario Harrison presents of a relatively homogeneous group achieving self-regulation through social pacts and groans of protests at meetings, this form of control runs counter to some of the realities of diversity in organizations as well as to the more rigorous protections against particularism that were the positive legacy of bureaucracy. I would hate to see the formation of democratic organizations that were exclusionary in their hiring (to foster homogeneity) or that used informal social pressure to evict or to intimidate those who fail to "trust" enough to support the will of the group.

I don't think that Harrison is unaware of these problems, only that she has downplayed them in favor of emphasizing the benefits and appeal of democratic organizations. I am curious, however, about the types of businesses or industries in which such democratic organizations could thrive, given the time pressures placed on decision making. Time is the ultimate competitive advantage these days—the current business environment rewards managers who can consistently make high-quality decisions with inadequate information and little opportunity to discuss the pros and cons with employees. Real democracy takes time, as every voice can claim a right to be heard. Organizations I have known that are most democratic (e.g., the Santa Monica, California, City Council) are nearly comic in this regard—their ideological support for self-expression leads predictably to citizens testifying weekly to alien invasions and the second coming of the messiah. But how and where would a similar set of values and practices work in industry? Is modern (or postmodern) capitalism really compatible with democracy?

As this question is no doubt an empirical one, I am especially intrigued by Harrison's assertion that democracy is constituted in interactional practices. She says very little about the nature of such practices, however; hence I would like to end this piece with a personal nomination of dialogue as a kind of democratic discourse.

DIALOGUE AS DEMOCRATIC DISCOURSE

> [Dialogue] is one of the richest activities that human beings can engage in. It is the thing that gives meaning to life, it's the sharing of humanity, it's creating something. And there is this magical thing in an organization, or in a team, or in a group, where you get unrestricted interaction, unrestricted dialog, and this synergy happening that results in more productivity, and satisfaction, and seemingly magical levels of output from a team. (Evered & Tannenbaum, 1992, p. 8)

Humans are neither entirely social nor entirely private. To be human means to live in between, to establish a sense of self apart from the world and a sense of self as part of the world (Eisenberg & Goodall, 1993). Along these lines, the central challenge facing all organizations is one of balance, between individual autonomy and agency, on the one hand, and social coordination and constraint, on the other. This challenge is magnified in democratic organizations where, at least in principle, the support for freedom of expression and diverse viewpoints is in some way expected to constitute a superior form of coordination.

But this is easier said than done. Few organizations have learned *how* to foster productive conflict and to remain profitable and competitive while at the same time promoting a diversity of opinions (and, in Harrison's terms, "minimizing deleterious psychological impacts on organizational members"). Few individuals are able to see beyond their personal worldviews to accept and understand the viewpoints of others. In the beginning of this commentary, I described a number of different approaches currently being taken to reconcile competitive pressures with empowerment. I now conclude with my own approach, which focuses specifically on promoting dialogue in organizations.

In my opinion, the litmus test for a democratic organization is its ability to handle diversity. It is currently in style to speak of "managing" diversity in organizations, but the meaning behind such statements is often more abstract, legalistic, or ideological than practical. A better question might be this: What practical steps can a democratic organization take to reap the benefits of its diverse membership? One answer is to promote dialogue. Doing so requires one to shape communication practices in a number of different ways, involving issues of voice, empathy, and experience. Each is described below.

First, it is well known that in organizations some people's voices count more than others. The first step in establishing dialogue (and, I would argue, democracy) is through the equalization of opportunities for employee voice. Much of the work on employee participation, empowerment, and involvement has this as a primary goal, and changes are made in job design and organizational structure to allow employees at all levels to speak their minds on important issues.

A second step in establishing dialogue in organizations is to promote empathy for differing ideas, opinions, and worldviews. Perhaps the greatest obstacle to progress in most organizations is the stubborn belief on the part of those in power that their view of organizational reality is the one, correct view. According to management theorist Peter Drucker (1993), most organizations today are in trouble because their fundamental "business theory" that worked some years ago no longer makes sense. The only way such theories can change is if people are willing to risk letting go of some of their most treasured beliefs and to truly listen to others who hold different positions. Listening skills must be learned. Many have the mistaken belief that simply bringing people together and giving them the opportunity to speak will lead to quality dialogue—in fact, this is only the first step. People must also learn to listen openly to others' ideas and opinions.

The third step in cultivating dialogue in organizations has to do with how the personal experiences of organizational members are handled in conversation. All too often, managers treat discussions with peers or subordinates as a kind of "marketplace of ideas" in which individuals critique others' perceptions in an attempt to win the argument and elevate their own point of view. In the process, individuals rarely speak from experience. They say things like the following: "We need a new compensation policy for these reasons . . ." rather than "The people in my work group feel underpaid and so do I."

Conversations about ideas usually alternate between constructive and destructive comments, often leading to some partial consensus on a course of action. Alternatively, a dialogue of experience leads people to speak from their experience and listen for the experiences of others, which may be very different than their own. This both limits defensiveness by reducing attacking communication and, more important, gives people insight into the ways in which others frame their opinions and behavior—the personal and cultural context that can help others seem different, yet sensible.

A dialogue of experience is additive. Each person's experience is a contribution to the whole, and, while others' experiences do indeed make one think differently about one's own, no person's experience can invalidate another's. Four different accounts of the same problem, if seen as complementary and not competing, can lead to a complex, sophisticated solution. What is more, there is no goal of consensus or integration of experience—in fact, the rich tapestry of experience that emerges from such dialogue properly resists such attempts at synthesis.

An example is in order. I once facilitated a weekend retreat for the executive team of a major construction company. The company had asked me to help them improve the quality of their communication, which translated into an attempt on the part of the vice-presidents to resist the president's autocratic, militaristic decision-making style. The first thing I did was to structure the meeting so that everyone had an equal chance to speak. While this was a step forward, most of the participants remained frustrated, because whatever they said was immediately judged by the president to be useless or impractical. Next, I taught them the principles of active listening and gave them ample opportunity to practice. While there were many fewer interruptions, I felt that their newfound "tolerance" for one another's opinions was more superficial than real. Then there was a turning point.

The conversation turned to the management abilities of one member of the team. There was a heated discussion, with radically different opinions on both sides. I stopped the conversation and asked them to switch from talking about "how the manager really is" to "your experience with the manager."

The consequences of this small change were remarkable. As each person told his or her experience with this manager, it became clear to all participants that the person in question behaved differently in different situations and that they were all partly "right" about him. When customers were present, he tended to act condescending to employees; with the boss present, he was formal and kept himself at a distance; one on one with direct reports, he was warm and supportive. The point I wish to make is that this complex view of "the real situation" and the excellent solutions that were tried as a result *did not and could not come out of the traditional kind of "meeting" common to most organizations*. It was only when people spoke from and listened to others' experiences that the fullest range of information about the situation became available. In the world of ideas and opinions, differences in experience get inappropriately transformed into differences of opinion, which in turn the group may try to "resolve."

In summary, Harrison has sounded the alarm for a more thoroughgoing consideration of alternative kinds of interdependence. She has described in detail some of the democratic organizational forms that are being tried today and drawn important distinctions among companies that might otherwise appear similar. Finally, she has opened the door for an analysis of the specific communication practices that constitute democratic organizing. I offer dialogue as one potentially fruitful set of practices; there are surely many others to be explored.

REFERENCES

Barley, S. (1986). Technology as an occasion for structuring: Evidence from observations of CT scanners and the social order of radiology departments. *Administrative Science Quarterly, 31*, 78-108.

Bellah, R., Madsen, R., Sullivan, W., Swidler, A., & Tipton, S. (1991). *The good society*. New York: Knopf.

Clegg, S. (1989). *Frameworks of power*. Newbury Park, CA: Sage.

Deetz, S. (1992). *Democracy in an age of corporate colonization*. Albany: State University New York Press.

Drucker, P. (1993, February 2). A turnaround primer. *Wall Street Journal*.

Eisenberg, E., & Goodall, H. L. (1993). *Organizational communication: Balancing creativity and constraint*. New York: St. Martin's Press.

Eisler, R. (1987). *The chalice and the blade*. San Francisco: Harper Collins.

Elden, M., & Levin, M. (1991). Cogenerative learning: Bringing participation into action research. In W. F. Whyte (Ed.), *Participatory action research* (pp. 127-142). Newbury Park, CA: Sage.

Evered, R., & Tannenbaum, R. (1992). A dialog on dialog. *Journal of Management Inquiry, 1*, 43-55.

Giddens, A. (1984). *The constitution of society*. Berkeley: University of California Press.

Lawler, E. (1986). *High involvement management*. San Francisco: Jossey-Bass.

Meyer, J., & Rowan, B. (1977). Institutionalized organizations: Formal structure as myth and ceremony. *American Journal of Sociology, 83*, 340-363.

Morgan, G. (1986). *Images of organization*. Newbury Park, CA: Sage.

Osterberg, R. (1992). A company without hierarchy. *At Work: Stories of Tomorrow's Workplace, 1*, 9-10.

Perrow, C. (1986). *Complex organizations: A critical essay* (3rd ed.). New York: Random House.

Peters, T. (1987). *Thriving on chaos*. New York: Knopf.

Redding, W. C. (1985). Stumbling toward identity: The emergence of organizational communication as a field of study. In R. McPhee & P. Tompkins (Eds.), *Organizational communication: Traditional themes and new directions* (pp. 15-54). Beverly Hills, CA: Sage.

Riley, P. (1983). A structurationist account of political cultures. *Administrative Science Quarterly, 28*, 414-437.

Weick, K. (1979). *The social psychology of organizing* (2nd ed.). Reading, MA: Addison-Wesley.

Wellins, R., Byham, W., & Wilson, J. (1991). *Empowered teams*. San Francisco: Jossey-Bass.

"Wego" Comes in Several Varieties and Is Not Simple

WILLIAM I. GORDEN
Kent State University

POWERFUL corporate interests in contemporary America reign supreme. Despite the U.S. system of citizen ownership, citizens are far distanced from citizen control. Ironically, of the 100% of the Americans who "own" immense resources, very few know how their possessions are managed; among these are federal lands, totaling one third of America, and the airwaves. Moreover, even those fortunate enough to have a stake in the trillions of dollars vested in pension funds, savings, insurance equities, and stocks do not control any of them. Corporations do (Nader, 1992). An elite 1% owns more than 90% of the rest of Americans combined (Brown, Flavin, & Kane, 1992; Dentzer, 1992; Fisher, 1992). As Nader (1992) argues, "Democracies do not thrive unattended. They are diminished by plutocracy and oligarchy, by political betrayals that feed public frustration and lead to resignation and then fatalism" (p. 653). His remedy is public citizenship: timely information, the technology to communicate with one another, and then mobilization for action and results.

This macrolandscape of U.S. society, with its long history of corporate colonialism (Deetz, 1992a) and popular frustrations with a "democratic" government fraught with favors for the privileged, can inform and serve as a backdrop for Harrison's discussion of communication and interdependence in democratic organization of the workplace. Harrison's look at the theory and practice that constitute democracy in the workplace, in particular those that are more or less employee owned, makes a splendid contribution. She addresses a topic that has received scant attention from the scholars of organization communication.

In our times, global market share is the prize that goes to high-speed management, those who get to market first and fast with new products and

Correspondence and requests for reprints: William I. Gorden, School of Speech Communication, Kent State University, Kent, OH 44242.

Communication Yearbook 17, pp. 285-297

with continuous reduction in cycle time. It is in such an economic environment (which Harrison does not describe) that she submits the proposition that employee-owned business is communication rich and therefore good. Contrarily, her argument implies that traditional corporate bureaucratic organization is not so good and its communication is impoverished. Harrison does not use the term *good* as I have. Rather, her argument for democratic enterprise organization is more implied. By *good,* she apparently means a workplace that is efficient and competitively viable while at the same time allowing for maximization of member input and self-actualization. Combining the concept of democratic practice with the need to be competitive, she describes employee-owned enterprise as structuring "routine practices that preserve equalized power relations . . . and allow conflict to occur while at the same time providing a way to allow decisions to be made with some degree of efficiency" (p. 267).

The inherent deficits of traditional bureaucratically managed employer-owned organization are more implied than developed: the greed that tends to be linked with a powerful elite, the domination by wealth and consequent maldistribution of resources, the exploitation of people and environment, the stifling of human community. The negative argument for democratic reform and connectedness rests upon the depravity of a system that fosters an ethic of personal advantage rather than a system that nurtures an ethic of well-being (Mitchell & Scott, 1990). Recovery will not come easily from recent decades of "speculative extravagances," "merger and acquisition mania," and a "binge of greed" that have resulted in an "economic hangover" (Galbraith, 1992, p. 6).

Harrison argues that the metaphor of structure is traditionally understood as girders of a building that hold a social collective together rather than as a dynamic transactive process that continuously creates and re-creates the organization and its structures. Rather, she favors Weick's (1969/1979) model of organizational interdependence whereby interlocking behavioral cycles are aggregated into stable subassemblies and complex patterns. To this organization conceptualization, Harrison would add Giddens's (1984) perspective that social systems are not so much themselves structures but are systems that *have* structures, which tend to reproduce themselves, and also Katz and Kahn's (1978) notion that it is interrelated "events rather than things which are structured" (p. 24).

Harrison characterizes bureaucracies as systems with asymmetrical distribution of authority, resources, and political inequality that typically restrict communication to certain channels, often avoiding face-to-face relations. Management's function is to provide information, to monitor, and to coordinate activity. The regulation or suppression of conflict is necessary in bureaucracy to have a smooth-running machine. Asymmetry of power between employer/management and workers resides in the possession of capital by employer/management and the difficulties of workers in organizing an effective voice.

The tenor that emerges in Harrison's work fluctuates between optimism and pessimism. The cooperative sectors of Europe and the growth of employee stock ownership plans within the United States are grist for optimism. Approximately 12 million U.S. employees are enrolled in ESOPs (Rosen & Young, 1991). But, of the 23 largest employee-owned companies with 10,000 or more employees, only 5 are employee majority owned. Most of the more than 12,000 ESOPs were created not because of "democratic ideologies" but to better deal with economic uncertainty (Bradley & Gelb, 1983). Moss (1991) concludes that "significant sharing of wealth, power and status between labor and management is not on the agenda of either U.S. corporations or the U.S. labor movement" (p. 199).

Social Darwinism appears not only to weed out less efficient enterprise, whether privately or collectively owned, that cannot compete but also applies within an enterprise. Employee-owned democratically structured enterprise tends to "degenerate" toward bureaucratic hierarchy and "greater equality" for some more than others. Ironically, as employee-owned organizations prosper, ownership may become more centralized, and the organizations become more attractive targets of private buyers. It is a frustrating picture that appears connected to society's need to curb human avarice, notwithstanding Kant's speculation that even a society of devils if arranged in opposition could develop a workable government (Kant, 1794/1963, p. 15).

Harrison acknowledges that organizational size and member competence variables, as predicted by the "iron law of oligopoly," play a crucial role: The larger the democratic entity, the more likely it is that the need for efficient communication and decision making will limit leadership to a representative elite, thus making a few more powerful than the many.

Two types of democratic workplaces are described by Harrison: Type 1—the participative cooperatives, where democracy is valued in itself—and Type 2—employee business acquired for financial survival and gain, where democracy is a pragmatic concern to protect one's interests. If democracy is to be reproduced, Harrison suggests, an alternative discourse must be generated to the language of bureaucratic hierarchy. That discourse must borrow from and in a sense co-opt the language of the dominant paradigm. Democratic systems, if they are to prosper, must be configured in communicative mechanisms that enable unhindered access to organizational information, foster homogeneity of purpose, and yet do not suppress dissent.

These amplifications to Harrison's essay made in this commentary focus upon four concerns: (a) Is the definition of democratic work organization sufficiently inclusive? (b) Does an underlying communication perspective explain why employee-owned organizations are communicatively rich? (c) Are employer-owned bureaucratic work organizations as communication-deprived as is implied? (d) What are the structures and attitudes conducive to creating and re-creating democratic processes in the workplace?

DEMOCRACY DEFINED

Harrison limits discussion of democratic organizations to Types 1 and 2; she does not address European codetermination and economic democracy. The economic setting for both types appears to be within a state that adopts a hands-off, you-are-on-your-own relationship to business enterprise. But there also are other economic-political possibilities, such as European mandated employee-employer codetermination. Such "democratizing" plans do not necessarily pertain to employee ownership, but they do mandate employee participation in decision making to some degree at various levels of management.

The Swedish model entails a small elite of wealthy families and banks that own almost all industry. Owner-employers have had a rather stable though recently fluctuating accommodation with strong union membership and political influence. I suggest the Swedish model is another version of democracy at work. State-fostered democratic dialogue at the plant level and legislated representative participation of employee unions and employers at the national level are manifestations of democratic practice. The Swedish state labor panel (made up of three judges representing the public and an equal number of representatives of the employer association and of employee unions) that sits in judgment of complaints of employers and labor is evenly balanced. The Swedish Wage Earner Fund, though far short of its original proposal, was set up to fund a pool of capital from industrial profits and to create a tangible form of worker stakeholdership and profit sharing. The current Swedish realignment of partisan politics, the disillusionment with union leadership, the employers association determination to decentralize collective bargaining and its withdrawal from participation in work environment agencies, despite capital's ascendent direction, must fit somewhere within the definition of democracy at work (Mahon, 1991).

Harrison ignores the issue of whether unions are a form of organizational democracy. Some unions cater to a privileged elite within their ranks and are notoriously undemocratic in their own election procedures, yet their very existence provides an organized and legitimate voice in the work environment. They provide mechanisms to resolve grievances, protect whistle-blowers, monitor safety, and negotiate wages and policies that affect job security. Unions are protective of hard-won rights to bargain. They have been wary of various versions of employee empowerment and workplace democracy, perhaps because they fear such will diminish union power and may cause workers to see unions as unnecessary (Moss, 1991). Union leaders, in view of management's often antiunion behavior and cavalier unilateral decisions to downsize, have been cynical about employee involvement/empowerment efforts. Some see them as manipulative and union busting. Teamster President Ron Carey says employee-involvement programs aim to "diminish the presence of the union" (Rose & Kotlowitz, 1992, p. A1). There is another reason unions may be hesitant about employee-owned firms. Because employee-owned firms generally are relatively small and lack the advantages of scale that are necessary for global competition, they sometimes pay less than unionized employer-owned firms. To pay employees less than industry norms undermines industrywide standards. That version of economic democracy works against union interests.

Unions' most important function is political, making workers more equal to the employers (Tyler, 1980). Their self-interest concerns extend far beyond local bargaining to lobbying for societal and environmental matters. If and when labor and environmentalists combine their political clout, the possibility increases that a state will require employers to calculate into their accounting the impact and costs of production upon the environment and upon people.

Unions' role in employee-owned enterprise is another issue that begs for attention. What is the role of a union in employee-owned companies? Does a union within an employee-owned company facilitate or frustrate democratizing structures? Is it different than its traditional adversarial role in employer-owned organizations? Bado and Logue's (1991) investigation of employee-owned firms found that those with "unionized hourly workers are generally better represented than the [unorganized] salaried" in their governing bodies (p. 16). These scholars also conclude that, without a contractual basis for enterprise democracy, individually "employees have no recourse if they are suspended or dissolved" (p. 16).

COMMUNICATION PERSPECTIVE

The communicative richness that Harrison asserts comes with democracy in the workplace appears to be based upon decision processes assumed to result in convergence of activity. The process is legitimized by an agreement to confer and debate policies that shape the employee-owned workplace. Access to information, influence, and persuasion are the implied vehicles of interdependence. Conflict is acknowledged as possible, although not desired, and is something that must not lead to gridlock and antagonism. If the structures of democracy are put in place and structure is understood as a dynamic process, then democracy should be continuously reproduced. In contrast to this influence and involvement conception of democracy, a different communicative perspective focuses on the equable collaborative participatory constitutive process (Deetz, 1992b). Democracy at work in this sense is understood as dissensus, reclaiming suppressed conflicts and hidden points of resistance, revealing value-laden practices that favor the interests of dominant groups, and giving voice to diverse and ignored stakeholders.

Modernists see democracy as a rhetorical marketplace and procedural counting of noses to reduce differences and create a common order. Those who feel alienated are so because they have been excluded from the process. They should fight to gain an identity and stay with the unitary structure.

A postmodernist communication perspective rather suggests that stable social networks are no longer a reality, that possibilities for creating identity are diminishing, that majority rule can be suffocating, and that workplace democracy provides little hope for impeding social disintegration (Westenholz, 1991). Democratic processes, Westenholz reasons, can cause corporate behavior to fall apart without the employees realizing it because, beneath the banner of reducing variations of behavior, employees see participation as serving different ends, such as in asserting themselves, furthering friendship, and making decisions. Postmodernists claim that, because it is impossible for those with different worlds that lack an understanding of each other to come to agreement, organizational divorce therefore may be the most viable alternative to the tyranny of a majority.

Dialectic is implied but does not appear integral to Harrison's considerations. Her perspective appears to be modern in that workplace democracy is pictured as a means for rationality to conquer irrationality. The functional purpose of communication richness appears to be grounded in what Deetz (1992b) terms a version of democracy centered in persuasion aimed at reproducing existing meanings (p. 11). When communication is understood as dialectic and constitutive negotiation in which dissensus is valued, there exists the potential for new meanings. From this perspective, "the democratic firm is a democratic social institution rather than a traditional piece of property" (Ellerman, 1990, pp. 211-212), but one with a divergent future.

BUREAUCRATIC DEMOCRATIZATION

Are traditional bureaucratic organizations communication impoverished? In the above dialectic democratic sense, they are. Yet employee involvement in decision making has increased in contemporary corporations. Admittedly, most of such efforts are efficiency motivated: to improve quality and to cut costs and enhance productivity. Involvement should not be confused with codetermination (Deetz, 1992b).

In corporate America, access to information pertaining to the total financial picture of a business generally is not available and only provided in part. Executives prefer to hide their high salaries and bonuses especially while cutting longtime employees. It is when times are tough that management paints a profit-loss picture for all employees to see, sometimes with an explicit threat to fix it, sell it, or close it! Yet it is in times of dwindling market share that managers of such companies draw Venn diagrams that acknowledge the overlapping circles of interest for management and labor. That common area of interest, it is stressed, is survival and that, in turn, calls for increased employee involvement in productivity, competitiveness, and continuous improvement in quality.

One must not overlook the managerial pragmatism of employer-owned corporations. Management interest in "empowerment" of employees is primarily economic. The case of Caterpillar is illustrative (Rose & Kotlowitz, 1992); an employee involvement program called the Employee Satisfaction Process was abandoned when the union struck over outsourcing of parts to low-wage foreign suppliers and management refused to go along with industrywide bargaining. When CAT began hiring permanent replacements, the union quickly called off the strike and capitulated to management's imposed terms of its contract offer. Some employees redefined ESP as "employees stop participating."

Employee involvement programs in traditional bureaucratic organizations, however, I suggest, do not always or entirely co-opt labor in management's interests. The walls between management and labor do begin to crumble when an organization encourages employee voice and team building.

Quality of work life (QWL) programs spring from the principle that employees given the opportunity for involvement and who are empowered thenceforth are highly motivated to perform (Kanter, Stein, & Brinkerhoff, 1982). Where QWL thrives, parallel structures to conventional line organization evolve. Whereas line organization with its long chain of command is focused primarily on production and reduction of uncertainty, QWL shortens the chain of command; is flexible; promotes job rotation, problem solving, and expanding opportunities; encourages employee "say"; and focuses more holistically on "organization." According to Kanter et al.'s research, the parallel structure that QWL can provide may be a significant organic democratizing answer to the question of how to reform conventional mechanistic organization. The widening role of employee involvement, continuous quality improvement, self-directed natural work groups, and the expansion of employee ownership (both majority and nonmajority ESOPs) are evidence that conventional bureaucratic organization is undergoing a democratizing change (McWhirter, 1991).

The thrust of many companies to involve and empower employees in decisions pertaining to their work is not all fluff. This is to argue that the reality of democracy within the workplace is not something that either *is* or *is not*. Rather, enriched communication and thus varying degrees of democracy have come—through government legislation, union negotiation, and management programs calculated to better competitiveness.

STRUCTURING DEMOCRATIC PROCESSES

What is the day-to-day stuff of which workplace democracy is created? This is a pivotal question that emerges in Harrison's speculation regarding the employee-owned industry. She wonders what the " 'rationalization' of processes of industrial democracy" (p. 270) is and what is used to cope with the "day-to-day exigencies of organizational life." This is of no or little concern to those breaking the new ground of employee ownership. Every effort to build an employee-owned business comes with the background imprint of traditional capitalistic workplace culture (of management preroga- tives, of alienation that has accumulated from being ordered, of punching in and out both physically and psychologically, and so on). Traditional organi- zations invest between an estimated $45 at the low end and $200 billion at the high end for employee training, most of which goes for management training. Employee-owned enterprise, because of its newness, requires an intensive educational effort involving training in the most effective processes for a democratically run workplace.

Recent studies show that ownership alone has little impact on performance. Corporate performance is, however, positively related to companies that have combined employee ownership with employee participation (Conte & Sve- jnar, 1990; General Accounting Office, 1987, 1990; Michigan Center for Employee Ownership & Gainsharing, 1990). Typically, employees in organi- zations where employee stock ownership plans are instituted are informed about the operations of the benefit plan—retirement of the owner, divestiture of a division, or the establishment of benefit plans. Information about the mechanics is, however, not enough.

Appreciation and enthusiasm for employee ownership evolve with learning how to participate actively in new democratic systems. Communication is the key that provides access to information and mechanisms for representative decision making. Business knowledge training enhances employee-owners' abil- ity to understand and monitor postings of annotated financial statements, oper- ating profits on all jobs, departmental productivity, and strategic priorities. It's a long process to educate employees about the complexities of ownership. That may include a broad range of skills needed to be competitive: from basic math and blueprint reading to a mini-MBA in accounting and inventory control.

The theory of employee ownership education is straightforward: Relevant information leads to understanding of sound business practices and motiva- tion, which in turn enables participation in the mechanisms of ownership. The combination of skills and *ownership*, in attitude and fact, results in improved productivity (Moody & Ivancic, 1991). Provided that employee-owners are empowered by attainment of adequate skills and participative know-how, this sequence leading to improved performance differs from that used in the traditional corporate setting in its meaningfulness: *Ownership* in this case is not a euphemistic word; participation in decision making and representation in the formulation of company strategy are not fiction.

Harrison reasons that bureaucratic systems minimize face-to-face interac- tion and that democratic systems are "rich in face-to-face interaction." We cannot yet say that employee-owned business is intrinsically communica- tively rich. Harrison's thesis begs for testing and methodological proposals that can best tease out its truth or falsity.

There are many questions: How does the structure-in-process and the process-in-structure work in employee-owned settings? Is there a decentering

(Derrida, 1978), a new authenticity, in sites where democracy is being worked out in practical ways? How does reciprocity work in employee-owned settings? Is the accumulation of "sting" (Linstead & Grafton-Small, 1992) resulting from being ordered and the redress of differences any different in traditional employer-owned than employee-owned business? Are the asymmetry, the deference, and inequities lessened? Is the "gaze" (Bentham's metaphor for surveillance; Letiche, 1990) different? Is compliance (Czarniawska-Joerges, 1992) more voluntary in employee-owned business?

Perhaps the larger issue is not micro but macro: Is workplace democracy viable within a capitalist system? Does capitalism foster the common good?

The argument for capitalism is straightforward. Its virtue is that it makes the individual responsible for deciding her or his own morality. Industry is virtue. Sloth is sin. Greed is supposed to be tempered by higher values that come from religion and traditional mores. Competitive markets weed out liars and cheaters. Theoretically, unethical behavior is costly in a competitive system. Consumers can boycott firms that spoil the environment or discriminate. This best possible capitalistic scenario argues that self-interest limits selfishness (Lappé, 1989).

Set against this line of argument are the grim realities of our capitalist system, one in which capitalism seeks out the low-wage suppliers, hires personnel from temporary employment agencies to escape paying benefits and health care, and has a widening gap between those at the top and at the bottom. Capitalism can well be blamed for the ethic of personal advantage and its ill consequences (Mitchell & Scott, 1990). In contrast, despite the gross failures of Western democracies colonized by big corporations (Deetz, 1992a), the democratic idea persists. Grassroots workplace democracy contains the seeds for a nurturing-caring ethic.

Democracy is an ethic of equal voice and collective good. It bears within it the balancing act of providing the well-being of the many and protecting the human dignity of the few and the less able. On the other hand, what makes workplace democracy problematic is the reality that enclaves of workplace democracy within a very competitive individualistic culture may not survive unless they too can function within a society shaped by a personal-advantage ethic.

Ethnographic studies of employee-owned organizations are few indeed. When such are conducted, most likely democratization will differ among various employee-owned work environments. Studies of organization will always be to a great extent not unlike John Saxe's "The Blind Men and the Elephant" and as Waldo (1961) suggested in his essay "Organization Theory: An Elephantine Problem." To see employee-owned companies as closed democratic systems, to see them as caged beasts in a zoo (Perrow, 1980), is to miss the culture that frustrates or facilitates democratization of lives.

Communication richness is not just increased frequency of face-to-face interaction on day-to-day tasks. Communication richness, rather, is having an equal say in decisions about one's work and life environment. Insight about how that is accomplished in employee-owned enterprise may entail what Czarniawska-Joerges (1992) describes as political anthropology. She reasons that, because organizations are complex, they look different when viewed from the top than when seen from the bottom, but, when seen through "narrative holograms," an "as if I were there" insightful feeling is possible (p. 222).

Such holograms have been presented by participant-observers (Burawoy, 1979; Philipsen, 1975) or even by researchers' reports of contrived simulations (Donnellson, Gray, & Bougon, 1986). Organizations are speech communities; symbols, meanings, premises, and rules reflect and reproduce an organization's ideology (Philipsen, 1992, p. 13).

The way democracy is realized in a Type 1, employee-owned cooperative-type organization, Harrison points out, is dependent upon the homogeneity of its members and upon small-world face-to-face interaction. Kanter's (1972) study of socialization tactics employed by communes provides insights, as other accounts of commune practices reveal that even in small member-owned organizations power comes to be vested in a capable charismatic few.

To understand how democracy is communicated in Type 2 employee-owned organizations, one must study their premises and processes. The premises and processes entail moral, economic, and political domains and are manifested in the variables pertaining to efficiency, equality, expertise and effort, and equity.

Efficiency

The notion that the workplace should not be divided between workers and owners cannot be based upon efficiency; however, efficiency does matter. The charge that workplace democracy requires untold hours of meeting time is justified. Establishing representative systems does take time. But traditional management systems also suffer from high administration costs. In U.S. manufacturing, until recent downsizing, there were 40 administrators for every 100 production workers (Melman, 1983). That is an abundance of oversight! Where workers are motivated, in sync, and committed to organizational values, there will be greater efficiency, waste cutting, increased energy, and less need for oversight. Ownership and sharing in the rewards are related to motivation, and motivation is linked to efficiency (Lappé, 1989).

When workers are owners and owners are workers, control mechanisms should differ from those in employer-owned organization. Anecdotal evidence supports this notion. Time clocks were eliminated, and a time sheet filled out by employees themselves was posted at one partially employee-owned factory. Special committees were charged with review of discipline, and employees said, "Before Karl used to come and tell us what he was going to do. Now we tell him what we want to do" (Ford, 1991).

Equality

Type 1 employee ownership is ideologically based. Ego is subordinated to "wego." The "good of all" in the collective means meeting the basic needs of each member and respect for each individual's dignity. Responsibilities and rewards are to be evenly proportioned. Type 2 employee ownership is founded upon the premise of equality but is modified by variables of investment (voting sometimes based upon the number of shares accumulated over one's tenure, which may differ). Equal opportunity to voice one's concerns, however, appears to be a fundamental premise of employee-owned companies.

Expertise and Effort

Wages within employee-owned firms generally are based upon the various expertise, skills, and effort required for certain jobs. Dirtier, riskier, heavier, and more stressful jobs involve additional factors that can modify the ideal of equal pay. The concept of comparable worth of jobs currently is not clearly of more concern in employee-owned than traditional employer-owned companies, but the premise of equality does make this a more natural concern of employee ownership. The notion of each individual who works to her or his capacity being rewarded equally is an ideal of communal life that should transfer to employee ownership.

Equity

Employer-owned firms are premised upon the belief that those with more capital invested and major management responsibilities should receive the lion's share of the rewards. Consequent disparities in rewards in traditional employer-owned organization are cause for four out of five employed in nonmanagement positions and over one half of managers to say that they are underrewarded for what they do (Huseman & Hatfield, 1989). The human tendency to see ourselves as more deserving than others may never be changed, but envious comparison should be lessened when power and profits are more equally distributed and based upon the productivity of the whole operation in employee-owned organizations rather than upon the divisive reward systems of individual competition.

Idealism, self-interest, and necessity make strange bedfellows. The utopian experiments of the 1800s and communal dropouts of the 1970s; the agricultural and producer cooperatives in the United States and abroad, such as the Spanish anarchists and the Israeli kibbutzim; the "every man a capitalist" rhetoric of San Francisco attorney and investment banker Louis Kelso and Louisiana populist politician Russell Long; the varied quality of work life efforts, Scanlon plans, and labor union organizing—each has contributed to an ongoing conversation. Essays such as Harrison's focus that conversation upon communication's inherent democratic character.

REFERENCES

Bado, J., & Logue, J. (1991). *Hard hats and hard decisions: The evolving union role in employee-owned firms.* Kent: Kent State University, Northeast Ohio Employee Ownership Center.

Bradley, K., & Gelb, A. (1983). *Worker capitalism: The new industrial revolution.* Cambridge: MIT Press.

Brown, L. R., Flavin, C., & Kane, H. (1992). *Vital signs: Trends that are shaping our future.* New York: Norton.

Burawoy, M. (1979). *Manufacturing consent.* Chicago: Chicago University Press.

Conte, M. A., & Svejnar, J. (1990). The performance effects of employee ownership plans. In A. A. Binder (Ed.), *Paying for productivity: A look at the evidence* (pp. 142-172). Washington, DC: Brookings.

Czarniawska-Joerges, B. (1992). *Exploring complex organizations.* Newbury Park, CA: Sage.

Deetz, S. (1992a). *Democracy in an age of corporate colonialism: Developments in communication and politics of everyday life.* Albany: State University of New York Press.

Deetz, S. (1992b, October). *Building a communication perspective in organization studies I: Foundations.* Paper presented at the Speech Communication Association, Chicago.

Dentzer, S. (1992, June 1). A wealth of difference. *U.S. News & World Report,* pp. 45-47.

Derrida, J. (1978). *Writing and difference.* London: Routledge & Kegan Paul.

Donnellson, A., Gray, B., & Bougon, M. G. (1986). Communication, meaning, and organized action. *Administrative Science Quarterly, 31,* 43-55.

Ellerman, D. P. (1990). *The democratic worker-owned firm: A new model for the East and West.* Boston: Unwin Hyman.

Fisher, A. B. (1992, June 29). The new debate over the very rich. *Fortune,* pp. 42-54.

Ford, S. (1991). *Better decisions via employee involvement: Employee participation at Reuther Mold Manufacturing.* Kent: Kent State University, Ohio Employee Ownership Center.

Galbraith, J. K. (1992). The economic hangover from a binge of greed. *Business and Society Review, 83,* 6-7.

General Accounting Office. (1987). *Employee stock ownership plans: Participants' benefits generally increased, but many plans terminated.* Washington, DC: Author.

General Accounting Office. (1990). *Employee stock ownership plans: Little evidence of effects on corporate performance.* Washington, DC: Author.

Huseman, R. C., & Hatfield, J. D. (1989). *Managing the equity factor.* Boston: Houghton-Mifflin.

Kant, I. (1963). *On history* (L. W. Beck, Ed.; L. W. Beck, R. E. Anchor, & E. R. Fackenheim, Trans.). Indianapolis: Bobbs-Merrill. (Original work published 1794)

Kanter, R. (1972). *Commitment and community: Communes and utopias in sociological perspective.* Cambridge, MA: Harvard University Press.

Kanter, R. M., Stein, B. A., & Brinkerhoff, D. W. (1982). Building participatory democracy within a conventional corporation. In F. Lindenfield & J. Rothschild-Whitt (Eds.), *Workplace democracy and social change* (pp. 371-382). Boston: Porter Sargent.

Katz, D., & Kahn, R. L. (1978). *The social psychology of organizations.* New York: John Wiley.

Lappé, F. M. (1989). *Rediscovering America's values.* New York: Ballantine.

Letiche, H. (1990). Five post-modern aphorisms for trainers. *Management Education and Development, 21*(3), 229-240.

Linstead, S., & Grafton-Small, R. (1992). On reading organizational culture. *Organizational Studies, 13*(3), 331-355.

Mahon, R. (1991). From solidaristic wages to solidaristic work: A post-Fordist historic compromise for Sweden? *Economic Analysis and Workers Management, 24,* 295-325.

McWhirter, D. A. (1991). Employee stock ownership plans in the United States. In C. Rosen & K. M. Young (Eds.), *Understanding employee ownership* (pp. 43-73). Ithaca, NY: ILR Press.

Melman, S. (1983). *Profits without production.* New York: Knopf.

Michigan Center for Employee Ownership and Gainsharing. (1990). *A study of employee ownership in Michigan.* Lansing, MI: Governor's Office for Job Training.

Mitchell, T. R., & Scott, W. G. (1990). America's problems and needed reforms: Confronting the ethic of personal advantage. *Academy of Management Executive, 4,* 23-35.

Moody, C., & Ivancic, C. (1991, May 15-17). *Understanding ownership: ESOP training in large employee-owned firms, owner education at Republic Engineered Steels, Inc.* Paper presented at the ESOP Association 14th Annual Convention, Washington, DC.

Moss, G. (1991). Employee ownership in the USA: A four-frame perspective. *Economic and Industrial Democracy, 12,* 187-202.

Nader, R. (1992, November 30). How Clinton can build democracy. *The Nation, 649,* 652-653.

Perrow, C. (1980). Zoo story or life in the organizational sandpit. In G. Salaman & K. Thompson (Eds.), *Control and ideology in organizations* (pp. 259-277). Cambridge: MIT Press.

Philipsen, G. (1975). Speaking "like a man" in Teamsterville: Culture patterns of role enactment in an urban neighborhood. *Quarterly Journal of Speech, 61,* 13-22.

Philipsen, G. (1992). *Speaking culturally: Explorations in social communication.* Albany: State University of New York.

Rose, R. L., & Kotlowitz, A. (1992, November 23). Back to bickering: Strife between VAW and Caterpillar blights promising labor idea. *Wall Street Journal,* pp. A1, A8, A9.

Rosen, C., & Young, K. (Eds.). (1991). *Understanding employee ownership.* Ithaca, NY: ILR Press.

Tyler, G. (1980). What do unions really do? *Dissent, 27,* 474.

Waldo, D. (1961). Organizational theory: An elephantine problem. *Public Administration Review, 21,* 210-225.

Weick, K. (1979). *The social psychology of organizing.* Reading, MA: Addison-Wesley. (Original work published 1969)

Westenholz, A. (1991). Democracy as "organizational divorce" and how the postmodern democracy is stifled by unity and majority. *Economic and Industrial Democracy, 12,* 173-186.

SECTION 2

TAKING MESSAGES SERIOUSLY

7 Discourse Features and Message Comprehension

DIANE M. BADZINSKI
University of Nebraska—Lincoln

MARY M. GILL
Buena Vista College

Our chapter concerns the impact of discourse features on comprehension and argues that much of current work underestimates the complexity of the relationship between features and message understanding. This underestimation results from oversimplifying the comprehension process, failing to recognize cues as possibly impairing understanding, and neglecting to challenge assumptions underlying comprehension models. In this manuscript, we define *comprehension,* offer a taxonomy of discourse features, examine various comprehension models, and demonstrate the need to study the relation between discourse features and comprehension within the framework of some theory associated with message understanding.

A NGELA Lansbury is perhaps best known for her award-winning role as Jessica Fletcher, a mature mystery writer masquerading as a detective's helper in the series *Murder, She Wrote.* Regardless of the episode, a murder is committed in which a friend of Jessica's is arrested. The episode is devoted to Jessica pointing out clues to a poor-sighted detective implicating other people who have motives for committing the crime. As clues are uncovered, Jessica has hunches about the identity of the murderer with more information unfolding during the episode to confirm or disconfirm her hunches. By carefully weighing available clues, Jessica ultimately solves the crime.

The steps in solving a mystery are not unlike the processes involved in constructing meaning. When confronted with a passage, individuals consider various information sources to construct working hypotheses or "hunches" about possible meanings. As more information is encountered, new hypotheses may be made with existing hunches abandoned or modified. After considering

Correspondence and requests for reprints: Diane M. Badzinski, 432 Oldfather, Department of Speech Communication, University of Nebraska, Lincoln, NE 68588-0329.

Communication Yearbook 17, pp. 301-332

available information, a hypothesis is selected that, at least in the reader's eyes, best captures the intended meaning.

Much empirical work is directed toward understanding the processes involved in constructing meaning. It is not our goal to review this rich body of literature (see Berger, 1989; van Dijk, 1987, 1988; van Dijk & Kintsch, 1983). We also make little distinction between reading and listening comprehension. Despite reading and listening differing in terms of information acquisition, it is generally assumed that the manner in which higher order processes are executed is similar whether the information is auditorially or visually presented (Colley, 1987) with the interactive nature of the process evident in both modes (Bostrom, 1990; Chafe & Tannen, 1987).

Our discussion concentrates on potential explanations accounting for the effect of discourse features on comprehension processes. This issue is raised by a variety of researchers in our field including those interested in how verbal and nonverbal behaviors relate to student learning (Gorham, 1988; Kelly & Gorham, 1988; Sanders & Wiseman, 1990), the influence of gestures on retrieving verbal messages (Woodall & Folger, 1985), and the impact of verbal, contextual, and extratextual cues on comprehending visual and print media (Cameron, Schleuder, & Thorson, 1991; Hoffner, Cantor, & Thorson, 1988; Thorson, Christ, & Caywood, 1991; Wilson & Weiss, 1991). Others study the role of cues on jurors' understanding of trial information (Badzinski & Pettus, 1992; Kaminski & Miller, 1984; V. L. Smith, 1991), children's understanding of narratives (Badzinski, 1991a, 1991b, 1992), consumers' understanding of product warning labels (Kelley, Gaidis, & Reingen, 1989), and couples' understanding of each other's remarks (Noller, 1984; Noller & Ruzzene, 1991; Sillars, Pike, Jones, & Murphy, 1984).

Throughout the essay, we argue that current work often underestimates the complexity of linking cues to comprehension. This tendency results from an oversimplification of the comprehension process, the failure to consider cues as enhancing and impairing comprehension, the tendency to study message understanding void of considering theories of comprehension, and a neglect of challenging the assumptions underlying models of text understanding.

COMPREHENSION: WHAT IS IT?

Most contemporary definitions of comprehension emphasize that meaning is constructed through a complex set of dynamic processes involving the integration of past experiences with text information. Although recent views accept this constructivist position, differences exist in the relative importance of various processes in understanding. For instance, some definitions stress the integration of information presented in the discourse claiming comprehension is a "cognitive process whereby individuals build meanings from either sounds in oral communication or visual markers in written communication" (Ellis, 1992, p. 202). Other definitions focus on the importance of background knowledge, defining comprehension as the "act of using prior knowledge to extract meaning from a message on the basis of its components (e.g., words or sentences) and the relations between these components" (Ratneshwar & Chaiken, 1991, p. 53). Yet others stress the integration of a variety of information sources. Wittrock (1990, p. 252), for example, defines comprehension as a process of "actively generating relations among the parts of the text and between the text and one's memories, knowledge, and experiences." Still others such as van Dijk (1988) point to the strategic and interactive nature of comprehension arguing that understanding is "a complex integrated process of strategic selection, retrieval, and application of various information sources in the construction of textual representations and models" (p. 148).

The definitions reviewed above prompt us to conceptualize comprehension in the following way:

> *Comprehension,* involving a set of cognitive processes, is the product of constructing meaning by implementing a set of strategies for selecting, retrieving, and integrating a number of information sources (e.g., background knowledge, textual features, memories, and emotions) to form a mental representation of the discourse that sufficiently captures the gist of the source's intent.

There are several key elements of our conceptualization that merit further attention.

Comprehension Is a Set of Cognitive Processes

Kintsch and Yarbrough (1982) claim that "comprehension is a commonsense term for a whole bundle of psychological processes, each of which must be evaluated separately" (p. 834). The view that comprehension consists of a collection of processes such as attention, retrieval, integration, and memory implies that any theory of comprehension must be sufficiently broad to capture the diverse processes. Another implication is that comprehension is often exploited by researchers purporting to tap text understanding while measuring only one of its many components. For example, the primary data on comprehension are subjects' recall and summaries of text events (Ericsson, 1988), which capture only a small part of the process. Although it is naive to assume that one measurement instrument could be devised to tap the entire process, researchers must not assert that "comprehension" is measured when only a part of the process is addressed. Our work, in fact, falls prey to this tendency by claiming to tap comprehension while addressing inference-making and recall, which are two of the many components involved in understanding.

Comprehension Is the Instantiation of a Set of Flexible Plans and Strategies

Strategies, which exist prior to the processing of incoming input, are a set of directions for making sense of a text and shaping what is processed (Fish, 1980). Strategies are used to attend to, select, retrieve, and integrate relevant information needed to construct meaning. Indeed, many communication scholars recognize that plans and strategies exert great influence on various comprehension processes (e.g., Berger & Jordan, 1992; Berger, Karol, & Jordan, 1989; Burke, 1986; Tracy, 1991; Waldron, 1990).

One assumption of conceptualizing comprehension as a strategy-driven activity is that message understanding will depend on one's knowledge, interests, and goals (van Dijk & Kintsch, 1983). This view implies that one cannot assume that an individual's primary goal upon confronting incoming stimuli is discourse understanding (O'Shea, Sindelar, & O'Shea, 1985). The position that comprehension is not a primary goal may explain why processors are often unable to recall much content (Keenan, MacWhinney, & Mayhew, 1977; Stafford & Daly, 1984).

A strategy-view approach also stresses that understanding is a highly mindful goal-directed event, requiring at least a minimal amount of awareness, intentionality, and effort. Strategies are not automatically activated but entail the intentional selection of appropriate plans. Thus one's plans provide the rationale for a particular strategy selection (Hobbs & Agar, 1985; Schank & Abelson, 1977). A strategy-driven approach, however, does not require selection to be a time-intensive and cognitively taxing activity; rather, strategies become highly automatic and cognitively efficient once part of a general knowledge system (Berger, 1989; van Dijk & Kintsch, 1983).

Comprehension Is an Active Meaning-Making Process

Early views conceptualized comprehension in terms of a shunting metaphor in which information is transferred unchanged from source to receiver via the written or spoken word (F. Smith, 1985; Straw & Bogdan, 1990). Accordingly, the source is responsible for encoding intent and the receiver is charged with the task of extracting intent. Thus comprehension is a passive, receptive activity requiring little more than extracting and digesting presented material.

The shunting metaphor was replaced with a mechanistic approach viewing comprehension as the "active consumption" of information. Text comprehension is achieved by the successful execution of a set of skills (e.g., paraphrasing, predicting story outcome) that are systematically and more or less automatically applied to all discourse (Dole, Duffy, Roehler, & Pearson, 1991). Although comprehension is no longer viewed as only a process of extracting meaning or the mastery of a set of skills, it should not be taken to mean that comprehension does not involve extracting meaning and acquiring a set of skills. Rather, comprehension is something much more—it is the active construction of meaning within the constraints set forth by the text and accomplished through a willingness to engage in meaning-making activities.

Comprehension Is the Construction of a Mental Representation

Comprehension involves building a cognitive representation, often called a "mental model," by integrating information presented in the text with general background knowledge and knowledge of other available information sources. The mental model constrains the amount of inferences needed to make the discourse coherent and provides the framework for evaluating and interpreting incoming information (Johnson-Laird, 1983; Morrow, Bower, & Greenspan, 1989; van Dijk & Kintsch, 1983). One builds a representation of a text from one of two broad approaches: a syntactic or bottom-up process in which interpretations are gradually built by identifying surface features (e.g., words, sounds) and connecting them to larger units (e.g., paragraphs, topics) or the semantic or top-down process in which comprehenders begin with an interpretation and use the framework to filter incoming information. Most scholars acknowledge that the construction of a mental model entails some combination of both processes (Ellis, 1992; Kellermann & Sleight, 1989).

Comprehension is, in fact, often described in terms of a construction process (Bartlett, 1932; Gernsbacher, 1990; Gernsbacher, Varner, & Faust, 1990; Spiro, 1980). Consider Gernsbacher et al.'s (1990) description of comprehension:

> The goal of comprehension is to build a cohesive, mental representation or "structure." The first process involved in building this structure is laying a foundation. The next process involves developing a model by mapping on incoming information when that information coheres or relates to previous information. However, if the incoming information is less coherent or related, comprehenders employ a different process: They shift to initiate a new substructure. (p. 431)

While the construction metaphor (e.g., laying a foundation, building a structure, constructing an interpretive framework) is a useful tool for describing some processes, the metaphor implies that the ultimate goal is the completed structure, at which time understanding is reached. The metaphor fails to capture the continual reevaluation of a representation and one's affective and behavioral reactions to the model. This serial depiction of text understanding has been abandoned in favor of a control system that generates strategies and plans for shaping meaning or a neural circuitry system in which pieces of information activate many paths of connection.

Comprehension Is a Process of Modifying and Matching Mental Models

Discourse comprehension involves planning, aligning, revising, and monitoring interpretations; hence cognitive representations must be viewed as having a draftlike quality—subject to revisions (Tierney & Gee, 1990; Tierney & Pearson, 1983). Glenberg, Meyer, and Lindem (1987) write: "Mental models are updatable: The representation is modified by the addition of new information, and that new information may require accommodation that produces a completely different interpretation of the events" (p. 69). The critical point is that comprehension does not end when all available information is received but involves continually reevaluating available input and integrating one's affective and behavioral responses as part of the interpretation.

The question becomes this: "Is it ever possible to state that comprehension has been attained?" The answer is the point at which one's interpretation is stabilized, following the processing of relevant information, provided that the constructed representation sufficiently captures the source's intent. This later requirement stresses that comprehension entails some sort of validation process through explicit (e.g., written tests, relevant topic extensions) or implicit (e.g., cultural norms) means. Although comprehension requires a sufficient match between two models, the degree of match is a negotiated process between source and receiver, with the source the ultimate decision maker.

Summary

Our conceptualization stresses that comprehension begins prior to encountering a particular text and continues beyond the consumption of available input. Meaning takes shape only through considering text precursors (e.g., attitudes, prior knowledge) and reactions to the discourse (e.g., affective evaluations). Any comprehension theory must consider the various components in the process and the relationships among those entities. Our goal now turns toward investigating a specific part of the comprehension process—the ways in which discourse features influence meaning construction.

DISCOURSE FEATURES: WHAT ARE THEY?

When examining research on discourse features, one factor is immediately apparent. Although discourse features are generally defined as devices or cues that affect message understanding by triggering particular text representations, numerous terms are used to identify discourse features. For example, *speech markers* (Giles & Coupland, 1991), *communication codes* (Ellis, 1992), *discourse pointers* (Carpenter & Just, 1977), *relevancy markers* (van Dijk, 1979), *contextual cues* (Dorr-Bremme, 1990; Gumperz, 1982), *cues* (Doelger, Hewes, & Graham, 1986; Kellermann & Sleight, 1989), and *discourse strategies* (Kintsch & Yarbrough, 1982) are a few terms used to refer to a concept similar to what we call discourse features or cues. Regardless of the term used, discourse features stem from the source, context, message, and receiver.

Although these divisions may conjure a linear model, we are concerned with isolating points during a transaction in which discourse features influence understanding and with the way these features interact in meaning-making. Hewes and Graham (1989) write: "A cue is not simply an objective property of message, but arises from a receiver's interpretation of the message content, form, and such contextual factors as the immediate definition of the situation and background knowledge, relational history, and any implicit goals attributed to the participants in the exchange" (p. 225). Indeed, it is the interaction among the set of cues that gives rise to interpretation.

Source Features

The importance of source cues was recognized in very early views of reading comprehension. During the nineteenth century, meaning resided in the author, and thus knowledge of the author was essential for the interpretive process. Straw and Bogdan (1990) note that "the primary knowledge needed by a reader in order to read, understand, and interpret text was perceived to be knowledge about the author, his or her life, his or her historical context, and his or her moral/philosophical stance" (p. 15). Although the central role of the author has declined in contemporary views, the importance of the source in constructing meaning must be recognized.

As presented in Table 1, source features provide information regarding source identity. For example, features including accent, speech rate, phonological variants, skin color, smiling, and gaze are markers of group identity (Bourhis & Giles, 1977; Giles & Coupland, 1991; Giles, Henwood, Coupland, Harriman, & Coupland, 1992; Gill, 1991; Gill & Badzinski, 1992). Other cues such as personal appearance, facial expressions, body movements, and language choices provide information about a person's credibility, attractiveness, intelligence, mood, character, and status (Bradac, Bowers, & Courtright, 1979; Bradac & Wisegarver, 1984; Burgoon, Birk, & Pfau, 1990; Mays, 1982; Scherer & Giles, 1979). Age and gender also effect the conclusions formed by listeners (Helfrich, 1979; P. M. Smith, 1979; Williams & Giles, 1991).

Despite the substantial work pointing to features signaling source characteristics and the importance of such features on source perception, little is known regarding their role on comprehension. This lack of knowledge is the result of neglecting to include comprehension as a dependent variable in much communication research. Source features must be evaluated as to their importance in constructing meaning.

Contextual Features

Communication scholars recognize the situated nature of interaction and call for more research focusing on contextual influences (Cody & McLaughlin, 1985; Giles & Hewstone, 1982; Haslett, 1986, 1987). Generally, the

TABLE 1
Classifying Discourse Features

Source Features
   Group/ethnic identity: race, gender, socioeconomic status, group affiliation
   History: topic knowledge, relationship with receiver, familiarity with content, knowledge
     of situation
   Personal features: power, warmth, enthusiasm, psychological profile, intelligence
   Disposition: goals, expectations, motivation, arousal, affective state
   Skills: ability to encode message, perspective-taking ability, flexibility, verbal proficiency
Contextual Features
   Physical setting: type of situation, people involved, norms
   Affective climate: mood, tension
Message Features
   Lexical: connectives, diversity of items, repetitions, paraphrases, restatements, coloring
   Syntactic: word order, sentence structure, dialect features, topicalization, sentence length
   Rhetorical: metaphors, humor, irony, question-asking, similes, tropes and figures, puns,
     hyperbole
   Paratextual: headings, bold type, illustrations, punctuations, type size, italics, underlining
   Paraverbal: facial/vocal expression, gestures, smiles, gaze, rate, fluency, intonation/
     vocalization patterns, volume, pitch, resonance
Receiver Features
   Group/ethnic identity: race, gender, socioeconomic status, group affiliation
   History: topic knowledge, relationship with source, familiarity with content, knowledge
     of situation
   Personal features: power, warmth, enthusiasm, psychological profile, intelligence
   Disposition: goals, expectations, motivation, arousal, affective state
   Skills: ability to decode message, integrate information, sensitivity to markers, memory ability

context includes an individual's prior knowledge about the physical setting. Such knowledge influences expectations about what will be occurring by providing relevant knowledge structures needed to comprehend the messages (Haslett, 1987).

Indeed, text understanding often requires information about the situation (e.g., Bower & Morrow, 1990; Bryant & Tversky, 1992; Glenberg, Meyer, & Lindem, 1987; Taylor & Tversky, 1992; van Dijk & Kintsch, 1983). Accordingly, van Dijk and Kintsch (1983) argue that meaning can be represented in terms of a situational model defined as a "cognitive representation of the events, actions, persons, and in general the situation that a text is all about" (pp. 11-12). Thus comprehension requires constructing a text representation and envisioning the physical properties conveyed by the text (Bower & Morrow, 1990; Gernsbacher, 1990; Morrow et al., 1989). Situational models assist in holding relevant information in working memory (Morrow, 1985; O'Brien & Albrecht, 1992) and are needed to accomplish goals and plans (Fletcher, 1986).

Sociolinguists and anthropologists also recognize the importance of contextual information in the interpretive process (e.g., Dorr-Bremme, 1990; Givon, 1989; Gumperz, 1982). Gumperz (1982) defines a contextual cue as "any feature of linguistic form that contributes to the signalling of contextual presuppositions" (p. 131). These cues are things such as shifts in voice tone and/or rhythm, switches in linguistic codes, dialects, speech style, and changes in various nonverbal expressive qualities of speakers. Gumperz (1982), and later Dorr-Bremme (1990), proposes that these features, which regulate the flow and content of discourse, are habitually but rarely consciously used. Of interest, Gumperz (1982) holds that a failure to react to a cue or acknowledge its functions results in misinterpretation that is regarded as "a social faux pas and leads to misjudgments of the speaker's intent; it is not likely to be identified as a mere linguistic error" (p. 132). The adverse consequences that arise with such a faux pas should readily point to the central role of context in assessing meaning.

Taking the lead from others (e.g., Forgas, 1983; Wish, Deutsch, & Kaplan, 1976), we divide contextual cues into aspects of the physical setting and affective climate. The physical properties include type of situation (e.g., formal/informal), number of people involved, and goals and expectations of such settings. Affective climate pertains to the general mood and tensions (e.g., friendly/hostile) characterizing the situation.

Message Features

In comparison to the scant research linking source and contextual cues to message understanding, substantial work centers on the link between message features and comprehension. A message perspective concentrates on features in the text that contribute to one's understanding of that text. This perspective emerged early in communication studies; rhetorical scholars were concerned with what language or message features aided comprehensibility (see Cooper, 1923; Wallace, 1978). For example, Bacon analyzed words and word combinations and their effect on interpretation and noted that "the ill and unfit choice of words wonderfully obstructs the understanding" (Wallace, 1978, p. 109). Cicero identified the usefulness of witticism and figures of speech to the understandability of a speaker's message (Rolfe, 1963). Examining the Roman system of style and figures of speech, Smith and Prince (1990) reported that "of particular importance to the Romans was the judicious use of tropes and figures, the manipulation of syntax, diction and meaning in order to catch attention, fascinate or elicit meaning" (p. 63).

Current perspectives identify more finely distinguished variables as message features. For example, Ellis (1992) calls these devices "communication codes," which comprise paraverbal cues (e.g., gestures, visual cues, and contextual information), lexical morphemes (e.g., nouns, verbs), and grammatical morphemes (e.g., *and, a*). Ellis argues that discourse features are "structure-carrying units" (p. 85) and that codes are formed, altered, and refined in interaction. Williams (1986) is similarly concerned with syntactic, graphic, lexical, semantic, and schematic signals as triggers to text understanding.

Another feature receiving a great deal of attention, presumably due to its central role in text understanding, is cohesive ties (Brown & Yule, 1983; Planalp, Graham, & Paulson, 1987; Villaume & Cegala, 1988). These devices take the form of reference, substitution, conjunction, ellipsis, and lexical cohesion (Halliday & Hasan, 1976). Although it is acknowledged that "in the absence of cohesive devices, discourse can still be considered meaningful," most agree that cohesive devices facilitate interpretive processes by signaling "connectivity, relatedness and pertinence" (Kellermann & Sleight, 1989, p. 102).

Other kinds of message features such as advance organizers (Mayer, 1980; Mayer & Bromage, 1980), typographic cues (Hartley, 1987), metaphors (Reynolds & Schwartz, 1983; Waggoner, Messe, & Palermo, 1985; Yarbrough & Gagne, 1987), accents (Gill, 1991; Gill & Badzinski, 1992), nonverbal immediacy behaviors (Christophel, 1990; Gorham, 1988), gestures (Woodall & Folger, 1985), language choices (Badzinski, 1989; Goetz, 1979), and vocalics (Badzinski, 1991a) also influence comprehension processes. Future work needs to move away from investigating isolated message features and focus on how these features interact with other information sources in determining meaning.

Receiver Features

One major movement in reading research asserts that meaning resides almost exclusively with the reader/receiver. This view stems from both reading comprehension theories that center on how meaning construction is a problem-solving activity and reading response theories that emphasize the reader's ability to evoke a variety of meanings from literary texts (Hynds, 1990; Straw & Bogdan, 1990).

Although there exists a movement to elevate the role of the reader, too much research in our discipline neglects the receiver (Hewes & Graham, 1989). Despite this tendency, research investigating the impact of receiver characteristics on comprehension is accumulating. For example, research documents that receivers' (a) goals and anxiety levels affect conversational recall (Stafford & Daly, 1984), (b) individual perceptions influence conversational recollections (Stafford, Waldron, & Infield, 1989), (c) prevailing attitudes determine what information will be attended to from a message (Bodenhausen & Lichtenstein, 1987), (d) levels of cognitive complexity affect information recall (Neuliep & Hazelton, 1986), and (e) degrees of high and low involvement influence the likelihood of providing elaborate conversational extensions (Cegala, 1981, 1984; Villaume & Cegala, 1988). Further, high self-monitors are better able to isolate important information, despite little evidence that high self-monitors process more information (Douglas, 1983).

To more fully understand the role of receiver cues, much more work needs to be done. As Colley (1987) notes, virtually nothing is known about the ways in which goals and other receiver characteristics bear on message comprehension. A focus on receiver characteristics may also assist in explaining individual differences in comprehension skills and why some populations have great difficulty monitoring their comprehension ability (Glenberg & Epstein, 1985; Glenberg, Sanocki, Epstein, & Morris, 1987; Maki & Berry, 1984).

In summary, isolating a taxonomy of discourse features, which no doubt is illustrative rather than exhaustive, is an important step in identifying information sources that are likely to affect comprehension. Although the current way of thinking is to focus on a single characteristic, research needs to examine the relative contributions of the different information sources on meaning construction and the functions of the various features at different stages of the comprehension process. In addition, more work should be devoted to stipulating the conditions in which, and the probability of which, a particular cue accesses the desired interpretation. To address this later concern, we report on several of our studies that investigate the likelihood that specific features activate particular interpretations.

CUES AND COMPREHENSION

How might discourse features serve to prompt the construction of a particular interpretation? Scholars suggest a variety of roles that cues perform in meaning construction. Discourse cues act as pieces of converging evidence biasing an individual toward making a particular text representation (Hayes-Roth & Thorndyke, 1979; Schmidt & Paris, 1983), affect the selection and coordination of relevant text information (Ryan & Ledger, 1984; Yuill & Joscelyne, 1988), and enhance an individual's motivation to process the material (Christophel, 1990; Kelley et al., 1989). Despite the different ways cues may influence interpretation, we concentrate our efforts on studying how discourse features affect the construction of text representations by facilitating inference making, memory for text material, and speed of message processing.

Inferential Processing

One primary function of discourse features is to guide the inference-making process. Indeed, meaning construction involves being able to make inferences to produce a coherent text base (Bower, Black, & Turner, 1979; Potts, Keenan, & Golding, 1988; van Dijk & Kintsch, 1983; Walker & Meyer, 1980). In some situations, a number of plausible, and perhaps competing, inferences could be made requiring an individual to select among a pool of possible alternatives. In these circumstances, discourse features provide valuable information regarding which relations will be made. More specifically, cues narrow the range of likely inferences, resulting in an increased probability that a particular inference will be made.

We have studied the extent to which discourse features affect the likelihood of drawing inferential relations. In one investigation (Badzinski, 1991a), children listened to stories in which narratives were told in a tone of voice that either strongly or weakly cued specific text interpretations. To illustrate, consider the following event recounted by a little girl named Laura: "Well, mom was at the kitchen table pouring chocolate milk into the glasses. But before mom could stop her, Fluffy jumped on the table and began leaping on the plates. She knocked one of the glasses." We predicted that the intensity of the story character's vocal expression would influence the likelihood that the passage would implicate information such as the milk spilled and that Laura's mother was angry. As expected, both first and third graders made more inferential ties with a strong than weak tone. Similarly, we found that elementary school age children made more such inferences with narratives in which the story characters' word choices were considered of high rather than low message intensity (Badzinski, 1989) and with narratives in which the emotional expression was consistent rather than inconsistent with story content (Badzinski, 1991b). Thus discourse cues clearly promoted the construction of text representations by influencing the probability of making particular inferential links.

Memory

Discourse features also serve to facilitate memory of text information. Clearly, individuals do not remember entire dialogues (Keenan et al., 1977; Stafford & Daly, 1984). Studies document that individuals are more likely to remember important material (Meyer, 1975). Even young children recall more information deemed high in importance (Lorch, Bellack, & Augsbach, 1987; Young & Schumacher, 1983; Yussen, Mathews, Buss, & Kane, 1980). This research led us to speculate that mechanisms that draw one's attention to important text information should also aid in accurate text recall.

To explore the effects of cues on recall, our studies were also designed to tap memory for explicit story content. The investigations yielded little support for the position that discourse features improve memory for text information. The vocal manipulations had little impact on children's memory for explicit ideas, especially measured by free and cued recall tasks (Badzinski, 1991a). Thus the results fail to support the thinking that discourse cues signal text importance, which, in turn, heightens memory of text concepts.

It is likely that the relationship between features and recall is more complex than proposed. Perhaps the relation between cues and memory should not be divorced from the above discussion pertaining to the impact of cues on inference-making. Some studies show that recall of text material correlates with an understanding of contextual inferences (Paris & Upton, 1976); thus features that prompt inferential processing are also likely to improve recall (Thompson & Myers, 1985). On the other hand, some findings show little or no effect of inference-making on factual recall (Mayer, 1979; Yuill & Josce-lyne, 1988). The results of our studies suggest that discourse features affect memory independently of their role in inference-making. Despite our work failing to support a direct relationship between cues and recall, we cannot yet dismiss this issue. The null results may be due to the relatively easy texts used in our studies and that the tasks involved immediate rather than delayed recall. It seems apparent that future work should consider the impact of cues on inferential processing controlling for memory of text concepts. Indeed, we need to question the extent to which separate processes (e.g., memory) should be studied independently of other processes (e.g., inferential processing). In short, the verdict is not yet rendered regarding the role of cues on memory.

Processing Speed

Third, discourse features facilitate the speed of processing text informa-tion. This proposed relationship is based on two lines of reasoning. One argument is simply that features signal text importance and that processing is quicker with information of high importance (Badzinski, 1989; Goetz, 1979). For example, Walker and Meyer (1980) report that inference-making is quicker for ideas high rather than low in structure. A second line of reasoning is that cues trigger the activation of implicit text ideas and that such concepts should be processed rather quickly. Thus processing speed is a direct function of the activation of implicit text concepts.

We find partial support for this position. Namely, reaction times in verify-ing implicit text ideas are quicker given stories in which vocal cues strongly cued particular associations (Badzinski, 1991a) and when vocal cues are consistent with text information (Badzinski, 1991b). When adults are asked to read children's stories containing lexical items of high or low message intensity, however, reaction times in drawing implicit relations do not vary as a function of the intensity manipulations (Badzinski, 1989). Age-related differences may be due to individual differences in perceptions of text difficulty. It seems reasonable to suspect that cues are more likely to affect processing speed among individuals who find the text difficult to compre-hend. It is important to keep in mind that the cues did influence the probability of drawing particular inferences among both the older and the younger subject populations. Without doubt, individuals at different ages and stages of devel-opment will not focus on the same cues in interpreting messages (Fleisher, 1988). Thus such differences are likely to influence the likelihood that the cues will facilitate processing speed; this conclusion suggests the need to study individual differences with regard to the importance of the various cues in message interpretation.

We have explored the extent to which discourse features guide text inter-pretation by controlling inference-making, potentially affecting information recall and facilitating ease of text processing. To more fully understand the impact of cues on message interpretation and to offer explanations for such relationships, these functions must be packaged in terms of some theory of message comprehension. We now turn to examining the adequacy of several theories for explaining the role of cues on message understanding. Our discussion is divided according to models proposing that text understanding requires some type of an executive controller and those models that reject the notion of a controller. The theories also differ in terms of the mechanism guiding interpretation and the role discourse features play in meaning construction.

MODELS OF COMPREHENSION

Executive Control Models

Executive control models point out that comprehension entails a number of processing components under the direction of some executive or higher order process. The controller is responsible for coordinating the vast number of components involved in understanding, in prioritizing the different processes, in allocating cognitive resources, and in selecting material needed to complete the representation (Britton & Glynn, 1987). A variety of mechanisms may serve as executive controllers including goals and plans, prior knowledge, cognitive knowledge structures (e.g., frames, scripts), or some combination of mechanisms.

Plans and strategies. Plan- and strategy-based approaches are goal-driven models in which texts are interpreted in relation to a plan (Bauman, 1991; Schank & Abelson, 1977). Plans specify "the actions necessary for the attainment of a goal or several goals" (Berger, 1988, p. 96) and involve prerequisites and effects. Prerequisites are the conditions that must exist prior to plan execution and effects are the outcomes after the plan has been executed (Litman & Allen, 1987).

One example of a plan-based approach was developed by Litman and Allen (1987) in which they model the link between plans and utterances. Their approach is described in terms of a stack metaphor; plans are ordered hierarchically with the top of the stack representing the current plan or the just-executed plan and the bottom of the stack containing the suspended or completed plans. The executive controller is the plan recognizer, charged with the tasks of identifying the plan and adding plans to the stack. In linking utterances to plans, the recognizer adheres to a set of rules. As a first attempt, the recognizer tries to fit incoming input to the current plan. If this attempt fails, the recognizer either modifies the plan or shifts to a new one. Thus comprehension processes are enhanced by plan continuation and dampened by plan shifts.[1]

Discourse features serve an important role in Litman and Allen's (1987) plan recognition model. The cues reinforce the plan or direct the recognizer to other plans. To illustrate, the lexical marker *by the way* introduces a topic shift. Such markers ease the recognition of topic continuations and shifts. Although the model accounts for lexical cues, other classes of features are not considered (Bauman, 1991).

Perhaps the most comprehensive plan-based approach to discourse understanding is van Dijk and Kintsch's model (1983). According to these authors, strategies are best thought of in terms of a theory of action. They write "a strategy is the idea of an agent about the best way to act in order to reach a goal" (van Dijk & Kintsch, 1983, pp. 64-65). Thus strategies, which are a part of a general knowledge system, are used to attain the goal of discourse comprehension. A basic assumption of their model is that people have the ability to flexibly use a variety of strategies to reach their goals. One component of their model holds that a small number of propositions are held in short-term memory. Because people have limited memory capacity, restricting the amount of information active in memory, the memory buffer maintains the relevant subset of information in short-term memory. Thus comprehension is facilitated if new information is semantically related to the propositions held in the short-term memory buffer. If long-term memory must be searched to make a connection, the process is impaired. The model contains various types of strategies including coherence strategies used to establish links between propositions and the leading-edge strategy used to select the contents in short-term memory. Discourse features play a prominent role by facilitating the strategies in a variety of ways including focusing attention on important concepts, providing cues for coherence, and suggesting plausible interpretations.

Memory structures. Another view of comprehension places memory as the primary building block by providing the foundation on which other information is mapped. Gernsbacher et al. (1990) state that comprehension is a process of laying a foundation, mapping information onto the structure, and initiating a new structure as incoming information fails to cohere. Thus text processing is initially slow during the foundation-laying stage, and incoming information consistent with the framework is processed more quickly than inconsistent information. Comprehension is also impaired after a new structure has been initiated. This expectation is formed on the notion that information from the initial framework is lost upon shifting to a new structure (Gernsbacher, 1990; Gernsbacher et al., 1990). This structure building framework proposes that information enhances comprehension upon activating memory cells consistent with the existing framework.

Memory structure models can be classified in roughly the same category as other knowledge structures such as schemas, scripts, frames, and story grammars (Bower et al., 1979; Johnson & Mandler, 1980; Minsky, 1975; Schank & Abelson, 1977; Thorndyke, 1977). These knowledge structures are used to provide the background for interpreting discourse, fill in missing or incomplete details, generate expectations, retrieve information from memory, and guide the sequence of processing (Colley, 1987; Graesser, 1981). In general, these types of structures provide the blueprint on which subsequent information is mapped. In turn, information consistent with the activated structure should be comprehended more quickly than information inconsistent with the given structure.

Generative processing. Wittrock's model of comprehension holds that cognitive and metacognitive processes shape meaning. His model contains four mechanisms guiding understanding: *motivation* or a desire to comprehend the material, *attention* to relevant information, *memory* for accessing stored knowledge, and *generation* of relations among text parts and between the text and prior knowledge (Wittrock, 1990). The mechanism foregrounded in the model is generation. He argues that characteristics of the discourse may stimulate generative processing. Accordingly, discourse features may be present but, to enhance understanding, one must invest effort to recognize the markers and use this information in drawing relations. Wittrock argues that comprehension is enhanced by constructing relationships—in activities such as generating titles and drawing illustrations—that are not otherwise made. Although features are available to prompt the meaning-making activity, the individual is accountable for using this information. Hence cue use rather than availability is essential for enhancing understanding.

Comparisons among the executive control models. The preceding models emphasize the need for an executive controller governing the comprehension process. The particular mechanism serving as the controller and the role of discourse features on text understanding distinguish the various models. In Litman and Allen's plan-based approach, discourse features function to continue or shift plans. Accordingly, plan continuation should ease comprehension and plan shift should impede the process. van Dijk and Kintsch's model suggests that features prompting a long-term memory search should hinder comprehension and that sources easily mapped with information residing in the short-term memory buffer should ease understanding. In contrast, the generative-processing model proposes that features stimulating the construction of relations among text ideas will enhance understanding. Finally, Gernsbacher's structure building framework holds that the features that activate information consistent with the memory structure will aid comprehension but a shifting of frameworks lessens understanding.

Both the plan and the structure building approaches hold that shifts adversely influence understanding. Shifting, however, may encourage entertaining connections not otherwise made—an activity favored by the generative-processing model. The plan and structure building approaches also emphasize quick reading times as a mark of comprehension. In contrast, generative processing is a time-engaging activity, suggesting that an increase in processing time should enhance comprehension. Future research testing these models should involve manipulating aspects of the executive controller (e.g., plans, generative activities, or memory structure) and measuring the changes in the ease of comprehension. Research might also assess how various information sources influence the executives in performing their tasks. Some questions that arise from these models include the following: How do plans and memory structures influence components of comprehension? What types of goals are likely to lead to high levels of understanding compared with those that interfere with the process? What types of information sources are likely to hinder the controller in performing its duties? And should reading time serve as the primary mark of comprehension? In short, the emphasis should be placed on how control mechanisms affect various processes involved in text understanding.

Alternative Models

In this section, three alternative models are described. Although the three models reject the notion of an executive controller, the models are different in the kinds of issues they raise. The first model, known as connectivist or parallel distributed processing model (PDP), addresses how discourse features affect on-line processing such as encoding information and drawing causal connections. The second model, a quantitative model proposed by Aaronson and Ferres (1986), identifies how discourse features affect different processing components—lexical, syntactic, and semantic levels. Finally, mathematical models, such as information integration theory, provide a useful methodology for assessing the relative importance of different features in constructing meaning. We describe the general ideas of these models in turn.

Connectivists. Connectivist models explicitly reject the need for a central processor, arguing that processing should not be conceptualized in terms of hierarchical steps or stages. Rather, connectivist models are a class of models, often referred to as parallel distributed processing models (PDP), that consist of processing units and connections among those units (Feldman, 1981; McClelland, 1988, 1990; McClelland, Rumelhart, & Hinton, 1986; Rumelhart, Hinton, & McClelland, 1986). The units are conceptual objects such as letters or words that simply receive information from other units and send input to other nearby units. Thus the processing units interact by sending excitatory and inhibitory signals to other units with the strength and the redundancy of the signals determining the likelihood of activating a particular pattern. In contrast to most executive models, knowledge is stored in the connections between the units rather than retrieved from memory. Hence learning is a process of activating the right set of connections, allowing new patterns to emerge or old patterns to be re-created.

To illustrate the general ideas of the connectivist framework, we offer a brief description of a model developed to examine one aspect of the reading process—visual word recognition and pronunciation (Patterson, Seidenberg, & McClelland, 1989). The model consists of units involving orthographic (word), phonological (sound), and hidden or unknown units and sets of connections between these different units. The units are encoded as a set of triplets, for instance, *MAK*. Thus the process begins with the presentation of an orthographic string, which in turn activates the potential hidden units. The unit most likely selected, in this case the letter *E* forming the word *MAKE*, is a function of the strength of the relationship between the different connections. Learning occurs through exposure to the orthographic strings followed by feedback assessing the difference between the correct activation and the unit activated.

One major advantage of connectivist models such as the word recognition model is their capacity to explain processes "on-line" (that is, at the time the stimulus is perceived); thus such models account for the rapid speed at which word recognition and pronunciation generally occur (Patterson et al., 1989). By allowing the strength of the connections between the different units to have varying weights, the models explain why certain units are activated and can predict the types of errors likely to be made. Such models also account for other comprehension processes such as inference-making. Through patterns of association like those advocated by PDP models, the models predict the types of connections that will be made to "fill in" missing details. A connectivist framework also provides an account of why certain discourse features prompt particular interpretations; that is, the features serve to excite or inhibit particular connections. As the strength and redundancy of the features increase, so should the likelihood that a particular connection will be activated.

Quantitative model. Aaronson and Ferres (1983a, 1983b, 1984, 1986) propose a model, referred to as a quantitative model, for describing the linguistic coding that occurs during reading. They propose that processing time, as measured by word-by-word reaction time data, is an additive function of three components: words, structure, and meaning. The by-product of these three processes is a coded representation of the discourse in active memory. The process begins with lexical coding—translating visual input to letters or syllables from which words are formed. At the point at which the lexical information is accessed, the reader retrieves relevant syntactic and semantic information from memory.

The second component is the coding of the structure, with the difficulty of coding dependent upon length and syntactic complexity. Although structure coding is one of three major processes, Aaronson and Ferres contend that, with relatively easy tasks, no time is spent coding structure. In such situations, one is able to skip this phase or at least perform the task simultaneously with the next process, provided that he or she has the skills to allow for immediate semantic processing.

The final process involves coding meaning. This process consists of tasks such as performing linguistic transformations, abstracting key concepts, "recod[ing] verbal information into visual images that idealize the original meaning or that contain features never presented and . . . provid[ing] an emphasis or . . . obtain[ing] compatibility with a previously established semantic framework" (Aaronson & Ferres, 1986, p. 94). As Aaronson and Ferres (1986) point out, the syntactic and semantic processors are analogous to van Dijk and Kintsch's (1983) distinction between microstructure (focus on small units such as words or phrases) and macrostructure (focus on the discourse as a whole), respectively.

The quantitative model is particularly appealing as it explicitly acknowledges that comprehension is a function of task type and the skills of the readers. For instance, the model holds that the time needed for coding structure is great for memory tasks and for children, at least compared with other types of comprehension tasks and older subjects. Thus processing times for the three components vary depending on the purposes of reading and the expertise of the individuals.

Although the role of discourse features in Aaronson and Ferres's model is not of explicit concern for these researchers, the model posits that the ease of lexical coding is greatly dependent on word frequency; thus the redundancy of text features should facilitate this stage of processing. Further, cue strength and frequency should aid semantic coding in a similar fashion to other general comprehension models; that is, the cues assist in identifying key concepts and integrating the material into the established framework. The quantitative model should also provide a useful framework for identifying how specific features affect particular processing units. For instance, situational features may aid primarily in semantic coding, whereas message features (e.g., punctuation marks, bold lettering, italics) assist primarily in syntactic processing.

Information integration theory. Unquestionably, there are many sources of information available to the reader to assist in forming an interpretation; thus the reader must determine the importance of the different features in making an overall assessment of the text. Anderson's information integration theory (Anderson, 1980, 1981, 1982) provides a framework for assessing the ways in which people integrate different information sources in making an interpretation. According to Anderson, people arrive at judgments by combining information according to mathematical principles. The various pieces of information are assigned a value; values are then weighted and combined according to mathematical rules such as the additive and averaging rules.

Although, at least to our knowledge, this theory has not been applied to issues addressed in this essay, the theory has been used to investigate many decision-making processes, including the importance of clothing/physical appearance cues in judgments of first impressions (Lennon, 1986), the role of biographical (e.g., hair color, height) and capability cues (e.g., educational level, recommendations) on the likelihood of hiring a job applicant (Schwartz & Norman, 1989), and children's ability to consider cues in making moral judgments (Surber, 1977), judgments of equity (Anderson & Butzin, 1978), and perceptual judgments of physical area (Mullet, Lautrey, & Glaser, 1989). To illustrate, Hoffner and Badzinski (1989) applied information integration theory to study children's reliance on situational and facial cues in making affective judgments. Children at four age levels were shown pictures in which facial and situational cues were congruent, incongruent, or presented alone. After examining the pictures, children assessed the emotion felt by the character in the pictures. Anderson's theory was used to test whether children rely primarily on facial, situational, or combined cues in making judgments. If the children are relying on one cue, then the effect of situational cues, for example, would be independent of the level of the facial cue. The averaging rule, on the other hand, would predict that the effects of each cue alone should be greater than situational and facial cues combined. By using this method, Hoffner and Badzinski (1989) report that children's reliance on facial cues in making affective judgments decreases with age, but the importance of situational cues increases.

Mathematical models, like that proposed by Anderson, may prove to be very profitable in detecting the relative importance of various discourse features in assessing meaning—an issue left unexplored by comprehension researchers. The model may also be adapted to distinguish between the importance of various discourse features (i.e., the weight of each source of information) and the relevance of the cues (i.e., the likelihood that the features will be considered) in constructing meaning (Schwartz & Norman, 1989). Finally, the framework could be used to assess how different populations or individuals with differing goals, for example, use information sources differently in message interpretation despite the individuals starting with identical texts.

Comparisons Among the Alternative Models

The alternative models reviewed take diverse approaches. The similarity among these models is that they all reject the notion of an executive. Features that take precedence in the absence of the executive control processor differentiate the alternative models. The connectivist model is concerned with the connections a receiver makes during the on-line processes of comprehension. In contrast, the quantitative model views comprehension as the successful completion of processing components. Both models hold that individuals may travel a number of different paths to arrive at meaning. Background knowledge, task demand, and individual differences are a few of the many factors that affect one's route to text understanding. The nature of the paths distinguish the models such that connectivist models hold that one's route is determined by the patterns of activation of simple processing units. On the other hand, the quantitative model proposes that individuals travel through lexical, structural, and semantic processors but traveling speed and the ultimate destination depend on linguistic characteristics of the text, task, and subject factors.

Information integration theory as a mathematical model is concerned with the weight or value assigned to the information sources. As the comprehension process is occurring, individuals may assign relatively more weight to the stimuli that have greatest significance for them. Thus someone especially attuned to nonverbal cues may assign greater weight to facial expressions than an individual who views such nonverbal expressions as providing little information of value.

Summary

We are excited about the comprehension models described above and the intriguing avenues of research generated from these models. Without doubt, the most appropriate theoretical framework depends on the interest of the investigator. Our concern is that, as communication scholars increasingly include comprehension as a dependent measure, the studies will be cast in terms of some theory of message understanding. We are afraid that the tendency will be to place the emphasis on a theory explaining the effects of the discourse feature, with substantially less focus on the comprehension variable. A study on the impact of nonverbal cues on message understanding, for instance, will be framed primarily in terms of a nonverbal rather than a comprehension theory. Granted, this practice stems from the researcher's heightened interest in the manipulated variable; however, its impact on comprehension processes may be more aptly explained from a theory of message understanding. It is our hope that comprehension is not simply viewed as a convenient dependent measure but is esteemed as the construct of interest, resulting in an effort to challenge and develop comprehension theories.

CHALLENGING COMPREHENSION THEORIES

In this section, we argue for the need to challenge current views and assumptions of comprehension models. One of those assumptions is that text understanding is a function of the strength and number of cues inviting a particular interpretation. Thus cue strength and redundancy determine the likelihood of drawing the intended meaning. Although this might often be the case, situations may exist in which discourse features impede rather than promote comprehension. For example, despite the belief that illustrations facilitate comprehension by making the information more appealing (Rose, 1986), promoting mental imagery (Pressley, Pigott, & Bryant, 1982), and aiding in the construction of a mental model (Glenberg & Langston, 1992), some work demonstrates that illustrations distract reader's attention from critical discourse, reducing one's understanding of the material (Rose, 1986; Rose & Furr, 1984).

Discourse features may also dampen understanding by providing one with too much assistance, which in turn reduces comprehension due to the low amount of processing effort. That is, the absence of cues prompts more in-depth processing of information, leading to enhanced comprehension (Maki, Foley, Kajer, Thompson, & Willert, 1990; McDaniel, Einstein, Dunay, & Cobb, 1986; McDaniel, Ryan, & Cunningham, 1989). In an interesting series of studies, Maki et al. (1990) designed paragraphs in which some of the letters were deleted. They reasoned that the paragraphs containing the deleted letters, as compared with intact paragraphs, would require more active processing, increasing the strength of the text representations. In support of their position, they found that respondents had better memory of paragraphs with deleted letters. This finding calls into question the assumption that comprehension is a function of the number of information pieces available.

A second assumption of many text comprehension models is that understanding entails constructing a single working interpretation with unfolding information prompting individuals to continue building upon the interpretation or abandoning it in favor of one that better fits available input. In fact, our opening remarks likening the comprehension process to solving a mystery may be disputed; rather than developing multiple hunches, it is generally assumed that people stick with only one hunch until incoming information suggests otherwise. Yet, recent work supports the possibility that individuals may construct several plausible text representations. Simpson, Peterson, Casteel, and Burgess (1989) argue that, "although context does not have an effect on the activation of potential targets, it does place constraints on the resolution of this candidate lists, and the eventual selection of a single candidate" (p. 95). That is, discourse features place constraints on the number of potential models rather than prompting a particular representation. Rueckl and Oden (1986), for example, found that the word *pain* rather than *pair* was more likely to be selected given the phrase "the arthritic had a _____ in his hand." In contrast, both *pain* and *pair* were plausible interpretations given the less constraining sentence "the shoemaker had a _____ in his hand." Hence the particular lexical item *arthritic* narrowed the pool of alternatives, cuing the word *pain*. Rather than constructing a particular representation, discourse cues serve to reduce or constrain the number of plausible models; hence comprehension may be best construed as a process of interpretation *reduction* rather than *construction*.

We sought to address this issue in a series of studies by examining the extent to which cues serve primarily to trigger particular interpretations or to reduce the number of plausible models (Badzinski, 1992; Badzinski & Gill, 1991). To address these contrasting positions, adults were instructed to read statements that either contained or did not contain a cue to interpretation (Badzinski & Gill, 1991). The construction of the statements involved inserting one adverb into each kernel statement (e.g., "Jennifer checked her spelling words" versus "Jennifer *carefully* checked her spelling words"). The participants assessed the plausibility of different event outcomes. One of the outcomes was considered plausible and consistent with the cue (e.g., "Jennifer passed her spelling test"). The other outcome was plausible but inconsistent with the cued interpretation (e.g., "Jennifer failed her spelling test").

To support the reduction model, the critical prediction is that the consistent outcomes should receive similar plausibility ratings among all participants regardless of whether they are given the cue-present or cue-absent statements. At the same time, the inconsistent outcomes should be perceived as less plausible by those participants given the cue-present statements. Such an interaction suggests that the pool of plausible models is judged to be smaller when the cues are present. In contrast, the study supports the position that cues trigger one representation provided that the consistent outcomes are more plausible in the presence of the cues while the inconsistent outcomes are still perceived as less likely in the presence of the cue.

The results of these three studies support the view that lexical cues serve as devices for reducing the number of plausible interpretations. Regardless of the presence or absence of the markings, the cue-consistent outcomes were viable accounts; however, respondents judged the cue-inconsistent outcomes less plausible given the cued statements. It is critical to remember that, if the cues instantiate one model, then the consistent outcomes would be more viable in the presence than in the absence of the lexical cues. This was not the case; the consistent outcomes were equally viable in the presence and absence of the cues. Such findings challenge the position that discourse features prompt the construction of one interpretation.

In the same series of studies, we also addressed the presupposition that accepting an interpretative framework is, for the most part, a rather cognitively easy task. Instead, we thought that accepting relevant interpretations may be more cognitively taxing than rejecting irrelevant outcomes, lending support for the view that individuals are hesitant in adapting one interpretive blueprint. Our investigations reveal that reaction times are quicker for the inconsistent (e.g., Jennifer failed her spelling test) than the consistent outcomes (e.g., Jennifer passed her spelling test). We reason that accepting an interpretation involves more cognitive resources than dismissing irrelevant ones. We consider our results in conjunction with the findings from Bauman's dissertation.

In her work, Bauman (1991) investigated whether reading times are shorter for topic (changing focuses or direction) or strategy shifts (modifying existing topic). She found that topic shifts took less time to process than strategy shifts. She proposed that modifying existing structures takes more processing time than activating new knowledge structures. Although it may be premature to speculate, individuals may be very flexible in terms of which knowledge system is operating, but altering a prevailing interpretation involves a great deal of cognitive energy. Thus an optimal strategy is to allow a pool of viable interpretations to remain in a "state of suspension" until a commitment to a particular system or interpretation is required. One could delay selecting an interpretation until all available information had been processed or until a selection was necessary to fulfill task demands (O'Brien, Shank, Myers, & Rayner, 1988). A less sophisticated strategy is to quickly adapt one interpretation or completely ignore incoming information sources. One advantage to delaying selection is that information discrepant with the interpretation would not demand its abandonment or the reconstruction of a new alternative.

We do not present our position lightly, as we realize that more evidence needs to be gathered that favors a conceptualization of comprehension as either a construction or a reduction process. Our point is that much work needs to be done to design studies that challenge current views of comprehension. We question the belief that comprehension entails the construction of one model. We also ask whether dismissing irrelevant outcomes or accepting an outcome involves more cognitive resources. Indeed, very basic tenets of the comprehension process deserve careful scrutiny.

CONCLUSIONS

In this chapter, we centered on the relationships between discourse features and comprehension. We began by arguing that meaning is continually negotiated, through a process of integrating knowledge sources with incoming information, to construct a text representation that mutually satisfies the parties in the exchange. This definition implies that comprehension is a dynamic, changeable function of human understanding. By employing strategies, we make mindful choices in the ultimate comprehension of a text. It is important, however, to view comprehension more broadly than being concerned with a particular event. Comprehension occurs prior to encountering a text and continues after the consumption of input.

The study of comprehension also requires careful construct development. As discussed earlier, researchers often claim to be examining comprehension while tapping only a small portion of that process. Future research must consider instrumentation to isolate the different processes involved in message understanding with a primary focus on the validity and reliability of such instruments (Bostrom, 1990; Bostrom & Waldhart, 1988). An intriguing approach may be the construction of a measure to identify the specific points in message processing at which comprehension is enhanced or hindered.

We underscore the need to consider the impact of source, context, message, and receiver characteristics on interpretive processes. A possible avenue of future work is to establish a hierarchical integration of the various information sources. Applying the mathematical model, one could isolate the features that have the greatest significance to message understanding. For example, what features are most important for comprehension to occur and how do they vary among individuals? Is the same process passed through for all individuals?

We give even greater emphasis, however, to the importance of explaining how these various pieces of information fit together in meaning construction.

To start addressing this issue, comprehension theories were presented focusing on their potential contributions to our knowledge of the link between discourse features and comprehension. It is this section that spawns the most exciting avenues for future work. Each of the different theoretical frameworks outlines a worthy research agenda—from the executive models pointing to the need to examine how higher order processes (e.g., goals, knowledge structures) affect message understanding to information integration theories providing a methodology for investigating the relative contributions of the different information sources.

The essay then concludes with a series of studies suggesting that message understanding might be more appropriately construed as a representation reduction rather than construction process. Although speculative at this point, the research demonstrates the importance of seriously challenging commonly held views of message understanding. Our hope is that communication researchers will become increasingly interested in testing, modifying, and developing theories explaining the diverse ways in which information sources affect our understanding of discourse.

NOTE

1. We would like to thank Isabelle Bauman for directing us to Litman and Allen's plan-based model. In her dissertation, Bauman tested several predictions derived from this model. She found that plan continuations were perceived as more coherent than strategy and topic shifts; however, reading time data failed to support the expectation that strategy shifts are easier to process than topic shifts.

REFERENCES

Aaronson, D., & Ferres, S. (1983a). Lexical categories and reading tasks. *Journal of Experimental Psychology: Human Perception and Performance, 9*, 675-699.

Aaronson, D., & Ferres, S. (1983b). A model for coding lexical categories during reading. *Journal of Experimental Psychology: Human Perception and Performance, 9*, 700-725.

Aaronson, D., & Ferres, S. (1984). Reading strategies for children and adults: Some empirical evidence. *Journal of Verbal Learning and Verbal Behavior, 23*, 189-220.

Aaronson, D., & Ferres, S. (1986). Reading strategies for children and adults: A quantitative model. *Psychological Review, 93*, 89-112.

Anderson, N. H. (1980). Information integration theory in developmental psychology. In F. Wilkening, J. Becker, & T. Trabasso (Eds.), *Information integration by children* (pp. 1-45). Hillsdale, NJ: Lawrence Erlbaum.

Anderson, N. H. (1981). *Foundations of information integration theory.* New York: Academic Press.

Anderson, N. H. (1982). *Methods of information integration theory.* New York: Academic Press.

Anderson, N. H., & Butzin, C. A. (1978). Integration theory applied to children's judgments of equity. *Developmental Psychology, 14*, 593-606.

Badzinski, D. M. (1989). Message intensity and cognitive representations of discourse: Effects on inferential processing. *Human Communication Research, 16*, 3-32.

Badzinski, D. M. (1991a). Children's cognitive representations of discourse: Effects of vocal cues on text comprehension. *Communication Research, 18,* 715-736.

Badzinski, D. M. (1991b). Vocal cues and children's understanding of narratives: Effects of incongruent cues on story comprehension. *Western Journal of Speech Communication, 55,* 198-214.

Badzinski, D. M. (1992). Message cues and narrative comprehension: A developmental study. *Communication Quarterly, 40,* 228-238.

Badzinski, D. M., & Gill, M. M. (1991, May). *Lexical cues and mental representations of discourse.* Paper presented at the annual meeting of the International Communication Association, Chicago.

Badzinski, D. M., & Pettus, A. B. (1992, November). *Nonverbal involvement and gender: Effects on jury decision processes.* Paper presented at the annual meeting of the Speech Communication Association, Chicago.

Bartlett, F. C. (1932). *Remembering: A study in experimental and social psychology.* Cambridge: Cambridge University Press.

Bauman, I. (1991). *Coherence and conversational comprehension: "What does that have to do with anything?"* Unpublished doctoral dissertation, University of Wisconsin—Madison.

Berger, C. R. (1988). Planning, affect, and social action generation. In L. Donohew, H. E. Sypher, & E. T. Higgins (Eds.), *Communication, social cognition, and affect* (pp. 93-116). Hillsdale, NJ: Lawrence Erlbaum.

Berger, C. R. (1989). Goals, plans, and discourse comprehension. In J. J. Bradac (Ed.), *Message effects in communication science* (pp. 75-101). Newbury Park, CA: Sage.

Berger, C. R., & Jordan, J. M. (1992). Planning sources, planning difficulty, and verbal fluency. *Communication Monographs, 59,* 130-149.

Berger, C. R., Karol, S. H., & Jordan, J. M. (1989). When a lot of knowledge is a dangerous thing: The debilitating effects of plan complexity on verbal fluency. *Human Communication Research, 16,* 91-116.

Bodenhausen, G. V., & Lichtenstein, M. (1987). Social stereotypes and information processing strategies: The impact of task complexity. *Journal of Personality and Social Psychology, 52,* 871-880.

Bostrom, R. N. (1990). *Listening behavior: Measurement and application.* New York: Guilford.

Bostrom, R. N., & Waldhart, E. S. (1988). Memory models and the measurement of listening. *Communication Education, 37,* 1-13.

Bourhis, R. Y., & Giles, H. (1977). The language of intergroup distinctiveness. In H. Giles (Ed.), *Language, ethnicity and intergroup relations* (pp. 119-135). London: Academic Press.

Bower, G. H., Black, J. B., & Turner, J. T. (1979). Scripts in text comprehension and memory. *Cognitive Psychology, 11,* 177-220.

Bower, G. H., & Morrow, D. G. (1990). Mental models in narrative comprehension. *Science, 247,* 44-48.

Bradac, J. J., Bowers, J. W., & Courtright, J. A. (1979). Three language variables in communication research: Intensity, immediacy, and diversity. *Human Communication Research, 5,* 257-269.

Bradac, J. J., & Wisegarver, R. (1984). Ascribed status, lexical diversity, and accent: Determinants of perceived status, solidarity, and control of speech style. *Journal of Language and Social Psychology, 3,* 239-255.

Britton, B. K., & Glynn, S. M. (1987). *Executive control processes in reading.* Hillsdale, NJ: Lawrence Erlbaum.

Brown, P., & Yule, G. (1983). *Discourse analysis.* Cambridge: Cambridge University Press.

Bryant, D. J., & Tversky, B. (1992). Internal and external spatial frameworks for representing described scenes. *Journal of Memory and Language, 31,* 74-98.

Burgoon, J. K., Birk, T., & Pfau, M. (1990). Nonverbal behaviors, persuasion and credibility. *Human Communication Research, 17,* 140-169.

Burke, J. A. (1986). Interacting plans in the accomplishment of a practical activity. In D. G. Ellis & W. A. Donohue (Eds.), *Contemporary issues in language and discourse production* (pp. 203-222). Hillsdale, NJ: Lawrence Erlbaum.

Cameron, G. T., Schleuder, J., & Thorson, E. (1991). The role of news teasers in processing TV news and commercials. *Communication Research, 18*, 667-684.

Carpenter, P. A., & Just, M. A. (1977). Integrative processes in comprehension. In D. LaBerge & J. Samuels (Eds.), *Basic processes in reading: Perception and communication* (pp. 217-241). Hillsdale, NJ: Lawrence Erlbaum.

Cegala, D. J. (1981). Interaction involvement: A cognitive dimension of communication competence. *Communication Education, 30*, 109-121.

Cegala, D. J. (1984). Affective and cognitive manifestations of interaction involvement during unstructured and competitive interactions. *Communication Monographs, 51*, 320-338.

Chafe, W., & Tannen, D. (1987). The relation between written and spoken language. *Annual Review of Anthropology, 16*, 383-407.

Christophel, D. M. (1990). The relationships among teacher immediacy behaviors, student motivation, and learning. *Communication Education, 39*, 323-340.

Cody, M. J., & McLaughlin, M. L. (1985). The situation as a construct in interpersonal communication research. In M. L. Knapp & G. R. Miller (Eds.), *Handbook of interpersonal communication* (pp. 263-312). Beverly Hills, CA: Sage.

Colley, A. M. (1987). Text comprehension. In J. R. Beech & A. M. Colley (Eds.), *Cognitive approaches to reading* (pp. 113-138). New York: John Wiley.

Cooper, L. (1923). *The poetics of Aristotle: Its meaning and influence.* Boston: Marshall Jones.

Doelger, J. A., Hewes, D. E., & Graham, M. L. (1986). Knowing when to "second-guess": The mindful analysis of messages. *Human Communication Research, 12*, 301-338.

Dole, J. A., Duffy, G. G., Roehler, L. R., & Pearson, P. D. (1991). Moving from the old to the new: Research on reading instruction. *Review of Educational Research, 61*, 239-264.

Dorr-Bremme, D. W. (1990). Contextualization cues in the classroom: Discourse regulation and social control functions. *Language in Society, 19*, 379-402.

Douglas, W. (1983). Scripts and self-monitoring: When does being a high self-monitor really make a difference? *Human Communication Research, 10*, 81-96.

Ellis, D. G. (1992). *From language to communication.* Hillsdale, NJ: Lawrence Erlbaum.

Ericsson, K. A. (1988). Concurrent verbal reports on text comprehension: A review. *Text, 8*, 295-325.

Feldman, J. A. (1981). A connectionist model of visual memory. In G. E. Hinton & J. A. Anderson (Eds.), *Parallel models of associative memory* (pp. 49-81). Hillsdale, NJ: Lawrence Erlbaum.

Fish, S. (1980). Interpreting the variorum. In J. P. Tompkins (Ed.), *Reader-response criticism: From formalism to post-structuralism* (pp. 164-184). Baltimore: John Hopkins University Press.

Fleisher, B. M. (1988). Oral reading cue strategies of better and poorer readers. *Reading Research and Instruction, 27*, 35-50.

Fletcher, C. R. (1986). Strategies for the allocation of short-term memory during comprehension. *Journal of Memory and Language, 25*, 43-58.

Forgas, J. (1983). Language, goals and situations. *Journal of Language and Social Psychology, 2*, 267-293.

Gernsbacher, M. A. (1990). *Language comprehension as structure building.* Hillsdale, NJ: Lawrence Erlbaum.

Gernsbacher, M. A., Varner, K. R., & Faust, M. E. (1990). Investigating differences in general comprehension skill. *Journal of Experimental Psychology: Learning, Memory and Cognition, 16*, 430-445.

Giles, H., & Coupland, N. (1991). *Language: Contexts and consequences.* Buckingham, England: Open University Press.

Giles, H., Henwood, K., Coupland, N., Harriman, J., & Coupland, J. (1992). Language attitudes and cognitive mediation. *Human Communication Research, 18*, 500-527.

Giles, H., & Hewstone, M. (1982). Cognitive structures, speech and social situations: Two integrative models. *Language Sciences, 4*, 188-219.

Gill, M. M. (1991). *Accents and stereotypes: Their effects on perceptions of teachers and lecture comprehension.* Unpublished doctoral dissertation, University of Nebraska—Lincoln.

Gill, M. M., & Badzinski, D. M. (1992). The impact of accent and status on information recall and perception formation. *Communication Reports, 5*, 99-106.

Givon, T. (1989). *Mind, code, and context.* Hillsdale, NJ: Lawrence Erlbaum.

Glenberg, A. M., & Epstein, W. (1985). Calibration of comprehension. *Journal of Experimental Psychology: Learning, Memory and Cognition, 11*, 702-718.

Glenberg, A. M., & Langston, W. E. (1992). Comprehension of illustrated text: Pictures help to build mental models. *Journal of Memory and Language, 31*, 129-151.

Glenberg, A. M., Meyer, M., & Lindem, K. (1987). Mental models contribute to foregrounding during text comprehension. *Journal of Memory and Language, 26*, 69-83.

Glenberg, A. M., Sanocki, T., Epstein, W., & Morris, C. (1987). Enhancing calibration of comprehension. *Journal of Experimental Psychology: General, 116*, 119-136.

Goetz, E. T. (1979). Inferring from text: Some factors influencing which inferences will be made. *Discourse Processes, 2*, 179-195.

Gorham, J. (1988). The relationship between verbal teacher immediacy behaviors and student learning. *Communication Education, 37*, 40-53.

Graesser, A. C. (1981). *Prose comprehension beyond the word.* New York: Springer.

Gumperz, J. J. (1982). *Discourse strategies.* New York: Cambridge University Press.

Halliday, M. A. K., & Hasan, R. (1976). *Cohesion in English.* London: Longman.

Hartley, J. (1987). Typography and executive control processes in reading. In B. K. Britton & S. M. Glynn (Eds.), *Executive control processes in reading* (pp. 57-79). Hillsdale, NJ: Lawrence Erlbaum.

Haslett, B. J. (1986). A critical analysis of van Dijk's theory of discourse. In B. Dervin & M. Voight (Eds.), *Progress in the communication sciences* (Vol. 7, pp. 153-193). Norwood, NJ: Ablex.

Haslett, B. J. (1987). *Communication: Strategic action in context.* Hillsdale, NJ: Lawrence Erlbaum.

Hayes-Roth, B., & Thorndyke, P. W. (1979). Integration of knowledge from text. *Journal of Verbal Learning and Verbal Behavior, 18*, 91-108.

Helfrich, H. (1979). Age markers in speech. In K. R. Scherer & H. Giles (Eds.), *Social markers in speech* (pp. 63-107). Cambridge: Cambridge University Press.

Hewes, D. E., & Graham, M. L. (1989). Second-guessing theory: Review and extension. In J. Anderson (Ed.), *Communication yearbook 12* (pp. 213-248). Newbury Park, CA: Sage.

Hobbs, J. R., & Agar, M. H. (1985). The coherence of incoherent discourse. *Journal of Language and Social Psychology, 4*, 213-232.

Hoffner, C., & Badzinski, D. M. (1989). Children's integration of facial and situational cues to emotion. *Child Development, 60*, 411-422.

Hoffner, C., Cantor, J., & Thorson, E. (1988). Children's understanding of narrative: Developmental differences in processing video and audio content. *Communication Research, 15*, 227-245.

Hynds, S. (1990). Reading as a social event: Comprehension and response in the text, classroom, and world. In D. Bogdan & S. B. Straw (Eds.), *Beyond communication: Reading comprehension and criticism* (pp. 237-256). Portsmouth, NH: Boynton.

Johnson, N. S., & Mandler, J. M. (1980). A tale of two structures: Underlying and surface forms in stories. *Poetics, 9*, 51-86.

Johnson-Laird, P. N. (1983). *Mental models: Toward a cognitive science of language, inference, and consciousness.* Cambridge: Cambridge University Press.

Kaminski, E. P., & Miller, G. R. (1984). How jurors respond to videotaped witnesses. *Journal of Communication, 34*, 88-98.

Keenan, J. M., MacWhinney, B.; & Mayhew, D. (1977). Pragmatics in memory: A study of natural conversations. *Journal of Verbal Learning and Verbal Behavior, 16,* 549-560.

Kellermann, K., & Sleight, C. (1989). Coherence: A meaningful adhesive for discourse. In J. A. Anderson (Ed.), *Communication yearbook 12* (pp. 95-129). Newbury Park, CA: Sage.

Kelley, G. A., Gaidis, W. C., & Reingen, P. H. (1989). The use of vivid stimuli to enhance comprehension of the content of product warning messages. *Journal of Consumer Affairs, 23,* 243-266.

Kelly, D. H., & Gorham, J. (1988). Effects of immediacy on recall information. *Communication Education, 37,* 198-207.

Kintsch, W., & Yarbrough, J. C. (1982). The role of rhetorical structure in text comprehension. *Journal of Educational Psychology, 74,* 828-834.

Lennon, S. J. (1986). Additivity of clothing cues in first impressions. *Social Behavior and Personality, 14,* 15-21.

Litman, D. J., & Allen, J. F. (1987). A plan recognition model for subdialogues in conversations. *Cognitive Science, 11,* 163-200.

Lorch, E. P., Bellack, D. R., & Augsbach, H. (1987). Young children's memory for televised stories: Effects of importance. *Child Development, 58,* 453-463.

Maki, R. H., & Berry, S. L. (1984). Metacomprehension of text material. *Journal of Experimental Psychology: Learning, Memory and Cognition, 10,* 663-679.

Maki, R. H., Foley, J. M., Kajer, W. K., Thompson, R. C., & Willert, M. G. (1990). Increased processing enhances calibration of comprehension. *Journal of Experimental Psychology: Learning, Memory and Cognition, 16,* 609-616.

Mayer, R. E. (1979). Can advance organizers influence meaningful learning? *Review of Educational Research, 49,* 371-383.

Mayer, R. E. (1980). Elaboration techniques that increase the meaningfulness of technical text: An experimental test of the learning strategy hypothesis. *Journal of Educational Psychology, 72,* 770-784.

Mayer, R. E., & Bromage, B. K. (1980). Different recall protocols for technical texts due to advance organizers. *Journal of Educational Psychology, 72,* 209-225.

Mays, D. V. (1982). Cross cultural social status perception in speech. *Studies in Second Language Acquisition, 5,* 52-64.

McClelland, J. L. (1988). Connectionist models and psychological evidence. *Journal of Memory and Language, 27,* 107-123.

McClelland, J. L. (1990). Parallel distributed processing: Implications for cognition and development. In R. G. M. Morris (Ed.), *Parallel distributed processing: Implications for psychology and neurobiology* (pp. 8-45). Oxford: Clarendon.

McClelland, J. L., Rumelhart, D. E., & Hinton, G. E. (1986). The appeal of parallel distributed processing. In J. L. McClelland & D. E. Rumelhart (Eds.), *Parallel distributed processing: Explorations in the microstructure of cognition* (pp. 3-44). Cambridge: MIT Press.

McDaniel, M. A., Einstein, G. O., Dunay, P. K., & Cobb, R. E. (1986). Encoding difficulty and memory: Toward a unified theory. *Journal of Memory and Language, 25,* 645-656.

McDaniel, M. A., Ryan, E. B., & Cunningham, C. J. (1989). Encoding difficulty and memory enhancement for young and older readers. *Psychology and Aging, 4,* 333-338.

Meyer, B. J. F. (1975). *The organization of prose and its effects on memory.* Amsterdam: North-Holland.

Minsky, M. (1975). A framework for the representation of knowledge. In P. Winston (Ed.), *The psychology of computer vision* (pp. 211-280). New York: McGraw-Hill.

Morrow, D. G. (1985). Prominent characters and events organize narrative understanding. *Journal of Memory and Language, 24,* 304-319.

Morrow, D. G., Bower, G. H., & Greenspan, S. L. (1989). Updating situation models during narrative comprehension. *Journal of Memory and Language, 28,* 292-312.

Morrow, D. G., Greenspan, S. L., & Bower, G. H. (1987). Accessibility and situation models in narrative comprehension. *Journal of Memory and Language, 26,* 165-187.

Mullet, E., Lautrey, J., & Glaser, P. L. (1989). Information integration in an area judgment task: Effect of aids on children's perceptual judgments. *Journal of Genetic Psychology, 150,* 375-388.

Neuliep, J. W., & Hazelton, V. (1986). Enhanced conversational recall and reduced conversational interference as a function of cognitive complexity. *Human Communication Research, 13,* 211-224.

Noller, P. (1984). *Nonverbal communication in marital interaction.* New York: Pergamon.

Noller, P., & Ruzzene, M. (1991). Communication in marriage: The influence of affect and cognition. In G. J. O. Fletcher & F. D. Fincham (Eds.), *Cognition in close relationships* (pp. 203-233). Hillsdale, NJ: Lawrence Erlbaum.

O'Brien, E. J., & Albrecht, J. E. (1992). Comprehension strategies in the development of a mental model. *Journal of Experimental Psychology: Learning, Memory and Cognition, 18,* 777-784.

O'Brien, E. J., Shank, D. M., Myers, J. L., & Rayner, K. (1988). Elaborative inferences during reading: Do they occur on-line? *Journal of Experimental Psychology: Learning, Memory and Cognition, 14,* 410-420.

O'Shea, L. J., Sindelar, P. T., & O'Shea, D. J. (1985). The effects of repeated readings and attentional cues on reading fluency and comprehension. *Journal of Reading Behavior, 17,* 129-142.

Paris, S. G., & Upton, L. R. (1976). Children's memory for inferential relationships in prose. *Child Development, 47,* 660-668.

Patterson, K., Seidenberg, M. S., & McClelland, J. L. (1989). Connections and disconnections: Acquiring dyslexia in a computational model of reading processes. In R. G. M. Morris (Ed.), *Parallel distributed processing: Implications for psychology and neurobiology* (pp. 131-181). Oxford: Clarendon.

Planalp, S., Graham, M., & Paulson, L. (1987). Cohesive devices in conversation. *Communication Monographs, 54,* 325-343.

Potts, G. R., Keenan, J. M., & Golding, J. M. (1988). Assessing the occurrence of elaborative inferences: Lexical decision versus naming. *Journal of Memory and Language, 27,* 399-415.

Pressley, M., Pigott, S., & Bryant, S. L. (1982). Picture content and preschoolers' learning from sentences. *Educational Communication and Technology Journal, 30,* 151-161.

Ratneshwar, S., & Chaiken, S. (1991). Comprehension's role in persuasion: The case of its moderating effect on the persuasive impact of source code. *Journal of Consumer Research, 18,* 52-62.

Reynolds, R. E., & Schwartz, R. M. (1983). Relation of metaphoric processing to comprehension and memory. *Journal of Educational Psychology, 75,* 450-459.

Rolfe, J. (1963). *Cicero and his influence.* New York: Cooper Square.

Rose, T. L. (1986). Effects of illustrations on reading comprehension of learning disabled students. *Journal of Learning Disabilities, 19,* 542-544.

Rose, T. L., & Furr, P. M. (1984). Negative effects of illustrations as word cues. *Journal of Learning Disabilities, 17,* 334-337.

Rueckl, J. G., & Oden, G. C. (1986). The integration of contextual and featural information during word identification. *Journal of Memory and Language, 25,* 445-460.

Rumelhart, D. E., Hinton, G. E., & McClelland, J. L. (1986). A general framework for parallel distributed processing. In J. L. McClelland & D. E. Rumelhart (Eds.), *Parallel distributed processing: Explorations in the microstructure of cognition* (pp. 45-76). Cambridge: MIT Press.

Ryan, E. B., & Ledger, G. W. (1984). Learning to attend to sentence structure: Links between metalinguistic development and reading. In J. Downing & R. Valtin (Eds.), *Language awareness and learning to read* (pp. 149-171). New York: Springer.

Sanders, J. A., & Wiseman, R. L. (1990). The effects of verbal and nonverbal teacher immediacy on perceived cognitive, affective, and behavioral learning in the multicultural classroom. *Communication Education, 39,* 341-353.

Schank, R. C., & Abelson, R. (1977). *Scripts, plans, goals and understanding.* Hillsdale, NJ: Lawrence Erlbaum.

Scherer, K. R., & Giles, H. (1979). *Social markers in speech.* Cambridge: Cambridge University Press.

Schmidt, C. R., & Paris, S. G. (1983). Children's use of successive clues to generate and monitor inferences. *Child Development, 54,* 742-759.

Schwartz, J. P., & Norman, K. L. (1989). Separating cue relevance from cue importance within models of judgment and decision making. *Organizational Behavior and Human Decision Making, 43,* 355-384.

Sillars, A. L., Pike, G. R., Jones, T. S., & Murphy, M. A. (1984). Communication and understanding in marriage. *Human Communication Research, 10,* 317-350.

Simpson, G. B., Peterson, R. R., Casteel, M. A., & Burgess, C. (1989). Lexical and sentence context effects in word recognition. *Journal of Experimental Psychology: Learning, Memory and Cognition, 15,* 88-97.

Smith, C. R., & Prince, P. (1990). Language choice expectation and the Roman notion of style. *Communication Education, 39,* 63-74.

Smith, F. (1985). A metaphor for literacy: Creating worlds or shunting information. In D. R. Olson, N. Torrance, & A. Hildyard (Eds.), *Literacy, language, and learning: The nature and consequences of reading and writing* (pp. 195-213). Cambridge: Cambridge University Press.

Smith, P. M. (1979). Sex markers in speech. In K. R. Scherer & H. Giles (Eds.), *Social markers in speech* (pp. 109-146). Cambridge: Cambridge University Press.

Smith, V. L. (1991). Impact of pretrial instruction on jurors' information processing and decision making. *Journal of Applied Psychology, 76,* 220-228.

Spiro, R. J. (1980). Constructive processes in prose comprehension and recall. In R. J. Spiro, B. C. Bruce, & W. F. Brewer (Eds.), *Theoretical issues in reading comprehension* (pp. 245-278). Hillsdale, NJ: Lawrence Erlbaum.

Stafford, L., & Daly, J. A. (1984). Conversational memory: The effects of recall mode and memory expectancies on remembrances of natural conversations. *Human Communication Research, 10,* 379-402.

Stafford, L., Waldron, V. R., & Infield, L. L. (1989). Actor-observer differences in conversational memory. *Human Communication Research, 15,* 590-611.

Straw, S. B., & Bogdan, D. (1990). Introduction. In D. Bogdan & S. B. Straw (Eds.), *Beyond communication: Reading comprehension and criticism* (pp. 1-18). Portsmouth, NH: Boynton.

Surber, C. F. (1977). Developmental processes in social inference: Averaging of intentions and consequences in moral judgments. *Developmental Psychology, 13,* 654-665.

Taylor, H. A., & Tversky, B. (1992). Spatial mental models derived from survey and route description. *Journal of Memory and Language, 31,* 261-292.

Thompson, J. G., & Myers, N. A. (1985). Inferences and recall at ages four and seven. *Child Development, 56,* 1134-1144.

Thorndyke, P. W. (1977). Cognitive structures in comprehension and memory of narrative discourse. *Cognitive Psychology, 9,* 77-110.

Thorson, E., Christ, W. G., & Caywood, C. (1991). Effects of issue-image strategies, attack and support appeals, music, and visual content in political commercials. *Journal of Broadcasting and Electronic Media, 35,* 465-486.

Tierney, R. J., & Gee, M. (1990). Reading comprehension: Readers, authors, and the world of the text. In D. Bogdan & S. B. Straw (Eds.), *Beyond communication: Reading comprehension and criticism* (pp. 197-235). Portsmouth, NH: Boynton.

Tierney, R. J., & Pearson, P. D. (1983). Toward a composing model of reading. *Language Arts, 60,* 568-580.

Tracy, K. (1991). *Understanding face-to-face interaction: Issues linking goals and discourse.* Hillsdale, NJ: Lawrence Erlbaum.

van Dijk, T. A. (1979). Relevance assignment in discourse comprehension. *Discourse Processes, 2,* 113-126.

van Dijk, T. A. (1987). *Communicating racism: Ethnic prejudice in thought and talk.* Newbury Park, CA: Sage.

van Dijk, T. A. (1988). *News as discourse.* Newbury Park, CA: Sage.

van Dijk, T. A., & Kintsch, W. (1983). *Strategies of discourse comprehension.* New York: Academic Press.

Villaume, W. A., & Cegala, D. J. (1988). Interaction involvement and discourse strategies: The patterned use of cohesive devices in conversation. *Communication Monographs, 55,* 22-40.

Waggoner, J. E., Messe, M. J., & Palermo, D. S. (1985). Grasping the meaning of metaphor: Story recall and comprehension. *Child Development, 56,* 1156-1166.

Waldron, V. R. (1990). Constrained rationality: Situational influences on information acquisition plans and tactics. *Communication Monographs, 57,* 184-201.

Walker, C. H., & Meyer, B. J. F. (1980). Integrating different types of information in text. *Journal of Verbal Learning and Verbal Behavior, 19,* 263-275.

Wallace, K. R. (1978). Francis Bacon on communication and rhetoric. In J. L. Golden, G. F. Berquist, & W. E. Coleman (Eds.), *Rhetoric of Western thought* (pp. 108-117). Dubuque, IA: Kendall.

Williams, A., & Giles, H. (1991). Sociopsychological perspectives on older people's language and communication. *Ageing and Society, 11,* 103-126.

Williams, J. P. (1986). Teaching children to identify the main ideas of expository texts. *Exceptional Children, 53,* 163-168.

Wilson, B. J., & Weiss, A. J. (1991). The effects of two reality explanations on children's reactions to a frightening movie scene. *Communication Monographs, 58,* 307-326.

Wish, M., Deutsch, M., & Kaplan, S. (1976). Perceived dimensions of interpersonal relations. *Journal of Personality and Social Psychology, 33,* 409-420.

Wittrock, M. C. (1990). Generative processes of comprehension. *Educational Psychologist, 24,* 345-376.

Woodall, W. G., & Folger, J. P. (1985). Nonverbal cue context and episodic memory: On the availability and endurance of nonverbal behaviors as retrieval cues. *Communication Monographs, 52,* 319-333.

Yarbrough, D. B., & Gagne, E. D. (1987). Metaphor and free recall of technical text. *Discourse Processes, 10,* 81-91.

Young, D. R., & Schumacher, G. M. (1983). Context effects in young children's sensitivity to the importance level of prose information. *Child Development, 54,* 1146-1156.

Yuill, N., & Joscelyne, T. (1988). Effect of organizational cues and strategies on good and poor comprehenders' story understanding. *Journal of Educational Psychology, 80,* 152-158.

Yussen, S. R., Mathews, S. R., Buss, R. R., & Kane, P. T. (1980). Developmental change in judging important and critical elements. *Developmental Psychology, 16,* 213-219.

Codes and
Pragmatic Comprehension

DONALD G. ELLIS
University of Hartford

T HE chapter by Badzinski and Gill is a useful and thorough cataloguing of numerous issues and variables that influence the process of comprehension. The breadth and inclusiveness of the essay are a real strength. Moreover, the authors appreciate the complexity of the problem and that future work must be based on sound theory. At stake is our understanding of the relationship between language and comprehension, a relationship that is inherently indeterminate and schematic. What follows below is not so much a critique of Badzinski and Gill's chapter as it is an extension of the issues. Although their chapter nicely specifies variables that influence the psycholinguistic process we call "comprehension," I found their discussion too reliant on the "objective" features of text and cognition and not reliant enough on the "subjective" experience of interactants. By subjective experience, I do not mean the one-time idiosyncratic meanings of individuals but the processes by which language users (communicators) assign conventional meanings to utterances—*pragmatic comprehension* (Ellis, 1992a, pp. 202-205).

ISSUES IN LANGUAGE AND COMPREHENSION

Any piece of language, regardless of length or complexity, that is used for any communicative purpose can be said to be *textual*. In other words, that language has sign value and is interpretable by some community of users. Signs can be of a certain type (iconic, symbolic; Eco, 1984), medium (language, painting, film; Mitchell, 1986), and compositional makeup (Tannen, 1982). The fact of their interpretability by a speech community situates a text within a social matrix that is responsible for its production and comprehen-

Correspondence and requests for reprints: Donald G. Ellis, Department of Communication, University of Hartford, West Hartford, CT 06117.

Communication Yearbook 17, pp. 333-343

sion. The objective and formal properties of a message are less important to the comprehension process than the pragmatic interpretive frames that arise from the speech community. This social orientation is what makes language, in addition to everything else it is, fundamentally and definitionally communicative (Bakhtin, 1986). This social orientation also means that the comprehension process is unavoidably schematic because gaps of indeterminacy must be continually filled.

The act of filling these gaps of indeterminacy is essentially the comprehension process. Badzinski and Gill focus on some elements that make up structures of comprehension but almost ignore the local management processes that result in comprehension. Moreover, Badzinski and Gill spend very little time, if any, on what is widely considered the central defining quality of a complete and coherent text—context. Linguistic devices, grammatical structures, and subject predilections cue communicative genres and frames for interpretation. But final comprehension is only in the union of language and context. Perhaps the purest form of propositional interpretations are the least context dependent, but even this is the subject of debate (Brown & Yule, 1983).

Communicative exchanges require broad considerations of context for comprehensibility. These include such processes as performance (Bauman, 1986), genre (Hanks, 1987), frame, and footing (Goffmann, 1981). Where formal linguistic approaches try to explain objective linguistic facts, these approaches relate form to social matrices. It is certainly impossible to properly discuss all of these perspectives, so I will concentrate on a midrange problem. I believe the comprehension issues most appropriate for communication theorists lie somewhere between linguistic formalism, which concentrates on many of the devices outlined by Badzinski and Gill, and what might be called radical sociology, which insists on reducing all comprehension to massively historicized phenomena. A better goal is to develop a stance in which to examine the interpenetration of the cognitive and the social. This completed task would include all manner of media and channels (oral, written, poetry, pictographic, painting, film), but I will focus on verbal text without attention to other forms. Yet there remains additional problems, all of which are ignored by Badzinski and Gill. Comprehension surely must differ, either slightly or considerably, according to the type of discourse. Is the process the same when processing literal from figurative meaning, monologue versus dialogue, or indirect and quoted speech?

POSITIONING MESSAGES

The comprehension process uses multiple cues and channels to remove indeterminacy. But positioning is the foremost task of comprehending a message. A piece of discourse is *positioned* when it is hinged to a locally defined social context. This context operates as a channel of information for the comprehender to establish an interpretation. Positioning an incomplete message by hinging it to a context is central to the comprehension process. In fact, social context is not and cannot be practically or theoretically independent from a message. All messages are necessarily assumed to be incomplete, and therefore positioning serves a constitutive function. Language is always evaluated according to its functions. That is why it has been possible in the cases of formal linguistics and transformational grammar to characterize language as an independent abstract system that served a mapping function. This allowed language to be analyzed as an isolated componential system governed by lawlike principles. But structuralism too understood the communicative function of language (Jakobson, 1960) and recognized that, as well as semantic interpretations (Hymes, 1974), even highly technical properties of messages could be delimited by social context.

By linking comprehension to the positioned message, we firm up the relationship between context and indeterminacy. The communicative function of a message regulates the interpretation of the message by establishing its position. This I believe is an important communication orientation. Formal linguistics starts from the objective compositional factors of a message and works outward toward the social realm. So phonetic, rhythmic, syntactic, and intertextual cohesive devices all help regulate textual positioning and the resultant comprehension. A communication perspective complements this line of work by joining individual interpretive schemes, intentionality, discourse routines, relational models, and so on to the text to fill gaps of indeterminacy.

Contexts are part of the comprehension process because they function as a type of metalanguage that describes, characterizes, explains, and refers to the message. Utterances such as "I wanna tell you a joke," "I have a secret to tell you," "This paper is a review of literature in interpersonal communication," "The meeting shall now come to order," "The word *book* is a noun," and various literary genres all function as a metalanguage that hinges complex linguistic structures to a context (Gumperz, 1982). Badzinski and Gill have teased out a number of devices that cue comprehension but they have not adequately explained how complex information structures correspond to actional wholes such as frames, general knowledge packets, and scenes of various types. Given the point I have made above, that messages are by definition indeterminate and schematic, then access to these actional wholes semantically positions a message and makes available additional information that is not expressed but nevertheless is available to the competent interpreter.

Contexts and Comprehension

One persistent problem with context analysis for positioning messages is the problem of how broad a context one must analyze in order to interpret a message. What information must an interpreter assemble from what variety of sources to position the message for comprehension? An acceptable model of comprehension must be able to account for the diversity of messages that vary along a continuum of highly context dependent to context independent. Some messages are extremely elliptical and only previous knowledge can fill the spaces necessary for understanding. Other messages are quite concrete and interpretation comes through very localized means. The speed and ease of comprehension are not necessarily related to local or global knowledge requirements. A technical text is a very circumscribed message but requires complex conceptual structures for comprehension. It can be comprehended quickly and easily by the right interpreter. A common road sign, on the other hand, also requires "broad" contextual knowledge, albeit not very complex, and can be understood equally as quickly.

I find the oft used distinction between local and global context cues for comprehension to be illustrative but awkward as an explanatory concept. No message-carrying text is an artifact divorced from the constraints of users, interpreters, and social conditions. Moreover, all texts require a interpreter and rely on the assignment of meanings based on the receiver's interaction with a text. These principles and processes are more important to pragmatic comprehension than the placement of interpretation cues on a local-global continuum. The problem is this: How does a hearer assign meaning to speaker utterances and thereby position the message such that the hearer knows the intent, purpose, or actional nature of the message?

Standard speech act theory treats a number of conditions for contextual interpretation as essentially cognitive. Assumptions such as (a) speaker knows x, (b) speaker believes y, (c) speaker wants z, (d) speaker believes that if a then b, and so on are primitives. But a pragmatic theory of comprehension must examine how these processes are assigned in communication; that is, in what contexts are they actually expressed? This brings us to the gap between language and meaning. Although the above are considered cognitive primitives, they are not literally necessary for interpretation. What a speaker actually knows, or thinks, or wants is unimportant as long as his or her communicative behavior is understood as exhibiting these cognitive conditions. One measure of the "success" of communication is the extent to which the content of these cognitive primitives is shared by participants in an interaction. For example, when two members of a communicative exchange share the nature of the social conditions that govern the pragmatic principles, there will be fewer misunderstandings, mishaps, and "social mistakes." When participants "share" the content of social rules such as politeness, power, authority, and personal relations, they use this to make interpretations about the context.

It is incumbent on communication scholars to struggle with issues in pragmatics to improve clarity and precision. Pragmatics, and its role in the comprehension process, has only recently been seriously acknowledged as necessary for a full account of communication. There was a time when pragmatics was considered the ragbag of linguistics, but more recently scholars have written that it is simply impossible to understand language unless we understand pragmatics: how language is used in communication (Leech, 1983). There are any number of good explications of context analysis (e.g., Ventola, 1987) so I will not dwell on it here. For example, van Dijk (1977) explains how contexts are necessary (although not sufficient) for comprehension. Pragmatic comprehension positions a message within the initial context of an utterance that is characterized by both action and the accumulation of information from earlier events and states. The participant's analyses then assign meaning on the basis of contextual features such as categories: private, public, institutional, informal. Contexts can also be factored into social categories such as positions, person characteristics, power relations, roles, and so on. van Dijk suggests that all of these are systematically related and constitute the context that defines an array of possible actions. All of this is organized in *frames*, which are "chunks" of knowledge organized around a concept. The power of frames is that they are conventional and specify "typical" and "cultural" characteristics, episodes, routines, and the like.

Text and Comprehension

Context provides the conditions and expectations for pragmatic comprehension. It serves as a macro-interpretive frame for speech participants. But final comprehension results from the interaction of context and text. Although each can be an interpretive frame for the other, the message function of communication is inextricably reliant on *language-in-use*. Badzinski and Gill orient their attention to the results of studies that examine rules of natural language processing and how phonological, morphological, and syntactic features stimulate cognitive responses. *Pragmatic comprehension* is more concerned with (a) the linguistic and discourse features that prompt the assignment of a speech act function to an utterance, (b) the internal textual cohesion mechanisms that assist with the tracking of information and the reference system of the text, and (c) the interpretive code of communicators that regulates meaning in on-line interaction.

Assignment of speech act function. During real-time interaction, the participants track unfolding discourse and make sense of (comprehend) the communication as they go along. The goals and intentions of a speaker are not always apparent. Contexts provide expectations about the goals, intentions, and rationales of speakers and therefore about speech acts. But actual language use is probably the most important source of information about how to comprehend a message. My goal here is to focus on how communicators use their real-time subjective experience to assign conventional meanings, such as speech acts and individual meanings. Surely the processing of grammatical units (words, sentences, and so on) is important but pragmatic comprehension is more concerned with illocutionary force.

Illocutionary force is determined at semantic, syntactic, lexical, and para-linguistic levels (van Dijk, 1977). An utterance such as *Take this one* carries a semantic structure that denotes a speaker and hearer and a line of action. The hearer knows that the utterance refers to an immediate action with respect to an object (chair). Given generalized world knowledge, the hearer knows that the utterance is a socially acceptable order to do something. Syntactically, the utterance is structured as an order because the sentence form has an understood "you" and an imperative structure; moreover, it is stated in the present tense. Lexically, this utterance is very simple in that it denotes actions such as *take* and then two deictic pronouns. These pronouns refer to some-thing in the environment. *This* directs the hearer's attention and *one* functions to point to the object in question. Finally, a hearer would get some assistance assigning a speech function from an array of paralinguistic activities such as deictic movements (e.g., pointing to an object), facial gestures, tone and stress, bodily movements, and the like.

This list in the above paragraph is not complete or particularly explicit, but it does show that numerous linguistic and paralinguistic indicators are nec-essary for pragmatic comprehension. No single indicator—as is the emphasis of Badzinski and Gill's review—is sufficient to establish comprehension. All indicators must be integrated with the context for interpretation. This is crucial because it is the difference between understanding *Take this one* as an "order" with all of the socially objectionable implications, or comprehending it as potentially a polite offer. The unstated relationship between the two individuals and the nature of the discourse routine will determine this differ-ence (Dummett, 1976). It is important to underscore here that the gaps of indeterminacy that position the message are filled pragmatically and not linguistically.

There is much we do not know about how incoming linguistic stimuli are processed psychologically. We do not know exactly what processes are involved, nor do we have much detail about how information is combined to form an impression. We do not know much about how information is stored and integrated with existing knowledge. But there are some assumptions that must be made about the cognitive foundation of pragmatic structures. First, the complexity of incoming linguistic stimuli must be reduced and assigned a "function." Badzinski and Gill (p. 307) are right to emphasize that linguistic cues probably constrain certain knowledge frames from moving into the foreground rather than "construct" representation. The mind must make a judgment as it encounters a mountain of information. It must process infor-mation and make decisions about relevance, urgency, meaning, and appropri-ateness, and it must do this under restrictions of time, circumstance, and storage capacity. It must be the case that hierarchical abstract knowledge structures are responsible for the storage of information about the structure of action, and these knowledge structures are "moved" into the foreground by linguistic devices and activated for interpretive work.

Unfolding text and pragmatic comprehension. Textual cohesion plays a role in how comprehension is accomplished pragmatically. Of course, Halliday and Hasan's (1976) work helped establish cohesion devices as a necessary machinery of texts. But they alone are not sufficient to achieve "texture" or the semantic unity that characterizes messages. Pragmatic comprehension views cohesion devices as the result of semantic relationships within a message. In the section above, we addressed the matter of assigning illocutionary force and the fact that this was highly dependent on global knowledge structures that were pragmatically determined. Now we come to how actual messages are understood through the interaction of these global knowledge structures and the reference cues in a text.

Halliday and Hasan (1976) explain that reference devices (e.g., reference, substitutions, and ellipses) are essentially instructions to go elsewhere in a text for meaning. But Hankamer and Sag (1976) and Sag and Hankamer (1984) demonstrate that theoretical explanations for linguistic devices in a text—cohesion devices or any other—are quite incomplete if they refer only to an idealized semantic system abstracted from the psychology of those who use them. In real-time interaction, communicators interpret messages by integrating information into foregrounded frames and by processing short-term functional information. Hankamer and Sag (1976) have argued that these interpretive processes fall into two classes, which are termed *deep* and *surface*. Deep processing is more pragmatically controlled. That is, understanding a communication is facilitated because the interactants have developed a cognitive model that they hold "in focus" and use for interpretation. The communicators know what a situation, and the talk embedded in the situation, is about. They know what point a speaker is making and what he or she is trying to do (see above). Deep interpretive processes have a long life in memory. Examples of specific anaphoric interpretations that rely on deep processes are pronouns (see example 1a), sentential *it* (see 1b), and the null complement (see 1c):

1. John ran a marathon.
   a. *He* did *it* because *he* felt ready
   b. *It* was a special experience
   c. He will run again when he can ø

To appreciate how deep reference that is highly pragmatically controlled is not subject to short-term recency effects, consider the following example from FCC safety instructions for using an answering machine:

2. a. This unit contains a Ringer Equivalence Number (REN). If requested please provide this information.
   b. To be certain of the number of devices you may connect to your line you should call your local telephone company. (some additional information)

    c. If you experience trouble contact Phonemate to obtain the name of your authorized dealer. (some additional information)

    d. Repairs can only be made by the manufacturer. (This followed by five more instructions)

    e. First check to see if *it* works.

The *it* refers to the answering machine, an element in the discourse model, which was evoked in the first sentence and foregrounded throughout the entire discourse so it may be referred to by an anaphoric *it*. Deep pragmatic processing requires some parallelism between the linguistic device and the foregrounded frame and, of course, some pragmatic means for the communicator to make the connection.

Surface comprehension processes use more immediate propositional representations. They are used for short-term information and interpretation and contribute to confusion and ambiguity if they occur too long after a specific propositional representation has registered with an interactant. Below are the most common examples. The ellipsis in example 3 and the gaps in 4 and 5 are more propositionally based and do *not* require an individual to establish a general cognitive model for interpretation with the text serving as a linking device to the model.

    3. David crashed the car. At least he said he did ∅.

    4. I'll wash the dishes, but ∅ not ∅ now.

    5. The ball hit his mother, and his mother ∅ me.

Consider the result if the sentence in example 2e had been the following elliptical reference.

    6. *OK, now you know how ∅. [∅ = operate the answering machine safely]

The confusion that would have resulted demonstrates how comprehending a message is dependent on interpretive strategies (e.g., surface and deep) that follow the assignment of illocutionary force, and these strategies are based on key elements of a text.

Codes and comprehension. Although we have touched upon two essential components of pragmatic comprehension—that is, the foregrounding of global meaning structures and the use of these structures in interpretation—I still believe it necessary to find a place for the highly subjective experiences of language users. In a series of studies and articles (Ellis, 1992a, 1992b; Ellis & Hamilton, 1985), I have tried to articulate a theory of codes that reflects the language user as a member of society with various social experiences. A full and principled theory of pragmatic comprehension must eventually include how individuals subjectively organize experience with reality and how these concepts inform the comprehension process. When a subjective concept is established, it by definition forms a sign relationship between the concept and the semantic reality that it represents. Concepts are organized experience that have been reduced to categories with names (Bolton, 1977). *Systems of concepts are codes.* These systems of concepts develop and evolve through diachronic change and learning to accommodate new experience. Just as adaptation is natural in the biological scenario, so too do systems of concepts change to suit contexts, individuals, historical developments, and cultural variation.

Codes are formed in interaction but the fact that so much communication is routinized and automatic (Kellermann, 1992) is evidence of strong convergence in concept formation. Communication and ease of comprehension improve to the extent that knowledge is shared and individuals have had corresponding interaction experiences. Codes become powerful factors in the comprehension process to the extent that they are responsive to particular group experiences. When specific codes express specialized group meanings such as those found in the patterns of talk used by groups such as doctors, criminals, students, age cohorts, and so on, then it becomes possible to comprehend subjective reality.

There is a psycholinguistic aspect of codes that focuses on the inner qualities of integrated networks of abstract constructs. These constructs are composed of the sign relationships discussed above and in Ellis (1992a). But this orientation is inadequate and must be complemented by a social orientation. A strong psychological perspective on codes fails to account for interactively produced meaning. If codes exist and only operate "within" individuals, then there is no place for the role of the real-time interaction that expresses subjective meaning. Communicators use the rules and conventions of the code to produce a message that will be comprehended properly, but these rules and conventions can only entail a probabilistic array of possible interpretations (Sanders, 1987). The psycholinguistic aspect of codes can account well enough for the propositional content and illocutionary force of a message. But an utterance also takes place within the context of an unfolding dialogue, and a *specific* interpretation results from connecting an utterance to other utterances and projecting interpretive consequences. The actual meaning of an utterance and its successful comprehension result from hinging a real-time utterance to the context of unfolding discourse.

This notion that utterances are constrained by the context of real-time discourse helps explain how codes are powerfully contextually sensitive. Pragmatic comprehension relies on specific lexical and syntactical forms of an utterance and their relationship to lexical and syntactic forms in other utterances. This relationship narrows or widens what can be said and influences the interpretation. Pragmatic comprehension includes the quasi decisions that communicators make at various junctures in the interaction. These decisions make psycholinguistic considerations secondary to concerns of relevance and correct interpretation. The *essential* social nature of codes is a necessary ingredient in a pragmatic theory of comprehension. As Bernstein (1975) argues, when communication patterns reflect shared experiences, they are internalized and sustained in language. This language is used in future interactions to activate codes and thereby regulate comprehension.

When we begin with the assumption that communication is indeterminate, the problems of comprehension get difficult. It is not that solipsism is inevitable but that these gaps of indeterminacy must be filled. In fact, these gaps are filled and it is our task to explain them. Future efforts in this area must work to develop common theories. As of now, I am reminded of the adolescent who can easily disassemble a car but cannot get it back together. It is certainly useful to have all the parts laid out in front of you, but the thing won't run unless you know how to connect them.

REFERENCES

Bakhtin, M. M. (1986). *Speech genres and other late essays* (V. W. McGee, Trans.). Austin: University of Texas Press.

Bauman, R. (1986). *Story, performance and event: Contextual studies of oral narrative.* Cambridge: Cambridge University Press.

Bernstein, B. (1975). *Class, codes and control* (Vol. 3). London: Routledge & Kegan Paul.

Bolton, N. (1977). *Concept formation.* Oxford: Pergamon.

Brown, G., & Yule, G. (1983). *Discourse analysis.* Cambridge: Cambridge University Press.

Dummett, M. (1976). What is a theory of meaning? (II). In G. Evans & J. McDowell (Eds.), *Truth and meaning* (pp. 67-137). Oxford: Clarendon.

Eco, U. (1984). *Semiotics and the philosophy of language.* Bloomington: Indiana University Press.

Ellis, D. G. (1992a). *From language to communication.* Hillsdale, NJ: Lawrence Erlbaum.

Ellis, D. G. (1992b). Syntactic and pragmatic codes in communication. *Communication Theory, 2,* 1-23.

Ellis, D. G., & Hamilton, M. (1985). Syntactic and pragmatic code usage in interpersonal communication. *Communication Monographs, 52,* 264-279.

Goffman, E. (1981). *Forms of talk.* Philadelphia: University of Pennsylvania Press.

Gumperz, J. (1982). *Discourse strategies.* Cambridge: Cambridge University Press.

Halliday, M. A. K., & Hasan, R. (1976). *Cohesion in English.* London: Longman.

Hankamer, J., & Sag, I. (1976). Deep and surface anaphora. *Linguistic Inquiry, 7,* 391-426.

Hanks, W. F. (1987). Discourse genres in a theory of practice. *American Ethnologist, 14,* 668-692.

Hymes, D. (1974). *Foundations in sociolinguistics.* Philadelphia: University of Pennsylvania Press.

Jakobson, R. (1960). Concluding statement: Linguistics and poetics. In T. A. Sebeok (Ed.), *Style in language* (pp. 350-377). Cambridge: MIT Press.

Kellermann, K. (1992). Communication: Inherently strategic and primarily automatic. *Communication Monographs, 59,* 288-300.

Leech, G. (1983). *Principles of pragmatics.* London: Longman.

Mitchell, W. J. T. (1986). *Iconology: Image, text, ideology.* Chicago: University of Chicago Press.

Sag, I. A., & Hankamer, J. (1984). Toward a theory of anaphoric processing. *Linguistics and Philosophy, 7,* 325-345.

Sanders, R. E. (1987). *Cognitive foundations of calculated speech.* Albany: State University of New York Press.

Tannen, D. (Ed.). (1982). *Analyzing discourse: Text and talk* (Georgetown University Round Table on Language and Linguistics). Washington, DC: Georgetown University Press.

van Dijk, T. A. (1977). Context and cognition: Knowledge frames and speech act comprehension. *Journal of Pragmatics, 1,* 211-232.

Ventola, E. (1987). *The structure of social interaction: A systematic approach to the semiotics of service encounters.* London: Francis Pinter.

8 Embodied Health and Constitutive Communication: Toward an Authentic Conceptualization of Health Communication

ERIC G. ZOOK
Pennsylvania State University

Health communication as a field of study has been traditionally ill-defined, focusing on health contexts and health-related content. By failing to adequately problematize the conception of health, these definitions confine communication to an ancillary position with respect to health professionals and institutions, emphasizing its instrumental managerial functions. Recent conceptions of health as a state of biological, psychological, and social well-being, however, place communication in the center of health as a central means whereby one can develop, maintain, and/or restore systemic integration. Such a conception, however, fails to ensure the promise of holistic health by retaining the biological function as the central concern of health care. As such, it promotes the idea of social engineering the self to match the dictates of specifically valued biological states. Therefore a phenomenological corrective is provided that defines health as "a state of ontological (i.e., meaningful) unity." This move grounds health within the *experience* of being-in-the-world, rather than privileging the object body, and suggests the need for a radical reconception of both health care and health communication.

THE field of health communication has grown significantly during its roughly 20 years of existence (Ray & Donohew, 1990). Indeed, given the concrete achievements of increasing emphasis on communication in both medical education and practice, the establishment of the journal of *Health Communication*, and growing membership in the health communication commissions of the Speech Communication Association and the International Communication Association, it is safe to say that the fledgling is no more. Efforts to provide a meaningful order to this adolescent burst of growth

Correspondence and requests for reprints: Eric G. Zook, Department of Speech Communication, 318 Sparks Building, Pennsylvania State University, University Park, PA 16802-5202.

Communication Yearbook 17, pp. 344-377

have been forthcoming in the form of in-depth reviews of research trends (Cassata, 1978, 1980; Costello, 1977; Finnegan & Viswanath, 1990; Kreps, 1988; Thompson, 1984) and reflective essays suggesting future directions for research (Arntson, 1985; Korsch, 1989; Kreps, 1989; Nussbaum, 1989; Pettegrew, 1988; Smith, 1989). These articles provide significant testament to the importance of communication in the management of health.

In the midst of all this activity, however, one can discern a troubling lack of critical reflection about the very notion of health toward which our efforts are aimed (Finnegan & Viswanath, 1990). Rather, we have moved straight to the project of improving health care, leaving it to others to define health, principally medical professionals. As such, we have engaged almost entirely in "administrative" research (Lazarsfeld, 1941) aimed at correcting the shortcomings of current medical practices (e.g., noncompliance, dissatisfaction, "knowledge gaps") rather than involving ourselves in questions regarding the ends of health care practices (though see Arntson, 1989).

The position developed here is that, by failing to engage in meaningful reflection on the nature of health, we have settled for a narrow *biological* conception. This has significantly reduced the scope and range of health communication research, leading us to: (a) focus inordinately on biomedical communication, particularly between physicians and patients (Smith, 1989; Thompson, 1984) and between public health agencies and the public (Freimuth, 1990); (b) emphasize formal contexts of biomedical care (Nussbaum, 1989); (c) stress the dissemination of formal biomedical information (Atkin, 1979; Wartella & Middlestadt, 1991); (d) rely primarily on social psychological theories of communication to the exclusion of broader theoretical perspectives (Nussbaum, 1989; Smith, 1989); and (e) rely on a narrow, instrumentalist conception of communication. As such, we have disregarded: (a) the extent to which individual states of health and illness are constituted through interpretation of biological, psychological, and social messages (Arntson & Droge, 1987; Good & Good, 1981; Stoeckle & Barsky, 1981) and (b) that normative standards for evaluating function at each of these levels are principally historical social creations rather than immutable "scientific" discoveries (Baron, 1985; Mishler, 1981). As such, we have fostered a perception of health communication as an important yet ancillary field of research, the purpose of which is to serve the interests of the lay public and the medical community toward sustaining and/or restoring biological health.[1]

To correct these deficiencies, two significant, simultaneous acts of retrenchment are necessary. First, we must embrace a definition of health that balances the concern of biological survival with concerns of personal and social, as well as societal, well-being. This is possible, however, only if we embrace as well a broader conception of communication wherein instrumental interests are balanced by emancipatory interests. This tandem action emphasizes the need for a concept of health (and health care) that answers to the human quest for *meaningful* rather than *mere* existence (Callahan, 1987).

Achievement of this goal, however, is severely constrained by the pervasive presumption of biological primacy in matters of health. That is, inasmuch as our experience of self and the world presupposes biological survival and function, the latter is accorded primordial, foundational status. On the strength of such, the medical community has traditionally recused itself of responsibility for anything beyond the body as object. Any attempt to develop a holistic conception of health that fails to temper this interpretation of the admittedly obvious necessity of biological survival must ultimately fail. Thus the bulk of this essay is devoted to extricating ourselves from such commitment. Its principal accomplishment then is the clearing of a small but crucial plot of ground upon which to elaborate an ontological conception of health. Though concrete suggestions concerning the nature of this wider project are provided, space precludes more than minimal indication of promising directions. More complete development of the themes introduced must await future work.

CONCEPTUALIZING HEALTH COMMUNICATION

At the outset, it is useful to examine briefly how we came to conceive ourselves in such a narrow fashion. In general, it appears to have been less a matter of conscious determination than of a rate of research that far outpaced conceptual and theoretical work. In particular, the problem can be traced significantly to our failure to adequately problematize the concept of health (Finnegan & Viswanath, 1990). This failure has left us open to—or more likely is the result of—the narrow biomedical emphasis on biological survival and function.

In contrast with the youthfulness of the field of health communication, the biomedical model has largely dominated thought about health for nearly four centuries (Rasmussen, 1975). Its success in the scientific development and application of knowledge concerning the biological base of our existence allowed a coalescing of "the power to heal" by a professionalized medical community, which then gained a near monopoly on "the right to heal" through legislative regulations (Starr, 1982).

The attractiveness of the biological conception of health has always been the firmness of its material presence (or absence) in the objective body. As such, it can pass the "verifiability" criterion that has so long marginalized mental dysfunction except in cases of proven biochemical agency. Just as important, however, is the primordial value accorded biology. The strength of the biomedical community has derived largely from its ability to effect cures of biological dysfunction. This ability still produces a level of awe, regardless of our increased cynicism and concern about the ultimate impact of high-tech biomedicine; when push comes to shove, medical professionals and scientific disciplines are accorded superior status in the social and academic hierarchy. After all, if biology is the seat of life, must not the sciences that study it and the professionals who practice it deserve greater esteem as well?

As researchers we have, like most citizens in the West (Engel, 1982), accepted the inherent logic of biological primacy and accordingly built our research upon it. The "givenness" of health as foundationally a question of biology is such that the few explicit definitions of health communication that do exist (Cassata, 1978; Costello, 1977; Kreps & Thornton, 1984; Ray & Donohew, 1990) appear to be merely an exercise in the obvious. That is, they appear largely an attempt to meet the pro forma conceptual requirement of any organized area of study, explicating "straightforward" but previously ignored links between communication and health. Such "definitions" are in effect little more than the elaboration of frameworks for organizing communication research in health care, road maps locating important intersections and bypasses.

This is clearly evident in what may be taken as the standard definition, presented by Cassata (1980; see also Kreps, 1988; Kreps & Thornton, 1984; Reardon, 1988). He defines health communication as "the study of communication parameters (levels, functions, and methodologies) applied in health situations/contexts" (p. 584). While establishing a broad agenda for applying communication to health, the two concepts are merely situated within a common domain (Peters, 1986), resting largely on how "health situations/ contexts" are defined. The tendency has been to specify *formal* medical care contexts (e.g., Pettegrew, 1988), which, however helpful for delimiting the field, is woefully inadequate and arbitrary. Furthermore, the agenda is tied firmly, albeit with implicit (unwarranted) confidence, to biological health. Even Cassata's (1980) incorporation of psychosocial influences is premised on their potential to interfere with biological health and recovery through the anchoring of "inappropriate" behaviors. An alternative emphasis on content (i.e., "health-related messages"; Ray & Donohew, 1990) retains "health" as a given and thus still succumbs to the biological presumption.

This uncritical acceptance of the biomedical vision of health commits us to a similar acceptance of its traditional ends (i.e., maintaining and/or restoring biological function). However much we have applied communication theory and process toward the goal of "rehumanizing" and enhancing the effectiveness of medical practice, we have questioned neither the presumption of biological primacy nor the scientific knowledge upon which this practice is founded. As such, we have effectively "medicalized" the field of health communication (Smith, 1989; Thompson, 1984) as is evidenced in the three principal areas of research pursued to date: (a) promotion of lifestyle behaviors conducive to the development and maintenance of biological health (e.g., adequate nutrition, exercise, safe sex), (b) improving compliance with therapeutic recommendations, and (c) strengthening the alliance between patients and medical professionals (Finnegan & Viswanath, 1990).[2]

This represents a clear devaluation of extrabiological dimensions of health (i.e., mental and social well-being), which helps explain the lack of attention to mental health workers (Thompson, 1984, 1990) as well as social workers and clergy—even allied medical staff, who are, after all, secondary to the true action taken or directed by physicians. With the exception of mass media studies, we have also overemphasized formal health care contexts (i.e., medical clinics and hospitals) to the exclusion of nonmedical settings, where we spend the *vast* majority of our time and where therefore most of our "health knowledge and behavior" are formed and enacted.

This narrow focus is increasingly inadequate in the face of significant and tumultuous changes affecting modern health care: growing awareness of the human costs exacted by our increasing technical ability to sustain biological life (Callahan, 1990; Reardon, 1988), the burgeoning costs of high-tech biomedical care (Callahan, 1990), recognition of the influence of behavioral choices on health and well-being (Finnegan & Viswanath, 1990), the increasing prominence and prevalence of chronic illness (Strauss & Corbin, 1988), rapid growth in the elderly population (Callahan, 1990), and the trend away from institutional care to outpatient treatment and home-based care (Corbin & Strauss, 1988). Such changes require that we focus attention not only on a broader range of health care professionals but on family members, friends, and the wider society as well (Ellis, Miller, & Given, 1989; Zook & Miller, 1992, 1993). The changing scene also impugns the validity and value of any attempt to contain health communication in a contextual fashion.

It would be unjust, nevertheless, to hold ourselves wholly accountable for these failings. Rather, we are guilty of having responded to the perceived needs of the lay public and medical practitioners in response to such "problems" as patient dissatisfaction, noncompliance, and "knowledge gaps." Recent calls for a more socially informed research agenda (e.g., lack of insurance, access, knowledge, self-efficacy; Arntson, 1989) continue to heed such voices. Though by no means unimportant, these continue to press a biological agenda that has long been in need of amendment.

If we are to render an adequate agenda for health communication research, however, it is necessary that our view of communication be up to the task. In short, we need to recognize the reciprocal relation between conceptions of communication and health: A truly holistic conception of health is sustainable only through an appreciation of communication's constitutive capability; conversely, an understanding of this constitutive function requires our advocacy for and adoption of a holistic conception of health.

RETHINKING COMMUNICATION

The need to reexamine how we, both as a community of researchers and a wider public, define health has become increasingly evident in the wake of developments that deconstruct the notion of an immutable, universal notion of reality (e.g., Berger & Luckmann, 1966; Kuhn, 1970; Rorty, 1979). This wide body of work impugns the correspondence notion of truth and thereby the traditional conception of communication as a conduit through which intentional states and meanings are passed (Axley, 1984). As such, we have long assumed that communication is *preceded* by reality, knowledge of which is ideally derived through "objective" strategies of logic and/or scientific empiricism. The technical sophistication of the biomedical understanding of bodily health and function is perhaps *the* exemplar of this. In attacking these assumptions, critics have emphasized the inherently linguistic—and thus the inescapably historicized and perspectival—nature of "reality." Truth is hereby rendered a matter of *coherence*, wherein discourse, and the tradition of which it is both product and producer (Gadamer, 1992; Rorty, 1989, 1991), is seen to *construct* reality through the creation of meanings. In this manner, discourse underlies even the cherished "materiality" of the body (Levin & Solomon, 1990; Rorty, 1991).

Although application varies widely, arguments for the constitutive nature of language derive fundamentally from the phenomenological insight into the intentionality of consciousness. The nature and implications of this insight have been well developed elsewhere (e.g., Deetz, 1978, 1992; Stewart & Mickunas, 1974) and will not be detailed here. A brief exegesis, however, is necessary.

The phenomenological insight, as formulated by Husserl (1962), is that consciousness, which forms the base for all knowledge, is *always* directed *toward* something. Though he retains the "polar structure of consciousness" (Stewart & Mickunas, 1974), Husserl dodges the dualistic dilemma of Descartes by revealing experience as the result of two "simultaneous 'movements': (a) an intending act, (*noesis*, the consciousness of) and (b) an intended object (*noema*, that which the consciousness is of). *The critical phenomenological insight is that neither can stand alone*" (Deetz, 1992, p. 120, italics added). It is important to note, however, that Husserl's observation does not imply an autonomous subject engaged in the observation of an empirical object. As Stewart and Mickunas (1974) stress, "The noetic-noematic structure . . . is the *condition* for the possibility of experiencing *both* the subject and the object; . . . they are two sides of the same coin" (pp. 37-38, italics added). In other words, our categorization of the world into subjective and objective entities is performed against their unity within lived experience and is therefore ever susceptible to misrepresentation.

Husserl (1962) thus exposes perceptual experience as the primordial fount from whence all knowledge of the world, including ourselves, is drawn. As such, it is both inappropriate and irresponsible to view communication as merely the jug that transports objective knowledge from the distilleries of logic and/or scientific empiricism. Rather, all understanding of reality is constructed linguistically, filtered through intentional interests, and thereby always partial. That is, because "raw" perceptual experience is meaningless, perception is formed (i.e., made sense of) interactively among "subjects" and "objects," emerging within language as a choice among possibilities. To accept "reality" as a social product is to recognize the existence of choice, of possibilities both not seen and not taken. That common sense suggests otherwise is but the result of institutionally suppressed conflict that naturalizes certain perceptions (Deetz, 1992; Habermas, 1968). Because the selection and sedimentation of perceptions rests principally on tradition (and as such is "arbitrary"), and because institutional forms of power (e.g., status, legal authority, expertise) are not equally distributed, the process is intrinsically political as well.[3] That is, the reification of certain perceptions inherently privileges certain experiences, persons, and societies. Because equal participation in the production and reproduction of social practices is thereby precluded, our challenge as citizens—but more explicitly as scholars—is to recover suppressed conflict, *to make perceptual choice as conscious, constant, and participative as possible* (Habermas, 1984, 1987).

This process allows for a more complete rendering of the nature of knowledge and human interests (Habermas, 1968). In particular, it allows us to acknowledge the instrumental value of empirical-analytic research without denigrating the practical importance of interpretive-hermeneutic research and the emancipatory value of critically-oriented research (Habermas, 1968). In short, the validity of all three forms of science is recognized as necessary to the project of human existence.[4]

Although much of this position has been worked out in other disciplines (Beniger, 1986; Hiley, Bohman, & Shusterman, 1991; Skinner, 1990), an increasing number of communication scholars (Deetz, 1992; Delia, O'Keefe, & O'Keefe, 1982; Fisher, 1987; Hyde, 1983; Hyde & Smith, 1979; Pearce, 1989; Pearce & Cronen, 1980; Scott, 1967, 1976) have applied these insights in a critical expansion of communication research.[5] Despite significant interest without and growing interest within, however, our discipline as a whole has been slow to grasp the full implication of these insights (Dervin, Grossberg, O'Keefe, & Wartella, 1989). In particular, those of us with a social scientific orientation, for all our increasing emphasis on interpretive research, have too long overemphasized empirical-analytic work at the expense of critically oriented research. Thus, while unfortunate, it is not surprising that much of the extant research in health communication has failed in this respect as well, especially because the majority of us studying in the area have our roots in the social science side of the discipline.

In short, the majority of our research in health has retained the conduit conception of communication. Communication is therefore merely (however crucial) a means of information exchange, variously educational or persuasive depending on source intentions, toward the ends of understanding and control with respect to issues of health. Even those studies that might be grouped under the general rubric "coordinated management of meaning," wherein meaning is a mutually negotiated accomplishment within interaction (e.g., Adelman, 1991; Ballard-Reisch, 1990; Sharf, 1990), amount principally to a more complex version of the conduit metaphor, with interactants attempting to uncover or establish truth through discourse.

Acknowledging communication's constitutive function does not invalidate "administrative" aims; rather, it subsumes them under a broader concern with the ends toward which communication practices and processes are directed. As such, constitutive communication can be conceived as a second-order instrumentalism, possessing the vital difference of emancipatory promise (or at least potential) to deliver us from confining social practices. That is, new realities arise in response to problems occurring in old ones (Kuhn, 1970; Rorty, 1979, 1989, 1991). In seeking to manage human affairs, we may alternatively apply or adapt standard practices *within* traditional frames; conversely, we may alter the frame and set about exploring and developing the new possibilities made visible thereby. This is the difference between the use of communication research to facilitate paternalistic medical care *or* to facilitate mutuality, versus shifting the frame from one to the other. The first is an administrative concern; the second, an emancipatory one. While we need not endorse the implication of some (e.g., Conquergood, 1991) that the only valid research is oppositional—in short, that researchers *must* side with the "oppressed" against the status quo—we must pay at *least* as much attention to this second function as we have to the first.

RETHINKING HEALTH

In turning to health and health care, both the need and the means for a critical assessment of the concept of "health" should be evident. This section examines three conceptions and their implications for communication research and practice: health as biological (i.e., a question of survival), health as biopsychosocial (i.e., a question of systemic integration), and health as ontological (i.e., a question of meaningful integration—that is, of *being* itself).

It is argued that the first two conceptions share a common limitation that renders them inadequate. That is, each maintains an *ontic* (Heidegger, 1962) orientation toward understanding and managing problems with health. In other words, each respectively emphasizes an *ontology* that merely inquires into the "what and why" of "reality" (Deetz, 1978). In the case of the biomedical model, the concern is with the what and why of biological function and modes of repair. Reformed biomedical *practice* places additional emphasis on the what and why of satisfactory care and effective patient education and persuasion. And, finally, the biopsychosocial model calls attention to the what and why of biochemical and behavioral mediation between mental and biological states.

Through incorporation of Heidegger's formulation of a fundamental ontology (i.e., explication of the meaning of Being), a truly holistic conception of ontological health is provided, which subordinates the ontic understanding of health developed in the prior models to the more encompassing project of securing authentic, meaningful existence. While the role of communication expands in necessary and significant directions within the biopsychosocial model, conceiving health as ontological requires a *quantum* leap forward in our thought and research.

The Biomedical Model and Bodily Health

Though widely criticized and less evident today in a "pure" form, the biomedical conception of health focuses solely on normative biological function. The validity of this conception rests on Cartesian dualism, which allows medicine to render the body an objective mechanism, shorn of the subjective vagaries of individual experience. Anchored by assumptions of ontological realism, biomedical science aims to discover the universal laws that organize and determine the desubjectified body. The corpus of knowledge generated thereby revolves around the understanding of normative physiological functioning, development of systematic and thorough nosologies of dysfunctional states, and determination of clinical interventions capable of physical reparation. The model is inherently instrumental, reducing the body to a site for regimen and control, without which health can be neither sustained nor restored (Freund, 1982).

Clinical medical practice derived from this conceptual model "naturally" emphasizes the symptomatic language of the body with which medical practitioners converse via the conceptual and theoretical frameworks of the physical sciences, aided by increasingly sophisticated diagnostic equipment. This technical dialogue is seen as the most efficient and accurate method for assessing physical dysfunction and guiding therapeutic choice. Consequently, the model fosters a habit of speaking past the patient to his or her body. Further, inasmuch as the existential complexity and concerns of the patient are viewed as tangential, the model is inherently *disease-based*. This formal exclusion of the patient's illness experience also promotes *doctor-centered* care by privileging the practitioner's superior technical expertise concerning bodily function (Levenstein et al., 1989; Smith & Pettegrew, 1986). The ideal patient in traditional biomedical practice is thus passive and compliant, one whose responsibilities are primarily those of seeking appropriate medical assistance as needed and complying with recommended therapies.

Clearly, the role accorded communication in this model is extremely limited (Smith & Pettegrew, 1986). It is conceived as a conduit through which a *minimal* amount of health-related information (e.g., patient symptoms) and directives (e.g., prescribed therapies) are passed for purposes of maintaining and repairing biological health. Because medical knowledge is derived through rigorous science (i.e., nonlinguistically), and greater value is accorded the "voice" of the body, verbal communication is at most the quiet handmaiden through which treatment proceeds.

Criticism

Traditional biomedical practice has been soundly castigated as both "de-humanizing" and out of step with the changing needs and concerns of its clients (Engel, 1977; McWhinney, 1989; Smith & Pettegrew, 1986). In particular, critics have taken issue with medical paternalism, clinical formality, overreliance on technology, and emphasis on cure over care. The latter in particular fails to recognize the importance of preventative behaviors as well as the more complex needs of the chronically ill. These faults within biomedicine have been particularly tied to increased consumer dissatisfaction with medical care, high levels of noncompliance (Miller, 1975), and reliance on alternative healers (Eisenberg et al., 1993). Although these "problems" provide an impetus for creating the biopsychosocial model (see below), it is instructive to realize that their resolution in no way requires such "elaborate" response.

In short, the brunt of criticism has been directed toward biomedical *practice*, leaving untouched its construal of the objective body. Although scientific training inherently tends to foster a detached clinical gaze, and medical education has often stressed the need to maintain clinical distance, issues of application are distinct from issues of biomedical truth. Thus negative dimensions of biomedical practice can be justifiably rendered as either an unintended side effect or a misguided, overly-zealous scientific attitude, either of which may be reformed *without* reformulating health itself. That is, though significant changes in practice appear necessary, these are largely surface level, centering on *stylistic* dimensions of care. Correcting these problems merely requires the acquisition of skills necessary to foster therapeutic relationships and provide effective patient education and health promotion. This perceived need makes communication scholars natural allies in the medical community's efforts to retool practitioners. Though still perceived as a conduit, such reformed biomedical practice accords communication greater significance and legitimacy by virtue of its capacity to facilitate effective, satisfactory care.

Incorporation of these changes within current medical practice has typically been claimed as the natural outgrowth of the biopsychosocial conception of health (McWhinney, 1989). As shown here, however, their implementation does *not* require a new conception of health. This recognition foreshadows the primary limitation of the biopsychosocial model—retention of the presumption of biological primacy.

The Biopsychosocial Turn Toward
"Holistic" Health

As noted above, the biopsychosocial (BPS) model (Engel, 1977, 1979, 1982) is designed to correct for the inherent reductionism of biomedical medicine. Toward this end, individual health is reconceived as the systemic integration of biological, psychological, and social forces (i.e., "psychobiological unity"). In formulating the model, Engel (1977) envisions a revised medical practice that is not only more humane but more effective as well.[6]

The argument for greater effectiveness derives from two related but distinct forms of causality not *explicitly* incorporated within the biomedical model: the material existence of biochemical pathways between mind and body, and the effect of psychological, social, and cultural variables on personal health behaviors. Only the first, however, presents an alteration in health per se. The argument is premised on research in neuroendocrinology showing the role of hormones in the development of physical ailments such as heart disease, hypertension, and ulcers (Freund, 1982). Hormones have also been linked to suppression of the body's immune system, thereby increasing susceptibility to a host of other diseases (Jemmott & Locke, 1984; Kaplan, 1991). Various forms of alternative medicine (i.e., mental imaging, hypnosis, and laughter therapy) suggest additional, though more vaguely specified, possibilities of relationships between mental and physical states (Gillick, 1985). Although supporting research remains tentative and controversial (Angell, 1985), the growing field of psychoneuroimmunology and the recent establishment of the Office for the Study of Unconventional Medical Practices by the National Institutes of Health appear likely to advance our understanding of both conventional and alternative forms of mind-body connection. As the existence and function of these pathways becomes clarified, medical competence will require attention to psychosocial issues to a much greater extent than at present.[7]

The second and more accepted route focuses on the indirect relationship between psychosocial variables and physical health. As such, it affirms biomedical understanding of the objective body and is *not* a reconceptualization of health. The argument here draws from a significant body of research supporting the influence of psychosocial variables on a variety of health-related outcomes (e.g., when individuals will view themselves—and/or come to be seen by others—as sick, what forms of advice will be sought, and levels of compliance with therapeutic recommendations). Particular attention has focused on the manner in which patients' self-perceptions and "commonsense" theories of disease etiology (Gillick, 1985) shape their behavior, often in ways that contravene medical recommendations. The former has produced a vast body of research emphasizing the importance of such personal constructs as self-efficacy (Bandura, 1977) and locus of control (Rotter, 1966); the latter has produced an awareness of the influence of patients' pseudoscientific (and therefore largely "erroneous") explanatory models of disease and the factors informing these models (e.g., ethnicity, culture, education, gender, and socioeconomic status; Ballard-Reisch, 1990; Gillick, 1985; Kleinman, 1988; Sharf, 1990). On the strength of such influence alone, a sound case is made for psychosocial medicine; we need not wait for further evidence of direct effects on health of biochemical pathways. Forthcoming evidence for the latter will merely strengthen the argument.

Overall, the BPS model's principal advance over the biomedical is its wider ontological (or, more truly, its *ontic*) concern with the material effects of psychosocial experience on biological function. As such, health is reconceived as adequate systemic integration. In the wake of disintegration, it is not enough merely to "cure" (i.e., reintegrate bodily function); rather, one requires "healing" (i.e., reintegration of body and self). As rendered by numerous researchers (most notably Brody, 1987; Charmaz, 1991; Kleinman, 1988), the distinction between curing and healing is the difference between biology and biography. Put briefly, these researchers address the significance of individual illness narratives for purposes of reorienting the self in the wake of systemic dysfunction. Though theoretically applicable to *all* disruptions, such research has centered on chronic and/or terminal conditions, which are by definition incurable.[8] Thus a curative emphasis gives way to care, and attention turns to facilitating self-narratives that make sense of biographical turning points represented by underlying dysfunctions. To paraphrase a quote attributed to Howard Brody (J. Foglio, personal communication, 1992), patients come to medical encounters saying, "Doctor, I'm sick," and asking, "Can you heal my story?"

The complex requirements of narrative healing are more fully appreciated by distinguishing between three traditionally synonymous concepts in accord with the biopsychosocial model (i.e., disease, illness, and sickness; Friedson, 1970; Kleinman, 1988). *Disease* is retained as the common referent for biological disruptions; *illness* is applied to the process of individual interpretation and response to dysfunctional states; and *sickness* refers to sociocultural perceptions of and responses to persons experiencing some level of dysfunction.

While a normative state of health presumes the adequate integration of body, self, and society, disintegration creates a complex problem (Robinson, 1990). It is possible, and tempting, to understand dysfunction as principally an *in*adequate integration across the three levels of experience. That is, ideally, biological dysfunction means that a disease is present, that individuals perceive and respond to this fact, and that others share and reinforce (i.e., co-construct) such response as appropriate through both direct social interaction and mediated cultural messages. As Kleinman (1988) points out, however—and as has been clearly evidenced by the highly charged debates concerning the nature and meaning of, as well as appropriate reactions to, HIV infection (Shilts, 1986; Sontag, 1989)—disease, illness, and sickness are

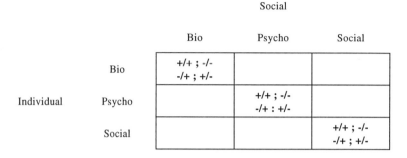

Figure 1. An intersubjective model of health.

far from necessarily integrated. Neither are they inherently copresent: One may be diseased without personal or social awareness of this state (e.g., an untested, asymptomatic HIV-positive individual), may perceive oneself as ill without any underlying disease or social recognition (e.g., the "worried well" with respect to AIDS), or may be seen by others to be diseased and/or ill without personally perceiving this (e.g., homosexuality perceived as biological or mental aberration). The problem of understanding dysfunction and determining appropriate response becomes thus a matter of socially negotiated consensus about the existence and etiology of a disintegrated systemic state (see Figure 1). As the model presented here is discussed in greater detail below, it will suffice to note that various forms of intersubjective agreement and disagreement may occur within as well as across the three levels of experience. As such, the model represents the basic agenda around which discourse and interaction proceed.

The implications of these insights for medical practice are significant (McWhinney, 1989). Specifically, it is now *requisite* that physicians elicit far greater information from patients than reports of physical symptoms, including their explanatory models (and attendant fears or concerns) and self-perception as well as valued activities or social requirements that may be impeded by, and therefore lower compliance with, certain forms of treatment. These issues amount to a patient "agenda," which may or may not be consistent with the physician's. Medical care thereby becomes a matter of *mutual negotiation* rather than a one-way, physician-directed exchange (Ballard-Reisch, 1990). This form of medical care has been alternatively construed as a *contractual* model (wherein both parties engage in explicit negotiation of actions and expectations) and a *covenant* model (which seeks to correct for the legalistic connotations of the former by emphasizing the importance of relational commitment and concern; Garrett, Baille, & Garrett, 1989). Medical providers are thus called upon to understand disease not in a decontextualized fashion but as it appears within the web of a patient's life. Attention to the "voice" of the body is balanced with attention to the voice of the patient. It is on *this* basis that the BPS model has been advocated and embraced as a means of rehumanizing medicine (McWhinney, 1989; Smith & Pettegrew, 1986).

As part of this rehumanizing drive, the BPS model also undermines the exclusive right of medicine to effect healing, opening the process to a wider interplay of significant (i.e., spouse, family, friends) and societal (e.g., counselors, chaplains, social workers) others. Medical professionals' expertise concerning normative biological function remains a variously relevant component of healing but is rendered one voice among many. Though the medical community will continue to urge that people heed that voice, it remains the case that people will, for reasons both sound and questionable to medical professionals, act within this multiplicity of voices.

Criticism

The BPS model has also opened medical practice more fully to the scrutiny and participation of humanistic (Pellegrino, 1979; Pellegrino & Thomasma, 1981) and social scientific (Eisenberg & Kleinman, 1981) disciplines. As noted earlier, the knowledge developed in these disciplines has been increasingly recognized as a necessary complement for biomedical competence (Engel, 1979; Pellegrino & Thomasma, 1981). While much of this "extramedical" research shares with health communication the aim of enhancing health care, researchers in other disciplines have more strongly defended the need to maintain an independent, critical stance (particularly Armstrong, 1987; see also Conrad & McGuire, 1981; Freund & McGuire, 1991; Gerhardt, 1989; Helman, 1990; Taussig, 1992). In this respect, they have done much more than we to emphasize the constructed nature not only of means and methods of care delivery (Conrad & Schneider, 1981; Freidson, 1981; Starr, 1982) but of human dysfunction as well (Baron, 1985; Laing, 1967; Mishler, 1981; Szasz, 1961). In short, the "objective" classifications of disease, illness, and sickness presumed within the BPS model are more accurately historical (thus arbitrary and political) constructions. This is not to deny that very real material outcomes (both positive and negative) are associated with such classifications. Indeed, it is this concrete effect that provides the impetus for an ongoing critical dialogue.

For all its improvements of medical practice, the failure of the BPS model to acknowledge the sociohistorical basis of "dysfunction" limits its value. Its substantive change in the conception of health (i.e., the mechanistic causality of biochemical links between mind and body) remains concerned with the objective body. Whether the emphasis is on the biochemical or the behavioral mind-body relationships (or both), the inclusion of psychosocial variables is justified largely on the basis of their impact on the object body. As such, the BPS conception of health actually provides the means to *further* the reach of biological concern into our lives by promoting a social engineering mentality both individually and collectively. Clearly, such a claim requires more explicit justification.

Engel (1973) directly denies that his aim is to overturn the biomedical model, arguing instead that we "retain what time has shown to be sound: the strength and vitality of the existing biomedical research and teaching. We must develop and add to this what has been missing: competent teaching and research in the psychosocial aspects of medicine" (p. 592). To overcome the traditional skepticism and quick dismissal of psychosocial medicine as "soft," as well as to meet professional and legal requirements of competency, scientific empiricism is retained as the method of choice for establishing the reality of biochemical and behavioral links between mind and body. To be sure, the securing of such evidence *is* necessary to the development of BPS medical practice. In the shuffle, however, the richness of the patient's voice gets reduced to a numerical abstraction, emasculating its wider value and importance.

More problematic is Engel's (1977) "resolution" of Cartesian dualism. In effect, reliance on systems theory does not resolve this dualism—rather, it provides a more complex dualism through emphasis on circular causality. While researchers and practitioners informed by a systems view of health may seek to pass back and forth with greater care and attention, they retain a language and sensibility that continues to hold humans now as body/now as mind in a more or less unsuccessful dialectical balance. Moreover, given that biological function is affirmed as the foundation of health, the BPS conception of health contains the potential to make the self a prisoner of the body as opposed to recognizing their mutual interest (Gadow, 1982).

This concern can be clarified by way of the increase in psychosocial education and training within medical education (Stewart & Roter, 1989). In particular, attention has focused on teaching the importance of patient beliefs and feelings about medical problems (Frankel & Beckman, 1989; Weston & Brown, 1989), and developing skills for eliciting such information during medical interviews (Cox, 1989; Katon & Kleinman, 1981). Such efforts still, however, take a backseat to the primary goal of developing biomedical competence (Smith & Pettegrew, 1986). As such, there is a temptation to reduce psychosocial variables to points of likely resistance that competent physicians must manage in order to achieve effective treatment. To secure appropriate patient behavior (i.e., compliance with medical recommendations), it is recommended that physicians diagnose and treat "dysfunctional" beliefs and attitudes held by patients, as well as the social situations in which they are embedded, that obstruct or impede medical treatment (Stewart & Roter, 1989).[9]

In such fashion, the biomedical commitment to biology remains the foundation of health care; *psychosocial* merely replaces *mind,* and dualism remains, though masked by the language of systems theory. This allows for— even leads us to—fall short of a truly holistic conception of ourselves, wherein concern for biological health and longevity is effectively tempered by concern for the *meaningfulness* of life. Although efforts to provide a balance between quality and quantity of life have increased (e.g., living wills, the Patient Bill of Rights, the Patient Self-Determination Act), the fact of our biological mortality continues to tip the balance toward extending life as long as possible. To the extent that psychosocial insights are applied within this assumptive field, it can be legitimately criticized as a means for co-opting the inherently "irrational" resistance of patients to the scientifically valid wisdom of medicine without sacrificing (and very likely *enhancing*) patient satisfaction in the process.

Such application of psychosocial knowledge clearly widens the scope and reach of medicine into our lives, suggesting the further medicalization of human experience (Illich, 1976; Taussig, 1992; Zaner, 1983). Rather than necessarily establishing a more humanistic appreciation for the complex project of human life, the BPS model thus provides the means whereby the lifeworld may be colonized (Habermas, 1987) for the sake of biological health. That is, the implication is that one needs to engineer a self—to enact a life—that is conducive to physical health and survival. To the extent that individuals who disregard preventative recommendations and develop costly impairments affect us all through increased insurance premiums and medical costs, the "need" to influence behavior through social pressure, even to the point of legal compulsion, is raised (Salmon, 1989).[10]

This attitude was cogently expressed in President Bush's remarks to the San Diego Rotary club in February 1992 (Jehl, 1992): "He suggested that health care costs to government and individuals would plummet if Americans would just take better care of themselves. 'If you exercise and eat right and don't smoke or abuse drugs and drink less, . . . you will live longer and Americans will live better' " (p. A18). This is by no means one person's opinion; it is the medical mantra with respect to preventive health behaviors (Angell, 1985; Salmon, 1989). Clearly, such logic ignores the presence of environmental stressors and social inequities that impede compliance as well as diverting criticism from communal inaction to "irresponsible" individual behavior. But more significant is the privileging of economic criteria as *the* standard by which to evaluate personal behavior, denying any wider existential benefit or worth derived from these (biologically) "unhealthy" habits.

Furthermore, while compliance reduces the likelihood of dying from such leading killers as cancer and heart disease, it no more ensures health and longevity than it would, in and of itself, reign in the explosive costs of health care. Sorting through the more nuanced and widely divergent opinions concerning what is and is not healthy with respect to diet and exercise could well consume our full attention (and *life*) without producing the desired biological effect (Becker, 1986; Giddens, 1991). And, regardless, the *quality* of life sustained thereby stands in need of critical examination and reflection.

That we all desire a long life is generally a safe, but by no means certain, assumption. To the extent that longevity comes at the expense of a "fully lived" experience or is seen to merely prolong undesirable states of being, the value of life's quantity diminishes. Ideally, our understanding (both "subjective" and "objective") of the body, and of the impact of life events and personal behaviors on bodily health, should allow us to strive for an appropriate balance between quantity and quality. But this understanding will never be complete, bounded as it is by upper limits of cultural, professional, and personal knowledge and willingness or ability to adhere to specific recommendations. Within these constraints, individual balance is always a unique accomplishment, enacted on a field of personal needs and desires interpenetrated by the needs and desires of others.

The vital issue is that we not foreclose personal choice more than absolutely necessary in light of legitimate societal concerns and despite the very real material outcomes (e.g., fiscal costs, disability, death) that attend particular choices. As active participants in the arena of health, communication researchers are obligated to maintain the integrity of this choice, striving to facilitate balance between not only the interests of patients and physicians but also the wider society wherein health behaviors, decisions, and effects play out. As such, our role is not necessarily—but neither does it preclude—the provision of specific solutions. Rather, we must seek to promote the ability of all voices and perspectives to be heard (Habermas, 1987). Our uppermost concern should be the elaboration of the greatest range of possibilities to which we may, as humans, aspire.

We fail to meet this obligation—sell ourselves and those we would assist far too short—if we settle for merely improving and extending medical care delivery. Even setting aside the important fact that not all dysfunction is biological (Cross National Collaborative Group, 1992), all medical care is not curative, or effective, for all people, and all treatment carries side effects that may outweigh benefits when assessed on the quality-quantity continuum. This is not to imply that we have pretended otherwise but merely to underscore our need to be coparticipants in health care, aligned with the "beneficent" interests of practitioners (theological and psychological as well as medical) but capable of assuming a critical stance toward their presumptions and practices and the ways of life promoted thereby.

While a *balanced* application of the BPS model *can* provide the basis for a wider research agenda, the limitations presented here suggest the need for a more secure and substantive position. To effectively conceive of individuals not as alternatively physical, psychological, and/or social beings but as all these at any and every instance, we must be more cognizant of the existential constraints and possibilities of ourselves as embodied beings. The remainder of this essay is devoted to articulating a framework for shaping health communication research around the wider ontological project that is the specific challenge of being human.

THE PHENOMENOLOGICAL EXTENSION AND ONTOLOGICAL HEALTH[11]

The ultimate value of the proposed framework derives from the effectiveness with which phenomenology cuts through the Gordian knot of Cartesian dualism through recognition of the intentional nature of all consciousness. Of greater interest, however, is the work of existential phenomenologists. This section explores the implications for health of Heidegger's (1962) distinction between ontic and ontological science, and his explication of the nature and modes of being-in-the-world. Gadamer's (1992) work on hermeneutics is used to extend Heidegger's work in support of the argument for ontological health, which replaces the presumption of biological primacy with a focus on authentic existence. As such, biography supersedes biology, requiring greater appreciation of the narrative unfolding and recounting of one's life. In this regard, Erik Erikson's (1963, 1968) epigenetic theory of psychosocial development is presented as a generic structural prototype for conceiving the lifelong pursuit of authentic existence.

The first order of business is to clarify the earlier charge that prevailing models of health have foundered on a merely ontic orientation. Heidegger (1962) categorizes as such any science that assays the nature of and relations between beings without raising the question of their Being as such. In presupposing this question, ontic sciences, however technically capable of advancing knowledge of causal relationships, are grounded in ignorance.[12] Furthermore, the tendency of these sciences to render human beings (i.e., *Dasein*) as simply one being among many fails to acknowledge the fact that Dasein is that being alone that concerns itself with its being as well as the being of other entities. It is left to phenomenology therefore to raise and address the question of Being as such, a project Heidegger (1962) conceives as a fundamental ontology. The first step in this project is an existential analytic of Dasein.

This analytic establishes three fundamental characteristics of Dasein's temporal being (Krell, 1977): "facticity" (i.e., historical being that is "thrown" into a world of significance), "existentiality" (i.e., being oriented toward a future of possibilities), and "ensnarement" (i.e., being caught up in the concerns and issues of the present). The particular threat to which Heidegger (1962) alerts us is the omnipresent tendency and temptation to live inauthentically, that is, in accord with the "dictatorship" of mass opinion that shapes one's choice of being-in-the-world. To live thus is to experience but a derivative world provided by an unquestioned, unappropriated tradition. To live authentically, Heidegger argues, is to (a) freely choose the situations in which we find ourselves (i.e., accept our "thrownness"), (b) possess authentic (i.e., personally derived) understanding of these situations, and (c) express this understanding in authentic language (Stewart & Mickunas, 1974). For Heidegger, authentic living (i.e., "being-in-truth") is *the* project of human existence. Inasmuch as we begin life inauthentically, relying on others to provide us with initial representations of meaning as well as material and emotional sustenance, authentic existence must be wrested from the grip of historicity. Further, there is never a point at which we may be said to have finally and fully achieved authenticity; rather, Dasein must constantly protect itself from the temptation to "fall" (i.e., descend) into taken-for-granted commonness.

This pursuit of authenticity requires the ability to uncover our world and our being through hermeneutical reflection. Gadamer's (1992) work on the interpretation of language is especially helpful in this respect. In particular, he provides a positive valuation of prejudice, which he conceives as the base of presuppositional knowledge (i.e., tradition), which is the only means whereby we can understand the world into which we are thrown. Without such prejudice, the world would be meaningless. Thus the inauthentic understanding with which we begin life provides us with a "historically effective consciousness" [13] (Wallis, 1991) that alone enables us to pursue authentic being.

Prejudice is not, however, infallible; its rendering of the world is always partial (i.e., perspectival) and thus inadequate in the face of experience. It becomes inhibiting therefore to the extent that we fix upon specific sedimented perceptions and close ourselves against the instruction of experience, refusing to recognize or be altered by it. It is only through openness to the clash of experience that we realize the inadequacies of our current prejudices through the appearance of other prejudicial possibilities (Deetz, 1978). This openness provides for the continuing evolution of prejudice, though of a circular form rather than advancing toward a final aperspectival understanding. In short, Gadamer (1992; as Heidegger before him) conceives human understanding as a hermeneutic circle whereby the authenticity of our being-in-the-world is constantly being reclaimed (without final success) from the pull of the common.

Gadamer's (1992) notion of understanding differs sharply from that normally invoked in communication research (Deetz, 1978). That is, he does not picture it as a translation of intentional states across the gulf between two autonomous subjects but as the communal development of new insights. Understanding is thus not about "putting oneself forward and successfully asserting one's point of view, but being transformed into a communion in which we do not remain what we were" (Gadamer, 1992, p. 379). In this respect, being is always ahead of itself, always a being-becoming, speaking and revealing more than it "knows" or "intends." Our understanding of self and the world is thus ever unfolding through interaction with the other beings, both animate and inanimate, that share our world.

A final characteristic of Gadamer's (1992) conception of understanding is that it is inherently linguistic. In accord with Husserl's noetic-noematic structure, he argues that language is not just one of man's possessions in the world; on it depends the fact that man has a world at all . . . language has no independent life apart from the world that comes to language within it. Not only is the world "world" only insofar as it comes into language, but language, too, has its real being only in the fact that the world is presented in it. Thus, that language is originally human means at the same time that man's being-in-the-world is primordially linguistic. (p. 443)

The immediate importance of the phenomenological work of Heidegger and Gadamer with respect to health is twofold. First, Gadamer (1992) enables us to understand conceptions of health as "prejudicial" (i.e., derived through and informed by tradition). As such, he provides the basis for ongoing critique of the sociohistorical conceptions of "dysfunctional" states, which may be more reified than real (Armstrong, 1987). Second, Heidegger's (1962) elaboration of Dasein's pursuit of authenticity enables us to temper concern over systemic dysfunction within the wider ontological project of existence. We may thus acknowledge our biological mortality but refrain from undue emphasis on it. In short, the notion of authenticity provides the necessary weight with which quality concerns can balance quantity concerns.

This position is anchored firmly in the phenomenological emphasis on the primordial nature of lived-body experience:

Whether it is a question of another's body or my own, I have no means of knowing the human body other than that of living it, which means taking up on my own account the drama which is being played out in it, and losing myself in it. I am my body, at least wholly to the extent that I possess experience, and yet at the same time my body is as it were a "natural" subject, a provisional sketch of my total being. Thus experience of one's own body runs counter to the reflective procedure which detaches subject and object from each other, and which gives us only the thought about the body, or the body as an idea, and not the experience of the body or the body in reality. (Merleau-Ponty, 1992, pp. 198-199)

Being-in-the-world is thus *being-embodied*. Our experience of the world arises first and foremost within the prereflective unity of body and self in lived experience. Embodiment thus precedes the more narrowly construed "body as idea (i.e., object)" that we find in both medical models. As such, the question of the *meaning* of our being is not merely *a* concern—it is *the* concern. Although the BPS model addresses the mental and social experience of the self in relation to dysfunction, it does not explicitly raise the question of what it is that being (i.e., Dasein) wishes to be. In this failure resides the concern that the application of BPS insights may actually advance the medicalization of the lifeworld. This threat can be countered effectively only to the extent that we occupy the phenomenological clearing. That is, only by making the meaning of being our central concern can we resist the logical force of social engineering. Only thus can biological interests be reduced to a necessary but insufficient constituent element of our individual and collective answers to the question of meaning.

We are now in a position to advance a definition of ontological health: the meaningful (i.e., authentic) embodiment of biological, psychological, and social experience (Pellegrino & Thomasma, 1981).[14] While knowledge as generated by the various ontic sciences (e.g., biology, chemistry, psychology, sociology, anthropology) of each of these levels of experience remains important, it is secondary to the pursuit of authentic being-in-the-world. In such a conception, communication is recognized as the means whereby we consciously understand, assess, and pursue authentic integration. This is not to argue that systemic integration occurs solely through communication; no attempt is made to claim the status of communication for nerve impulses, hormones, and other forms of physiological regulation. The argument is, rather, that, in our constant immersion in the lived world, we are varyingly attuned to biological and social messages that alternatively alert and assure us about the adequacy of our being. To be in a normal state of health means that our integration is adequate enough to recede into the background, forming the presumptive field upon which we pursue transbodily and transpersonal purposes (Pellegrino, 1979).

While the experience of felt stress and bodily aches or pains signal integrational strain, it is only in the wake of significant ontological rupture that we become fully aware of the tenuousness with which ourselves and our world are bound. Such rupture—whether occurring in ourselves or in significant others with and around whom we have built our lives, whether perceived to be physical or psychological in origin—throws into relief and potentially invalidates the habitual patterns and meaning of our existence.[15] In the case of acute ruptures, we may reasonably expect to resume our prior state of being after a time of treatment and recuperation.[16] For ruptures that obstruct such return (e.g., chronic or terminal illness), we face the task of adapting our being-in-the-world to new constraints. Ontological health for the chronically ill is available through development of a new normative integration that is acceptable to the individual whose being thereby incorporates an obstinate material condition.[17] A perceived inability to maintain or pursue an authentic life following a permanent dysfunction, however, may well erase one's desire to live (Brody, 1987). Ontological health for the terminally ill, however paradoxical sounding, may be attained through orienting toward death in an authentic, personally meaningful manner. This may vary from a stark refusal to go "gentle into that good night" to a calm acceptance (Kubler-Ross, 1969). Even in death, the pursuit of authenticity promotes resistance to attempts to "normalize" or "script" experience (Feigenberg, 1980).

The centrality of the meaning of being in ontological health shifts attention from biology to biography at the individual level (and in a much more complete manner than within the BPS model) and from science to cultural history on the collective level. As an individual, my "life plan" (Brody, 1987) provides direction for my life, providing for a contextual interpretation of my past, present, and future states of existence. That is, the being that I currently am is construed narratively upon the ground provided by my lived history and my anticipation of to-be-lived possibilities. This is, however, no solipsistic endeavor. Rather, I take up possibilities through membership in a social community where I assume various roles and engage in relevant behaviors that commit me to be that which I am by virtue of such performances. My available options, however, are limited in numerous ways, not the least of which is my birth to a specific set of parents within a specific community and culture at a specific time in human history. Thus my individual biography is written within a cultural horizon that constrains my choices even as it provides the frame that makes those choices both possible and meaningful (Gergen & Davis, 1985).

In addition to providing me with a delimited set of possibilities upon which my ontological formation occurs, those whom I value, and the culture within which we communally reside, provide me with numerous *evaluative* responses that shape my choice among those possibilities, affirming or disconfirming the "rightness" and "worthiness" of the ontological project in which I am engaged, the being that I am becoming. With respect to ontological ruptures, I rely on input from others to aid in my interpretation of and response toward the impairment. In the event of chronic or terminal impairment, I rely on others in reorienting my being toward projects that remain both *possible*—within reach of my newly constrained grasp—and *worthwhile* (Brody, 1987; Kleinman, 1988; Lyman, 1990; Richardson, 1990).

To better understand the development, maintenance, and adaptation of ontological health in relation to biological, psychological, and social contingencies, it is useful to turn to theories of human development. While numerous theories have been developed, Erik Erikson's (1963, 1968) epigenetic theory of psychosocial development is particularly relevant. Specifically, his elaboration of "normative life crises" allows us to situate "nonnormative" systemic dysfunction within a process of "normal" ontological development. Erikson (1968) formulates eight normative crises, each representing a struggle to achieve a balance between qualities of polar opposition (i.e., trust versus mistrust, autonomy versus shame/doubt, initiative versus guilt, industriousness versus inferiority, identity cohesion versus role confusion, intimacy versus isolation, generativity versus stagnation, and integrity versus despair). Each stage is viewed as a key turning point in individual development. Erikson (1968) argues that successful resolution of each crisis facilitates further growth through the development of the virtues (i.e., hope, will, purpose, competence, fidelity, love, care, and wisdom) necessary to meet the unique challenges of later life stages. Conversely, unsuccessful resolution (i.e., adoption of one polar extreme) within a given stage is argued to impede the further development of a healthy, integrated personality.

The postmodernist impulse is to dismiss such a theory as merely a masculine, politically-oriented, ethnocentric attempt to constrain individual possibilities of being through pursuit of a unitary construction of developmental experience. Erikson (1963), however, emphatically rejects any attempt to regard his theory as a prescription for development. As well, Erikson leaves room for individual and cultural variation with respect to the manner in which the normative crises are encountered and resolved. As such, Erikson's "stages" are better viewed as a series of questions to which individuals respond over the course of their existence, crafting thereby a biographical account of their being-in-the-world. In addition, empirical research suggests that the issues involved in the various "stages" may be addressed at any point in life rather than in a necessary sequence or at a specific age (Whitbourne, Zuschlag, Elliot, & Waterman, 1992) and that their "resolution" is not necessarily "final" (Novak, 1985-1986).

Despite additional, pertinent feminist criticism,[18] the value of a basic framework for ordering the life course warrants revision rather than rejection. The inherent limitations of our prejudicial understanding are, after all, fodder for the hermeneutic conversation within which we are all always engaged. The importance of theories of human development is not the extent to which they "get things right" but the extent to which they provide a means of organizing our experience, even if only as something that we resist. The ultimate worth of Erikson's theory (or any other developmental theory), particularly in relation to ontological health, is the extent to which it facilitates our pursuit of authentic being.

Before explicitly drawing the implications of ontological health for health communication research, one further issue of importance must be noted. That is, when conceived within Dasein's wider ontological project, biologically negative behaviors (e.g., drinking, smoking) may actually serve a *positive* function. Rather than merely being behaviors one enjoys for the pleasure or experience derived thereby (though such is not to be lightly dismissed), such behavior may actually *advance* one's ontological project: Alcohol may allow the shy individual to overcome inhibition that limits his or her social interaction; a cigarette break may provide the overly-stressed individual the strength to meet situational demands. The point is that *all* behaviors possess ontological value, a fact that is typically overlooked in the promotion of preventive health behavior. Of course, many biologically negative behaviors are an inauthentic response to peer pressure and media messages. Furthermore, conscious behavioral choices may become inauthentic (i.e., habituated) and persist long after their specific ontological function passes (e.g., the shy individual may overcome his or her self-consciousness but persist in an excessive use of alcohol).

Nonetheless, recognition of the ontological value of behaviors requires: (a) that we accept that individuals do not merely behave in order to stay alive, (b) that we be realistic about what we can expect from health education campaigns, and, most important, (c) that we be fully aware of what we are asking of, and attempting to do to or with, individuals targeted by such campaigns—nothing less than the engineering of identity and experience on the basis of normative models of predominantly biological health.

A NEW DEFINITION OF
HEALTH COMMUNICATION

It has been argued that health is best conceived from a truly ontological stance. Inasmuch as one's being-in-the-world is developed and maintained through both *intra-* and *inter*subjective processes, ontological health is a substantively communicative/linguistic accomplishment. In contrast to an ancillary role, communication lies in the very midst of health and illness, providing constitutive as well as instrumental force. Rather than serving merely as a conduit for the passage of "objective" knowledge and intentional states, communication is *the* means whereby we pursue authenticity, whereby we construct our world and our being-in-the-world. In this regard, communication possesses literal therapeutic value. In short, therapy becomes disabused of its predominant connotations of pharmacology, surgery, and behavioral modification, expanding to a meaningful incorporation of music, art, literature, dialogue—and even, if we perform our task well, scholarly articles.

Health communication is thus more appropriately defined as *the study of personal and sociocultural symbol usage for purposes of developing, maintaining, and adapting ontological health.* While ontological disruption may originate primarily from physical or psychosocial dysfunction, emphasis remains on the unity of lived-body experience. As such, we may still distinguish heart attacks from anxiety attacks without denigrating the lived experience of either or both events.

Returning to the model presented in Figure 1, a more complete agenda may now be established for health communication research. As noted above, intersubjective agreement and disagreement occur within and across biological, psychological, and social levels of experience. Negotiation for purposes of coordination occurs with respect to three fundamental concerns: (a) the *presence* of a particular embodied state of being (with varying degrees of integrational adequacy), (b) the *evaluation* (e.g., good/bad, functional/dysfunctional) of this state of being, and (c) the *ontological* nature of this state of being. The advantage of the proposed ontological conception of health over those presented by the biomedical and BPS models is that it is the only one to *formally* recognize the importance of all *three* concerns. The principal function of health communication research within this conception is the study and facilitation of social discussion in and around these three questions, at both administrative and constitutive levels of analysis. That is, though we will always be interested in furthering human understanding with respect to health, there should be times when our aim is merely to facilitate the application of given conceptions and others when we seek to critique existing conceptions so as to reopen or disclose unrecognized or marginalized possibilities. Only through addressing each of these concerns will we have a comprehensive, meaningful, and ethical agenda for pursuing health communication research.[19]

Clearly, the inherent promise of this expanded definition is its greatest potential weakness as well. In short, it is difficult to discern what forms and aspects of communication do not impinge upon, for good or ill, one's ontological health. For surely all situations within which we find ourselves hold the potential to destroy ontological health, although this occurs with surprising infrequency. Common instances of "losing face" that occur through embarrassing "slips" of the tongue or body, or even the more self-threatening receipt of negative social evaluation, are typically incapable of fundamentally rupturing our current state of being. To the extent that we find ourselves under a steady barrage of self-disconfirming social messages, incapable of making ourselves "at home" in interaction, or too often unsuccessful in shaping interaction toward fulfillment of personal goals and desires, however, our ontological integrity may suffer (e.g., through low self-esteem and self-efficacy). Inasmuch as all of these have been associated with the development of physiological dysfunction, as well as being potentially negative states in their own right, issues of health are clearly relevant.

The ontological conception of health thus shares the characteristic risk of overinclusion with Gregory Bateson's (1972) conception of "mind"—both threaten to be so pervasive as to elude effective understanding and management. Therefore the temptation to establish more clearly defined boundaries is great, perhaps even necessary. However, we must not sacrifice the complexity of lived experience merely for the sake of tidy research. Our highest responsibility is to participate in the ongoing recovery and dialogue through which individual and social understanding unfolds in the pursuit of authentic existence.

It is necessary to emphasize that what I have called administrative research retains its importance and value. There is still much to learn with respect to facilitating patient understanding of diagnoses, discerning the impact of interaction styles, the relationships between personal characteristics and health behavior, the components of effective and ethical health education campaigns, and so forth. But, more important, we need to understand the role of communication in constituting individual and public conceptions of health as well as the health care structures and practices through which care is managed and practiced. We need, that is, to develop better understanding of the role of communication in determining the ends of human life as well as the means.

The need to embrace this larger project with respect to health is poignantly underscored by a recent international study on rates of depression (Cross National Collaborative Group, 1992). Although the prevalence of depression increases with age, the study garnered significant attention for its finding that rates of depression were increasing among young people.[20] Moreover, "in some countries the likelihood that people born after 1955 will suffer a major depression—not just sadness, but a paralyzing listlessness, dejection and self-deprecation, as well as an overwhelming sense of hopelessness—at some point in life is more than three times greater than for their grandparents' generation" (Goleman, 1992, p. C1).

The researchers suggest a number of theories to explain these sharp increases. In general, they tie depression to a combination of psychological stress and biological vulnerability. Though some people are believed to be genetically susceptible to depression, other theories focus on characteristics of modernity: erosion of the nuclear family, ascendance of individualism, waning of larger beliefs in religion—in general, a loss of resources to facilitate coping with life crises. Higher rates of depression among women in the United States are further connected with the dual burdens of work and family and the existence of an unrealizable ideal of feminine beauty.

Underlying each of these explanations is the commonality of what we might call ontological illness. In short, while one must interpret such data with caution, it would appear that, for all its technical successes, and despite Heidegger's call for a return to the question of the meaning of Being, modern society continues to remain more capable of meeting the technical than the symbolic requirements of human existence. The temptation to soothe ontological anxiety with antidepressants (Goleman, 1992, cites a physician who assures us that such treatment is effective in 80% of depression cases) reveals the muteness of modernity with respect to meaningful existence. In this regard, it is fitting to close with the following quote by Deetz (1992):

> The present concern with "what is and why" needs to be subsumed and redirected by the joint question of "how it came about and what can it be?" The concern for the possibilities of life should not be left to the poets, planners, and politicians, but should be directly connected with those most focused on the actualities of life. The opening of life-possibilities based in and relevant to the real human condition requires a self-awareness which destroys the myth of objective consciousness and reconsiders what prejudices should be controlled. The social service of the study of communication will come, if it does, more from the creation of new forms of human relationships than the ability to control toward particular existing forms. (p. 23)

NOTES

1. Anyone familiar with medical research sociology, anthropology, and psychology will quickly realize that these charges are inapplicable outside the boundaries of the communication discipline (e.g., Freund & McGuire, 1991; Gerhardt, 1989; Helman, 1990). Researchers in these disciplines have already developed the significant critical literature missing in our own. This essay then is directed mainly toward health-related research as it has emerged within the discipline of communication. The hope is not simply to call us into the wider conversation going on outside our workshop but to foster less presumptuous and more ethically informed research.

2. Due to space limitations, I have removed a section advancing in more complete fashion the evidence for this claim. Though this creates a weakness in the current work, it is my belief that anyone familiar with the research being done in health communication will not find the claim unreasonable.

3. This perceptual choice is directed by institutional practices (i.e., tradition) and, over time, "certain perceptions become protected as common sense, with social order, legitimate knowledge, and personal identities invested in them" (Deetz, 1992, p. 116).

4. It is particularly useful for our discipline as a means for integrating the perceived rift that has historically separated social scientific and rhetorical approaches to the study of communication, erupting with sufficient regularity in a fruitless debate about which is *the* appropriate and/or most meaningful method.

It further requires scholars of all stripes to engage in a significantly different form of reflexive self-criticism than mandated by empirical-analytical science alone. That is, we must take greater responsibility for the experiences we privilege during the construction of our theories.

5. This clearly is not an exhaustive list. Many within the communication discipline have addressed the claims of critical theory and poststructuralism, both for and against. I have, however, noted here those persons who have fashioned particularly cogent interpretations of theory with implications for communication research.

6. In fact, the two cannot truly be separated given the significant relationship between satisfaction and compliance and willingness to use formal medical care for health problems (Campion, 1993).

7. Regardless of the findings, it is likely that the public, stirred by such authors as Norman Cousins (1979, 1984) and Bernie Siegel (1986, 1989), will retain significant faith in such pathways and maintain reliance on alternative forms of medicine (Barasch, 1992; Eisenberg et al., 1993).

8. While we have much to learn from the extensive research on illness narratives, it has to date failed to explicate the biographical implications of acute dysfunction. In short, existing research in illness narratives has focused on chronic illness, due to the obvious fact that one's self is forced to reformulate itself by the materiality of a persistent biological condition. We need to focus more on the larger *life* narrative, however, and recognize that even acute ailments, particularly those that are life threatening, can have a significant influence on the development of our life in the wake of such events.

9. Another significant application of BPS medicine has been the development of interdisciplinary health care teams (Cline, 1990). The aim is to produce an informative dialogue among various professionals with expertise relevant to the various dimensions of patients, ideally resulting in a holistic representation of the patient. The success of such group constructions of the patient remains unclear, however. That is, further research is required into the question of whether the holistic construction theoretically available within the team itself is internalized, or even internalizable, by individual members. To the extent that medical professionals simply or principally assign nondisease issues to other members of the team who are, after all, specialists in those areas, the desired results of holistic care are unlikely to be realized (Spitzer & Roberts, 1980; Wise, 1972). Furthermore, this attempt to grasp the complexity of systemic integration still enacts the dualism of systems theory. Moreover, from a critical perspective, such teams can be seen as a more powerful response to the perceived complexity of understanding and controlling psychosocial resistance.

10. Of course, concern that helpless patients may be led to act against their will is no more justified than similar concerns expressed in hypodermic models of mass media use; people possess marvelous reserves of resistance with which to frustrate even the most well-intentioned efforts on their behalf. Such concern is further tempered by the increasing willingness to accept quality-of-life arguments as justifiable reasons to avoid and/or suspend aggressive medical care. But the meager legal protection of patient rights to self-determination largely applies only to those in the final days of their life; hospice is available only for those within 6 months of dying; suicide remains irrational to most of us except, perhaps, among those in the grip of a painful terminal illness. The greatest danger for incursion into the lifeworld, however, lies in the emphasis on *preventive* health behaviors.

Though our libertarian tradition might otherwise secure the right of individuals to engage in biologically negative behaviors, it does not obviate the still-felt sense that such actions are, at minimum, irrational. Moreover, in the face of arguments that advance a greater public good, this tradition stands aside (Leichter, 1991; Salmon, 1989). In either case, behaviors conceived to be biologically negative are ever susceptible to social control without due regard for the ontological impact, to both the individual and the society, of such action.

11. There is already an extensive body of phenomenological analyses of health and medicine that supports the value of such a turn within health communication. In particular, the reader is referred to Kestenbaum (1982) and Pellegrino and Thomasma (1981).

12. *"All ontology, no matter how rich and tightly knit a system of categories it has at its disposal, remains fundamentally blind and perverts its innermost intent if it has not previously clarified the meaning of Being sufficiently and grasped this clarification as its fundamental task"* (Heidegger, 1962, p. 53, italics in original).

13. Wallis (1991) argues for this translation over the traditional one of "historically effect*ed* consciousness" to temper the overly deterministic tone of the latter.

14. Pellegrino and Thomasma (1981) provide a significant and important reconstruction of medical practice around phenomenological insights, which contains the basic ontological definition of health presented here. Their retention of biological primacy, however, clouds the effectiveness of their support for individuals' rights to self-determination. Without tempering the biological presumption, the logic of personal resistance to recommended medical actions remains inferior to that guiding scientific medicine. To the extent that patient resistance might persist in the face of medical pressure, such "inferior" biographical logic may yet succumb to pressure from family and friends, whose biographical selves are implicated in the existence of the patient and who therefore have a vested interest in the latter's continued survival.

15. To the extent that this confronts us with the realization of our ultimate death, we become what Heidegger (1962) refers to as "being-unto-death." As such, death "reveals itself as the *most proper, nonrelational, insurmountable possibility* of Dasein, . . . the possibility of being no longer able to be 'there' " (quoted in Krell, 1977, p. 23, italics in original).

16. It is again important to note, however, that this "return to normalcy" is not necessarily, or always, so easy as is commonly believed. Each experience in life plays its part in shaping who we have been, currently are, and will one day be and should not be downplayed simply because its direct significance cannot be immediately or fully appreciated.

17. The ability to live authentically is in no way limited by functional restrictions; paraplegics and epileptics can achieve authenticity while many "normally" functioning individuals can easily fail to do so. That is, we are "thrown" into impaired states of being in the same way we are thrown into life, and we face the same challenge of reclaiming ourselves through linguistic constructions. The case is admittedly less clear with respect to mental illness and impairment.

18. Feminist scholars have particularly criticized Erikson on a number of points: his "masculine" emphasis on individuation to the greater exclusion of the "feminine" emphasis on attachment (Gilligan, 1982), his overemphasis on the biological reproductive capacity of women (Gergen, 1990), his normative privileging of heterosexuality (Franz & White, 1985; Gergen, 1990), and his emphasis on the division of sexual activity by sex, which is too easily extended to a division of other roles by sex (i.e., household and economic roles; Franz & White, 1985). Though acknowledging these criticisms, Franz and White (1985) argue that "the major shortcoming of Erikson's theory is not, as some feminists have argued, that it is a male theory, but that it fails to account adequately for the processes of interpersonal attachment to the development of *both* males and females" (p. 224, italics added). These authors provide a two-path model of development that elaborates separate but interconnected strands of individuation and attachment. This provides a strengthened framework within which to engage the conversation of our individual and collective lives, allowing for new forms of integration, and thus being, for both women *and* men.

19. The greatest lack in this essay is the inability to develop in any meaningful sense the ethical implications of an ontological conception of health. Though implicitly pervading the full length of the work, it requires much more attention than I have been able to devote to it and requires

future clarification to secure the arguments I have advanced thus far. The interested reader, however, may refer to the works of Daniel Callahan (1990, 1987) and Howard Brody (1987) for significant presentation of the issues that are immediately relevant to an ethics of ontological health.

20. This reaction suggests the problematic acceptance that depression is part and parcel of growing old in modern society. A more humane stance would be to address the conditions that would allow the elderly to remain vitally involved in the human community rather than becoming superfluous. Of course, the growing numbers of elderly have allowed their acquisition of significant political power, but such should not be the only or primary means for involvement to offset diminishing function in later years.

REFERENCES

Adelman, M. B. (1991). Play and incongruity: Framing safe-sex talk. *Health Communication, 3*(3), 139-156.

Angell, M. (1985). Disease as a reflection of the psyche. *The New England Journal of Medicine, 326*(24), 1570-1572.

Armstrong, D. (1987). Theoretical tension in biopsychosocial medicine. *Social Science and Medicine, 25*(11), 1213-1218.

Arntson, P. (1985). Future research in health communication. *Journal of Applied Communication Research, 13*, 118-130.

Arntson, P. (1989). Improving citizen's health competencies. *Health Communication, 1*(1), 29-34.

Arntson, P., & Droge, D. (1987). Social support in self-help groups: The role of communication in enabling perceptions of control. In T. L. Albrecht & M. B. Adelman (Eds.), *Communicating social support* (pp. 148-171). Newbury Park, CA: Sage.

Atkin, C. K. (1979). Research evidence on mass mediated health communication campaigns. In D. Nimmo (Ed.), *Communication yearbook 3* (pp. 655-668). New Brunswick, NJ: Transaction.

Axley, S. (1984). Managerial and organizational communication in terms of the conduit metaphor. *Academy of Management Review, 9*, 428-437.

Ballard-Reisch, D. S. (1990). A model of participative decision making for physician-patient interaction. *Health Communication, 2*(2), 91-104.

Bandura, A. (1977). Self-efficacy: Toward a unifying theory of behavioral change. *Psychological Review, 84*, 191-215.

Barasch, D. S. (1992, October). The mainstreaming of alternative medicine. *The New York Times Magazine* (Part 2), pp. 6-9, 36, 38.

Baron, R. J. (1985). An introduction to medical phenomenology: I can't hear you while I'm listening. *Annals of Internal Medicine, 103*, 606-611.

Bateson, G. (1972). *Steps to an ecology of mind.* New York: Ballantine.

Becker, M. (1986). The tyranny of health promotion. *Public Health Reviews, 14*, 15-25.

Beniger, J. (1986). Information and communication: The new convergence. *Communication Research, 15*, 198-218.

Berger, P. L., & Luckmann, T. (1966). *The social construction of reality: A treatise in the sociology of knowledge.* New York: Anchor.

Brody, H. (1987). *Stories of sickness.* New Haven, CT: Yale University Press.

Callahan, D. (1987). *Setting limits: Medical goals in an aging society.* New York: Simon & Schuster.

Callahan, D. (1990). *What kind of life: A challenging exploration of the goals of medicine.* New York: Simon & Schuster.

Campion, E. W. (1993). Why unconventional medicine? *The New England Journal of Medicine, 328*, 281-282.

Cassata, D. M. (1978). Health communication theory and research: An overview of the communication specialist interface. In B. Ruben (Ed.), *Communication yearbook 2* (pp. 495-503). New Brunswick, NJ: Transaction.

Cassata, D. M. (1980). Health communication theory and research: A definitional overview. In D. Nimmo (Ed.), *Communication yearbook 4* (pp. 583-589). New Brunswick, NJ: Transaction.

Charmaz, K. (1991). *Good days, bad days: The self in chronic illness and time.* New Brunswick, NJ: Rutgers University Press.

Cline, R. (1990). Small group communication in health care. In E. B. Ray & L. Donohew (Eds.), *Communication and health.* Hillsdale, NJ: Lawrence Erlbaum.

Conquergood, D. (1991). Rethinking ethnography: Towards a critical cultural politics. *Communication Monographs, 58*(2), 179-194.

Conrad, P., & McGuire, M. B. (1981). *The sociology of health and illness: Critical perspectives.* New York: St. Martin.

Conrad, P., & Schneider, J. W. (1981). Professionalization, monopoly, and the structure of medical practice. In P. Conrad & R. Kern (Eds.), *The sociology of health and illness: Critical perspectives* (pp. 155-164). New York: St. Martin.

Corbin, J., & Strauss, A. (1988). *Unending work and care: Managing chronic illness at home.* San Francisco: Jossey-Bass.

Costello, D. E. (1977). Health communication theory and research: An overview. In B. Ruben (Ed.), *Communication yearbook 1* (pp. 557-567). New Brunswick, NJ: Transaction-International Communication Association.

Cousins, N. (1979). *Anatomy of an illness as perceived by the patient.* New York: Bantam.

Cousins, N. (1984). *The healing heart.* New York: Avon.

Cox, A. (1989). Eliciting patients' feelings. In M. Stewart & D. Roter (Eds.), *Communicating with medical patients* (pp. 99-106). Newbury Park, CA: Sage.

Cross National Collaborative Group. (1992). The changing rate of major depression. *JAMA, 268*(21), 3098-3105.

Deetz, S. (1978). Conceptualizing human understanding: Gadamer's hermeneutics and American communication research. *Communication Quarterly, 26,* 12-23.

Deetz, S. (1992). *Democracy in an age of corporate colonization: Developments in communication and the politics of everyday life.* Albany: State University of New York Press.

Delia, J. G., O'Keefe, B. J., & O'Keefe, D. J. (1982). The constructivist approach to communication. In F. E. X. Dance (Ed.), *Human communication theory* (pp. 147-191). New York: Harper & Row.

Dervin, B., Grossberg, L., O'Keefe, B. J., & Wartella, E. (1989). *Rethinking communication: Vol. 1. Paradigm issues.* Newbury Park, CA: Sage.

Eisenberg, D. M., Kessler, R. C., Foster, C., Norlock, F. E., Calkins, D. R., & Delbanco, T. L. (1993). Unconventional medicine in the United States: Prevalence, costs, and patterns of use. *The New England Journal Medicine, 328,* 246-252.

Eisenberg, L., & Kleinman, A. (1981). *The relevance of social science for medicine.* Dordrecht, Holland: D. Reidel.

Ellis, B. H., Miller, K. I., & Given, C. W. (1989). Caregivers in home health care situations. *Health Communication, 1*(4), 207-226.

Engel, G. L. (1973). Enduring attributes of medicine relevant for the education of physicians. *Annals of Internal Medicine, 78,* 587-593.

Engel, G. L. (1977). The need for a new medical model: A challenge for biomedicine. *Science, 196,* 129-136.

Engel, G. L. (1979). The biopsychosocial model and the education of health professionals. *Annals of the New York Academy of Sciences, 310,* 169-181.

Engel, G. L. (1982). The biopsychosocial model and medical education: Who are to be the teachers? *The New England Journal of Medicine, 306*(13), 802-805.

Erikson, E. (1963). *Childhood and society.* New York: W. Norton.

Erikson, E. (1968). *Identity: Youth and crisis*. New York: Norton.

Feigenberg, L. (1980). *Terminal care: Friendship contracts with dying cancer patients*. New York: Brunner/Mazel.

Finnegan, J. R., & Viswanath, K. (1990). Health and communication: Medical and public health influences on the research agenda. In E. B. Ray & L. Donohew (Eds.), *Communication and health* (pp. 9-24). Hillsdale, NJ: Lawrence Erlbaum.

Fisher, W. R. (1987). *Human communication as narration: Toward a philosophy of reason, value and action*. Columbia: University of South Columbia Press.

Frankel, R., & Beckman, H. (1989). Evaluating the patient's primary problem. In M. Stewart & D. Roter (Eds.), *Communicating with medical patients* (pp. 86-98). Newbury Park, CA: Sage.

Franz, C. E., & White, K. M. (1985). Individuation and attachment in personality development: Extending Erikson's theory. *Journal of Personality, 53*(2), 224-226.

Freidson, E. (1981). Professional dominance and the ordering of health services: Some consequences. In P. Conrad & R. Kern (Eds.), *The sociology of health and illness: Critical perspectives* (pp. 184-197). New York: St. Martin.

Freimuth, V. S. (1990). The chronically uninformed: Closing the knowledge gap in health. In E. B. Ray & L. Donohew (Eds.), *Communication and health: Systems and applications* (pp. 171-186). Hillsdale, NJ: Lawrence Erlbaum.

Freund, P. E. S. (1982). *The civilized body*. Philadelphia: Temple University Press.

Freund, P. E. S., & McGuire, M. B. (1991). *Health, illness, and the social body: A critical sociology*. Englewood Cliffs, NJ: Prentice-Hall.

Friedson, E. (1970). *Profession of medicine: A study of the sociology of applied knowledge*. New York: Harper & Row.

Gadamer, H. G. (1992). *Truth and method* (J. Weinsheimer & D. G. Marshall, Trans.; 2nd rev. ed.). New York: Crossroad.

Gadow, S. (1982). Body and self: A dialectic. In V. Kestenbaum (Ed.), *The humanity of the ill: Phenomenological perspectives*. Knoxville: University of Tennessee Press.

Garrett, T. M., Baille, H. W., & Garrett, R. M. (1989). *Health care ethics: Principles and problems*. Englewood Cliffs, NJ: Prentice-Hall.

Gergen, K. J., & Davis, K. E. (1985). *The social construction of the person*. New York: Springer-Verlag.

Gergen, M. M. (1990). Finished at 40: Women's development within the patriarchy. *Psychology of Women Quarterly, 14*, 471-493.

Gerhardt, U. (1989). *Ideas about illness*. New York: New York University Press.

Giddens, A. (1991). *Modernity and self-identity: Self and society in the later modern age*. Stanford, CA: Stanford University Press.

Gillick, M. R. (1985). Common-sense models of health and disease. *The New England Journal of Medicine, 313*, 700-703.

Gilligan, C. (1982). *In a different voice: Psychological theory and women's development*. Cambridge, MA: Harvard University Press.

Goleman, D. (1992, December 8). A rising cost of modernity: Depression. *The New York Times*, p. C1.

Good, B. J., & Good, M. D. (1981). The meaning of symptoms: A cultural hermeneutic model for clinical practice. In L. Eisenberg & A. Kleinman (Eds.), *The relevance of social science for medicine* (pp. 165-196). Dordrecht, Holland: D. Reidel.

Habermas, J. (1968). *Knowledge and human interests* (J. Shapiro, Trans.). Boston: Beacon.

Habermas, J. (1984). *The theory of communicative action: Vol. 1. Reason and the rationalization of society* (T. McCarthy, Trans.). Boston: Beacon.

Habermas, J. (1987). *The theory of communicative action: Vol. 2. Lifeworld and system* (T. McCarthy, Trans.). Boston: Beacon.

Heidegger, M. (1962). *Being and time* (J. MacQuarrie & E. Robinson, Trans.). New York: Harper & Row.

Helman, C. G. (1990). *Culture, health and illness* (2nd ed.). London: Wright.

Hiley, D. R., Bohman, J. F., & Shusterman, R. (1991). *The interpretive turn: Philosophy, science, culture.* Ithaca, NY: Cornell University Press.

Husserl, E. (1962). *Ideas: A general introduction to pure phenomenology* (W. R. B. Gibson, Trans.). London: Collier-Macmillan.

Hyde, M. J. (1983). Rhetorically, man dwells: On the making-known function of discourse. *Communication, 7,* 201-220.

Hyde, M. J., & Smith, C. R. (1979). Hermeneutics and rhetoric: A seen but unobserved relationship. *Quarterly Journal of Speech, 65*(4), 347-363.

Illich, I. (1976). *Medical nemesis.* New York: Pantheon.

Jehl, D. (1992, February 8). Bush talks up his health care plan in San Diego visit. *Los Angeles Times,* p. A18.

Jemmott, J. B., III, & Locke, S. E. (1984). Psychosocial factors, immunologic mediation and human susceptibility: How much do we know? *Psychological Bulletin, 95*(1), 78-108.

Kaplan, H. B. (1991). Social psychology of the immune system: A conceptual framework and review of the literature. *Social Science and Medicine, 33*(8), 909-923.

Katon, W., & Kleinman, A. (1981). Doctor-patient negotiation and other social science strategies in patient care. In L. Eisenberg & A. Kleinman (Eds.), *The relevance of social science for medicine* (pp. 253-279). Dordrecht, Holland: D. Reidel.

Kestenbaum, V. (1982). *The humanity of the ill: Phenomenological perspectives.* Knoxville: University of Tennessee Press.

Kleinman, A. (1988). *The illness narratives: Suffering, healing and the human condition.* New York: Basic Books.

Korsch, B. M. (1989). Current issues in health communication. *Health Communication, 1*(1), 5-9.

Krell, D. F. (1977). General introduction: "The question of being." In D. F. Krel (Ed.), *Martin Heidegger: Basic writings.* San Francisco: Harper.

Kreps, G. L. (1988). The pervasive role of information in health and health care: Implications for health communication policy. In J. Anderson (Ed.), *Communication yearbook 11* (pp. 238-276). Newbury Park, CA: Sage.

Kreps, G. L. (1989). Setting the agenda for health communication research and development: Scholarship that can make a difference. *Health Communication, 1*(1), 11-15.

Kreps, G. L., & Thornton, B. C. (1984). *Health communication: Theory and practice.* New York: Longman.

Kubler-Ross, E. (1969). *On death and dying.* New York: Macmillan.

Kuhn, T. S. (1970). *The structure of scientific revolutions* (2nd ed., enlarged). Chicago: University of Chicago Press.

Laing, R. D. (1967). *The politics of experience.* New York: Pantheon.

Lazarsfeld, P. F. (1941). Remarks on administrative and critical communication. *Studies in Philosophy and Social Science, 9,* 2-16.

Leichter, H. M. (1991). *Free to be foolish: Politics and health promotion in the United States and Great Britain.* Princeton, NJ: Princeton University Press.

Levenstein, J. H., Brown, J. B., Weston, W. W., Stewart, M. McCracken, E. C., & McWhinney, I. (1989). Patient-centered clinical interviewing. In M. Stewart & D. Roter (Eds.), *Communicating with medical patients* (pp. 107-120). Newbury Park, CA: Sage.

Levin, D. M., & Solomon, G. F. (1990). The discursive formation of the body in the history of medicine. *The Journal of Medicine and Philosophy, 15,* 515-537.

Lyman, M. J. (1990). Examining support in context: A redefinition from the cancer patient's perspective. *Sociology of Health and Illness, 12*(2), 169-194.

McWhinney, I. (1989). The need for a transformed medical model. In M. Stewart & D. Roter (Eds.), *Communicating with medical patients* (pp. 25-40). Newbury Park, CA: Sage.

Merleau-Ponty, M. (1992). *Phenomenology of perception* (C. Smith, Trans.). London: Routledge.

Miller, W. D. (1975). Drug usage: Compliance of patients with instructions on medicine. *Journal of American Osteopath Association, 75*, 401-404.

Mishler, E. (1981). Viewpoint: Critical perspectives on the biomedical model. In E. Mishler, L. R. Amarasingham, S. T. Hauser, S. D. Osherson, N. E. Waxler, & R. Liem (Eds.), *Social contexts of health, illness, and patient care.* Cambridge: Cambridge University Press.

Novak, M. (1985-1986). Biography after the end of metaphysics: A critique of epigenetic evolution. *International Journal of Aging and Human Development, 22*(3), 189-204.

Nussbaum, J. F. (1989). Directions for research within health communication. *Health Communication, 1*(1), 35-40.

Pearce, W. B. (1989). *Communication and the human condition.* Carbondale: Southern Illinois University Press.

Pearce, W. B., & Cronen, V. (1980). *Communication, action, and meaning.* New York: Praeger.

Pellegrino, E. D. (1979). *Humanism and the physician.* Knoxville: University of Tennessee Press.

Pellegrino, E. D., & Thomasma, D. C. (1981). *A philosophical basis of medical practice: Toward a philosophy and ethic of the healing professions.* New York: Oxford University Press.

Peters, J. (1986). Institutional sources of intellectual poverty in communication research. *Communication Research, 13*, 527-559.

Pettegrew, L. S. (1988). Theoretical plurality in health communication. In J. Anderson (Ed.), *Communication yearbook 11* (pp. 298-308). Newbury Park, CA: Sage.

Rasmussen, H. (1975). Medical education: Revolution or reaction. *The Pharos, 38*, 53-59.

Ray, E. B., & Donohew, L. (1990). *Communication and health: Systems and applications.* Hillsdale, NJ: Lawrence Erlbaum.

Reardon, K. K. (1988). The role of persuasion in health promotion and disease prevention: Review and commentary. In J. Anderson (Ed.), *Communication yearbook 11* (pp. 277-297). Newbury Park, CA: Sage.

Richardson, L. (1990). Narrative and sociology. *Journal of Contemporary Ethnography, 19*(1), 116-135.

Robinson, I. (1990). Personal narratives, social careers, and medical courses: Analysing life trajectories in autobiographies of people with multiple sclerosis. *Social Science and Medicine, 30*(11), 1173-1186.

Rorty, R. (1979). *Philosophy and the mirror of nature.* Princeton, NJ: Princeton University Press.

Rorty, R. (1989). *Contingency, irony and solidarity.* New York: Oxford University Press.

Rorty, R. (1991). *Truth, objectivity and relativism.* New York: Oxford University Press.

Rotter, J. (1966). Generalized expectancies for internal versus external locus of control of reinforcement. *Psychological Monographs, 80*(1), 1-28.

Salmon, C. T. (1989). Campaigns for social "improvement": An overview of values, rationales, and impacts. In C. T. Salmon (Ed.), *Information campaigns: Balancing social values and social change* (pp. 19-53). Newbury Park, CA: Sage.

Scott, R. L. (1967). On viewing rhetoric as epistemic. *Central States Speech Journal, 18*, 9-17.

Scott, R. L. (1976). On viewing rhetoric as epistemic: Ten years later. *Central States Speech Journal, 27*, 258-266.

Sharf, B. F. (1990). Physician-patient communication as interpersonal rhetoric: A narrative approach. *Health Communication, 2*(4), 217-231.

Shilts, R. (1986). *And the band played on.* New York: St. Martin.

Siegel, B. S. (1986). *Love, medicine, and miracles: Lessons learned about self-healing from a surgeon's experience with exceptional patients.* New York: Harper & Row.

Siegel, B. S. (1989). *Peace, love and healing—Bodymind communication and the path to self-healing: An exploration.* New York: Harper & Row.

Skinner, Q. (1990). *The return of grand theory in the human sciences.* Cambridge: Cambridge University Press.

Smith, D. H. (1989). Studying health communication: An agenda for the future. *Health Communication, 1*(1), 17-27.

Smith, D. H., & Pettegrew, L. S. (1986). Mutual persuasion as a model for doctor-patient communication. *Theoretical Medicine, 7*, 127-146.

Sontag, S. (1989). *AIDS and its metaphors.* New York: Farrar, Strauss, & Giroux.

Spitzer, W. O., & Roberts, R. (1980). Twelve questions about health care teams. *Journal of Community Health, 6*(1), 1-5.

Starr, P. (1982). *The social transformation of American medicine.* New York: Basic Books.

Stewart, D., & Mickunas, A. (1974). *Exploring phenomenology: A guide to the field and its literature.* Chicago: American Library Association.

Stewart, M., & Roter, D. (1989). *Communicating with medical patients.* Newbury Park, CA: Sage.

Stoeckle, J. D., & Barsky, A. J. (1981). Attributions: Uses of social science knowledge in the "doctoring" of primary care. In L. Eisenberg & A. Kleinman (Eds.), *The relevance of social science for medicine* (pp. 223-240). Dordrecht, Holland: D. Reidel.

Strauss, A., & Corbin, J. (1988). *Shaping a new health care system.* San Francisco: Jossey-Bass.

Szasz, T. S. (1961). *The myth of mental illness: Foundations of a theory of personal conduct.* New York: Hoeber-Harper.

Taussig, M. (1992). *The nervous system.* New York: Routledge.

Thompson, T. L. (1984). The invisible helping hand: The role of communication in the health and social service professions. *Communication Quarterly, 32*(2), 148-163.

Thompson, T. L. (1990). Patient health care: Issues in interpersonal communication. In E. B. Ray & L. Donohew (Eds.), *Communication and health* (pp. 27-50). Hillsdale, NJ: Lawrence Erlbaum.

Wallis, J. (1991). *The hermeneutics of life history: Personal achievement and history in Gadamer, Habermas, and Erikson.* Evanston, IL: Northwestern University Press.

Wartella, E., & Middlestadt, S. (1991). The evolution of models of mass communication. *Health Communication, 3*(4), 205-215.

Weston, W. W., & Brown, J. B. (1989). The importance of patients' beliefs. In M. Stewart & D. Roter (Eds.), *Communicating with medical patients* (pp. 77-86). Newbury Park, CA: Sage.

Whitbourne, S. K., Zuschlag, M. K., Elliot, L. B., & Waterman, A. S. (1992). Psychosocial development in adulthood: A 22-year sequential study. *Journal of Personality and Social Psychology, 63*(2), 260-271.

Wise, H. (1972). The primary health care team. *Archives of Internal Medicine, 130*, 438-444.

Zaner, R. M. (1983). Flirtations or engagements? Prolegomenon to a philosophy of medicine. In W. L. McBride & C. O. Schrag (Eds.), *Phenomenology in a pluralistic context.* Albany: State University of New York Press.

Zook, E. G., & Miller, K. I. (1992). *Care partner involvement and communication in the illness management systems of AIDS patients.* Paper presented at the annual convention of the International Communication Association, Miami.

Zook, E. G., & Miller, K. I. (1993). The role of care partners in managing AIDS patients' illness: Toward a triadic model of health care delivery. In S. C. Ratzan (Ed.), *AIDS: Effective health communication for the 90's.* Washington, DC: Taylor & Francis.

An Invitation to Leap from a Trinitarian Ontology in Health Communication Research to a Spiritually Inclusive Quatrain

MARIA CRISTINA GONZÁLEZ
Arizona State University

T HE task of writing this commentary was simultaneously enticing and threatening as I prepared to do so. Reading Eric Zook's essay, I related to much of what he had to say. In 1987 I remembered a conversation with Gary Kreps in which we discussed the need for a critical review of literature of the work that had been done in health communication. He agreed that the movement of our work in this area had been somewhat limited and that future research needed to move in new directions. I did not do such a review; rather, I chose to effectively withdraw from debate and contemplate what it was about the hundreds of papers I had reviewed for both the International Communication Association Division and the Speech Communication Association Commission on Health Communication over a period of 3 to 4 years that left me feeling something was "missing."

Around that time, I picked up a copy of Heidegger's *What Is Called Thinking?* (1968) from a discount bin in a bookstore in Princeton. Although it had been a while since I had "thought" about this collection of lectures, I found myself remembering bits and pieces of its wisdom as I prepared to write this commentary. The text is quite metaphysical; those things about which we "choose" to think are in a sense *drawing* us toward them because of the fact that they elude us. In our doing of research, we are drawn by questions that, if answered, we hope will aid us in our piecemeal attempts to arrive at truths. Perhaps in our discourse regarding the enterprise of health communication, we have been consumed by the guiding cultural themes of instrumentalism

Correspondence and requests for reprints: Maria Cristina González, Department of Communication, Arizona State University, Tempe, AZ 85287-1205.

Communication Yearbook 17, pp. 378-387

and profits. Certainly, Eric Zook invites us to consider the effects of such emphases on our research and resulting knowledge in the area of health communication.

For Heidegger (1968, Lecture II), there is an integral relationship between thought and poesy in our attempts to uncover truths. As we take the critical lens and apply it to our study of health communication, it is the heart of this relationship that I think has been avoided in our research: the uncovering of truths, where "truth means the disclosure of what keeps itself concealed" (Heidegger, 1968, p. 19). Perhaps the communal common "sense" discerned in a review of health communication literature is merely that "institutional naturalization of specific perceptions" (Deetz, 1992) that Zook highlights for us. These naturalized perceptions lead us to believe we are seeing what is really there when we look at health communication. What is really there is rooted in an ontology that, as do all ontologies, creates circular confirming perceptions. Therefore, when we seek truth within the confines of accepted ontology, we miss that truth that is *concealed* through our very lenses. As Zook says, as researchers, our challenge is "*to make perceptual choice as conscious, constant, and participative as possible*" (p. 350). Let us not miss the revolutionary implications of such a statement. Conscious and participative perceptual choice requires that the sacred walls that limit our views not merely be acknowledged but, in fact, at some point, be torn down.

An anticipated, well-socialized, academically impulsive response to the statement that we are seeking the disclosure of concealed truths is that this is *obviously* what drives good research. Such superficial avowals keep us from critically examining the possibility that the sacred walls around our research enterprise might in fact isolate us from the vision that would lead us to that which "keeps itself concealed." Zook's plea for an inclusive biopsychosocial approach to health communication research is in many ways an attempt to tear down our sacred walls so that alternative visions might be possible. When we tear down these walls, we are in fact dealing with issues of ontology; we challenge the very ways we have framed reality. Still, what I would like to suggest with this commentary is that, while we accept the premises Zook has laid out for us, we do so only as a preliminary step toward an enterprise of radically transforming the ontology of our research to include more than the biological, more than the psychological, and more than the social. I invite us to consider the *spiritual* dimension of health communication experience as equally valid. I ask that we consider that the very fact that it is not included in views of holism is because it is not traditionally acceptable. I ask, in the spirit of Heidegger, that we consider that the absence of the spiritual from our literature be considered the indicator that it is in fact that which should be drawing us.

There are many reasons that spirituality has not been given equal status with the biological, psychological, and social aspects of health communication. These reasons are well entrenched historically in real institutional/political battles, nationalistic ideology, and scientific mythologies. But, beyond these reasons, to whose influence I will give some attention later, there are real practical issues to studying the spiritual dimension of communication experience, and these create special challenges in research. As such, spirituality has been conceptualized as a form of coping mechanism, as psychoses, or as the manipulative domain of religious organizations. Framed as such, it can be handled in our research as an extraneous factor or socially constructed artifact. Such a frame, however, does not grant the spiritual the sort of status of reality that those things biological, social, and psychological share in our research. As such, our traditional ontology, and even that sort of holistic ontology proposed by Zook, does not grant spirituality real status.

Tradition, however, is contextual, and if we allow ourselves to expand the boundaries of time, culture, and experience, there are, in fact, traditions that are rooted in an ontology that grants things spiritual definite reality (Grof & Grof, 1990; Guerra, 1969; Koss-Chioino, 1992). If we allow ourselves to examine our own domain, that of the study of health communication, within a greater context of tradition and meaning, we find that the very focus of our enterprise is itself rooted in acknowledgment and incorporation of the spiritual. Both words, *health* and *communication,* have etymological histories replete with spiritual references. In transforming the meaning of *health* to the success of the medical profession and process, and that of *communication* to the instrumental use of language toward the goals of the medical process, we focus so narrowly that we miss an unbelievably rich field of experience.

It is my primary premise that the spiritual is a natural dimension of human experience, equally as valid as (a) biophysical, (b) socioemotional, and (c) psychorational experiences (our "sacred trinity"). The exclusion of spirituality from the literature and research of health communication does not consist of lack of acknowledgment but in its not being granted dimensional status equal to the trinity. Social science has enabled this to occur with great facility in our work. We have managed to find ways to measure phenomena that we classify as psychological and social. The spiritual—not fitting into "the notion of acceptable reality [that] was narrowed to include only those aspects of existence that are material, tangible, and measurable"—has been "exiled from the modern scientific worldview" (Grof & Grof, 1990), including that of health communication. Its simple (or perhaps not so simple) exile from study on its own grounds does not obviate the necessity to explore it. To quote Heidegger (1968): "In fact, what withdraws may even concern and claim man more essentially than anything present that strikes and touches him. Being struck by actuality is what we like to regard as constitutive of the actuality of the actual. However, in being struck by what is actual, man may be debarred precisely from what concerns and touches him—touches him in the surely mysterious way of escaping him by its withdrawal" (p. 9).

Simply because the spiritual has been avoided, and perhaps because it is so difficult to approach, is not sufficient justification for its relegation to that which we do not study. The schemas that we now have for the study of health communication, including that proposed by Zook (although, of interest, I believe he is approaching those same elusive aspects of communication that draw my attention) do not adequately account for the metaphysical phenomena that take place in that arena we call health communication. Even in anthropological approaches to topics of health communication (Hahn & Gaines, 1985), the placement of spirituality as a dimension of culture does not give it the status validity that would allow for explanations of health phenomena to be rooted in spirit. The introduction of spirituality as a valid dimension of experience would, in my opinion, aid in the development of true understanding of what it is we do when we communicate, what it is we do when we heal. It is much more than the use of words and medical technique/ology.

It is my further premise that, because spirituality is a natural dimension of experience, those schemas that we have developed for the study of human communication that relegate it to a position somewhat secondary to that of the "sacred trinity," while perhaps preventing us from explicitly acknowledging the valid force of this dimension, have *not* resulted in its *absence*. Rather, my second premise is that the spiritual dimension has been *displaced*. As such, evidence of it can be found in the ways in which we treat aspects of the health communication context. For example, when Zook mentions that health communication literature has not looked sufficiently at ancillary care providers, including clergy, the spiritual domain of such a role is totally overlooked in favor of the psychological and social. By focusing on networks of social support as a category, many of the aspects of highly spiritual (not religious) interaction are not able to be studied. Spiritual functions are categorized according to attributes within the measurable domains of the psychological and the social. Unfortunately, such displacement does not allow for the treatment of the metaphysical, the unmeasurable, the truly spiritual dimension of much health communication. Such displacement, while allowing for the maintenance of the dimension, does not allow for its full manifestation. Many of the problems that we encounter in the context of health communication can be explained through the incorporation of the fourth dimension of spirituality into our research. How, then, do we approach this challenge? To again quote Heidegger (1968), "There is no bridge here— only the leap" (p. 8). It is perhaps because we determine the validity of that which we study through our existing ontology that we are able to maintain the exclusion of phenomena that require alterations to that ontology in order to be granted validity.

Hence we, those of us who come from the sciences, must endure what is shocking and strange about thinking—assuming we are ready to learn thinking. To learn means to make everything we do answer to whatever essentials address themselves to us at the given moment. . . . It is important above all that on the way on which we set out when we learn to think, we do not deceive ourselves and rashly bypass the pressing questions; on the contrary, we must allow ourselves to become involved in questions that seek what no inventiveness can find. Especially we moderns can learn only if we always unlearn at the same time. Applied to the matter before us: we can learn thinking only if we radically unlearn what thinking has been traditionally. To do that, we must at the same time come to know it. (Heidegger, 1968, p. 8)

One of the obstacles confronting scholars who might wish to include the spiritual in their study of health communication phenomena is the need to *define* the spiritual so as to *recognize and identify* it. The sequential order of first defining, then recognizing and identifying, a phenomena, prior to *understanding and explaining* it, is an example of what I often term *positivistic residue*. At times we are plagued by the power of repetition. We are, in fact, like mere creatures of habit when it comes to thinking. The paradox of studying the spiritual is that one must "come to know it" before being able to study it. This is a radical rupture in the status quo of methodology. Before attempting to explain, recognize, or identify the spiritual, one must have some sort of experiential understanding. This is literally backward from traditional positivist approaches to research, although perhaps more in synchrony with naturalist/constructivist (Guba, 1990) approaches, which allow for inductive, grounded explanations to emerge during the research process.

One of the most common problems that surfaces when facing the relativist ontology of constructivist approaches to research is what I commonly refer to as *relativistic paralysis*. As we attempt to incorporate spirituality into the study of health communication, I am convinced that we will be faced with those who will claim that their scholarship cannot be evaluated, on the grounds that it is their own experience, that "you had to be there to understand." I would argue that such expressions create dialogical paralysis, that scholarly dialogue cannot proceed behind the protective cloak of relativism and exclusive personal experience and insight. If we are to incorporate the study of spirituality as a valid dimension of human experience in health communication, we will have to expect that those who claim they have identified something "spiritual" demonstrate how it is that they came to this conclusion. It is here that the remnants of our "sacred walls" of institutional naturalization can often become obstacles. The religious is automatically called spiritual, the ritualistic and ceremonial is assumed spiritual, the simply inexplicable "must be" spiritual. Because the religious, the ritualistic, and the ceremonial have so often been categorized as spiritual within the confines of the biopsychosocial model, it is tempting to automatically refer to them as manifestations of the spiritual dimension. But are they?

If we are to approach the spiritual as a valid dimension, what characterizes "spirit"? If we do not exert the same amount of care and attention to the understanding of this dimension, then we risk creating an intellectual arena into which that called spiritual will rapidly be devoured by the lions that evaluate good scholarship. If we allow spirituality to be cloaked in the protective discourse of the relativism of personal experience, we eliminate the possibility of mutual understanding.

There is a bit of paradox in this. For if spirit cannot be defined until experienced, then where do we begin? If our efforts existed in a scholarly vacuum, perhaps this could be considered a more genuine articulation. We are, in fact, surrounded by vast amounts of literature by persons who have devoted themselves and their lives to the study of things spiritual. To presume that as scholars of communication we would have to start from ground zero would indeed be naive. "Our demons are our own limitations, which shut us off from the realization of the ubiquity of the spirit" (Campbell, in Maher & Briggs, 1988, p. 28). In the same ways that we have availed ourselves of the medical, psychological, and sociological literatures in the study of health communication, we should expose ourselves to the literatures that attempt to explore and explain that which is spiritual.

Bloch (1986) examines, among many things, the use of the term *spirit* by Hegel (1952) in *Phenomenology of Spirit*. Hegel was critical of phrenology and physiognomy and even more so of the attempts to impute causal or lawlike generalizations to phenomena that were not determinate in nature (MacIntyre, 1972/1984). To Hegel, spirit is a sort of collective unconscious oath, a "law of the heart"; furthermore, spirit is "reality as dialectical reason, reason as dialectical reality" (Bloch, 1986, pp. 121-128). I would like to take these notions of spirit and apply them to an analysis of a phenomenon frequently studied in health communication: the power relationship between the physician and patient. In doing so, I hope to exemplify, though necessarily briefly for purposes of this commentary, the type of analysis that I think would be possible if spirituality were considered to be a valid fourth dimension.

If in fact the dimension of spirituality has through a process of displacement found itself to manifest in the dimensions of biophysicality, psychorationality, and socioemotionality (B-P-S, the three dimensions of reality within what I will call a Trinitarian Ontology), it is first important to situate the ideology of medicine within these three dimensions. I will then explore how communication responds to challenges situated within an ideology posed by the Trinitarian Ontology.

Why do I introduce the notion of ideology? Mumby (1987) writes that ideology has been treated in neo-Marxist literature as an "intrinsic part of the process by which social actors are integrated into extant power structures" (p. 117). Mumby claims that ideology provides persons with a sense of the limits and possibilities of the social world in which they are social actors. As such, ideology would seem to provide a sort of "cultural map" by which individuals situate their reality. Ontology would therefore necessarily precede the development of ideologies, providing the reality for which the ideological mappings are provided. As such, a critical examination of ideology that does not itself examine the ontology within which particular ideologies come to exist could not fully offer an enlightened eye. To do so, a vision of an alternative ontology should be available. By viewing the ideology of medicine first through the eyes of a Trinitarian Ontology that necessarily displaces spiritual experience within the domains of three validated dimensions (B-P-S), we can see how the role of physician-as-god could logically come to exist. Within the ideology of medicine, the doctor's socialization into the role of physician is all but sacred:

> Because "being a doctor" contributes so decisively to good medical care, everyone, laymen as well as doctors, should see to it that nothing interferes with its development, particularly that none of the many changes taking place in medical education and in medical practice destroy the conditions necessary for it to develop . . . it is exceedingly dangerous . . . to do anything to destroy the doctor's sense of his special . . . attitude toward patient care, his sense of himself as an exception. (Bird, 1973, p. 17)

The physician is enacting the displaced deity from the spiritual dimension. Medical ideology defines the enemy as disease; the ultimate enemy is death. The physician is armed with power, which is defined as medical knowledge and skill. In the words of one medical resident, "But being a doctor, you don't make mistakes. You have to, in a sense, be God" (González, 1986). When a physician fails—that is, when a patient dies—medical ideology does not allow for any explanation other than the scientific. The disease/injury exceeded the abilities of the physician and/or the potential of medical knowledge and skill. If the ability to deal with death were purely psychorational, this ought to be enough. But it is not enough for human beings who seek *spiritual* answers to such a question. The Trinitarian Ontology does not provide the spiritual answers, although it might suggest that persons who construct social realities including constructs to account for death fare better spiritually than those who don't (Feifel, 1977). It is my belief that the reason we see so much wrath vented against physicians is that they have been cast in the role of the deity but within an ideology that does not allow for spiritual transcendence. The ideology is limited by its ontological roots. Ideologies do not exist in isolation, however, and because we exist within a system structured highly by the influence of capitalist ideology, it is not surprising that anger at the failing deity is translated into attempts to be paid for one's loss. Still, however, spiritual transcendence has not been accomplished.

If, in this particular case, we focus on attempting to improve patient satisfaction so that the chances of lawsuits are decreased, our health communication research might lead us into training doctors how to communicate with their patients who are dying. This approaches the problem from within the Trinitarian Ontology, treating communication as socioemotional, dealing with psychorational aspects of the biophysical reality of treating a patient who is dying. Notice that simple logical consistency in explanation and strategy does not ever explain to us why certain patients transcend their own impending deaths, why certain families transcend the failure of medical practice to heal a dying relative. Why is that?

Returning to Bloch's interpretation of Hegel: *Spirit is a rationality of dialectical reason.* If we allow this to be the definition of that which exists within the spiritual dimension, how can this enlighten us in our study of health communication? In the particular example provided, I would say it is because spirit allows for the transcendence of the duality of life and death. Spirit, if it is indeed a rationality of dialectical reasoning, is that which allows us to transcend all duality into an experience of unity. This is where naive ponderings on the nature of dialectics in communication have greatly missed the boat that would have taken them in the direction of spirituality. Dialectics are not merely experiences of opposition. They are not about choices between privacy and openness in interpersonal communication; they are not about differences in collectivism and individualism in intercultural communication; and they are not about choices between health-promoting and destructive behaviors in health communication. Dialectics and dialectical reasoning are about the *understanding* of privacy through an understanding of openness, the *understanding* of collectivism through an understanding of individualism, the *understanding* of healthy behaviors through the understanding of destructive behaviors. *Spirituality* is experienced in this dialectical reasoning when the duality is suddenly experienced as unity. The duality is transcended. This is what happens when healing takes place. This is what happens when genuine dialogue (Buber, 1966) takes place. The experience of healing is spiritual. While physical intervention, rational strategy, and social interaction might necessarily precede it, the transcendental experience that characterizes what we have called "patient satisfaction" or "understanding" is by nature *spiritual*. In our communication, when we transcend such dualities as doctor-patient, husband-wife, teacher-student, and arrive at the transcendent reality of their unity, that is when we have experienced the spiritual dimension. Zook approaches this reality when he discusses Gadamer's (1992) conception of human understanding as "being transformed into a communion in which we do not remain what we are" (p. 362).

There is much that is unexplained when we deal with topics of healing and human communication. Perhaps it is because we have sought that explanation within walls that have kept the answers out of sight. Perhaps it is because those walls have led us to believe our answers had to come from within them. While Zook offers us an alternative to the emphasis on the biological aspects of health communication by incorporation of the psychosocial, it is an incorporation that falls within the already accepted domains of social science research. It would not necessarily result in the sort of radical transformation in the direction of research of those aspects of health communication that I feel he and I agree should be studied. I do not believe it is any coincidence that Martin Buber was a highly spiritual man when he wrote about the nature of dialogue and the inseparable "I-Thou" that is present in such true communication. I do not believe it is coincidence that John Powell (1969), who speaks of "peak communication" when two persons totally understand one another, almost in a form of ecstatic communication, was himself committed to a life as a Jesuit scholar approaching the topic of interpersonal communication from a spiritual perspective. As long as these spiritual aspects of communication continue to be relegated to dimensions that do not allow their full exploration in their own domain, however, we deny ourselves the potential knowledge resources that could be developed through accepted research.

More and more physicians are acknowledging the role of the spiritual in healing the psychological and physical diseases of human beings (Grof, 1990; Siegel, 1986). While we may be able to account for the success of more tangible forms of communication with our traditional Trinitarian Ontology, I suggest that we adopt a fourth dimension and, in the spirit of Martin Heidegger, who saw the relationship between the search for truth and poesy, that this *quatrain* allow us to approach the questions that have eluded us in our study of health communication. We need not abandon those instrumental and biomedical concerns that have been the focus of our research for so long, but this Ontology of Four Dimensions allows us not to be limited by those seemingly natural habits of perception that have prevented us from obtaining answers to questions outside the realm of the biopsychosocial.

REFERENCES

Bird, B. (1973). *Talking with patients* (2nd ed.). Philadelphia: J. B. Lippincott.

Bloch, E. (1986). *Natural law and human dignity.* Cambridge: MIT Press.

Buber, M. (1966). *The way of response: Martin Buber.* (N. N. Glatzer, Ed.). New York: Schocken.

Deetz, S. (1992). *Democracy in an age of corporate colonization: Developments in communication and the politics of everyday life.* Albany: State University of New York Press.

Feifel, H. (1977). Death and dying in modern America. *Death Education, 1,* 5-14.

Gadamer, H. G. (1992). *Truth and method* (J. Weinsheimer & D. G. Marshall, Trans.; 2nd rev. ed.). New York: Crossroad.

González, M. C. (1986). *Communication with patients who are dying: The effects of medical education.* Unpublished dissertation, University of Texas, Austin.

Grof, S. (1990). God in the laboratory. In C. Grof & S. Grof, *The stormy search for the self.* New York: Tarcher/Perigree.

Grof, C., & Grof, S. (1990). *The stormy search for the self.* New York: Tarcher/Perigree.

Guba, E. G. (1990). The alternative paradigm dialog. In E. G. Guba (Ed.), *The paradigm dialog* (pp. 17-27). Newbury Park, CA: Sage.

Guerra, F. (1969). The role of religion in Spanish American medicine. In F. N. L. Poynter (Ed.), *Medicine and culture.* London: Frank Cottrel.

Hahn, R. A., & Gaines, A. D. (1985). *Physicians of Western medicine: Anthropological approaches to theory and practice.* Boston: D. Reidel.

Hegel, G. W. F. (1952). *Phenomenology of spirit* (A. V. Miller, Trans.). Oxford: Oxford University Press.

Heidegger, M. (1968). *What is called thinking?* New York: Harper & Row.

Koss-Chioino, J. (1992). *Women as healer, women as patients: Mental health care and traditional healing in Puerto Rico*. Boulder, CO: Westview.

MacIntyre, A. (1984). Hegel: On faces and skulls. In T. Honderich (Ed.), *Philosophy through its past*. New York: Penguin. (Original essay published 1972)

Maher, J. M., & Briggs, D. (Eds.). (1988). *An open life: Joseph Campbell in conversation with Michael Toms*. Burdett, NY: Larson.

Mumby, D. (1987). The political function of narrative in organizations. *Communication Monographs, 54*, 113-127.

Powell, J. (1969). *Why am I afraid to tell you who I am?* Valencia, CA: Tabor.

Siegel, B. S. (1986). *Love, medicine, and miracles: Lessons learned about self-healing from a surgeon's experience with exceptional patients*. New York: Harper & Row.

9 Once More, *With Feeling*: Reconsidering the Role of Emotion in Work

VINCENT R. WALDRON
Arizona State University West

The role of emotion in the workplace has been the subject of a series of provocative studies (Hochschild, 1983; Van Maanen & Kunda, 1989). This essay locates research on organizational emotion in the larger traditions of emotion research and argues that the communicative aspects of emotion have been understudied. Existing research on the subject is divided into three themes: the emotional labor and attendant psychological costs that characterize some occupations, the use of emotional expression as a tool for the achievement of management objectives, and the role of culture in shaping the emotional lives of members. Three broad areas requiring study by communication researchers are explored. First, the substantial literature on organizational regulation of emotional display is reviewed and criticized for implicitly casting communication in the role of "emotional packaging." Second, possibilities for studying the process of emotional interpretation are presented, with particular emphasis on the constitutive and heuristic rules used by organizational members. Third, tactical uses and organizational functions of organizational emotion are explored, with the role of emotional communication in defining work relationships most emphasized. Finally, a call for more message-based research is issued.

Former Pilot: I remember low-level flight in the Air Force. . . . You're strapped into the jet, in tight formation with the other guys . . . screaming across the face of the earth, it seems like 10 feet off the ground. You're totally dependent on the instruments. . . . One wrong move up, down, or sideways and presto! you're dead, smashed into a mountain or something . . . and that's the end of you.
One day we're sitting in this training session listening to cockpit tapes. One guy on the tape watched his buddy eat it. . . . One minute he was on his wing, the next minute he was up in smoke. We're listening to the tape and the guy is cryin' and screamin' cause his buddy crashed. We couldn't believe it!

Correspondence and requests for reprints: Vincent R. Waldron, Communication Studies, 4701 Thunderbird Road, P.O. Box 37100, Arizona State University West, Phoenix, AZ 85069-7100.

Communication Yearbook 17, pp. 388-416

| Interviewer: | Pretty scary, I guess. |
| Pilot: | Scary? We were embarrassed. I mean nobody wants their friend to die. But geeze, you don't *cry* about it. Not on the cockpit tape! Not if you want to be a pilot. |

THIS seasoned pilot belongs to one of the few professions that demand emotional self-control as a prerequisite to physical survival (Waldron, 1986), but emotional control is an integral, if less dramatic, part of the work performed by most organization members. The excerpt above illustrates a principle intuitively apparent to members of many professions: that control of emotion (feelings, affective responses) is required for *social* survival at work. If one hopes to occupy the role of pilot (manager, clerk, physician) and to remain in good standing in the fraternity of pilots (professors, clergy, airline attendants), then one must learn the emotional rules of the profession. Emotion is very much a part of the task and social components of work.

Historical overviews of trends in organizational theory and rhetoric indicate that emotion, broadly defined, has periodically captured the attention of organizational scholars and practitioners (Barley & Kunda, 1992; Bendix, 1956). The predominant concern, however, has been with relatively mild and diffuse affective reactions to working conditions or, as with human relations theorists, the meeting of workers' "higher order" needs. Indeed, researchers have long been concerned with emotion as a pleasant (e.g., job satisfaction; for reviews, see Isen & Baron, 1991; Locke, 1976) or unpleasant (e.g., "burnout"; Maslach, 1982) psychological side effect of work. Historically, prescriptions for controlling emotional side effects have included carefully administered doses of management consideration, vacation time, worker participation, job enrichment, and the like.

Emotion has also been a prominent tool of management control. The arousal of worker passions has been viewed as a preliminary step in the process of cultivating motivation, loyalty, and commitment. Of course, since Cicero, emotion has been a valued implement in the persuader's toolbox, the means by which audiences' grip on their opinions is pried loose through appeals to hope, fear, or pride (for a review, see Hyde, 1984). As organizational theorists have noted (Barley & Kunda, 1992; Barley, Meyer, & Cash, 1988; Van Maanen & Kunda, 1989), an obvious recent instance of this phenomenon in the organizational arena involves organizations bent on building "strong cultures," in which symbols, rituals, and other cultural components are orchestrated in an attempt to manipulate member emotions and foster member commitment to organizational objectives.

In historical perspective, then, worker emotion has been prominent in the theory and practice of management, but it has been viewed primarily as a kind of undeveloped management resource, ideally developed and controlled by adjustments in work practices or management exhortation. These treatments of emotion are limited in that they fail to address the variety and intensity of emotion as it arises "naturally" from work, without management prompting. Nor do they acknowledge the proactive (rather than reactive) aspects of workplace emotion: attempts by members to express, repress, and fabricate emotion as part of their tasks, routine interactions, and work relationships; the communication processes used by members to interpret the emotional experiences and expressions of themselves and others; member uses of emotion language; the means by which organizational control of emotion is reinforced or resisted in the behavior of members. In short, the possibility that the *performance* of emotion might be an integral part of working has only recently received the attention of organizational researchers (but see Pacanowsky & Trujillo, 1983).

Indeed, most workers would not recognize the sanitized and seemingly emotionless work environments depicted in much recent scholarly organizational writing. Smitten by metaphors of the machine, the computer, the brain (Morgan, 1986), organizational researchers have too often culled out and discarded large portions of workers' emotional lives—perhaps the most human and vitalizing elements of work. Even theorists who view organizational practices as less than rational (Simon, 1976, 1989; Staw, 1980; Weick, 1979) are wedded to information-processing perspectives. To the extent that theorizing eventually contributes to the way organizations are viewed by members (see Knights & Morgan, 1991), this limited view of emotion reinforces a potentially unhealthy rationalist fiction among practitioners—that unsolicited emotion has no legitimate place, indeed, should not exist, at work. The enormous effort expended by many organizations to control the emotions of members is implicitly supported, but the emotional costs of work are underestimated and the communication processes through which emotion is created, expressed, and interpreted in the organization are understudied. Perhaps it is because we work in institutions where emotional displays are viewed as "unprofessional" that we have produced research that at least implicitly values emotional disengagement over emotional involvement. Boldly stated, "The *professionals*, . . . [live] in the ghetto of objectivity. He [*sic*] is the distinctively "disengaged" man and is therefore liable to become the tool of a degenerate humanity" (Helmut Thielicke, *Nihilism*, quoted in Scott & Hart, 1979, p. 130).

Fortunately, the uncritical acceptance of rationalist assumptions by organizational researchers (but see Mumby & Putnam, 1992) is countered by a growing body of provocative research documenting the prevalence of emotion in the routine activities of many organizations and their members (e.g., Hochschild, 1979, 1983; Rafaeli & Sutton, 1987, 1989, 1990; Sandelands & Buckner, 1989; Sutton, 1991; Van Maanen & Kunda, 1989). Perhaps because it allows the reader to make an emotional (not just intellectual) connection to his or her own work experiences, this literature makes stimulating reading. Moreover, it directs attention to the rich and complex interaction between organizational communication and organizational emotion, yielding in the process enough research questions to keep a large contingent of communication researchers busy for the near future. My purpose in this essay is to provide some initial direction to this group. I do so by locating research on organizational emotion in the broader stream of research on emotion and then briefly reviewing the important studies and themes in the organizational emotion literature. Next, I try to show where communication theory and research fit into the organizational emotion puzzle and argue that organizational communication researchers should address the symbolic and functional aspects of emotion. In outlining a communication-oriented view of organizational emotion, I pose research questions regarding the regulative, interpretative, and strategic influences of communication on organizational emotion. Finally, I explore the potential functions, intended and unintended, of emotion in the workplace, with an emphasis on the role of emotion in defining organizational relationships.

THEORETICAL FOUNDATIONS OF
ORGANIZATIONAL EMOTION RESEARCH

Space limitations allow only the briefest foray into the vast history of emotion theory and research. Hochschild (1983), in an appendix, and Bowers, Metts, and Duncanson (1985) provide more thorough reviews. Scientific interest in emotion can be traced to the early work of such influential scholars as William James (1884) and Charles Darwin (1872). The intellectual legacy of these theorists is evident in recent scholarly controversy, much of which focuses on the nature, structure, and physiological correlates of psychological emotional experience. For example, the primacy and importance of the "steps" of emotional experience listed below have been the subject of much emotion research (Lazarus, 1982, 1984; Zajonc, 1980, 1984):

1. meet a bear → 2. appraise as dangerous → 3. physiological arousal →
4. flight → 5. fear

Organization members rarely encounter bears (of course, bears sometimes disguise themselves as coworkers, bosses, or customers), but, for illustrative purposes, Step 1 has traditionally represented a prototypical encounter with an emotion-provoking stimulus. The Darwinian tradition associates emotion with innate physiological responses to environmental stimuli that facilitate survival of the organism. Modern theorists loosely associated with this camp (e.g., Izard, 1977; Tomkins, 1980) generally view primary emotions as "preprogrammed" organismic reactions to certain encountered situations. Theory in this tradition excludes Step 2 above, connecting Step 1 directly to Steps 3, 4, or 5, depending on the particular theorist. In contrast, what survives from James's view (essentially the five-step process shown above) is the belief that emotion involves a cognitively mediated response to physiological arousal. For some theorists (e.g., Schacter & Singer, 1962), Steps 2 and 3 are reversed, such that a generic response of physiological arousal is associated with the appropriate emotion label through cognitive appraisal of the immediate environment ("that is a bear, so I guess I am feeling fear"). Others (Arnold, 1970; Crawford, Kippax, Onyx, Gault, & Benton, 1992; Lazarus, 1991) emphasize the importance of memory and appraisal processes in producing physiological and behavioral responses to emotion. Supplementing these organismic and cognitive perspectives on emotion is a third tradition of emotion research that focuses on social and symbolic aspects of emotion. It is most obviously relevant to organizational emotion. This work focuses attention on the role that cultures and communities play in shaping members' interpretations of emotional events and experiences (Step 2) and members' communicative responses to such events (Step 4). It includes emotion theories previously labeled "psychosocial" (Bowers et al., 1985) and "social constructionist" (Harré, 1986).

Although a number of theorists have proposed decidedly social or cultural views of emotion (Averhill, 1982, 1986; Crawford et al., 1992; Denzin, 1983; de Rivera, 1977; Harré, 1986), these writers are united by the belief that emotions are not simply sensations automatically experienced in response to bears (and other stimulus conditions). Instead, they argue that emotional experience can emerge from the application of cultural understandings to each social situation (for variations on this general theme, see Lutz & White, 1986). An emotional experience can be viewed as an active interpretation and response to the events, people, and objects in a given situation (de Rivera, 1977). The performance of emotion is one means by which cultural agreements are enacted, negotiated, and created. Theorists in this camp often accept arguments that some emotions are characterized by predictable physiological disturbances and behavioral responses (see Collier, 1985; Ekman, Friesen, & Ellsworth, 1972), but they provide evidence that emotion is in part culturally, rather than biologically, determined. In this regard, they note that a given physiological state can be cognitively attributed to multiple emotions (Averhill, 1980a); that no particular feeling or neurophysiological response is associated with such social emotions as loneliness (L. Wood, 1986), pride, chagrin, or hope (Harré, 1986); that, without regard to an individual's state of arousal, cultural agreements prohibit the experience or expression of some emotions in some situations (Averhill, 1986; e.g., one cannot feel proud of a personal failure); and that certain emotions apparently exist in some cultures but not in others (Lutz, 1986). For example, Morsbach and Tyler (1986) report that the Japanese nourish an emotional experience similar to "sweet dependence," while Western cultures suppress this experience from early childhood.

Thus, at least among these emotion theorists, the rules and social agreements that govern how emotions are experienced and expressed are more appropriate subjects of study than the physiological nuances of emotion. The means by which expectations regarding emotion are negotiated, conveyed, and confirmed within a social community are of more importance than the unmediated nonverbal behaviors that signal the experience of emotion. Ultimately, the question "What is emotion?" becomes less important than such questions as these: "How is emotion performed by members of a particular community?" "What are the accepted causes of emotion?" "How is emotion collectively interpreted?" "How are emotions regulated by the community?" "What functions do emotional controls serve within a community?" (See Harré, 1986.)

These questions direct attention to the communicative dimensions of emotion. To view emotion as a performance is to acknowledge that emotion is intertwined with self-presentation. As Goffman (1955) argues, we are emotionally invested in our self-presentations; our emotions are in part responses to the acceptance or rejection by others of our projected selves. Moreover, experiencing certain emotions, or at least acting like we do, is part of what others expect of us in social situations (Goffman, 1956, 1959). Emotional performance enacts cultural expectations, is coordinated with those with whom we share the social situation, and helps others understand how we perceive social situations (Goffman, 1967). All of these activities are important in organizations. These communicative aspects of emotion are perhaps most salient at work, where emotion is typically subject to organizational regulation; the interdependence of members makes it likely that emotional performances will be witnessed by attentive and critical audiences; and the acceptance of emotional performances (by customers, supervisors, coworkers) has consequences not only for our psyches but also for our careers.

THE ORGANIZATIONAL EMOTION
LITERATURE: THREE THEMES

Evidence that organizations are potentially rich settings for the study of the social aspects of emotion is found in the rapidly expanding body of recent literature on organizational emotion. First, in contrast to the traditional views of emotion as a reaction to work, emotion has been conceptualized as an integral part of the labor required of some workers. From this perspective, the internalization of occupational and organizational norms, the fabrication and repression of emotion, *are* the work. The psychological cost to workers of such emotional labor is a primary concern. A second theme focuses on the instrumental role of emotional expression in achieving the goals of organizations and individual workers. Displays of emotion for external audiences and the tactical uses of emotion by workers are central. Organizational benefits rather than psychological costs of emotional performance are emphasized. A third theme involves the cultural understandings that shape the emotional lives of organization members. As mentioned above, some organizational writers advocate culture-building, viewing cultural manipulation as a source of emotional invigoration for the work force. But recent work takes a more skeptical view, emphasizing the active role that members may play in resisting and working around cultural controls on emotion.

Emotion as the Work

Much of the current interest in organizational emotion is attributable to Hochschild's (1983) insightful and detailed description of emotional labor in the airline industry. She notes that the flight attendants do physical and mental labor when pushing service carts through the aisles or preparing for emergency landings and evacuations. But flights attendants are "also doing something more, something I define as *emotional labor*. This labor requires one to induce or suppress feeling in order to sustain the outward countenance that produces the proper state of mind in others" (pp. 6-7).

For Hochschild (1983), emotion is not a reaction to work, it *is* the work. Airline attendants, as do most service workers, sell their emotional exertions for wages, just as physical laborers sell their physical exertions. Emotional labor involves the suppression of authentic emotion and the expression of false emotion to create an illusion for customers. But, with experience, attendants also learn how to fool themselves about their true feelings. Hochschild (1983) quotes a flight attendant to provide an example of the "deep acting" used by service professionals to feel the emotions their organizations require. This attendant describes how she seeks resemblances between passenger characteristics and people she knows well: *"You see your sister's eyes in someone sitting at that seat"* (p. 105). She thinks of the cabin as her living room. "When someone drops in [at home] you may not know them, but you get something for them. You put that on a grand scale—thirty-six passengers per flight attendant—but *it's the same feeling"* (p. 105).

Theorists from Freud (1926/1961) to Darwin (1872) have described emotion as a kind of warning system, alerting individuals to situations or people that are dangerous, prompting them to reconsider their actions or the actions of others, keeping us in touch with our individuality. But, according to Hochschild (1983), excessive manipulation of emotions for commercial purposes (*transmutation* is her term) dulls this signal function of emotion, leaving workers potentially estranged from themselves. She argues that "emotional dissonance," the product of a prolonged difference between "feeling and feigning," eventually takes a psychological toll on service workers. Hochschild argues further that, in using worker emotions as instruments of production, much as manufacturing organizations once used the bodies of child laborers, service organizations exploit and dehumanize their workers.

Hochschild's (1983) study of airline attendants should encourage communication researchers to examine closely the emotional labor performed in other occupations. Hochschild (1983) also studied bill collectors, as did

Sutton (1991). But most research has examined professions where emotional labor is obvious, visible, or dramatic. Numerous writers have provided research and anecdotal data documenting the emotional labor of physicians, who must deal with death and grief on a frequent basis (Bell, 1984; Daniels, 1960; Klein, 1981; Lief & Fox, 1963). The "death telling" work of nurses, police officers, and clergy has received some attention (Clark & Labeff, 1982; J. Wood, 1975). Hochschild (1983) emphasizes, however, that emotion work is a relatively ordinary activity. The routine, behind-the-scenes performance of emotional labor by ordinary workers in ordinary jobs has yet to be fully described. In addition, descriptive communication studies of "typical" managers and subordinates could provide useful data about the prominence, quality, and costs of emotional labor in the routine work lives of workers who interact not primarily with customers but with each other.

The Organizational Uses of Emotional Expression

Hochschild's (1983) wide-ranging and rich sociological description of emotional labor describes organizational attempts to control both the private and the public lives of members and emphasizes the potential personal and societal costs of emotional exploitation. A second research theme concerns the utility of emotional display in achieving management-prescribed objectives (Rafaeli, 1989; Rafaeli & Sutton, 1987, 1989, 1990; Sutton, 1991; Sutton & Rafaeli, 1988). Increased interest in emotional expression is due in part to the growth of service industries as well as the belief among practitioners and scholars that the interaction between service provider and service receiver is the economic battleground of the future (Albrecht, 1988; Albrecht & Zemke, 1985; Czepiel, Solomon, & Suprenant, 1985; Lash, 1989; Peters, 1988). This published work makes clear that service organizations spend enormous amounts of money and effort to ensure that workers express emotion in a manner consistent with organizational prescriptions for good service.

In positing an initial theoretical framework for understanding emotional display, Rafaeli and Sutton (1987) argue that organization members express emotion in accordance with role expectations. These expectations are internalized as the member is recruited, socialized, and rewarded by the organization. Interactions with other members yield feedback about the appropriateness of emotional displays. Properly expressed emotions are posited to yield both organizational outcomes (e.g., short- or long-term gains in sales, improved reputation among customers, and individual outcomes, such as improved financial status through increased tipping by customers).

In a study of convenience store clerks, Sutton and Rafaeli (1988) found the relationship between displayed positive emotion and organizational sales to be complex. Contrary to expectation, clerks in the busiest stores were not the cheeriest, despite substantial organizational effort to orchestrate such good cheer. Apparently, only clerks in slow stores adhered to organizational pre-scriptions. Sutton and Rafaeli's (1988) admirable reanalysis of the data pertaining to their unconfirmed expectations supports a more strategic view of emotional expression than is evident in their original model. Rather than simply conforming to management role prescriptions, members may adjust emotional displays based on the requirements of the immediate work environ-ment, their personal objectives, and the objectives of the audience (custom-ers). The emotional communication of the convenience store clerks studied by Sutton and Rafaeli (1988) was apparently less influenced by organiza-tional goals (produce a positive "emotional front") than by personal goals (conserve physical and emotional resources, avoid customer hostility) and customer goals (minimize waiting time).

This strategic theme is evident in their qualitatively rich analyses of bill collectors and interrogators (Rafaeli & Sutton, 1991; Sutton, 1991). The empha-sis here is on emotional display as a tool of social influence. Building on the work of Cialdini (1984), Rafaeli and Sutton (1991) argue that social influence is enhanced when the target's attention is directed to the contrast between a positive and a negative emotional display. Accordingly, the emotional positiveness of a friendly interrogator is particularly salient when contrasted with the angry tone of another unfriendly interrogator. The target feels a certain obligation to the friendly investigator. From their qualitative data, these researchers derive five variations on this "good cop, bad cop" technique.

The work of Rafaeli and Sutton, and other management theorists who have conceptualized emotion-related display as instrumental to the achievement of valued outcomes (e.g., Garrity & Degelman, 1990; Stephen & Zweigenhaft, 1986; Tidd & Lockard, 1978; Whyte, 1948), is especially provocative, largely because it is grounded in the real-world activities of workers who routinely manage their emotions for personal and organizational gain. It establishes that emotional communication has important economic and practical uses and that organizations expend considerable effort to influence such communica-tion. Investigation of the communication components of Rafaeli and Sutton's (1987) descriptive model of emotional expression has barely begun. Ques-tions awaiting answers include these: How are organizational expectations about emotional expressions communicated during socialization? What are the sources of these expectations? What communication skills or attributes do employers seek when recruiting emotional laborers? What kinds of inter-actions with coworkers result in the adjustment of emotional behavior? What are the personal consequences for members of prolonged emotional labor?

Regarding this last point, researchers might look more critically than Rafaeli and Sutton (1987) have at the potentially negative effects of organi-zationally prescribed emotional display. Perhaps the most compelling point of the study of convenience store clerks (Sutton & Rafaeli, 1988) is *not* the irony of an organization expending tremendous effort to orchestrate emo-tional behavior without first confirming that such behavior would facilitate sales. It is the willingness of an employer to manipulate with cash incentives and monitoring regimes the emotional lives of low-power members, without first considering the work circumstances that could make worker compliance impossible (e.g., the sales pace of the store). Critical investigations of the value attached by management to emotional labor and the potentially exploitative uses of emotional communication and emotion workers would be valuable supplements to this research tradition (for one critical perspective, see Mumby & Putnam, 1992).

Control of the Heart:
Cultural Manipulation of Emotion

Van Maanen and Kunda's (1989) examination of cultural "control of the heart" at Disneyland and an anonymous high-technology firm is the study that most defines a potentially influential third approach to the study of emotion at work. Rather than focus on emotion as a component of task performance or on instrumental expression of emotion, these authors direct attention to the cultural understandings and collective activities that shape the emotional lives of members (for an extensive review of anthropological perspectives on emotion and culture, see Lutz & White, 1986). They see emotional control as the potentially "dark side" of organizational culture, the product of a "culture cult" running amuck, as organizations attempt to bolster the confidence, identification, and commitment of members.[1] "In essence, we think that much of the organizational culture discourse inside organizations masks managerial attempts to control not only what employees say and do but also what they feel" (p. 52).

The emphasis on ritual and collective, rather than individual, emotion is one distinguishing feature of this perspective. Rituals are symbolic and rule-governed activities that can encourage members to value certain thoughts, objects, or feelings (Lukes, 1975; Lutz & White, 1986). Rituals allow members of a community to reaffirm their commonality, but they also provide managers a unique opportunity to regulate and prioritize the emotions of members (Van Maanen & Kunda, 1989). Members can be expected to profess allegiance to organizational values by collectively displaying appropriate emotion at formal rituals (e.g., sales rallies, awards banquets) and in response to organizational stories, myths, and symbols. In addition, emotional controls may be promulgated by coworkers through more informal workplace rituals (e.g., Roy, 1959) and in the treatment that cultural rebels and outcasts receive from coworkers (Van Maanen & Kunda, 1989). Organizations recognized as having strong cultures (e.g., Disneyland) are those most likely to concoct rituals, job descriptions, and evaluation systems that seek to control not only the bodies and minds of members but also the emotions they feel at work.

Research in the cultural vein will be most useful if it looks beyond the obvious cultural forms of emotional control (formal ceremonies, slogans, symbols) to the more subtle yet pervasive means by which emotional life is structured. The discourse of organizational emotion, including the emotion words used by members to make sense of their organizational experiences, is one indication of how cultural prescriptions have seeped into the emotional lives of members (Harré, 1986). Boland and Hoffman's (1983) description and analysis of humor in a machine shop is one of a precious few ethnographies documenting the routine performances of emotion by members of a work culture. Investigations of the organizational root metaphors (Smith & Eisenberg, 1987) and unobtrusive controls that shape member values (Tompkins & Cheney, 1985) could provide insight into the cultural understandings that govern emotion. Finally, as Van Maanen and Kunda (1989) make clear, members are unlikely to passively accept attempts to manipulate their emotions. They may fake what they are supposed to feel and resist in subtle ways or privately mock the rituals they are supposed to take seriously. How individual workers and organizational subcultures resist emotion control, and their success at doing so, should be a primary research interest of those embracing the culture metaphor.

TOWARD A COMMUNICATION PERSPECTIVE

The three traditions described above have obvious communication implications. Yet, rather than simply extend existing research traditions, a communication-based perspective should offer alternative and potentially richer research questions to guide the study of organizational emotion. A communication perspective brings to the foreground the symbolic, negotiated, and strategic aspects of emotion. At a minimum, such a perspective directs attention away from the individual psychology of emotion to the social agreements and the collective processes through which emotion is regulated and interpreted. From a communication perspective, emotion could be construed not just as a reaction but also as a performance (Goffman, 1967; Pacanowsky & Trujillo, 1983)—a rhetorical act, specially adapted to achieve certain objectives in the presence of a specific organizational audience. Emotion can be construed as a symbolic resource; emotion words, memories of past emotional events, and emotion rules are all drawn upon by members as they create messages. A communication perspective permits emotional experiences to be viewed not just as isolated events fixed in a place and time but as topics of continuing discussion such that emotion is reinterpreted and reexperienced across the life course of relationships, work groups, and whole organizations.

Most of these "communication" possibilities have received at least some attention in the literature, and some have been directly addressed by sociologists (Goffman, 1955, 1959, 1967) and organizational theorists writing from interactionist (e.g., Van Maanen, 1979) and information-processing perspectives (e.g., Weick, 1979). Without duplicating this existing work, my intention in the remainder of this essay is to explore three broad areas of inquiry most likely to benefit from study by communication researchers. The first involves the organizational regulation of members' emotional expressions, an area that has drawn considerable attention from organizational researchers. Despite its obvious concern with communicative aspects of emotion, I criticize this body of research for at least implicitly accepting a metaphor of communication as "emotional packaging," its portrayal of emotional expression as a passive rule-dictated activity, and its almost exclusive concern with external audiences. The second broad area involves less studied issues of emotional interpretation. Here I pose a series of research questions pertaining to rules and processes used by members to make sense of their emotional experiences and expressions and those of others. Finally, I examine the potential uses and functions of emotion for organizational members, focusing largely on the tactical deployment of emotion within work relationships.

Regulation: Communication as "Emotional Packaging"

Organizational researchers have often portrayed communication as the process by which genuine, real, or felt emotion is translated into organizationally acceptable emotional expressions (Hochschild, 1983; Rafaeli & Sutton, 1987; Van Maanen & Kunda, 1989; Waldron & Krone, 1991). Communication imposes regulation on felt emotion through "feeling rules." Some researchers emphasize that these emotional translations may yield positive organizational outcomes (Sutton & Rafaeli, 1988) while others lament the potentially negative personal consequences, including self-estrangement (Hochschild, 1983) and emotional numbness (Van Maanen & Kunda, 1989). This regulative aspect of communication is the instrument of what Van Maanen and Kunda (1989) call the "dark side" of organizational culture.

Unfortunately, the dichotomous portrayal of emotion as real or expressed, private or public, genuine or fabricated, lends itself to oversimplification of the role of communication processes in the emotional lives of organization members. Too often in this literature, communication is cast in the familiar, but potentially unsavory, role of emotional "packaging"—the symbolic means by which genuine feelings are disguised and by which organizationally appropriate, but insincere, emotions are fabricated and displayed.

Of the work reviewed in this essay, Hochschild's (1983) depiction of emotional labor illustrates best the multiple influences of language and communication on the experience of workplace emotion. It is somewhat ironic, then, that numerous examples of the "emotional packaging" assumption appear in her work. Illustrative is Hochschild's (1983, p. 112) analysis of an amusing story related to new recruits by a veteran flight attendant (acting as a trainer at the time of the telling). The woman describes how she was handing a dinner tray to a man in a window seat when a woman sitting in the aisle seat "snitched the man's dessert." The flight attendant reportedly responded politely, "I notice this man's dessert is on your tray." This response (which implies that the dessert descended upon the tray through some amazing accident) apparently masked the emotions (amusement? disgust?) the flight attendant felt toward the offending passenger. For Hochschild, "Emotion work has been accomplished, but it has hidden its tracks with words" (p. 112).

Of course, communication *does* play the role of emotional packaging, and the regulative rules and practices that encourage workers to hide or display emotions should be of concern to communication researchers. As Hochschild's (1983) portrayal makes so clear, the packaging of emotion is, quite literally, the work performed by airline attendants, bill collectors, and other service professionals. The emotional packaging metaphor resounds in the large body of research focused on organizational regulations governing the emotional displays of clerks toward customers (Czepiel, Solomon, & Suprenant, 1985; Komaki, Blood, & Holder, 1980; Rafaeli & Sutton, 1990; Shamir, 1983; Tidd & Lockard, 1978). Particularly in this work, the packaging metaphor overshadows other potentially important influences of communication on emotion (e.g., negotiating cultural expectations regarding emotional display, interpreting the emotional displays of others, re-creating past emotional experiences, eliciting emotion in others). Researchers might find it useful to identify and use metaphors that bring these processes to the foreground.

In addition to balking at the conceptual limitations imposed by the emotional packaging metaphor, communication scholars might object to (a) the implicit assumption that emotional communication is a passive, rule-dictated process and (b) the nearly exclusive focus on external audiences. Regarding the first of these, the implicit assumption guiding some studies is that members step into their roles and execute emotion in a reactive, stimulus-response process of rule execution. Although employers may operate on this assumption ("If the customer complains, smile cheerfully and apologize" is the reminder given clerks at a nationally known discount retailer in my area), it seems unlikely that this model of communication fully applies even in highly structured service encounters. The earlier-discussed finding of Sutton and Rafaeli (1988) is illustrative. Convenience store clerks adjusted their emotional displays to the pace and pressure of the store rather than robotically exhibiting good cheer under all conditions. In other words, they strategically adapted emotional regulations to their work environments.

The second limiting factor, the assumption of external audiences, is a side effect of the tendency to focus almost exclusively on the regulation of emotion during the performance of service work. Apparently because the most visible emotional labor involves interaction with external audiences (e.g., customers, patients), the role of emotional regulation inside the organization, in managing coworker relationships (but see Van Maanen & Kunda's, 1989, analysis of "Tech"), has received less attention. This inordinate concern with external audiences is partially accounted for by the potentially dramatic nature of such externally directed emotion work as "death telling" (Clark & Labeff, 1982), policing (Martin, 1980), and corrections work (Waldron & Krone, 1991). Similarly, the highly visible emotional choreography that characterizes work at Disneyland probably accounts in part for its pervasiveness in the applied and scholarly organizational literature (e.g., Peters & Waterman, 1982; Smith & Eisenberg, 1987; Van Maanen & Kunda, 1989). Despite the intuitive appeal of such emotion-laden tasks, the most impactful emotion work may have little to do with the task itself. For example, when parole officers were asked to describe emotional workplace events, Waldron and Krone (1991) found that only a third were directly task related. The majority involved emotional encounters with coworkers, the organizational bureaucracy, or unfair cultural practices. In other words, the emotion rules that regulated members' potentially hostile responses to organizational and relational injustices were more in evidence than task-related rules, despite the emotionally demanding nature of corrections work.

In studying the organizational regulation of emotional expression, researchers should look to the job descriptions, company handbooks, and training procedures that describe the rules governing emotional labor.[2] Examination of the formal and informal criteria applied in performance appraisals and job interviews may reveal which types of emotions are sought and which are devalued. Basic descriptive work on the character of such rules is needed, as are studies investigating whether the display rules enforced by organizations have negative or positive consequences for the organization and for individual workers. Communication researchers could contribute to this literature by examining whether members actually conform to regulative emotional rules in their interactions and by describing how workers compensate for, circumvent, or modify such rules on the job. Both Hochschild (1983) and Van Maanen and Kunda (1989) describe instances of emotional laborers extracting secret revenge from emotionally demanding customers (e.g., airline attendants described "accidentally" spilling drinks onto passengers' laps; Disneyland ride operators used an overly snug "seat belt squeeze" when preparing obnoxious riders for departure). But what are the more constructive verbal equivalents of these revenge moves? The message strategies used by members to express emotion within the constraints imposed by organizational and relational rules should be examined. How and why do some workers excel at (and enjoy) emotional labor? Finally, emotional expression with coworkers and supervisors and other members of the internal audience and the relational consequences of such expressions should be investigated.

Interpretation: Creating the Meaning of Organizational Emotion

Organizations influence not only how members express emotion but also how they assign meaning to the emotional experiences of themselves and

TABLE 1
Sample Research Questions Pertaining to the Rules of Emotional
Interpretation and Three Interpretative Tasks

Emotion Rules	Interpretative Tasks		
	Assessment	Evaluation	Explanation
Constitutive	What counts as "genuine" emotion?	What counts as positive or negative emotion?	Does getting emotional count as an excuse or explanation for behavior or events?
Regulative	What emotions are members not allowed to "see" in coworkers?	What emotional qualities can inform public and private evaluations of coworkers?	Which explanations for emotional displays are acceptable for different types of members (e.g., male/female, leader/member)?
Heuristic	Do emotion labels vary with the audience (e.g., "pissed-off" to coworkers; "concerned" to supervisor)?	How are negative/positive emotional displays overlooked or magnified to meet managerial goals?	How do members manage relational perceptions by offering accounts of how emotions felt toward coworkers (hostility, affection) developed?

others. Members discover and create these meanings through interaction and through observation of other members. The left side of the matrix in Table 1 describes types of rules that might influence emotional interpretations in the organizational setting (see Averhill, 1980a, 1986; Harris & Cronen, 1979). Across the top of the matrix are three types of emotion tasks that are likely to involve communication. Members *assess* the qualities of emotional experiences, interactions, and expressions; *evaluate* these experiences as positive, negative, or neutral; and *explain* (or justify) the reasons for emotional displays. Each of these activities could be subject to the communication rules that partially constitute an organization's culture. The intersections of the matrix in Table 1 yield numerous research questions that have yet to be addressed by organizational communication researchers.

Constitutive rules. Constitutive rules (Pearce, 1976), while familiar to organizational communication researchers (Harris & Cronen, 1979), have not often been invoked by emotion researchers (but see Averhill, 1986; Lazarus, 1991; Levy, 1973). Constitutive rules are the social understandings that members of a community use to determine what "counts" as emotion or as an emotional event. Organizationally influenced constitutive rules might color member assessments of their own feelings and the feelings of others. For example, organizations could instill in members a relatively narrow definition of what counts as "pride." No matter what their felt sensations, organization members might interpret as pride only those feelings experienced after certain organizational objectives are met. An athlete can learn to associate pride more with winning than with performing skillfully. Clerks might be taught that their feeling about an obnoxious customer is not really anger but familial concern (Hochschild, 1983). Organizations could conceivably convince members that the unsettled feelings that accompany organizational change should be interpreted as excitement, not fear. Constitutive rules could be used by members to assess the significance of emotional interaction. How intense, lengthy, or expressive does a monologue have to be before it is construed to be unacceptably emotional? At what point does the boss's expression of criticism become a tirade?

The extent to which a feeling is thought to be voluntary or involuntary may influence such assessments. Averhill (1980a) implies that experiences judged to be beyond one's control are given the status of genuine emotions, or "passions" (for an alternative perspective on the "cultural performance" of passion, see Pacanowsky & Trujillo, 1983). Accordingly, members may distinguish between emotional states that they "feel" and emotional states that they "do." The latter are emotional performances, executed as part of the work role or job description or to achieve some desired effect. Perhaps one sign that workers have been thoroughly socialized is the involuntary experience of emotions that they previously performed only at the bequest of the organization. Cultural rituals and ceremonies may be designed in part to create the experience of involuntary emotion (see Van Maanen & Kunda, 1989).

The experience of being overwhelmed by emotion at work may be relatively rare and, for that reason, interpreted as powerful or significant. The war stories told by organizational veterans often include this kind of emotional component, particularly in professions like police work (Van Maanen, 1973, 1978) where emotional self-control is a critical job skill. The involuntary quality of emotion may convince organization members to excuse behavior that would otherwise be unacceptable in the organization. Impolite or irresponsible behavior may be attributed to or temporarily explained by such statements as these: "I lost my head" or "I lost my grip." Such statements direct attention to the rules of emotional explanation and attribution. Waldron (1989) reported that supervisors, presumed to be thoroughly socialized, justified their emotional behavior by referencing organizational rules and objectives ("He was repeatedly late, so I had to get angry at him"). Nonsupervisors attributed their emotions to breeches of the general cultural rules governing interpersonal conduct ("He insulted me. When someone does that they really don't deserve your respect"). Disloyal coworkers ("back stabbers") and betrayals of confidence by friends also were cited as reasons for becoming intensely emotional at work. To the extent that cultural subgroups (supervisors/subordinates, males/females) accept different reasons as legitimate causes for emotion, misunderstanding and conflict might be expected to develop.

Constitutive rules may be consulted to determine if a coworker's emotional expression is genuine or not. In some organizational cultures, genuine emotion may be admirable. Those individuals perceived to be "laying it on the line," "cutting through the crap," and "letting their hair down" may be valued for their emotional frankness. "Letting off steam" may be accepted practice in some organizational circles. In contrast, a coworker suspected of false emotion may not be trusted. Members labeled "brownnosers" or "two-faced" are typically suspected of displaying false enthusiasm, sincerity, or affection.

More often, the involuntary quality of genuine emotion is associated with negative meanings. Coworkers perceived to be in the "grip" of involuntary emotion are likely to be labeled "out of control" or "hysterical." The author has attended more than one meeting where an angry outburst of a coworker has left the room in stunned silence. In fact, the very word *outburst* implies that emotion is an uncontrolled dangerous force waiting to break through the walls of organizational reason. Organizational communication researchers might use the stories told about emotional episodes and the emotion words used by organization members (for research examples in the interpersonal literature, see Shimanoff, 1985a, 1985b) as indications of the constitutive rules prevailing in a given culture (Harré, 1986).

Regulative rules. Regulative rules apply most obviously to the regulation of emotional expression, as described above. Yet organizations also regulate how members interpret emotion. Hochschild's (1983) airline attendants were encouraged to invoke metaphors and analogies to help them make the "right" emotion assessments. Complaining passengers were to be viewed as frightened or cranky "children." The aircraft pilot quoted at the beginning of this essay evaluated crying, even under the most trying of circumstances, as a sign of weakness. Emotional evaluation is routinely regulated by service organizations. Workers are often discouraged from evaluating negatively even the most outrageous and angry customer ("the customer is always right").

Regulative rules are invoked when workers offer (or choose not to offer) explanations for their emotional acts. Waldron and Krone (1991) described messages that members chose not to deliver during emotional encounters evaluated as negative or positive. A substantial number of these undelivered messages involved justification of emotional responses or protests of organizational or relational practices. Workers apparently felt that openly attributing their emotions to unjust practices was prohibited and potentially damaging to their careers. With regard to positive emotions, the individual who receives a big raise must not appear overly joyful in front of less fortunate coworkers, if he or she hopes to avoid certain inquiries ("So, what are *you* so happy about?"). Of course, such emotions might be displayed deliberately to encourage such curiosity. But, in most organizations, the emotion rules call for modesty in these situations.

These rules of emotional explanation are sometimes explicitly commented upon in collective, public forums where members jointly reconstruct emotional events and their causes (see Pacanowsky & Trujillo, 1983; Weick, 1979). In "bitch sessions," members rehash emotionally negative work events (e.g., layoffs) and construct mutually acceptable explanations for their occurrence (e.g., "you can't trust management"). Building on the existing work on organizational ritual (e.g., Trice & Beyer, 1984), communication researchers should identify other forums for collective emotional explanation and examine the communication process through which such explanations are negotiated. Collective reconstruction of emotional memories has been advocated as a method for researching the social significance of emotion within cultural subgroups (Crawford et al., 1992).

Heuristic rules. With experience, organization members develop emotional "rules of thumb." These are strategic rules of use, adapted to an individual's unique position in a culture (Averhill, 1986). Heuristics can be emotional shortcuts, efficient replacements for the rules prescribed by the organization, but still designed to further individual or organizational objectives. For example, despite organizational prescriptions limiting the expression of organizational emotion, managers might strategically overlook the emotional outbursts of certain talented employees in the interest of sustaining productivity. Food servers learn that management-prescribed cheerfulness ("Hi! My name is Bob and I am your server tonight!") is evaluated positively by certain types of customers and negatively by others. Coaches might strategically attribute the football team's first-half failure to cowardliness to provoke a more emotionally charged second-half performance from certain players.

Workers also apply heuristics to advance their individual agendas or protect themselves. An individual may learn that an appropriately timed tantrum or subtle display of tears typically is interpreted sympathetically by coworkers or that a certain communication pattern is almost always a sign that the boss is upset. The text of interviews of four veteran female employees reported as part of a larger study of relationship maintenance tactics used by women and men suggests heuristic rules were applied to interpret the sexually tinged humor of male coworkers (Waldron, Foreman, & Miller, 1993).[3] The women apparently detected and managed sexually threatening encounters with the male employees by selectively ignoring or acknowledging that the comments were acceptable forms of humor.

As these examples suggest, heuristics provide a kind of specialized emotional expertise. They facilitate rapid assessment of frequently encountered emotional displays and help workers predict the emotional responses of others. A rich source of data on expressive and interpretive heuristics are expert emotional laborers, akin to the "compliance professionals" studied by Cialdini (1984). Existing studies of experienced bill collectors (Hochschild, 1983; Rafaeli & Sutton, 1991) suggest these professionals are adept at interpreting the emotional reactions of debtors. These initial studies are a promising beginning for researchers interested in emotional heuristics, but studies of the more "ordinary" emotional expertise developed by veterans of nearly any job requiring social interaction would be useful in this regard.

The Tactical Uses and
Organizational Functions of Emotion

It has been argued in this essay that the quality of emotional experience is, at least in part, culturally determined. Emotion is not simply a biologically based reaction to stimulus events but, instead, a symbolically mediated and socially negotiated experience. Armon-Jones (1986) argues that, for this position to be tenable, the cultural functions of emotion must be established. She notes that social constructionists see emotion as a means of sustaining the social structure of a community. Emotions are felt and expressed when social agreements are violated or affirmed.

In this section, I review some potential functions of organizational emotion. The discussion is limited in several ways. First, my intention is to stimulate new thinking on such functions rather than to provide an exhaustive list. Second, I emphasize the intended uses of emotion. It is obvious, however, that emotional experiences and displays have simultaneous intended and unintended effects. Third, due to the potential importance of emotion in work relationships (and because much of my own work is focused on the relational context), I emphasize the relational functions of organizational emotion over other types. Of course, emotion also functions at individual, group, and organizational levels of analysis, and I do not mean to understate the importance of current and future research directed at those levels.

Task achievement. The previously discussed studies of convenience store clerks (Sutton & Rafaeli, 1988), airline attendants (Hochschild, 1983), and interrogators (Rafaeli & Sutton, 1991) all operate on the assumption that emotion is used intentionally to facilitate the accomplishment of task objectives. Emotional display is a means of obtaining compliance, sales, tips, or customer satisfaction. Of course, the use of emotion (e.g., fear) to facilitate the performance of communication tasks (e.g., persuasion) has been a traditional concern in the communication literature (Hyde, 1984). More recently, however, theorists studying social influence (for example) have fruitfully conceptualized communication as serving multiple goals simultaneously (Dillard, Segrin, & Harden, 1989). Conceptualizing communication situations in terms of relational, identity, and personal objectives, as well as task objectives, may yield a more complex understanding of the strategic emotional messages produced by workers and the potential consequences of such displays. Researchers using such a theoretical perspective are better able to assess the multiple rhetorical requirements of emotional communication tasks and to develop a more elaborated model of competent emotional expression.

If emotional communication is conceptualized solely in terms of its task function, researchers run the risk of creating a potentially endless set of atheoretical tactic taxonomies, one for each task situation. The proliferation of such taxonomies in the organizational compliance-gaining literature (for a review, see Hellweg, Geist, Jorgenson, & White-Mills, 1990) is convincing evidence that more integrated and parsimonious approaches are needed. While one might argue that work situations are characterized primarily by task objectives, the bulk of the literature reviewed for this essay operates from an implicitly multifunctional view of communication. For example, authors offering advice on the desired outcomes of service interactions stress the simultaneous achievement of task objectives (e.g., sales) and relational objectives (e.g., maintaining long-term relationships with customers; Albrecht, 1988; Albrecht & Zemke, 1985; Lash, 1989; Peters, 1988), although they rarely address objectives related to maintaining worker identity.

Relationship definition. The expression of emotion at work can be an integral part of defining, maintaining, and reformulating relationships. The relationship definition function of emotion has been understudied in the organizational literature. Organizations use ceremonies (e.g., welcoming parties for new members) to create collective experiences of positive emotion that may form the foundation for work relationships (Van Maanen & Kunda, 1989). Shared emotional experiences, whether negative or positive, may prompt organization members to form personal relationships where none existed or to more carefully control their contacts with coworkers. Waldron and Krone (1991) reported that intense positive and negative emotional experiences sometimes prompted members to redefine their relationships from "friends" to "just coworkers" or vice versa. In a later study, Waldron (1991) found that the regulation of positive and negative emotion was reportedly used by subordinates to maintain acceptably defined relationships with supervisors.

Relationships with supervisors and coworker peers are primary sources of expectations regarding organizational emotion. As primary socialization agents (Jablin, 1987), supervisors are particularly influential in setting the emotional tone of work relationships. Supervisors evoke member emotions as a means of motivating (pride), coercing (fear), or calming (relief) them. Subordinates become attuned to the emotional cues displayed by the boss before proceeding with certain "risky" communication tasks, including the establishment of upward influence (Waldron, Hunt, & Dsilva, in press). They may also manipulate the boss's emotional state through the withholding of some messages (e.g., bad news) and the expression of others (small talk, compliments, self-disclosure).

Coworker peers are the informal emotional enforcers of organizational culture (Van Maanen & Kunda, 1989), sanctioning some emotional displays and discouraging others. Roy's early (1959) description of "banana time" and other rituals in a manufacturing firm shows how coworkers expect certain kinds of emotional displays from new members. Individuals capable of positively manipulating the emotions of others may receive considerable positive reinforcement from peers. The company "clown" would be the most obvious example. The sharing of genuine emotion with coworkers (joy, affection, sadness) is no doubt an important and attractive feature of work. Because of the great amount of time and effort invested in work and the interdependent nature of many jobs, the workplace provides numerous opportunities for emotional attachments to develop.

Finally, emotion is used to define relationships with customers and clients. For example, by creating experiences of positive emotion (e.g., through compliments or references to common experiences), salespeople may convince customers to view them as friends, with all the attendant obligations (Cialdini, 1988, pp. 160-168).

Defining the moral order. Emotion functions to preserve and alter the moral order of an organization. Member interpretations and expressions of emotion both reflect and confirm cultural and relational agreements and rules. Such utterances as "I had a right to be angry"; "he was wrong to feel that way"; and "that's nothing to feel proud of" all link emotion to the organizational system of values, rights, and obligations. It is unacceptable to be angry with a coworker unless she or he has broken some organizational rule. The anger functions to protest perceived violations of the moral order and to reassert it. In contrast, expressions of positive emotion may affirm the moral order.

The signal function of emotion, traditionally discussed in terms of an alarm system located within the individual psyche (Freud, 1926/1961; Hochschild, 1983), may operate similarly within organizations and work relationships. Individual or collective experiences of frustration, guilt, or fear signal that something is morally amiss in the organization. Workers may experience guilt when their organizations produce products or services (e.g., nuclear weapons, cigarettes) they find morally repugnant (see Davis, 1983). The means by which organizations attempt to control such feelings should be of interest to researchers. The dulling of the signal function of emotion may account for certain grave errors in organizational decision making. Mumby and Putnam (1992) speculate that the *Challenger* tragedy may have been averted had engineers felt they could question the launch decision without being perceived as irrational. In suppressing the fears of engineers, NASA and its contractors apparently silenced the organizational conscience.

Less dramatic examples of the morality function of emotion can be located in the work histories of most organization members. Parole officers participating in a study of emotional work events (Waldron & Krone, 1991) reported that some of their most intense emotions were not the fear, frustration, and sadness accompanying their daily interactions with parolees. Instead, they cited their negative feelings toward the unjust practices of their organization and supervisors. One young woman's account illustrates the multilayered relationship of emotion and organizational injustice:

> A group of women parole officers were discussing possible promotions when our regional supervisor came into the room and told us outright, he would *not* promote a woman within the agency because "Women cannot handle a supervisor's position. All they do is cry." . . . My expectations and hopes of ever being promoted were destroyed. I was angry, hurt, and humiliated.

At one level, this supervisor's stereotyped notions about female emotionality obviously perpetrate injustice in this organization. At another level, the experience of emotion by the female member functions to alarm her (and potentially her organization) to the existence of unjust practices. Finally, at a third level, the suppression of emotions like anger, hurt, humiliation (common in this organization) is also functional, in that it allows immoral practices to go unquestioned.

Employee handbooks, peer pressure, coercion, banishment, and rewards also function to define the moral order. But when individual members stop feeling and expressing emotional responses to injustice, organizations lose a potentially valuable barometer of organizational fairness. This was obvious when members of the same corrections organization described the socialization messages they had received about how to deal with emotional experiences like the gross injustice described above. Member reports indicated that "go with the flow," "take it in stride," "don't make waves" were typical messages.

Sustaining power relations. Individuals granted position power by their organizations can use their positions to elicit emotional responses in the less powerful. For example, public recognition of subordinates typically results in positive feelings. The attribution of these feelings to the actions of the powerful serves to reinforce the hierarchy (in addition to sanctioning the behavior of the subordinate). Of course, less desirable emotions can also be manipulated. Embarrassing others is one way to remind them of who is in charge (Goffman, 1956). In a study of intentional embarrassment at work (Sharkey & Waldron, 1991), subordinates who had been publicly embarrassed by supervisors typically perceived that the supervisors were seeking to assert their position power (although some perceived the embarrassment as an attempt to build solidarity). One rather blatant example involved the intense embarrassment experienced by the employee of a father-son team of undertakers. "While in front of a large room of people at a funeral, we were about to close the casket for the final time. The father indicated that I should fold the 'throw' and place it in the casket. The son felt this was his job, and after I had placed the throw in the casket, he yanked it out, folded it his *way,* and replaced it."

Personal engagement/disengagement. Kahn (1990) views emotion as one means by which persons invest themselves in their work roles and relationships and make meaningful connections with their organizations. Personal engagement is the expression of a person's "preferred self" in work tasks, relationships, and role performances. As part of engagement, the expression of emotion energizes role performance. Behaviors associated with personal engagement "bring alive" the relation of self to role, connecting the individual with the organization. In contrast, personal disengagement disconnects the self, emotionally, cognitively, and behaviorally from roles and relationships. Much of what has been described in the literature as emotional labor (Hochschild, 1983) arguably promotes personal disengagement. The role of communication behaviors in facilitating *engagement* has yet to be studied but obviously represents one of the more important avenues of organizational emotion research. In a preliminary study, communicative responses to emotional work situations were identified along an engagement/disengagement continuum (Waldron, Bussey, & Myers, 1992). Disengaging message behavior involved emotional withdrawal, denial, substitution of acceptable emotions for felt emotions (e.g., anger to "concern"), and venting of emotion without regard for work role expectations. Engaging behaviors expressed actual felt emotion but did so in a manner that preserved work relationships, organizational goals, and work role identities.

In describing organizational communication as cultural performance, Pacanowsky and Trujillo (1983) offer an alternative perspective. They suggest that the storytelling and repartee of members is used to enliven routine activities. Even members who perform the most mundane of tasks impassion their work experience with metaphors and language that emphasize the occasional glory, risk, competition, or tragedy associated with their jobs, occupations, and organizations. This emotion-provoking language presumably helps members to remain personally engaged in their roles and encourages them to prepare for those future occasions when work again will be nonroutine.

Promoting organizational and personal health. The expression of emotion may function to relieve the tensions that inevitably emerge when organizational subcultures clash, personalities conflict, and resources are scarce. Organizations and their members may, rightly or wrongly, perceive expressions of positive emotion by workers ("the troops are happy"), and certainly customers, as signs of good organizational health. Expressions of humor appear to play a role in relieving organizational tensions (Boland & Hoffman, 1983). Van Maanen (1986; Van Maanen & Kunda, 1989) views rituals, like the drinking sessions of Scotland Yard detectives, as the social channels through which organizational emotion is vented. Teasing may be one way organizational members get others to "lighten up" emotionally (Sharkey & Waldron, 1991). Veteran female managers of a manufacturing firm found their younger female colleagues to be too serious for their own good and urged them to "laugh off" the sexual bantering they encountered on the shop floor (Waldron et al., in press). In general, there exists a belief by researchers and organizational members that positive emotion "wards off" bad organizational and individual health, although this belief would benefit from critical examination. Although the use of ritual and ceremony to promote positive, "healthy" emotion has received some research attention, the perceived causes, frequency, and function of intense positive emotions (e.g., joy) have not been fully studied (but see Abramis, 1988; Averhill, 1980b; Waldron & Krone, 1991). Member beliefs about the role of positive emotion in organizational life and the interpersonal messages through which those emotions are created and expressed require research attention.

CONCLUSION

In summary, I have suggested in this essay that, although organizational theory has not ignored emotion, it has failed to fully appreciate the complexity of workplace emotion and the role of communication in its expression and interpretation. I have argued that social and cultural theories of emotion may be most useful to organizational communication researchers. Recent research, found mainly in the management and sociology literatures, has focused on three related themes: the psychological costs of emotion work, the organizational benefits accrued from members' emotional displays, and the role of organizational culture in shaping members' emotional lives. The communicative aspects of emotion, particularly its regulation, interpretation, and uses and functions, were identified as potentially rich areas of future study.

My overriding intentions in this essay were to stimulate interest in the communicative aspects of organizational emotion and to provide initial direction to the research effort. Readers who review the existing literature are likely to find themselves "personally engaged," both intellectually *and* emotionally. Organizational emotion researchers have provided a rich and broad descriptive base on which studies focused more narrowly on communication issues can be built. Their data have an undeniable aura of ecological validity.

Emotion, communication, and organization are three complexly interwoven processes. I have only begun to identify some of the points at which communication researchers might apply their expertise to shed light on the weaving process. Perhaps the most immediate need is for theory and research that focus squarely on messages and their role in interpreting, expressing, and using emotion in organizational contexts. Descriptive studies that document the frequency and nature of emotional messages and encounters in the ordinary activities of workers would provide useful baseline data. The interpersonal communication strategies, tactics, and discourse associated with organizational emotion have only received the attention of a few scholars thus far (Hochschild, 1983; Rafaeli & Sutton, 1991). The messages used by members when they offer assessments, evaluations, and explanations for their emotional displays and the displays of others should be studied, with special attention given to how these messages serve individual, relational, and organizational purposes.

Studies of the socialization messages used to convey organizational and coworker expectations about emotion, and teach members how to manage their emotions at work, have yet to be fully explored. Communication used by members collectively to reconstruct and make sense of emotional events requires additional study. Critical work has already begun (Mumby & Putnam, 1992), but the substantial communicative investment made by organizations seeking to privilege selected types of emotional experiences and expressions should be subjected to additional critical scrutiny. In sum, there is good reason to put our minds (and hearts) to the task of studying organizational emotion.

NOTES

1. Obviously, many practitioners and some theorists take a less cynical view. Moreover, control is only one of the many issues implied by the use of the culture metaphor. The role of culture in organizational theory and discourse has been addressed thoroughly elsewhere (Barley & Kunda, 1992; Barley et al., 1988).

2. A semianonymous reviewer rightly notes that I emphasize internal organizational processes here to the exclusion of extraorganizational and occupational influences (e.g., business schools, popular books, professional associations). I have narrowed the field in this way not to unduly reify the boundaries of "the organization" but simply because space limitations prohibit my addressing the relevant but vast literatures pertaining to socialization and occupational training. Van Maanen and Barley (1984) and Jablin (1987) offer pertinent analyses.

3. Waldron et al. (in press) report only selected portions of the interviews and do not analyze the data for evidence of heuristic rules.

REFERENCES

Abramis, D. J. (1988, August). *The "up-side" of emotions in work: Joy, excitement, humor, play, and fun.* Paper presented at the annual meeting of the Academy of Management, Anaheim, CA.

Albrecht, K. (1988). *At America's service: How corporations can revolutionize the way they treat their customers.* Homewood, IL: Dow Jones-Irwin.

Albrecht, K., & Zemke, R. (1985). *Service America! Doing business in the new economy.* Homewood, IL: Dow Jones-Irwin.

Armon-Jones, C. (1986). The social functions of emotion. In R. Harré (Ed.), *The social construction of emotions* (pp. 57-82). Oxford: Basil Blackwell.

Arnold, M. B. (1970). Perennial problems in the field of emotion. In M. B. Arnold (Ed.), *Feelings and emotions: The Loyola symposium.* New York: Academic Press.

Averhill, J. (1980a). A constructivist view of emotion. In R. Plutchik & H. Kellerman (Eds.), *Emotion: Theory, research, and experience* (pp. 305-339). New York: Academic Press.

Averhill, J. (1980b). On the paucity of positive emotions. In K. R. Blankenstein, P. Pliner, & J. Polivy (Eds.), *Advances in the study of communication and affect* (Vol. 6, pp. 7-45). New York: Plenum.

Averhill, J. (1982). *Anger and aggression: An essay in emotion.* New York: Springer-Verlag.

Averhill, J. (1986). The acquisition of emotions during adulthood. In R. Harré (Ed.), *The social construction of emotions.* Oxford: Basil Blackwell.

Barley, S. R., & Kunda, G. (1992). Design and devotion: Surges of rational and normative idealogies of control in managerial discourse. *Administrative Science Quarterly, 37*, 363-399.

Barley, S. R., Meyer, G., & Cash, D. C. (1988). Cultures of culture: Academics, practitioners, and the pragmatics of control. *Administrative Science Quarterly, 33*, 24-60.

Bell, M. (1984). Teaching of the heart. *Journal of the American Medical Association, 252*, 26-84.

Bendix, R. (1956). *Work and authority in industry: Ideologies of management in the course of industrialization.* New York: Harper & Row.

Boland, R. J., & Hoffman, R. (1983). Humor in a machine shop: An interpretation of symbolic action. In L. Pondy, P. Frost, G. Morgan, & T. Dandridge (Eds.), *Organizational symbolism* (pp. 187-198). Greenwich, CT: JAI.

Bowers, J. W., Metts, S. M., & Duncanson, W. T. (1985). Emotion and interpersonal communication. In M. L. Knapp & G. R. Miller (Eds.), *Handbook of interpersonal communication* (pp. 500-550). Beverly Hills, CA: Sage.

Cialdini, R. B. (1984). *Influence: The new psychology of modern persuasion.* New York: Quill.

Cialdini, R. B. (1988). *Influence: Science and practice* (2nd ed.). New York: Harper Collins.

Clark, R. E., & LaBeff, E. E. (1982). Death telling: Managing the delivery of bad news. *Journal of Health and Social Behavior, 23*, 366-380.

Collier, G. (1985). *Emotional expression.* Hillsdale, NJ: Lawrence Erlbaum.

Crawford, J., Kippax, S., Onyx, J., Gault, U., & Benton, P. (1992). *Emotion and gender.* Newbury Park, CA: Sage.

Czepiel, J., Solomon, M. R., & Suprenant, C. (1985). *The service encounter: Managing employee interaction in service businesses.* Lexington, MA: Lexington.

Daniels, M. J. (1960). Affect and its control in the medical intern. *American Journal of Sociology, 86*, 259-267.

Darwin, C. (1872). *Expressions of emotions in man and animals.* London: John Murray.

Davis, J. (1983). Work on weapons pains the conscience of some engineers. In P. J. Frost, V. F. Mitchell, & W. Nordance (Eds.), *Organizational reality: Reports from the firing line* (pp. 224-228). Glenview, IL: Scott, Foresman.

Denzin, N. K. (1983). A note on emotionality, self and interaction. *American Journal of Sociology, 89*, 402-409.

de Rivera, J. (1977). *A structural theory of the emotions.* New York: International Universities Press.

Dillard, J. P., Segrin, C., & Harden, J. M. (1989). Primary and secondary goals in the production of interpersonal influence messages. *Communication Monographs, 56*, 19-38.

Ekman, P., Friesen, W. V., & Ellsworth, P. (1972). *Emotion in the human face: Guidelines for research and an integration of findings.* New York: Pergamon.

Freud, S. (1961). Inhibitions, symptoms, and anxiety. In J. Strachey (Ed. and Trans.), *The standard edition of the complete psychological works of Sigmund Freud* (Vol. 20, pp. 77-176). London: Hogarth. (Original work published 1926)

Garrity, K., & Degelman, D. (1990). Effect of server introduction on restaurant tipping. *Journal of Applied Social Psychology, 20*, 168-172.

Goffman, E. (1955). On face work. *Psychiatry, 18*, 215-236.

Goffman, E. (1956). Embarrassment and social organization. *American Journal of Sociology, 62*, 264-274.

Goffman, E. (1959). *The presentation of self in everyday life.* New York: Doubleday Anchor.

Goffman, E. (1967). *Interaction ritual.* New York: Doubleday Anchor.

Harré, R. (1986). An outline of the social constructionist viewpoint. In R. Harré (Ed.), *The social construction of emotions* (pp. 2-14). Oxford: Basil Blackwell.

Harris, L., & Cronen, V. E. (1979). A rules-based model for the analysis and evaluation of organizational communication. *Communication Quarterly, 27*, 12-28.

Hellweg, S. A., Geist, P. A., Jorgenson, P. F., & White-Mills, K. (1990). An analysis of compliance-gaining instrumentation in the organizational communication literature. *Management Communication Quarterly, 4*, 244-271.

Hochschild, A. R. (1979). Emotion work, feeling rules and social structure. *American Journal of Sociology, 85,* 551-575.

Hochschild, A. R. (1983). *The managed heart.* Berkeley: University of California Press.

Hyde, M. J. (1984). Emotion and human communication: A rhetorical, scientific, and philosophical picture. *Communication Quarterly, 32,* 120-132.

Isen, A. M., & Baron, R. A. (1991). Positive affect as a factor in organizational behavior. In L. L. Cummings & B. M. Staw (Eds.), *Research in organizational behavior* (Vol. 13, pp. 1-54). Greenwich, CT: JAI.

Izard, C. (1977). *Human emotions.* New York: Plenum.

Jablin, F. M. (1987). Organizational assimilation, entry and exit. In F. M. Jablin, L. L. Putnam, K. H. Roberts, & L. W. Porter (Eds.), *Handbook of organizational communication* (pp. 679-740). Newbury Park, CA: Sage.

James, W. (1884). What is an emotion? *Mind, 9,* 188-205.

Kahn, W. A. (1990). Psychological conditions of personal engagement and disengagement at work. *Academy of Management Journal, 33,* 692-724.

Klein, K. (1981). *Getting better.* Boston: Little, Brown.

Knights, D., & Morgan, G. (1991). Corporate strategy, organizations, and subjectivity: A critique. *Organization Studies, 12,* 251-273.

Komaki, J., Blood, M. R., & Holder, D. (1980). Fostering friendliness in a fast food franchise. *Journal of Organizational Behavior Management, 2,* 151-164.

Lash, L. (1989). *The complete guide to customer service.* New York: John Wiley.

Lazarus, R. S. (1982). Thoughts on the relations between emotion and cognition. *American Psychologist, 37,* 1019-1024.

Lazarus, R. (1984). On the primacy of cognition. *American Psychologist, 39,* 124-129.

Lazarus, R. S. (1991). Progress on a cognitive-motivational-relational theory of emotion. *American Psychologist, 46,* 819-834.

Levy, R. I. (1973). *Tahitians: Mind and experience in the Society Islands.* Chicago: University of Chicago Press.

Lief, H. I., & Fox, R. C. (1963). Training for a "detached concern" in medical studies. In H. I. Lief, V. F. Lief, & R. F. Lief (Eds.), *The psychological basis for medical practice.* New York: Harper & Row.

Locke, E. A. (1976). The nature and causes of job satisfaction. In M. Dunnette (Ed.), *Handbook of industrial and organizational psychology* (pp. 1297-1350). Chicago: Rand McNally.

Lukes, S. (1975). Political ritual and social integration. *Sociology, 9,* 289-308.

Lutz, C. (1986). The domain of emotion words on Ifaluk. In R. Harré (Ed.), *The social construction of emotions* (pp. 267-288). Oxford: Basil Blackwell.

Lutz, C., & White, G. (1986). The anthropology of emotions. *Annual Review of Anthropology, 32,* 357-404.

Martin, S. E. (1980). *Breaking and entering: Policewomen on patrol.* Berkeley: University of California Press.

Maslach, C. (1982). Understanding burnout: Definitional issues in analyzing a complex phenomenon. In W. S. Paine (Ed.), *Job stress and burnout* (pp. 111-124). Beverly Hills, CA: Sage.

Morgan, G. (1986). *Images of organization.* Newbury Park, CA: Sage.

Morsbach, H., & Tyler, W. J. (1986). A Japanese emotion: Amae. In R. Harré (Ed.), *The social construction of emotions* (pp. 289-307). Oxford: Basil Blackwell.

Mumby, D. K., & Putnam, L. L. (1992). The politics of emotion: A feminist reading of bounded rationality. *Academy of Management Review, 17,* 465-486.

Pacanowsky, M. E., & Trujillo, N. (1983). Organizational communication as cultural performance. *Communication Monographs, 50,* 126-147.

Pearce, W. B. (1976). The coordinated management of meaning: A rules-based theory of interpersonal communication. In G. R. Miller (Ed.), *Explorations in interpersonal communication* (pp. 17-35). Beverly Hills, CA: Sage.

Peters, T. (1988). *Thriving on chaos: Handbook for management revolution.* New York: Knopf.

Peters, T., & Waterman, R. (1982). *In search of excellence.* New York: Harper & Row.

Rafaeli, A. (1989). When cashiers meet customers: An analysis of the role of supermarket cashiers. *Academy of Management Journal, 32,* 245-273.

Rafaeli, A., & Sutton, R. I. (1987). Expression of emotion as part of the work role. *Academy of Management Review, 12,* 23-37.

Rafaeli, A., & Sutton, R. I. (1989). The expression of emotion in organizational life. In L. L. Cummings & B. M. Staw (Eds.), *Research in organizational behavior* (Vol. 11, pp. 1-42). Greenwich, CT: JAI.

Rafaeli, A., & Sutton, R. I. (1990). Busy stores and demanding customers: How do they affect the display of positive emotion? *Academy of Management Journal, 33,* 623-637.

Rafaeli, A., & Sutton, R. I. (1991). Emotional contrast strategies as means of social influence: Lessons from criminal interrogators and bill collectors. *Academy of Management Journal, 34,* 749-775.

Roy, D. (1959). Bananatime. *Human Organization, 18,* 158-168.

Sandelands, L. E., & Buckner, G. C. (1989). Aesthetic experience and the psychology of work feelings. In L. L. Cummings & B. M. Staw (Eds.), *Research in organizational behavior* (Vol. 11, pp. 105-132). Greenwich, CT: JAI.

Schacter, S., & Singer, J. E. (1962). Cognitive, social, and physiological determinants of emotional state. *Psychological Review, 69,* 379-399.

Scott, W. G., & Hart, D. K. (1979). *Organizational America.* Boston: Houghton Mifflin.

Shamir, B. (1983). A note on tipping and employee perceptions and attitudes. *Journal of Occupational Psychology, 56,* 255-259.

Sharkey, W. F., & Waldron, V. (1991, November). *Subordinates' perceptions of intentional embarrassment in the workplace.* Paper presented at the annual conference of the Speech Communication Association, Chicago.

Shimanoff, S. B. (1985a). The role of gender in linguistic references to emotive states. *Communication Quarterly, 31,* 174-179.

Shimanoff, S. B. (1985b). Expressing emotions in words: Verbal patterns of interaction. *Journal of Communication, 35,* 16-31.

Simon, H. (1976). *Administrative behavior* (3rd ed.). New York: Free Press.

Simon, H. (1989). Making management decisions: The role of intuition and emotion. In W. H. Agor (Ed.), *Intuition in organizations* (pp. 23-39). Newbury Park, CA: Sage.

Smith, R. C., & Eisenberg, E. M. (1987). Conflict at Disneyland: A root-metaphor analysis. *Communication Monographs, 54,* 367-380.

Staw, B. M. (1980). Rationality and justification in organizational life. In L. Cummings & B. Staw (Eds.), *Research in organizational behavior* (Vol. 2, pp. 45-80). Greenwich, CT: JAI.

Stephen, R., & Zweigenhaft, R. L. (1986). Effect on tipping of a waitress touching male and female customers. *The Journal of Social Psychology, 126,* 141-142.

Sutton, R. I. (1991). Maintaining norms about expressed emotions: The case of bill collectors. *Administrative Science Quarterly, 36,* 245-268.

Sutton, R. I., & Rafaeli, A. (1988). Untangling the relationship between displayed emotions and organizational sales: The case of convenience stores. *Academy of Management Journal, 31,* 461-487.

Tidd, K. L., & Lockard, J. S. (1978). Monetary significance of the affiliative smile. *Bulletin of the Psychonomic Society, 11,* 344-346.

Tomkins, S. S. (1980). Affect as amplification: Some modifications in theory. In R. Plutchik & H. Kellerman (Eds.), *Emotion: Theory, research, and experience* (pp. 141-164). New York: Academic Press.

Tompkins, P. K., & Cheney, G. (1985). Communication and unobtrusive control in contemporary organizations. In R. D. McPhee & P. K. Tompkins (Eds.), *Organizational communication: Traditional themes and new directions* (pp. 179-210). Beverly Hills, CA: Sage.

Trice, H. M., & Beyer, J. M. (1984). Studying organizational culture through rites and ceremonies. *Academy of Management Review, 9*, 653-669.

Van Maanen, J. (1973). Observations on the making of policemen. *Human Organizations, 32*, 407-417.

Van Maanen, J. (1978). "The asshole." In P. K. Manning & J. Van Mannen (Eds.), *Policing*. New York: Random House.

Van Maanen, J. (1979). The self, the situation and the rules of interpersonal relations. In W. Bennis, J. Van Maanen, & E. H. Schein (Eds.), *Essays in interpersonal dynamics*. Homewood, IL: Dorsey.

Van Mannen, J. (1986). Power in the bottle. In S. Srivasta (Ed.), *Executive power*. San Francisco: Jossey-Bass.

Van Maanen, J., & Barley, S. R. (1984). Occupational communities. In B. Staw & L. L. Cummings (Eds.), *Research in organizational behavior* (Vol. 6, pp. 287-365). Greenwich, CT: JAI.

Van Maanen, J., & Kunda, G. (1989). Real feelings: Emotional expression and organizational culture. In L. L. Cummings & B. M. Staw (Eds.), *Research in organizational behavior* (Vol. 11, pp. 43-104). Greenwich, CT: JAI.

Waldron, V. (1986). *Knowledge acquistion interviews with former military pilots*. Dallas: Texas Instruments, Inc.

Waldron, V. (1989). Emotional encounters in the workplace: A social constructionist perspective. *The Speech Communication Annual, 4*, 73-95.

Waldron, V. (1991). Achieving communication goals in superior-subordinate relationships: The multi-functionality of upward maintenance tactics. *Communication Monographs, 51*, 274-287.

Waldron, V., Bussey, J., & Myers, S. (1992). *Communicating emotion in the organization*. Unpublished manuscript, University of Kentucky, Department of Communication.

Waldron, V., Foreman, C., & Miller, R. (1993). Managing gender conflicts in the supervisory relationship: Relationship definition strategies used by women and men. In G. Kreps (Ed.), *Sexual harassment: Communication implications* (pp. 234-256). Cresskill, NJ: Hampton.

Waldron, V., Hunt, M. H., & Dsilva, M. (in press). Toward a threat management model of upward communication: A study of influence and maintenance tactics in the leader-member dyad. *Communication Studies*.

Waldron, V., & Krone, K. J. (1991). The experience and expression of emotion in the workplace: A study of a corrections organization. *Management Communication Quarterly, 4*, 287-309.

Weick, K. (1979). *The social psychology of organizing* (2nd ed.). Reading, MA: Addison-Wesley.

Whyte, W. F. (1948). *Human relations in the restaurant industry*. New York: McGraw-Hill.

Wood, J. (1975). The structure of concern: The ministry in death-related situations. *Urban Life, 4*, 369-384.

Wood, L. A. (1986). Loneliness. In R. Harré (Ed.), *The social construction of emotions* (pp. 184-208). Oxford: Basil Blackwell.

Zajonc, R. (1980). Feeling and thinking. *American Psychologist, 35*, 151-175.

Zajonc, R. (1984). On the primacy of affect. *American Psychologist, 39*, 117-123.

Is Emotional Expression Repression Oppression? Myths of Organizational Affective Regulation

CHARLES CONRAD
KIM WITTE
Texas A&M University

TO begin, we found Waldron's essay to be excellent. It was a comprehensive, insightful, and well-written exposition of the current state of emotion communication in the workplace. He extends his previous work by developing new ways to conceptualize the communication of emotion in organizational settings. In addition, he offers new directions for research that should yield important information about organizational regulation of affect.

One point with which we take issue, however, is the tendency for many organizational researchers, including Waldron, to posit a false dichotomy in terms of organizational regulation of emotion. The dichotomy assumes that affect rules are beneficial to the organization and detrimental to the individual. This false dichotomy, however, takes (a) a simplistic view of employees, assuming that emotional regulation is inherently harmful and that workers are unable to act in ways that create positive outcomes, and (b) a simplistic view of affect rules, assuming that these rules are unambiguous and internally consistent.

Organization researchers currently give us a picture of employees as passive victims of organization emotional control processes. We propose an alternative frame, which argues that, while controlling employees may be the

AUTHORS' NOTE: We are grateful to Beth Le Poire for her suggestions.

Correspondence and requests for reprints: Charles Conrad, Department of Speech Communication, Texas A&M University, College Station, Texas 77843-4234.

Communication Yearbook 17, pp. 417-428

intent of display rules, what display rules really do is give parameters within which employees can manage emotionality and the stresses related to it.

Much research has focused on the negative outcomes occurring from organizational regulation of emotion, but little theoretical or empirical work has focused on the positive outcomes from emotional regulation. First, we will present why and how organizational regulation of emotion can lead to positive outcomes for employees. Then we will examine how employees retain their autonomy and work within organizational affect rules to achieve their goals.

POSITIVE OUTCOMES FROM
ORGANIZATIONAL REGULATION OF EMOTION

Waldron emphasizes the personal and societal "costs" of regulating emotional communication in the organization. Implicit throughout the essay is the notion that expression of emotions is good and that constraint on emotions in the workplace is bad. For example, Waldron notes that the "enormous effort expended by many organizations to control the emotions of members is implicitly supported, but the emotional costs of work are underestimated." Further, he quotes Thielicke (*Nihilism*) to emphasize the undesirable nature of emotional regulation and display rules by organizations ("[The professional] is the distinctively 'disengaged' man and is therefore liable to become the tool of a degenerate humanity"; p. 390).

But, is emotional regulation in the workplace all that bad? Does it lead to stressed-out employees who fail to produce? Do those employees who are subject to strict emotional display rules suffer psychologically? While employees can define display rules negatively with negative outcomes, it will be argued here that employees also can define display rules positively with positive outcomes. More specifically, an examination of the emotion and health literature suggests that regulation of emotion and display rules is adaptive, is essential to a properly functioning organization, and can lead to positive outcomes for both the individual and the organization. Waldron does call for more research examining "whether the display rules enforced by organizations have negative or positive consequences for the organization and for individual workers" (p. 401). It is clear, however, that the positive consequences of organizational regulation of emotions have been underemphasized, if not dismissed altogether, in the organization and emotion communication literature.

Organizational Researchers' Depictions of
Emotional Regulation

This section of our commentary argues against the implicit but prevailing view that emotional regulation or control at the workplace is harmful. First, we will outline how researchers up to now have argued that emotional regulation is harmful to the individual and society. Then we will question these assumptions by showing how the health and emotion research suggests that emotional regulation and display rules are in fact beneficial. Finally, we will offer directions for future research by providing a theoretical framework that addresses how regulation of emotional communication within the organization can lead to healthier and more productive employees.

Employees are depicted as being harmed by organizational regulation of emotions in three ways. First, emotional labor, where employees' expression of emotions *is* their work, is presented as causing psychological damage to service workers. That is, individuals who must suppress "authentic emotion" and express "false emotion to create an illusion for customers" are portrayed as being exploited and dehumanized. Second, emotional display rules are presented as limiting emotional expression. Putting limits on emotional expression is implicitly assumed to be harmful. For example, Waldron calls for more research into the "negative effects of organizationally prescribed emotional display." Third, organizations that engage in "emotional control" of their employees are portrayed as being malevolent in some way (i.e., having a "dark side"). Specifically, Waldron suggests that "organizations recognized as having strong cultures (e.g., Disneyland) are those most likely to concoct rituals, job descriptions, and evaluation systems that seek to control not only the bodies and minds of members but also the emotions they feel at work" (p. 397). Thus the current organizational literature focuses on the harmful effects of emotional labor, emotional display rules, and emotional control.

Emotional Expression and Health

Is the regulation of emotion through display rules inherently harmful to the employee? The literature on emotional influences on health would suggest otherwise. First, the literature suggests that modulation of emotional expression leads to the most healthy individuals (Hollan, 1992). Many folk medicine systems around the world have long held that strong expression of emotions leads to physiological damage (Hollan, 1992; Witte, 1991). The scientific evidence supports the view that too strong an expression of emotion results in the release of certain hormones or chemicals that can harm the body (Justice, 1987). The expression of negative emotions can be especially damaging to the individual (Justice, 1987; Lazarus & Folkman, 1984). Thus controlled and balanced emotions for the individual are essential to physical and mental health (Justice, 1987; Moos, 1984). When employees are directed to act in a certain emotional manner, the entire organization benefits because the organization maintains an emotional equilibrium where individuals can achieve the greatest level of productivity. In contrast, when employees are "allowed" to express their emotions, especially negative emotions, a spiral can develop where those employees who previously were satisfied with their environment become dissatisfied. In addition, allowing employees to express hostility or anger may contribute to an unpleasant and tense atmosphere within the organization, making work more stressful and difficult. Finally, the health of employees can be adversely affected by the expression of negative emotions. Justice (1987) reported studies finding that "if a substantial number of people on a job start seeing their employer as uncaring or nonsupportive and the work as stressful, boring or meaningless, then the chances for 'mass illness' increase greatly" (p. 179). Conversely, when employees are directed to maintain positive, balanced, and pleasant emotional expressions (e.g., Disneyland), the result is a better work environment and healthier employees. For example, many scholars have found that people who maintain a positive outlook on life have greater immune functioning and less illness (e.g., Justice, 1987; Maes, Spielberger, Defares, & Sarason, 1988; Stone, Cohen, Adler, & associates, 1979).

But does the *legislation* of positive emotion have detrimental effects on the individual? Probably not, according to the emotion and health literature. Research has shown that the mere act of saying positive things or acting cheerful even if one does not feel cheerful leads to healthier individuals (Dillon, Minchoff, & Baker, 1985-1986; Justice, 1987; Zajonc, 1985). This raises a provocative question. If one is directed to communicate in a positive and pleasant manner as part of an organization's display rules, will one's physiological status be altered? Psychophysiological research suggests that how one acts and what one says definitely influence physiological responses (e.g., Dillon et al., 1985-1986; Justice, 1987; Zajonc, 1985). For example, Zajonc (1985) found that, when individuals assumed happy facial expressions, favorable neurotransmitters were released and there was increased blood flow to the brain. Additionally, Justice (1987) cites another study that found, when patients at a nursing home were taught to make positive statements to themselves when faced with a stressor, they had fewer physical symptoms and an improvement in stress hormone levels. Finally, other studies have revealed improved immune status when subjects were directed to smile, make positive statements, or act in a cheerful manner (Dillon et al., 1985-1986; Justice, 1987; Lazarus & Folkman, 1984; Zajonc, 1985). Of course, Norman Cousins (1976) and TV guru Bill Moyers have long argued that making humorous statements and remaining positive leads to better health. In light of this research, organizational control of emotional expression and regulation of emotional communications could be adaptive. This research suggests that employees who are directed to smile, act cheerful, and say positive things would in fact be affecting their physiological states, resulting in physically and mentally healthier employees. Thus it appears that organizational control of emotions would be beneficial to the employee.

Using Self-Perception Theory to
Explain Positive Outcomes

One theoretical framework that can be used to explain the positive effects of emotional regulation by the organization is self-perception theory, which argues that we infer our attitudes and beliefs from our behaviors or actions (Bem, 1967). Individuals try to explain why they say certain things or why they act in certain manners. That is, they search for an attribution for their actions. In the same vein, employees must generate reasons within themselves for why they act certain ways toward customers or clients or why they say certain things. When employees' internal cues for saying something or acting in a certain way are weak, or when the reason for or meaning of their emotions is ambiguous, they search for explanations in their environment to explain their behavior or feelings (Bem, 1967). Employees are not given large extrinsic rewards for acting in accordance with company policy (i.e., no raises or promotions directly linked to acting appropriately within company guidelines). Thus employees must generate explanations for why they act the way they do on the job. Even if employees say they acted a certain way because their employer directed them to do so, positive behavioral and emotional changes can still take place. For example, recent research has shown that, by virtue of speaking something or acting in a certain way, subtle changes take place in line with those "directed actions." For example, Rhodewalt and Comer (1979) found that, when subjects were subtly manipulated to smile while writing a counterattitudinal essay, they reported a more positive mood and greater attitude change than subjects who were subtly manipulated to frown. Additionally, the physiological and emotion research outlined earlier suggests that, when individuals start acting cheerful and positive, they start feeling cheerful and positive.

Organizational Stress Versus Organizational
Regulation of Emotion

One reason that "emotional regulation" has been presumed to be negative by researchers is that many have failed to distinguish emotional regulation from other constructs. For example, it is important to separate the concept of organizational stress from the concept of organizational regulation of emotion. Organizational display rules can provide appropriate outlets for employees to relieve their work-related stress. The structure or type of job *can* lead to stress and pent-up emotions. But, the expression of pent-up emotions outside of accepted display rules at the workplace is ultimately damaging to employees because expressed strong negative emotion can lead to dissatisfaction among those who were formerly satisfied. In addition, it can lead to a depressing or hostile atmosphere. The work site is not the place to express emotional outbursts stemming from job-related stress, but it is the place to problem solve to change work site stressors. For example, employees must be able to make work-related suggestions to improve the environment, product, and procedures so as to decrease work-related stress (Johansson & Gardell, 1988), but employees can still do this while maintaining organizational emotional display rules. In short, organizational stress cannot be avoided, but cultural rules of emotional expression may help to minimize the effects of stressful workplace situations.

Summary

In sum, we have argued that organizational controls of emotional display rules and labor can be adaptive and lead to healthier and happier organizations and employees. Job-related stressors must be addressed and solved and the atmosphere must remain pleasant, however, if the organization is to remain healthy. As Lazarus and Folkman (1984) noted, "Just as negative emotions can result in damaging hormonal secretion patterns, positive ones might produce biochemical substances having protective tissue effects, perhaps warding off disease or even facilitating recovery and health" (p. 314). We believe that positive outcomes can and do occur as a result of organizational regulation of emotion.

EMOTIONS AND SOCIAL/ORGANIZATIONAL CONTROL

As Waldron notes briefly, social actors experience emotions within particular cultural and societal situations that provide them with guidelines and constraints about (a) when to feel (what we will label "feeling rules"), (b) what and how to label the physiological states that we call feelings ("emotion" or "labeling" rules), and (c) when and how to display those emotions ("display" rules).[1] In the remainder of this essay, we will concentrate our attention on (a) feeling and emotion rules and (b) on the ways in which the social and organizational structuring of emotional displays influence those constructs.[2]

Feeling, Emotion, and Display Rules

Many scholars have recognized the role that social structures play in the processes through which people label physiological states ("feelings"). Far fewer have examined the role of social processes in arousal itself. The arousal of social feelings[3] depends on the expectations that we hold about social situations and on our focus of attention in feeling-evoking contexts (Franks, 1985). Feeling rules channel our subjective experiences, telling us *when* we should feel and *when* we should interpret our physiological states as emotional (Hochschild, 1975). Because these expectations are grounded in the socially constructed selves that we bring into feeling situations (Ashforth &

Humphreys, 1993), they vary across individuals and across cultural differentia like race, ethnicity, gender, and class (Mills, 1940; Shott, 1979). So some actors may view repeated television scenes of ethnic cleansing in Bosnia-Herzegovina with strong feelings[4] while others may not have an affective response to these geographically distant and personally irrelevant events. Thus to accuse managers of being "unfeeling" during reductions in force may not only be a moral accusation, it may be an empirically accurate statement. Because they are social constructions, feeling rules also may be patterned in predictable ways. For example, people near the top of social/cultural hierarchies seem to be more likely to focus their attention on dimensions of an affective situation that raise issues of equity/inequity than do people closer to the bottom. Inequitable situations seem to generate feelings for middle- and upper-class women but not for women from lower socioeconomic groups (Hochschild, 1975). In short, "prior expectations are part and parcel of what we see, and in the same way they are part of what we feel" (Hochschild, 1983, p. 221).

Of course, more attention has been paid to societal influences on the labeling of feeling. The link between feeling/experience and emotion is inherently mediated by our symbol systems, although that mediation may be instantaneous and nonconscious (Langer, 1967). Within the limits set by cultural expectations and meaning systems, we construct our emotions: "Internal states and cues [that is, *feelings*], necessary as they are for affective experience, do not in themselves establish feeling, for it is the actor's definitions and interpretations that give physiological states their emotional significance or nonsignificance" (Shott, 1979, p. 1323). Emotions are not automatic, physiological consequences but complex constructs influenced by learning, interpretation, and social influence.

But, emotional experience is inherently ambiguous, and it is in the ambiguities among self, society, and symbolic action that societal power relationships operate (Conrad & Ryan, 1985). Ambiguity results in part from the nature of affective experience. Scholars have recognized, at least since Cannon (1927), that physiological states ("feelings") are so similar that we cannot differentiate among them. Although it seems that some feelings are less ambiguous than others (sexual arousal, hunger, pain, and thirst seem to be less ambiguous than depression or anger; Shott, 1979, p. 1319, note 2), people must actively seek out situational cues and interpret those cues through their own frames of reference to apply emotional labels (Schachter & Singer, 1962).

A second source of ambiguity is the complex, socially constructed character of emotional labels:

> Anger, resentment, indignation, contempt, guilt, and anguish all correspond to
> different patterns of focus on the *cause* of frustration and on my relation to this
> cause. If I feel as powerful or more powerful than the blameworthy party on whom

I focus, we say I feel *anger.* If I see the causal agent as very much more powerful than myself, we say I feel *fear. . . . Indignation* is a name for adding a focus on a thing that is disapproved of; *contempt* is a name for adding a focus on one's social or moral superiority. *Guilt* is a name for seeing ourselves as the author of an unwanted event. *Envy* is a name for noting what we do not have but want and noting further that another has it. *Jealousy* is a name for a focus on the threat to something that we already suppose we possess. . . . As in the case of all emotions, too, what is noted is experienced as *relevant to the self.* (Hochschild, 1983, p. 226)

Not only do actors need to choose emotional labels for their feelings, they also must legitimize those labels within a particular social/cultural context.[5]

A third source of ambiguity in emotional labeling results from the embeddedness of emotional experience: "Let us say that a man becomes violently angry when insulted. What, in his cultural milieu, constitutes an insult? As his anger rises, does he recodify the reality to which he responds? Does some feature of the social context aid or inhibit him in this? Simultaneous to his outburst, does he react with shame or pride at the anger?" (Hochschild, 1983, pp. 211-212). Feelings and emotions emerge, develop, and are transformed through interactions. The nature of interpersonal interaction adds ambiguity to emotional experience. The inherent ambiguity of emotion/labeling rules allows social and organizational display rules to be flexible. But, as we will argue in the final section of this essay, this ambiguity also provides "space" within which employees can (and do) resist organizational emotional control.

The final type of socially constructed affect rules are those influencing the display of emotion.[6] Cultural factors create a social value/cost for the display of emotions, and these values/costs differ for members of different races, classes, genders, or ethnic groups—it is more expensive for Connecticut Yankees to express anger than for Southern Italians to do so and less expensive for Latinas than for Southern belles (Hochschild, 1975). Feelings can be commoditized, although to different degrees for members of different social classes. For example, middle-class parents seem to be more concerned with controlling their children's feelings than are lower-class parents, and prepare them for unobtrusive, emotion-centered forms of organizational control by using, and thus normalizing, appeals to feelings. In contrast, lower-class parents are more concerned with the control of behavior and use/normalize overt behavioral controls (Bernstein, 1971; Hochschild, 1979; Kohn, 1963). People with higher social status (e.g., physicians, bill collectors, and police interrogators) are able to violate display rules with impunity while people of lower social status or formal power are more tightly constrained (Ashforth & Humphrey, 1993). Similarly, the constraining power of display rules seems to be influenced by task structure and organizational rank. Employees whose tasks involve high levels of interaction with either coworkers or outsiders are tightly constrained. Employees in the middle of organizational hierarchies are more limited than those near the top (where privilege allows them to be violated) or the bottom (where behavioral forms of control are dominant; Van Maanen & Kunda, 1989).

Emotion Control as a Site of Resistance

The focus of existing treatments of organizational emotion is on the ways in which feeling, emotion, and display rules function as a mechanism of social control. A typical conclusion is offered by Van Maanen and Kunda (1989):

> In sum, these heralded corporate cultures are of a very conscious sort. They are organized and fine-tuned with considerable attention to detail. Emotions are involved [because] employees attach themselves to these organizations and their respective parts in many ways—through the establishment of close friendships; the acceptance of company standards for proper performance and attitude; the willingness to draw values and a sense of what is important in the world in line with corporate objectives and working principles; the ability to enjoy and support the ritual occasions that go with membership; and the ever-present desire to talk with other members and come to collective assessments of just what is going on in the organization. . . . [Intentional culture manipulation] is powerful because it seemingly aims at a deeper level of employee compliance (i.e., emotional) than other forms of control. (p. 88)

A more sophisticated analysis of the emotional control process suggests that employees vary in their responsiveness to affect rules. For example, Waldron, following Sutton and Rafaeli, suggests that actors simultaneously consider managerial role prescriptions/proscriptions, personal goals, client goals, and attributes of particular work situations in deciding when and how to respond to display rules (p. 18). Hochschild (1975) suggests that employees differ in the extent to which they have internalized affect rules. Ashforth and Humphrey (1993), following Turner (1976), suggest that people who believe that one's "real" self must be discovered through spontaneous actions that may violate institutional constraints[7] are less prone to accept affect rules than people whose self-conceptions are more tightly linked to their institutional membership.

Although an improvement over the "emotion control as monolith" perspective, these views are problematic in two ways. They provide no analysis of why some employees are more capable of resisting than others, largely because they provide analyses of affective control that deemphasize or ignore broader cultural processes. Resistance occurs because the mode of control is flawed in some way, for the normal response is to succumb.[8]

An alternative perspective would suggest that resistance is inherent in the exercise of emotional control (Foucault, 1977, 1980). The *opportunity* to resist is embedded in the complexity and ambiguity of social emotions. Heller (1985) notes that

> disgust, eroticism, fear, gaiety, and sadness, as well as bodily pain and rage, are not only "socialized" but serve as *means* for socialization at the same time. They

are instruments and weapons of culture, [but can be] directed and used against each other. Disgust is used against eroticism, eroticism is "used" against fear, bodily pain against rage, rage against fear and so on. (p. 6)

As Waldron and others have noted, affect rules serve as processes of social and organizational control. But affect rules are resources that are complex, ambiguous, and malleable. They are resources that can be employed by any social actor to empower him- or herself; they need not function solely as instruments of managerial control.[9]

The *incentive* to resist social/organizational affect rules is inherent in the selves of cultural actors/employees. Hochschild (1983) concludes that "institutional rules run deep but so does the self that struggles with and against them" (p. 219). Societal groups *do* contend for access to means of production, means of violence, *and* means of "emotion production." The latter struggle occurs over and through rituals that are designed to forge emotional solidarity.[10] Clearly, this solidarity can in turn be used against other groups or for establishing status hierarchies that can lead to the domination of subordinates (Collins, 1975). Elites, and social groups in general, struggle to assert the legitimacy of preferred feeling, labeling, and framing rules. But the struggle *is* a struggle. Resistance is inherent in the process of emotion control: "Not simply the evocation of emotion but laws governing it can become, in varying degrees, the arena of political struggle" (Hochschild, 1979, p. 568).

CONCLUSION

Waldron's essay has provided an invaluable integration of research on emotion and emotional display from a variety of theoretical perspectives. Its signal strength is its suggestion that the management of emotions is a central element of processes of unobtrusive organizational control. Although we have expressed the concern that existing models of organizational emotional control underestimate employees' capacities to benefit from and resist those rules, we are convinced that dealing with the issues raised in Waldron's essay is necessary for developing comprehensive theories of social and organizational power.

NOTES

1. We hesitate to use the term *rules* because we define the term quite differently than the "rules theorists" that Waldron cites. Our definition is grounded in Anthony Giddens's (1979, 1984) conceptualization of social rules as sedimented patterns of communicative interaction that have a cognitive dimension but are not essentially cognitive constructs.

2. Throughout the commentary, we will assume that there is a duality of emotional structure (Giddens, 1979, 1984), through which affect rules guide and constrain emotional displays, which in turn reproduce or transform affect rules. As Franks (1985) concludes: "Structural accounts of emotions must show the steps by which emotional experience is constrained and shaped by the

possibilities offered by the social, physical, and biological environments of selves, as well as how individuals' active daily involvements in constructing emotions, work upward to reconfirm, maintain, and change structures" (p. 162).

3. In using the term *social feelings,* we are intentionally hedging on the issue of the possibility of innate feeling responses, implicitly recognizing that some fight-flight responses in situations of physical pain/danger may be biologically based. The possibility of feelings that are not symbolically mediated has been a matter of substantial controversy, dating back at least to Marx's differentiation of "social" and "natural" needs in *The Manuscripts of 1844* and subsequent argument that even "natural" needs are socially constructed in *Grundrisse* and *Das Kapital.*

4. We subsequently may label the feelings that are elicited "horror" at the loss of life or "anger" at the Serb's continued defiance of the demands of Western Europeans and Americans, or a variety of other things depending on our individual socially constructed expectations and focus of attention.

5. The means of legitimizing particular labels may be asymmetrically distributed within a culture. Hochschild (1975) notes that "I quit graduate school because I fell in love" is more easily legitimized by women than men. Women are more likely to label an affective response to an abuse suffered at work "being upset" or being "disappointed" and less likely to label it "anger" than men. The difference is important because the former labels tend to generate self-directed action (self-recrimination or depression) while the latter label generates other-direction acting. The feeling itself may not be related to gender, but the labeling is related to a social/cultural ideology about what men and women should and should not feel (Hochschild, 1979, pp. 566-567).

6. Hochschild (1975) notes that the "social constructedness" of emotional rules is much clearer in the case of display rules than in the case of feeling or emotional/labeling rules.

7. Their label is the "impulsive" self. They also suggest that some people "habitualize" affect rules more completely than others and that highly habitualized people are more responsive to affect rules than other people are.

8. A more sophisticated version of this position, and an extended treatment of the key social emotions of shame and guilt, has been developed by Heller (1985): "If external authority is only partly internalized *and* shame is interpreted intersubjectively, the practice of submission can trigger guilt feelings transformed into grudges, resentment or hatred against the authority the subject succumbed to. The interpretation of shame becomes 'ideological' if the actor discharges his or her shame by imputing to the external authority aggression against his [*sic*] family, profession, race, class, sex or community. Shame is thus channeled through projection, and resentment becomes projective" (p. 23).

9. This is a crucial difference between Waldron's conception of "social rules," which, grounded in "rules theories" of communication, conceives of them as independent of communicative action and asymmetrically available to different social actors, and our perspective, which is based on Giddens's notion of social "rules" as embedded in social action and therefore available to all social actors. In the former notion, transformation of affect rules through the action of relatively powerless employees is impossible; in the latter perspective, both reproduction and transformation of affect rules can occur.

10. For an analysis of the relationship between emotion control and organizational ritual, see Van Maanen and Kunda (1989) and Lukes (1974).

REFERENCES

Ashforth, B. E., & Humphrey, R. H. (1993). Emotional labor in service roles: The influence of identity. *The Academy of Management Review, 18,* 88-115.

Bem, D. J. (1967). Self-perception: An alternative interpretation of cognitive dissonance phenomena. *Psychological Review, 74,* 183-200.

Bernstein, B. (1971). *Class, codes and control.* New York: Schocken.

Cannon, W. B. (1927). The James-Lange theory of emotion. *American Journal of Psychology, 39,* 106-124.

Collins, R. (1975). *Conflict sociology.* New York: Academic Press.

Conrad, C., & Ryan, M. (1985). Power, praxis and person in social and organizational theory. In P. Tompkins & R. McPhee (Eds.), *Organizational communication.* Beverly Hills, CA: Sage.

Cousins, N. (1976). Anatomy of an illness (as perceived by the patient). *The New England Journal of Medicine, 295,* 1458-1463.

Dillon, K. M., Minchoff, B., & Baker, K. H. (1985-1986). Positive emotional states and enhancement of the immune system. *International Journal of Psychiatry in Medicine, 15,* 13-18.

Foucault, M. (1977). *Discipline and punish.* Harmondsworth, England: Penguin.

Foucault, M. (1980). *Power/knowledge* (C. Gordon, Trans.). Brighton, England: Harvester.

Franks, D. (1985). Introduction [to the special issue on the sociology of emotions]. *Symbolic Interaction, 8,* 161-170.

Giddens, A. (1979). *Central problems in social theory.* Berkeley: University of California Press.

Giddens, A. (1984). *The constitution of society.* Berkeley: University of California Press.

Heller, A. (1985). *The power of shame: A rational perspective.* London: Routledge & Kegan Paul.

Hochschild, A. R. (1975). The sociology of feeling and emotion. In M. Millman & R. Moss Kanter (Eds.), *Another voice* (pp. 280-307). Garden City, NY: Anchor.

Hochschild, A. R. (1979). Emotion work, feeling rules and social structure. *American Journal of Sociology, 85,* 551-575.

Hochschild, A. R. (1983). *The managed heart.* Berkeley: University of California Press.

Hollan, D. (1992). Emotion work and the value of emotional equanimity among the Toraja. *Ethnology, 31,* 45-56.

Johansson, G., & Gardell, B. (1988). Work-health relations as mediated through stress reactions and job socialization. In S. Maes, C. D. Spielberger, P. B. Defares, & I. G. Sarason (Eds.), *Topics in health psychology* (pp. 271-285). Chichester, England: John Wiley.

Justice, B. (1987). *Who gets sick: Thinking and health.* Houston, TX: Peak.

Kohn, M. (1963). Social class and the exercise of parental authority. In N. Smelser & W. Smelser (Eds.), *Personality and social systems* (pp. 297-313). New York: John Wiley.

Langer, S. (1967). *Mind: An essay on human feeling, I.* Baltimore: Johns Hopkins University Press.

Lazarus, R. S., & Folkman, S. (1984). Coping and adaptation. In W. D. Gentry (Ed.), *Handbook of behavioral medicine* (pp. 282-325). New York: Guilford.

Lukes, S. (1974). *Power: A radical view.* London: Macmillan.

Maes, S., Spielberger, C. D., Defares, P. B., & Sarason, I. G. (1988). *Topics in health psychology.* Chichester, England: John Wiley.

Mills, C. W. (1940). Situated actions and vocabularies of motive. *American Sociological Review, 5,* 904-913.

Moos, R. H. (1984). Social-ecological perspectives on health. In W. D. Gentry (Ed.), *Handbook of behavioral medicine* (pp. 523-547). New York: Guilford.

Rhodewalt, F., & Comer, R. (1979). Induced-compliance attitude change: Once more with feeling. *Journal of Experimental Social Psychology, 15,* 35-47.

Schachter, S., & Singer, J. E. (1962). Cognitive, social, and physiological determinants of emotional state. *Psychological Review, 69,* 121-128.

Shott, S. (1979). Emotion and social life. *American Journal of Sociology, 84,* 1317-1334.

Stone, G. C., Cohen, F., Adler, N. E., & associates. (1979). *Health psychology: A handbook.* San Francisco: Jossey-Bass.

Turner, R. H. (1976). The real self: From institution to impulse. *American Journal of Sociology, 81,* 989-1016.

Van Maanen, J., & Kunda, G. (1989). "Real feelings": Emotional expression and organizational culture. *Research in Organizational Behavior, 11,* 43-103.

Witte, K. (1991). The role of culture in health and disease. In L. A. Samovar & R. E. Porter (Eds.), *Intercultural communication: A reader* (6th ed., pp. 199-207). Belmont, CA: Wadsworth.

Zajonc, R. B. (1985). Emotion and facial efference: A theory reclaimed. *Science, 228,* 15-21.

SECTION 3

MEDIA, CULTURE, AND DIVERSITY

10   Does TV Belong in the Classroom? Cognitive Consequences of Visual "Literacy"

PAUL MESSARIS
University of Pennsylvania

In the face of mounting support (on the part of academic writers, if not the general public) for an increased emphasis on visual media in primary and secondary education, this essay examines one of the major arguments accompanying this trend, namely, the idea that visual "literacy" (in the sense of fluency regarding the conventions of visual communication) leads to a more general enhancement of cognitive skills. The possibility that a specifically visual, TV-based educational program may have a broader, positive impact on the quality of thought is examined with regard to four areas of cognition: the formation of conceptual categories, analytic reasoning, spatial intelligence, and abstractive/analogical thinking.

IN the course of an essay containing detailed prescriptions for a revival of the nation's economy, Felix Rohatyn, who had been a principal architect of the plan that saved New York City from financial collapse in the 1970s, makes the following recommendation: "Beginning in kindergarten, the use of computers, television, and VCRs in the teaching process should be part of any program to improve learning and reverse the high dropout rates of our public school system" (Rohatyn, 1991, p. 9). This statement may be an extreme example of faith in the educational possibilities of television, but a more qualified belief in television's potential contribution to schooling is present in much academic writing on education. On the other hand, to many parents and teachers, this attitude must surely seem perverse. In the eyes of many, television is *the* great enemy of formal education. From such a perspective, what sense can it make to suggest that we should deliberately increase this medium's presence in our schools?

Arguments in favor of the classroom use of television have taken at least three relatively distinct forms. One line of argument entails an essentially

Correspondence and requests for reprints: Paul Messaris, 3620 Walnut Street, Annenberg School for Communication, University of Pennsylvania, Philadelphia, PA 19104-6220.

Communication Yearbook 17, pp. 431-452

defensive stance toward television, predicated on the need to teach children how to be critical viewers. The other two sets of arguments are both based on a more positive view of the medium: On the one hand, it has been proposed that, for some subjects that students are taught in school, television may be able to convey the content more clearly or more engagingly than a teacher alone could; on the other hand, it has been hypothesized that, independent of content, engagement with the medium's formal characteristics may contribute to the development of a distinct set of mental skills applicable not just to television or to other visual media but also to the viewer's dealings with her or his broader (nonmediated) environment. It is this third kind of proposition that I want to address in this essay. As a prelude to assessing the merits of this line of reasoning about television in the classroom, however, it may be helpful to take a quick look at the other two.

The idea that schools should assume responsibility for teaching students how to be critical consumers of television has received much support in recent years (e.g., see Alex, 1989; Brown, 1991; Davies, 1991; Lloyd-Kolkin & Turner, 1989; Sneed, Wulfemeyer, Van Ommeren, & Riffe, 1989), in concert with growing public concern about the potentially manipulative uses of visual media (see Messaris, 1990, 1992). Advocacy in this area is often buttressed by references to the fact that other countries have given critical-viewing education considerable support, as indicated by the following excerpt from UNESCO's 1982 Declaration on Media Education: "The school and the family share the responsibility of preparing the young person for living in a world of powerful images, words and sounds. Children and adults need to be literate in all three of these symbol systems, and this will require some reassessment of educational priorities." It would be difficult, indeed, to find much dissent from this view among communication scholars. It is all the more important therefore to stress the fact that available empirical evidence on the actual outcome of media education programs is not very encouraging. Even the most meticulously designed programs (e.g., Dorr, Graves, & Phelps, 1980; Singer, Zuckerman, & Singer, 1980) have found that, while children will readily absorb information about how television works, that knowledge cannot be counted on to enhance critical viewing. Furthermore, a recent study with college students has found no relationship between critical viewing and a background in media studies (Tatlow, 1992). Instead, this study's findings suggest that *general* critical-thinking ability may lead to critical viewing, independent of specific knowledge about media. In other words, rather than commit resources to media-based curricular innovations, perhaps the best way to encourage students to be critical about television is to emphasize critical thinking in all aspects of their education.

Although the movement in favor of critical-viewing education appears to be intensifying, currently existing instances of in-class television use are much more likely to involve the transmission of information than the inculcation of critical-viewing skills. By implication, then, the justification for this use of television corresponds to the second item on our list, namely, the idea that some academically relevant subjects are most effectively conveyed by television or through a combination of television and oral instruction by a teacher. The use of television along these lines is widespread, in large part because of the availability of subsidized services such as that of Whittle Communications, which gives schools television sets, as well as VCRs and other equipment, in exchange for an agreement to broadcast *Channel One,* a 12-minute news program including 2 minutes of commercials. It is reported that, during the current school year (1992-1993), this service is being used in 10,200 schools (both public and private), with a total enrollment of 6.8 million students in grades 6 through 12 (Toch, 1992, p. 86). A 15-minute newscast without commercials, *CNN Newsroom,* is available free of charge to 25,000 schools, and it is also included in a larger package of free programming (including material produced by C-Span, Arts & Entertainment, Black Entertainment Television, and other sources), which Tele-Communications, Inc. (a cable operator) provides to 5,000 schools (Wulfemeyer & Mueller, 1992, p. 726). Use of in-school television to broadcast news and public affairs programming has also been characteristic of the experience of other countries (e.g., see Greenfield, 1984, pp. 168-169).

In principle, at least, there can be little doubt about the potential social significance of the information conveyed by such programs. For example, Whittle Communications has recently sent a correspondent to Africa to report on such matters as the drought in Mozambique or AIDS in Uganda, as experienced by young people living through these ordeals themselves (Brozan, 1992, p. 20). If used appropriately, information of this kind can presumably play an important role in promoting what should be one of the major goals of education, namely, the development of insight into the conditions of the lives of people unlike oneself. At the same time, however, there is reason to be skeptical about other aspects of this material. The kind of programming provided by such sources as *Channel One* is typically modeled on the format of regular broadcast television. This means that, while these programs may do a good job of conveying descriptive information—the details of a particular event or situation—they are much less likely to provide an adequate framework for an analytic understanding of cause, effect, and context. In principle, of course, it could be argued that analysis can be furnished by the teacher. As Neuman (1991) has argued, even regular home TV viewing can be educational if parents create an appropriate context (see also Messaris, 1983). In practice, however, bridging the gap between ordinary home-viewing habits and the intellectual demands of the classroom situation can be quite problematic. For example, in a thoughtful discussion of her own experiences with the use of visual material in the classroom, Greenfield (1984, pp. 169-171) notes that even college students have a tendency to treat video and film "as breaks in the class, opportunities to 'space out' " (p. 170). Consequently, while it may make sense, in the abstract, to argue in favor of an increased role for television as a conveyor of information in the classroom, the likely nature of concrete applications of this idea should give one pause.

In both of the areas that we have reviewed thus far, then, there is reason to doubt whether the claims that have been made for classroom uses of television are likely to be matched by the actual consequences of these uses. With this note of caution as a backdrop, I would now like to turn our focus on the principal subject of this essay, namely, the last of the three pro-TV arguments described earlier. The basic premise of this final argument is the idea that, in addition to conveying information, television can also cultivate the viewer's cognitive skills. Accordingly, in examining the merits of this position, I want to address the following questions: Does experience in the visual conventions of television—or, to use an increasingly popular term, visual *literacy*—have broader cognitive consequences in terms of a child's (or older viewer's) ways of perceiving and thinking about unmediated reality? In teaching a child about the formal characteristics of the medium, are we also enhancing certain aspects of her or his more general cognitive development?

While this aspect of television's potential contribution to education has received considerable attention from writers concerned specifically with visual media, the broader theoretical ancestry of the ideas with which we shall be dealing goes back to previous work in the study of spoken language. In particular, it was from students of language that contemporary media theorists derived the core notion that a medium's formal conventions play an active role in structuring the thought processes of that medium's users. With regard to spoken language, this notion can be traced back at least as early as the writings of the German philologist Wilhelm von Humboldt (1767-1835), who developed the notion in the course of an attempt to categorize the grammatical characteristics of a broad sample of the world's languages. Humboldt's analysis (1836/1988) of the grammars of such widely differing languages as Chinese, Kawi (used in Java), Latin, and Sanskrit, examined in relation to the cultures with which they were associated, led him to the conclusion that, far from being a passive recorder of reality and instrument of thought, language is actually constitutive of its users' perceptual and cognitive skills. As a man of his time, Humboldt also added to this conclusion the contention that the grammatical characteristics of the Indo-European family of languages (to which most contemporary European languages belong) render them superior to other languages as vehicles for the exploration of reality.

Stripped of this ethnocentric appendage, Humboldt's ideas about the cognitive implications of linguistic form have been echoed and amplified in the writings of several generations of linguists (most prominently, Edward Sapir, 1921, and Ferdinand de Saussure, 1959), and, since the 1940s, they have percolated into the broader academic discourse under the impetus of the well-known series of popularizing articles by Benjamin Lee Whorf (1956, pp. 207-245). Incidentally, it is worth noting that, in direct contrast to Humboldt's position on the relative merits of the European languages, Whorf argued that certain grammatical features of the Hopi language make it a better instrument than English for a variety of scientific and technical applications (Whorf, 1956, pp. 55-56).

Going beyond spoken language, now, one can distinguish between two rather different pathways through which the idea we are concerned with—that is, the idea that a medium's formal features may shape the forms of thought—has come to be applied to other modes of communication. One of these pathways has sought to link cognition to the technical characteristics of media—to such matters, that is, as the degree of resolution in a visual image or the speed of transmission and the availability of feedback in any particular medium. This is the kind of approach that is most prominently associated with the name Marshall McLuhan (1964). Although McLuhan's writings were clearly not designed to yield coherent, testable propositions, related ideas—not necessarily derived from his work—have been developed more systematically by other investigators. The bulk of this scholarship has dealt with the cognitive consequences of literacy—not in terms of grammar, as in the Whorfian model, but with regard to such issues as the durability of various written media (Innis, 1951), the ease with which any particular script can be learned (Goody & Watt, 1972), or the simple fact that writing makes thought available for repeated scrutiny and reflection.

This latter point was a major focus of a landmark study by Scribner and Cole (1981), which sought to determine whether the acquisition of literacy might affect the user's style of deductive reasoning. This study, conducted in Liberia, required its subjects to respond to syllogisms of the following sort: "All women who live in Monrovia are married. Kemu is not married. Does Kemu live in Monrovia?" The hypothesis was that the detached, reflective style of thought assumed to be cultivated by literacy would manifest itself in a greater tendency for premise-based answers (e.g., "You said all women who live in Monrovia are married")—as opposed to context-based answers (e.g., "I don't know Kemu")—among literate subjects. In fact, however, the study's findings did not support this hypothesis. While the subjects' responses did appear to be affected by the presence or absence of formal (secular) schooling (with its attendant emphasis on premise-based problem solving), literacy in and of itself did not have the expected effect. This finding should be contrasted with the fact that the Whorfian hypothesis about language per se—that is, its internal structure rather than the properties of its mediated forms—has received repeated confirmation in cross-cultural studies of physical and social perception. (See Lakoff, 1987, for a review of recent work in this area. Some of this work will also be discussed below.) This discrepancy in the empirical findings may be one reason that attempts to go beyond language in the search for secondary cognitive consequences of communication have tended to take a "Whorfian" route (emphasizing internal message structure) more frequently than the route of technological determinism (emphasizing the channel through which a message is carried).

A major step in the evolution of scholarly interest in the structural characteristics and cognitive consequences of nonlinguistic modes of communication came with the publication, in 1974, of *Media and Symbols*, a collection of essays edited by David Olson. The central theoretical premise uniting the voices of this collection's contributors may be summarized as follows: Each of the principal modes of human communication—such as language, music, or body motion—is characterized by a distinct set of semantic and syntactic properties; consequently, the development of fluency in any one mode amounts to the acquisition of a distinct way of engaging with reality. In other words, whereas earlier work in linguistics had emphasized the structural differences among individual languages, the focus in the Olson volume was on global differences between language as a whole and the various other modes. As a corollary of the idea that each mode confers on its users a unique set of mental tools for understanding and acting upon the environment, it was also argued that a well-rounded education should be multimodal and should reject the heavy emphasis on language that is typical of current practice.

These ideas were developed further in the work of Howard Gardner, who argued that different modes of communication are paths to different kinds of intelligence. Gardner's "theory of multiple intelligences," and the concomitant belief that schools should train students in a broad variety of communicational forms, have become extremely influential, not only on academic theorists but also among educational practitioners. For example, a *Newsweek* cover story on excellence in education describes a program in Pittsburgh's public schools that is directly based on Gardner's theories (Chideya, 1991). The program, which is in place in all the middle and secondary schools in the city, encompasses training in music and visual art, as well as creative writing, and Gardner is quoted as giving the following synopsis of its goals: "art for art's sake and art for *mind's* sake" (Chideya, 1991, p. 61, italics in the original). This idea is also expressed more succinctly in *Newsweek's* caption for a picture of students learning pottery in one of the classes described in the article: "Throwing a pot is another form of intelligence" (p. 61).

It is precisely this kind of assertion that I would like to scrutinize in the discussion that follows—not in reference to pottery, of course, but with regard to television. In one sense, it is self-evidently true that the creation and appreciation of a pot or any other work of visual art require sets of skills (mental and manual) that may reasonably be thought of as forms or aspects of intelligence. But is it also true that skills of this sort have *broader* consequences in terms of their possessor's dealings with her or his real, unmediated environment? Does television "literacy" make a child more adept at perceiving and thinking about anything other than television itself? In addressing these questions, I will begin by comparing the cognitive consequences of visual "literacy" with those of the acquisition of language proper. Then I will examine the type of consequence that has been the focus of most of the previous work in this area: spatial intelligence. Finally, I will discuss the possibility that experience with visual media may lead to an enhancement of the viewer's capacity for abstraction and analogical thinking.

IMAGES VERSUS WORDS

As I have indicated, the idea that a particular communication system's syntactic and semantic conventions may play a formative role in shaping its users' thought processes was originally formulated with reference to spoken language. In seeking to examine the validity of this idea with regard to images, it may be useful to begin with a direct comparison between these two modes of communication. To what extent might a viewer's experience with visual communication cultivate mental habits paralleling those that may be imputed to the learning of a language? As a first step in answering this question, I want to make a distinction between two rather different functions or aspects of communication, which I shall label, very simply, *analysis* and *description. Description* entails an account of a particular series of events or of the features of a particular object or situation. *Analysis* differs from description in two major ways that concern us here: First, it often deals with generalities, with classes of objects, situations, or events, rather than individual cases; second, and more important, rather than simply reporting events or the characteristics of objects or situations, it is concerned with establishing the conditions under which these events or characteristics can be expected to occur. Both description and analysis are routine and, sometimes, overlapping features of our use of language. For example, in a single stretch of conversation, we might describe the harrowing circumstances of a family member's recent hospitalization and then go on to discuss the probable causes of her or his ailment, the effectiveness of various known cures, the likelihood that new cures will be found, and so on. But how compatible are these two functions of communication with the characteristics of images?

As far as what I am calling description is concerned, I do not think there could be much argument on this question. Conveying information about the features of particular objects or the details of particular events is so central a part of what we do with images that even raising the question in this connection may seem peculiar. When it comes to analysis, however, it seems to me that we face a very different situation. *Analysis,* in the sense in which I am using the term here, often deals with general categories rather than individual items, and it is characterized by a focus on causality, contingent relationships, hypotheticals, estimates of likelihood, and so on. For all these aspects of meaning, verbal language contains conventions (individual terms or syntactic devices) that indicate explicitly what kind of statement is being made. In the case of images, however, such conventions are almost totally lacking.

The reason for the word *almost* in the previous sentence is that images do seem to have a limited capacity for certain kinds of explicit generalizations.

For example, the generic images of men and women on bathroom doors, or the generic cigarette in "no-smoking" signs, are explicit symbols for classes of objects rather than for any individual man, woman, or cigarette. But the range of generic images is limited to the world of concrete objects or events (e.g., we can show an individual cause of illness—say, a picture of someone smoking—but there can be no generic image corresponding to the abstract term *cause*); and, within that world, it is further limited to classes of *similar* objects or events (i.e., we can have a generic "person" and a generic "cigarette" but not a generic "object"). In the absence of explicit means for conveying generalizations, the creators of images will sometimes use such devices as a sequence of individual cases, on the basis of which the viewer her- or himself is supposed to infer the implied generalization. To take an example from the world of advertising (in which analytic statements are hardly a primary concern, of course), a much-analyzed campaign for AT&T featured an ad in which several individual people were shown communicating with their loved ones over the telephone, the implied message being of course that AT&T brings "people," in general, together (see Arlen, 1980, for a detailed discussion of this ad campaign).

Similar devices are routinely used as substitutes for at least some of the other types of meanings that images cannot express explicitly. For example, a recent TV ad consists of a number of vignettes in which husbands or wives who are initially reluctant to return their spouses' early-morning affections become extremely responsive after using Scope mouthwash. This "before-after" contrast as a symbol of causal transformation has become highly conventionalized in visual advertising, and it might seem that here, at least, we do have an adequate visual equivalent of a feature of analytic language. In my view, however, the equivalence is, at best, very weak. For one thing, there is evidence that the kind of visual device we are considering here—that is, a juxtaposition of images from which the viewer is supposed to infer a causal claim or other type of analytic statement—can be problematic even for experienced viewers (people who watch TV regularly) unless it is accompanied by narration or a caption that makes the point verbally (see Messaris & Nielsen, 1989).

More significant, however, the reason these devices are poor substitutes for genuine analytic discourse—and the reason my examples had to be drawn from the "quasi-analytic" area of advertising—is that the real world is rarely as uniform or as predictable as the world of advertising. The type of device used in the AT&T and Scope ads, a series of vignettes in which the product brings about a desirable outcome, may be an adequate tool of analytic communication when all events in a certain category are similar or when a certain cause always has the same effect. But the moment we go beyond such a simple state of affairs, we run into trouble. For example, how would we use this type of device to convey the following, fairly routine analytic statement: "This product is not always effective, but it is more effective than its com-

petitors"? Would we start with a series of nine effective before-after sequences, add one ineffective one, and then contrast this with another batch of
before-after sequences for each of the competitors? I think this example has
already brought us well into the realm of absurdity, even though we have
barely begun to penetrate the extraordinary range of complexity of which
analytic language is capable.

With respect to the topic of visual "literacy," then, I would argue that,
whatever other benefits students might receive from a more visually oriented
educational system, a new analytic "language" is not likely to be one of them.
On the other hand, perhaps a more appropriate place to look for cognitive
consequences of visual "literacy" would be the descriptive function of communication, an area in which images are very much at home. In discussing
the cognitive implications of the descriptive symbol systems of images, let
us begin once again with a comparison between images and language. In its
descriptive aspects, as a system of symbols for representing the objects and
events of the world around us, language is sometimes seen as conferring upon
its users a "worldview," a distinctive slant or perspective on those objects and
events. The reasoning behind this assumption about language is based on the
fact that the connection between words and the things they stand for is
arbitrary, in the sense that there is no resemblance between the symbol and
its referent. In the absence of such a resemblance, linguistic communication
depends on the establishment of a relatively fixed set of categories and labels for
the phenomena to which it will make reference. What this amounts to is the
imposition on reality of a set of distinctions and categories, and, because any two
languages may differ with regard to the distinctions they "choose" to make, their
users' views of reality could conceivably be shaped accordingly.

Perhaps the best-documented example of this kind of difference between
languages is the fact that the number of basic color terms in some languages
is much smaller than that which a speaker of English takes for granted (e.g.,
there are languages with only two color terms, *black* and *white*), but equally
clear instances of divergent linguistic classification systems can be found in
various languages' terminologies for shape and size, for animals and plants,
and for space and time. It is sometimes assumed that, in and of themselves,
these differences prove the contention that language shapes worldview, and
more than one prominent anthropologist has used language as the basis for
descriptions of such things as the "primitive mind" or the "Oriental view of
reality." At the same time, however, there have also been several attempts,
over the years, to test the consequences of terminological differences empirically (beginning with such studies as Carroll & Casagrande, 1958, and
including, more recently, the work of researchers such as Kay & Kempton,
1984). This research suggests that, while the idea that language differences
lead to radically different conceptions of reality may be a romantic exaggeration, a smaller scale "fine-tuning" of people's sensitivities to shape or color
or whatever, does seem to occur. Furthermore, there is also evidence that

cross-cultural differences in systems of linguistic representation of reality may reflect the different requirements of various cultures' physical and social environments (e.g., see Berlin & Kay, 1969). In this sense, then, a language's representational system can be seen as a means of adapting a growing child's cognitive/perceptual framework to the task of life in a particular cultural milieu.

Keeping in mind this background material about language, we can now go on to look at images. The idea that the representational conventions of a culture's images might shape the worldview of the members of that culture— or, more precisely, the children growing up in that culture—may seem, on the face of it, an obvious proposition. In this obviousness, however, there is also the danger of tautology, that is, of seeing the images themselves as evidence of the worldview. I have insisted on the importance of outlining the equivalent notions in the case of language because it seems to me that these can serve as our guide regarding the kinds of criteria we should apply in our examination of images. As I hope my discussion of language made clear, the notion that a representational system might shape its users' worldview is contingent on the presence, within that system, of a particular way of "carving up" an area of reality, such as a particular way of dividing up the color spectrum, a particular way of classifying shapes, and so on. Applying this criterion to images, we would be led to look for instances in which a certain representational style made a consistent set of distinctions within the flux of experience.

Examples of this kind of thing are not hard to find. As far as color is concerned, there are numerous instances of pictorial style in which the spectrum is consistently reduced to a palette of no more than three or four encompassing terms (e.g., archaic Greek vase painting, seventeenth-century Japanese prints, Native American art of the Pacific Northwest coast). A more complicated and, perhaps, more interesting example is described in a classic cross-cultural study of art styles by John L. Fischer (1961). In a comparison between relatively egalitarian and relatively hierarchical societies, Fischer found that the art of the former was characterized by the repetition of similar design elements (people, animals, or abstract figures), while the art of the latter was characterized by the presence of a variety of different elements. The obvious hypothesis that emerges from this finding is that these art styles might have served to "bias" social perspectives in the direction of lesser or greater awareness of interpersonal differences, respectively.

Cases such as the one described by Fischer are certainly most intriguing, and, because the concept of "worldview" is often associated with social perception rather than with physical perception, this seems to be a particularly apt illustration of the process whose existence we are considering. I think we have to be very cautious in generalizing from such an example, however. While at least some pictorial styles evidently do meet the criterion of a distinctive partitioning of reality, our discussion of language points to two further considerations that may be appreciably more problematic. First of all, it should be recalled that in the case of language the presence of a fixed categorization scheme is an unavoidable necessity, arising from the arbitrary nature of linguistic signification. As Saint-Martin (1990) has argued, however, images are substantially analogical representations of the things they stand for, and this has a crucial implication. It means that, in principle, images are capable of representing the entire range of variation in a realm of experience and need not be confined to collapsing this range into a more limited number of categories. Thus, while certain visual styles may exercise consistent limitations in their color palettes or in the range of variation of pictured objects' shapes, no visual style *has* to exercise such limitations in any particular area of representation; and, in a medium such as TV, whose images are almost always the products of photographic technology, lack of such limitations is surely the rule rather than the exception.

In other words, what I am suggesting is that a child growing up with the mass-mediated visuals of today's world is not being exposed to the kind of consistent partitioning of visual experience from which a "biasing" of vision might be expected to arise. Let me be the first to acknowledge, however, that the argument I have just made applies only to the *representational conventions* of images, in other words, that aspect of images for which linguistic analogies are usually thought most appropriate and that visual "literacy" training is typically concerned with. If, on the other hand, we were to examine the *narrative content* of television or other visual media, I have little doubt that we would encounter any number of category schemes with a potential for structuring audiences' worldviews, most notably, perhaps, the typical action drama's assignment of most of humanity to the category of not-hero.

A second reason for skepticism regarding the potential effects of images on viewers' perceptual frameworks stems from another important difference between images and language. Language is a mode of communication that all fully socialized people participate in routinely and actively, as both producers and receivers of messages. On the other hand, in most societies—and certainly in all modern industrialized societies—the routine production of images is the province of a relatively small number of individuals and organizations, while the bulk of the population is confined most of the time to the role of receiver. In the case of language therefore, the categories of the representational system have a force and an obligatory character that, as far as most people are concerned, is missing from images. In other words, if internalization of the categories of a representational system is contingent on active use of those categories, the kind of shaping of cognitive/perceptual frameworks that appears to be attributable to language may be considerably less likely to occur in the case of images.

With respect to visual "literacy," what all this means is that the view of images as a form of language is probably not a very useful analogy in thinking about the benefits of a visual education. Making students more aware of the representational conventions of images is not likely to give them access to an analytic apparatus that they would otherwise have lacked, and it does not seem very likely to lead to the kind of adaptive restructuring of cognitive/perceptual frameworks that appears to occur in the case of "real" language. Furthermore, such visual training is also not likely to make much difference to students' ability to extract descriptive information from images, because the representational conventions of images, unlike those of language, are typically based on informational cues that people learn to deal with in their everyday encounters with their real visual environments (Gibson, 1982; Messaris, in press). If linguistic analogy is not the way to go in searching for possible cognitive consequences of visual education, is there another avenue of exploring these issues that might be more productive?

SPATIAL INTELLIGENCE

What may seem to be the obvious answer to the question raised above is suggested by the work of Howard Gardner and others on the nature of human intelligence. As indicated earlier, Gardner (1983) has argued that intelligence should be thought of not as a single phenomenon but as comprising a number of distinct types of mental ability, such as linguistic intelligence, mathematical intelligence, musical intelligence, and so forth. In Gardner's theory, these various forms of intelligence are typically associated with distinct symbol systems, but the match is not always precise. In particular, while there is no specifically pictorial intelligence in Gardner's system, there is a more encompassing category, which he calls "spatial intelligence." At the heart of spatial intelligence is the ability to envision mentally the relationships among objects or parts of objects in three-dimensional space (e.g., what a particular structure might look like from various angles of view, how well one shape might mesh with or fit into another), and it should be clear that this form of intelligence plays a role not only in art (painting, sculpture, dance) but also in geometrical thinking, in the design and construction of any solid object (furniture, buildings, machinery), and in much of our everyday interaction with our physical environment. Because vision is so important to these skills and spatial intelligence contributes to picture-making ability, might spatial intelligence be an area of cognitive functioning that is enhanced by experience with images?

This is the one aspect of our general topic on which there happens to be a small body of directly relevant empirical work, in the form of several studies of children's responses to visual media. The common focus of these studies is on the ability of motion pictures (including television) to represent different points of view in succession (e.g., to switch from a frontal view of a person to a side view). As Hobbs, Frost, Davis, and Stauffer (1988) have shown, a viewer's ability to produce a coherent mental representation of on-screen space from such a succession of views is most probably an extension of the real-world cognitive skill involved in generating an integrated conception of our surroundings from the partial evidence of our successive glances. Given that this real-world cognitive skill must be "stretched" somewhat—and often quite considerably—to fit the demands of television and film, it seems reasonable to assume that this may be another area in which enhanced "literacy" in visual media might entail a reciprocal enhancement of spatial intelligence. One piece of evidence with a bearing on this proposition is a study by Comuntzis (1987), which found a positive relationship between children's scores on spatial-intelligence tasks and their ability to make sense of editing involving successive over-the-shoulder shots. Although Comuntzis was concerned with spatial intelligence as the causal agent rather than as the effect, it is conceivable that her findings may be the result of reciprocal influences. Other studies in this area, however, have dealt directly with the causal sequence we are concerned with here.

In a widely cited experiment by Salomon (1979), children were shown images of familiar objects, presented in a variety of ways. One group of children saw a movie, in which the camera gradually swings around from the initial point of view to a reverse angle. In a second experimental condition, the reversal in angle of view was accomplished by switching from one still image to another. After repeated exposure to one of the presentational modes, each child was tested as to her or his ability to perform the angle-reversal mentally. The test employed was a variant of one of the standard tests of spatial intelligence, namely, the "three-mountain test," in which children are shown a picture of a person looking at a mountainous landscape and then asked to pick out, from a variety of alternatives, the picture that most accurately corresponds to that person's point of view.

In Salomon's study, the children in the moving-camera condition did better on this test than the children in the two-image condition. Salomon bases his explanation of this finding on the notion that the former situation "models" the cognitive process that is required of the subject in the three-mountain tests, whereas the latter situation "short-circuits" it. He also contrasts these two possibilities with a third, which he labels "activation," represented in his study by an experimental condition in which children were shown only a single image of the initial view of the objects. Children in this third condition did somewhat better on the three-mountain test than the children who saw the two different images, and Salomon indicates that this finding is accounted for by the superior performance of those children in the single-image group who were already relatively high in spatial intelligence. For these children, Salomon argues, the single image served as an activator of abilities that were high enough not to require the fuller treatment of the modeling condition.

The implications of all this for the process of everyday TV viewing outside the experimental laboratory are unclear. On the one hand, it could be argued that, because most types of television programming typically present space through editing—that is, as shown in Salomon's two-image condition—rather than in a single static shot or through continuous camera movement, the viewer's processes of spatial cognition are being continually short-circuited and might actually be expected to atrophy in cases of heavy TV exposure. On the other hand, however, it is possible that the short-circuiting condition in Salomon's experiment failed to match the results of the others not because it was too weak a stimulus but because it was too challenging. In other words, the instantaneous reversal of camera angle in the two-image condition might have been too demanding for the children in this study, all of whom were second graders, and the attendant confusion might have prevented the children who saw this version from benefiting as much as their counterparts in the other two conditions. This interpretation is consistent with Salomon's observation that a few children whose spatial-intelligence abilities were relatively high to begin with did seem to benefit from seeing the two-image presentation.

These issues have also been explored in a more natural setting in a study by Forbes and Lonner (1980; see also Lonner, Thorndike, Forbes, & Ashworth, 1985). This study was conducted at the time of the introduction of satellite TV programming to certain parts of Alaska that had previously not had a regular television service. By testing children in these areas and comparing their performance to that of matched samples in places where television had not yet arrived, the researchers were able to get a sense of the effects of the new medium. The study employed several standard tests of cognitive abilities, focusing both on visual and on linguistic skills. Unfortunately, however, the results that most directly concern us here were inconsistent. While the children from the areas with satellite reception tended to do worse than the other children on some tests of spatial intelligence, a different analysis of the children's scores, with individual exposure to television as the independent variable, yielded an opposite pattern of findings. As the reason for this disparity in the results is unclear, this study does little to modify the picture that Salomon's research left us with.

One final set of findings should be mentioned briefly before we conclude our examination of this area. In an informal study of the impact of television on spatial intelligence, Wachtel (1984) examined the historical trends in Swiss children's scores on the three-mountain test in relation to the introduction of television to Switzerland. He found that there had been a pronounced *decrease* in these scores over the period during which television became an established medium in that country. Of course, as Wachtel himself acknowledges, it is impossible to infer a causal connection from data of this kind, especially given the fact that the testing procedures were not stable over time. His discussion of these findings, however, contains a pair of interesting observations that amplify and extend Salomon's point about short-circuiting.

Wachtel notes that (a) television editing does not provide the full range of visual and kinesthetic experience that real-world changes in point of view provide, and (b) the TV viewer is confronted with a preorganized sequence of points of view rather than a space that she or he can actively explore. The latter argument is particularly telling. There is a well-known body of research in developmental psychology that has demonstrated that the early development of visual skills goes hand in hand with the active, physical exploration of the environment and is severely stunted in the absence of such exploration (e.g., see Gregory, 1977). It is conceivable, of course, that, once the initial foundation of spatial intelligence has been laid, subsequent development might be less dependent on self-directed, physical movement through a real three-dimensional environment. Salomon's findings in the modeling condition would certainly suggest as much. Nevertheless, on balance, it seems fair to say that neither the empirical evidence we have reviewed nor the theoretical arguments we have considered build a particularly strong case in favor of the idea that experience as a spectator of still pictures or film and television is a significant contributor to general spatial intelligence.

FROM CONCRETE TO ABSTRACT TO ANALOGY

Up to this point, then, our search for broader cognitive consequences of visual "literacy" has not been especially fruitful. There is one more possibility that remains to be explored. We began by looking at images in comparison to language, and then we went on to examine them in terms of the specifically visual area of spatial intelligence. We will now return to matters related to language once again, but this time our focus will be on the interplay between words and images rather than on their unique characteristics and separate functions. When visuals are combined with a verbal narration, the sequencing of the images is often governed by what the words are doing. This situation is especially prevalent in informational films and TV programs (e.g., news shows and documentaries), where it is indeed the norm. In such cases, the main function of the images is to portray the people, places, and events referred to in the verbal narrative, and the interpretational process that is called for by the visuals is arguably only an extension of the act of attending to a spoken narrative accompanied by pointing, physical imitation, and other forms of visual illustration. Furthermore, research on people's responses to TV news has found that, when the visuals do not match the verbal narrative closely enough, they tend to be dropped from the viewer's/listener's mental processing of incoming information (Grimes, 1989).

All of this suggests that the interaction between words and images in the typical news program, documentary, and so on is probably not much of a stimulus for the development of cognitive skills beyond those involved in following a verbal description. In fact, one could even argue that the presence of the visuals in these kinds of situations actually impedes the development of audience members' mental abilities, because there is considerable evidence that the addition of pictures to a verbal story suppresses the listener's imaginative reconstruction of the events referred to in the narrative (Greenfield & Beagles-Roos, 1988; Meringoff et al., 1983; Williams & Harrison, 1986). Not all combinations of words and images, however, follow the pattern with which we have been concerned up to this point, that is, a "literal" match between the visual illustration and the subject of the verbal narration. Even in typical informational genres, the visual-verbal connection is sometimes quite abstract, and, when that happens, the possibilities for broader cognitive involvement on the viewer's part become more pronounced. As an example of these possibilities, let us take a brief look at the structure of a widely aired commercial for Smuckers, a popular brand of fruit preserves.

This 30-second commercial begins with a brief opening shot of a picturesque landscape, accompanied by soft music that keeps playing as the commercial continues. Over this musical background, a man's voice goes through a list of what it takes to produce a product as good as this particular brand of preserves. Each of the ingredients he mentions is paired to an image on the screen. In the following transcription of the voice-over sound track, the image that accompanies each item will be listed after the line that mentions it: "If you could taste time" (man walking across a wide expanse of cultivated land), "caring" (man tending a fruit tree), "dedication" (man carefully stacking one crate of fruit above another); "if you could taste the sun" (cherries sparkling in sunlight), "rain" (berries moist from rain), "fresh air" (a farmyard scene: children clambering over a fence, horses in background); "if you could taste tradition" (an older farmer talking to a younger one), "and pride" (plump strawberries), "this is what it would taste like every time" (display of the preserves).

It should be obvious from the very first line spoken by the narrator that the relationship between images and words in this commercial is quite different from the ones we have been discussing thus far. Before, we were concerned with images that were direct representations of concrete objects mentioned in the narration: a particular person, a particular place, a particular action. Now, on the other hand, the narration itself makes it clear that one should not expect concrete correlatives in the images. "If you could taste time, care, dedication," the narrator says, but obviously one cannot—not just because these things aren't edible, but because they aren't concrete objects at all. With the exception of rain and the sun, all the "ingredients" referred to in the verbal sound track are abstractions.

In and of itself, the abstractness of the things mentioned in the speaker's words virtually eliminates any possibility of a direct relationship between these words and the accompanying visuals. The reason for this is that visuals of the kind we are dealing with here, that is, pictures produced by a camera rather than by hand, are almost inevitably images of concrete, particular objects and events. In other words, a camera has to record whatever is in front of the lens when the button is pressed, and what is in front of the lens has got to be some specific slice of concrete reality. It is true, of course, that specificity and concreteness can be obscured through manipulations of focus or other such means, and it is always possible to produce a camera image of abstract graphics—although even then it is not clear that one could obtain a direct match with a verbal abstraction. But the typical photographic image, in commercial television at least, is of the kind that is used in this commercial: a picture of a particular scene, which existed in reality at a particular time and place (even if that place was a studio). It follows, then, that this commercial's visuals cannot correspond directly to the abstractions of the verbal sound track. Consequently, in place of the kind of redundancy between words and pictures that we often get in news stories, this commercial confronts us with a very different order of relationship.

The general principle behind this relationship is fairly straightforward: For every abstraction mentioned on the sound track, we get an image of a concrete situation exemplifying that abstraction. Thus, when the speaker refers to "time" as something that goes into making the preserves, we see a concrete instance of a time-consuming activity (walking across a wide field); when the speaker mentions "tradition," we see a specific example of the sort of incident out of which a tradition emerges (an older man passing knowledge on to a younger one); and so forth. Of interest, this general principle seems to be in evidence even in two cases, the references to "the sun" and "rain," in which the words could have been interpreted at a concrete level and "visualized" directly—as is done, in fact, with the words "fresh air," which are paired to a shot of just that (framed, of course, by the farmyard setting that testifies to the air's purity). Instead of such a direct approach, what we get in the case of "the sun" is an image (sunshine playing off fruit) that encourages a more abstract interpretation of what is being implied—not literally "the sun" but its effect on fruit—and the same goes for the image corresponding to rain (fruit dripping with moisture).

With regard to word-image relationships, then, the basic interpretive task that confronts the viewer in this commercial is that of bridging two levels of representation, the abstractions in the sound track and the concrete representations of the visuals. How might we account for a viewer's ability to perform such a task, and what cognitive skills might the demands of this situation bring into play? On the one hand, the interpretive process demanded by this type of editing could be viewed as being largely a matter of experience with other uses of abstraction in the voice-over narration of visual media. For example, a nature documentary might accompany footage of wolves hunting caribou with a verbal disquisition on ecological balance; a children's program might use a skit featuring popular puppet characters to reinforce verbal exhortations about the importance of sharing; and a political advertisement for an incumbent president might pair images of happy and industrious citizens with a verbal paean to the spirit of renewal achieved during his or her first term in office. It can also be argued that there is a parallel between these kinds of situations and certain uses of labels, captions, or other accompanying text in the case of still pictures, as, for example, when the label *American Gothic,* which, technically speaking, describes a style of midwestern architecture, is attached to a painting of a somber-faced rural couple. On the other hand, however, it is possible that the intellectual skills that are brought into play in such circumstances, whether with moving pictures or still images, are not confined to these circumstances alone. Rather, it may be the case that these skills are related to aptitude for abstract reasoning in a more general sense, and it is further conceivable that the act of interpreting visual-verbal juxtapositions of this sort serves to extend the interpreter's abstract thinking abilities rather than merely drawing on them passively.

In this connection, it is worth noting that, aside from these visual-verbal juxtapositions, there is at least one other type of cinematic construction in whose interpretation the capacity to "see" abstract qualities in concrete images no doubt plays a major role. What I have in mind here is exemplified rather elegantly in a brief sequence from Kon Ichikawa's *The Makioka Sisters* (1983). Close to the end of this film, there is a scene in which an unmarried woman, who has endured a series of disappointing attempts at third-party matchmaking, finally meets a suitor she finds attractive. As she faces this man for the first time, Ichikawa's camera travels from a shot of her to a shot of wind-ruffled foliage—with red colors prominent—in the window behind her. To interpret this juxtaposition in the manner that the director presumably intended, the viewer must be able to perceive in each of the two images a cluster of abstract qualities, such as invigoration or warmth, that they both have in common. In other words, the ability to perceive these abstract qualities forms the basis for seeing an analogy between the two images.

Analogical constructions of this sort are clearly an important element of some forms of purely "propositional" editing (e.g., the series of Exxon commercials in which speeding cars are intercut with charging tigers, a device whose sole intent is to imply an analogy), but they also may be present in situations in which propositionality is a less obvious feature of the editing, such as the oft-cited sequence in *2001* in which a prehuman primate who has just learned to use tools throws a bone in the air and the scene switches to a space station spinning in the void. Furthermore, as this example from *2001* may suggest, the kind of mental operation that these analogical constructions demand of the viewer is obviously a very significant ingredient of everyday or real-world intelligence, as opposed to specifically cinematic "literacy." The frame of mind that can see the wealth of similarities between an ape-man's bone/axe and a space station is an integral part of both the poetic and the scientific process, and in fact it can be argued that analogical thinking of this order is a prime mover of intellectual advances, because it allows for the lessons learned in one context to be expanded to another.

At least in principle, then, an argument can be made in favor of the notion that some aspects of visual interpretation may have a parallel in viewers' *more general* skills of abstraction and analogical thinking. But is there any good reason to suppose that experience in the former actually enhances the latter? Some empirical evidence with a possible bearing, although not a direct one, on this supposition comes from a study in which undergraduate students with varying degrees of film-related experience were asked to interpret a 10-minute fiction film (Messaris, 1981). In one of the scenes of this film, the protagonist, a fashionably dressed young woman, was shown walking into a clothing store, but the shot of her going through the door (which was taken from outside the store) was followed immediately, via match-cutting, by a shot of her entering a church. In designing this study, it had seemed to me that no viewer could possibly miss the far-from-subtle implications of this analogical construction. And yet, to my considerable surprise, it turned out that only among students who had taken film courses or had actually made films themselves was there any significant level of awareness of the analogy. Among the other students, the most frequent interpretation of this sequence was purely narrative, that is, the transition was seen as a simple scene change from one location to another. What this suggests, then, is that viewers with special film-related experience may be more sensitive to analogy and its attendant abstractions than "ordinary" viewers.

The problem with this finding, of course, is that viewers were interpreting a ready-made analogy in a movie rather than situations encountered in reality. It is conceivable that the differences between the ordinary viewers and the viewers with film experience were caused primarily by differential sensitivity to the implications of match-cutting rather than differential awareness of the analogy itself. More important, even if we do conclude that awareness of the analogy itself was the deciding factor in this case, we might still want to question whether this intellectual aptitude would extend to the world outside of movies. Here our earlier discussion of spatial intelligence might be of some relevance. As I pointed out in connection with the research of Salomon and Wachtel, it is a standard assumption in the area of developmental psychology that active exploration of reality is necessary for the development of mental skills. When a viewer is faced with an analogical construction in a film or TV program, determining the basis of the analogy may be a challenge, but the initial work of bringing together the two terms of the analogy has already been done by someone else. The same goes for the kinds of visual-verbal constructions that we discussed earlier: The pairing of an abstract narration or caption with a concrete image may stimulate the viewer to see an abstraction where she or he would otherwise not have been aware of one, but the nature of that abstraction has already been set by the words. All of this suggests that the idea of a connection between cinematic or pictorial experience and extracinematic or extrapictorial abstractive/analogical skills must remain very tentative.

CONCLUSIONS

We have examined a number of possible connections between experience with TV or other visual media—visual "literacy"—and the cultivation of broader mental aptitudes. It was argued that visual "literacy" is unlikely to enhance a viewer's skills in analytic thinking and that—however counterintuitive this conclusion may seem—the representational conventions of contemporary visual media are unlikely to shape the perceiver's "worldview." A tighter connection can be drawn, in principle, between visual "literacy" and spatial intelligence. The empirical evidence on this point is equivocal, however. Finally, it was suggested that certain aspects of visual "syntax" and of the interaction between images and voice-over narration (or verbal captions) may contribute to the development of abstractive/analogical thinking, although the argument in support of such a possibility is by no means unproblematic.

What are the broader implications of these observations? From a theoretical point of view, it seems to me that the various kinds of connections between images and thought processes that we have considered here remain very intriguing, even if there is good reason to be skeptical about some (or all) of them. As I indicated at the outset, however, the issues we have been examining also have substantial practical implications, in terms of the ongoing national debate about the future direction of the educational system in the United States. With regard to the practical side of these issues, then, I would lay particular stress on the tentative nature of the assumptions that have been advanced or reviewed here. To the extent that arguments for TV-based visual education are predicated on an expectation of broader intellectual consequences, I would suggest that such educational efforts more than likely will lead to disappointment. Furthermore, as noted earlier, serious questions can also be raised about the other major premises of visual education advocacy, namely, its putative contribution to critical viewing and to the transmission of educational information. Under the circumstances, it may be appropriate to conclude by broadening the context of this discussion to encompass one further point: According to current estimates, U.S. employers are spending approximately $100 billion a year retraining high school graduates in "basic skills" (Beardsley, 1992, p. 103). Prescriptions for TV-based educational reform might do well to weigh this additional fact against any hoped-for benefits of classroom television.

REFERENCES

Alex, N. K. (1989, September). How to "read" television: Teaching students to view critically. *ERIC Clearinghouse Digest*, pp. 1-4.

Arlen, M. J. (1980). *Thirty seconds.* New York: Penguin.

Beardsley, T. (1992). Teaching real science. *Scientific American, 267*(4), 98-108.

Berlin, B., & Kay, P. (1969). *Basic color terms: Their universality and evolution.* Berkeley: University of California Press.

Brown, J. (1991). *Television "critical viewing skills" education: Major literacy projects in the United States and selected countries.* Hillsdale, NJ: Lawrence Erlbaum.

Brozan, N. (1992, August 15). Chronicle. *The New York Times,* sec. 1, p. 20.

Carroll, J. B., & Casagrande, J. B. (1958). The function of language classification in behavior. In E. E. Maccoby, T. M. Newcomb, & E. L. Hartley (Eds.), *Readings in social psychology* (3rd ed., pp. 18-31). New York: Holt, Rinehart & Winston.

Chideya, F. (1991, December 2). Surely for the spirit, but also for the mind. *Newsweek,* p. 61.

Comuntzis, G. M. (1987, July 26-29). *Children's comprehension of changing viewpoints in visual presentations.* Paper presented at the Visual Communication Conference, Alta, UT.

Davies, J. (1991, Second quarter). Linking media literacy to critical thinking: An opportunity for education. *Telemedium,* pp. 3-4.

Dorr, A., Graves, S. B., & Phelps, E. (1980). Television literacy for young children. *Journal of Communication, 30*(3), 71-83.

Fischer, J. L. (1961). Art styles as cultural cognitive maps. *American Anthropologist, 63,* 79-93.

Forbes, N., & Lonner, W. J. (1980). *The sociocultural and cognitive effects of commercial television on previously television-naive rural Alaskan children* (Final report, NSF Grant No. BNS-78-25687). Washington, DC: National Science Foundation.

Gardner, H. (1983). *Frames of mind: The theory of multiple intelligences.* New York: Basic Books.

Gibson, J. J. (1982). *Reasons for realism: Selected essays of James J. Gibson* (E. Reed & R. Jones, Eds.). Hillsdale, NJ: Lawrence Erlbaum.

Goody, J., & Watt, I. (1972). The consequences of literacy. In P. P. Giglioli (Ed.), *Language and social context* (pp. 311-357). New York: Penguin.

Greenfield, P. M. (1984). *Mind and media: The effects of television, video games, and computers.* Cambridge, MA: Harvard University Press.

Greenfield, P., & Beagles-Roos, J. (1988). Radio vs. television: Their cognitive impact on children of different socioeconomic and ethnic groups. *Journal of Communication, 38*(2), 71-92.

Gregory, R. L. (1977). *Eye and brain: The psychology of seeing* (3rd ed.). New York: McGraw-Hill.

Grimes, T. (1989, August 10-13). *The consequences of "grabbing B-roll" in television news: Why semantic audio and video redundancy is crucial to recognition.* Paper presented to the Association for Education in Journalism and Mass Communication, Washington, DC.

Hobbs, R., Frost, R., Davis, A., & Stauffer, J. (1988). How first-time viewers comprehend editing conventions. *Journal of Communication, 38*(4), 50-60.

Humboldt, W. von (1988). *On language: The diversity of human language-structure and its influence on the mental development of mankind* (P. Heath, Trans.). New York: Cambridge University Press. (Original work published 1836)

Innis, H. A. (1951). *The bias of communication.* Toronto: University of Toronto Press.

Kay, P., & Kempton, W. (1984). What is the Sapir-Whorf hypothesis? *American Anthropologist, 86*(1), 65-79.

Lakoff, G. (1987). *Women, fire, and dangerous things: What categories reveal about the mind.* Chicago: University of Chicago Press.

Lloyd-Kolkin, D., & Turner, K. (1989, October 30). *Media literacy education needs for elementary schools: A survey.* Paper presented to the International Visual Literacy Association, Scottsdale, AZ.

Lonner, W. J., Thorndike, R. M., Forbes, N. E., & Ashworth, C. (1985). The influence of television on measured cognitive abilities: A study with Native Alaskan children. *Journal of Cross-Cultural Psychology, 16*(3), 355-380.

McLuhan, M. (1964). *Understanding media: The extensions of man.* New York: McGraw-Hill.

Meringoff, L. K., Vibbert, M. M., Char, C. A., Fernie, D. E., Banker, G. S., & Gardner, H. (1983). How is children's learning from television distinctive? Exploiting the medium methodologically. In J. Bryant & D. R. Anderson (Eds.), *Children's understanding of television: Research on attention and comprehension* (pp. 151-179). New York: Academic Press.

Messaris, P. (1981). The film audience's awareness of the production process. *Journal of the University Film Association, 33*(4), 53-56.

Messaris, P. (1983). Family conversations about television. *Journal of Family Issues, 4*(2), 293-308.

Messaris, P. (1990). Ethics in visual communication. (Broadcast Education Association's) *Feedback, 31*(4), 2-5, 22-24.

Messaris, P. (1992). Visual "manipulation": Visual means of affecting responses to images. *Communication, 13*, 181-195.

Messaris, P. (in press). Visual "literacy": A theoretical synthesis. *Communication Theory.*

Messaris, P., & Nielsen, K. (1989, August 10-13). *Viewers' interpretations of associational montage: The influence of "visual literacy" and educational background.* Paper presented to the Association for Education in Journalism and Mass Communication, Washington, DC.

Neuman, S. B. (1991). *Literacy in the television age: The myth of the TV effect.* Norwood, NJ: Ablex.

Olson, D. R. (Ed.). (1974). *Media and symbols: The forms of expression, communication, and education* (Yearbook of the National Society for the Study of Education). Chicago: University of Chicago Press.

Rohatyn, F. (1991). The new domestic order? *The New York Review of Books, 38*(19), 6-10.

Saint-Martin, F. (1990). *Semiotics of visual language.* Bloomington: Indiana University Press.

Salomon, G. (1979). *Interaction of media, cognition, and learning: An exploration of how symbolic forms cultivate mental skills and affect knowledge acquisition.* San Francisco: Jossey-Bass.

Sapir, E. (1921). *Language.* New York: Harcourt, Brace.

Saussure, F. de (1959). *Course in general linguistics* (C. Bally & A. Sechehaye, Eds.; W. Baskin, Trans.). New York: McGraw-Hill.

Scribner, S., & Cole, M. (1981). *The psychology of literacy.* Cambridge, MA: Harvard University Press.

Singer, D. G., Zuckerman, D. M., & Singer, J. L. (1980). Helping elementary school children learn about TV. *Journal of Communication, 30*(3), 84-93.

Sneed, D., Wulfemeyer, T., Van Ommeren, R., & Riffe, D. (1989, August 10-13). *Media literacy ignored: A qualitative call for the introduction of media studies across the high school social sciences curriculum.* Paper presented to the Association for Education in Journalism and Mass Communication, Washington, DC.

Tatlow, R. (1992). *Media literacy vs. critical thinking: Which is a better predictor of critical viewing skills?* Unpublished master's thesis, University of Pennsylvania, Annenberg School for Communication.

Toch, T. (1992, November 9). Homeroom sweepstakes. *U.S. News & World Report,* pp. 86-89.

Wachtel, E. (1984). The impact of television on space conception. In S. Thomas (Ed.), *Studies in mass communication and technology: Selected proceedings from the Fourth International Conference on Culture and Communication* (pp. 168-174). Norwood, NJ: Ablex.

Whorf, B. L. (1956). *Language, thought, and reality: Selected writings of Benjamin Lee Whorf* (J. B. Carroll, Ed.). Cambridge: MIT Press.

Williams, T. M., & Harrison, L. F. (1986). Television and cognitive development. In T. M. Williams (Ed.), *The impact of television: A natural experiment in three communities.* New York: Academic Press.

Wulfemeyer, K. T., & Mueller, B. (1992). Channel One and commercials in classrooms: Advertising content aimed at students. *Journalism Quarterly, 69*(3), 724-742.

Pedagogical Issues in
U.S. Media Education

RENÉE HOBBS
Babson College

IT'S a child with a thousand names: critical viewing, visual literacy, media education, media literacy, media studies, and more. But if we are to ask the question, "Does TV belong in the classroom?" it is essential to explore the full range of possible meanings associated with the process of using a television set in an elementary or secondary classroom, most of which, at the current time, do not go far beyond the delivery system model provided for by the label "educational technology," where television is merely a tool to teach traditional subject matter (Dorr & Brannon, 1992).

In an article on education reform, Ted Sizer (1992) wonders, "Can we change the very nature of what it is to watch TV? Can the incentives for a student's use of that medium be made powerful so that 'watching a television program' is an active engaging experience?" (p. 26). In considering the specific dimensions of *visual literacy, media literacy,* and its companion phrases, this commentary examines how these concepts are instantiated in classroom activity and how the practice of considering media as an object of inquiry differs from the educational practices that use television as a tool. In doing this, we can better understand the larger context in which Messaris presents his analysis of one of these concepts: visual literacy.

Messaris makes three fundamental points concerning the concept of visual literacy: (a) There are more important differences than similarities when linguistic symbol systems and pictorially based systems are compared; (b) viewers' exposure to media-specific symbol systems may impair, not improve, spatial intelligence because experiential manipulation is not activated in the process of watching film or television; and (c) film and television provide a range of relatively complex relationships between images and

Correspondence and requests for reprints: Renée Hobbs, Babson College, Babson Park, MA 02157-0310.

Communication Yearbook 17, pp. 453-466

words, which may or may not affect the cognitive skills of abstraction and generalization. All in all, Messaris provides a valuable and much-needed critique of the media and cognitive skills theory, which has been taken as an article of faith since the late 1970s by scholars with interests in media and developmental psychology. The groundwork for this theoretical approach began midcentury, when art historians, aesthetic philosophers, and educational psychologists began to develop a new form of discourse based on analysis of media symbol systems that was explicitly aimed at furthering our understanding of the nature of artistic and pictorial modes of expression (Arnheim, 1969; Cassirer, 1953; Goodman, 1968; Langer, 1942).

During the 1970s and 1980s, a different set of questions about media symbol systems emerged. Based on sociopolitical analysis of the mass media, scholars in Great Britain and the United States broadened the framework for analyzing media away from a philosophical and psychological perspective to consider economic, political, and sociological factors and examine how institutional power is manifested and elaborated through symbolic expression in mass media and how meaning is created and shared (Ewen & Ewen, 1982; Fiske & Hartley, 1978; Hall, 1973). Of interest, concepts that place mass media in sociopolitical context have been notably absent from instructional curricula in critical-viewing skills education (Brown, 1991), perhaps because of the dominance and unchallenged acceptance of the "visual thinking" perspective throughout the 1970s. In the 1980s, as Canadian, British, and U.S. educators began to apply some of these concepts in their work with secondary students in schools, the term *media literacy* emerged anew—but, to this day, the term still carries a multiplicity of meanings that reflect the various theoretical stances that now exist regarding the mass media in society.

MEDIA LITERACY:
DEFINITIONS AND THEORETICAL LINEAGE

Messaris defines visual literacy as experience with and knowledge about the conventions of pictures, film, and television. In this regard, he singles out for attention one of the four theoretical traditions for media literacy education in the United States (Anderson, 1983). As Messaris clearly notes, the visual literacy model of media education focuses exclusively on aesthetic technique, not content, and is concerned with the examination of how formal features of the structure of a message have impact on viewers. Dorr and Brannon (1992) identify this approach as a "code-based" perspective, noting that "the focus is on teaching students how to attribute meaning to symbols and how to use these symbols to construct meaningful communications . . . for example, some television literacy curricula teach young children about filmic codes such as cuts that mean a change in time, place or perspective" (pp. 304-305).

The visual literacy model focuses on the decoding processes involved in the interpretation of editing techniques, special effects, camera angles, the use of music, and so on. The visual literacy approach is also conducive to encoding or production activities that explore the construction of messages by examining how small variations on the aesthetic design and structure of messages alter message reception.

From an educational standpoint, such efforts to introduce these concepts into the classroom failed, largely for two reasons. First, the visual literacy approach was based upon the false assumption that people needed to learn to read the symbols of visual imagery in the same way people must learn to read linguistic symbols. Although long a product of folklore in the field of media studies, it has been found through extensive naturalistic fieldwork with a group of people in Northwest Kenya with no prior experience with pictorial or visual media that first-time viewers were readily able to decode complex editing conventions, including flashbacks, point-of-view editing, and other manipulations of time and space when the message content was moderately familiar (Hobbs & Frost, 1991; Hobbs, Frost, Stauffer, & Davis, 1988). Adults do not need much experience or exposure to the conventions of film and television to effectively extract meaning from mediated messages, which accounts in part for the rapid dissemination of the technology of television and video to almost every corner of the planet. Very young children's occasional difficulties in comprehending editing that manipulates time (Collins, 1983) is most certainly due to their limited cognitive skills, not their lack of experience with the medium.

Another weakness with the visual literacy approach in education centers on the questionable value of applying concepts of visual literacy to hands-on production activities. This approach gradually became embedded in the vocational education framework for teaching television production both at the college level and down into the large secondary schools, which resulted from the shift in journalism schools and education schools after World War II when demand for pragmatic real-world skills led to enormous growth in education within vocational and professional fields, including business, journalism, and education (Lazerson & Grubb, 1974). Non-college-bound high school students, in particular, still learn concepts of visual literacy like the 180-degree rule or names for various editing techniques as some of the "tricks of the trade" in the construction of film and television. Messaris points out how limited such knowledge is and how unrelated it is to the complex process of critical viewing.

In 1983 Cassidy and Knowlton, after a thorough exploration of the evidence that supports visual literacy, argued that

> there is little in the relevant cross-cultural or developmental literature to substantiate the contention that people need to be taught how to interpret pictures. . . . As we delved ever more deeply into the quagmire that is visual literacy, it became

ever clearer that the VL metaphor lacks any redeeming value. Indeed, this
metaphor has had an insidious influence in that it has sometimes given scholars
in the field a "set" to search for similarities between the digital and iconic
systems, resulting in a neglect of the differences. (p. 88)

But, while Messaris uses similar evidence to argue that the entire enterprise
of television in the classroom is suspect because of the inadequacy of conceptualizations of visual literacy, it is important to recognize that the visual literacy
approach is but one of a number of concomitant theoretical strands in the
efforts to teach about media in elementary and secondary classrooms.

James Anderson (1983) identifies two other traditions that lay claim to the
"media literacy" concept as it has evolved since the invention of film at the
turn of the twentieth century, both of which spring directly from social-scientific approaches to media study. The effects (or protectionist) model teaches
skills of media literacy by focusing on the presentation of material that helps
protect or inoculate children from the vast array of negative effects, including
violence, stereotyping, and so on, while the "uses and gratifications" model
is based on helping children to identify their motivations and satisfactions in
watching television. Reflecting their powerful ambivalence about mass media
and popular culture, elementary and secondary teachers feel most comfortable with these two perspectives on media literacy, evident in surveys of
educators that consistently find high levels of concern about the negative
impact of television on social attitudes, interest in how to modify students'
viewing choices, and concern about television's contribution to declines in
attention, perseverance, and reasoning skills (Hobbs, 1992; Kozoil, 1989;
Wulfemeyer, 1990). While still popular among American educators, this
model has been almost completely rejected by educators in Great Britain, who
point to concerns about class bias and elitism in identifying the fallacies of
the protectionist model of media literacy (Alvarado & Boyd-Barrett, 1992).

Yet another competing tradition in the media literacy lineage has been
called by Anderson the "cultural understanding" model. This approach uses
television as a vital source of information about the culture, "composed of
the shared values, ideas and symbols by which individuals are joined as a
people" (Anderson, 1983, p. 303), focusing on the application of techniques
of literary criticism to media "texts." In Piette's (1992) analysis of U.S. and
European media education curricula, he elaborates additional models for
media education based on critical theory, semiology, and cultural studies,
which are evident in media literacy curricula from Finland, Great Britain, and
Switzerland.

It is important to recognize that each of these models claims to instantiate
the phrases *critical-viewing skills, media literacy*, and *visual literacy,* yet
each comes from the distinctly different intellectual traditions of aesthetics,
philosophy and semiotics, social science, literary criticism, and the humanities. One of the reasons for the lack of coherence in the scholarly literature

and the stagnation of efforts to implement media education in U.S. schools is important definitional problems, which are still widely evident today. For example, journalism educators who specialize in graphic design have begun adopting the terms *visual communication* and *visual cognition* in their efforts to get more attention to college-level courses that focus on design issues in media production. Clearly, there is not yet any systematic consensus among the academic community about what needs to be taught and learned about images produced and consumed via media for either general or professional programs. Without initiatives to develop consensus among the scholarly community, educational discourse will be slowed.

THE CURRICULUM OF MEDIA LITERACY: WHAT DO STUDENTS NEED TO KNOW?

In contrast to the United States, there is considerable consistency among educators in other English-speaking nations, especially in Great Britain, Canada, and Australia, about the concepts that might be deemed central to the process of critical viewing, which all include at least the following elements: (a) awareness of the *constructed nature of representations* in both print and visual media; (b) knowledge about the economic and political context in which media messages are produced by a number of different *institutions* with specific objectives and goals; (c) awareness and knowledge about the ways in which *audiences construct meaning* from messages and about the variety of processes of selecting, interpreting, and making use of messages in various forms. All of these concepts are basic issues in media study that students would be unlikely to appreciate without systematic exposure and exploration; but note that the traditional conceptualization of visual literacy makes use only of the first of these three.

Researchers have long been interested in the extent to which people are able to evaluate the "reality" of the images provided by film and television (Berger & Luckmann, 1966; Hawkins & Pingree, 1981) and the question remains increasingly paradoxical and troublesome for media scholars. But one of the reasons that media education continues to receive renewed interest by educators is that images are processed like real stimuli—and we tend to continually forget that they are constructed representations. Unlike print, where the reader cannot escape the fact that information is being transmitted through a medium, viewers of film and television find it easy to process visual media with little awareness of the constructed nature of the form, and many U.S. viewers are so unconsciously habituated to the form of television that its conventions and representations seem "natural," so much so that television that uses a different set of conventions (like some video art) is intolerable for many viewers (Hobbs, 1991). Teachers are not much more sensitive to this issue, as Masterman notes that "a major problem facing those who wish to develop the study of the media in schools is that one of their fundamental assumptions—that the media are signifying practices or symbolic systems which need to be actively read—flies in the face of many people's common sense understanding of the media as largely unproblematic purveyors of experience" (p. 6).

Messaris provides a potent argument against the visual determinism arguments that suppose that exposure to a particular set of visual conventions creates a set of visual "biases" in perceptual and cognitive skills, noting that the analogical nature of images means that, unlike language, images do not need to collapse information into a limited set of categories. But, while exposure to specific image-based conventions may not shape cognitive skills in a way that creates a certain " 'biasing' of vision" (Messaris, p. 441), repeated and habitual exposure to conventions of film and television does shape viewer expectations, which are a critical component of message reception (Hobbs, 1991).

The second concept put forward as essential is an understanding of the political and economic context in which media institutions operate. According to Masterman (1985),

> What is important, in other words, is for any pupil or student to know enough about, say, the Official Secrets Act, the influence of sources, the structural influence of advertising upon the media, the law of libel, the growth of public relations, institutional self-censorship and general patterns of ownership and control to be able to recognize them in play within a particular text. (p. 71)

One of the complexities of teaching about political and economic influences in media studies is that, while they are critically important forces operating on the media products we consume each day, these influences are covert, long term, and diffused throughout the culture, so that it is not easy to point to direct and specific connections between them and the media texts we consume (Masterman, 1985, p. 74).

What we know for certain is the widespread public ignorance of Americans in terms of basic knowledge of the political or economic issues central to the mass media. In a random telephone survey of 250 adults, 80% identified "sponsors" or "advertisers" as the source of revenue for broadcasters, but only 61% could explain where advertisers got their money, with almost 40% of adults unable to make the point that consumers pay for television indirectly through the purchase of goods and services (Hobbs, 1993). While media literacy intervention efforts of the 1970s talked about the importance of teaching about media economics, only recently have U.S. curriculum developers actually put forward approaches to introducing these concepts to young people (Hobbs & Miller, in press; Lloyd-Kolkin & Tyner, 1991).

The third concept put forward as essential is an understanding of how audiences negotiate meaning in media, moving beyond the social-scientific framework of the uses and gratifications paradigm, which simply posits the viewer as potentially active and identifies different types of behavior which motivate individuals to sit in front of the screen. The theoretical lineage of this approach comes directly from new directions in literary criticism, which has moved away from traditional models that subordinate the reader to "the twin authorities of authorship and the text itself" (Masterman, 1985, p. 215). Pedagogically, the goal of this approach is to strengthen students' awareness of their own process of constructing meaning from textual messages in a variety of forms. Unlike the media education models that rely on the uses and gratifications paradigm, the study of audience's interpretations of media products has powerful potential to reshape education more broadly. Masterman (1985) suggests that

> if meaning resides, not within the text itself, but in the interaction between audiences and text, then this holds true not simply in front of the television screen, but within every classroom. . . . Differential decodings, traditionally either repressed or treated as a "problem" to be overcome through the combined authorities of teacher, author and text, can now be given the fullest articulation as reflections or refractions of important subcultural differences with the group. (p. 218)

Masterman points media literacy education firmly toward the direction of some school reform efforts, which emphasize empowering students; changing authority relationships between students, teachers, and administrators; and the active project-centered and interdisciplinary approach to education (Sizer, 1992).

Note that none of the three concepts of representation, institution, or audience articulated above has much relationship to the model of media literacy generated in the 1970s by American scholars (see Brown, 1991, for review) but are based on the intellectual traditions of other nations: Canadian communication scholarship (McLuhan and Innis) and British cultural studies (particularly the Centre for Contemporary Cultural Studies, Birmingham University). Whether it is possible for U.S. teachers to master these concepts and transmit them to students is, of course, the major question to be addressed to communication scholars interested in media education at the elementary and secondary levels.

INSTRUCTIONAL METHODS OF MEDIA LITERACY: WHAT DO STUDENTS NEED TO DO?

In recent years, the classic debate John Dewey (1938) initiated early in the twentieth century has been renewed, as educators evaluate the relative value of traditional approaches, which emphasize the goal of education to be the inculcation of organized bodies of knowledge, as in recent efforts to promote "cultural literacy" versus more "progressive" approaches, which emphasize the student as an active creator of knowledge and present the goal of education as not merely to create efficient workers, parents, or citizens but "to make human beings who will life to the fullest, who will continually add to the quality and meaning of their experience, and who will participate with their fellow human beings in the building of a good society" (Cremin, 1990, p. 125).

The two dominant instructional methods in media literacy consist of "textual readings" of media products, using key concepts of representations, audience, institutions, genre, and other concepts to deconstruct and provide negotiated or oppositional readings to media texts, and "practical work," hands-on activities that give students experience in designing, creating, and producing a media message to experience how these concepts get articulated in practice. Predictably, in the United States, textual reading occurs in language arts, English, or social studies classes, while practical work occurs in journalism or in video production classes, the latter of which are found usually within vocational education programs. Most high school video production courses are designed for non-college-bound or "at-risk" students, designed to keep kids in school without being unduly taxing on their intellectual skills.

Among scholars and practitioners of media education in Europe and Canada, there has been considerable debate about the merits of hands-on experience as a contributor to the development of critical-viewing skills. While it seems obvious to many that hands-on work in the construction of media products has educational value, there are a number of problematic issues that arise when practical work involving print or video production is introduced into a K-12 classroom. In the United States, video production work has been "variously exploited to motivate alienated under-achievers, to extend self-expression and to develop individual creativity as ends in themselves" (Grahame, 1990, p. 148). In fact, educators have been taking advantage of hands-on production activities as strategies to keep children interested in school since the 1880s, when the vocational education movement began its ascendancy in U.S. schools (Lazerson & Grubb, 1974).

Such work in secondary classrooms, often identified as "media arts," generally concentrates on the technical skills of production. Due to differential funding and teacher training, which has existed since the 1930s, "a dual system of schools" gradually became established, with vocational programs and general education programs increasingly separated and remote from each other (Russell, 1938). Where video production activity does occur in U.S. schools, it is more often than not concerned with mastery of the technical skills of production and the creation of video materials that the school administration deems useful (for example, the taping of football games, the use of videotaped morning announcements, a videotaped public relations piece for the school).

One of the most potent barriers to the more widespread introduction of practical work into the 7-12 curriculum is the management of the school and the structure of the school day, where 45-minute periods and large class sizes make it difficult to provide students with hands-on experience in creating, designing, and producing video projects.

In addition, there is little research on whether the pedagogy of video production activity as it is currently constituted in U.S. public schools has any meaningful impact on reasoning, communication, or critical-viewing skills. Why? Because student work involving video production has many learning objectives and skill outcomes, it is often difficult to assess exactly what has been learned. Students may learn the skills of group communication and teamwork, working under a deadline, creative problem solving, and oral and written communication skills—but such skills are notoriously difficult to assess using traditional methods of inquiry across large samples of students when instructional methods vary enormously. And, because such courses are taught by vocational education teachers without certification in English, video production courses generally do not count toward the requirements needed for entrance into college, so there has been little institutional concern for assessment.

Strangely enough, in some schools, the funding source for media teachers comes from the local cable franchise firms, who often provide staff support, video equipment, studio construction, mobile vans, and other material resources to high schools as part of the franchise agreement. In these situations, media teachers are dually responsible both to the school administration and to the cable companies, a truly awkward and difficult situation that may limit media teachers' autonomy and flexibility.

After more than a decade of fierce budget cuts, most video production teachers feel their positions within the school community are marginal. Yet good work is still occurring in U.S. schools, with students actively producing, making, and analyzing media messages in ways that clearly extend their creative and expressive skills, their oral and written communication skills, and in ways that give them more fully informed understanding of the functions of mass media in our society. For example, nonprofit arts and educational organizations, such as the Educational Video Center in New York City, have developed teacher education programs and direct intervention with at-risk youth that involve video production activities that strengthen students' communication, reasoning, and problem-solving skills. Media teachers in the state of New York have organized to share ideas across districts and are beginning to see themselves as distinct from media specialists, who are predominantly school librarians with responsibility for nonprint materials and audiovisual equipment who have become increasingly interested in improved delivery systems for traditional subject matter, including hypercard stacks, multimedia, CD-ROM, and other tools (Weller & Burcham, 1990).

Media literacy education is not confined to instruction that centers on video production, however. Using primarily the instructional technique of "textual reading," language arts and social studies teachers make use of some key concepts of media literacy in the context of their existing curricula. In a survey of 159 social studies teachers in California, teachers indicated the topics that were most likely to be included in their work with secondary students (Wulfemeyer, 1990). General information about the news media was the most commonly taught topic, with 17% of teachers including this in their curriculum. Other topics included units on advertising (11%), analyses of propaganda (10%), analyses of bias (9%), and discussions of the power and influence of mass media (4%).

While teachers overwhelmingly believed in the importance of including media studies in the secondary curriculum, 40% of the respondents indicated they did not include any material on the subject due to lack of time or space in the curriculum. Wulfemeyer estimates that this finding represents an overgenerous percentage, given the response rate of 50% to the survey instrument. In addition, the results of Wulfemeyer's survey show that most teachers believe that they're qualified to teach about the mass media, yet only 34% had any college training that helped them develop this expertise.

Such evidence parallels similar findings by Kozoil (1989), whose survey of 104 secondary teachers in Maryland found that language arts teachers also see the importance of including media literacy concepts in their curriculum but are inhibited by three factors: the absence of outcomes relevant to media literacy in the state's instructional objectives, lack of teaching materials and training, and lack of time and space in the existing curricula. Curricular materials developed by language arts teachers and circulated by associations such as the National Council of Teachers of English suggests that, among English teachers, analyses of film are most popular, especially curricular materials that compare and contrast written narratives with film versions. In addition, analysis of advertising is also a common thread in the approach language arts teachers use in the teaching of media literacy.

Sadly, the high levels of isolation that exist within many secondary school communities means that only in rare instances do teachers collaborate or share expertise to develop new curriculum, materials, or initiatives within or between schools. Although many large public high schools have motivated and capable teachers among the social studies, language arts, visual or performing arts, and video production staff, there have been few initiatives in the United States that take advantage of the cross-fertilization that occurs when teachers get together to share ideas. However, in August of 1993, one hundred secondary school teachers, scholars, and school administrators attended the Institute on Media Education at Harvard Graduate School of Education, a week-long initiative to promote new leadership in media education among K-12 educators.

TEACHING WITH MEDIA VERSUS
TEACHING ABOUT MEDIA

A number of opportunities and barriers exist that make it difficult to predict the growth of media literacy programs in U.S. schools. One of the most paradoxical is the increased availability to teachers of video playback equipment and instructional materials suitable for use in the classroom. While most educators trumpet the improvements in access to technology and video software, which are due primarily to the phenomenal growth in the deregulated cable television industry of the 1980s and the development of new services to sell young audiences to advertisers (like Whittle Communications' *Channel One*), Messaris has identified the dangers in the use of television simply as a conveyor of information. For example, he notes with alarm the vast increase in the amount of televised materials now available to teachers for the purposes of conveying information about science, geography, mathematics, and other subject areas and students' tendency to "glaze over" when the video screen turns on in the classroom. In wondering about the cognitive skills developed by students' use of television in the classroom, Messaris follows the arguments laid forth by Postman (1985), who charges that learning from television is inferior to learning from print because it is "less likely than print to cultivate higher-order, inferential thinking" (p. 152) perhaps because televised information relies on iconic symbols that are not intellectually demanding or perhaps because television, in its particular form, has a systematic bias in favor of presenting information in a way that is fragmented, oversimplified, and visually appealing.

Clearly, one of the most significant barriers in implementing media education is the difficulty of separating the concepts of "teaching with media" and "teaching about media," which are wedded firmly together in the minds of many educators and scholars. Even Messaris glides too easily between these two very distinct approaches to the use of media in classrooms. Although Postman (1985) decries the use of television in schools as a tool for conveying subject matter, he does call for teaching about media to be made a priority of education reform quite directly when he writes: "It is an acknowledged task of schools to assist the young in learning how to interpret the symbols of their culture. That this task should now require that they distance themselves from their forms of information is not so bizarre an enterprise that we cannot hope for its inclusion in the curriculum; even hope that it will be placed at the center of the curriculum" (p. 163).

But how to distance ourselves from our forms of information? Embedded firmly within the education establishment, there now exist more than 14,000 library media specialists, one in almost every school district in the United States, whose positions are defined as promoting the use of media to convey subject matter and to organize and manage nonprint materials (Weller & Burcham, 1990). Imagine the difficulty of valorizing the "teaching about media" approach—the very heart of media literacy—when such a constituency exists primarily to maintain the current conceptualizations of media use in classrooms. Each year, the media specialist, persuaded by the trade show huckster, allures administrators and teachers alike with the promise of new media, including computers, interactive satellite communication for distance learning, hypercard stacks, laser videodiscs, and other tools consisting of expensive hardware and limited and often poor quality software. These items are intensively promoted as necessary for administrators to purchase to be considered a "leading-edge" school (Stover, 1990), and, each year, such efforts to market new products insistently and continuously push educators to conceptualize media as merely a vehicle for delivering information.

A number of small but influential voices in the education reform movement seem to acknowledge the importance of moving away from the technology-driven delivery system model, focusing on the development of students' critical thinking and communication skills and realigning the environment of the school with the culture in which students and citizens live. In a recent essay, Ted Sizer (1992) wrote:

> It is difficult to persuade young people to read carefully and hard, to respect serious academic demands, to tell the truth and not to cheat, to understand the differences among people and to make the best of them—in a word, to take even the practical, civic life of the mind seriously—if the culture outside the school does otherwise. One cannot reform the school if the older folk in the community by their actions signal contempt for the desired school values. (p. 27)

In Great Britain and Canada, it is widely held that media education is a central component of both school reform and social change, because, in the process of helping students acquire critical distance from forms of information and entertainment presented by the mass media, students develop strategies for questioning, problem solving, and reasoning that can be applied to all information forms, subject areas, and situations (Lusted, 1990). But, in the United States, without leadership and support from committed administrators at the federal, state, and district levels, media literacy is likely to continue to exist only in isolated classrooms where individual teachers have taken the personal initiative to experiment and explore. Why? The basic premises of media literacy education serve to alter existing relationships between student and teacher, open to question the unchallenged "content delivery" approaches which have dominated in the nineteenth and twentieth centuries (Apple, 1990), and engage in the process of "demythologizing information" (Postman, 1985), something that schools have never been able to do. Scholars interested in the intersection of media and education can play a fruitful role in examining more closely the patterns and practices that might nurture and sustain this dynamic and complex process.

REFERENCES

Alvarado, M., & Boyd-Barrett, O. (1992). *Media education.* London: British Film Institute.

Anderson, J. A. (1983). Television literacy and the critical viewer. In J. Bryant & D. Anderson (Eds.), *Children's understanding of television: Research on children's attention and comprehension.* New York: Academic Press.

Apple, M. W. (1990). *Ideology and curriculum* (2nd ed.). New York: Routledge.

Arnheim, R. (1969). *Visual thinking.* Berkeley: University of California Press.

Berger, P., & Luckmann, T. (1966). *The social construction of reality.* Garden City, NY: Doubleday.

Brown, J. A. (1991). *Television "critical viewing skills" education.* Hillsdale, NJ: Lawrence Erlbaum.

Cassidy, M. F., & Knowlton, J. Q. (1983). Visual literacy: A failed metaphor? *Educational Communication and Technology Journal, 31*(2), 67-90.

Cassirer, E. (1953). *Philosophy of symbolic forms.* New Haven, CT: Yale University Press.

Collins, W. A. (1983). Interpretation and inference in children's television viewing. In J. Bryant & D. R. Anderson (Eds.), *Children's understanding of television: Research on attention and comprehension.* New York: Academic Press.

Cremin, L. A. (1990). *Popular education and its discontents.* New York: Harper and Row.

Dewey, J. (1938). *Experience and education.* New York: Macmillan.

Dorr, A., & Brannon, C. (1992, March 18-20). Media education in American schools at the end of the twentieth century. In *Medienkompetenz als Herausforderung an Schule und Bildung* (Proceedings of media education conference). Gutersloh, Germany: Bertelsmann Foundation.

Ewen, S., & Ewen, E. (1982). *Channels of desire: Mass images and the shaping of American consciousness.* New York: McGraw-Hill.

Fiske, J., & Hartley, J. (1978). *Reading television.* New York: Routledge.

Goodman, N. (1968). *Languages of art.* Indianapolis: Bobbs-Merrill.

Grahame, J. (1990). The production process. In D. Lusted (Ed.) *The meda studies book: A guide for teachers.* London: Routledge.

Hall, S. (1973). *Encoding and decoding in the television discourse* (Occasional Papers no. 7). Birmingham: Birmingham University, Center for Contemporary Cultural Studies.

Hawkins, R., & Pingree, S. (1981). Using television to construct social reality. *Journal of Broadcasting, 25*(3), 347-364.

Hobbs, R. (1991). Television and the shaping of cognitive skills. In A. M. Olson, C. Parr, & D. Parr (Eds.), *Video icons and values.* Albany: State University of New York Press.

Hobbs, R. (1992). *Obstacles to effective use of television in the classroom.* Paper presented at the 9th International Conference on Technology and Education, Paris, France.

Hobbs, R. (1993). *Public knowledge about television.* Manuscript in progress.

Hobbs, R., & Frost, R. (1991). Comprehension of editing conventions by African tribal villagers. In F. Korzenny & S. Ting-Toomey (Eds.), *Mass media effects across cultures* (pp. 110-129). Newbury Park, CA: Sage.

Hobbs, R., Frost, R., Stauffer, J., & Davis, A. (1988). How first time viewers comprehend editing. *Journal of Communication, 38*(4), 50-60.

Hobbs, R., & Miller, B. (in press). *TV eye: A curriculum for the media arts.* Boston: Boston Film/Video Foundation.

Koziol, R. (1989). *English/language arts teachers' views on mass media consumption education in Maryland high schools.* Paper presented at the annual meeting of the Association for Education in Journalism and Mass Communication.

Langer, S. (1942). *Philosophy in a new key.* Cambridge, MA: Harvard University Press.

Lazerson, M., & Grubb, W. N. (1974). *American education and vocationalism.* New York: Teachers College Press.

Lloyd-Kolkin, D., & Tyner, K. (1991). *Media and you: An elementary media literacy curriculum.* Englewood Cliffs, NJ: Educational Technology.

Lusted, D. (1990). *The media studies book.* London: Routledge.

Masterman, L. (1985). *Teaching the media.* London: Routledge.

Piette, J. (1992, March 18-20). Teaching television critical viewing skills: From theory to practice to theory. In *Medienkompetenz als Herausforderung an Schule und Bildung* (Proceedings of media education conference). Gutersloh, Germany: Bertelsmann Foundation.

Postman, N. (1985). *Amusing ourselves to death.* New York: Viking.

Russell, J. D. (1938). *Vocational education* (Staff Study No. 8). Washington, DC: Advisory Committee on Education.

Sizer, T. (1992, November). School reform: What's missing. *World Monitor,* pp. 20-27.

Stover, N. (1990). Principals and programmers: Partners in the use of technology. *NASSP Bulletin, 74*(528), 72-77.

Weller, D., & Burcham, C. (1990). Roles of Georgia media specialists perceived by teachers, principals and media specialists. *Perceptual and Motor Skills, 70*(3), 1360-1362.

Wulfemeyer, T. (1990). *Mass media instruction in high school social science classes: A survey of Southern California teachers.* Paper presented at the annual meeting of the Association for Education in Journalism and Mass Communication.

Coming to Terms With Television

AIMÉE DORR
University of California, Los Angeles

P AUL Messaris's disquisition on the cognitive consequences of visual literacy and on television's place in the classroom manages to be simultaneously engaging and negative. Put most baldly, he asks and answers seven questions:

> Does experience with images (or television) influence viewers' conceptual categories? No.
>
> Does it influence their analytic reasoning? No.
>
> Does it influence their spatial intelligence? No.
>
> Does it influence their abstractive or analogical thinking? Maybe.
>
> Is promoting students' mental skills a good reason to put television in classrooms? No.
>
> Is improving their instruction in traditional subject matter areas a good reason? No.
>
> Is teaching them critical-viewing skills a good reason? No.

Most of the essay is devoted to the explication and argumentation that lead to Messaris's answers to the first four questions. Taken together, conceptual categories, analytic reasoning, spatial intelligence, and abstractive or analogical thinking constitute the mental skills referred to in the fifth question. This and the last two questions begin and end the chapter and provide something of a motivational justification for exploring the first four.

Messaris raises a raft of provocative issues in the description and analysis that lead to his fundamentally negative conclusions about the possible cognitive consequences of what he calls visual literacy. Central to his line of reasoning are five issues: What is visual literacy? How does it develop? What is television? What promotes cognitive functioning? Are cognitive skills domain specific? These issues have engaged good minds for decades. Not one

Correspondence and requests for reprints: Aimée Dorr, Graduate School of Education, 405 Hilgard Ave., University of California, Los Angeles, CA 90024-1301.

Communication Yearbook 17, pp. 467-480

has yet been resolved. Messaris explicitly or implicitly takes a position on each one as he works toward his conclusions about the cognitive consequences of visual literacy. Had he taken other stands, from among those advocated by other scholars and to varying degrees supported by empirical research, his conclusions might have been different. Part of the appeal of this chapter comes from the extent to which Messaris's analyses provoke renewed consideration of what remain highly intriguing issues.

Most of my commentary will be devoted to presenting alternative perspectives on the five issues I regard as most central to Messaris's argument and most open to debate. Because of space limitations, I mostly leave it to the reader to work out the implications of the various stands for his or her conclusions either about the cognitive consequences of visual literacy or about research that needs to be done to clarify matters. My commentary concludes with a brief discussion of what Messaris's chapter does and does not offer the reader and a few suggestions about where we should go in considering the cognitive consequences of visual literacy and in deciding whether television belongs in classrooms.

WHAT IS VISUAL LITERACY?

There is no one well-accepted conceptualization of visual literacy. Many if not most writers (e.g., Dondis, 1973; Sinatra, 1986; Suhor & Little, 1988; Wileman, 1980) propose something akin to Braden and Hortin's (1982) "ability to understand and to use images, including the ability to think, learn, and express one's self in terms of visuals" (p. 41). Visual literacy proponents focus on drawings, paintings, graphs, charts, signs, and so forth, representations that rely almost exclusively on visual elements for expression and communication. Messaris, however, seems to equate visual literacy with television literacy. His most explicit statements of his conceptualization of visual literacy are at the beginning and end of the chapter: "Does experience in the visual conventions of television—or, to use an increasingly popular term, visual *literacy*—have broader cognitive consequences . . .?" (p. 434) and "we have examined a number of possible connections between experience with TV or other visual media—visual 'literacy'—and the cultivation of broader mental aptitudes" (p. 450).

Television combines images with linguistic features consistently and with print occasionally. Messaris uses the word-image combination to great advantage in his analysis of abstractive/analogical thinking. Television's joining of words and images provides the user with a very different interpretive task, "literacy event" if you will, than does a purely visual representation or a purely linguistic representation. Some would argue that the joining also leads television creators to use a different visual code than would be found in representations that had no recourse to language. Presumably, then, television viewing might require or cultivate a different kind of literacy than would interaction with purely visual systems. Many signify this possibility by using terms such as *television literacy* or *media literacy,* rather than *visual literacy,* when considering any of television's representational systems, including its visual system. Given the differing technological elements and content options, most television literacy goals and curricula look rather different than most visual literacy goals and curricula (for comparisons of different literacies, see Dorr, in press, and Dorr & Brannon, 1993; for examples of television literacy goals and curricula, see J. A. Anderson, 1983; Anderson & Ploghoft, 1980; J. A. Brown, 1991; Corder-Bolz, 1982; Dorr, Graves, & Phelps, 1980; Piette, 1993).

Television, as Messaris notes, is also primarily a one-sided medium. Most people interpret television content created by a privileged few; rarely, if ever, do most people create such content. From the perspective of visual literacy advocates, then, half of their conceptualization—the ability to create visual representations—is missing when television is considered a domain of visual literacy. Some advocates might even argue that, if television is included among the visual media, then most people cannot be visually literate because they do not create visual communications using television. Television literacy advocates rarely have this dilemma because few include the ability to send messages via television as part of literacy.

A further consideration in conceptualizing any kind of literacy is identifying the types or levels of knowledge and skill that represent different degrees of literacy attainment. At one point, Messaris suggests that visual literacy is greater awareness "of the representational conventions of images" (p. 442), but he otherwise has little to say about the specifics of what he calls visual literacy. Does it include having concepts and vocabulary for visual styles or visual codes or visual symbols? Does it include having aesthetic standards? Does it include being able to make sense of representational and nonrepresentational visual images or analogical and nonanalogical visual images? Does it require meeting some minimal standards of knowledge or performance? Can visual literacy be scaled? These are difficult issues for visual literacy scholars; however, direct tests of the consequences of any literacy require some means either of identifying people who are and are not literate or of ordering people from more to less literate.

HOW DOES VISUAL LITERACY DEVELOP?

A perennial issue in education and development is the extent to which skills and abilities are or can be acquired through ordinary everyday interactions in normal human environments. For example, must children be taught language? Or do they pick it up naturally as they listen to and interact with others in situations where language is an important part of what is happening? Similarly, does visual literacy develop of its own accord in visually rich environments or must it be taught? Many argue that instruction leads to notable improvements in visual literacy, media literacy, television literacy, computer literacy, and traditional print literacy—improvements that do not ordinarily develop through everyday experience alone. They acknowledge that some basic literacy develops without deliberate instruction. Their conceptualization of true literacy, however, entails concepts, vocabulary, knowledge, skills, standards, and self-awareness that have not been shown to develop, or to develop sufficiently, during most Americans' everyday interactions with their environments (e.g., Culbertson, 1986; Dondis, 1973; Dorr, 1993; Graham, 1981; Hill, 1992; Olson, 1988).

Messaris seems to agree that true visual literacy arises from activities that are somehow more than or different from those of everyday life. At one point he asks, "In teaching a child about the formal characteristics of the medium, are we also enhancing certain aspects of her or his more general cognitive development?" (p. 434). He also reports a very interesting study in which only those undergraduates who had taken film courses or made films themselves recognized analogical cutting and juxtaposition in a film (Messaris, 1981). Much of the research he reviews, however, examines the degree of relationship between a subject's television viewing and his or her mental skills rather than that between the subject's measured visual literacy and mental skills. For example, one study contrasts Alaskan children with and without access to television via satellite and another contrasts a control group and three groups of children exposed repeatedly to audiovisual presentations of different processes for seeing objects from multiple perspectives. Messaris treats all such work as tests of whether visual literacy promotes mental skills. Yet many of these studies did not use an independent assessment of each subject's visual or television literacy, and many scholars would doubt that viewing patterns were themselves a good indicator of literacy status. There is, in fact, some research indicating that greater viewing is associated with less medium sophistication (e.g., Rossiter & Robertson, 1977). Such findings should make us wary about using amount of everyday viewing experience as a proxy measure for degree of literacy.

WHAT IS TELEVISION?

Like the fabled blind men's elephant, television's diverse attributes permit dramatically diverse characterizations of the medium. None can be said to be wrong; many could be misleading. One who knows an elephant only by its tail will fail to appreciate the damage the strong legs can do and the lift the trunk can manage. A simple amalgamation of an elephant's features fails to capture what it is able to do when the single elements are coordinated together, what distinct subcultures can arise in the different environments in which elephants live, and what remarkable events occur with particular combinations of capabilities, subcultures, and happenstance. Consider, for example, the recent news report of a single female elephant who butted, pushed, delayed, and ultimately derailed a train after her baby had been frightened by another train that had preceded this one down the track. No one would predict this after feeling her tail!

The literature is replete with characterizations of television. Consider just a few examples. McLuhan (1964) focused on the physical characteristics of the television signal, how these had to be processed by viewers to produce images, and what the likely consequences of this were for human cultures. Recent innovations, several of which are treated as television-like by researchers and laity alike, have provoked renewed interest in technical features of television: How are the physical capabilities for remote control, off-air taping, tape rental, cable access, increased numbers of channels, high definition television, and higher quality sound used by viewers and what difference does such usage make? (see, for example, the 1990 special issue of *Communication Research,* Vol. 17, no. 1). Some scholars (e.g., Anderson & Lorch, 1983; Huston & Wright, 1989; Salomon, 1979) have focused on the formal features of television, the use and meaning of various visual production techniques (e.g., cuts, zooms, pans, fades, slow motion) and sound qualities (e.g., slow, languorous music). Many have equated television with its content (e.g., Greenberg, 1980; Lesser, 1974; Malamuth & Donnerstein, 1984). Sometimes, as with soft pornography or commercial advertising, a particular type of content—most often disapproved of content—is emphasized. Occasionally, laudable content or the mix of content options is the focus. Television has also been considered to be an activity. Sometimes the activity is that of attending or not, processing content or not, constructing meaning or not (e.g., Anderson & Lorch, 1983; Anderson, Lorch, Field, & Sanders, 1981; Campbell, Wright, & Huston, 1987). Other times the activity is that of investment of time, with the consequent possibility of time taken away from reading, homework, informal social interaction, formal organizations, and so forth (e.g., Medrich, Roizen, Rubin, & Buckley, 1982; Robinson, 1977; Williams, 1986).

Television is simultaneously all these things. An unresolved question is whether and when the impact of any part, any particular perspective or characteristic, can be accurately or fully understood in isolation. The formal features of television, for a first example, are rarely used in isolation from or in direct contradiction to content. Camera work, editing techniques, and audio features are employed in conjunction with visual representation, dialogue, commentary, story line, and other content elements to teach, inform, entertain, uplift, or persuade. Often enough, formal features simply reinforce or restate what is also represented in the content. Moreover, correct interpretation of formal features often requires attention to and comprehension of content elements. Formal features ordinarily have multiple possible meanings, as do words, and their correct interpretation requires sensitivity to the context of their use. As a second example, the technological capabilities of different delivery options (e.g., VHF, UHF, cable, VCR) tend to coexist with variations in content or content options. Video recorders are most frequently used to play rented or purchased movies. Each cable channel is likely to offer single-theme content: news, country music, religion, children's fare, telemarketing, Spanish-language programming, and so forth. Each VHF channel tends to offer network or independent programming of "considerable" variety in terms of genre and target audience. It is an open question, one I consider well worth pursuing, whether we are led astray by limited characterizations of what are in reality the correlated and coordinated features of television.

Messaris's view of the television beast is mostly implicit in his argument. In considering its effects on viewers' conceptual categories and analytic reasoning, he treats television as a purely visual system and contrasts it to language, ignoring the fact that the visual and linguistic elements of television are ordinarily coordinated and all evidence indicates that both are processed by viewers. For these two mental skills, Messaris argues that television images succeed in description, "simply reporting events or the characteristics of objects or situations" (p. 437), but largely fail in analysis, which "often deals with generalities . . . and . . . establishing the conditions under which . . . events or characteristics can be expected to occur" (p. 437). This seems to suggest that television content is primarily descriptive, in some sense veridical with objective reality. Most critics of television per se and most advocates of visual or television literacy argue otherwise, contending that television's images—like all visual images—are representations that some people create and that all people must learn to interpret (e.g., Olson, 1988). In this section, Messaris also asserts that television does not have a "consistent partitioning of visual experience from which a 'biasing' of vision might be expected to arise" (p. 441). Others disagree. Cross-cultural researchers, in particular, have identified differences in visual elements of television and film, differences they regard as meaningful expressions of cultural differences (e.g., Worth & Adair, 1972). In considering television's effects on viewers' spatial intelligence, Messaris again treats television as a purely visual system; the research that is reviewed includes studies that used 3½-minute black-and-white videos (with audio), films, slides, and broadcast television. Television becomes a visual and auditory system when Messaris considers the fourth mental skill, abstractive or analogical thinking. Most of the research cited in this section is about television and video; one of the most pertinent studies (Messaris, 1981) is about films. Whether television includes UHF, VHF, cable, and VCRs is never clear. Whether or when studies using slides, specially made videos, film, or photographs have direct implications for television effects is never clear. One's assessment of the implications of television for various mental skills will surely vary depending on which of these many television-like things are included, and which excluded, from one's definition of television and depending on whether the full range of television's features, or a limited subset such as the visual elements, is included.

WHAT PROMOTES COGNITIVE FUNCTIONING?

The means by which mental skills, or cognitive functions, develop has been a concern for millennia and a subject of basic research for perhaps a century. There is much evidence, as Messaris notes, that physical engagement with a three-dimensional environment is essential for early development of the visual system. He ignores, however, equally strong evidence that certain visual functions appear to be wired in (e.g., Haith, 1980) and that mental skills also develop through engagement with iconic and symbolic representations. Three respected scholars and their many current adherents are well known for their work in the latter area. Piagetian theory and research (e.g., Piaget & Inhelder, 1969) have maintained that the semiotic function (which includes language) "allows the representative evocation of objects and events not perceived at that particular moment . . . and makes thought possible by providing it with an unlimited field of application" (p. 91). Bruner (1964) has argued that there are "three systems of processing information by which human beings construct models of their world: through action, through imagery, and through language" (p. 1). For him, the course of cognitive growth is from action to icon to symbol, with symbolic systems (language being the preeminent one), not actions, being essential for the "unlocking and amplification of human intellectual powers" (p. 15). Vygotsky (1962) and later neo-Vygotskian researchers have also argued that, with development, inner speech, not external action, becomes a crucial tool in cognition.

These lines of research, among others, offer considerable evidence that movement in a three-dimensional world and manipulation of three-dimensional objects are not the only means for developing mental skills, cognitive structures, or intellectual functions. After a certain point rather early in development, movement and manipulation in the three-dimensional world are unlikely to be the most prevalent developmental influence in symbol-rich, literate cultures such as our own. Relationships among actual objects, icons, and symbolic representations, causes of growth in ability to use them, and the place of concrete experience in representational systems and mental operations are matters of some debate in the literature, but the ability of human beings to develop mental skills without recourse to action in a three-dimensional world is not much disputed in many well-respected theoretical systems. In these theoretical formulations, there is plenty of conceptual room for television's representational system to influence viewers' mental skills. Whether there is evidence for such influence is another matter.

At times in the argumentation, Messaris seems to back away from the requirement of involvement in a three-dimensional world for mental skill development. For example, according to Messaris, category formation, one of the four mental skills considered in his essay, comes from active use of a representational system that includes categories. He is not explicit about what constitutes active use, but one surmises he means using a representational system and its categories to construct one's own communications. The meaning of "active" use of television and the evidence for it have been a matter of some debate. Noting that television viewing involves nothing more than processing of auditory and visual signals chosen by others and transmitted at their chosen pace, critics of television have asserted that viewing is a passive activity. Researchers find that viewing is usually an active process in which one attends to, selects, encodes, and—most important—makes sense of television's auditory and visual signals—hardly passive endeavors. Young children's patterns of attention to television content varying in comprehensibility and their misunderstandings of television content suggest that they have been actively constructing meaning for what they view (e.g., D. R. Anderson et al., 1981; Campbell et al., 1987; Dorr, 1980, 1983). Thus television viewing involves active processing of its signals. It is possible, however, that these meaning-making activities are insufficient to induce internalization of whatever categories are embodied in television's representational system. The jury is still out on the kinds and amounts of activity needed for various types of learning.

In reference to television images (which the public rarely creates), Messaris poses this problem: "If internalization of the categories of a representational system is contingent on active use of those categories, the kind of shaping of cognitive/perceptual frameworks that appears to be attributable to language may be considerably less likely to occur in the case of images" (p. 441). By "active," he seems to mean use of the representational system to construct one's own messages. His underlying presumption is that linguistically based categories arise only if one uses language to speak. This is by no means a universally accepted tenet. Noam Chomsky (1957) is perhaps the best known proponent of the view that much of language structure is innate and universal. Following this line of thought, Gazzaniga (1992) recently elaborated the biological basis for linguistic or cognitive concepts: "Concept- and language-specific circuits resulting from thousands and thousands of years of evolution are available to humans. As environment interacts with a brain with these capacities, the system responds in an orderly way, storing the information that will guide the circuits into action specific to that environment" (p. 94). In this theoretical framework, one definitely needs experience with the symbol system to activate the mental structure, but there is no apparent requirement that experience should be that of production rather than of reception.

ARE COGNITIVE SKILLS DOMAIN SPECIFIC?

Hypothetically, the cognitive consequences of visual literacy could pertain—if they pertained at all—only while one is engaged with visual representations, or they could be more widespread. Increased television literacy could enhance the mental skills involved in making sense of or in constructing messages with television without influencing "similar" mental skills involved in using other symbol systems or in interacting in a three-dimensional world. Alternatively, mental skills developed through experience with television could transfer to other domains. Like most, but not all, scholars interested in the cognitive consequences of visual literacy, Messaris focuses on the possibilities of transfer of mental skills from one domain, television, to other domains.

The domain specificity of mental skills and the problems of transfer of training are central issues in education. Much has been written on the difficulty of obtaining transfer and the challenge involved in training for it (e.g., Brown & Campione, 1984; Perkins & Salomon, 1989; Resnick, 1987). Research on the topic has included work on problem-solving strategies, analogical reasoning, and other mental skills similar to those Messaris considers. Transfer is rarely easily achieved or broadly applied. It is more likely if initial skill acquisition involves multiple differing examples, self-monitoring, and metacognition (reflective processes of the type promoted during formal visual literacy instruction) and results in the learner having formed a schema for the skill. In a new domain, when transfer could occur, it is more likely if people are helped to recognize the relevance of previous learning to this new situation, are able to map the significant elements of the original situation onto the new one, and are self-monitoring and metacognitively active. The difficulties with transfer and the demonstrated variability of mental performance across domains have led some scholars to question whether mental skills and content knowledge are intertwined rather than separate and whether mental skills are therefore always somewhat domain specific (e.g., Ennis, 1989; Glaser, 1984). From this perspective, mental skills must be relearned as they operate within each particular domain. Basic and applied research in education and psychology thus strongly suggests that the cognitive consequences of visual literacy (the transfer of visual literacy mental skills to other domains) should be sought in situations with some very particular characteristics. Much of the research Messaris cites did not employ situations such as these. Perhaps we should not expect this research to yield strong evidence in support of the transfer of visual literacy skills to other domains.

Howard Gardner's proposed multiple intelligences are yet another version of this same debate about the domain specificity of mental skills. As Messaris explains, Gardner (1983) argues that there are several different types of mental ability rather than some sort of pervasive general intelligence. Gardner treats these intelligences rather like mental skills in separate domains, domains often identified by the use of different symbol systems. He does not argue much for a general underlying intelligence or for its appearance in similar levels of skilled performance across different systems. Others would (for reviews of various positions, see Gardner, 1983; Sternberg, 1985). Empirical evidence can be marshalled to support and refute both positions.

Messaris's implicit assumption that visual literacy mental skills could generalize or transfer easily to other domains sparks renewed consideration of what has been a long-standing debate among those investigating intelligence, mental skills, and cognitive capabilities.

WHAT'S BEEN DONE HERE?

The role of television in schooling and the cognitive consequences of its use are intriguing topics. Messaris has written provocatively about them. His perspectives are forcefully presented. The reader cannot help but feel challenged to ponder the issues and sketch out new research. The real strength of Messaris's work is in the many issues it raises, the particular perspectives it offers, the thought it provokes. We easily appreciate these strengths; we need also to recognize associated limitations.

Messaris's essay is not a review chapter. A full range of theoretical perspectives is not presented. In the preceding sections, I have illustrated this for the five issues I considered most central to Messaris's line of reasoning and most open to debate. Similar illustrations could have been offered for other issues brought up in this chapter (e.g., the connections between language and thought, the influence of media on creativity). In making his points, Messaris cites supportive research, but one has the sense that there was little effort to amass, describe, and evaluate all relevant research. For example, the section on spatial intelligence reports one study from Salomon (1979) and omits at least six others. One also has the sense that Messaris was selective in the findings he used. To stay with Salomon for an example, the perspective-taking study had a no-treatment control group as well as the three groups Messaris describes. On the total score for the dependent measure, the control group did significantly less well than the short-circuiting group, suggesting that the short-circuiting condition was beneficial to second graders even if less beneficial than the activation and modeling conditions. Also, when scores on the four most difficult items were used, the modeling condition, not the activation condition, was the best. Finally, Salomon is not very interested in the fact that children who were more skilled at pretest did better later; rather, he argues for an aptitude-treatment interaction in which less skilled children were helped most by conditions that showed them how to perform the skill, and more skilled children, by conditions that led them to practice the skill. Messaris has brought a wealth of scholarly literature to bear on his consideration of the cognitive consequences of what he calls visual literacy, but the quantity and range of literature should not lead one to assume that his is a review chapter. It is a think piece.

Three types of thinking are employed to evaluate television's influence on four mental skills. For the first two mental skills, conceptual categories and analytic reasoning, Messaris's rhetorical approach is to compare the extent to which words and images can be used for analysis and description. He concludes that

> the view of images as a form of language is probably not a very useful analogy in thinking about the benefits of a visual education. Making students more aware of the representational conventions of images is not likely to give them access to an analytic apparatus that they would otherwise have lacked, and it does not seem very likely to lead to the kind of adaptive restructuring of cognitive/perceptual frameworks that appears to occur in the case of "real" language. (pp. 441-442)

For the third mental skill, spatial intelligence, Messaris relies primarily on the findings from five pieces of empirical research. He concludes, "On balance, it seems fair to say that neither the empirical evidence we have reviewed nor the theoretical arguments we have considered build a particularly strong case in favor of the idea that experience as a spectator of still pictures or film and television is a significant contributor to general spatial intelligence" (p. 445). For the fourth mental skill, abstractive/analogical thinking, Messaris argues primarily from example. After analyzing the interpretive tasks required by one television commercial and by a cinematic construction used in two films, Messaris concludes that "the idea of a connection between cinematic or pictorial experience and extracinematic or extrapictorial abstractive/analogical skills must remain very tentative" (p. 449). Messaris uses these three approaches well. One cannot help but wish to see what would have resulted if he had applied all three to each of the four mental skills.

WHAT'S NEXT?

Like Messaris, I find that "the various kinds of connections between images and thought processes that we have considered here remain very intriguing" (p. 450). His analyses have only heightened my interest. They offer the reader a rich vein to be mined for inspiration and guidance. If they yield renewed analyzing, theorizing, and researching, then they will have indeed been the mother lode. If, however, they are used to support his concluding suggestion that there is little reason to put television in schools and much reason not to do so, then the vein will have yielded more tailings than ore.

In beginning and ending the chapter, Messaris offers three good justifications for putting television in elementary and secondary classrooms. Only one of them—promoting students' mental skills—is seriously considered in the chapter. The other two justifications receive cursory, even haphazard, evaluation. Still other justifications, for example, cost-effectiveness or television's ability to present educationally important material that students would not otherwise experience in their classrooms, are never even brought up. A serious answer to the question, "Does TV Belong in the Classroom?" requires much more information and analysis than one chapter could possibly offer. Let us, then, reserve for another time this first part of Messaris's two-part title and, instead, appreciate the power of the exposition of the second part—"Cognitive Consequences of Visual 'Literacy.' "

REFERENCES

Anderson, D. R., & Lorch, E. P. (1983). Looking at television: Action or reaction? In J. Bryant & D. R. Anderson (Eds.), *Children's understanding of television: Research on attention and comprehension* (pp. 1-33). New York: Academic Press.

Anderson, D. R., Lorch, E. P., Field, D. E., & Sanders, J. (1981). The effects of TV program comprehensibility on preschool children's visual attention to television. *Child Development, 52,* 151-157.

Anderson, J. A. (1983). Television literacy and the critical viewer. In J. Bryant & D. R. Anderson (Eds.), *Children's understanding of television: Research on attention and comprehension* (pp. 297-327). New York: Academic Press.

Anderson, J. A., & Ploghoft, M. (1980). Receivership skills: The television experience. In D. Nimmo (Ed.), *Communication yearbook 4.* New Brunswick, NJ: Transaction.

Braden, R. A., & Hortin, J. A. (1982). Identifying the theoretical foundations of visual literacy. *Journal of Visual Verbal Languaging, 2*(2), 37-42.

Brown, A. L., & Campione, J. C. (1984). Three faces of transfer: Implications for early competence, individual differences, and instructions. In M. E. Lamb, A. L. Brown, & B. Rogoff (Eds.), *Advances in developmental psychology* (Vol. 2, pp. 143-192). Hillsdale, NJ: Lawrence Erlbaum.

Brown, J. A. (1991). *Television "critical viewing skills" education: Major media literacy projects in the United States and selected countries.* Hillsdale, NJ: Lawrence Erlbaum.

Bruner, J. S. (1964). The course of cognitive growth. *American Psychologist, 19,* 1-15.

Campbell, T. A., Wright, J. C., & Huston, A. C. (1987). Form cues and content difficulty as determinants of children's cognitive processing of televised educational messages. *Journal of Experimental Child Psychology, 43,* 311-327.

Chomsky, N. (1957). *Syntactic structures.* The Hague, the Netherlands: Mouton.

Corder-Bolz, C. R. (1982). Television literacy and critical television viewing skills. In D. Pearl, L. Bouthilet, & J. Lazar (Eds.), *Television and behavior: Ten years of scientific progress and implications for the eighties: Vol. 2. Technical reviews* (DHHS Publication No. ADM 82-1196, pp. 91-102). Washington, DC: Government Printing Office.

Culbertson, J. (1986). Whither computer literacy? In J. A. Culbertson & L. L. Cunningham (Eds.), *Microcomputers and education: Eighty-fifth yearbook of the National Society for the Study of Education* (pp. 109-131). Chicago: University of Chicago Press.

Dondis, D. (1973). *A primer of visual literacy.* Cambridge: MIT Press.

Dorr, A. (1980). When I was a child, I thought as a child. In S. B. Withey & R. P. Abeles (Eds.), *Television and social behavior: Beyond violence and children* (pp. 191-230). Hillsdale, NJ: Lawrence Erlbaum.

Dorr, A. (1983). No short cuts to judging reality. In J. Bryant & D. R. Anderson (Eds.), *Children's understanding of television: Research on attention and comprehension* (pp. 199-220). New York: Academic Press.

Dorr, A. (1993). Media literacy for modern America. In *Media competency as a challenge to school and education* (pp. 217-236). Gutersloh, Germany: Bertelsmann Foundation.

Dorr, A. (in press). What constitutes literacy in a culture with diverse and changing means of communication? In D. Keller-Cohen (Ed.), *Literacy: Interdisciplinary conversations*. Cresskill, NJ: Hampton.

Dorr, A., & Brannon, C. (1993). Media education in American schools at the end of the twentieth century. In *Media competency as a challenge to school and education* (pp. 71-105). Gutersloh, Germany: Bertelsmann Foundation.

Dorr, A., Graves, S. B., & Phelps, E. (1980). Television literacy for young children. *Journal of Communication, 30*(3), 71-83.

Ennis, R. H. (1989). Critical thinking and subject specificity: Clarification and needed research. *Educational Researcher, 18*(3), 4-10.

Gardner, H. (1983). *Frames of mind: The theory of multiple intelligences*. New York: Basic Books.

Gazzaniga, M. S. (1992). *Nature's mind: The biological roots of thinking, emotions, sexuality, language, and intelligence*. New York: Basic Books.

Glaser, R. (1984). Education and thinking: The role of knowledge. *American Psychologist, 39*, 93-104.

Graham, P. A. (1981). Literacy: A goal for secondary schools. *Daedalus, 110*, 119-134.

Greenberg, B. S. (Ed.). (1980). *Life on television: Content analyses of U.S. TV drama*. Norwood, NJ: Ablex.

Haith, M. M. (1980). *Rules that babies look by*. Hillsdale, NJ: Lawrence Erlbaum.

Hill, M. (1992). The new literacy. *Electronic Learning, 12*(1), 28-34.

Huston, A. C., & Wright, J. C. (1989). The forms of television and the child viewer. In G. Comstock (Ed.), *Public communication and behavior* (Vol. 2, pp. 103-159). New York: Academic Press.

Lesser, G. S. (1974). *Children and television: Lessons from Sesame Street*. New York: Random House.

Malamuth, N. M., & Donnerstein, E. (Eds.). (1984). *Pornography and sexual aggression*. New York: Academic Press.

McLuhan, M. (1964). *Understanding media: The extensions of man*. New York: McGraw-Hill.

Medrich, E. A., Roizen, J. A., Rubin, V., & Buckley, S. (1982). *The serious business of growing up: A study of children's lives outside school*. Berkeley: University of California Press.

Messaris, P. (1981). The film audience's awareness of the production process. *Journal of the University Film Association, 33*(4), 53-56.

Olson, D. R. (1988). Mind and media: The epistemic functions of literacy. *Journal of Communication, 38*(3), 27-36.

Perkins, D. N., & Salomon, G. (1989). Are cognitive skills context-bound? *Educational Researcher, 18*, 16-25.

Piaget, J., & Inhelder, B. (1969). *The psychology of the child*. New York: Basic Books.

Piette, J. (1993). Teaching television critical viewing skills: From theory to practice to theory. In *Media competency as a challenge to school and education* (pp. 147-165). Gutersloh, Germany: Bertelsmann Foundation.

Resnick, L. B. (1987). *Education and learning to think*. Washington, DC: National Academy Press.

Robinson, J. P. (1977). *How Americans use time: A social-psychological analysis of everyday behavior*. New York: Praeger.

Rossiter, J. R., & Robertson, T. S. (1977). Children's responsiveness to commercials. *Journal of Communication, 27*, 101-106.

Salomon, G. (1979). *Interaction of media, cognition, and learning*. San Francisco: Jossey-Bass.

Sinatra, R. (1986). *Visual literacy connections to thinking, reading and writing*. Springfield, IL: Charles C Thomas.

Sternberg, R. (1985). *Beyond IQ*. Cambridge: Cambridge University Press.

Suhor, C., & Little, D. (1988). Visual literacy and print literacy: Theoretical considerations and points of contact. *Reading Psychology: An International Quarterly, 9,* 469-481.

Vygotsky, L. S. (1962). *Thought and language.* Cambridge: MIT Press.

Wileman, R. E. (1980). *Exercises in visual thinking.* New York: Hastings House.

Williams, T. M. (Ed.). (1986). *The impact of television: A natural experiment in three communities.* New York: Academic Press.

Worth, S., & Adair, J. (1972). *Through Navajo eyes: An exploration of anthropology and film communication.* Bloomington: Indiana University Press.

11 Market Censorship Revisited: Press Freedom, Journalistic Practices, and the Emerging World Order

SUE CURRY JANSEN
Muhlenberg College

This essay undertakes a wide-ranging assessment of the ways current transformations in global political formations are being configured within Western news discourses. Inspired by but not modeled after Raymond Williams's (1976) *Keywords*, this analysis identifies some of the structures, conditions, and theoretical issues that need to be addressed to construct a vocabulary of key terms in the current interpretive crises. Situated within the assumptions of media-critical theory, it examines the relevance of recent feminist and philosophical approaches to metaphor, how terms become naturalized in political discourse, key terms in post-cold war political linguistics, and their implications for democracy and the critical spirit.

RAYMOND Williams begins *Keywords: A Vocabulary of Culture and Society* (1976) with a brief autobiographical story. Returning to Cambridge in 1945 after 4½ years of military service during World War II, Williams reports that he experienced a profound sense of estrangement. All of the familiar faces were gone and everything seemed different. After many disorienting days, he encountered an old acquaintance who had also just returned from the army. They eagerly shared their impressions of the strange new world around them. Then Williams writes, "We both said, in effect simultaneously: 'The fact is, they just don't speak the same language.' " (p. 9).

Williams, of course, used scholarship to cope with his disorientation. He undertook a review, or, to use a more fashionable term, a *genealogy,* of the formation of key terms and concepts in the English language. Originally intended to serve as an appendix to *Culture and Society* (1958), Williams

Correspondence and requests for reprints: Sue Curry Jansen, Communication Studies, Muhlenberg College, Allentown, PA 18104.

Communication Yearbook 17, pp. 481-504

subsequently spent 25 years revising and refining his vocabulary of keywords before it was finally published in 1976.

According to Williams (1976), each of the 155 "keywords" he examined "virtually forced itself" on his attention because the problems of its meanings appeared to be inseparable from the problems it was being used to discuss. According to Williams, the words are "key" in two connected senses: "They are significant, binding words in certain activities and their interpretation" and "they are significant, indicative words in certain forms of thought" (p. 13).

Williams made modest claims for his compilation. Acknowledging that it was neither thorough nor neutral, he invited readers to become collaborators in the work. Indeed, he even convinced the publisher of the original edition to include blank pages to encourage readers to make their own notes as well as to signal both that the inquiry remained open and that the author solicited corrections and amendments for future editions. Williams himself continued work on the project throughout his life. His final public lecture, "When Was Modernism?" which explicated postmodernism as an enemy ideological formation, was in many ways the coda of this endeavor.

Raymond Williams died in January 1988 at the age of 66. In the 5 years that have passed since Williams's death, planet Earth has undergone epochal transformations that appear to be rivaled in scale only by the revolutionary political and cultural developments that precipitated the Western Enlightenment and the birth of modern political cultures in the eighteenth century.

These transformations have been accompanied by changes in the languages, categories, and assumptions of contemporary politics and culture. These changes are so dramatic that E. P. Thompson (1990) claims history is now turning "on a new hinge" (p. 117).

Thompson's assessment may be premature. Some suggest that the old hinge of ethnic tribal conflict, frozen in place since World War I by the long winter of Soviet repression, has simply reasserted itself in the wake of the collapse of communism, and that, as a result, the twentieth century is ending much the way it begun. Moreover, as David Harvey (1989) points out, "There is always a danger of confusing the transitory and the ephemeral with more fundamental transformations in political-economic life" (p. 124). Nevertheless I think it is possible to assert, with some confidence, that the press and the official sources that supply it with information are experiencing profound interpretive crises because the political ideologies and rhetorics secured by the mythologies of the cold war have lost their resonance. The old political mythos, based upon polarized, binary, categorical structures, have collapsed, but the new discursive system (or systems) for making sense of world politics is still struggling to be born.

When he was president of the "new," now former, Czechoslovakia, Václav Havel emphasized this radical discontinuity, this epistemological rupture, in political narratives in an op-ed editorial in *The New York Times*, "The End of the Modern Era" (1992). Havel maintains that the collapse of communism has not only profoundly challenged the assumptions of our (Eurocentric) political and social theories, it has also undermined the foundations of rational inquiry:

> The end of Communism has brought a major era in human history to an end. It has brought an end not just to the 19th and 20th centuries but to the modern age as a whole. . . . The large paradox at the moment is that man—a great collector of information—is well aware of all of this, yet is absolutely incapable of dealing with the danger. (p. E15)

The altered political landscape of the 1990s is far more bewildering than the milieu Williams encountered at the dawn of the cold war. Presidents, premiers, policymakers, political pundits, and managers of paranational corporations—not just returning soldiers and old reds—are now disoriented and actively engaged in mass-mediated races to locate, secure, name, and claim key formations in this brave new world *dis*/order.

THE INTERPRETIVE CRISIS:
TRANSCRIBING FIELD NOTES

This essay will examine some of the discursive practices and framing devices that Western policymakers, social theorists, and media organizations are using to attempt to make sense of these changes. Most current scholarship and speculation focus on how these transformations are altering institutions and structures of knowledge in the former Soviet Union and Soviet-bloc nations and how the emerging nations of Eastern Europe are being repositioned in relation to the West.

My work gives some attention to these questions, but its primary focus is on how these changes are altering discussions of and warrants for freedom of expression and the production of knowledge within Liberal (or post-Liberal) democracies, especially the United States. More specifically, I will argue that these changes are accompanied by or precipitating domestic changes within Liberal democracies that have, to date, attracted relatively little systematic commentary or analysis. These changes appear to be further eroding the remaining residues of Enlightenment-based concepts of participatory democracy and press freedom while, at the same time, creating some openings for new forms of critical discourse.

My agenda is modest, sometimes painfully so. It identifies some of the constituents of the current interpretive crises and explores some of their implications for social theory. It offers no sure recipes for resolving the crises. Moreover, it underscores the significance of these crises and the importance of critical engagement with them but also profiles some of the obstacles to this engagement. In short, it examines some of the elements necessary to critical analysis of a fairly narrow and elite form of communication—international news—in light of the dissolution of its master narrative or defining trope, "the Cold War."

My analysis takes international news as a site where government, corporate, and media elites communicate with one another, compete for control over national and international agenda-setting processes, and rationalize and seek to legitimate political and corporate policies and practices.

I recognize that most news consumers, at least in the United States, do not invest very heavily in consumption of international news, that they do not regard it as having much relevance to their daily experience, and that they do not conceive of themselves as participants in either the events or the discourses of international news. Moreover, I acknowledge the accuracy of these structural assessments. Most citizens are seldom more than spectators or eavesdroppers on these conversations of political and journalistic elites. Nevertheless, this form of spectatorship offers one of the few open windows routinely available for observing elite thinking about global issues, even if these windows are usually tightly screened ideologically.

My effort to make sense of some field notes on international news recorded during the interpretive crisis precipitated by the end of the cold war is inspired by, but not modeled after, Williams's "Introduction" to *Keywords*. My transcriptions of these notes identify some of the structures, conditions, and theoretical issues that, I think, need to be addressed in attempts to construct a vocabulary of "key terms" in current public (mediated) discourses about post-cold war configurations of global power. Unlike Williams's inquiry, however, my assessment is not informed or tested by the perspective of time. It is an initial draft, a set of field notes, prepared during a period when the grounds and parameters, not just the vocabularies, of public discourse are shifting very rapidly. Moreover, it is a study in contemporary political linguistics with only modest gestures toward historical semantics. Although I cannot give the reader the gift of blank pages, my effort is, of course, much more partial, arbitrary, and incomplete than Williams's.

My argument is secured by five interrelated textual moves. The first part, "Media-Critical Theory and Political Discourse," situates the inquiry within the assumptions and precedents of media-critical theory. The second part, "The Winner Names the Age," establishes the relevance of recent philosophical and feminist studies of metaphor to analysis of keywords in contemporary political discourse. The third part, "Hanging the New Hinge of History," considers some of the processes whereby terms become naturalized and amplified in mass-mediated forms of political discourse. In the fourth part, "Keywords and Information Markets," some key terms in contemporary, post-cold war, political discourse are identified and briefly examined. The final section assesses some of the implications of what Herbert Marcuse (1969, p. 73) called "political linguistics" for Liberal or post-Liberal concepts of press freedom.

MEDIA-CRITICAL THEORY AND
POLITICAL DISCOURSE

The designation *media-critical theory* is used here to signal affiliation with dialectical approaches to critique that recognize both (a) the importance of sociological analysis of formations and structures of power and knowledge, including the power of media, media organizations, and their positioning within market systems, and (b) the significance of cultural analysis of the complex hegemonic and sometimes counterhegemonic processes whereby mediated messages acquire meaning and exercise influence in socially stratified, heterogeneous industrial societies. The term is also intended to convey a continued appreciation of the critical spirit of the Frankfurt tradition, especially its insistence that it is only "by the refusal to celebrate the present" that the possibility of a more humane future might be preserved (Jay, 1973, p. 299).

The hyphenated form *media-critical* is intended to convey an inclusive, eclectic, perhaps even somewhat preemptive positioning: one that attempts to foreground what Hanno Hardt (1992) characterizes as "a notion of critique that is inherent in the idea of democracy and can be defined as thinking about freedom and responsibility and the contribution that intellectual pursuits can make to the welfare of society" (p. xi). For the purposes of this inquiry, I relegate to secondary consideration current struggles for theoretical and epistemological purity within and among various theory groups in the field that have been set in motion by what Jürgen Habermas (1972) has called the linguistic turn in contemporary scholarship.

The Critical Spirit

Both levels of engagement with the critical spirit are necessary and useful. Nevertheless, I believe the current context requires theoretical flexibility, even some compromise, for three interrelated reasons. First, this flexibility is a pragmatic, even a strategic, stance. What is at stake in current struggles to define the future is nothing less than the idea (and/or ideology) of democracy itself and with it, of course, the survival of any viable form of political critique. To defer critical engagement until more reliable tools for cultural analysis are available is therefore not only irresponsible but dangerous.

Second, currently ascendant approaches to the problem of meaning and the rhetoric of inquiry can easily disable interventions in these struggles. Constructivism, poststructuralism, and most versions of the ubiquitous and polymorphous postmodernism persuasively display the follies of naive realism. These positions support profound doubts about referentiality: about the ways words may be said to refer to the world (Benson, 1992; Eco, 1986). For those "stuck in the post," Williams's *Keywords* can only be read as exercise of "naive realism" (A. O'Connor, 1989). To seek to emulate that work today is not only to invite a similar indictment in the court of philosophy but to do so with wanton and reckless abandon.

Third, those engaged in realpolitik and the media organizations that represent their activities as "news" are not deterred by the problem of referentiality, by postmodern ennui, or by the prospect of the philosopher's stick. To the contrary, their struggles are aggressive, strategic, and institutionally routinized. Moreover, they command the material and organizational resources that ensure mass distribution of their messages. Whether motivated by naive or crackpot realism, Machiavellian calculation, or market considerations, they are fully engaged in struggles to locate—when possible, even to create—capture, colonize, and control keywords within the referential fields that define, construct, and cultivate hegemonic constructions of social reality.

In sum, I recognize that the referents of "events" represented in mass media are always linguistically mediated. This antifoundational recognition is, however, tempered by a strategic form of sociological realism that embraces the venerable Thomas Theorem: If a situation is defined as real, it is real in its consequences (Merton, 1968). Powerful forces are currently proclaiming the emergence of new global realities. These proclamations have real consequences for realpolitiks.

The New Hinge of History

The new hinge of history is being defined now. The current moment of hegemonic disjuncture, if not rupture, presents extraordinary challenges as well as extraordinary opportunities for both critical communication scholarship and counterhegemonic struggles.

Our options are, however, limited. We can remain at the post, aspiring to the wisdom of gods and the purity of angels. Or we can accept our limits, acknowledge the paradoxical character of our activity, and craft our conceptual tools in the trenches. In this essay, I take the low road.

In doing so, I emulate feminist theorists like Sandra Harding and Donna Haraway, who have been to "the post" but are not stuck there. These scholars have engaged fully in current dialogues on postmodernism and standpoint epistemologies without being disabled by philosophical or political uncertainties. Their critiques of key terms and concepts in the discourses of Western thought, such as *objectivity* and *rationality,* do not only expose the ideological limitations of current constructions of these terms. They also recognize the political and rhetorical resonance of these concepts and consequently refuse to surrender them to the opposition. Instead, they treat them as "indigenous" cultural resources of the West (to use Harding's, 1992, term), and they try to retool these concepts to serve more inclusive and just ends. Thus, for example, Haraway (1988) defends the objectivity of "socially situated knowledge" and Harding (1991) develops the concept of "strong objectivity." In short, they do what Williams did, but they do it from positions beyond the "post."

THE WINNER NAMES THE AGE:
LINGUISTICS AS THE
"ARMOR OF THE ESTABLISHMENT"[1]

Herbert Marcuse (1969) described "political linguistics" as the "armor of the establishment." He maintained that "one of the most effective rights of the Sovereign is the right to establish enforceable definitions of words" (p. 73). Williams (1976) acknowledged that he found his interests in historical semantics "closely echoed" in some of the later works of the Frankfurt school, which combine "analysis of key words or key terms with key concepts" (p. 22). Williams was presumably referring, at least in part, to Marcuse's analysis of political language.

Neither Marcuse nor Williams intended their decodings to serve only, or perhaps even primarily, as academic exercises. Both saw their critiques of political linguistics as acts of resistance and even as potential admission tickets to emancipatory praxis. Marcuse made this explicit by linking the idea of political linguistics to linguistic therapy. He acknowledged that the idea of linguistic therapy is a utopian vision, whereby art and politics—what he later called "the aesthetic dimension" (Marcuse, 1978)—combine to rescue key-words from the control of hegemonic forces and recruit them to the service of emancipatory ends. He offered no recipes for organizing these rescue missions, but he did provide some lucid examples, such as the refusal and inversion of the language of oppression by black civil rights leaders in the United States during the 1960s, a form of semantic intervention that, for a time, replaced resignation with a collective vision of transcendence.

On the surface, Williams's project is more esoteric: to chart historical changes in the range of meanings ascribed to key terms that are also associated with, or indicators of, shifting social formations. Yet, Williams's genealogies were also politically charged. He saw them as means to raising consciousness of the social conflicts present in and sometimes papered over by changes in usage (A. O'Connor, 1989).

Feminist Contributions to Political Linguistics

Feminist approaches to historical semantics and linguistic therapy (see Haraway, 1988, 1989; Harding, 1986, 1991; Kellcr, 1985; and many others) owe more to the linguistic insurrections of Mary Daly (1973, 1979; and others) than to either Williams or Marcuse. Feminist studies of language are nevertheless relevant to this argument because they demonstrate that studies in political linguistics are not merely exercises in negative dialectics or utopian forms of wordplay.

Within feminist studies, semantic digs have been used both to organize research projects and to formulate policy recommendations. Thus, for example, feminist research in the history of science, especially the work of Carolyn

Merchant (1980), Evelyn Fox Keller (1985), and Susan Bordo (1986), has systematically attended to the use of language, particularly metaphors, in scientific discourse. It has documented the sexual and sexist character of the founding metaphors of Western science. This, in turn, has provided rationales for political activism that has produced some modest transformations in pedagogies in science and mathematics and in research practices in science in the United States. Thus, for example, the National Institutes of Health has changed its research protocols to include women in health research, and the National Endowment in the Humanities recently (1991) sponsored a summer institute on science as culture practice that produced a document that encouraged integration of gender issues in science and technology programs in higher education. For fuller development of these ideas, see Glazer, Heath, Jansen, Lewis, and Rooney (1991).

Feminist inquiries in historical semantics differ from the studies of Williams and Marcuse by virtue of the fact that they are informed by a sociology of knowledge and a methodology, the so-called strong program (Bloor, 1977) of the Edinborough School, that was explicitly formulated to decode and critique the discourse and epistemological foundations of scientific objectivity.[2] The Frankfurt tradition of critical theory, especially the work of Horkheimer and Adorno, was also committed to radical critique of Western dualism and instrumentalism; however, the arguments of critical theory were framed within the meta- and "master" narrative conventions of traditional philosophy (Fraser, 1989; Jamieson, 1981).

Metaphor and Scientific Objectivity

In contrast, the research agenda of the "strong program" of the sociology of knowledge was undertaken by scholars, trained in traditional scientific fields, who applied the analytic tools developed by the "ordinary language" philosophers, especially Austin and Searle, to the study of scientific discourse. The strong program examined the scientific careers of specific words, metaphors, and models. Eventually, those associated with the strong program enlarged their inquiries to include ethnographic studies of scientific talk, texts, and practices. In short, the strong program operates at a relatively low level of abstraction and therefore has been able to provide detailed maps of the ways specific scientists construct rhetorics of objectivity to advance specific interpretations of nature. The strong program has demonstrated that metaphors play crucial roles in the construction of scientific texts. David Bloor (1977) describes metaphors as the primary agents of ideological and social transfer in scientific discourse. Working independently but along parallel lines, feminists are using similar forms of textual analysis to decode and map patriarchal markers in the discourses of modern science, philosophy, and political discourse.

Social studies of science have demonstrated that in scientific revolutions, as in political revolutions, the winner takes custody of the conceptual Armor and redeploys it to the service of its cause. These studies have shown that "mobile armies of metaphors" (Nietzsche—see Rorty, 1986, p. 3) provide the rhetorical assault troops necessary to achieve and maintain paradigmatic dominance. That is, the strong program has demonstrated that metaphors empower scientific vision; they provide the scaffolding for arguments, color the language of assertion, put poetry in the paradigms, and guide inquiry. In short, they make science possible. And, contrary to the tenets of older theories of knowledge, the processes by which they achieve this empowerment are rational because, as Mary Hesse (1966) points out, "rationality consists just in the continuous adaptation of our language to our continually expanding world, and metaphor is one of the chief means by which this is accomplished" (p. 177).

What holds for scientific narratives applies with even greater force to news narratives because scientific storytelling is constrained by nonhuman phenomena and actions while most news stories are fully embedded within the hermeneutic circle of human agency and interests. Metaphor is the chief means by which the referents of President Bush's "New World Order" and President Clinton's "new world" (see the 1993 inaugural address)—both hyperbolic if not counterfactual metaphors—are conceptualized and colonized. Metaphors are therefore significant indexical markers of keywords in current struggles to name and claim the political future.

The next section explores some of the ways "mobile armies of metaphors" function within political discourse: how they are represented within the "objective" genres of news narratives and how they become naturalized within hegemonic discourse practices.

HANGING THE NEW HINGE OF HISTORY: METAPHORS, FRAMES, AND NEWS PARADIGMS

Hyperbole appears to be a constituent of all forms of power knowledge. As James Baldwin put it in an address to the National Press Club (Washington, D.C., December 10, 1986), "Every society has a model of itself, and everyone of those models is false." Socrates, Plato, Aristotle, Machiavelli, Marx, Burke, Bentham, Gramsci, Habermas, Foucault, Rorty, and hundreds of other students of political and social theory have examined the meanings and implications of the disparity between theory and practices for both the governed and their governors.

The ability to effectively recruit and strategically position "mobile armies of metaphors" to fill and police the resulting voids is, of course, the hallmark of effective statecraft. And, conversely, the commitments of democratic covenants to closing the gaps that separate theory and practice provide the historic justification for protections of free speech and freedom of the press in democratic societies. Thus, for example, Thomas Jefferson's salutary description of the mission of the free press has become a sacred canon of the professional ideology of journalism: "The basis of our government being the opinion of the people, the first object should be to keep that right; and were it left to me to decide whether we should have a government without newspapers or newspapers without government, I should not hesitate to prefer the latter."

Metaphor and Journalistic Objectivity

The political press envisioned by Jefferson and James Madison is, of course, history. It was replaced in the United States and in most other parts of the world by the commercial press (D. Schiller, 1981; Schudson, 1978). The commercial press has not entirely relinquished its claims to service as the watchdog of democracy; however, profit, not politics, has become its primary master (Jansen, 1988). So much so that A. J. Leibling's dictum, "Freedom of the press belongs to the man who owns one," is almost as well known today as Jefferson's apology for an adversarial press.

The commercial press secured its claims to authority by embracing the rhetoric, though not the methodology, of scientific objectivity. The ideological constituents of this rhetoric have always been relatively transparent. Gaye Tuchman (1972) characterized journalistic objectivity as a "strategic ritual." Dan Schiller (1981) characterized it as a "cultural form" and a "myth" in Barthes's (1972) sense. Nevertheless, Herbert Gans (1979) contends that journalism is "the strongest remaining bastion of logical positivism in America" (p. 184). Following Harding (1992), I would characterize journalistic objectivity as one of the "indigenous" resources of the Western press: flawed, incomplete, and hyperbolic but also harboring a tarnished fragment of democratic idealism that continues to value the quest for something more than and better than simply reproducing hegemonic definitions of social order. In short, I suggest that this strategic ritual is a democratic accomplishment, albeit an imperfect one, *as well as* an ideological cover, and that its functions and promises can best be plumbed by adopting what feminist epistemologies conceive of as both/and logics, logics that acknowledge the Janus-headed character of most powerful ideas.

News as a Cultural Form

Since the early 1970s, a virtual cottage industry in news analysis and critique has developed both within communication research and in the alternative press. This work has examined the historical origins, ideological foundations, organizational routines, narrative structures, and most recently the gendered constituents of journalistic objectivity (see, for example, Gans, 1979; Hartley, 1982; Rakow & Kranich, 1991; D. Schiller, 1981; Tuchman, 1972; and many others).

There are a number of reasons that news analysis became a growth industry during the last quarter of the twentieth century. The primary reason is, however, the increased presence, visibility, and social power of the mass media. As Stuart Hall (1977) points out, "Quantitatively and qualitatively, in twentieth century advanced capitalism, the media have established a decisive and fundamental leadership in the cultural sphere. . . . They have progressively colonized the cultural and ideological sphere" (pp. 340-341).

Initially, critiques of this colonization sought simply to document the ideological constituents of the framing conventions, narrative structures, and organizational practices used to accomplish the strategic rituals of objectivity (Gans, 1979; Gitlin, 1980; Tuchman, 1972; and others). That is, they demonstrated that news is made, not discovered, and that it is generally made in ways that are congruent with the dominant system of signification in the society that produces it. This was a crucial critical move because news is represented and marketed as a univocal and naturalistic rendering of events. Critical studies of news production demonstrated that news is, and must be, a historically and socially situated cultural form. In short, this early work not only exposed the presence of cultural values and ideological biases in the social construction of news, it also documented the historically dependent character of the concept of journalistic objectivity itself.

More recent communication research has built upon these foundations. Conceptualizing news (like science) as mediated by "paradigms," and "facts" as rule governed and paradigm dependent, this work opens up new avenues for inquiry (Corcoran, 1991; Hackett, 1984; and others). It also underscores the importance of analyzing the visual constituents of news narratives including the functions visual metaphors perform in enhancing the intertextual, polysemic, and, with them, hegemonic dimensions of mass communication (Halliday, Jansen, & Schneider, 1992; Medhurst & Benson, 1991).

Despite its debts to the work of Thomas Kuhn (1970), to my knowledge, this research has not been influenced by either feminist epistemologies or the strong program in the sociology of knowledge. Yet, it does foreshadow the possibility of developing forms of critical news analysis that illuminate both the sociological and the rhetorical dimensions of political discourse.

Framing Conventions

By exploring the founding metaphors that secure political visions, communication scholars can begin to track the roles framing devices play in naturalizing and cultivating hegemonic constructions of social reality. The "paradigmatic crisis" produced by the collapse of communism has, for example, rendered visible long established and largely unquestioned media practices for gathering, organizing, and constructing international news. For over 40 years in U.S. news organizations, the master trope, "the Cold War," provided the news net, the bifurcated categorical structures, and the framing devices for conceptualizing international news (Corcoran, 1991; Halliday et al., 1992; Thompson, 1990).

During the period of open hegemonic rupture that extended from the fall of the Berlin Wall in 1988 until the start of the Persian Gulf War in January 1991, this paradigmatic crisis was evident as routine Manichaean strategies for encoding foreign news seemed increasingly to invite, even court, ironic decodings. The spirit of the times was captured in newspaper headers such as "The loss of an enemy is a frightful thing" (*The Washington Post*, October 12, 1989) and "Three European views on the risks of peace" (*The New York Times*, March 12, 1989). Similarly, the struggle to find new ways of organizing representations of events in Eastern Europe was transparently played out in the pages of *The New York Times*, which first embraced metaphors of natural disasters in its running headers, such as *collapse, earthquake, storm,* then shifted for several months to evolutionary metaphors. In short, for a time, "media frames," not just mediated events, acquired news value. And no appeals to the strategic rituals of journalistic objectivity could conceal their social, cultural, historical, rhetorical, and mythic character.

Derived from Wittgenstein's linguistic philosophy, the concept of "frame analysis" was, of course, introduced into sociology by Erving Goffman (1974). It gained currency in news analysis as a result of the contributions of Gaye Tuchman (1978), Stuart Hall (1980), and Todd Gitlin (1980). Gitlin (1980) defines "media frames" as "persistent patterns of cognition, interpretation, and presentation, of selection, emphasis, and exclusion, by which symbol-handlers routinely organize discourse, whether verbal or visual" (p. 7). According to Gitlin, these frames are normally "unspoken and unacknowledged" devices that organize the world for both journalists and, to a significant degree, for those who rely on their reports. Media frames are what "makes the world beyond direct experience look natural" (p. 6). They endow messages with "an eery substance in the real world, standing outside their ostensible makers and confronting them as alien forces" (p. 2).

Within news analysis, the framing process is seen as a site of contention and a source of hegemonic power. For this reason, framing conventions have attracted a great deal of critical attention. Gitlin, for example, demonstrated how major media used "frames" derived from crime reporting to (mis)represent the antiwar movement. In short, frames have usually been analyzed as conduits of ideological distortion.

Critical scholarship in news analyses, like Raymond Williams's study *Keywords*, generally have been launched from counterhegemonic (left or left-Liberal) positions. As a result, they sometimes appear to be coming from less contaminated (because less immediately materially invested) epistemological positions. This perception, in turn, has continued to nourish the impossible dream of escaping from what Nietzsche called the "prison-house" of language. It has kept alive the realist's dream of stripping away the frames and apprehending the real "facts," the real "reality." And it has done this despite the phenomenological disclaimers of its more philosophically sophisticated practitioners.

Focusing on the role metaphors play in securing news paradigms and in advancing intextuality and polysemy bypasses this temptation. It serves as a constant reminder of the mediated character of *all* communication. It provides the critical resources necessary to identify and analyze "the armor of the establishment" as well as to envision alternative or counterhegemonic frames for interpreting events. In short, it acknowledges that frames are sense-making devices—"semiotic technologies" (Haraway, 1988) or conceptual lenses—that expand human vision by narrowing it.

The Problem of Relativism

This approach to critical media studies recognizes that real "reality" exists but also that it can only be apprehended from "God's eye" and that it therefore lies beyond the ken of media scholarship. Feminist standpoint epistemologies demonstrate that this discovery is the beginning, not the end, of the quest for rational and objective knowledge. According to Haraway (1988), "The alternative to relativism is not totalization and single vision, which is always finally the unmarked category [of the dominant group] whose power depends on systematic narrowing and obscuring." Rather, "it is precisely in the politics and epistemology of partial perspectives that the possibility of sustained, rational, objective inquiry rests" (p. 584; for further development of these ideas, see also Jansen, 1989).

What critical-media theory can do therefore is recognize the radical historical contingency of all knowledge and set itself the task of identifying the rhetorical and social constituents of media frames as well as tracking how they operate within fields of power relations. Analysis of the roles metaphors play both in securing news "paradigms" and in acting as agents of "ideological transfer" would appear to be a very important part of this task in an era where mass media play central roles in cultivating hegemonic constructions of social reality. Metaphors do the "border crossings" that take messages of elites from think tanks to speeches, headlines, sound bytes, sitcoms, and advertising slogans. Defining, master, or mythic tropes like "the Cold War" or its would-be successor, "the New World Order," are generative structures. These root metaphors shape, instantiate, strategically position, and ensure both the authority and the mobility of keywords in ascendent forms of political discourse. They propel the conceptual leaps necessary to capture, contain, and communicate new realities but do so by foreclosing alternative formulations. The mythos buried in these root metaphors readily call up and thereby privilege certain constellations of words and word associations that operate in the political linguistics in the ways Lakoff and Johnson's (1980) "metaphors that we live by" operate in the conversations of everyday life. This is how "key" words become both/and "significant, binding words in certain activities and their interpretation" and "significant, indicative words in certain forms of thought" (Williams, 1976, p. 13).

KEYWORDS AND INFORMATION MARKETS

Williams's lament, "They just don't speak the same language," assumes new significance in the emerging global marketplace. Political discourse is deliberately, carefully, cautiously, and collectively constructed in the media culture of late-twentieth-century industrial societies. Television, advertising, public relations, litigation, and political action committees have largely eliminated spontaneity from the speech of U.S. politicians and policymakers. What little spontaneity remains survives in the netherworld of revealing misstatements, slips, and errant "off-the-record" statements that are breached onto the record.

Writing from a neoconservative standpoint, Irving Lois Horowitz (1991) acknowledges, "Every epoch redefines what of the past remains relevant and what needs to be discarded" (p. 27). What distinguishes current forms of revisionism, according to Horowitz, is, however, "the hyper-consciousness with which this cultural redefinition is being constructed." This hyperconsciousness extends to the ways policy positions are constructed, commodified, and marketed for media consumption, that is, the ways they are preframed and packaged as sound bytes. It also largely determines how these messages are disseminated, often simultaneously, through many different media "windows" in efforts to "bandwagon" public opinion. Successful media plans for the distribution of informational and policy positions now involve deliberate (and sometimes deliberately deceitful) exploitations of the ambiguity and polysemy that make commercial media, especially television, accessible to heterogeneous mass audiences.

Much has been written about the privatization of public resources, spaces, media, and information in Liberal democracies (Elliott, 1983; Smythe, 1981; and many others). This privatization movement has, of course, been accompanied by ideologies and policies (Thatcherism, Reaganomics) that valorize the rationality and wisdom of the marketplace. Mainstream Western media organizations have largely filtered their framings of the collapse of the former Soviet Union within the assumptions of these ascendant and still largely unchallenged discursive screens. Market terms—in the case of the former Soviet bloc, development of market economies, and, in the instance of the United States, attending to national and trade deficits—seem to have largely replaced political definitions of the relations of the old cold war rivals in international news constructions. Reports from the East configure resurgence of ethnic rivalries as obstacles to the development of market-based economies. In the United States, discussions of the national deficit, taxes, entitlements, and the spiraling costs of health care—economic issues of unquestionable importance—dominate or, more accurately, supplant political discourse.

These structural transformations in global capitalism, long in the making in the West but significantly accelerated in the 1980s, have been theorized by neoconservatives as a transition to postindustrialism, by the left as a move to post-Fordism, and by many of all ideological gradations as the advent of an information or postmodern age. Writing from a neo-Marxian position, David Harvey (1989, p. 123) describes this transformation in capitalist expansion as involving a new configuration, which he calls "flexible accumulation." It is "characterized by more flexible labour processes and markets, of geographical mobility and rapid shifts in consumption practices." Within this configuration, access to and control over accurate and up-to-date information as well as capacities for instant data analysis become highly valued commodities. The value of scientific knowledge to global competitiveness is also increased; and control "over information flow and over the vehicles for propagation of popular taste and culture have likewise become vital weapons in competitive struggle" (Harvey, 1989, p. 160).

The commodification of culture, including political discourse, makes explorations of political linguistics more difficult than they were when Williams began his work in 1945. Print-based references like the *Oxford English Dictionary* are largely irrelevant to the task at hand. Television has turned up the heat and hyped the pace of political discourse. It has also cut the cord that, in the early years of the medium, made visual images extensions or exemplifications of print narratives. Media cultures privilege visual images and increasingly draw upon the distinctive "grammars" of their "languages" to communicate and cultivate their messages.

The disjunctive narratives of the new media culture are not random, scattered, or meaningless as some (print-biased) postmodernist and postreferential theorists suggest. To the contrary, the MTV-ing of political discourse represents, in the cultural sphere, what the political economy models of communication, developed by the late Dallas Smythe, Herbert Schiller, and others, have long described within the structures of media markets.

In this discursive form, as in scientific discourse, metaphor acts as the agent of ideological transfer. Metaphor is the boundary crosser, mediator, epoxy, and occasional translator that makes the new form of individualized and consumerist communication and sense-making processes of the media culture possible. The new forms of sense-making are not forms that print-based thinkers and democrats like Williams or I comfortably recognize as rational in Hesse's sense (see the section in this essay, "The Winner Names the Age"). Yet, in mediated discourse, as in scientific discourse, metaphor does facilitate "an adaptation of our language to our continually expanding world" (Hesse, 1966, p. 177). This adaptation may more closely approximate *rationalization* (in Max Weber's, 1947, sense of that term) than it does the substantive kind of rationality valued by philosophers like Hesse, but it is nevertheless responsive to the changing material, social, and cultural arrangements of our time.

Agenda-Setting Technologies

The new discursive forms of media cultures have been implicated in undermining the print-based binary logic that secured cold war mythology.

Some analysts see them as contributing factors in the collapse of communism (Thompson, 1990; Wilson, 1992). The friendly imperialism of the glamorous visual imagery produced and CNN-ed throughout the world by Western media cultures are seen as having cultivated desires for consumer products that state-controlled production systems could not and would not satisfy.

What was framed in the Western press as a clamor for democracy can perhaps be more plausibly reframed as a clamor for Western technologies and consumer goods, especially communication technologies, computers, VCRs, FAX: what Ithiel de Sola Poole (1983), in my view mistakenly, called "the technologies of freedom" and what I would call the technologies of consumerism. Like all technologies, the designs of commercial technologies transmit more than just the material cultural markers imprinted in transistors and circuits. They also carry social values and designs for living. They are, as Dallas Smythe (1981) put it, agenda setters and teaching machines. These technologies make it easier to say and do some things while making it difficult, although not impossible, to do others.

Within the media cultures, this agenda-setting process becomes a major site of cultural contest. Thus, for example, at one point during the 1992 U.S. presidential election campaign, former Vice President Dan Quayle appeared to be running against Candice Bergen, the actress who plays the lead role in a popular television series, rather than Democratic contenders Bill Clinton and Al Gore. Charging that Bergen's character Murphy Brown is responsible for undermining family values, Quayle's position was a direct extension and reflection of the new post-cold war agendas of conservative think tanks and policymakers. This agenda casts the entertainment industry and popular culture in the role of prime mover in America's cultural malaise and crisis of leadership. It also deflects attention away from critical analysis of the high levels of hegemonic closure that now operate within elite news media in the United States: a closure that was apparent in the responses of most major media organizations to government censorship and press controls during the Persian Gulf War.

To be sure, this closure is not complete. The credibility and "strategic rituals" of the Western news media are dependent on circulation of some counterhegemonic messages. Proactive conservative lobbies, think tanks, and media, including the growing conservative presence in cable broadcasting (for example, the news programming and analysis on Pat Robertson's Christian Broadcasting Network), appear to be committed to finding ways to exercise greater control over the flow of counterhegemonic messages (J. J. O'Connor, 1992). In attempting to retain their autonomy as commercial enterprises as well as their ideological attachments to their historical mission as watchdogs, mainstream media organizations increasingly possess but seldom overtly exercise the power to undermine the authority and legitimacy of governments (Entman, 1989). This culture power is largely contained and disciplined by elite media organization's dependence upon official sources and increasingly conservative think tanks for information (Soley, 1992). The

"End of History" debate (discussed in the second part of this essay) as well as press coverage of the Persian Gulf War are striking examples of the ways this dependence works.

Think Tanks and Sound Bytes

In identifying the keywords that are both "significant, binding words in certain activities and their interpretation" and "significant, indicative words in certain forms of thought" in the United States, it is increasingly necessary to track their migration from think tank to sound byte. Lawrence Soley (1992) has documented the growing reliance of elite journalists on think tanks, especially conservative think tanks, as news sources by comparing a sample of news reports from 1979-1980 with a comparable sample for 1987-1988. Washington-based think tanks, addressing national and international issues, are supplemented by regional institutes and foundations that supply the local press with information on domestic and regional economic and social issues. Soley has also examined the increasing presence of journalists as fellows-in-residence at these think tanks, which are generously funded by corporate contributions. Unlike academic knowledge producers, whose intellectual autonomy is protected, at least in theory, by academic freedom and tenure, the knowledge producers supported by think tanks must return to positions in commercial media after a year or two in residence. For this reason, Soley points out, they do not "want to be identified with unpopular political positions, such as supporting Nicaragua's Sandinista government" (Soley, 1992, p. 64). Within this context, the meanings of, and relationships among, "knowledge," "research," and the always problematic pursuit of "objectivity" are highly responsive to market conditions.

As a result of the growing dependence of news media on private, corporate-funded, data and policy sources, many—perhaps even most—of the keywords that have acquired currency within U.S. political discourse since the early 1980s have been fabricated within conservative think tanks like the Heritage Foundation, American Enterprise Institute, Cato Institute, Olin Foundation, Council for Social and Economic Studies, Hudson Institute, Foreign Policy Institute, National Institute for Public Policy, and others. Moreover, these organizations are playing crucial roles in supplying expertise, planning resources, and conceptual maps for restructuring and privatizing the state economies of the nations of Eastern Europe and the former Soviet Union. Indeed, some cynical (counterhegemonic) readings of the process suggest that Western experts are supplying Russian President Boris Yeltsin with media consultants and a new "made-for-TV" persona.

Keywords in a Global Village

The definitions of democracy and freedom that are being exported by these think tanks to former communist nations conflate *democracy* and *capitalism*:

terms that always coexisted in modern Western Liberal societies in uneasy and occasionally conflictual unions (Bowles & Gintis, 1986; Jansen, 1988). Within this new vocabulary, *the* keyword of Liberalism—*democracy*—is increasingly drained of its critical, resistant resources and becomes fully synonymous with free enterprise and consumer sovereignty. Here a set of terms—*freedom of expression* and *freedom of choice*—that were borrowed from politics and used metaphorically by U.S. manufacturers and advertisers in the early part of this century to herald the promises of consumerism become literalized. The equation of free/private enterprise and freedom from government regulation with political freedom by conservative consultants and advisers reinforces one-dimensional interpretations of democracy.

When such interpretations become naturalized within the political discourse of leaders and citizens of Eastern Europe and the former Soviet Union—people who have little access to or presumably interest in the prehistory or metaphoric associations of the languages of Western democracy—the meaning of democracy changes. Freedom of choice becomes the freedom to choose between SONY, IBM, Zenith, or Toshiba. When this political discourse is reimported as "news" from Eastern Europe and represented in Western news media, virtually all residue of its site of origination—U.S. think tanks—has been scrubbed away. To be sure, this import also bears the imprimatur of its reception and reinterpretation from the perspectives of the experiences and national identities of the former communist nations. Nevertheless, the naturalization of market-based definitions of democracy within the reportage that have come out of these nations since the late 1980s, and that have circulated widely in the Western press, have presumably also contributed to domestic redefinitions of these terms.

The following examples illustrate the way this migratory process works. When, for example, representatives of the American Enterprise Institute appear on U.S. television informational programs like *Nightline* or *The McNeil-Lehrer NewsHour*, their affiliations are noted, and sometimes moderated, if not always countered, by an expert representing an alternative position. This practice is a lingering residue of the FCC fairness doctrine, which mandated that information carriers using the public airwaves strive to achieve "balance" in the presentation of political views. Always problematic in theory and practice, this mandate nevertheless reinforced strategic rituals of objectivity.

Exporting and Importing Facts

When, in contrast, positions developed in U.S. think tanks are refracted back to the United States from Eastern Europe, the signatures of the expertise of the American Enterprise Institute or the RAND Corporation are no longer attached. For example, in the period immediately following the dismantling of the Berlin Wall, when Gorbachev or Yeltsin's advisers issued policy positions after meetings with former U.S. Secretary of State James Baker's staff and their advisers, they were articulating Soviet or Russian positions, not RAND positions. These articulations become "fact," and, within the rituals of U.S. journalistic objectivity, facts do not require the same kinds of signatures as "opinions." By framing their reportage within the established structures of news narratives and relying on routine news-gathering practices—in short, by conducting "business as usual"—U.S. news organizations are thereby valorizing rather than monitoring U.S. foreign policy.

The U.S. news media are also, implicitly, contributing to a kind of collective social amnesia regarding the history and constituents of Liberal democracy. That is, they are providing their readers/audiences with unreflexive representations of the views that U.S. foreign policy experts and corporate developers are exporting to countries that do not have established institutional structures for regulating, monitoring, taxing, or resisting privatizing initiatives. In doing so, they are also further eroding their own, already severely compromised, ideological claims to autonomy: claims that provided the historical warrant for privileging press freedom in the First Amendment to the U.S. Constitution.

Perhaps no term, phrase, or metaphor better displays the *hyperconscious* effort, by those in power, to redefine social reality and cultivate new keywords within contemporary political discourse than the Bush Administration's counterfactual valorizations of *the New World Order* (NWO). Political slogans have, of course, been a characteristic of U.S. politics since the American Revolution. Manifest Destiny, the New Deal, the Square Deal, the New Frontier, and of course the Cold War are all master tropes that advanced visions of American futures. Moreover, *the Cold War* was a media-made term, coined by journalist Walter Lipmann in response to Winston Churchill's announcement on March 5, 1946, in a speech in Fulton, Missouri, that an "iron curtain" had descended upon Europe.

The New World Order

The concept of a "new world order" has, however, been articulated within a new communication environment: one in which hyperconscious myth-making has immediate and global resonances. Moreover, the New World Order and the occasion of its articulation represent extraordinarily innovative exercises in political linguistics for several reasons.

First, its articulation, in a televised speech by U.S. President George Bush on January 17, 1991, 2 days into the Persian Gulf War, when television audiences throughout the world were acutely attentive to U.S. news, ensured unprecedented levels of immediate global visibility.

Second, coupling the articulation of this vision with the announcement of massive bombing of Iraq elevates to the level of political praxis poststructuralist doubts about the ways words may be said to refer to the world. So much so that Herbert Schiller (1991) suggests that President Bush's assertion that mass bombing of urban centers constitutes "the rule of law, not the law of the jungle" raises a "psychiatric question" (p. 12).

Third, the term represents a hyperconscious attempt to appropriate counterhegemonic languages and practices at a number of levels. Schiller examines the most immediate and obvious antecedents of the term in United Nations initiatives, the New International Economic Order, and the New International Information Order. Responding to pressures from Third World nations, NIEO and the NIIO were designed to redistribute both economic and information resources in ways that redressed some of the enormous inequities between industrialized societies and the rest of the world. Supported by more than 125 nations, these initiatives were opposed by the United States and largely ignored by U.S. media (Schiller, 1991). The NWO also appropriates the language of another and less well-known but prestigious international effort. The World Order Models Project, founded in 1966, which publishes the journal *Alternatives* is a transnational association of scholars and political figures engaged in research, education, dialogue, and publication of materials aimed at "promoting a just world peace." Its advisory board includes, among many others, left and liberal social reformers like Paulo Freire, Elise Boulding, and Henryk Skolimowski. In addition, the NWO appropriates or piggybacks onto the language of U.S. government-sponsored 1492-1992 commemorations of Columbus's "discovery" of the new world. The term, of course, also has other less salutary historical associations in the rhetorics of both Mussolini and Hitler, who used the term extensively (Rundle, 1992).

Fourth, these appropriations have amplified the resonance, ambiguity, and polysemy of the NWO but also of course its openness to ironic renderings.

Fifth, the Bush administration's articulations of the vision of the NWO was accompanied by sophisticated scripting of visual representations, especially during the Persian Gulf War, where sets, video technology, and mythic narrative patterns, developed for television coverage of sports, specifically football, were simulated in military "press briefings." These briefings were actually live U.S. government broadcasts directly to the people of the "global village," which were, presumably, intended to negate the power of journalistic mediation. The sporting metaphor extended to visuals. So that, for example, photo opportunities were effectively used to convey the layers of hierarchy and the distributions of power as well as the gender order of the NWO. Not only were Saudi military press officers used at some news conferences, formally posed official photographs of the coalition military leadership carefully replicated structures of global power with Western troops centrally positioned, Middle Eastern figures at the near periphery, and Third World representatives at the margins (Jansen & Sabo, 1992).

The war naturalized the NWO metaphor. It became familiar furniture in editorial headers and talk show conversation. It also quickly infiltrated the language of the television talk show circuit. After the war, the press transferred this framing to analysis of events—the destabilization and disorder—in the then Soviet Union. The resonance of the phrase appears to owe as much to its openness to ironic inversions as to its "bandwagoning" effects. Moreover, the vastness and vagueness of its terms permit an unusually broad range of meanings to find refuge under its umbrella. So much so that the titular author of the concept has been plausibly charged with misunderstanding it. Thus Lester Thurow (C-SPAN, *Booknotes,* May 31, 1992), charges President Bush—"the Cold War President"—understands less about the new world order than most policy analysts because he conceives of it primarily as a military phenomena when actually the most dramatic structural transformations are occurring in global market systems, not in military formations. This example is doubly significant because it is one of hundreds that demonstrate the migration and naturalization of the metaphor, NWO, in the statements and publications of would-be oppositional mediated voices and publications.[3] As yet, it is too early to tell whether President Bill Clinton's speechwriters will be able to effectively mobilize new metaphors to describe the transformations in international political formations. In Clinton's inaugural address, they appeared to be trying to erase former President Bush's imprimatur from the slippery NWO metaphor by simply referring to "the new order."

This brief analysis of the NWO only scratches the surface. It demonstrates that the term is not new, that the "world" it evokes is highly selective both economically and geographically, and that the "order" it valorizes, so far, has no material referents. In Williams's sense, the NWO constitutes an exemplary case of a set of keywords that disorient because the problems of their meanings are inseparable from the problems they are being used to discuss.

The difference between this set of keywords and the keywords that troubled Williams in 1945 is that the obfuscation that accompanies their articulation is deliberate, hyperconscious. Some other keywords in contemporary mediated political vocabularies that warrant further examination in light of the above conditions are *freedom* including *freedom of the press* and *free market; competitiveness; democracy; history; evolution; environment; energy; public/private dualisms; science and technology; knowledge/information; media culture/popular culture; totalitarianism,* and *authoritarianism.* Analysis of the inversions and migratory patterns of these terms is beyond the scope of this essay. It is, however, a task of significant importance both to media-critical theory and to the preservation (or recovery) of democracy as a political, as opposed to a purely economic, form.

Democracy and the Critical Spirit

When Herbert Marcuse wrote *One-Dimensional Man* in 1964, the book's title and its argument were correctly criticized as hyperbolic. The thesis he put forth is still somewhat overdetermined, but current structural relationships for the production and distribution of knowledge and their representations in news media now come much nearer to approximating Marcuse's model. Ironically, conservative think tanks mastered Marcuse's lessons on political linguistics and are now very effectively practicing what he preached against. Meanwhile, many of his erstwhile friends on the left, who first embraced and then abandoned his critical insights regarding media cultures, are now devoting enormous intellectual resources and energies to the pursuit of residues of political resistance in products of the U.S. entertainment industry like Madonna, soap operas, hip-hop, and heavy metal.

In a speech to the European Bank for Reconstruction and Development, Jacques Attali (1991) described the new global market formation in these terms: "The world is becoming an ideologically homogeneous market where life is being organized around common consumer desires, whether or not those desires can be fulfilled" (p. 422; Wilson, 1992, pp. 209-210). Within this new postindustrial or post-Fordian world order, political candidates, positions, and programs are brought to market like music videos, waffle irons, and dandruff shampoos.

Whether the keyword of Euro-American political linguistics during the first half of the twentieth century, *democracy,* will retain its historic resonance within this new world order is open to question. Citizens and scholars committed to its preservation would be well-advised to accept Hanno Hardt's (1992) challenge to recover the critical spirit "that is inherent in the idea of democracy and [that] can be defined as thinking about freedom and responsibility and the contribution that intellectual pursuits can make to the welfare of society" (p. xi).

NOTES

1. The title for this section is based on the title of Lillian Smith's (1978) book; the subtitle is from Marcuse (1969).

2. While feminist work in science has been influenced significantly by the strong program in the sociology of knowledge, the strong program remains virtually untouched by feminism.

3. Many left-oriented publications have contributed to amplification of the term: some in literal ways, others with irony and inversion. For example, the *Socialist Register* devoted an entire issue to the NWO in 1992, while in March 1991 *Marxism Today* published several articles under the header, "New World Order: War of the Imagination."

REFERENCES

Attali, J. (1991, May 1). The European Bank for Reconstruction and Development. *Vital Speeches, 57,* 422.

Baldwin, J. (1986, December 10). [Address at the National Press Club, Washington, DC].

Barthes, R. (1972). *Mythologies* (A. Laver, Trans.). New York: Hill and Lang.

Benson, T. (1992). Communication and the circle of learning. *Quarterly Journal of Speech, 78,* 238-275.

Bloor, D. (1977). *Knowledge and social inquiry.* London: Routledge & Kegan Paul.

Bordo, S. (1986). The Cartesian masculization of thought. *Signs, 11*(3), 439-456.

Bowles, S., & Gintis, H. (1986). *Democracy and capitalism, property, community, and the contradictions of modern social thought.* New York: Basic Books.

Corcoran, F. (1991). KAL 007 and the Evil Empire: Mediated disaster and forms of rationalization. In M. J. Medhurst & T. W. Benson (Eds.), *Rhetorical dimensions in media* (pp. 162-182). Dubuque, IA: Kendall/Hunt.

Daly, M. (1973). *Beyond god the father: Toward a philosophy of women's liberation.* Boston: Beacon.

Daly, M. (1979). *Gyn-ecology: The metaethics of radical feminism.* Boston: Beacon.

Eco, U. (1986). *Semiotics and the philosophy of language.* Bloomington: Indiana University Press.

Elliott, P. (1983). Intellectuals, the "information society" and the disappearance of the public sphere. In E. Wartella, D. C. Whitney, & S. Windahl (Eds.), *Mass communication review yearbook* (Vol. 4, 569-579). Beverly Hills, CA: Sage.

Entman, R. M. (1989). *Democracy without citizens: Media and the decay of American politics.* New York: Oxford University Press.

Fraser, N. (1989). *Unruly practices: Power, discourse and gender in contemporary social theory.* Minneapolis: University of Minnesota Press.

Gans, H. (1979). *Deciding what's news.* New York: Pantheon.

Gitlin, T. (1980). *The whole world is watching: Mass media in the making and unmaking of the new left.* Berkeley: University of California Press.

Glazer, G., Heath, D., Jansen, S. C., Lewis, J., & Rooney, P. (1991). STA and gender. In S. Fuller & S. Raman (Eds.), *Teaching science and technology studies: A guide for curricular planners* (pp. 15-23). Blacksburg: Virginia Polytechnic Institute and State University.

Goffman, E. (1974). *Frame analysis.* New York: Harper & Row.

Habermas, J. (1972). *Knowledge and human interests.* Boston: Beacon.

Hackett, R. A. (1984). Decline of a paradigm? Bias and objectivity in news media studies. *Critical Studies in Mass Communication, 1,* 229-259.

Hall, S. (1977). Culture, the media, and the ideological effect. In J. Curran, M. Gurevitch, & J. Woolacott (Eds.), *Mass communication and society* (pp. 340-341). London: Arnold.

Hall, S. (1980). Encoding and decoding in the television discourse. In S. Hall, D. Hobson, A. Lowe, & P. Willis (Eds.), *Culture, media, language* (pp. 128-138). London: Hutchinson.

Halliday, J., Jansen, S. C., & Schneider, J. (1992). Framing the crisis in Eastern Europe. In M. Raboy & B. Dagenis (Eds.), *Media, culture and democracy: Mass communication and the disruption of social order* (pp. 63-78). London: Sage.

Haraway, D. (1988). Situated knowledge: The science question in feminism and privilege of partial perspective. *Feminist Studies, 14*(3), 575-599.

Haraway, D. (1989). *Primate visions: Gender, race, and nature in the world of modern science.* New York: Routledge.

Harding, S. (1986). *The science question in feminism.* Ithaca, NY: Cornell University Press.

Harding, S. (1991). *Whose science? Whose knowledge? Thinking from women's lives.* Ithaca, NY: Cornell University Press.

Harding, S. (1992, April 26). [Presentation to the Women's Professional Group, Muhlenberg College, Allentown, PA].

Hardt, H. (1992). *Critical communication studies: Communication, history and theory in America.* London: Routledge.

Hartley, J. (1982). *Understanding news.* London: Methuen.

Harvey, D. (1989). *The condition of postmodernity.* Oxford: Basil Blackwell.

Havel, V. (1992, March 1). The end of the modern era. *The New York Times*, p. E-15.

Hesse, M. (1966). *Models and analogies in science.* South Bend, IN: Notre Dame Press.

Horowitz, I. L. (1991). The new nihilism. *Transaction: Social Science and Modern Society, 29*(1), 27-32.

Jamieson, F. (1981). *The political unconscious: Narrative as a socially symbolic act.* Ithaca, NY: Cornell University Press.

Jansen, S. C. (1988). *Censorship: The knot that binds power and knowledge.* New York: Oxford University Press.

Jansen, S. C. (1989). Gender and the information society: A socially structured silence. *Journal of Communication, 39*(3), 196-215.

Jansen, S. C., & Sabo, D. F. (1992, May). *Sport/war: The gender order, the Persian Gulf War, and the new world order.* Paper presented at the annual meetings of the International Communication Association, Miami, FL.

Jay, M. (1973). *The dialectical imagination: A history of the Frankfurt school and the Institute of Social Research, 1923-1950.* Boston: Little, Brown.

Keller, E. F. (1985). *Reflections on gender and science.* New Haven, CT: Yale University Press.

Kuhn, T. S. (1970). *The structure of scientific revolutions.* Chicago: University of Chicago Press.

Lakoff, G., & Johnson, M. (1980). *Metaphors we live by.* Chicago: University of Chicago Press.

Marcuse, H. (1964). *One-dimensional man.* Boston: Beacon.

Marcuse, H. (1969). *An essay on liberation.* Boston: Beacon.

Marcuse, H. (1978). *The aesthetic dimension: Toward a critique of Marxist aesthetics.* Boston: Beacon.

Medhurst, M. J., & Benson, T. W. (1991). *Rhetorical dimensions in media.* Dubuque, IA: Kendall/Hunt.

Merchant, C. (1980). *The death of nature: Women, ecology and the scientific revolution.* New York: Harper & Row.

Merton, R. K. (1968). *Social theory and social structure.* Glencoe, IL: Free Press.

National Endowment in the Humanities (summer institute). (1991). *Science as culture.* Middletown, CT: Wesleyan University.

O'Connor, A. (1989). *Raymond Williams: Writing, culture, politics.* New York: Basil Blackwell.

O'Connor, J. J. (1992, June 14). For the right, TV is half the battle. *The New York Times,* sec. 12, p. 1.

Poole, I. S. (1983). *Technologies of freedom.* Cambridge, MA: Harvard University, Belknap Press.

Rakow, L., & Kranich, K. (1991). Woman as sign in TV news. *Journal of Communication, 41*(1), 8-23.

Rorty, R. (1986, April 17). The contingency of language. *London Review of Books, 17,* 3-6.

Rundle, G. (1992). A new world order. *Left Curve, 6,* 4-8.

Schiller, D. (1981). *Objectivity and the news: The public and the rise of commercial journalism.* Philadelphia: University of Pennsylvania Press.

Schiller, H. (1991, February). Whose new world order? *Lies of Our Times,* pp. 12-13.

Schudson, M. (1978). *Discovering the news.* New York: Basic Books.

Smith, L. (1978). *The winner names the age.* New York: Norton.

Smythe, D. W. (1981). *Dependency road: Communication, capitalism, consciousness, and Canada.* Norwood, NJ: Ablex.

Soley, L. (1992). *The news shapers: The sources who explain the news.* New York: Praeger.

Thompson, E. P. (1990, January 29). END and the beginning: History turns on a new hinge. *The Nation,* pp. 117-118, 120-122.

Thurow, L. (1992, May 31). *Booknotes.* C-SPAN.

Tuchman, G. (1972). Objectivity as strategic ritual: An examination of newsmen's notions of objectivity. *American Journal of Sociology, 77*(4), 660-679.

Tuchman, G. (1978). *Making news.* New York: Free Press.

Weber, M. (1947). *Theory of social and economic organization.* Glencoe, IL: Free Press.

Williams, R. (1958). *Culture and society 1780-1950.* London: Chatto and Windus.

Williams, R. (1976). *Keywords: A vocabulary of culture and society.* New York: Oxford University Press.

Wilson, R. (1992). Techno-euphoria and the discourse of the American sublime. *Boundary 2, 19*(1), 204-229.

Communication Technology as a Metaphor of Power

JOHN J. PAULY

Saint Louis University

L ET me respond to Sue Curry Jansen's tale of a dark New World Order with a lighter story of my own. For the last 2 years, my former university has invited a veritable host of scholars, journalists, diplomats, economists, and assorted glitterati to town for a conference on international affairs. This conference has been a big-think production from first to last—lots of geopolitical speculation, lots of publicity, lots of opportunities for hobnobbing alumni and trustees. Its function has been to display the university president's commitment to "globalization" and—nominally—to educate faculty, students, and the community.

There has been just one problem: Students rarely attend any sessions of the conference, much to the dismay of the president. It is not that students are uninterested in international affairs. They regularly enroll in courses in intercultural communication, everyday life in the Third World, the politics of China, or the history of South Africa. More students are seriously studying foreign languages than at any time in my 25 years in universities. Students turn out in significant numbers to attend Amnesty International meetings or to support service projects in Central America. But, even after being hectored by faculty and administrators, they refuse to attend the international affairs conference.

Is the problem that students are apathetic and provincial, as many of my colleagues believe? Or do students cynically recognize that such conferences are designed to guarantee their attendance but exclude their participation? Students, after all, have little say about the speakers invited or the topics chosen, and the format of the conference discourages engagement with the

Correspondence and requests for reprints: John J. Pauly, Department of Communication, Saint Louis University, St. Louis, MO 63108.

Communication Yearbook 17, pp. 505-510

audience. As a result, students exercise the only power left them: They refuse their presence. Students got our disinvitation but decided not to attend our party.

This modest parable usefully balances Sue Jansen's account of power in our age. There is little doubt that modern elites behave in just the way Jansen has described—turning the world into markets, insinuating their views into every conversation, clearing a space for capital in everyday life. Having dismissed citizens as participants, however, elites must always reassemble the public as a chorus to lend legitimacy to their own accomplishments. It is not enough, as Max Weber noted, for rich people to be rich; they must get everyone else to agree that they *deserve* to be rich. Thus elites now devote much energy to producing a public that ratifies their actions—through polls, press conferences, educational campaigns, and various other forms of compulsory communication. After each barrage of information, however, the disenfranchised climb out of their bunkers and go about their business. In some sense, the media now need us more than we need them.

As a loyal son of Chicago, I enjoy a good con as well as the next person, and so I admit a certain dazed respect for the chicanery of the elites that Jansen describes. But I do not take their claims of intellectual authority or moral grandeur very seriously; nor do I think that the sheer scale of their ambition will guarantee their success. Jansen, too, recognizes the possibility of failure, but her description speaks more eloquently of domination. Like Milton, she has given the devil all the best lines. Her project is to describe the forms of social control likely to emerge in a post-cold war world. She hopes to demonstrate the power of metaphors by tracing the paths of "ideological transfer"—from the intentions of the powerful, by way of the channels of production and dissemination, through narrative practices, and into the behavior and attitudes of the audience.

Jansen reminds us that the end of the cold war signals a moment of profound change. The breakup of older colonial empires, following World War II, is now nearly complete in Africa, Asia, and Eastern Europe. Without a shared enemy, we struggle to articulate a sense of national identity. Without the corporate welfare payments provided by a permanent military state, the economy founders. We imagine ourselves victors at the dawn of a new day but spend our nights counting our losses. And we fear that one of those losses may be democracy itself, as William Greider (1992) has recently argued:

> The permanent mobilization has altered democratic relationships profoundly, concentrating power in remote and unaccountable places, institutionalizing secrecy, fostering gross public deception and hypocrisy. It violated law in ways that have become habitual. It assigned great questions of national purpose to a militarized policy elite. It centralized political power in the presidency at the expense of every other democratic institution. (p. 360)

For Greider, the central question of the post-cold war age is this: Who will tell the people that their hopes of democracy have been betrayed? Jansen shares this gloomy assessment (as do I) and finds little cause for hope. She stresses the enormity of the forces at work, the subtle powers of the enemy, and the relentless coalescence of a new system of domination. She expresses an understandable frustration with the self-satisfied role of the postmodern intellectual, particularly those communication scholars who study residual cultural forms such as "Madonna, soap operas, hip-hop, and heavy metal" (p. 502). In the end, Jansen offers little solace beyond a call to "recover the critical spirit."

What is it about critical theory that compels it to haunt this morbid ground? Why does such theory always imagine power as that which tattoos our wrist and sends us off to the work camp? For a time, critical theory offered a bracing alternative to the functionalism that once dominated U.S. social science. It forcefully argued that functionalism amounted to little more than an apology for the status quo, a naive insistence, in the face of blatant force and fraud, that consensus governs American society. Critical theory noted that pluralists left no room for irreconcilable differences. All groups played their role, and the system would efficiently monitor and readjust intergroup differences.

Today, oddly enough, critical theory has come to invent its own form of functionalism. It now resembles the older style of social science it once critiqued, not in its politics, worldview, or conclusions but in its style of analysis. Critical theory and functionalism both assume that different institutions play identifiable roles in maintaining the totality of society, though neither fully specifies what that totality is. Both believe that only those who grasp society as a whole can exercise intellectual authority, and so both tend to overestimate the power of elites. Both show a certain contempt for the uncritical masses and remain indifferent to the evidence of personal experience. And both display an insensitivity to the artful ambiguities of narrative.

In short, I myself find it difficult to discover in critical theory the spirit of solidarity, mutual aid, and tolerance needed to sustain democracy. So I propose to reinterpret Sue Jansen's essay in terms that are more idiosyncratically my own. In the process, I hope to honor her essay's most worthy impulses, but in terms that recognize the possibility of democratic renewal.

Let us start with her judgment of our own historical moment. What does that moment look like to the powerful groups that Jansen describes? Do political and economic elites now feel themselves ascendant, exhilarated at the prospect of a new imperial age? Quite the contrary: U.S. intellectuals of the center and right, for example, are suffering from a premature case of the fin de siècle blues. A few years ago, as the Soviet Union was breaking up, the Berlin Wall falling, and Iraqis dying with admirable efficiency, these same intellectuals subjected the country to an endless litany of fatuous and self-serving eulogies to the American way. Everywhere now, however, the talk is of ruin, of America's declining wealth and influence, its loss of national mission and civic virtue, its inability to reinvigorate its economy or educate its children, its steady drift toward class warfare. Conservative intellectuals' prideful arguments about "the end of history" have now soured. Far from acting self-assured, power everywhere finds itself disputed, divided, and desperate.

Not surprising, talk about communication often figures in this discourse of decline. By this account, when the national interest can no longer be equated with national security, the country devolves into a Babel of chattering tribes. In the absence of widely accepted principles by which to adjudicate differences, politics turns into a free-for-all and respect for authority declines. Political leaders find themselves stymied by the unregulated demands of contentious single-issue interest groups. Conservatives and liberals may disagree about how to cast the roles in this drama, but they largely agree on the plot.

Jansen speaks of this moment—quite properly, I think—as a series of "interpretive crises," a void into which powerful institutions hope to insert their own meanings. For her, metaphors chosen by the media are powerful weapons in mobilizing citizens. As do most critical theorists, she asks us to imagine an ominous chain of command and influence that connects large-scale economic and political structures to small turns of phrase and, ultimately, to habits of mind.

There is a different way in which we might speak of media power, however. Instead of stressing the power of metaphors, we might speak of communication as itself a metaphor of power. James Carey (1990a, 1990b) has argued that communication technology is perhaps the root metaphor of modern societies, a very totem of social order. Rather than look for power in the metaphors of the moment, we might focus on communication technology as a metaphor for the social order that elites hope to design and control. Thus the new role of writing, reading, and printing sustained eighteenth-century bourgeois intellectuals' faith in the public sphere, and the digital computer sustains the twenty-first-century knowledge elites' vision of an information society. The very nature of modern intellectuals' work encourages them to pledge allegiance to one or more technologies—to the book as repository of Western thought, or the daily newspaper as watchdog of government, or the computer as database. In each case, communication technology metonymically represents the architects of the system—as men of letters, as well-informed citizens, as programmers—and synecdochically represents the social whole, offering a blueprint for the world that intellectuals hope to dream into existence.

This way of talking about social order in terms of communication may seem characteristically American. Lewis Lapham (1986) made this very point a few years ago in a provocative and subtle essay titled "Paper Moons." In that piece for *Harper's* magazine, Lapham reported his encounter with an "intellectual mercenary" named Townsend, a consultant who during the 1980s had enlisted in the campaign to promote the Strategic Defense Initiative and supply-side economics. Townsend and his fellow mercenaries have now been invited to help the federal government solve its trade imbalance. Townsend is holding forth at the bar, matching wits with his fellow consultants, when he asks, "What is it that Americans know how to make and sell better than anybody else in the world?" His fellow consultants guess: "fast-food restaurants," "fashion," "videotapes," "ammunition," but Townsend just shakes his head. Then he answers his own question: What product do Americans make the best? "Metaphors," Townsend replies. "Metaphors and images and expectations."

What American cultural empire sells, in short, is the dream of cultural empire. Our fevered talk about "the media" testifies to our lavish (and characteristically American) hope of remaking the world by rewiring social relations. To be sure, Jansen senses what is at stake in this debate. She understands that U.S. media conglomerates are busily assembling the infrastructure through which they hope to sell packaged information and entertainment worldwide. She also recognizes that, in a world of large-scale media, the division of symbolic labor between producers and consumers will loom larger and constitute a new class distinction.

What she sees less clearly, I would argue, is the likely source of communication technology's most powerful effects. The most profound ideological effects may be exercised not through the content of media products but by changes in the very infrastructure of everyday life. Like the students at my university, we will always be able to marshall irony and indifference to shield ourselves from media bias. But how will we defend ourselves against a global business system that conjoins computer networks and satellite communication? It is this prospect—of a computer-powered global market in capital, labor, and intelligence—that undermines our ability to control our own destiny. It is this prospect, and the possibility that the United States will lose this new economic war, that is scaring U.S. intellectuals.

It is always useful, as Jansen advises, to maintain a sense of skepticism, and where possible to contest others' images of us. But, in the days ahead, such action will not be nearly enough to protect U.S. democracy. The new metaphors of power are embedded in the communication technologies themselves and in the social relations they prefigure. Resistance will need to take many forms. It may appear as a new Luddism, a defense of countervailing oral traditions, a principled indifference, or a program of ridicule and satire.

Above all, we should remember that our problems are not unprecedented and that the history of oppositional social movements offers strategies for the future. Such movements have themselves been a characteristic outcome of the communication revolution. They exemplify what Carey (1969) has called the centrifugal force of communication, the tendency of the new technologies to articulate and join special-interest groups across space. These movements have historically put international communication in the service of difference, tolerance, and brotherhood.

Above all, for our purposes here, these movements have imagined an alternative "new world order," parallel to the emerging global marketplace but not dependent upon it. Long before the lines of commerce were fully established or the modern techniques of marketing fully exploited, social movements were establishing international communities of sympathy and interest. New technologies of communication have expanded and enabled such movements but have never subsumed them. All of the grand modern campaigns for justice—to end slavery, lynching, Jim Crow, and apartheid; to win the vote and contraception rights for women; to demand an 8-hour day and combat the depredations of capital; to ban nuclear weapons; to protect prisoners of conscience; to limit environmental pollution—have begun with local acts of courage, then echoed into the far corners of the earth.

This is why the end-of-history arguments ring hollow to me and why I remain more guardedly optimistic than Jansen. U.S. intellectuals of the center and right, fearing that the United States will no longer dominate the new world order, despair of any future whatsoever. But democratic renewal never comes from that quarter anyway, as Greider (1992) has argued:

> This renewal, if it comes, will not come from books. A democratic insurgency does not begin with ideas, as intellectuals presume, or even with great political leaders who seize the moment. It originates among the ordinary people who find the will to engage themselves with their surrounding reality and to question the conflict between what they are told and what they see and experience. (p. 410)

When power admits to being so divided, so vulnerable, so surprisingly at risk, then there is good reason for the rest of us to keep hope alive.

REFERENCES

Carey, J. W. (1969). The communications revolution and the professional communicator. *Sociological Review Monograph, 13,* 23-38.

Carey, J. W. (1990a). The language of technology: Talk, text and template as metaphors for communication. In M. J. Medhurst, A. Gonzalez, & T. R. Peterson (Eds.), *Communication and the culture of technology* (pp. 19-39). Pullman: Washington State University Press.

Carey, J. W. (1990b). Technology as a totem for culture. *American Journalism, 7,* 242-251.

Greider, W. (1992). *Who will tell the people.* New York: Simon & Schuster.

Lapham, L. (1986, December). Paper moons. *Harper's,* pp. 8-10.

12 Interethnic Communication: The Context and the Behavior

YOUNG YUN KIM
University of Oklahoma

Issues of ethnicity and interethnic interaction have been extensively investigated across social science disciplines for several decades. This essay presents an overview of some of the concepts that are prominent in the literature and proposes a conceptual framework in which many of the existing concepts can be integrated from a communication viewpoint. The current description of interethnic communication is grounded in some of the metatheoretical assumptions of pragmatism and systems theory, which emphasize the inseparability and interdependence of the context and the behavior of communication in any given interethnic encounter. Based on this perspective, interethnic communication is conceptualized in the form of a transactional matrix that consists of the behavior (encoding and decoding) and three layers of the context: the communicator, the situation, and the environment.

ETHNIC passions continue to boil around the globe. Hardly any day passes without reports of some new incidents of interethnic conflict. Many of the major conflicts today are being fought *within* states, engendered by issues of ethnicity—from the long-festering conflicts in places like Northern Ireland and South Africa to the new or renewed violence erupting in the Balkans and beyond. The continuing salience of ethnicity is accompanied by an increasing polyethnic norm of human society: Today fewer than 10% of the 186 countries are ethnically homogeneous and the rest are multiethnic states (Talbott, 1992). The "average" U.S. citizen, by 2056, is predicted to trace his or her descent to Africa, Asia, the Hispanic world, the Pacific Islands, or Arabia if current trends in immigration and birthrates persist (Talbott, 1992). This changing interethnic landscape has been accompanied by an explosion of books discussing various societal strains as ethnic groups that cling to their units of identity clash in neighborhoods, college campuses, and business organizations (e.g., Schlesinger, 1992; Terkel, 1992).

Even though issues of ethnicity are of universal concern, each locale, each encounter, and each individual presents a unique set of conditions that define

Correspondence and requests for reprints: Young Yun Kim, Department of Communication, 610 Elm Avenue, Room 101, University of Oklahoma, Norman, OK 73109-0335.

Communication Yearbook 17, pp. 511-538

the overall meaning of a particular interethnic interface. Many kinds of interethnic experiences and expressions are seen—public and private, explosive and subtle, conflictual and cooperative, violent and peaceful, hateful and caring. To the extent that interethnic dynamics can be generalized across individuals, situations, and societies, however, social scientists have attempted to find ways to explain how, why, and with what effects different ethnic groups and individuals interact with one another. Extensive and diverse academic descriptions and explanations have been proposed across disciplines over the past several decades. Indeed, the literature on interethnic relations presents a wide variety of concepts, definitions, perspectives, theories, and research findings. The largest body of theoretical and research studies exists in psychology and sociology and, to a lesser extent, in history, anthropology, political science, and sociolinguistics. Across the disciplines, the most prominent issue has been the various aspects of interethnic relationships: how conflict arises, how such conflicts can be eased, and how cooperative relationships can be promoted.

BUILDING AN INTEGRATIVE FRAME

Communication as a discipline is relatively new to the field of interethnic relations. This means that communication researchers have opportunities to learn from the body of knowledge and insights that are available today. We should make an effort to partake in the investigation of interethnic relations in ways that build on the existing interdisciplinary knowledge and, at the same time, to make our contributions with an emphasis on communication. This essay is an attempt to address this need. It presents a brief overview of the relevant literature across social sciences and, in doing so, proposes a communication-based conceptual framework within which many of the existing concepts and issues can be integrated. Because of the vastness and complexity of the field, and for the sake of brevity, citations of sources in this essay are selectively limited and not all-inclusive.

Description of Key Terms

The term *ethnicity* needs elaboration. Social scientists began using the word in the 1930s and 1940s in terms of national and cultural origin (Nash, 1989, p. 1). Today, *ethnicity* is commonly associated not only with cultural and national origin but with racial, religious, and linguistic origins as well (Gordon, 1981; Nash, 1989; Smith, 1981). In the sociological tradition, *ethnicity* has been used primarily as a label to designate a social *group* and to distinguish it from other social groups, based on such indicators as race, religion, language, national origin, or combinations of them. In this group-level definition, ethnicity becomes the "objective" character, quality, or condition of belonging to a social group as well as an individual's membership in an ethnic group. Most of the sociological discussions of ethnicity have employed ethnicity or ethnic group in a domestic context. This is the way, for instance, sociologists such as Glazer and Moynihan (1975) have investigated the phenomenon of ethnic "stratification" in the United States.

Cultural approaches to ethnicity emphasize the common life patterns, practices, and symbols that collectively connote a kind of temporal continuity or common "tradition" linking its members to a common future (Hsu, 1971; Nash, 1989). Some of the recent ethnographic studies in communication have taken such approaches, including the studies investigating communication patterns of American Indians by Wieder and Pratt (1990), of African Americans by Daniel and Smitherman (1990) and Kochman (1981, 1986), and of some of the mainstream American communities (Carbaugh, 1990; Philipsen, 1989). Like sociological approaches, cultural approaches view ethnicity primarily as a group-level phenomenon that, in essence, can be described in terms of its core, defining the group's life patterns by including language, behavior, norms, beliefs, myths, and values as well as the forms and practices of social institutions. These cultural patterns of ethnicity comprise *ethnic markers* (Nash, 1989), that is, symbolic (e.g., emblems such as flags, crosses, anthems, folk songs, folk gestures and movements, folk dances, and decorative objects) and physical/material features (e.g., skin color, dress, and food). Such ethnic markers represent within-group commonalities and between-group differences in individuals' backgrounds.

On the other hand, psychological studies have defined ethnicity primarily in terms of the "subjective"—often "unconscious" and "irrational" (or emotional) identification of individuals with an ethnic group and not with other groups, that is, the identity experienced by the group members. Social identity theory of intergroup behavior (Tajfel, 1974, 1978, 1982; Turner, 1975), for instance, has served as a basis for many experimental studies (e.g., Giles & Bourhis, 1976; Giles & Saint-Jacques, 1979) and has provided a systematic explanation of the way ethnic and other group identities are played out in individuals. The theory postulates that an individual's personal identity is based, in part, on membership in significant social categories along with the value and emotional significance attached to that membership.

In this regard, *ethnic identity* subsumes the related concept, *ethnic identification*—or a conscious act of identifying oneself with one's ethnic group— as well as the attributes of the ethnicity (group characteristics). Although often viewed as distinct phenomena, ethnicity and ethnic identity are empirically inseparable: They are two aspects of the same phenomenon, as the collective (ethnicity) and the individual experiences of it (ethnic or ethnolinguistic identity) mutually define each other. Whether strong or weak, some degree of inseparable relationship exists between an ethnic group and its members, and the concept that ties the individual member to the group is ethnic identity. Some scholars view ethnicity as the manifestation of a "primordial" tie that is embedded in the deep core of personhood. Yinger (1986), for instance, sees ethnic attachment as a "genuine culture" that forms the person's "basic identity" during the earliest periods of socialization, serving as a source of ethnic group strength. For De Vos (1990), ethnic identity is based on "the emotionally profound 'self'-awareness of parentage and a concomitant mythology of discrete origin" (p. 14).

The term *ethnolinguistic identity* has been used among some investigators who have conducted social psychological and sociolinguistic studies of intergroup conversational analysis (e.g., Gumperz & Cook-Gumperz, 1982), bilingualism (e.g., Bourhis, 1979; Clément & Noels, 1991; Landry & Allard, 1991; J. Ross, 1979), intergroup behavior (e.g., Giles & Johnson, 1987; Gudykunst & Gumbs, 1989; Lambert, 1979; Turner & Giles, 1981), and the role of language in the formation of ethnic identity (e.g., Heller, 1987).

Interethnic communication, then, is viewed as distinct from (intra)ethnic communication in that the psychological orientation taken by at least one interactant is based on ethnicity and ethnic identity (Collier & Thomas, 1988). As articulated extensively in studies of social identity theory, interethnic interactants tend to see themselves, as well as their interaction partners, in light of the respective ethnic *group membership* (Brewer, 1986; Brewer & Miller, 1984; Gudykunst, 1988a, 1988b; Kim, 1986, 1987; E. Ross, 1988; Tajfel, 1974; Turner & Giles, 1981). The impact of ethnicity in shaping identities and interethnic communication behavior varies across situations: Ethnicity can be critical, totally insignificant, or have a whole range of effects in between. Such variable presence and manifestation of ethnicity and ethnic identity in interethnic encounters has been described in terms of the intergroup-interpersonal continuum (e.g., Brewer & Miller, 1984; Tajfel, 1970, 1982; Turner & Giles, 1981). As Tajfel and Turner (1986) note,

> At one extreme . . . is the interaction between two or more individuals which is fully determined by their interpersonal relationships and individual characteristics and not at all affected by various social groups or categories in which they respectively belong. The other extreme consists of interactions between two or more individuals (or groups of individuals) which are fully determined by their respective memberships of various social groups or categories, and not at all affected by the individual personal relationship between the people involved. (p. 8)

Toward Interdisciplinary Integration

The diverse approaches to interethnic relations that have been taken across various social science disciplines have resulted in a rich body of information but one that is lacking in a comprehensive or interdisciplinary integration. Investigators in each discipline generally have limited their approaches to their respective research foci. In reality, interethnic phenomena involve all of the academic concerns across disciplines simultaneously, and any single perspective cannot fully, and thus realistically, explain them. My investigation echoes the view of Blalock (1982) and others, who have pointed out the serious need to provide a "big picture" or "theoretical road map" in this very complex and divergent area of study.

Recently, however, the field has shown a strong trend toward an interdisciplinary synthesis of perspectives in formulating theories and models designed to explain interethnic phenomena. Increasingly, efforts have been made with an emphasis on developing multidimensional conceptualizations that incorporate explanatory factors drawn from more than one discipline. A significant integrative approach was taken by Tajfel and his associates (Tajfel, 1974; Tajfel & Turner, 1986) in developing his theory of social identity and intergroup relations by taking into account the structural conditions of the society such as its minority-majority status.

Subsequent theoretical developments based on Tajfel's theory have continued his interdisciplinary tradition. The speech accommodation theory (Giles & Smith, 1979) and the ethnolinguistic identity theory of intergroup behavior (Giles & Johnson, 1987), for example, explain the "convergent" and "divergent" language behaviors of individuals in intergroup encounters, incorporating the structural/situational conditions, as well as the psychological ones, of group identity. The original speech accommodation theory has been broadened and revised into communication accommodation theory (Gallois, Franklyn, Giles, & Coupland, 1988). Here, the authors emphasize the role of the situation (such as degree of intergroup salience, dependence, and solidarity) and individual factors (such as social and personal identity) in constraining both speaker behavior and receiver attributions. The authors also emphasize the importance of interpersonal and intergroup salience in explaining the progress of a two-person intergroup interaction and the decisions the interactants make about their communication strategies (such as convergent and divergent strategies).

Related synthesizing efforts have been made in the area of ethnolinguistic identity and intergroup behavior. Clément and Noels (1991), for example, have examined situational norms, along with individuals' identity choice, in explaining the development of bilingualism. Here, situational norms include the extent to which the social milieu encourages or opposes both of the identities involved ("language institutional equality"), and the language status in the minority individual's home town, as well as the historical evolution of the minority ethnolinguistic status. Additional integrative approaches to explaining various intergroup behaviors have been offered by Bourhis (1979), Brewer and Miller (1984), De Vos (1990), Gudykunst and Lim (1986), Hewstone and Giles (1986), Landry and Allard (1991), Phinney and Rosenthal (1992), and Van Dijk (1987), among others.

The available integrative approaches to interethnic relations offer a substantial amount of interdisciplinary insights. They provide a broad basis on which I attempt to propose a more general description of interethnic communication. The current work, then, is intended as a continuation of the ongoing collective effort to move toward a comprehensive understanding of the way ethnicity is played out in human interaction.

An Organizing Framework

The current approach to interethnic communication is grounded in meta-theoretical assumptions derived from the perspectives of pragmatism and of systems theory. Communication is viewed as a phenomenon of action (and interaction) in which "all communication practices point beyond themselves to (and derive their meaning from) sets of contexts" (Cronen, Chen, & Pearce, 1988, p. 67). Similarly, in Bateson's (1972) words, "without context, there is no communication" (p. 402), and in Givón's (1989) metaphor, "A picture is not fully specified unless its frame is also specified" (p. 2).

The activities of encoding and decoding compose the communication *behavior*, and the conditions that "surround" this process are labeled here as the communication *context*. *Decoding* refers to the taking in and the process-ing of information from the environment, which may include one or more persons in a face-to-face contact or in some mediated form such as a book, a television show, or a movie. *Encoding* is used to refer to the sending out of verbal and nonverbal messages to the environment. As such, the process of encoding and decoding and the context constitute a basic communication *system*, in which we deal with sequences that resemble "stimulus and re-sponse" rather than "cause and effect" (Bateson, 1972; Watzlawick, Beavin, & Jackson, 1967). In many of the approaches that are based on positivistic assumptions, intergroup phenomena have been seen as linked together by one-directional cause and effect, and the resulting picture is of complexly branching and interconnecting reciprocal chains of causation. In the current approach, however, all contexts, personal and social, are viewed to arise through, and are sustained and altered by, behavior—the same as behavior is guided by context. Predictability in a given communication event, then, is explored by identifying what Bateson (1972) refers to as the "redundant patterns" in the action/interaction and in the context (p. 399). Using Bateson's metaphor, the current approach to searching for communication patterns can be compared to the way we try to select a piece for a given position in a jigsaw puzzle by looking at all of the identifiable patterns holistically.

Based on these pragmatist-systemic assumptions about communication, and mindful of the current purpose of an interdisciplinary integration, this investigator describes interethnic communication in Figure 1 in the most general and simplest way so that isomorphic patterns among various existing concepts across disciplines can be "seen" without being prematurely re-stricted by specificity or confused by complexity. Accordingly, this descrip-tion focuses on a system of a single person communicating interethnically, although implicitly present in this single-person communication system are one or more people with whom the person communicates. This system is

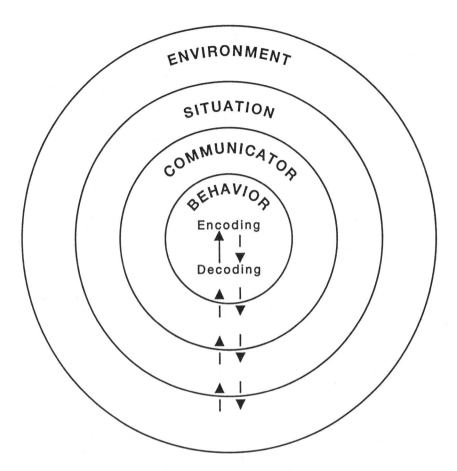

Figure 1. An organizing scheme for studying interethnic communication.

organized in a hierarchical arrangement made out of a progression of three levels of context. Each level acts as a metalevel, or context, to the sublevel(s) embedded within it (Givón, 1989; Ruben & Kim, 1975). Although temporality is built into the reality of any communication system, we artificially stop the action for the sake of examining and analyzing it cross-sectionally— rather like stopping a motion picture so that we can study a single frame at a particular moment.

Figure 1 thus serves as an organizing framework in the form of a *multilayered transactional matrix* of interethnic communication represented as a set of circles. At the core of this matrix are the activities of *encoding and decoding behavior*. Surrounding the core are three layers of the *context* that encircle the communication behavior. The first layer is the *communicator*— the densest locus of structure that guides, and is guided by, the communicator's encoding and decoding behavior. At this level, we are interested in what is traditionally called the "mind"—which organizes and processes incoming verbal and nonverbal information into forms of meaningful messages. Next comes the *situation*, that is, the immediate social milieu created when the communicator interfaces with one or more persons either face-to-face or through a mediating channel. Surrounding the situational level is the larger social milieu, which is referred to here as the *environment*. This environmental context, of course, includes many sublevels—from the suborganizational, organizational, through the community, to the national and international levels.

Note that these three levels of context (and the many sublevels thereof) are sets of "gradation, continuum and non-discreteness" (Givón, 1989, p. 5), unlike in nonpragmatic approaches to descriptions that have always assumed that categories are discrete. Because one level acts as the metalevel and/or the sublevel in this approach, the current scheme needs to be viewed as one of "mapping" or a "rigorous metaphor" (Bateson, 1972, p. 404) that is designed to serve as a simplified, yet integrative, approximation of the way an individual's interethnic communication is played out in reality. The layers represented here generally correspond to a group of concepts that have served as frequent objects of inquiry across disciplines, as highlighted in the following four sections.

THE BEHAVIOR

Various types of interethnic encoding and decoding behavior have been investigated extensively in social psychology, in sociolinguistics, and, more recently, in communication. A great deal of information and insight are available in the literature to help us understand some of the patterns of behavior that are prominent in interethnic encounters.

Decoding

One of the most widely investigated aspects of decoding is the *categorization* of information about or from out-group members. The term *stereotyping* is a more popularized term for the same phenomenon. Studies of social cognition, ethnic identity, and intergroup behavior have documented extensively that people tend to perceive out-group members based on simplistic and categorical manners and that such decoding is closely associated with *depersonalization* or *deindividuation* (Tajfel, 1970), that is, to stereotype them as "undifferentiated items in a unified social category" and thus to perceive them not as individuals but as "group representatives" (Turner, 1982, p. 28). According to Oddou and Medenhall (1984), simplistic categorization is also characterized by a cognitive tendency to *accentuate differences* and *deaccentuate similarities* between one's own group and an out-group.

Along with categorization and related concepts, *bias in attribution* has been identified as a conspicuous feature of intergroup decoding (Jaspers & Hewstone, 1982). This notion comes from attribution theorists such as Heider (1958), who proposed that the behavior of a person could be causally linked to the actor's personality, to the environment, or to a combination of both. Subsequent research has shown a tendency for people to underestimate the importance of situational causes in making inferences about others' negative behavior, an effect labeled the "fundamental attribution error" by L. Ross (1977). The fundamental attribution error becomes what Pettigrew (1979) calls the *"ultimate attribution error"* when this involves a positive bias toward one's own group and a negative bias toward out-group members. These phenomena have been found to be particularly significant in interethnic situations, as has been articulated in social identity theory.

Gumperz's (1978) conversational analysis of interethnic conversations between English speakers and Asian Indians demonstrates the power that biased interethnic attribution has to bring about serious consequences of "communication breakdowns." Similarly, Hopper (1986) coins the term *shibboleth schema* based on a biblical tale to illustrate the tendency of *prejudicial listening*, a tendency to interpret dialectic differences as being defective and therefore as objects of hostility and discrimination. Volkan (1992) adds to this observation a psychoanalytic explanation of biased interethnic attribution based on the notion of *projection*, a tendency that leads to ego-defensive reactions such as feelings of inferiority or superiority, avoidance, suspicion, and paranoia. Kim (1991b) calls such biased cognitive responses an element of *intergroup posturing*.

These and related concepts in the literature are counterbalanced by other concepts with opposite meanings. Billig (1987), for example, employs the concepts *particularization* and *decategorization* in discussing intergroup perception. Langer (1989) uses a more global term, *mindfulness*, to refer to a pattern of perception and thought that seeks a finer cognitive discrimination and more creative ways of interpreting information about and from out-group members. Other terms such as *personalization* (Kim, 1992a) and *differentiation* (Brewer & Miller, 1988) refer to the style of decoding that is more complex, refined, and less biased.

Encoding

An extensive amount of attention has been given to encoding behavior, particularly to language behavior, in sociolinguistic and social psychological studies. Based on speech accommodation theory and social identity theory, Giles, Bourhis, and Taylor (1977) examine *convergent and divergent behaviors* in relation to a perceived threat to one's ethnic identity and to the nature of power relationships between one's own ethnic group and that of the other. (See, also, related studies including Giles, Mulac, Bradac, & Johnson, 1987;

Giles & Smith, 1979.) A concept associated with divergent behavior is the overt *expressions of communicative distance* (Lambert, 1979; Lukens, 1979; Peng, 1974) or *border rituals* (Volkan, 1992), which concern the way speakers manipulate linguistic and other speech variants, either to increase or to decrease the psychological distance between themselves and others.

Yet other studies have documented various forms of *prejudiced talk* (Van Dijk, 1987) with varying degrees of emotional intensity and explicitness— from the subtle expressions such as "you people" to more blatant uses of *ethnophaulism* reflected in derogatory and dehumanizing *ethnic labels and jokes* (Allen, 1983; Gadfields, Giles, Bourhis, & Tajfel, 1979; Kirkland, Greenberg, & Pyszczynski, 1987; McConahay & Hough, 1976; Van Dijk, 1987). Similar observations have been made regarding *nonverbal expressions of prejudice* as well. Feldman (1985), for instance, suggests that interethnic conflicts are expressed, often covertly and subtly, through such nonverbal behaviors as voice tone, physical distance, avoidance of eye contact, and frozen facial expressions, especially when explicit forms of prejudice against out-group members are no longer sanctioned by the society at large. (See, also, Hanna, 1986.)

Countering these and related concepts is the potentially useful notion of "message complexity" that has been developed in constructivist approaches to communication (Delia, 1976). According to Applegate and Sypher (1988), a more sophisticated message behavior of this type generally requires speakers to recognize another person's perspectives and to exploit communication as a means of negotiating the definition of social situations between persons. This more complex message behavior is reflected in *person-centered messages* (Applegate & Delia, 1980; Applegate & Sypher, 1988; Burleson, 1987), which reflect a quality of communication that is responsive to the aims and behavioral styles of one's interactional partner and the topic or content of a message being communicated as well as that which seeks to enhance interpersonal relationships or create positive interpersonal identities. In addition, Kim (1992a), expanding on Hall's (1976, 1983) studies of cross-cultural differences in "synching" patterns, has proposed the practice of *mirroring* and *complementing* verbal and nonverbal styles between culturally diverse interaction partners to create a harmonious and cooperative interpersonal milieu.

From the above review, the various concepts depicting aspects of interethnic encoding and decoding seem to fall along a bipolar continuum of *association* and *dissociation*. The associative behaviors include the types of behavior that facilitate the communication process by increasing the likelihood of mutual understanding, cooperation, and the "coming together" of the involved persons into a constructive relationship, while the dissociative behavioral patterns include the types of behavior that contribute to misunderstanding, competition, and the "coming apart" of the relationship. Table 1 summarizes the various concepts of interethnic encoding and decoding and organizes them into these two interrelated categories: association and dissociation.

TABLE 1
Concept Related to Associative and Dissociative Interethnic
Communication Behavior

	Association	*Dissociation*
Decoding	Particularization	Categorization
	Decategorization	Stereotyping
	Personalization	Depersonalization
	Differentiation	Projection
	Accentuating similarities	Accentuating differences
	Mindfulness	Ultimate attribution error
		Communicative distance
		Intergroup posturing
Encoding	Convergence	Divergence
	Person-centered message	Prejudiced talk
	Personalized communication	Ethnic labels
	Mirroring/complementing	Ethnophaulism
		Body rituals
		Nonverbal expressions of communicative distance/prejudice

THE COMMUNICATOR

We now move to the first layer of communication context, the communicator. As previously noted, the communicator serves as the most immediate context for specific encoding and decoding behaviors. The communicator is examined here in terms of the relatively stable psychological attributes, or "routinized" patterns in one's "personality structure" (Givón, 1989).

Cognitive Structure

One of the psychological attributes of the communicator often examined in studies of interethnic relations is the degree of *complexity* in his or her cognitive structure, which is responsible for the way the communicator processes information (Applegate & Sypher, 1988; Delia, 1976; Kelly, 1955). Individuals of high cognitive complexity have been observed to use more refined, personalized, associative verbal messages. On the other hand, low cognitive complexity has been linked to erroneous generalizations, biased attributions, psychological distancing, impersonality, ignorance, and stereotype-based expectancies (Allport, 1954; Brewer & Miller, 1988; Gudykunst & Lim, 1986; Hamilton, Sherman, & Ruvolo, 1990; Tajfel & Turner, 1986). A related theoretical view has been provided by those who explain individual differences in intergroup attitude in terms of the role of *category width* (Detweiler, 1986). Studies have indicated that narrow categorizers tend to make more negative and confident attributions about out-group members. Low cognitive complexity has also been linked to an *authoritarian personality*

(Adorno et al., 1950), which reflects the decoding pattern of a simplistic, rigid categorization of people and ideas.

Identity

Several characteristics of the communicator's identity vis-à-vis his or her ethnicity are viewed as linked to encoding and decoding behavior. In particular, *ethnic commitment* (Giles & Johnson, 1986), *psychological distinctiveness* (Bourhis, Giles, Leyens, & Tajfel, 1979), or *in-group loyalty* (Brewer & Miller, 1988; Brown & Turner, 1981) have been found to facilitate dissociative decoding patterns such as biased attribution, psychological distance, and divergent behavior. In addition, the *insecurity* (Kim, 1989) the communicator feels in his or her ethnicity, *status anxiety* (De Vos, 1990), and *perceived threat* (Bourhis et al., 1979) have been identified as being related to divergent intergroup behavior, experiences of marginality (Taft, 1977), as well as hostility and aggression (Berkowitz, 1962), discrimination (Brewer & Miller, 1984, 1988), and stereotyping (Francis, 1976) of out-group members.

Bias

Closely related to the strength of one's commitment and sense of security in one's identity is the degree of intergroup bias that is frequently reflected in a negative *prejudice* one holds against out-groups and a positive prejudice toward one's own group (Billig et al., 1988; Brewer & Miller, 1984; Milner, 1973). Other similar terms have been used as well, such as *in-group favoritism* (Kim, 1989), *ethnocentrism* (Brewer & Campbell, 1976; Pettigrew, 1979; L. Ross, 1977; Sumner, 1906), *intergroup hostility* (Turner, 1982), *discrimination* (Smitherman-Donaldson & Van Dijk, 1988), and *racism* (Essed, 1991; Van Dijk, 1987, 1991; Volkan, 1992). Commonly, these terms imply beliefs and feelings about in-groups and out-groups that are irrational and unjustifiable. In extreme cases, people permit themselves to engage in severe dissociative behaviors including extreme violence (Volkan, 1992).

Associated Concepts

Concepts that counter the above communicator attributes are "intercultural identity" (Kim, 1991a, 1992b) and related concepts such as "multicultural man" (Adler, 1982), "double-swing" (Yoshikawa, 1986), "humanocentrism" (Gittler, 1974), and "moral inclusion" (Opotow, 1990). Each of these concepts reflects the vital component of a level of intellectual and emotional maturity that allows an outlook of interethnic accommodation and integration. Additionally, two general concepts of personality, *openness* and *strength*, have been proposed as important to the communicator's psychological resources for meeting the challenges of communicating with cultural strangers and for the development of an intercultural identity (Kim, 1988, 1992b; Kim & Ruben, 1988). These two concepts are closely associated with many other concepts that have been employed in the literature, such as patience, flexibility, sensitivity, receptiveness, and sociability.

The above concepts describe some of the more prominent aspects of the communicator—cognitive structure, identity, bias, and related attributes. Together, they offer a tentative psychological profile of the communicator whose encoding and decoding behaviors are likely to be associative or dissociative.

THE SITUATION

Next to the communicator is the situation of the interethnic encounter itself, whether it occurs face-to-face or via mediating channels. Each encounter presents a unique set of circumstances created by the interface of the interactants. Some of these conditions that have been emphasized in social psychological studies are discussed below in relation to their importance in understanding associative and dissociative encoding and decoding behavior.

Ethnic Heterogeneity

By definition, an interethnic encounter presents a level of heterogeneity, particularly in the interactants' ethnic characteristics (Sarbaugh, 1988). Because of the *cultural and language differences* in an interethnic encounter, the communicator is presented with a degree of challenges. Research has reported, for example, on added anxiety (Stephan & Stephan, 1985) and uncertainty, or lack of attributional confidence (Gudykunst, 1988b). "Miscommunication" occurs frequently due to differences in the interactants' language competencies and styles (Banks & Baker, 1991; Gass & Varonis, 1991). Heterogeneous encounters are also likely to increase the *incompatibility of interests and values* between the interactants, accentuating their feeling of psychological distance and inhibiting their ability to form consensus or seek common goals. Sociolinguistic and communication studies have examined some distinct features of communication behavior that are correlated with interethnic conflict. Gumperz (1978), for example, has focused on interethnic differences in the linguistic pragmatic features of verbal messages that contribute to interethnic communication "breakdowns" in key social situations such as job interviews. Rubin (1986) analyzes conflicts in classrooms where the discrepancies between the teacher's and students' communication behaviors create opportunities for misunderstanding and discrimination. Others have analyzed cultural differences in the way conflict is experienced and managed in different ethnic groups (e.g., Kochman, 1981; Ting-Toomey, 1988).

Ethnic Salience

Closely related to ethnic heterogeneity, the notion of ethnic salience has received close attention in the literature. *Ethnic salience* is defined here as the degree to which the interactants are self-conscious of each other's ethnic identity. Interethnic salience thus gives the encounter an "intergroup" character, which is accompanied by the dissociative encoding and decoding behaviors discussed previously (such as stereotyping, biased attribution, intergroup posturing, and verbal and nonverbal behaviors of divergence and communicative distance). Ethnic salience is mainly a function of the *distinctiveness between the discernible ethnic markers* of the interactants in a given encounter, such as distinct physical and behavioral features and conspicuous speech patterns (Worchel, 1979, p. 272). Often, some of the more obvious but superficial differences (e.g., skin color and speech accents) block the communicator from "seeing" less conspicuous aspects of an out-group member who, in fact, shares many similarities with him or her.

Studies have observed that ethnic salience is primarily a function of *ethnic composition* in the immediate and larger social milieu relative to the ethnic composition of the encounter itself (Brewer & Miller, 1988, p. 174). For example, the encounter between a Japanese and an African American in a predominantly African American community is likely to present strong ethnic salience. On the other hand, the same two persons' encounter would entail a weaker interethnic salience if it were to take place in a community where both groups are more or less equally represented. The so-called solo effect (Taylor, Fiske, Etcoff, & Ruderman, 1978) illustrates this observation.

Interaction Structure

Social encounters operate according to some form of structure that organizes the way interactions are carried out. The interaction structure provides each communicator with "guidelines" for encoding and decoding. One such structural guideline is provided by a *superordinate goal* beyond each party's own interests. Researchers have observed that the presence of such a goal provides a climate of interdependence and cooperation facilitating associative behaviors between interactants and, at the same time, discourages prejudice (Worchel, 1986). Also, Brewer and Miller (1988) argue that associative behaviors such as personalized decoding, rather than stereotypical categorization, are more likely to occur when the interaction is structured to promote an *interpersonal* and *cooperative* relational orientation rather than a *task-oriented* and *competitive* one between the involved parties.

An additional interactional condition that clearly influences the interethnic communication process has been identified in the relative status positions of interactants in an encounter. The term *status* is employed here broadly, whether in the symbolic sense of "importance," "worth," and "respectability" or in the practical sense of formal position and control. The role of relative status positions has been examined in terms of an *asymmetric power structure* (Brewer & Miller, 1984) or *power differentials* (Sachdev & Bourhis, 1985, 1987). For instance, studies with the "minimal intergroup situation" (e.g, Brewer, 1979; Turner, 1978) have generally indicated that differential treatment of groups by the experimenter increases interethnic conflict in the form of unfavorable discrimination against out-group members. Studies by Sachdev and Bourhis (1985, 1987) report a significant increase in unfavorable out-group discrimination when the perceived power differentials are greater, particularly among those who hold equal or superior positions.

The conditions reviewed here provide insights into the interaction situation and its potential influence on the encoding and decoding patterns. These conditions, collectively, provide a profile of the immediate milieu where individual communicators engage in associative or dissociative communication behaviors. Such academic insights into the situational conditions of interethnic communication provide a basis on which a multicultural classroom, for example, can be designed and managed.

THE ENVIRONMENT

As has been discussed above, social psychological studies have studied interethnic interaction phenomena focusing primarily on the first two levels of communication context: psychological and situational. In this section, some of the key concepts characterizing the environmental context discussed primarily in sociological literature are identified. Each of these conditions is relevant to various sublevels of the social environment, from the national (and international) environments to neighborhoods and organizations, and directly or indirectly influence, and are influenced by, all other conditions of the interethnic communication system we have discussed so far.

Institutional Equity/Inequity

One of the environmental factors crucial to understanding many of the contemporary incidents of interethnic conflict is the history of interethnic group relations. Particularly crucial in this regard is the *history of subjugation* of one ethnic group by another. Often, subjugation has taken the form of political, economic, and cultural domination through slavery, colonization, or military conquest. As Tagil (1984) argues, ethnic conflict can be explained based on the principle of "ethnoregionalism" in historical and geographic contexts. In this perspective, interethnic conflict is viewed as a conflict concerning the rights of an ethnic group to influence or control development within a certain state or region. Because it is believed that an ethnic group has the right to live on or possess territory that its members traditionally claim as their own, any historical injustice from the viewpoint of a subjugated ethnic group cannot be easily erased from the collective memory, contributing to contemporary interethnic encounters.

Many historical accounts have been written on the topic of colonization and its subsequent influences on interethnic discrimination and mistrust. In the case of West Indian immigrants living in England, for instance, the traditional colonial "Imperial Mythology" and the hegemonic tendencies of whites against nonwhite immigrants have been observed to be prevalent even today (see Rex, 1976; Richmond, 1986; Stone, 1985). Similar historical influences on contemporary interethnic power relationships can also be found in many other societies, including the situations of Native Americans and blacks in the United States, Koreans in Japan, and Palestinians in Israel, to name only a few.

Contemporary institutional inequity is reflected in patterns of the *stratification* of ethnic groups by socioeconomic class. Some scholars have argued that capitalistic economic systems exploit ethnic minorities (see Wolpe, 1986). Hechter (1975) uses the term *internal colonialism* to explain structural discrimination in the division of labor imposed on the "peripheral regions" (such as ethnic minorities) of a country, so that core or dominant regions keep for themselves the major manufacturing, commercial, and banking roles and delegate to the peripheral regions the least profitable kinds of work. Walker and Pettigrew (1984) theorized that, under an inequitable societal condition, subordinate groups' ethnic actions express their comparative feelings of dissatisfaction, or *fraternalistic relative deprivation*, along with their claims to social parity over the political, economic, social, and cultural structures of their society (Baker, 1983; Blalock, 1982). Rigid socioeconomic stratification along ethnic lines is also emphasized in Tajfel's (1978) social identity theory of intergroup relations. Tajfel places particular emphasis on structural conflicts of interest between social groups as a critical determinant of "category salience" in intergroup interaction.

Interethnic inequity in a society is reflected in its *laws and rules*, which, in turn, mirror the majority of the citizens' acceptance as a form of the status quo ("the way things are"). As such, changes in institutional equity in a given society are accompanied by changes in the law or other judicial actions. U.S. society, for instance, has undergone a significant transformation toward an increasing institutional equity among its majority and minority groups. Critical to the transformation has been a series of legal actions, such as the U.S. Supreme Court's 1954 ruling against racially segregated public schools. Many of these formal barriers persist, as demonstrated by the continuing patterns of intense racial discrimination in housing. Yet, enough progress has been made in some institutions, notably in education and employment, to introduce a second-generation set of less formal obstacles to ethnic minority inclusion (see Pettigrew & Martin, 1989).

Conditions of institutional inequity that pertain to interethnic communication are reflected in the "mainstream" *cultural ideology* of a given society and its subsocieties (such as a local community). Certain societies may legitimize discriminatory actions against certain minority groups, while others may punish such actions. Terms such as *assimilationism, pluralism, integrationism, separatism,* and *humanocentrism* as well as popular expressions such as *racist society, institutional racism, melting pot, tossed salad,* and *political correctness* represent different ideological views. By and large, the ideology of a given culture is further mirrored in its *official language policies* (such as monolingualism and bilingualism) and by mainstream institutions such as the government, mass media, and educational systems. *Mass media practices,* in particular, have been examined in research for the interethnic stereotypes and prejudices they carry to the public (Corea, 1990; Van Dijk, 1991; Wilson & Gutiérrez, 1985).

Institutional inequity in a given society may be intensified in times of *environmental stress* (Volkan, 1992), that is, when the society undergoes certain challenging circumstances caused by economic hardship, shortage of resources, or involvement in an international crisis (Olzak, 1987; Olzak & Nagel, 1986). Olzak and Nagel (1986) observe that such environmental stress tends to intensify competitive intergroup relations in a society. Others have observed that, under stressful circumstances, more than the usual level of dissociative interethnic behaviors are enacted (Stone, 1985; Volkan, 1992).

Ethnic Group Strength

In addition to the overall structural inequity in an environment that involves a communicator, the literature suggests a linkage between the collective strength of the communicator's ethnic group, political and otherwise, to his or her associative or dissociative interethnic communication behaviors. As the ethnic group becomes stronger in its relative status or power, the communicator's relative status in a given interethnic encounter is likely to become stronger as well, thereby influencing the previously discussed situational condition, the power differential, between the communicator and the interaction partner. A stronger ethnic group is further likely to encourage the maintenance of ethnicity and ethnic identity in the individual and discourage assimilation into the society at large (Breton, Isajiw, Kalbach, & Reitz, 1990; Kim, 1988). Empirical evidence reported by Gallois and Pittam (1991), for example, shows that, in Australia, adolescents in the Greek immigrant community, which is more cohesive and organized than is the Italian, placed more emphasis on their ethnic identity and on maintaining their heritage than did Italian Australian adolescents. Also, the researchers found that Greek Australian adolescents placed less emphasis on adapting to the dominant Australian culture at large.

Sociologists have provided explanations of differential strengths of ethnic groups according to evolutionary stages. Clarke and Obler (1976), for example, theorize that ethnic action evolves in a three-stage development: (a) the initial stage of *economic development*, which occurs upon arrival of the group until they become an integral part of the permanent economy; (b) the second stage of community building, or the development of community *leadership and institutional resources* used to assert the group's interests; and (c) the third stage of *aggressive self-assertion* that develops into the group's conventional use of the existing political system. As an ethnic group grows from its initial, economic adjustment stage to the later stages of community building and political self-assertion, it will increasingly show a group strength with which it may manipulate its cultural identity or ethnicity for the benefit of the group's interests. Breton (1964), Keyes (1981), and Marwell, Oliver, and Prahl (1988) have articulated similar views on the developmental process of ethnic groups and their increased political mobilization to assert and protect their collective interests.

Crucial to the developmental process of ethnic groups are the functions of *ethnic communication systems* such as ethnic media and community organizations (e.g., ethnic churches and social clubs). As Marwell et al. (1988) observe in their theory of the "critical mass," the potential for organizing a group depends on the social ties in the group through which collective actions are made possible. In this regard, media that are developed within an ethnic group are particularly crucial to the group's development by facilitating information gathering and the dissemination of information, reinforcing the group's identity, and frequently acting as the group's representative and liaison to the larger society (Kim, 1988).

A similar social psychological concept, *ethnolinguistic vitality* or *objective ethnolinguistic vitality* (compared with the "subjective ethnolinguistic vitality" concept discussed previously), has been extensively investigated as an important characteristic of ethnic group strength (see Giles, Rosenthal, & Young, 1985; Giles et al., 1977). This phenomenon has been assessed by Giles et al. (1977) based on (a) the status of a language in a community; (b) the absolute and relative number of its speakers (demographic characteristics); and (c) the institutional support (e.g., governmental services, schools, mass media) for the language. Linking this concept to intergroup relations theory (Tajfel, 1974) and speech accommodation theory (Giles, 1977; Giles & Smith, 1979), Giles and his associates (1977) theorized that the vitality of an ethnic language, in conjunction with the interactants' power differentials, influences their convergent or divergent speech behaviors. For example, a speaker who perceives the subordinate position of his or her group as illegitimate would be more likely to diverge from the speech patterns of the interaction partner.

Another social psychological explanation was provided by Blalock (1982) supporting the current theoretical linkage between subordinate group strength and interethnic conflict. In explaining the motivational basis of taking actions in interethnic conflict situations, Blalock presented two key concepts—subjective expected utilities (SEU) and subjective probability (SP). Based on the view of individuals as "rational" actors who enact behaviors based on SEU and SP, Blalock proposed that ethnic individuals will make behavioral choices if (a) they attach subjective values to the goals or outcomes of a certain behavior (such as avoiding or engaging in conflict) and (b) if their subjective utility associated with the behavior is high (i.e., a behavior will be enacted if it involves a high subjective probability). Applying these two conditions to interethnic communication situations, we can infer that, when there is a disagreement or conflict of interest in an encounter, the communicator whose ethnic group strength is greater is more likely to engage in dissociative encoding and decoding behaviors as such actions are perceived to be both desirable (or higher in SEU) and effectual (or higher in SP).

Interethnic Contact

Research has examined the environmental conditions for interethnic communication in terms of the extent of contact between different ethnic individuals. Arrangements such as integrated schools and neighborhoods in urban centers allow for maximum contact and interaction, while others such as ethnic neighborhoods and certain exclusive social clubs provide the least amount of *interaction potential* in one's personal network (Kim, 1986, 1987). Because segregated settings do not allow opportunities for communication, they have been viewed as negatively contributing to interethnic relations by "cementing" any existing hostility or prejudice (Worchel, 1979). Frequent contact, on the other hand, has been viewed as providing opportunities to reduce conflict and promote interethnic understanding, as postulated in the contact hypothesis (Amir, 1969). This straightforward linkage between *segregation* and conflict, or between contact and reduced conflict, has been a main theoretical source for the proponents of school and neighborhood integration.

The picture provided by research, however, is not so straightforward. Research has shown that, at least in the short run, intergroup contact is just as likely to heighten conflict as it is to reduce it. Worchel (1979), for example, reported that, in some cases, integrated apartment buildings led to a decrease in favorable racial attitudes. Although it appears that contact alone may not be a sufficient condition for conflict reduction, it is likely to reduce conflict in the long run. Similarly, segregation is likely to increase interethnic conflict in the long run, as it discourages ethnic groups from reducing their stereotypical perceptions and in-group biases. Validation of these hypotheses will require studies designed to test long-term changes rather than conventional short-term experimental designs.

On the whole, the conditions of institutional inequity, subordinate group strength, and interethnic contact discussed so far in this section influence (and are influenced by) the situational conditions of ethnic heterogeneity, ethnic salience, and interaction structure, which we discussed in the preceding section. These conditions provide a tentative profile of an environment that potentially facilitates or hinders the associative (or dissociative) interethnic behaviors of each individual communicator.

CONCLUSIONS

As shown throughout this work, the study of interethnic relations has made much progress over the past several decades. Across disciplines, many useful concepts, theories, and research findings have been accumulated, some of which have been discussed in this overview. The current conceptualization of interethnic communication has been offered as an initial organizing scheme for integrating the rich and yet often divergent theoretical and empirical information and insights that are currently available in various social science disciplines. This conceptual framework is grounded in some of the meta-theoretical assumptions of pragmatics and systems theory, which emphasize that the context and the behavior are inseparably intertwined in a given communication system and that, together, the context and the behavior operate in reality in a transactional, multidimensional, and holistic manner.

Table 2 summarizes the key concepts associated with the three layers of the interethnic communication context (the communicator, the situation, and the environment) that have been identified in this interdisciplinary overview. These concepts, collectively, provide an integrative profile of the context in which specific associative or dissociative encoding/decoding behaviors can be explained. Taken together, all of the behavioral and contextual patterns that have been discussed offer a tentative conceptual mapping of the current state of the art in the field of interethnic communication. Much more work is needed to improve on this mapping so that we can describe and explain—with greater consistency, specificity, and realism—what appear to be the infinitely varied ways in which interethnic communication is enacted.

Questions still need to be raised about the role of interethnic communication in the long-term evolution of the communicator and the environment. By and large, reliable principles concerning long-term insights on the nature of interethnic relations have escaped most researchers. A predominant assumption in previous studies has been that conflict is an undesirable "problem" that needs to be diminished. Although such may be clearly the case in many situations, the "problem" may be little more than a function of a particular ideological viewpoint, a lack of tolerance for ambiguity, or short-sightedness (Ruben, 1978).

In this regard, the systems-theoretic perspective offers potential benefits: It encourages us to view conflict as arising whenever there are discrepancies between the needs and capacities of the system and the environment. The system experiencing conflict then acts on the discrepancy, striving to adapt to the new reality by closing the gap, as it were. Conflict, then, can be viewed as a crucial force for the system's change, growth, and evolution as well as a defense against its stagnation, detachment, and entropy. Indeed, at least in the

TABLE 2
Dimensions, Factors, and Associated Concepts of the Context
of Interethnic Communication

Dimensions	Factors	Associated Concepts
The Communicator	Cognitive structure	Cognitive complexity Category width
	Identity	In-group loyalty Psychological distinctiveness Identity security/insecurity Intercultural identity Openness/strength
	Bias	Prejudice In-group favoritism Ethnocentrism Hostility Discrimination Racism
The Situation	Ethnic heterogeneity	Cultural/behavioral difference Cultural/behavioral compatibility
	Ethnic salience	Distinctiveness of ethnic markers Solo effect
	Interaction structure	Superordinate goal Interpersonal/cooperative orientation Power differential
The Environment	Institutional equity	History of subjugation Internal colonialism Ethnic stratification Fraternalistic relative deprivation Laws/rules Cultural ideology Language policy Media practice Environmental stress
	Ethnic group strength	Economic development Leadership/institutional resources Collective self-assertion Ethnic communication system Ethnolinguistic vitality
	Interethnic contact	Interaction potential Segregation/contact

United States, interethnic conflict experiences have brought the society to new stages of self-awareness and a broadened integration and democracy in spite of the many temporary stresses and pains that many have had to endure (Himes, 1974).

As such, determinations as to whether an interethnic conflict is good or bad, or functional or dysfunctional, must be based not on how it feels to social scientists, a particular ethnic person or group, or even to the public at large, but on what functions it serves for the evolutionary change in the communicator, the society, and even the international community as a whole. This theoretical placement of conflict in the context of long-term adaptation and change in communication systems can be particularly profitable for the purpose of developing social and personal mechanisms for building a true "community" in which a "humanocentric" ideology (Gittler, 1974) is cultivated side by side with pluralism and ethnic diversities are effectively coordinated into an enriching and integrative common system for all.

On the level of individuals, also, interethnic communication experiences need to be viewed not only as problematic but as growth facilitating (Kim, 1988, 1992b; Kim & Ruben, 1988). In light of the increasing clashes of individuals with rigid cultural identities in the United States and elsewhere, a case can be made for social scientists to extend the conventional fixed views of ethnic identity and to examine the experiences of numerous people whose identities, through intense and often stressful interethnic contacts, have moved beyond the perimeters of their original ethnic identity in the direction of increasing intercultural identity. It is mainly these and other like-minded persons of intercultural identity upon whose shoulders a culturally diverse society has to lean for its continued evolution as a single entity. In the end, they are the ones who can bridge divisions along ethnic lines, who can help make interethnic communication work, and whose work is vitally needed to create a community among divergent identities.

REFERENCES

Adler, P. (1982). Beyond cultural identity: Reflections on cultural and multicultural man. In L. Samovar & R. Porter (Eds.), *Intercultural communication: A reader* (3rd ed., pp. 389-408). Belmont, CA: Wadsworth.

Adorno, T., et al. (1950). *The authoritarian personality*. New York: Harper & Row.

Allen, I. (1983). *The language of ethnic conflict: Social organization and lexical culture*. New York: Columbia University Press.

Allport, G. (1954). *The nature of prejudice*. Reading, MA: Addison-Wesley.

Amir, Y. (1969). Contact hypothesis in ethnic relations. *Psychological Bulletin, 7*(5), 319-342.

Applegate, J., & Delia, J. (1980). Person-centered speech, psychological development, and the context of language usage. In R. St. Clair & H. Giles (Eds.), *The social and psychological contexts of language* (pp. 245-282). Hillsdale, NJ: Lawrence Erlbaum.

Applegate, J., & Sypher, H. (1988). A constructivist theory of communication and culture. In Y. Kim & W. Gudykunst (Eds.), *Theories in intercultural communication* (pp. 41-65). Newbury Park, CA: Sage.

Baker, D. (1983). *Race, ethnicity and power*. Boston: Routledge.

Banks, S., Ge, G., & Baker, J. (1991). Intercultural encounters and miscommunication. In N. Coupland, H. Giles, & J. Wiemann (Eds.), *"Miscommunication" and problematic talk* (pp. 103-120). Newbury Park, CA: Sage.

Bateson, G. (1972). *Steps to an ecology of mind.* New York: Ballantine.

Berkowitz, L. (1962). *Aggression: A social psychological analysis.* New York: McGraw-Hill.

Billig, M. (1987). *Arguing and thinking: A rhetorical approach to social psychology.* New York: Cambridge University Press.

Billig, M., Condon, S., Edwards, D., Gane, M., Middleton, D., & Radley, A. (1988). *Ideological dilemmas.* Newbury Park, CA: Sage.

Blalock, H. (1982). *Race and ethnic relations.* Englewood Cliffs, NJ: Prentice-Hall.

Bourhis, R. (1979). Language in ethnic interaction: A social psychological approach. In H. Giles & B. Saint-Jacques (Eds.), *Language and ethnic relations* (pp. 117-141). New York: Pergamon.

Bourhis, R., Giles, H., Leyens, J., & Tajfel, H. (1979). Psychological distinctiveness: Language divergence in Belgium. In H. Giles & R. St. Clair (Eds.), *Language and social psychology* (pp. 158-185). Oxford: Basil Blackwell.

Breton, R. (1964). Institutional completeness of ethnic communities and the personal relations of immigrants. *American Journal of Sociology, 70*(2), 193-205.

Breton, R., Isajiw, W., Kalbach, W., & Reitz, J. (1990). *Ethnic identity and equality: Varieties of experiences in a Canadian city.* Toronto: University of Toronto Press.

Brewer, M. (1979). Ingroup bias in the minimal intergroup situation: A cognitive-motivational analysis. *Psychological Bulletin, 86,* 307-324.

Brewer, M. (1986). The role of ethnocentrism in intergroup conflict. In S. Worchel & W. Austin (Eds.), *Psychology of intergroup relations* (2nd ed., pp. 288-304). Chicago: Nelson-Hall.

Brewer, M., & Campbell, D. (1976). *Ethnocentrism and intergroup attitudes: East African evidence.* New York: John Wiley.

Brewer, M., & Miller, N. (1984). Beyond the contact hypothesis: Theoretical perspectives on desegregation. In N. Miller & M. Brewer (Eds.), *Groups in contact: The psychology of desegregation* (pp. 281-302). New York: Academic Press.

Brewer, M., & Miller, N. (1988). Contact and cooperation: When do they work? In P. Katz & D. Taylor (Eds.), *Eliminating racism* (pp. 315-326). Newbury Park, CA: Sage.

Brown, P., & Turner, J. (1981). Interpersonal and intergroup behavior. In J. Turner & H. Giles (Eds.), *Intergroup behavior* (pp. 33-65). Chicago: University of Chicago Press.

Burleson, B. (1987). Cognitive complexity. In J. McCrosky & J. Daley (Eds.), *Personality and interpersonal communication* (pp. 305-349). Beverly Hills, CA: Sage.

Carbaugh, D. (Ed.). (1990). *Cultural communication and intercultural contact.* Hillsdale, NJ: Lawrence Erlbaum.

Clarke, S., & Obler, J. (1976). Ethnic conflict, community-building, and the emergence of ethnic political traditions in the United States. In S. Clarke & J. Obler (Eds.), *Urban ethnic conflicts: A comparative perspective* (pp. 1-34). Chapel Hill: University of North Carolina Press.

Clément, R., & Noels, K. (1991, August). *Ethnolinguistic vitality, language and identity.* Paper presented at the 4th International Conference on Language and Social Psychology, Santa Barbara, CA.

Collier, M., & Thomas, M. (1988). Cultural identity: An interpretive perspective. In Y. Kim & W. Gudykunst (Eds.), *Theories in intercultural communication* (pp. 99-120). Newbury Park, CA: Sage.

Corea, A. (1990). Racism in the American way of media. In J. Downing, A. Mohammadi, & A. Sreberny-Mohammadi (Eds.), *Questioning the media: A critical introduction* (pp. 255-266). Newbury Park, CA: Sage.

Cronen, V., Chen, V., & Pearce, W. (1988). Coordinated management of meaning: A critical theory. In Y. Kim & W. Gudykunst (Eds.), *Theories in intercultural communication* (pp. 66-98). Newbury Park, CA: Sage.

Daniel, J., & Smitherman, G. (1990). How I got over: Communication dynamics in the black community. In D. Carbaugh (Ed.), *Cultural communication and intercultural contact* (pp. 25-40). Hillsdale, NJ: Lawrence Erlbaum.

Delia, J. (1976). A constructivist analysis of the concept of credibility. *Quarterly Journal of Speech, 63,* 66-83.

Detweiler, R. (1986). Categorization, attribution and intergroup communication. In W. Gudykunst (Ed.), *Intergroup communication* (pp. 62-73). London: Edward Arnold.

De Vos, G. (1990). Self in society: A multilevel, psychocultural analysis. In G. A. De Vos & M. Suárez-Orozco (Eds.), *Status inequality: The self in culture* (pp. 17-74). Newbury Park, CA: Sage.

Essed, P. (1991). *Understanding everyday racism.* Newbury Park, CA: Sage.

Feldman, R. S. (1985). Nonverbal behavior, race, and the classroom teacher. *Theory into Practice, 24,* 45-49.

Francis, E. (1976). *Interethnic relations.* New York: Elsevier.

Gadfields, N., Giles, H., Bourhis, R. Y., & Tajfel, H. (1979). Dynamics of humor in ethnic group relations. *Ethnicity, 6,* 373-382.

Gallois, C., Franklyn, A., Giles, H., & Coupland, N. (1988). Communication accommodation in intercultural encounters. In Y. Kim & W. Gudykunst (Eds.), *Theories in intercultural communication* (pp. 157-185). Newbury Park, CA: Sage.

Gallois, C., & Pittam, J. (1991, May). *Ethnolinguistic vitality in multicultural/monolingual Australia: Perceptions of Vietnamese and Anglo-Australians.* Paper presented at the annual conference of the International Communication Association, Chicago.

Gass, S., & Varonis, E. (1991). Miscommunication in nonnative speaker discourse. In N. Coupland, H. Giles, & J. Wiemann (Eds.), *"Miscommunication" and problematic talk* (pp. 121-145). Newbury Park, CA: Sage.

Giles, H. (1977). Social psychology and applied linguistics: Towards an integrative approach. *ITL: Review of Applied Linguistics, 33,* 27-42.

Giles, H., & Bourhis, R. (1976). Voice and social categorisation in Britain. *Communication Monographs, 43,* 108-114.

Giles, H., Bourhis, R., & Taylor, D. (1977). Towards a theory of language in ethnic group relations. In H. Giles (Ed.), *Language, ethnicity and intergroup relations* (pp. 307-348). London: Academic Press.

Giles, H., & Johnson, P. (1986). Perceived threat, ethnic commitment, and interethnic language behavior. In Y. Kim (Ed.), *Interethnic communication* (pp. 91-116). Newbury Park, CA: Sage.

Giles, H., & Johnson, P. (1987). Ethnolinguistic identity theory: A social psychological approach to language maintenance. *International Journal of Social Language, 68,* 69-99.

Giles, H., Mulac, A., Bradac, J., & Johnson, P. (1987). Speech accommodation theory: The first decade and beyond. In M. McLaughlin (Ed.), *Communication yearbook 10.* Newbury Park, CA: Sage.

Giles, H., Rosenthal, D. A., & Young, L. (1985). Perceived ethnolinguistic vitality: The Anglo- and Greek-Australian setting. *Journal of Multilingual and Multicultural Development, 6,* 253-269.

Giles, H., & Saint-Jacques, B. (Eds.). (1979). *Language and ethnic relations.* New York: Pergamon.

Giles, H., & Smith, P. (1979). Accommodation theory: Optimal levels of convergence. In H. Giles & R. St. Clair (Eds.), *Language and social psychology* (pp. 45-65). Baltimore, MD: University Park Press.

Gittler, J. (1974). Cultural pluralism in contemporary American society: An analysis and a proposal. *International Journal of Group Relations, 4*(3), 322-345.

Givón, T. (1989). *Mind, code and context.* Hillsdale, NJ: Lawrence Erlbaum.

Glazer, N., & Moynihan, D. (1975). *Ethnicity: Theory and experience.* Cambridge, MA: Harvard University Press.

Gordon, M. (1981). Models of pluralism: The new American dilemma. *Annals of the American Academy of Political and Social Science, 454,* 178-188.

Gudykunst, W. (Ed.). (1988a). *Language and ethnic identity.* Clevedon, England: Multilingual Matters.

Gudykunst, W. (1988b). Uncertainty and anxiety. In Y. Kim & W. Gudykunst (Eds.), *Theories in intercultural communication* (pp. 123-156). Newbury Park, CA: Sage.

Gudykunst, W., & Gumbs, L. (1989). Social cognition and intergroup communication. In M. Asante & W. Gudykunst (Eds.), *Handbook of international and intercultural communication* (pp. 204-224). Newbury Park, CA: Sage.

Gudykunst, W., & Lim, T. (1986). A perspective for the study of intergroup communication. In W. Gudykunst (Ed.), *Intergroup communication* (pp. 1-9). Baltimore: Edward Arnold.

Gumperz, J. (1978). The conversational analysis of interethnic communication. In E. Ross (Ed.), *Interethnic communication* (pp. 13-31). Athens: University of Georgia Press.

Gumperz, J., & Cook-Gumperz, J. (1982). Introduction: Language and the communication of social identity. In J. Gumperz (Ed.), *Language and social identity* (pp. 1-21). New York: Cambridge University Press.

Hall, E. (1976). *Beyond culture*. New York: Anchor.

Hall, E. (1983). *The dance of life*. New York: Anchor.

Hamilton, D., Sherman, S., & Ruvolo, C. (1990). Stereotype-based expectancies: Effects on information processing and social behavior. *Journal of Social Issues, 46*(2), 35-59.

Hanna, J. (1986). Interethnic communication in children's dance, play and protest. In Y. Kim (Ed.), *Interethinc communication: Current research* (pp. 137-198). Newbury Park, CA: Sage.

Hechter, M. (1975). *Internal colonialism: The Celtic fringe in British national development, 1536-1966*. Berkeley: University of California Press.

Heider, F. (1958). *The psychology of interpersonal relations*. New York: John Wiley.

Heller, M. (1987). The role of language in the formation of ethnic identity. In J. Phinney & M. Rotheram (Eds.), *Children's ethnic socialization: Pluralism and development* (pp. 180-200). Newbury Park, CA: Sage.

Hewstone, M., & Giles, H. (1986). Social groups and social stereotypes in intergroup communication: A review and model of intergroup communication breakdown. In W. Gudykunst (Ed.), *Intergroup communication* (pp. 10-26). London: Edward Arnold.

Himes, J. (1974). *Racial and ethnic relations*. Dubuque, IA: William C Brown.

Hopper, R. (1986). Speech evaluation of intergroup dialect differences: The shibboleth schema. In W. Gudykunst (Ed.), *Intergroup communication* (pp. 127-136). London: Edward Arnold.

Hsu, F. (1971). *The challenge of the American dream: The Chinese in the United States*. Belmont, CA: Wadsworth.

Jaspers, J., & Hewstone, M. (1982). Cross-cultural interaction, social attribution and inter-group relations. In S. Bochner (Ed.), *Cultures in contact* (pp. 127-156). Elmsford, NY: Pergamon.

Kelly, G. (1955). *The psychology of personal constructs*. New York: Norton.

Keyes, C. (1981). The dialectic of ethnic change. In C. Keyes (Ed.), *Ethnic change* (pp. 3-30). Seattle: University of Washington Press.

Kim, Y. (1986). Understanding the social context of intergroup communication: A personal network theory. In W. Gudykunst (Ed.), *Intergroup communication* (pp. 86-95). London: Edward Arnold.

Kim, Y. (1987). Facilitating immigrant adaptation: The role of communication. In T. Albrecht & M. Adelman (Eds.), *Communicating social support* (pp. 192-211). Newbury Park, CA: Sage.

Kim, Y. (1988). *Communication and cross-cultural adaptation: An integrative theory*. Clevedon, England: Multilingual Matters.

Kim, Y. (1989). Interethnic conflict: An interdisciplinary review. In J. Gittler (Ed.), *The annual review of conflict knowledge and conflict resolution* (Vol. 1, pp. 101-125). New York: Garland.

Kim, Y. (1991a). Intercultural personhood: An integration of Eastern and Western perspectives. In L. Samovar & R. Porter (Eds.), *Intercultural communication: A reader* (6th ed., pp. 401-410). Belmont, CA: Wadsworth.

Kim, Y. (1991b). Intercultural communication competence. In S. Ting-Toomey & F. Korzenny (Eds.), *Cross-cultural interpersonal communication* (pp. 259-275). Newbury Park, CA: Sage.

Kim, Y. (1992a). Synchrony and intercultural communication. In D. Crookall & K. Arai (Eds.), *Global interdependence: Simulation and gaming perspectives* (pp. 99-105). New York: Springer-Verlag.

Kim, Y. (1992b, May). *Development of intercultural identity*. Paper presented at the annual convention of the International Communication Association, Miami, FL.

Kim, Y., & Ruben, B. (1988). Intercultural transformation: A systems theory. In Y. Kim & W. Gudykunst (Eds.), *Theories in intercultural communication* (pp. 299-321). Newbury Park, CA: Sage.

Kirkland, S., Greenberg, J., & Pyszczynski, T. (1987). Further evidence of the deleterious effects of overheard DELs: Derogation beyond the target. *Personality and Social Psychological Bulletin, 13*, 126-227.

Kochman, T. (1981). *Black and white styles in conflict*. Chicago: University of Chicago Press.

Kochman, T. (1986). Black verbal dueling strategies in interethnic communication. In Y. Kim (Ed.), *Interethnic communication: Current research* (pp. 136-157). Newbury Park, CA: Sage.

Lambert, W. (1979). Language as a factor in intergroup relations. In H. Giles & R. St. Clair (Eds.), *Language and social psychology* (pp. 186-192). Baltimore: University Park Press.

Landry, R., & Allard, R. (1991, August). *Ethnolinguistic vitality and substractive identity*. Paper presented at the 4th International Conference on Language and Social Psychology, Santa Barbara, CA.

Langer, E. (1989). *Mindfulness*. Reading, MA: Addison-Wesley.

Lukens, J. (1979). Interethnic conflict and communicative distance. In H. Giles & B. Saint-Jacques (Eds.), *Language and ethnic relations* (pp. 143-158). New York: Pergamon.

Marwell, G., Oliver, P., & Prahl, R. (1988, November). Social networks and collective action: A theory of the critical mass. III. *American Journal of Sociology, 94*(3), 502-534.

McConahay, J., & Hough, J. (1976). Symbolic racism. *Journal of Social Issues, 32*, 23-45.

Milner, D. (1973). Racial identification and preference in "black" British children. *European Journal of Social Psychology, 3*, 281-295.

Nash, M. (1989). *The cauldron of ethnicity in the modern world*. Chicago: University of Chicago Press.

Oddou, G., & Mendenhall, M. (1984). Person perception in cross-cultural settings. *International Journal of Intercultural Relations, 8*, 77-96.

Olzak, S. (1987). Causes of ethnic conflict and protest in urban America, 1877-1889. *Social Science Research, 16*, 185-210.

Olzak, S., & Nagel, J. (Eds.). (1986). *Competitive ethnic relations*. New York: Academic Press.

Opotow, S. (1990). Moral exclusion and injustice. *Journal of Social Issues, 46*(1), 1-20.

Peng, F. (1974). Communicative distance. *Language Sciences, 31*, 32-38.

Pettigrew, T. (1979). The ultimate attribution error: Extending Allport's cognitive analysis of prejudice. *Personality and Social Psychology Bulletin, 5*, 461-476.

Pettigrew, T., & Martin, J. (1989). Organizational inclusion of minority groups: A social psychological analysis. In J. Van Oudenhoven & T. Willemsen (Eds.), *Ethnic minorities: Social psychological perspectives* (pp. 169-200). Berwyn, PA: Swets North America.

Philipsen, G. (1989). Speech and the communal function in four cultures. In S. Ting-Toomey & F. Korzenny (Eds.), *Language, communication, and culture* (pp. 79-92). Newbury Park, CA: Sage.

Phinney, J., & Rosenthal, D. (1992). Ethnic identity in adolescence: Process, context, and outcome. In G. Adams, T. Gullota, & R. Montemayor (Eds.), *Adolescent identity formation* (pp. 145-172). Newbury Park, CA: Sage.

Rex, J. (1976). Racial conflict in the city: The experiences of Birmingham, England from 1952-1975. In S. Clarke & J. Obler (Eds.), *Urban ethnic conflict: A comparative perspective* (pp. 132-163). Chapel Hill: University of North Carolina Press.

Richmond, A. (1986). Racial conflict in Britain. *Contemporary Sociology, 9*(2), 184-187.

Ross, E. (Ed.). (1988). *Interethnic communication*. Athens: University of Georgia Press.

Ross, J. (1979). Language and the mobilization of ethnic identity. In H. Giles & B. Saint-Jacques (Eds.), *Language and ethnic relations* (pp. 1-13). New York: Pergamon.

Ross, L. (1977). The intuitive psychologist and his shortcomings: Distortions in the attribution process. In L. Berkowitz (Ed.), *Advances in experimental social psychology* (Vol. 10, pp. 174-220). New York: Academic Press.

Ruben, B. (1978). Communication and conflict: A system-theoretic perspective. *Quarterly Journal of Speech, 64,* 211-232.

Ruben, B., & Kim, J. (Eds.). (1975). *General systems theory and human communication.* Rochelle Park, NJ: Hayden.

Rubin, D. (1986). Nobody play by the rules he know: Ethnocentric interferences in classroom questioning events. In Y. Kim (Ed.), *Interethnic communication* (pp. 159-175). Newbury Park, CA: Sage.

Sachdev, I., & Bourhis, R. (1985). Social categorization and power differentials in group relations. *European Journal of Social Psychology, 15,* 415-434.

Sachdev, I., & Bourhis, R. (1987). Status differentials and intergroup behavior. *European Journal of Social Psychology, 17,* 277-293.

Sarbaugh, L. (1988). *Intercultural communication* (2nd ed.). New Brunswick, NJ: Hayden.

Schlesinger, A. (1992). *The disuniting of America: Reflections on a multicultural society.* New York: Norton.

Smith, A. (1981). *The ethnic revival in the modern world.* Cambridge: Cambridge University Press.

Smitherman-Donaldson, G., & Van Dijk, T. (Eds.). (1988). *Discourse and discrimination.* Detroit: Wayne State University Press.

Stephan, W., & Stephan, C. (1985). Intergroup anxiety. *Journal of Social Issues, 41*(3), 157-175.

Stone, J. (1985). *Racial conflict in contemporary society.* Cambridge, MA: Harvard University Press.

Sumner, G. (1906). *Folkways.* Boston: Ginn.

Taft, R. (1977). Coping with unfamiliar culture. In N. Warren (Ed.), *Studies in cross-cultural psychology* (Vol. 1, pp. 121-153). New York: Academic Press.

Tagil, S. (Ed.). (1984). *Regions in upheaval: Ethnic conflict and political mobilization.* Stockholm: Esselte Studium.

Tajfel, H. (1970). Experiments in intergroup discrimination. *Scientific American, 223*(2), 96-102.

Tajfel, H. (1974). Social identity and intergroup behavior. *Social Science Information, 13,* 65-93.

Tajfel, H. (Ed.). (1978). *Differentiation between groups: Studies in the social psychology of intergroup relations.* New York: Academic Press.

Tajfel, H. (Ed.). (1982). *Social identity and intergroup relations.* Cambridge: Cambridge University Press.

Tajfel, H., & Turner, J. (1986). The social identity theory of intergroup behavior. In S. Worchel & W. Austin (Eds.), *Psychology of intergroup relations* (2nd ed., pp. 7-17). Chicago: Nelson-Hall.

Talbott, S. (1992, July 20). The birth of the global nation. *Time,* p. 70.

Taylor, S., Fiske, S., Etcoff, N., & Ruderman, A. (1978). Categorical and contextual bases of person memory and stereotyping. *Journal of Personality and Social Psychology, 36,* 778-793.

Terkel, S. (1992). *Race.* New York: New Press.

Ting-Toomey, S. (1986). Conflict communication styles in black and white subjective cultures. In Y. Kim (Ed.), *Interethnic communication: Current research* (pp. 75-88). Newbury Park, CA: Sage.

Ting-Toomey, S. (1988). Intercultural conflict styles: A face-negotiation theory. In Y. Kim & W. Gudykunst (Eds.), *Theories in intercultural communication* (pp. 213-235). Newbury Park, CA: Sage.

Turner, J. (1975). Social comparison and social identity: Some prospects for intergroup behavior. *European Journal of Social Psychology, 5,* 5-34.

Turner, J. (1978). Social categorization and social discrimination in a minimal group paradigm. In H. Tajfel (Ed.), *Differentiation between social groups* (pp. 101-140). New York: Academic Press.

Turner, J. (1982). Towards a cognitive redefinition of the social group. In H. Tajfel (Ed.), *Social identity and intergroup relations* (pp. 15-40). Cambridge: Cambridge University Press.

Turner, J., & Giles, H. (Eds.). (1981). *Intergroup behavior*. Chicago: University of Chicago Press.

Van Dijk, T. (1987). *Communicating racism: Ethnic prejudice in thought and talk*. Newbury Park, CA: Sage.

Van Dijk, T. (1991). *Racism and the press*. New York: Routledge.

Volkan, V. (1992, December). Ethnonationalistic rituals: An introduction. *Mind & Human Interaction, 4*(1), 3-19.

Walker, I., & Pettigrew, T. (1984). Relative deprivation theory: An overview and conceptual critique. *British Journal of Social Psychology, 23*, 301-310.

Watzlawick, P., Beavin, J., & Jackson, D. (1967). *The pragmatics of human communication*. New York: Norton.

Wieder, D., & Pratt, S. (1990). On being a recognizable Indian among Indians. In D. Carbaugh (Ed.), *Cultural communication and intercultural contact* (pp. 45-64). Hillsdale, NJ: Lawrence Erlbaum.

Wilson, C., & Gutiérrez, F. (1985). *Minorities and media*. Beverly Hills, CA: Sage.

Wolpe, H. (1986). Class concepts, class struggle and racism. In J. Rex & D. Mason (Eds.), *Theories of race and ethnic relations* (pp. 110-130). New York: Cambridge University Press.

Worchel, S. (1979). Cooperation and the reduction of intergroup conflict: Some determining factors. In W. Austin & S. Worchel (Eds.), *The social psychology of intergroup relations* (pp. 262-273). Monterey, CA: Brooks/Cole.

Worchel, S. (1986). The role of cooperation in reducing intergroup conflict. In S. Worchel & W. Austin (Eds.), *Psychology of intergroup relations* (2nd ed., pp. 288-304). Chicago: Nelson-Hall.

Yinger, J. (1986). Intersection strands in the theorisation of race and ethnic relations. In J. Rex & D. Mason (Eds.), *Theories of race and ethnic relations* (pp. 20-41). New York: Cambridge University Press.

Yoshikawa, M. (1986). Cross-cultural adaptation and perceptual development. In Y. Kim (Ed.), *Cross-cultural adaptation: Current research* (pp. 140-148). Newbury Park, CA: Sage.

Deconstructing the "Big Picture": Perspectives and Layers of Interethnic Communication

RICHARD CLÉMENT
University of Ottawa

HOWARD GILES
University of California, Santa Barbara

IN her essay, Kim seeks to elaborate a truly comprehensive framework integrating concepts from various disciplines with a view to describing interethnic relations from a communication viewpoint. While subscribing to the boundary assumptions of a pragmatic-systemic approach, she seeks to describe interethnic communication "in the most general and simplest way so that isomorphic patterns among various existing concepts across disciplines can be 'seen' without being prematurely restricted by specificity" (p. 516). Whereas we welcome attempts at multidisciplinary integration, we feel uncomfortable about the particular directions taken by Kim if they are accepted uncritically. The lack of rigorous "specificity" may result in limited heuristic usefulness. Nevertheless, we share her interest in developing conceptual road maps and our position, which follows our critique of Kim's below, is complementary to the spirit of hers.

How does one study interethnic relations, specifically, from a communication perspective? Kim's introductory section makes reference to the concept of ethnic group membership, but the consequences of this for a pragmatic-systemic approach to interethnic communication are never really articulated. Admittedly, it is useful, for pedagogical and taxonomic purposes, to illustrate how different disciplines deal with the relationships between different ethnic groups. That notwithstanding, however, a descriptive representation of these multiple perspectives, even using schematic representations, does not easily

Correspondence and requests for reprints: Howard Giles, Department of Communication, University of California, Santa Barbara, CA 93106-4020.

Communication Yearbook 17, pp. 539-550

translate into an explanatory research-generating framework for promoting the significance of a unique communication perspective. Paradoxically, this is seemingly at odds with Kim's (e.g., 1988) previous and important explorations of how communication phenomena and processes are *fundamental* to understanding immigrants' successful adaptation to a host culture.

In the absence of a specific definition of what the communication approach is, there is therefore no reason to accept encoding-decoding as *the* core of the model. Whereas social psychologists would probably find themselves at ease with individualistic behavior being at the focus, there is no reason to believe that sociologists or anthropologists would likewise concur. Sharing values and symbols may do little to explain interethnic conflict. Rather, structural inequalities and their transmission and reproduction may, on many occasions, be at the core of the model. In other words, understanding the differential communicative beliefs and habits that characterize cultural groups in contact can sometimes have negligible social benefits in alleviating intergroup conflict if the socioeconomic (and other) power discrepancies (as, say, in the LA riots) are left, conveniently, sidestepped and unanalyzed by communication scholars. It may well be that communicating effectively and honestly about such discrepancies—the discourse of conflict—is more of a key issue for us to confront as the core of a model than any (dichotomous) associative or dissociative interpersonal inclinations.

The main instrument in Kim's approach to explaining interethnic communication is what she claims to be a "multilayered transactional matrix" functionally integrating a variety of sources; for us, this achieves a mere juxtaposition of constructs from different disciplines. As a result, two orders of contexts are completely confounded. The first one concerns the context in which the individual evolves with its multiple discursive, cognitive, interpersonal, situational, and societal facets. The second one is the disciplinary context of explanation adopted by the investigator. The result of using the latter to represent the former is a rather disjointed system lacking a common language for linking processes at the different levels. We see two related undesirable consequences of this.

First, the effort made to achieve interdisciplinarity also results in much redundancy. Take, for example, "ethnic identity" (from the communicator), "ethnic salience" (from the situation), and "ethnolinguistic vitality" (from the environment). The three concepts, as scientific constructs, are obviously not identical. The disciplinary and paradigmatic context of their definition confers on them some theoretical distinction. Yet, we surmise that the functions these constructs play in their respective paradigms are identical; they are essentially parallel explanations of the same phenomenon: the differential potency of ethnic groups. Unless they can be shown to act as reciprocal moderators or mediators (in a systemic sense) of some behaviors (in a pragmatic sense), they do not constitute different layers of the so-called transactional matrix.

Second, it is difficult to understand the rationale underlying what distinctively belongs in each of Kim's layers (i.e., the figure and tables). Under the aegis of the pragmatic assumption, we would expect to find explicit reference to communication behaviors and their function at *all* levels of the model (see Watzlawick, Beavin, & Jackson, 1967). In fact, apart from the phenomena described under "encoding," little is said about communication behavior and processes. Furthermore, at all levels of the framework, reference is made to what would be individual (intrapsychic) characteristics or processes: categorization, attribution for decoding; cognitive structure, ethnic identity, prejudice for the communicator; ethnic heterogeneity (as perceived), ethnic salience for the situation, and relative deprivation; subjective expected utility and subjective probability for the environment. All of these, we suggest *are part of* the communicator, the "mind" (p. 518) to use Kim's terms. The rest—essentially the structure of the situation and the factors included under the objective version of ethnolinguistic vitality—constitute the environmental and situational context.

A secondary problem to Kim's approach is related to the extent to which she upholds her own epistemological choices. Apart from the fact that the inclusion of mentalistic processes does not seem to correspond to a pragmatic approach to context and cross-cultural communication anyway (see Auer & DiLuzio, 1992; Blommaert & Verschueren, 1987), their introduction here is made without regard to the systemic assumption. Claiming that "each level acts as a metalevel, or context, to the sublevel(s) embedded within it" (p. 517) is a rather imprecise way of mapping out relationships in any predictive fashion. The same can be said of the unspecified relationships between elements appearing at each level of the framework. If the goal here is to remind us that everything may act on everything, the point is, of course, well taken. But let us remember that the assumptions of systems theory are here used as meta-assumptions (see Kim, 1988). Unless their applications and specifications to interethnic communication are articulated, this provides at best an underspecified model.

In her attempt at providing a "big picture," Kim may have sensitized readers to the possibility of apprehending interethnic communication from numerous vantage points. We, however, believe that her attempts fall short of providing what would become a distinctly communication perspective because of her focus on the rival disciplines rather than on the phenomena of interest. We do not seek here to provide a full-fledged explanatory framework but, like Kim, seek to point to boundary conditions and definitions that we feel would contribute more readily to generating relevant research questions. Following the above critique of Kim's, our approach hinges on a clear distinction between the disciplinary context of explanation and the contextual levels at which the individual may operate. While grounding our position in current research and theorizing, we aim to more clearly delineate the characteristics of a communication approach. We also would like to show how the domains of disciplines and families of disciplines (here called "perspec-tives") are not necessarily limited to specific layers of the communication episode. Following through, we would now like to describe three perspec-tives: the communication, the individual, and the environment.

A CONSTRUCTIVE DECONSTRUCTION

The Communication

Interethnic communication is an instance of intercultural communication. It concerns the exchange of symbols between members of cultural groups who, at the time the exchange takes place, are culturally different because they belong to different ethnic groups. We agree with Kim that communica-tion is interethnic when at least one interactant construes him- or herself in a way that is based on ethnicity or ethnic identity. Likewise, following Tajfel and Turner (1979), we agree that ethnicity may not always be at issue in all interpersonal encounters. Contrary to Kim's assumption, however, the inter-group versus interpersonal stances are not inevitably and always at opposite ends of a continuum: A particular interaction episode may involve *both* a high degree of personal involvement and a high degree of ethnic involvement. For example, Israeli and Arab diplomats could value personal relationships that could facilitate open discussion of group-level military and social conflicts plaguing their societies. Conversely, feeling threatened as a minority ethnic group member could also have severe personal implications.

Furthermore, the enactment of ethnicities may induce communication whose "core" far exceeds the immediate contextual parameters of the inter-actants. Ideological discussions elaborated within an ethnic stance between individuals, whether face-to-face or through the media, are not just interindi-vidual communications. They are reflections of a wider context. To under-stand interethnic communication (and, for that matter, intercultural commu-nication), it is important to analyze interactions independently from the apparent limits of the situation in which they take place. Interethnic commu-nication may convey all the "levels" or layers of representation from the very intimate to the most public, from the very specific to the very general. At the extreme, interethnic interaction may have nothing to do with the participants as individuals.

Strategies used to convey what may be seen as multilayered discourse may correspond to those identified by Kim as encoding behavior. In her view, these varied strategies fall along a bipolar continuum of association and dissocia-tion, referring to their essentially constructive or destructive effects on an interpersonal relationship. Notwithstanding our preceding argument about levels of communication and understanding, association-dissociation may label appropriately the outcome of an interaction. We, however, feel that it is overly simplistic to associate specific strategies with each outcome (see Kim's Table 1).

Auer (1992) shows how Bach uses abrupt harmonic switches to alter the meaning of the sung words and, in this particular instance, change a prayer into mockery. Likewise, for natural languages, the functions and effects of utterances are inseparable from the interaction of the verbal, nonverbal, and paraverbal strategies used to convey them. Argyle and Dean's (1965) research is a good example of how verbal and nonverbal modalities may compensate each other to adjust to the desired level of intimacy. Within the verbal mode, converging linguistically while using abusive language may have a doubly dissociative effect. Likewise, code switching toward the other interactant's language, while at the same time introducing words from one's own language (i.e., code mixing away from), may markedly alter the effects of the discourse.

In addition to textual context and interaction effects, a positive outcome of interethnic communication may require both associative and dissociative strategies. Following Hewstone and Brown's (1986) theory of intergroup contact, the dissolution of harmful out-group images requires that interactants from different ethnic groups see each other as *typical* representatives of their groups reflecting complementary positions that cannot be discounted as "exceptions." Understanding interethnic communication therefore requires (in our view) a less segregated representation of behavior than that proposed by Kim. Interethnic communication plays out much more than the encounter between two associating or dissociating individuals. It is an exchange of their multilayered representations of themselves via strategies whose impact is fostered by their particular combinations.

Our view of interethnic communication therefore calls for research aimed at studying discursive strategies in view of delineating their functions. Within a pragmatic-systemic approach, we would argue that all of the so-called layers of context would be reflected in these strategies and their active effects, which would consequently define the domain of our research program. Because we are also interested in how communication would be related to such *outcomes* as identity (e.g., Clément & Noels, 1992; Giles & Coupland, 1991), adjustment and adaptation (e.g., Kim, 1988; Mogghaddam, Taylor, & Wright, 1993), and inter-cultural-interpersonal communication (e.g., H. J. Kim, 1991), it would seem appropriate also to comment on the relevant mentalistic functions of communicators and on the interfaces between them and their behavior.

The Communicator

Many of the phenomena included by Kim under "encoding" we have accepted as being part of communication behavior, although not exactly in the same fashion as what was proposed. We, however, and as above, take exception to labeling as communication *behavior* such processes as categorization, stereotyping, attribution, and so forth. They are operations of "the mind." Furthermore, we wish to argue that these processes, to the extent that they are relevant, are conceptually indistinguishable from what Kim attributes to "the communicator." For convenience, we will discuss separately the important characteristics of the otherwise functionally related cognitive and motivational processes.

Cognitive processes relevant to communication as social acts correspond, in our view, to those that are relevant to any social act. They include the functions of categories, schemas, scripts—inferential heuristics that have been described elsewhere (see Fiske & Taylor, 1991) as fulfilling the functions of decoding and encoding. Utterances in an interethnic context may require competence in another language but, at least from a functional perspective, such knowledge may be treated as any other information. Two phenomena may, however, be particularly relevant to the production and outcome of interethnic interaction because of their immediate consequences for ethnic interaction and also because of the wider implications for the nature of the individual mediational process.

The first phenomenon is related to the distinction between category-based and individuated information processing. Both Brewer (1988) and Fiske and Neuberg (1990) propose theoretical frameworks wherein impression formation can result from the categorization of the target object or the "piecemeal" integration of an attribute analysis of that object. It is argued that the impression formed of an interlocutor may be based on the attributes pertaining to the category to which that interlocutor is assigned or may be a function of the "integration" of the separate reactions to each of his or her characteristics. Whether one or the other approach is taken would result in quite different and at times conflictual interpretations of the information at hand. In the context of interethnic interaction, one's social category may be completely discounted. Furthermore, should the goal of interethnic communication be the achievement of harmony, as in cross-cultural contact programs, this may not happen if an individuated processing is involved as opposed to a category-based processing. The interactants would then fail to generalize a positive interpersonal impression to all members of the other ethnic group (see also Hewstone & Brown, 1986).

Whereas the category versus individuated processing distinction focuses on impression formation and its eventual impact on interethnic communication, the second phenomenon deals, conversely, with the influence of communication on the emergence of meaning. In a series of experiments conducted under the so-called communication game paradigm, Higgins and his colleagues (Higgins, 1992) have shown that communicators systematically adapt the content of their communications to their audience's characteristics through a variety of discursive strategies. Furthermore, as a result of such "tuning," the communicators will actually distort their own meaning of an event to be concordant with what they previously communicated. This version of "saying is believing" supports, in a sense, Kim's argument in favor of the bidirectional exchange between communication and the communicator. Taken together with the previous categorization-individuation distinction, however, the communication game would suggest a level of cognitive interaction and processing that is not present in Kim's dichotomous caricature of the decoding-encoding sequence.

Most of the items included by Kim under "decoding" and "communicator" are, we would argue, motivational influences. Of course, none of the above cognitive processes is devoid of such influences. Brewer (1988), for example, considers self-involvement to be a condition for promoting individuated processing. The type of traits (e.g., authoritarianism) and attitudes (e.g., prejudice, ethnic identity) that Kim describes are part of a family of affective characteristics that influence attention and what information will be processed at the cognitive level (see Fiske & Neuberg, 1990). Moreover, attentional processes must be viewed as active. As shown by Lee and Boster (1991), individuals actively seek and elicit new information.

But ethnically relevant traits and attitudes may not be the only affective aspects acting as motivational supports. As shown in the context of studies of second language acquisition and usage (see Gardner, 1985), attitudes and values provide the affective background to orient the communicator toward or away from interethnic contact situations. When such contact is possible, self-confidence (Gardner & Clément, 1990) and anxiety-reduction strategies (see Gudykunst, 1993; McIntyre & Gardner, 1991) would appear to be the most relevant affective processes. Thus, whereas more remote attitudes, values, and traits may foster attentional orientation and initial information gathering, subsequent phases of the interaction are more directly controlled by immediate self-presentation and uncertainty reduction motives. This does not mean that attitudes are not involved in the management of interaction. As shown by Higgins (1992), characteristics of the communication influence subsequent beliefs.

Our representation of the interethnic communicator therefore involves intimately intertwined motivational and cognitive processes. Just as we claimed that communication behavior included all of Kim's layers, we would argue that motivational and cognitive processes operate on materials that range from the very intimate and interpersonal information to structural and macrosocial characteristics. Thus the mind itself is a "multilayered transactional matrix" and, from a psychological point of view, it and its relationship to communication could define our field of investigation. Our further understanding of the conditions under which interethnic communication may evolve and be influenced—as well as the societal impact of our research— may, however, require some reference to operational definitions of the context *other* than those privileged under a pragmatic-communication or constructivist-psychological approach.

The Environment

In view of heuristic simplicity, it could be argued that none of the factors pertaining to communication behavior or psychological processes should find their way into an account of environmental aspects. Thus we would exclude from such an account all aspects of the situation and the environment whose definition hinges on their subjective recognition by the communicator. These would include aspects such as ethnic salience, relative deprivation, and Blalock's (1982) conception of motivation as psychological processes of the level we have described in the preceding section. That is not to say, however, that anthropological or sociological descriptions of interethnic encounters are truncated. Any one of these other disciplines could provide a multilayered account of interethnic communication describing the individual as well as the collectivity. Using them to represent only the "wider" societal context does not do justice to their intended scope of application. We should further realize that, in borrowing specific constructs from these approaches without their theoretical context, we are in effect reifying them, that is, giving them a status of objective reality that they did not have as constructs in their original discipline. One consequence of this is that our description of the environment, while acknowledging the contribution of other disciplines, may do little in terms of explaining what we are really interested in—namely, interethnic communication.

A good example of this is our use of the various formulations that refer to objective definitions of power differentials between ethnic groups. As a case in point, ethnolinguistic vitality, under its objective operational definition, has been shown to be related to a variety of interethnic phenomena (e.g., Bourhis & Sachdev, 1984; Clément & Noels, 1992). It is, however, not a construct that has yet been shown to be related closely to actual communication behaviors. It seems therefore that ethnolinguistic vitality, situational distribution of power, and other "objective" environmental characteristics would be mediated by other constructs. What would really be important, perhaps provocatively for some, is the extent to which this information is attended to by the communicator, thus returning to our psychological account of context. Or it also may be that the construct itself is ill-suited to explain what we have so far described as an active symbol manipulation and exchange process.

Consequently, we would suggest that looking at the extraindividual and extracommunication environment might better be accomplished through an examination of communication networks (e.g., Kim, 1988; Rogers & Kincaid, 1981). Although still an "importation," communication networks represent the actual linguistic environment of the communicator, lending themselves to the type of analysis used for the communication and the communicator. In a manner consistent with our representation of the communicator as an active information seeker, the network also represents the environment created by communication activities. It also exerts influence on the individual through such characteristics as its size, density, and multiplexity. It therefore bears a systemic relationship with the individual communicators constituting it. Finally, it can be represented as including a number of ethnically defined subnetworks, each of which can be characterized structurally as being more or less influential. As a conceptual tool, we would argue that it accounts equally well for individually centered and societal descriptions of the environment.

Obviously, macrosocial conditions such as the relative demographic importance of different ethnic groups, their relative power, and institutional representation will constitute boundary conditions defining the limits of any one network and promoting specific structural characteristics. Knowing these relationships may be important for ethnic or linguistic policymaking. Our argument, however, is that mapping out the communication network begins to serve as a first conceptual step for our understanding of communication behavior and its personal and societal consequences.

CONCLUSION

While stating our position, we have made use of widely available theoretical positions and research findings. Theories with developing empirical traditions are "out there" as reflected in Kim and Gudykunst's (1988) collection of them. It would have been informative had Kim, at the outset, provided a critical view of the state of the art as a backdrop to understanding the need for her approach. Nonetheless, her essay is an ambitious attempt at providing a comprehensive framework for studying interethnic communication, drawing upon the constructs of other disciplines. Moreover, it will probably suit the tastes of some who may now call upon constructs they hitherto would never have encountered. Consequentially, such enrichments of designs may themselves lead to incisive theory-building and compelling findings, therefore making Kim's contribution a watershed in the field. We would take nothing but delight by such a vindication of her position.

Nevertheless, and to summarize, we find her position problematic on many counts. We remain unconvinced that the approach is a parsimonious heuristic that can be as useful to understanding the interethnic dynamics of communication in face-to-face interactions as it can in other domains such as media effects, organizations, health contexts, and so forth. The identification of the different "layers" of the individual communicator with a hierarchy of disciplines results in conceptual confusion and redundancy. Relatedly, we are also reticent to accept her approach because of problems attending (a) the distinctiveness of her levels (e.g., Can we really differentiate en- from decoding, communication from the latter, the former from the environment?); (b) the hierarchy of her levels in that the focus on the core (in Kim's terms "associative" versus "dissociative" strategies) may be simplistic to the extent that often fundamental social inequities are more responsible for interethnic conflict than any communicative practices and values; and (c) the role of communication processes and variables and their assumed central roles for better understanding interethnic relations (How, when, and why?).

Our deconstruction led us to elaborate an approach that, while opening disciplinary access to *all* layers of interethnic communication, highlighted what we saw as more clearly defined perspectives from which to view it: the communication behavior, the communicator, and the environment. On the basis of this metatheoretical heuristic, we can now proffer the following propositions about rules for deriving middle-range theories and, eventually, the development of a research agenda:

1. Investigating interethnic interaction as *communication* must necessarily focus on the symbolic exchange between two "ethnically" defined individuals.
2. The explanation of the interchange must rely on a definition of the context as encompassing layers that may vary from the most immediate text-bound attributes to the most general societal conditions. The influence of these layers on meaning must be understood to be a function of their interaction.
3. Each and every layer of the context may be found within each and every explanatory perspective (i.e., the communication, the communicator, and the environment).
4. The choice of a particular perspective should be coherent with the epistemological choices made by the investigators, given a specific definition of their problems.
5. The importation of constructs from one perspective to another should only be done following (a) a careful conceptual recontextualization of the construct to ensure its compatibility with the basic tenets and assumptions of the host perspective and (b) an equally careful study of the redundancy and/or incoherence of the prospective construct with existing ones.

This is not to say that the application of these rules will readily fulfill Kim's hope that such quests can lead to promoting the intercultural person as transcending unnecessary ethnic conflicts. In addition to raising the specter of structural inequities standing in the way and often being the core of disputes and hostilities, we see problems with this solution also and have some cautionary remarks. First, the pressures on becoming bicultural are usually (and sadly) unidirectional and placed on the shoulders of low-power collectivities. One can accept the notion, of say, Vietnamese Australians and Urdu Britons, but what are the possibilities for the reverse? In other words, how many Australians and white Britons, as we write, are prepared to learn the other language and become bicultural? These issues become all the more acute in multiethnic and multilingual contexts, which, after all, define most interethnic settings. Second, even those illustrative of a unidirectional accommodation, such as Indian Britons, may actually be in the process of forming a new contrastive identity that is not so much an intercultural identity as it is a third creative amalgam, differentiating itself in valued ways from both Anglo and Indian societies, communication patterns, and traditions. Third, we need to shy away—perhaps taxonomically initially—from any monolith of an intercultural identity. These will likely be quite different depending on the political-economic-histories operating between different groups. Put another way, a Serb-Croat intercultural identity will be different than a Jewish-Arabic intercultural identity, that is, even if they can be sanctioned at all by any of the groups involved under currently prevailing circumstances.

In conclusion, we find Kim's position important to the extent of provoking debate on what kinds of theory in interethnic communication we are seeking that will ultimately guide research. In this sense, maybe our own commentary here will provoke further consideration of these matters rather than our being seduced into accepting the previous conceptualization as a kind of panacea. Moreover, it may be necessary to endure the cycle of deconstructing "big pictures" before we can actually feel confident about locating the theoretical Holy Grail.

REFERENCES

Argyle, M., & Dean, J. (1965). Eye contact, distance and affiliation. *Sociometry, 28,* 289-304.

Auer, P. (1992). Introduction: John Gumperz' approach to contextualisation. In P. Auer & A. Di Luzio (Eds.), *The contextualisation of language* (pp. 1-37). Amsterdam: Benjamins.

Auer, P., & DiLuzio, A. (Eds.). (1992). *The contextualisation of language.* Amsterdam: Benjamins.

Blalock, H. (1982). *Race and ethnic relations.* Englewood Cliffs, NJ: Prentice-Hall.

Blommaert, J., & Verschueren, J. (1987). *The pragmatics of international and intercultural communication.* Amsterdam: Benjamins.

Bourhis, R. Y., & Sachdev, L. (1984). Vitality perceptions and language attitude: Some Canadian data. *Journal of Language and Social Psychology, 3,* 97-126.

Brewer, M. B. (1988). A dual process model of impression formation. In T. K. Srull & R. S. Wyer (Eds.), *Advances in social cognition: Vol. 1. A dual model of impression formation* (pp. 1-36). Hillsdale, NJ: Lawrence Erlbaum.

Clément, R., & Noels, K. A. (1992). Towards a situated approach to ethnolinguistic identity: The effects of status on individuals and groups. *Journal of Language and Social Psychology, 11,* 203-232.

Fiske, S. T., & Neuberg, S. L. (1990). A continuum of impression formation, from category-based to individuating processes: Influences of information and motivation on attention and interpretation. In M. P. Zanna (Ed.), *Advances in Experimental Social Psychology, 23,* 1-74.

Fiske, S. T., & Taylor, S. E. (1991). *Social cognition.* New York: McGraw-Hill.

Gardner, R. C. (1985). *Social psychological aspects of second language learning.* London: Edward Arnold.

Gardner, R. C., & Clément, R. (1990). Social psychological perspectives on second language acquisition. In H. Giles & P. Robinson (Eds.), *The handbook of language and social psychology.* London: John Wiley.

Giles, H., & Coupland, J. (1991). *Language: Contexts and consequences.* Pacific Grove, CA: Brooks/Cole.

Gudykunst, W. B. (1993). Toward a theory of effective interpersonal and intergroup communication: An anxiety/uncertainty management (AUM) perspective. In R. L. Wiseman & J. Koester (Eds.), *Intercultural communicative competence* (pp. 33-71). Newbury Park, CA: Sage.

Hewstone, M. R. C., & Brown, R. J. (1986). Contact is not enough: An intergroup perspective on the contact hypothesis. In M. R. C. Hewstone & R. J. Brown (Eds.), *Contact and conflict in intergroup encounters* (pp. 1-44). Oxford: Basil Blackwell.

Higgins, E. T. (1992). Achieving "shared reality" in the communication game: A social action that creates meaning. *Journal of Language and Social Psychology, 11,* 107-131.

Kim, H. J. (1991). Influence of language and similarity on initial intercultural attraction. In S. Ting-Toomey & F. Korzenny (Eds.), *Cross-cultural interpersonal communication* (pp. 213-229). Newbury Park, CA: Sage.

Kim, Y. Y. (1988). *Communication and cross-cultural adaptation: An integrative theory.* Clevedon, England: Multilingual Matters.

Kim, Y. Y., & Gudykunst, W. B. (1988). *Cross-cultural adaptation.* Newbury Park, CA: Sage.

Lee, H. O., & Boster, F. J. (1991). Social information for uncertainty reduction during initial interactions. In S. Ting-Toomey & F. Korzenny (Eds.), *Cross-cultural interpersonal communication* (pp. 189-212). Newbury Park, CA: Sage.

McIntyre, P. D., & Gardner, R. C. (1991). Methods and results in the study of anxiety and language learning: A review of the literature. *Language Learning, 41,* 85-117.

Mogghaddam, F. M., Taylor, D. M., & Wright, S. C. (1993). *Social psychology in cross-cultural perspective.* New York: Freeman.

Rogers, E. M., & Kincaid, D. L. (1981). *Communication networks: Toward a new paradigm for research.* New York: Free Press.

Tajfel, H., & Turner, J. C. (1979). An integrative theory of intergroup conflict. In W. C. Austin & S. Worchel (Eds.), *The social psychology of intergroup relation* (pp. 33-53). Monterey, CA: Brooks/Cole.

Watzlawick, P., Beavin, J. H., & Jackson, D. (1967). *Pragmatics of human communication.* New York: Norton.

Interethnic Communication and Cross-Paradigm Borrowing: A Disciplinary Response

VERNON E. CRONEN
University of Massachusetts

I N her essay, Professor Young Yun Kim has brought together a variety of literatures in support of a new model and description. Her effort is sparked by a concern for the problems of interethnic understanding in the United States and around the world. The urgency of the situation described in her essay ought to be taken seriously by all of us in the profession.

We do not need foreign examples to remind us of the problems of multicultural living. The Los Angeles riots of last summer witnessed not only violence between African Americans and whites but also between African Americans and Korean Americans. The American experiment is in large measure concerned with the possibilities of creating a single state without being a single nation. How we are doing at our great task is reflected in the news daily.

While I share Professor Kim's social concerns, I want to raise a number of questions that I hope Kim and others will find useful. This critique takes two perspectives. I will raise questions about the internal coherence of her model, and I will argue that there is little place for communication in such a model. These two lines of criticism are related in this way: Kim strives to discern what will be most useful in the varied work on interethnic communication. In doing so, she takes a field rather than a disciplinary view of communication. By a "field view," I mean the idea that communication is a set of phenomena that may be understood from a variety of scholarly traditions, each with its own claims about what the primary social process is. In traditional psychology, for example, the primary social process is individual psyche. By a disciplinary view, I mean the idea that communication is not only a set of phenomena worthy of study but also a unique set of traditions

Correspondence and requests for reprints: Vernon E. Cronen, Department of Communication, University of Massachusetts, Amherst, MA 01003.

Communication Yearbook 17, pp. 551-562

in which communication is taken to be the primary social process and thus the organizing locus of theoretical work.

Kim's work seems an attempt to cross the field-disciplinary distinction. She proposes what at first looks like a communication-centered model and intends to use it for organizing data from other disciplines. Her goal is interdisciplinary integration. Kim accepts much of the structural sociological and particularly the traditional psychological work relevant to her concern. The result of this eclecticism, however, is a set of three unproductive tensions in her essay: (a) the commitment to both Batesonian systems theory and pragmatist thought, (b) the brief overview of communication as an interactive process versus the model of interethnic communication in Figure 1, and (c) the commitment to creating a communication theory but a review of literature from different orientations.

This commentary is a call to Professor Kim and others to stop stirring around in the scrap heaps of other disciplines and explore what the *discipline* of communication has to offer. We ought to read what is written in other disciplines but not fill our theories with their findings, particularly when those other disciplines do not take communication seriously as *the primary social process* (Harré, 1984; Pearce & Cronen, 1980).

PRAGMATISM PLUS SYSTEM THEORY *AND* PRAGMATISM VERSUS SYSTEM THEORY

Early in her essay, Kim endorses taking a communication orientation based on ideas derived from systems theory and the heritage of American philosophical pragmatism. The kind of systems theory she has in mind is shown by her citation of Gregory Bateson (1972) and Watzlawick, Beavin, and Jackson (1967). It is not as easy, however, to infer which of the pragmatists were influential for her. Her commitment to theory-building clearly rules out the pragmatism of Richard Rorty. I will guess that she is thinking about the work running through William James, John Dewey, and George Herbert Mead, for they placed social interaction at the center of things. If I am correct in this characterization, then there is a tension between pragmatism and systems theory that needs attention.

Bateson thought of communication as patterns of message exchange. Each message, he thought, had two levels—command and report. The first formed a context for the second in a way that closely parallels John Searle's (1969) equally famous "F(p)" formulation. Bateson's view of message exchange is prone to the same critique as Searle's, however (Baker & Hacker, 1984), and is not compatible with pragmatic ideas. (See also Cronen, Pearce, & Xi, 1989-1990; James, cited in Gunn, 1991.)

Moreover, Bateson and Watzlawick's stress on homeostatic regulation is not readily compatible with the pragmatists' stress on the open, unfinished quality of interaction (Dewey, 1929; James, 1909). Indeed, within the community of family therapists that developed from the work of Bateson and the Mental Research Institute, there has been a distinct movement away from the cybernetic emphasis of systems theory toward a more discursive point of view (Anderson & Goolishian, 1988). Lynn Hoffman (1991) describes this movement as one *away* from the idea of component persons integrated by message exchanges and *toward* an emphasis on the way stories and interactive narrative constructions constitute and reconstitute persons and families.

This problem of compatibility is manifest in Kim's endorsement of Bateson's "jigsaw puzzle" metaphor for understanding "redundant" patterns of practice. Bateson's view is not sufficiently liberated from the psychological paradigm that pragmatist philosophers criticized. William James identified what he called "the psychologists' fallacy." That fallacy is thinking that concepts that may be employed to make sense of a finished process are necessarily the ones that best serve us when we want to understand a process in the making. The model of communication at play in Bateson's view assumes there must be intact patterns to find. We can know the meaning of a message if we find its place in a pattern. But, as family therapists inspired by Bateson learned, when we have identified the pattern post hoc, it is all too tempting to think that the actors had some preexisting "need" for it that functions to achieve a preexisting goal. This homeostatic view would be quite consistent with the cybernetic side of systems theory.

Many of our actions are not highly ritualized. We make our way, acting into the actions of others, trying to make sense for ourselves and others while keeping a place of significance and honor in the conversation (Harré, 1984). This opens up the *ubiquity* of unanticipated consequences. Yes, we are often informed by stories we know about how certain episodes go, and stories about the persons with whom we are conversing, and yes persons can get "stuck" in redundant patterns based on these stories. The stories that inform actors' abilities, however, may not be very well formed. Our ideas about another ethnic group may be fragmentary and come together only in the course of an important interaction or over several interactions. In other words, there may be no *preexisting* "jigsaw puzzle" or homeostatic setting to study.

This is important when we think about ethnic relationships on a university campus. Many freshmen come with only fragmentary bits of stories about other groups; some of those "bits" of narrative may even be contradictory. I overheard two fathers of university students discussing their concerns about Jewish professors. One repeated the story that Jews are money-hungry capitalists *and* the story that Jews are dangerous socialists. The other agreed and said he wondered just how they could be both—"Just what are they up to?" What comes together for the children of these parents is going to be worked through without those students necessarily having much of a preexisting agenda or even an inkling that stories of ethnic differences will be of any import for their college experience.

Political scientists Susanne H. Rudolph and Lloyd I. Rudolph (1993) have recently made a similar argument about worldwide ethnic conflicts and the ethnic problems of India in particular. They argue that ethnic traditions are multivocal. There are Hindu traditions, for example, that both naturalize and demonize other groups. They analyzed Muslim-Hindu relations historically without assuming at the beginning that mutual hatred was simply built-in. They conclude, "Which identities become relevant for politics is not predetermined by some primordial ancientness. They are crafted in benign and malignant ways in print and electronic media, in textbooks and advertising, in India's T.V. megaseries and American talkshows, in campaign strategies, in all the places and ways that self and other, us and them, are represented in an expanding public culture" (p. 29).

Notice how the historical treatment places emphasis on the unfinished quality of experience and highlights situated communication practices in which ethnicity is formed. If one were to adopt the pragmatic tradition, one would have to give a privileged place to the ideas of "acting into," "unanticipated consequences," and "tensions between stories lived and stories told" (Pearce, 1989) over preestablished patterns and homeostatic settings. The meaning of an utterance would have to be seen as always undergoing elaboration, reinstantiation, and/or reinterpretation. When there is redundancy, the researcher with a pragmatic point of view would investigate how such redundancy is accomplished in spite of the daily changes in life's course and the place (perhaps changing place) of such redundancies in the experience of actors.

All of this suggests the need for a closer description of what is taken from systems theory and pragmatism. Although there are important points of contact between them, neither is univocal and there are many consequential points of difference.

THE DESCRIPTION OF COMMUNICATION AND
THE MODEL OF INTERETHNIC COMMUNICATION

I have more in common with the brief description of communication that Kim offers in the first paragraph under the heading "An Organizing Framework" (p. 516) than I have with what comes immediately after as she details her model of interethnic communication. If one takes seriously the idea that communication is the primary social process, one could not present the model that follows. Kim cites an essay of which I am coauthor (Cronen, Chen, & Pearce, 1988) as saying that "communication practices point beyond themselves to (and derive their meaning from) sets of contexts" (p. 67). Little is made of the context in which my colleagues and I wrote that phrase, however. We stressed that each action influences the affordances and constraints for *other* actors. These conjoint practices reflexively form, extend, and alter contexts. Other topics of concern—such as ways of thinking, what psychologists call "consciousness," forms of selfhood, cultural understandings, perception, and the like—were subordinated to descriptions of a conjoint active process.

By contrast, in Kim's essay, the "communication process" gets a psychological reduction. Indeed, the center of the model is the *single* individual communicator. Communication becomes a merely mental process—"the activities of encoding and decoding."[1] Decoding is "taking in and the processing" while encoding is sending out "messages to the environment" (p. 516). It is not trivial to say that I do not send out messages to the environment. When I communicate, I have to "act into" (to use John Shotter's felicitous phrase) the practices of another so as make coherent connections in a moral order. Even if I am engaged in a private soliloquy, that practice is modeled on practices developed in conjoint action (Dewey, 1929; Shotter, 1984). Moreover, private action always comes at a particular time in the course of our lives, when *this* and *that* have been going on. Persons learn how to think as they are confronted with the problems of making coherent connections into social action (Becker, 1971; Shotter, 1984).

While I agree with Professor Pearce's argument, in his commentary on John Shotter and Kenneth Gergen in this volume, that they do not there present a detailed constructionist view of communication, they do indeed present arguments about why communication as joint action, not individual mentation, ought to be at the center of social thought. Gergen's and particularly Shotter's ideas are more clearly in the camp of communication than is the Kim model. I commend their essay to the reader's close attention as an argument against any model in which levels of context affect the individual knower, while communication is reduced to the mental processes of interpreting and sending.

John Dewey (1929) protested against the reduction of communication to "some psychic peculiarity, such as the tendency to 'outer expression' of 'inner' states" (p. 169). This is not the place to develop Dewey's conception of communication, but the interested reader might begin with his chapter "Nature and Communication" in *Experience and Nature* (1929) or the first chapter of *Democracy and Education* (1916) to see how far removed he was from Kim's model.[2]

An important feature of pragmatism is that it treats communication as having both a discursive-instrumental aspect and a consummatory-aesthetic aspect. Bateson paid little attention to this and Watzlawick et al. (1967) ignored it. Dewey, however, (1929) observed how crucial the aesthetic is for understanding human interaction and offered some provocative ways of conceptualizing it *within* the context of communicative practices. Nowhere in Kim's review is there attention to what is loved, hated, profoundly beautiful, or grotesquely ugly. Yet, so much of ethnicity interaction depends on this. The use of music by young African Americans, for example, has become a matter of conflict on city streets and in housing units. This is not merely a matter of nonverbal cues. It amounts to learning how to have and evoke the consummatory experiences of everyday activity without which we would not be describing human life.

While Kim's model does not seem to reflect pragmatism, I do not see much of systems theory in its current state of development. Obviously, Kim intends to develop the model further and only then will we know how or whether such notions as reflexivity, boundary, homeostasis, second cybernetics, or other systems concepts will be incorporated.

THE REVIEW OF LITERATURE:
WHAT HAPPENED TO COMMUNICATION?

I fear that Professor Kim's work exhibits the assumption that theoretical differences are matters of compatibility and that communication is a sort of crossroad where literatures from various disciplines meet on common concerns. Kim's literature review provides a valuable service for those who share the "field" perspective on communication. Kim's generosity to our disciplinary competitors, however, leads away form her own initial description of communication.

Kim is aware that she is drawing largely form the positivistic-variable testing literature, much of it from psychology. When taking such a position, one must be careful because the various contributions one wishes to integrate may reflect *incommensurable* orientations that cannot be integrated into our own discipline without a thorough *reworking* of those contributions. It is the view of logical positivism that all theoretical issues can be translated into a common, theory-neutral, variable analytic language. Since the publication of Thomas Kuhn's (1962) *The Structure of Scientific Revolutions*, however, an avalanche of work has discredited this view. (See Bernstein, 1985; Rorty, 1979; Taylor, 1985.) Given that both Bateson and the pragmatists rejected the positivist notion of theory-building, the reader would expect to find reformulations of psychological and sociological material into a new systemic or pragmatist perspective, rejecting some things and recasting others. Unfortunately, no such detailed work is done.

I do not intend a detailed review of Kim's interpretation of the data. My concern is with fostering communication theory, not with theories *about* communication from other disciplinary orientations. I hope what follows will be read as an effort to cure people in communication of both psychology and sociology. Failing that, I hope to sharpen the distinctiveness of a communication perspective so that some hard choices can be made.

In Kim's model, we are harkened to attend to "behavior." In the literature chosen for review, however, individual "messages" are discussed on the basis of whether they reflect "stereotyping," "prejudicial listening," "intergroup posturing," "person centeredness," and so on. A good deal of attention is also given to that offspring of Descartes and artificial intelligence named "cognitive structure." Communication is reduced to frequencies of behaviors that can be classified in certain ways. Consequently, communication can be of only secondary concern. It is merely the outcome of mystical cognitive operations and orientations.

There is really no analysis of communication to be found in Kim's chapter. In a communication perspective, one would expect to find discussions of how patterns of joint practice work within ethnic communities and in discussions across such community boundaries. That, at least, would be compatible with Bateson, but no such analysis is given.

To be fair, Professor Kim does discuss the communication "situation" and includes the subtopic "interactional structure." What promises to be a communication perspective, however, receives the psychological reduction. Interactive patterns are not discussed, only "orientations" and other mentalistic processes to which psychologists have appealed to account post hoc for patterns of interaction. "Interpersonal" and "cooperative" *orientations* along with "personalized decodings" are identified as producing more desirable interaction structures as compared with "task-oriented" and "competitive orientations" and "stereotyped" decodings. From a communication perspective, one must wonder about such one-way unsituated claims. How is "orientation" created and what sort of a concept is this? Is it a mental state, an element in a cognitive schema, or a general conclusion the *researcher* makes about past practices? As a communication researcher, I can only imagine using the term *orientation* as shorthand for agents' emergent positionings in situated activity. Such activity is not typically under the full control of one actor.

As for the practice of what the psychologists have called "stereotyping" behavior, that is somehow connected to their underdefined notion of "orientation." Many years ago, George Herbert Mead observed that category names have their function not primarily as a naming of things in the world but as *actions* that enter into practices with others (Mead, 1939). Following that lead, a communication researcher would be interested in much more than calling this or that "stereotyping." Years ago such traditional naming of behavior instead of explanation was called "Bubba psychology"—the kind of explanation a grandmother might give—which would be wrong. To understand stereotyping, a communication theorist would *not* inquire into what it "really is" but would want to know how expressions so described are used in discursive patterns. He or she would try to learn the "grammar" of such expressions, that is, how other elements of discourse may be coherently connected with it in one utterance and in responses by others. How does using stereotypical expression create obligations, legitimations, and prohibitions for "going on" in discursive practices? What prior and future utterances or actions legitimize its use and allow its use to be coherent? In other words, how does the utterance work in the making of social life? With all its limitations, Bateson's "jigsaw" metaphor is a better basis of understanding stereotyping than the classifying of utterances.

Notice in the foregoing that I am not discounting the importance of what the psychologists have called stereotyping. What I have tried to illustrate is how that phenomenon can be recast into a communication-centered research project of a very different kind. There are a variety of communication-oriented methodologies that have been advanced for such work. These *nonpsy*chological alternatives include coordinated management of meaning theory's episode analysis (Pearce & Cronen, 1980), adjacency pairs analysis (Schegloff, 1972), accounts in sequence analysis (Potter & Wetherell, 1987), narrative analysis (Fisher, 1987), and ethnography of cultural communication practices (Carbaugh, 1990).

Imposing hypothetical situations would make the psychologists' generalizations appear ludicrous if Kim's account of the seriousness of the current situation were not so accurate and compelling. For example, if we are conducting peace negotiations to stop war across ethnic neighborhoods, or trying to adjust living conditions in a multicultural college dormitory to prevent a fight tomorrow, we had better have a "task orientation," even if there is some *general* negative correlation between task orientation and desirable interethnic interactions.

My own reading of recent research in the tradition of "ethnolinguistic vitality" discussed by Kim suggests it too could be profitably recast in a communication orientation. My reason for thinking so is based on the fact that the same variables do not predict "vitality" for all groups. Because the real interests of these researchers are not in a psychological state but in real practices that preserve and develop cultural heritage, a turn to looking at the grammar or practices might help to organize this work in new ways. One could investigate what practices are opened up when the ethnic language is used. This could include the aesthetic dimension of using the language. Does it seem out of place or out of character to use the ethnic language? Does it facilitate emotional patterns that are not built into the rhythms and sounds of the language of the larger culture? I shall, however, limit my comments on this particular topic in deference to Professor Giles, who has been so intimately connected with this work.

The psychological emphasis of Kim's review is also shown by her endorsement of Tajfel and Turner's (1986) continuum from interpersonal orientations to intergroup orientations. Neither pragmatists nor system theorists typically organize concepts into variable-like continua, and for good reason. The opposite of treating someone as a negative stereotype is not treating him or her as an individual in a unique interpersonal interaction. In many institutional situations, there is no available information for doing so, and to get it would be an invasion of privacy. The opposite is to treat the other as having connections of race, ethnicity, community, and gender that deserve our respect.

The idea that the more personalized we are the better interactional patterns will be is a reflection of the older notion derived from Bacon, Descartes, and Locke that individuation and distance from one's ethnic and cultural roots is liberating and productive of creativity. The critique of this view in recent decades has been taken seriously by almost all social theorists except traditional psychologists and other "psychophiles." There is no simple "creativity" outside of culture, and, indeed, individuality is created in social practices informed by one or more traditions (Becker, 1971; Geertz, 1973). In addition to the academic literature on this point, we can look to the instructive turn of the U.S. civil rights movement. The civil rights movement learned from hard experience that talking about being treated as individuals who just "happen" to be black could not succeed. The "I'm white inside" approach (exemplified in the old song, "What Did I Do to Be So Black and Blue") was replaced by an insistence on the importance of and respect for black culture. The idea of a continuum from interpersonal to intergroup such that more of one amounts to less of the other is based on a psychological story and sanctified by certain psychometric methods that have little use outside of laboratory situations. I am not more unique and creative the more I separate from my own heritage. One of the abilities I hope I have developed in the practices afforded by my traditions is that of making some moves on them, but that is quite different than becoming more and more separated from them.

Not all the literature Kim summarizes is from a psychological orientation. Her turn to the sociological literature gets her no closer to communication, however. Clarke and Obler (1976) are cited for their stage analysis, as if Giddens's (1984, p. 12) attack had never been made. Kim also reviews some of the literature on power differentials and governmental/institutional practices. This is all well and good, but how does any of this affect the individual at the center of her model? Without such integration, it is not possible to tell how this sociological work is connected to her understanding of the communication process in any way other than the one-way causal determinism she wishes to reject. Here the underdevelopment of her model along either systemic or pragmatist lines is telling.

There is one final point to make about the incommensurability of the research orientations combined here. The traditional social science literatures assume a separation of the knower and the known modeled on the relationship of a physical scientist to nature. There, communication is simply the object of study. The systemic orientation, however, evolved in the direction of using the idea of second cybernetics in which the observer must be part of the analysis. The pragmatic orientation has moved in the direction of considering the researcher as telling another story about social interaction from a unique perspective. Like second-order cybernetics, this development in applied pragmatism rejects the old systems notion of a "meta" position, in the sense of having a superior position from which to observe, as well as the notion of objectivity essential to the positivist orientation. Both of these developments suggest a different way of describing what theories do and how data ought to be analyzed because they recognize the action of research as integral to the primary process of communication. Research then becomes a joining with subjects in particular kinds of communication.

SO WHAT'S THE BIG DEAL?

What I have told is a cautionary tale. When we read the literatures of other disciplines, we must be careful to discern that which is a turn away from the traditions of an older discipline to a communication perspective and that which is an effort to explain communication from a tradition that names something other than communication as the primary social process.

Left without any way to describe *how* structural or psychological processes are created in communication practices, ethnic relations seem doomed to conflict. Philosopher Richard Rorty (1983) argued as much, saying that, because each ethnic group constitutes its own discursive community, that which makes sense does so only inside the logic of that language-using community. The most we can do is stand aside from other groups and offer respect at a distance. Clifford Geertz (1986) described Rorty's notion as "making the world safe for condescension." The problem with Rorty's view is that he sees the individual as operating in a community of individuals each enclosed by language, institutions, and practices that create a logic of action. In excellent critiques of Rorty, both Clifford Geertz (1983) and Giles Gunn (1991) attack him for misunderstanding the way language works. Taking the pragmatist perspective, Gunn notes that communication is not circumscribed by community practices but only informed by them. Intrinsic to communication is the pointing beyond, acting into streams of action not of our own making. Pearce (1989) described the problem of intercultural and interethnic communication as privileging coordination over the coherence of our prior stories. He observes that tension between the coherence of prior stories and coordination of interaction is a ubiquitous feature of communication. If we are to avoid throwing up our hands in the face of diversity, we need a way of understanding communication that is focused on these efforts to muddle through, even with incomplete understandings. Such productive studies, I think, necessitate a distinctly disciplinary approach to interethnic communication.

NOTES

1. I will here pass over the important argument about describing any part of the communication process as "encoding" and "decoding." Such a description presupposes the dubious idea that persons are repositories of "ideas" that must be "encoded" into language and decoded from language into ideas. For a critique, see Baker and Hacker (1984) and Edwards (1985).

2. In the development of coordinated management of meaning theory, Barnett Pearce and I had to deal with this same conflict in the mid-1980s. Our resolutions have been on the side of the pragmatist philosophers.

REFERENCES

Anderson, H., & Goolishian, H. (1988). Human systems as linguistic systems. *Family Process, 27,* 371-395.

Baker, G. P., & Hacker, P. M. S. (1984). *Language, sense and nonsense.* Oxford: Basil Blackwell.

Bateson, G. (1972). *Steps to an ecology of mind.* New York: Ballantine.

Becker, E. (1971). *The birth and death of meaning.* New York: Free Press.

Bernstein, R. (1985). *Beyond objectivism and relativism.* Philadelphia: University of Pennsylvania Press.

Carbaugh, D. (1990). Toward a perspective on cultural communication and intercultural contact. *Semiotica, 80,* 15-35.

Clarke, S., & Obler, J. (1976). Ethnic conflict, community-building, and the emergence of ethnic political traditions in the United States. In S. Clarke & J. Obler (Eds.), *Urban ethnic conflicts: A comparative perspective* (pp. 1-34). Chapel Hill: University of North Carolina Press.

Cronen, V., Chen, V., & Pearce, W. B. (1988). Coordinated management of meaning: A critical theory. In Y. Kim & W. Gudykunst (Eds.), *Theories in intercultural communication* (pp. 66-98). Newbury Park, CA: Sage.

Cronen, V., Pearce, W. B., & Xi, C. (1989-1990). The meaning of "meaning" in the CMM analysis of communication: A comparison of two traditions. *Research on Language and Social Interaction, 23,* 1-40.

Dewey, J. (1916). *Democracy and education.* New York: Macmillan.

Dewey, J. (1929). *Experience and nature.* New York: Dover.

Edwards, J. (1985). *Ethics without philosophy.* Tampa: University of South Florida Press.

Fisher, W. (1987). *Human communication as narration: Toward a philosophy of reason, value and action.* Columbia: University of South Carolina Press.

Geertz, C. (1973). *The interpretation of cultures.* New York: Basic Books.

Geertz, C. (1986). The uses of diversity. *Michigan Quarterly Review, 25,* 111.

Giddens, A. (1984). *The constitution of society.* Berkeley: University of California Press.

Gunn, G. (1991). *Thinking across the American grain.* Chicago: Chicago University Press.

Harré, R. (1984). *Personal being.* Cambridge, MA: Harvard University Press.

Hoffman, L. (1991). A reflexive stance for family therapy. *Journal of Strategic and Systemic, 10,* 4-16.

James, W. (1909). *The meaning of truth.* Cambridge, MA: Harvard University Press.

Kuhn, T. (1962). *The structure of scientific revolutions.* Chicago: University of Chicago Press.

Mead, G. (1939). *The philosophy of the act.* Chicago: University of Chicago Press.

Pearce, W. (1989). *Communication and the human condition.* Carbondale: Southern Illinois University Press.

Pearce, W., & Cronen, V. (1980). *Communication, meaning and action.* New York: Praeger.

Potter, J., & Wetherell, M. (1987). *Discourse and social psychology.* Beverly Hills, CA: Sage.

Rorty, R. (1979). *Philosophy and the mirror of nature.* Princeton, NJ: Princeton University Press.

Rorty, R. (1983). Postmodern bourgeois liberalism. *Journal of Philosophy, 80,* 583-589.

Rudolph, S., & Rudolph, L. (1993, March 22). Modern hate. *New Republic,* pp. 24-30.

Schegloff, E. (1972). Sequencing in conversational openings. In J. Gumperz & D. Hymes (Eds.), *Directions in psycholinguistics* (pp. 346-380). New York: Holt.

Searle, J. (1969). *Speech acts.* Cambridge: Cambridge University Press.

Shotter, J. (1984). *Social accountability and selfhood.* Oxford: Basil Blackwell.

Tajfel, H., & Turner, J. (1986). The social identity theory in intergroup behavior. In S. Worchel & W. Austin (Eds.), *Psychology of intergroup relations* (2nd ed., pp. 7-17). Chicago: Nelson-Hall.

Taylor, C. (1985). *Philosophy and the human sciences.* Cambridge: Cambridge University Press.

Watzlawick, P., Beavin, J., & Jackson, D. (1967). *The pragmatics of human communication.* New York: Norton.

SECTION 4

EDITOR'S POSTSCRIPT

13 Future of the Discipline: The Challenges, the Research, and the Social Contribution

STANLEY A. DEETZ
Rutgers University

C LEARLY, communication studies has an identity, and in many senses we are doing well. Many feel that we have had our paradigm dialogues, displayed our mutual respect, and that it is time to go back to our work (and our associations with each group's preferred other disciplines). But identity is not just something one gets; it is best thought of in terms of constant invention regarding changing environments. I think it is worth the time to be continually self-reflective as a field in regard to our current environment.

Certainly, there are daily concerns we all continue to face. When I filled out my Fulbright application, I could not indicate my discipline or peer group, rather I had to choose among journalism, sociology, and business administration. There is no GRE in communication. Communication programs are not well respected on most campuses. Our basic texts are horrible. Not only are they shallow but even in the "communication theory" texts there is information theory, psychological theory, sociological theory, and even physiological theory but rarely any communication theory. Our journals are uneven at best. We have no more than a handful of major theorists in our departments and, of interest, they are more often cited by others than by ourselves. And, finally, when people ask my mother what I do, she tells them I am a psychologist. Despite my best efforts at explaining, I don't criticize her, after all, one of my best department colleagues is described as a psychologist every time he is on television. I've played the tunes. We're a small discipline, we're new—perhaps in our adolescence, perhaps we have not attracted the best minds, our diversity is a strength, or the communications industry has definitional authority. But, finally, these are neither the issues nor the reasons. I think these are by-products, that is, secondary effects of what is really at stake, our products.

Disciplines and schools of thought develop and become central by virtue of the social problems they address (Coleman, 1980). Unfortunately, communication

Correspondence and requests for reprints: Stanley A. Deetz, Department of Communication, Rutgers University, New Brunswick, NJ 08903-5067.

Communication Yearbook 17, pp. 565-600

studies has rarely provided productive new conceptions of problems and many studies only provide technical answers to problems as formulated by others. I recall a reporter approaching a colleague after a convention panel on a timely issue and asking what had been concluded. The colleague rightfully replied that we had heard a paper on topics x, y, and z. I doubt that the reporter ever came back. I believe that we as part of a world community have an identifiable set of social problems for which communication studies provides our best conception and chance for a meaningful response. If we as a field make a good move on these, the other things fall into place. If we don't, our petty disciplinary and ego concerns are the least of our problems. These are significant social issues for us as members of the wider community and our responsibility as professionals. To deal with such concerns, we must work to fulfill developmental trends in the field since the 1960s. Communication studies must be more completely severed from "informational" conceptions where meanings are assumed to be already existing and must provide "communication" explanations of processes of meaning development and the social production of perceptions, identities, social structures, and affective responses. Reminiscent of Steinbeck, an adolescent becomes an adult when an adult is needed. An adult is needed. We've had our liberal "brother can you spare a dime" period.[1] It's time to get to work.

In the few pages here, I do not intend to cut new ground as much as to contextualize what the past 25 years of reconceptualization offer us and the social problems we face. Essentially, I will argue that if we are to have a social effect we must focus more deeply on communication as a constitutive process rather than a phenomenon, work from an intent to foster codetermination rather than control, and embrace a pragmatist's understanding of the nature of theory and research in regard to social issues. In many respects, I believe that the postmodern (and largely communication) theorists have defined our situation usefully but have often failed to provide an affirmative response, a response our future must provide. In this essay, I wish to (a) characterize the nature of a discipline and argue that communication studies is central and ubiquitous but often not practiced in departments of communication, (b) describe how the move from information-based to communication-based conceptions of human interaction provides a new disciplinary "problematization," (c) develop four central social changes that place demands on the use of communication explanations and direct how we should study communication, and (4) discuss how we could conceptualize alternative research programs from a communication perspective.

A COMMUNICATION DISCIPLINE?

Answers to questions regarding the identity and impact of the field are largely dependent on the conception of "field." The slipperiness of terms like *fields, areas of study, disciplines,* and even *departments* lends ambiguity to any discussion of "our" situation and future because who and what is included (and excluded) and which organizing principles are salient remains unclear. The difficulty is not solved by definitions because these are essentially contested terms for which the definition provides part of the answer (Gallie, 1955-1956). This is not merely a nomenclature squabble; the conception of a difference allows a differentiation—to see something that is difficult to see in its absence. I wish to claim that communication has emerged as a core discipline in our contemporary context owing to the peculiar nature of contemporary social problems. But the practice of the discipline is diffused across traditional academic divisions and departments, hence weakening the contribution to a social response to these problems. And, further, unfortunately, researchers in departments of communication have often been among the last to grasp the significance of this emerging discipline owing to their commitments to focusing on technical, administrative problems and variable analytic studies in topical areas rather than on general social concerns. To clarify what this means, allow me to briefly sketch a conception of *discipline.*

The term commonly focuses our attention to the world in three distinct ways. Discipline$_1$ displays a world organized into academic units. As such, the concept focuses on professional concerns and the administration of grants and teaching personnel. Discipline$_1$ is better referred to as an academic unit. Discipline$_2$ displays a world organized around topical interests. Communication studies is a discipline$_2$ to the extent that communication is treated as a distinct phenomenon capable of being topically subdivided. Discipline$_2$ is best thought of as a field of study. Discipline$_3$ displays a world organized around competing modes of explanation. Communication is a discipline$_3$ to the extent that it presents a relatively organized way of attending to the world that explains how things come to be the way they are.

While "strong" disciplines are disciplines in all three senses, the third sense is the critical one. It is in this third sense that I claim that communication is a central discipline but often not practiced by people in communication departments and doing communication studies. Members of communication departments most often have thought of us as the field of communication studies (discipline$_2$) rather than as a discipline$_3$.[2] Ironically, scholars in other fields of study have rapidly grasped the importance of communication-textual-interactive-semiotic explanations. Whether social constructionist or interaction process work in psychology, ethnomethodology or structuration work in sociology, interactional studies in accounting, or cultural studies in English, others see the potential clearly. While many of the best theorists in communication departments are working to further these understandings,[3] the vast majority of the teachers and practitioners in the field (given their applied roots in psychologically oriented persuasion studies, newswriting, or public speaking, their social control orientation, and their atheoretical borrowing of concepts from other disciplines) have been among the slowest to see the significance of these developments. This is especially true in our textbooks. *If we are to make our full social contribution, we have to move from studying "communication" phenomena as formed and explained psychologically, sociologically, and economically, and produce studies that study psychological, sociological, and economic phenomena as formed and explained communicationally.*

Communication as a Disciplinary Mode of Explanation

Disciplines[3] arise when existing modes of explanation fail to provide compelling guidance for responses to a central set of new social issues. In these contexts, what is socially problematic becomes defined in the same process as the new mode of explanation. The combination of changing events and social conceptions leads to a new "problematization." A discipline differs from a field or area of study in that its set of conceptions and practices are guided by an anomalous problem rather than centered on predefined phenomena or sets of topics. For example, as is well known, psychology emerged as a particular way of accounting for hidden causes for individual behavior and sociology emerged concerned with social integration and control during the emergence of gesellschaft over gemeinschaft social configurations. Psychological and sociological explanations thus joined goal-driven, economic, spiritual, physiological, chemical, and physical ones in providing ways of thinking about and attending to the social and physical world with recipes for conception and response. While psychological and sociological disciplinary status and impact were solidified with the development of academic divisions and defined topical areas, their generative power derived from the way they entered everyday thinking as a way of producing new phenomena of interest and new conceptions of problems (Gergen, 1978). As such, they were used across fields of study including communication. In many senses, they epitomize "modernist" social science, and they have difficulties to the extent that the modern period's conceptions and problems disappear.

Communication explanations could be identified by the 1880s but were clear by the late 1920s with the emergence of social constructionist positions in authors like Heidegger, Wittgenstein, Mead, Whorf, and Dewey. These periods showed the gradual understanding, and resulting social crises, of cultural relativism whereby sociological and psychological explanatory factors were seen as abstractions that could be shown as derived from specific patterns of interaction. The "linguistic turn" in philosophy where language replaced consciousness as the core philosophical problem and the everyday social challenge to grounding cultural difference in a natural order served as the most technical and most immediate evidences of this change. Inherent in these positions is a challenge to any unitary social order. Crisis potential is present in this reconception much as it was with the development of the idea of hidden causes or contrived (mechanical) social structures. The depression, war, and resultant dislocations gave no place for such a fundamental crisis and conditionally reenacted explanations that provided a basis for social control.

The 1960s again produced the conditions for a rearticulation of a communicational view of the world. Both the autonomous person with his or her personal feelings and the social order itself were read as the result of particular power-laden social processes. The presence of particular linguistic distinctions and the conception of communication as a transmission or influence process were seen as social constructions that were used to stop more open social discussion and development. The groups most disadvantaged in these processes, of course, yelled loudest but were not necessarily in a good position to change these insights into a disciplinary way of thinking and acting. Yet the women's, black, student, worker, and antiwar movements reference a moment when public concern shifted from modernist conceptions of entryism, integration, and personal rights of expression within existing codes to a concern with difference, group autonomy, and social questions whose meanings are spoken in *whose* codes (Baudrillard, 1975). The revival of American pragmatism and European writings as varied as those of Bakhtin, Bourdieu, Derrida, Foucault, Habermas, Kristeva, Luhmann, and Lyotard would read these events in deeper terms of representation and communication than was popular before. Today these writings and their interpretations are often loosely held together by the term *cultural studies* but clearly they are theoretically broader than that. The rather macrosociological concerns that make such a term appropriate can also lead us to miss what is at stake—a new look at life as a constitutive communication process.

Barriers to Communication as a Discipline

A number of forces have worked against the development of communication explanations much as religious groups fought the development of psychological explanations at the turn of the last century. Psychological explanations were thought to undermine concepts of autonomy and responsibility essential to dominant religious doctrine. Communication explanations cast adrift the social order with its assumed natural basis for asymmetrical identities and social structure. In the post-1960s period, the prospect of personal identity, knowledge, and social structure giving way to perpetual renegotiation, and redifferentiation, was frightening enough to lead to considerable backlash. Most in our society have accepted the problematic that is core to communication explanation, but different groups, dominant in specific ways, wish more that the problems would go away than wish to deal with them. Dominant groups have tended to continue to advance social science research based in philosophies of social order and control (Henriques, Hallway, Urwin, Venn, & Walkerdine, 1984). Clearly, so-called communication studies has accepted prediction and control as central desires of its theory and research and, up until recently, maintained cozy relations with dominant groups, whether the administrative research tradition in mass media studies, managerialism in organizational studies, assimilation conceptions in intercultural studies, or compliance gaining in interpersonal studies (see Deetz, 1992a, chap. 4, for development; also Hamnett, Porter, Singh, & Kumar, 1984; Peters, 1986).

The reification of life processes together with these control-centered conceptions and research methods made developing communication explanations difficult. Early in this century, positivistic philosophies of science and the hope for certainty led researchers away from disciplinary disputes over alternative modes of explanation to a presumed value-neutral faith in the "reality" of the object and to explanatory reductionism. With these conceptions, the objects produced by psychological or sociological disciplinary practices became treated as independent psychological and sociological objects. These disciplinary practices were also taken on by those doing communication studies. While the more recent ethnographic studies have done so more subtly, many carry the same "realist" legacy. The legendary "elephant" was seen as real and fixed in form with each blind man (discipline) merely having a piece of the puzzle, which they unfortunately generalized to the whole. In such a context, the popularity of interdisciplinary studies is understandable and supports the expressed (though rarely believed) idea that communication studies was really better than the old disciplines. The conception of communication phenomena was as unproblematically assumed as the story's elephant—an object simply there in fixed form simply waiting to be discovered in its fullness. The assumed constancy of the object denied the most basic empirical communication questions: How are objects constituted for a social community and how are different potential interests represented in that process?

Unfortunately, with such conceptions, professed interdisciplinarity became a conceptually confused inclusion of differently produced variables rather than multiple ways of thinking through a problem (see Albert et al.'s, 1986, treatment of problems with both monist and pluralist approaches to theorizing). Members of departments of communication have by default often moved from being topically specialized scholars doing psychological explanations or versions of literary criticism to an interdisciplinary (in this weak sense) field of study focused on isolated topics. Communication studies manifests fully Kelly's (1970) description of the chief epistemological assumption of the behavior sciences as "accumulative fragmentalism." Both professional associations and textbooks divided the field into specialty literatures around topics like mass media, organizations, and interpersonal communication and overlooked the presence of theoretical perspectives that crossed the areas. The appeal of eclecticism and paradigm discussions displayed the academic equivalent of what Geertz (1983) called a sterile exoticism—"cosmopolitan without context" and "parochial without tears."

The praise of shallow interdisciplinarity is often both an excuse for not developing, and a block to developing, communication disciplinary explanations.[4] Interdisciplinary work properly is not antidisciplinary but requires the development of productive disciplines, otherwise interdisciplinary work becomes superficial and uninformed—a mere debate of opinions. Interdisciplinary work promises a problem-centered approach not encumbered by the parochial nature of "disciplines." Unfortunately, the use of the same word, *discipline,* tripped us up. It is not modes of explanation that are parochial but academic departments. What we need is an understanding of disciplines as holistic but complementary (Albert et al., 1986). Disciplines are attempts at explaining a totality: There are not psychological or sociological things; there are things that are constituted by thinking and talking about things psychologically or sociologically. Any world admits of being constituted and explained in any discipline's terms. Complementarity allows us to reconstitute the world in ways that are more or less useful in particular times and places. The choice of a mode of explanation is a situational one based on our problem—a problem a disciplinary way of thinking helped produce. Newtonian physics failed not because it did not help us measure our world (it did and most of us still think in that way daily—and every generation must be taught again of its limitations) but because we wanted to do other things.[5] If we center on problems and remove the limiting quality of academic departments (historically merely an administrative span-of-control issue anyway) and flourish in developing communication explanations for the problems for which it helps, we will get much further (and probably acquire some respect for the academic departments in the process because they won't go away).

While the dialogue and ferment of the past decade gave an opening for new conceptions, the sterility of phenomena-/topical-centered research leaves paradigm dialogue a mere pluralism. Only in dealing with choice making regarding problems in the necessary contingent conditions of social life does the difference of different modes of explanation stand out and make a difference. Mere paradigmatic pluralism makes it impossible to adjudicate conflicting knowledge claims and values because they reference not the common social problem but the incommensurable technical language and procedures of their makers.

Building a *discipline* in the strong sense of the term requires unpacking (inventing/discovering) a "problematization" composed of (a) specifying a way of thinking/acting/talking that leads to a particular type of attending to the world and (b) specifying what is socially problematic in such a world. I will start with a specification of what it is to attend to the world communicationally. This will include initially contrasting an informational view of human interaction explained externally to a communicational view explained internally, displaying how an informational view of human interaction remains dominant in our contemporary world and then more fully developing the conceptual and research agenda of a communication discipline. After this

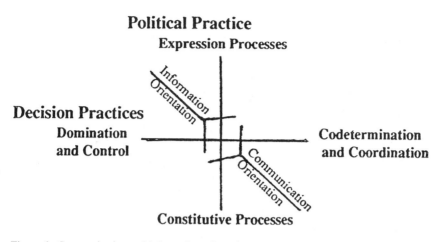

Figure 1. Communication and information orientations.

I will discuss our current set of social problems with reference to communication disciplinary practices.

CONTOURS OF ATTENDING COMMUNICATIONALLY

At issue in the difference between an information and a communication perspective is both what messages do and how joint action is decisionally produced. Many members of communication departments attend psychologically or sociologically to human interaction as an information process.[6] This contrasts with attending communicationally along both a *political practice* and a *decision practice* dimension. The *political practice* dimension is treated here as a conception of the pragmatic force of messages ranging from a focus on *expression processes* to a focus on *constitutive processes*. The *decision practice* dimension is a conception of how difference in a community is handled ranging from a focus on *processes of control and domination* to a focus on *processes of negotiation and codetermination*. See Figure 1.

The first dimension I refer to as *political practice* because it deals with what messages are considered to do in the social world. At one extreme, messages are considered *expressions*. In this conception, messages are to represent something that is absent or make public that which was private. The media of expression themselves are seen as relatively neutral or transparent or at least capable of being made so in an ideal world through definitions or removal of ideology. The expression conception draws attention to interaction primarily in reproductive terms—expression enables reproduction of meanings, perceptions, or feelings that reside independently somewhere else. In the *constitutive* conception, messages are an active part of the production of meaning, perceptions, and feelings. Rather than being neutral or even potentially so, discursive processes of making distinctions, attending to the world in particular ways, or producing an individual identity are active and fundamental. From a constitutive conception, all *expression* is derived from a more fundamental set of discursive practices in which the things that are to be expressed by messages are *constitutively* produced through messages. Informational approaches to interaction study have tended to be guided by a conception of messages as expression, and communication approaches by a conception of messages as *constitutive*.

The second dimension recognizes that differences exist in communities and that these differences are resolved in some way in making collective decisions. Clearly, if there were not such differences and a desire for collective action, a fundamental reason for human interaction would be gone. Whether we consider expression or constitutive practices, the decision practices can be relatively open and participatory or closed and exclusive. Habermas (1979, 1984) provided the most complete modern conception of this difference in his analysis of difference between strategic action aimed at control and communicative action aimed at reaching understanding. The open inclusionary practices will be called political *codetermination* directed by *coordination* and the closed exclusionary ones will be called political *domination* directed by *control*. Informational approaches to interaction study have tended to be guided by the desire to extend control, and communication approaches, to extend codetermination.

The nature of this difference and its consequences become clearer in epitomizing the ideal types in the quadrants provided in Figure 2. To aid identification, I have called dominating (control-directed) expression practices *strategy*; codetermining (coordination-directed) expression practices *involvement*; dominating (control-directed) constitutive practices *consent*; and codetermining (coordination-directed) constitutive practices *participation*.[7] Researchers in departments of communication differ in the extent to which they study strategy, involvement, consent, or participation. Because these dimensions are continua, from an information perspective, we often see direct strategies moving to involvement or consent as they become more complex, and from a communication perspective, we see concern with consent and involvement moving toward participation as they become more complex.

Allow me to sketch the difference between an information and a communication conception of interaction in terms of these dimensions to help specify what is unique about attending communicationally before looking to each in more depth to show why the difference matters. Initially, I believe that we can all agree that a human interaction process is a relation among people in a social community about an inner and outer world making decisions via particular systems of expression for the purposes of collective action. What this means, however, is very different if we take an informational rather than communicational perspective on the interaction.

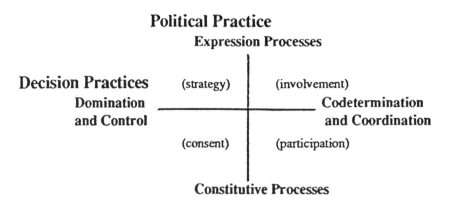

Figure 2. Political decision making.

NOTE: Two-dimensional typifications:

A. *Strategy* (dominant expression) is usually direct and visible, often based on the types of power Weber discussed and often uses rewards, propaganda, coercion, and manipulation for control. Information is knowingly distributed in line with dominant group interests. Control is of motivation, attitudes, and action.

B. *Involvement* (negotiation expression) is seen as based on the better argument, expertise, and ascertaining the better of competing existing positions. Eighteenth-century conceptions of rights, representation, and state political democracy are applied, including marketplace of ideas and freedom of speech. Information is widely distributed though the processes of information formation are rarely explored. Contestation of dominant position is governed by due process and finally voting.

C. *Consent* (dominant constitution) is indirect and often unnoticed through ideological formations, common sense, routines and standard practices, naturalization, and discipline in Foucault's sense. Control is of the grounds or based for action choices. When hegemonic, contestation appears irrational and ill-formed. Information may be widely distributed but its constitution may evidence systematic distortion. Conflict is often suppressed and invisible though evidenced by unfocused resistance.

D. *Participation* (negotiative constitution) is based on giving voice to difference, negotiation of values and decisional premises, and the production of new integrative positions. Contestation of dominant positions is open and is conducted through processes approaching those described by Habermas as the "ideal speech situation." New positions are generated out of the "subject matter" or "otherness" following processes approaching those described by Gadamer as "genuine conversation."

The Informational View Expanded

An "informational" view specifies personal expression as the political practice and specifies control through influence as the decision practice. If we take this view to be the description of human interaction suggested above, we get some interesting specifications. Most basically, expression produces a set of knowledge claims—claims of truthfulness (an adequate report of the inner world), of truth (an adequate report of the outer world), of propriety (an adequate enactment of shared definitions of self, other, and social norms), and of intelligibility (an adequate use of the means of expression; see Habermas, 1984, 1987). A problem with any one of these claims would specify a class of information (though often called "communication") problems.

Such expressions enter collective decision making by means of being directed at others, that is, being transmitted to and understood by (or at least affecting) others. Using this "informational" conception, people on the streets as well as researchers in departments of communication think about human interaction in terms of message expression and transmission. At the most extreme, the interaction process is thought of in terms of the "conduit" metaphor exemplified in figurative extensions of "information theory" (Axley, 1984). Conceptions of feedback, psychological interpretation processes, multiple meanings, and so forth demonstrate the complexity of this process but rarely change the essential problematic. The point of research is to specify factors (and their relations) that affect this expression, transmission, understanding, and influence process. From such a perspective, we can define a set of phenomena worthy of study and areas of meaningful professional intervention but not a mode of explanation, for each of the problems would require an explanation from outside the process (a problem of self-understanding, of proper perception, of socialization, or of linguistic competence).

Certainly, for most of the twentieth century, academic departments of communication have had their conceptions directed by eighteenth-century notions of the autonomous individual (with known self-interests, representational conceptions of language, and free speech) engaging in the attempt to influence others (see Deetz, 1992a, chap. 4; Peters, 1986). While those aiming for autocratic control or liberal democracy may have used these conceptions differently (an issue to be taken up regarding decision practices), most shared this basic conception of individual expression as self-evident and unquestioned. With such assumptions, it is clear why the field would see its modern origins in the practice of journalism and public speaking; why it traces its classical origins to an odd reading of Aristotle's work on rhetoric rather than his works on conversation, ethics, or politics; why psychological explanations have been so widely used; why persuasion and effect studies have filled the journal pages; and why even interpersonal trust is most often studied in regard to compliance gaining.

Informational views of interaction processes with their emphasis on expressionist political practice align well with the concern with control. This is partly because the concern with the fidelity of reproductive processes favors reproducing what dominant groups have produced, partly a result of the control orientation of external explanatory processes, and partly a result of the use of these concepts by those in power seeking to maintain social order (see, for development, Hamnett et al., 1984; Peters, 1986). Therefore information-oriented studies of human interaction tend to quickly be reduced to studies of strategy—something that the Michigan State "school" has presented as the exclusive purpose of communication for years and that is advanced to a complete expression in Beniger (1986) and Berger and Chaffee (1987).

This is not to suggest that there have not been important critiques of the focus on *strategy* from within the informational view. When the control orientation (particularly when practiced by dominant groups) as the decision practice has been challenged, both researchers and everyday people have tended to put emphasis on greater *involvement* most often from a humanist philosophy. Even the development of the call for representational government in the American revolution and the subsequent enactment of the Bill of Rights demonstrate an expressionist conception of messages contextualized by an interest in codetermination. The more recent use of humanistic psychology to respond to the persuasion focus of the field in the 1960s is a parallel case. Many of the contemporary attempts to look at reader/listener/audience interpretive processes are simply more sophisticated ways of assuring that the *decisional practices* involve more meanings, perceptions, and feelings rather than challenging the information viewpoint. The frequent discussions of greater public access to data bases and information systems, for example, fail to have democratic potential if data and information are already constituted in ways favoring dominant group interests.

Ultimately, most of these changes do not even challenge the *control* orientation. They encourage the diffusion of control across more of the population and ultimately count on some invisible hand to take everyone's control attempts and to produce out of them a unified positive collective choice. Neither humanist expressionism (best espoused in interpersonal textbooks and by Phil Donahue) nor an adversarial model (practiced by media issue polarization and the legal profession) fundamentally challenge the basic model. And each will be shown as leaving us less able to deal with contemporary social problems.

Less frequent, but other informational positions have maintained the control orientation but rejected expressionism. This has most often been an implicit rather than explicit move because the explicit attention to constitutive processes would undermine the most basic way that controlling constitutive processes (manufacturing consent) works—proclaiming a constructed order to be a natural order. But the development of things like cultural management programs in business and spin doctors in media suggest that many dominant groups have found that the best way to get their meanings across is to get target audiences to produce them themselves—control constitutive process so that people's thoughts and perceptions "spontaneously" arise rather than using direct influence or expression control.

A Communicational Perspective

A communicational analysis is not just a more sophisticated reformation or critique of an informational perspective. The building of a communicational perspective is rooted in early twentieth-century studies in philosophy and linguistics that showed that the eighteenth-century conceptions of person, perception, language, and politics missed key processes in social life and hampered our ability to solve contemporary social problems. These new conceptions set the ground for the formal beginning of a communication discipline[3] in the 1960s. Both the autonomous subject and the representational view of language were questioned by scholars as varied as Peirce, Heidegger, and

Wittgenstein. In different ways, they showed communication as a constitutive process and reclaimed the central concern with the interaction process as a site of meaning production. From this, they gave rise to a much more fundamental understanding of communication and politics. In terms of representational practices, the influence-centered, informational view that focused on meaning transmission within a code is replaced by a concern with alternative codes and how they constitute different human subjects and meanings. Choices within politically defined contexts shifted to concern with the constitution of political contexts. Concern with effective use of language changed to questions of whose language it was, its social/historical partialities, and means of reclaiming alternative voices.

From a communication standpoint, we would have to say that each of an informational view's presumed autonomous elements—an inner world, outer world, social relations, means of expression—is not only a product of prior communicative processes but requires reproduction (or enactment) to function in any particular context. Whatever stability each has is only by virtue of an appeal to the communicative processes that underlie them. A communication perspective therefore does not move from a person with meanings to their social reproduction but looks at the social production of meaning between individuals. The core political practice then is not perception, meaning, or emotional expression but perception, meaning, and emotion constitution, and the core decision practice is not the influence of messages on others but the question of who participated in what ways in the constitution of meaning. The humanistic psychologist's conception of "meaning is in people" is replaced by the communication question: "Whose meanings are in people?" Each of these elements of interaction can be explained through understanding their relations of production and reproduction (Deetz, 1992a; Giddens, 1984). Communication is about collaborative collective constructions of self, other, and world in the process of making collective decisions (Shotter, 1987). This includes the production and reproduction of personal identities, social knowledge, and social structures (Shotter & Gergen, this volume). As interaction process researchers would argue, communication explains psychological and sociological variables rather than being explained by them (e.g., Watzlawick, Beavin, & Jackson, 1967; and others). From a communication perspective, the political attention is on describing how the inner world, outer world, social relations, and means of expression are reciprocally constituted with the interactional process as its own best explanation. In this sense, if psychological explanations explain individual behavior using goals, reinforcements, needs, and drives, and sociological explanations explain collective action using economic class difference, social structures, and forms of integration, then communication explanations explain political practice by showing how goals, needs, reinforcements, drives, economic class, social structures, and forms of integration are produced and reproduced in interaction.

The attention to decision practice is also different. From an informational perspective, study of decision practices describes how autonomous individuals or groups have influence through advancing their claims with success being explained by reason, psychological or sociological variables, or information controls. From a communicational perspective, the concern with decision practice focuses on who participated in the constitutive practices and whether codetermination took place. Because the questions being determined in decisional practices regard what we will become as people and what kind of world we will live in and because the communication perspective would see any externally based answer to these questions as based in some group's prior construction, the decision practice difference is best conceptualized in moral terms granting all positions an equal right to codetermination.[8]

Theories from a communication perspective thus, like the foundations of information theories, have an intrinsic moral dimension. Morally, psychology pursues reflective autonomy, sociology pursues legitimate social order, and communication pursues equitable participation. Implicitly or explicitly, most Enlightenment modes of explanations, like the psychological and sociological disciplinary practices grounding information studies, were instrumental-technical in character and aimed at furthering control over nature and people based in superior knowing or expertise. This contrasted with pre-Enlightenment explanation that tended to work toward unity with nature, even though what was "natural" was clearly often conceptualized for control purposes. Post-Enlightenment communication explanations break with each of these traditions. They claim no certain foundation whether in method or nature. Rather, life continues to be an open choice. The question is how these choices should be made. The negotiations in social interaction itself, rather than an external universal, provide the only grounding for this choice context. Neither morality nor truth escapes perpetual negotiation; the problem is how to keep this negotiation process open rather than falling to forces outside of it (see Deetz, 1990, 1992a, chap. 6). Open participatory democracy supersedes all other goals of communication. From a communication perspective, efficiency, effectiveness, and information transfer cannot stand alone but are interpreted within the promotion or demise of participation. Communication research thus is about the creation of more participatory communication practices and the critique and/or deconstruction of control processes. Therefore the participative ethics intrinsic to communicative processes provides a preferable foundation to that provided by any dominant group interest (see Apel, 1979; Deetz, 1992a, chap. 6; Habermas, 1984).

Self-critique within the communication perspective like that within the information perspective comes from individuals more concerned with *involvement* or with *consent*. But the logic of these critiques is quite different. Individuals who have focused most heavily on consent tend to emphasize the potential difficulties of supporting liberal democracy, especially its potential for co-optation. The ones focusing more heavily on *involvement* suggest that the loss of respect for individual agency overlooks the positive effects on *participation* of Enlightenment democracy, leads to cynicism and potentially passivity, and cuts researchers off from fundamental values of society, thus reducing their impact (Blumler, 1983; Carey, 1992). The fights over their differences can easily hide what they share; both desire the critique of manufactured consent and greater involvement of diverse social groups in the constitution of society. Allow me to spend a moment on each.

Communication Participation Through Critique of
Consent and Wider Group Involvement

While information studies focus on the expression and distribution of meaning and judge the effectiveness of interaction based on criteria from strategic control (sometimes accomplished through expressionist involvement or manufactured consent), communication studies focuses on *participation* in the social production of the world, people, and meanings. The concern is with both the critique of *consent* and providing more *involvement*. The purpose of the communication discipline properly would be to describe and explain how *consent* and *involvement* operate in political decision practices in providing or limiting *participation*.

Critiquing consent. The critique of consent is a critical issue across topical areas in communication departments and is a key conception in any general theory of communication. Focusing on consent processes displays the manner people often fail to act in what would appear to an outsider (and to themselves in other contexts) to be in their own interests. One of the reasons that family therapy has so widely used communicational explanations is its usefulness of understanding consent in family systems, for example. Family violence is clearly an interpersonal political process but is not usually a control process in any simple way, nor are there simple nonartifactual psychological conditions for it (e.g., low self-esteem is not a thing that explains interaction, it is a produced and reproduced position in interacting, including descriptions of self to a psychologist). Patterns of interaction are not sociological facts, they must be communicationally reproduced across generations and contexts. The continued production and reproduction of individuals and their interpretive processes as *consent* in the violent system is both a compelling explanation and useful guidance for intervention (Harris, Alexander, McNamee, Stanback, & Kang, 1984). Similar examples exist in other areas. Because the various authors writing from a "cultural studies" perspective have written so widely on the process of consent, especially regarding mass media, I will be brief here.

The greatest threat to *participation* does not come in the form of the lack of opportunity for involvement, because that would most likely be directly resisted, but in *consent*. The treatment of consent has followed three quite distinct traditions. Perhaps the most widely used analytic procedure has been ideological critique. Ideological critique was developed by German scholars in the 1920s and 1930s in response to both the failure of Marxian economic analysis to account for new systems of domination and the lack of organized worker resistance, and the capacity of Hitler to use the culture industries to produce consent to national policies through appeals to existing social value premises. The media concern with the way an audience is transformed into a mass is the clearest legacy of this tradition. Such a position continues to have impact on mass media and organizational studies (Deetz, 1992b; McLuskie, 1992). More recently, ideological critique has been greatly enriched and freed from much of its Marxist heritage through Habermas's (1984, 1987) conception of systematically distorted communication, which focuses far more directly on constitutive and regulative communication processes (see Thompson, 1984, 1991). Work of this type is starting to have impact in communication perspectives on medical practices (Turow, 1989), community planning (Forrester, 1989), and the more technical areas like information systems (Lyytinen, 1992).

Partly from the oversimplicity of the early ideological critique writings, many researchers during the past 20 years have found Gramsci's (1971) conception of hegemony more useful in studying consent processes. Hegemony is conceptualized as a complex web of conceptual and material arrangements producing the very fabric of everyday life, the perception of events, the presence of commonsense knowledge, and what is now called conventional wisdom. Smart (1986) conceptualized it well, suggesting that hegemony constitutes a form of social cohesion "most effectively by way of practices, techniques, and methods which infiltrate minds and bodies, cultural practices which cultivate behaviors and beliefs, tastes, desires, and needs as seemingly naturally occurring qualities and properties embodied in the psychic and physical reality (or 'truth') of the subject" (p. 160). Gramsci's interest was in providing a general social theory of domination rather than a theory of communication, but both conceptual and extensive empirical work have been spun out of the synthetic work of Hall (e.g., 1989). The use of the term *hegemony* in the study of mass media and corporate organizations has focused on cultural arrangements and the role of media, education, and intellectuals in providing support for economic and legal conditions. Hegemony suggests the complex process by which domination is transformed into civic cooperation. Generally, we would expect dominance-seeking groups to move from *strategy* to *involvement* if constitutive control processes in the form of hegemony are present. This relation probably accounts for the observation that participation and individual autonomy appear to have increased in interpersonal relations, corporate organizations, and media choice today while processes of control and compliance appear tighter than ever before (see Czarniawska-Joerges, 1988). So-called empowerment and participation plans may in fact most often occur in situations of hegemony. Communication analyses have worked to demonstrate how these complex processes work. The concern is not with the inactivity of the audience, for example, but what it does when it is active. Much of this work has begun to look more like ideological critique as it has become more popular (see Carey, 1992) owing to misunderstanding and the desire by some groups to focus on external factors as explaining these complex coding and translation processes. Without a sophisticated communication theory, concern with processes of *consent* are quickly transformed into concerns with strategy.

Partly because of this, recently more authors have evoked some version of Foucault's (1980) conception of a strategic apparatus. The focus here is on the constitutive micropractices by which the human subject, "knowledge," and collective decisions are momentarily produced. Clearly, these practices are not intentional in any simple sense. The apparatus is composed of linguistic distinctions, institutional arrangements, and various routines. Each of these may be conflictual (rather than harmonious as hegemony would suggest) and put into play for very different reasons, but the outcome is to constitute a particular type of person and social decision and to exclude, deny, or marginalize others. The production of opposition and conflicts would be seen to be as much a part of the consent process as the production of integration and order. The apparatus web requires active complicity by all groups—there is a dialectic of control—but also delimits and limits dominant groups. Communication researchers, in looking at such constitutive processes, are not so much interested in the production of a dominant culture as in the cultural fragmentation and dispersion, micro-control processes, and places of resistance (Deetz, 1992b).

Enhancing involvement. Clearly, as a communication perspective interested in constitutive processes has developed, it has been primarily oppositional in its focus on processes of consent. As Carey (1992) suggests, it has been limited because it has not developed a positive alternative practice that could appeal to a wide spectrum of people (p. 61). Clearly, there are reasons for this. Most writers are cautious about either usual programmatic alternative: greater democracy through an enlightened public or a socially planned utopian ideal. Expressionist involvement is hollow because most domination happens in the constitution of knowledge, perception, and common sense and these become invisible in such a program. Utopian positions, as appealing as they may be, are ultimately simply different control mechanisms by different elites.

The positive alternative—*constitutive codetermination*—as a participatory democracy is still very difficult to work out in either conception or practice. The various critical and postmodern writers who have been so good at critique and deconstruction of dominant formations have provided less on this point. Clearly, silenced and marginalized voices must be recovered before any serious discussion is possible, but the emphasis on redifferentiated expressions of class, gender, sexual preference, and ethnicity becomes meaningless without the hope of a discussion to produce a codetermined future. This requires expanding *involvement* to help produce *participation.* The difficulties of articulating such a position are probably as great as early revolutionary writers found in expressing concepts of liberal expressionist democracy, and with as much opposition from the business, state, and intellectual communities, but also as important. A carefully developed conception of codeterminative constitutive processes based in a communication theory may well be as important to the next century as the conception of free speech and representation based in natural rights of the autonomous individual has been to the past two. Many authors are making attempts through conceptions of "recovery of otherness," "third-culture building," "ideal speech situations," and "genuine conversations" (see Belay, 1993; Casmir, 1993; Deetz, 1990; Shuter, 1993). The theoretical diversity of such positions is useful and points to the possibility of important theoretical debate within a communication perspective.

A Difference That Makes a Difference?

I hope that it is clear that the difference between focusing on the political decision practices in informational terms or in communicational ones is not a mere academic squabble. Without a careful understanding of this difference between expression and constitutive practices and between control and codeterminitive decision practices, human beings lose a clear understanding of how they actively engage in the production of knowledge and the very realities of life, thus hampering their ability to build satisfying systems and institutions. As Boland (1987) described the concern:

> At issue is the nature of language and human communication, and their role in our social construction of the everyday world. The problem that concerns us here is the way our images of information without in-formation [constitutive processes] lead to an ignorance of language and our human search for meaning which together deny the very possibility of human communication. The process of constructing the social world is a process of language and communication. Our distorted images of information and communication, and their widespread use to understand our everyday world, threaten our ability to construct and reconstruct it in humanly satisfying ways. (p. 366)

Communication studies in contrast tends to try to advance *participation* primarily through the critique of consent and enhanced involvement while information studies advances strategy often through manufacturing consent and facilitating expressionist *involvement*. The collapse of communication concerns into information ones by researchers leads them to aid dominating groups (Boland, 1979). Information studies (self-asserted as communication studies) is thus often proclaimed as practical by dominant groups while they are clearly impractical if we consider the full range of people involved and the wide social interests. Codeterminative constitutive processes serve as explanations for psychological, sociological, or economic claims and aim at the reconstruction of the psychology, social structure, and economy of societies. Because constitutive processes always underlie expression processes, much is often missed by those who study only strategy in either its direct or its derived forms. The more heterogeneous the society, the greater the potential significance of that missed and the greater the moral violation by control processes. And yet ordinary citizens and researchers in departments of communication have continued a dominant/dominating tradition, but not without costs.

Certainly one of the reasons the information view could be sustained in a democratic society has been the superficial understanding of contemporary politics as well as of human interaction itself. As suggested earlier, by extending eighteenth-century conceptions of person, perception, and language, which are the basis for information conceptions of interaction, political processes are generally reduced to the expression of self-interests aiming at consensus through producing agreement and/or voting. This is a very weak conception of politics and provides a fundamentally flawed basis for democracy (see Barber, 1984; Deetz, 1992a), including the production of special-interest politics. But, from at least the Greeks to the current time, competing with this view of politics as opinion expression has been a dialectic one that argues that interaction can be a constitutive, codeterminative process giving rise to a truth beyond that previously understood by any participant. In this view, the limitations of self-interest expression and resolution of differing opinions become possible in the communicative community that can exceed individual-centered politics. Thus we have always had two visions of democracy and communication, one centered in the free subject and persuasive potential aiming at reproducing existing meanings and the other centered in the interaction process itself and its constitutive potential aimed at producing particular types of human subjects and new meaning.

Failing to develop the second view leads to constant misrecognitions and a weakened participation in public choice. For example, many corporate organizations have implemented employee empowerment and "participation" programs. Nearly all, however, are information-based involvement rather than communication-based participation plans. The issue is not just the label. Without conceptualizing and analyzing the possibility of a dominant constitutive process (consent), it is impossible to determine whose and what interests the employee is representing (Deetz, 1992b). Lower-level employees may be simply mouthing what upper management would have said (Weick, 1987, for example, argues that confidence that this will happen is prerequisite to all employee involvement programs). Their involvement hides the lack of open participation. The practical and moral difficulties of this omission would seem less in an egalitarian homogeneous society because we might expect an earlier participation that provided an open codetermination of the constitutive consent. But in a heterogeneous society, particularly if there are great social asymmetries, one might well assume that consent is often manufactured or orchestrated through various constitutive processes.

The distinction has equally clear practical significance in other areas. For example, when disadvantaged groups focus on expression in the absence of concern with constitutive processes, they often fail to achieve representation even when they are influential. Feminists have argued this around concepts of "entryism." The employment of a female anchorperson or the personal success of a female corporate manager does not necessarily mean that the interests of women have been advanced, especially if the price for a woman to advance is to think and talk like a man. Or, further, the confusion between a concern with expression processes and constitutive processes was core to the media misrecognition of political correctness issues. By using what I will call *involvement* concepts, they saw PC in terms of issues of free speech and the marketplace of ideas rather than a communicational inclusive versus exclusive set of constitutive processes. The attempt by authors like Stanley Fish to provide a more inclusive participatory constitutive process was read as an exclusionary violation of free speech (Whitney & Wartella, 1992). Given that the U.S. Constitution is based on the same eighteenth-century concepts of representational language and informational interaction as the conceptions used by those concerned with expression processes, it is not surprising that many attempts to foster wider constitutive political participation are ruled constitutional violations. Information-based *involvement* democracy is quite different than communication-based *participatory* democracy (Barber, 1984). Communication professionals have been far less than proactive in bringing democracy in line with contemporary understandings. The professed fear of making the communication process and its study political has hidden the ways it is already political and the real fears of what the public would do if they understood the current politics. This is particularly acute in our current context.

OUR CURRENT SOCIAL PROBLEMATIC

In looking at the formation of a discipline₃, coextensive with the formulation of a way of attending to the world is the constitution of a social problematic. As I have suggested, this is neither a causal relation going from a way of attending to problem conception nor one from problem situation to a way of attending. They historically arise together as a problematization in a competitive environment of alternative attentions and problems. And, as the pragmatists argued, the basic question is not that one is right but what kind of people do we want to become and what kind of world do we wish to live in. We recognize that the world is changing in fundamental ways; the issue of what is problematic is largely a question of how we perceive the changes and which goals we pursue. The communication discipline is part of that debate and we each take a position whether we want to or not.

Rather than entering that debate, much of the field still clutches to a presumed neutral informational view of human interaction. But this has not just been for petty academic gains. It undermines our common purpose and leads to a misrecognition of our situation. There is probably nothing that various groups composing the communication field share more completely than their dedication to the public forum—to create an informed, discerning, articulate public that can negotiate the meaning of events and choose a common future. Our current period of internationalization, respect for cultural diversity, and declining public institutions calls for a position of leadership both appropriate to our sensibilities and of great social purpose. Instead, concerns with such issues are often marginalized by a dominant minority scholarly vision (reproduced in textbooks and by teachers) driven by a 1970-style technological futurism that tried to glorify itself by the proclamation of an "information age" over an age of service and negotiation, which focused on office automation and control systems over workplace diversity and employee participation and valued codified expertise over collective decision making. Many of us see a vision of social contribution to solving the dominant problems of our time, a vision of the cultivation of taste, critical judgment, and reclaimed public choice.

In my view, the focus on communication as a "constitutive, explanatory" process will continue to be fueled by four interrelated emerging social understandings that are experienced as a problem on the way to a future (see, for complementary development, Berman, 1982; Crook, Pakulski, & Waters, 1992; Featherstone, 1988). At root, contemporary Western society has lost its four foundations or centers: (a) the unitary-autonomous person, (b) an integrative social order, (c) an objective external world, and (d) a progress-driven cybernetic. We can either try to recover these foundations as those with vested interests do or we can embrace a new way of living without foundations. Modernist disciplines have each tried to recover the foundation in their realm: psychology with a centered-adjusted individual, sociology with a legitimate social order, analytic philosophy with a scientific method, and economics with market rationality (see Ramos, 1981). Communication, as the first discipline after modernity, seeks to aid the codetermination process in a world without centers, a world that happily survives with perpetual negotiation of the various bases for identity, social order, knowledge, and policy.

Identity Negotiation

In a traditional world, identity was a relatively simple thing, because the life narratives were simple and the situated person was subject-ed (and sub-jected) with minimal role conflict. In primary institutional processes (family and community), one came to reproduce the principal scripts that would order the world and self for life. It is simple to see that mobility, occupational change, cross-cultural contact, and so forth would make changing identities, role conflict, and role negotiation a way of life for modern people. As is clear from many literatures, the human subject is subject to so many discourses that personal fragmentation (Gergen, 1991; Gergen & Davis, 1986) and loss of self (Berger, Berger, & Kellner, 1973) is a way of life. What it is to be authentic or truthful in expression of an inner world is increasingly problematic as everyday people feel, which is also developed in the literature, that even the most basic feelings of the insides are arbitrary social constructions (Harré, 1986; Hochschild, 1983). Lifelong learning is not just for occupational role changes but to stay a viable human being. To accomplish this, secondary institutional processes have often replaced primary ones (e.g., therapist over friends, school over parents). Informational approaches in the field confronted the problematic either as increased *involvement* emphasizing authenticity and self-expressionism (the *Donahue* show), through increased *strategy* emphasizing image construction and impression management, or as increased *consent* through cultural management. But these approaches create a limited social sphere (Habermas, 1975, 1984) and support an increasingly colonized world (Deetz, 1992a). Communication analysis would emphasize progressive self-differentiation, self-redifferentiation, and identity negotiation as an ongoing process in all interaction. The conception of "process subjectivity" invites a responsive self, living the many me's in a dynamic relation with others (Epstein, 1988; Weedon, 1987). Gergen's (1991) conception of "multiphrenia" and Bakhtin's conception of "heteroglossia" have both been productively used to develop such a conception of identity for communication study.

Social Order Negotiation

We have long talked about the melting pot and many today seem to lament that the pot has cracked. A liberal social order and its tolerances were essential to the development of modern states, but no one ever doubted the integrative and colonizing forces that came with them. While differences were marginalized and suppressed, they were not eliminated. With the worldwide women's movement, internationalization of media and business interests, and decline of the state, pluralism as a world movement is a force to be taken as seriously as colonization (Barber, 1992). Multiculturalism is not merely a longing of the left; it will not go away. Power is likely to be shared in the future and everyone will probably work with and certainly have to deal with people who are culturally different. The integrative approach to life—"we may be multiracial but we will not be multicultural," or "I don't care what you are, you can succeed as long as you are like me"—approach to affirmative action and diversity training will probably not work even if we wanted it to. The informational approach to intercultural communication was always integrative-cultural control. Whether we like it or not, human interaction (whether between men and women or other social groupings) will only rarely work from an assumption of shared values and consensus on meaning construction; interaction will more often have to produce these for the purposes at hand.

"Not getting it" is the beginning of mutual enrichment, not simply a reason to recognize important differences. Neither organizations nor governments are likely to be assumed to be legitimate; legitimacy will be a constant production. And, further, we will come to find that the preservation of difference and the finding of means for difference to be retained are as essential to communication and social order as integration and finding a common ground.

Knowledge Negotiation

Gradually public understanding has come to accept what scholars have known for some time: Objectivity was oversold for the sake of prestige for clusters of elite researchers, journalists, teachers, and owners of knowledge. There are not facts, only artifacts produced from political social processes. In addition, mediated experience (via any number of technologies and storytellers) will increasingly exceed any "direct" sensory experience. The combination of the two assure that the social negotiation of knowledge claims and experience itself will have to follow lines in which the appeal to an "objective" outside will be seen as a particular rhetorical ploy (Simon, 1991). This change is not complete and should not be misunderstood.

First, clearly, there are questions that admit of empirical answers and it would be silly to argue about them without making observations. But let's be clear about what this means. The question of socially "what something is" is as empirical as the question of "how many are there" (see Deetz, 1992a, chap. 3). And, further, the process of counting presupposes an active communication process by which a value-laden discourse is constructed with sufficient nonempirically based agreement that we can constitute objects in the same way (Apel, 1972, 1979). Objectivity is an issue of a shared discourse, not of nature's preference for certain descriptions (see Rorty, 1979, 1989, for development). Clearly, this is why accounting theorists are all seeming to become communication theorists (see Arrington & Puxty, 1991; Power & Laughlin, 1992, or any issue of *Accounting, Organizations and Society*). They seem to do better communication theory than members of departments of communication. They have to; accounting matters while most of our studies have not.

Second, the public really wants to believe in an independent reality. The general appreciation of an antirhetoric rhetoric (Ross Perot), the fascination with amateur video shows, docudrama, and reporterless-style news are all genuine attempts to get behind the social construction. But they cannot. Nobody can. The combination of a belief in *a* "reality" *and* cynicism is disastrous for a democracy. The belief that all claims are merely opinions is used to stop discussions rather than start them (Deetz, 1992a, chap. 7). The public is in as bad a place as "representational" researchers. Having only objectivity and relativism available to them, they fail to understand negotiation and codetermination (Bernstein, 1984, 1992). Only discussion can give a truth because the physical world cannot.

Third, the modern university and the scholarly community have the most to lose by this change if they do not reform themselves. The university sold itself as a way to get information to an information-poor society. But, while students may lack basic skills, they are not information poor. If anything, they are saturated (Gergen, 1991). There is rarely an important topic covered in a communication department that has not already been exhaustively covered in newspapers, magazines, films, and on television. Both media and other corporate organizations are faster and better resourced than universities. If it is important, it is exhausted before we can gear up to do it. Doing adminis-trative-style research may get some grant money, but usually it is its "objec-tivity" as a rhetorical move that is bought because other institutions could do the work of data collection faster and better themselves. Codified knowledge as information becomes an increasingly irrelevant myth no matter how many textbooks we sell. The Enlightenment university is too slow for the contem-porary world. Education as information giving is dead and students know it. The issue of learning is not the codified but the process of codification. Concepts cannot simply name abstract variables, they must be windows on the world. The university needs to enrich the natural vocabulary so that complexity can be understood and codetermination made possible, things that are against the control interest of other institutions.

The decline of foundational thinking will only continue. Constitutive processes are becoming more central in the work world. Virtual reality is upon us and not only as a technological feat. As work becomes more service and "knowledge" centered, it becomes increasingly difficult to base judgments on objects; corporate image construction far exceeds substance as a concern; and the construction of personal identity is core to the modern corporation. Mass media will continue to be a primary constructor of knowledge, emo-tions, and events of the world, even if in the guise of faceless news. Even in information systems, control processes are clearly becoming more dependent on the construction of the information artifact and less on its distribution (Zmud, 1990). If the field were to do nothing other than help the society understand the communicative constitution of knowledge, we would perform a major function.

Policy Negotiation

In traditional societies, policies were rare because dominant values and people served alongside nature as cybernetic centers directing the system along some course toward a future. With the development of the state and organizational complexity, explicitly formulated policies were central to social planning. As Beniger (1986) rightly points out, organizational com-plexity gave rise to the policy center and information control mechanisms of today. As more new technologies are available and pluralism increases, we will have more difference of position and less voluntary compliance along the line of dominant values, hence the need for explicit policy debate will become greater. Any policy decision in the contemporary context, because it is arbitrary and seen as such, requires the explicit building of consensus. Even values widely assumed to be shared such as consumerism and progrowth attitudes are likely to be more fully questioned as ecological crises become greater and more parts of the world expect equality. We would expect not only a greater number of positions on each social problem but also a greater number of differences in the definition of what is a problem. In this situation, it is not surprising that many tried to depoliticize these issues through deregulation and a hope for a marketplace solution. Dollar (yen, mark) voting appeared preferable to policy debate. Clearly, the marketplace solution failed miserably in many regards (Barlett & Steele, 1992; Schmookler, 1992). More information will not settle the debates, for the issue is one of meaning, not admitting of artifactual solutions. Social and political policies related to communication increasingly will have to consider the process of meaning construction rather than systems of expression and transmission.

RESEARCH FROM A COMMUNICATION PERSPECTIVE

The development of a communication perspective requires a reconsideration of the research process itself. Most "empiricist" and "neopositivist" research processes like the informational perspective in communication studies are based on eighteenth-century philosophical treatments of language and perception. Further, modern ethnography has to see itself as a cultural artifact of nineteenth-century European conceptions of mentalistic interpretive processes even as it attempts to display other cultures in their own terms. Both are directed by a psychologically based representational philosophy attempting to mirror independently existing fully constituted objects or unifiable internal states. Conceptions of operationalization, "objectivity," and lawlike relations are merely the most obvious implications of the continuation of this perspective. While most contemporary researchers have given up faith in the foundations required for these methods, many still practiced them either through a conception of methodological determinism or blind conventionalism. The continued grounding of these practices and alternative choices in psychological/informational rather than communication disciplinary conceptions leads to the continuation of irrelevant fights over the relative objectivity or subjectivity of studies and the misunderstanding of recent research methods (see Apel, 1972; Bernstein, 1984). Allow me first to take a look at the unproductive subjective/objective discussion and then develop a communication-based set of distinctions among different research programs.

The Subjective-Objective Problem

Most information-centered studies looking at communication as a phenomenon assume a basic psychological distinction between an interior and an exterior world. Phenomena can be either interior or exterior. And the research process is seen as directed by either the interior (thus subjective) or the exterior (thus objective). Codified, and often quantified, studies get the privileged objective label because they are a double (both method and phenomenon) exterior. But the labeling and conception are easily shown to be misleading. Even "neutral" research classificatory devices like Burrell and Morgan's (1979) often perpetuate the problems. First, most of the communication-based approaches to communication studies rely on philosophical foundations that explicitly deny the subject-object (interior-exterior) split through different concepts of language and experience and through demonstrating the abstract and politically motivated conception of the difference. Without a metaphysical separation between subjects and objects, the whole meaning of objectivity and subjectivity is gone. The subjective-objective conception thus, rather than describing a meaningful difference, reproduces a neopositivist's philosophy of science view of the world and obscures the nature of other research programs. While few claim to be positivists anymore (given 50 years of critique), the inability to give up the subject-object split (even given 100 years of critique) leaves most researchers still practicing a kind of neopositivism. These researchers have been described as functionalists, covering law theorists, or simply practicing the variable analytic tradition. I describe such researchers as "normative" to emphasize the centrality of codification and the search for regularity (see Deetz, 1973).

Further, even if we retain a subjective-objective conception though stripped of neopositivists' conceptions, it is precisely normative practices that Husserl and others have shown to be the most "subjective" because their concepts and methods are held a priori, are unknown projections of their own way of encountering the world, constitute the world as observed, and are not subject to the "objection" of possible alternatively constituted worlds (see Deetz, 1973, 1982, for development). Probabilistic and lawlike claims are artifacts of a particular peer group-shared language game or set of constitutive activities. Questions of which problems to research, relevancy, and translation back to the subject's world have always posed constitutive and value-laden issues at the very heart of any normative research that intends to have a social effect (Gergen, 1978). And, further yet, the control orientation of this group can be seen as a thrusting of their group's desires over and against an existing outside. In both respects, in practice, so-called interpretivists and others often labeled as subjective have the better claim to objectivity through the way they allow alternative language games and the possibility of alternative constructions denying both normative conceptions and preferred methods.

The retention of the conception of subject-object separation has led to the continuation of rather silly conflicts and equally silly presumed relations between so-called qualitative and quantitative research. Normative researchers often reduce the difference to different ways to collect data and thereby retain the dream of triangularization. This of course hides the real conflict. More important than data collection techniques are the questions asked and the intent of analysis. At root, what the research is trying to do is different. The modes of analysis do not work from different points of view on the same thing; they are looking at different things for different reasons. The qualitative-quantitative difference could be retained if normative researchers saw their produced objects as objects of a constant external world and interpretivists saw their objects as socially constructed, but in neither case does the private-subjective experience of one or the other influence more strongly. Both kinds of objects are socially shared, historically produced, and general to a social group. Because both can accept objects as constituted as given (as in any "realist" description) rather then explore their constitution, positivist conceptions and assumptions are not unique to normative researchers but are often present for interpretivists also.

Alternatives From a Communication Perspective

Starting from a communication rather than a psychologically based informational perspective fundamentally changes the dimensions of contrast among different research programs. I will suggest two dimensions of contrast. The first dimension focuses on the origin of concepts and problem statements as part of the constitutive process in research. Differences among research perspectives can be shown by contrasting "situated/emergent" conceptions with "a priori/elite" ones. The second dimension focuses on whether the conceptions and research practices aim at a coherent representation or the display of difference. These differences among research perspectives can be shown by contrasting "consensus" and "dissensus" seeking. The two dimensions together attempt to show what is communicationally negotiable and not in research practice, how communication representations are organized, and the anticipated political outcome of the research activity (whether or not that usually happens). Figure 3 pictorially represents these dimensions and possible typifications. Again I see these dimensions as analytic ideal types mapping out two distinct continua. The typifications do not name a coherent quadrant but a position loading heavily on an end of both dimensions.

Situated/emergent-a priori/elite. Focusing on the origin of concepts and problems using a dimension of "situated/emergent-a priori/elite" allows three advantages. First, it acknowledges linguistic/social constructivism in all research positions and directs attention to whose concepts are used in object production and determination of what is problematic (see Deetz, 1973). Thus

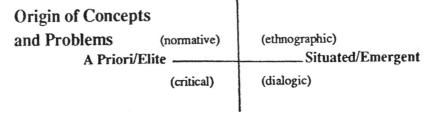

Figure 3. Types of research from the metatheory of representational practices.

NOTE: Two-dimensional typifications:

A. *Normative descriptive and experimental studies.* Goal: To display probabilistic and lawlike relations among produced but presumed real objects of the world.

B. *Ethnographic studies.* Goal: To display unified, consensual culture. To show how particular realities are socially produced and maintained through norms, rituals, and so on. Method: Ethnography.

C. *Critical studies.* Goal: To demonstrate and critique forms of domination and asymmetry. To show how reality can become systematically distorted and to produce opposition to domination therein. Method: Ideological critique.

D. *Dialogic studies.* Goal: To reclaim conflicts suppressed in everyday life realities. To show the partiality (the incompleteness and one sidedness) of reality and the hidden points of resistance and complexity. To negotiate mutually enriching language and conceptions. Method: Deconstruction and participatory research.

two possible extreme research positions would be (a), on the a priori-elite side, the test of a theoretically derived claim through a forced choice instrument and (b), on the situated-local side, a participatory ethnographic rearticulation of the multiple voices of a native culture. It would be difficult to say which is more objective, but they are different in a way that makes a difference. One research program starts with a set of concepts and applies them to the world; the other hermeneutically works to develop conceptions that display the site community's concepts in a way that makes them available to other cultures—a monological versus dialogical approach. With this difference, it is clear why ethnographers are spending so much time working on the role of the researcher these days. The traditional "realist" tale had a strong functionalist/normative bent that limited the potential of ethnographic research. Often either the research community or site community's conceptions were accepted a priori, hence the research oscillated between two privileges rather than retaining the distanciation necessary for productive (rather than reproductive) hermeneutic third-realm understanding.

Second, the focus on the origin of concepts lends clarity to the distinction between two very different kinds of knowledge. A priori-elite conceptions lead to the development of "theoretical codified" knowledge, a kind of book knowledge. Situated-emergent conceptions lead to the development of "practical" knowledge, a kind of street wisdom. This is the type of reformation in research that the pragmatists had in mind. As they argued, a vocabulary is a kind of resting place, a momentary dropping out of life. A basic point of research is to enrich the natural language, to give new and more interesting ways of thinking and talking about things (Rorty, 1979).

Third, reconceptualizing this dimension allows us to more easily see that both the application and the discovery of concepts can demonstrate implicit or explicit political alliances with different groups in society. In light of the participatory ideal, the understanding of political alliance is central to a communication understanding of research. For example, to the extent that organizational researchers' concepts align with managerial conceptions and problem statements (or mass communication with media industries) and are applied a priori in studies, the knowledge claims are intrinsically biased toward certain interests as they are applied within the site community. The knowledge claims become part of the same process that is being studied, reproducing both worldviews (and their appearance as person-world production) and these interests. And the sometime ethnographic fascination with the margins of white, middle-class society demonstrates a quite different political stance intrinsic to the methods of research. In either case, the declaration of objectivity and realism only heightens the effect and buries the political issue deeper. It becomes a constitutive political process rather than just an influence or expression one.

Consensus-dissensus. The "consensus-dissensus" dimension is similar to the "regulation-radical change" dimension of Burrell and Morgan (1979) and popular with sociologists. I will discuss the dimension here as communicational "consensus or dissensus" producing. Following the conception of communication used here, *consensus* or *dissensus* should not be understood as agreement and disagreement but as presentation of unity or of difference.

The difference in orientation displayed by this dimension is often demonstrated in the theory of language accepted by the researcher. Representational consensus seekers emphasize the need for definitions and see the primary function of words as naming a concept or category of things already in the world. Following from this, they seek to produce theories that "mirror" relations that are presumed to exist in the world (see Rorty, 1979). Consensus approaches seek generalizations and ground their validity in representational accuracy regarding a population. Dissensus approaches see words in a Heideggarian sense of striking a difference, thus producing a distinction in the world introducing the possible subsequent categorization in a derivative sense. Dissensus seekers pursue insight and look for analytic differences that were not seen before. The "mirror" gives way to the "lens" as the metaphor noting the shifting analytic attempt to see what could not be seen before. The existence of one, of the possibility that was not seen, rather than probability of things already constructed, is of primary interest. For dissensus, the generative capacity (the ability to challenge guiding assumptions and values) of an observation is more important than representational validity (see Gergen,

1978; Rorty, 1989). For example, consensus orientations in cultural studies seek to discover the organizational culture or cultures. Dissensus orientations show the fragmentation inherent in any claim of culture and the work required for site subjects to maintain coherence as well as subjects' own forms of resistance. Consensus orientations tend to seek role and identity classifications to relate to other variables; dissensus orientations see identity as multiple, conflictual, and in process.

While these differences can be characterized clearly in abstraction, in continuous time, every consensus arises out of and falls to dissensus, and every dissensus gives away to emerging (if temporary) consensus. The issue is not the ultimate outcome desired or likely but which part of this flow through time is claimed in the research process. For example, while critical theorists clearly seek a social consensus that is more rational, their research tries to produce this through the creation of dissensus in place of a dominant order. Ideological critique in the negative dialectic is to reclaim conflict and destroy a false order rather than produce a new one. Thus I place them on the dissensus end. Critical theories differ from many postmodern positions primarily in whether dissensus is produced by the use of elite understandings and procedures (as in Habermas, 1984, 1987) or in a deconstructive process whereby elite conceptions are unmasked to allow the elements to overcome existing conceptions of them within particular sites (Laclau & Mouffe, 1985). The dialogical outcome requires a constant dedifferentiation and redifferentiation for the sake of demythologizing and enriching natural language and the most basic and certain experiences of everyday life.

Information and Communication Orientations in Research

The difference between information-based, externally explained studies and communication-based, intrinsically explained studies can be mapped here again. The control and reproductive character of information studies lends it well to the fixity and elitism of normative studies with a connection to dominant configurations. The productive and codeterminative qualities of communication studies lend it to dialogical conceptions. It is of little surprise that people aligned here have been the most concerned about the development of communication explanations or that critical theorists have moved in this direction as they have taken the "linguistic turn" more seriously.

Like before, the interest is not just in the overall contrast but also in the way the orientation directs movement. (See Figure 4.) Researchers with an informational orientation have moved to more interpretive and critical studies but they have carried with them a more basic normative orientation. For example, interpretivists from this perspective may privilege the concepts of the native culture over emergent conceptions or may hold on to normative conditions of validation and representation as seen in things like "grounded theory." An information-based critical theory may limit critical theory to a

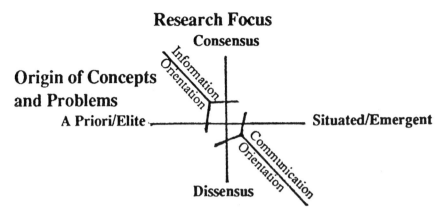

Figure 4. Types of research from information and communication perspective.

rationalist philosophy concerned principally with information distribution and reaching agreement.

The communication perspective fits comfortably in the dialogical sector focusing on a participatory research practice working with emergent conceptions and fostering diversity. As it reconstitutes the interpretivists, the concern is with seeing unified culture but to always see it in the context of suppression of difference and as temporary. As it reforms critical theory, it displays the need for a set of analytic moves to free any research program from conceptual blinders but struggles to avoid the elitism often connected with that.

Finally, does this suggest that a communication perspective is opposed to quantitative research? No, not at all. While an informational orientation and the quantitative research programs connected to it oppose a communication orientation because their assumptions must deny the constitution process, the relation is not reciprocal. Rather than denying information transfer or quantitative research, communication orientation shows them to be derived from more fundamental communication processes but quite appropriate within contexts. The move to quantification from a communication perspective is quite different than quantification from an information perspective.

In communication-based studies, quantitative analysis is a situated slice of the total research process arising out of and returning to constitutive processes. Unfortunately, these processes are either dismissed or treated sloppily by those who currently take this slice as the whole science (see Berger & Chaffee, 1987). Clearly, from a communication perspective, every language, set of concepts, or set of variables are a temporary resting place in the process of reconstitution. As Hall (1981) argued, "Almost every fixed inventory will betray us" (p. 235). Codification, quantification, and information arise out of constitutive communication processes, and quantitative research is possible only so long as we have agreement on processes of phenomenon constitution. But agreement is a consent process implementing the values of a particular peer group. Such agreements have no right to privilege but are assertions in larger codeterminative conversations. Attempts to claim such assertions as autonomous, universal, or objective hamper this codeterminative conversation. They are artifacts and as such they can be useful. The trouble arises in trying to make them more than that. There are interesting questions that are answered through normative-style research, especially if conducted with a communication understanding, but they always arise out of and must return to a communication context.

CONCLUSION

Communication studies for years have missed language-based control politics by pursuing neutral information studies. Studies have focused on compliance gaining, possession, and distribution of information, presentation skills, and decisional influence. Because their conception of communication was shallow and control oriented, they generally did not understand how these practices worked against interest representation and rationality, either in explicit influence processes or in more basic constitutive processes. Communication-based analyses can aid the understanding of these practices by making clearer the link between different social groups' representation and the fulfillment of the various outcomes. Psychological, economic, and sociological explanations tend to externalize the sources of power relations and hide the microprocesses of the actual exercise of power. By using a communication-based analysis, more can be understood. The intent is not to make communication studies value-laden but to recognize that it already is. It is political; let us make it a good politics. Morally and practically, we must expand the capacity to represent a wider segment of society and their values. If our loss of centers is not to lead to increased fragmentation, a new politics of control, or greater physical and symbolic violence, we must take seriously the issues of participation developed in a systematic and complete theory of communication.

NOTES

1. Thanks to Larry Fry for this expression.

2. Other social science disciplines began with a mode of explanation that led to departmentalization, teaching positions, and professions. As we began the other way around, our conceptions have often been less sophisticated and our theories and models have been more often pedagogical devices than research positions. Additionally, this situation led to our preoccupation with defining the phenomenon of communication for the sake of defining the field in contrast to others. The unique phenomenon was both the easiest and the most superficial difference and was

used to justify existing departments and research programs rather than articulate a way of thinking that would found them.

3. Such theorists in some areas may even be dominant, but the dominance is thin. While cultural studies is accepted and practiced in our pluralism, generally it is treated as one more approach to communication phenomena rather than as a challenge to our way of thinking about human interaction. Nor do I wish to suggest that communication merely followed other fields as Burgoon (1992) recently suggested (I assume the essay was more tongue in cheek than serious, however). In the late 1960s, some communication researchers were as quick as members in other departments to grasp the renewed significance of the communication-centered work of the pragmatists and the importance of the new communication-based theories in Europe. In fact, I suspect the data would suggest almost equal proportions of members of English, sociology, psychology, and communication departments taking these issues seriously. We have overlooked many of our best theoretical contributions. Pearce (1989), for example, developed a communication-based theory of interpersonal interaction that is widely used by psychologists, while most interpersonal communication researchers continue to do psychological studies and cite psychologists.

4. In suggesting a distinct communication perspective, I understand that I may be accused of committing the sin of being exclusionary. I hope it is understood that I really don't care whether most people in communication departments do communication or psychological explanations or that psychologists now often do communication explanations. But when the desire to make sure everyone feels at home means that we cannot conceptualize a new mode of explanation, the real exclusion is of a way of thinking that is central to the social community. No one in the field loses by naming it "communication." Additionally, to specify a communication mode of explanation doesn't suggest a particular theory. There are probably as many theories using communication explanations as there are using psychological ones. Showing what they share can foster new differentiations and theoretical pluralism.

Further, the field is currently not without its more subtle but effective exclusions. For example, interaction process theories went out of fashion in the research side of the field, not because they were false or weak but because they did not generate what had come to be defined as "research" for places like *HCR*. Many of the theoretical and research contributions of these theories continue to be very valuable in family therapy and interpersonal textbooks, but you cannot publish the case study-style of research in the journals of the communication field. In fact, the only line of research published from this perspective violated all the interactional process theoretical provisions—that is, Millar and Rogers. Such practices of exclusion have lead *HCR* to be probably the least useful and respected SCA or ICA journal to the majority of the field.

5. I am not going to suggest that what I will call an informational orientation has not done interesting things for us, or psychological explanations for that matter—simply that today our problems are more usefully approached from a different perspective.

6. Of course, Carey (1975, 1989) has provided an excellent discussion of the difference between an informational and a cultural perspective. His "ritual" conception is quite different than a "constitutive" conception and I will not try to compare and contrast them here. The differences between an informational and communication perspective have long historical roots in the influence and participation differences in Greek thought. It is an essential tension that each generation and group will have to reestablish in light of their situation.

7. Terminology is very difficult around these issues. For example, if I read him right, de Certeau (1984) describes what I have called *strategy* as *tactics*, and what I have called *consent* he names *strategy*. The trick is to find terms that can be stripped of some of their baggage and still help attend to the difference of note. The chosen ones would appear adequately sensitizing to accomplish that.

8. While the moral preference for codetermination is intrinsic to communication practice and the social community, control processes are not always illegitimate. Crises and short time frames can lead people to openly subordinate themselves for the possible short-term efficiencies; for example, even democratic people in the state political practice accept special conditions in time

of war. But, as every democratic people also know, constant crisis and increasingly shortened time frames are usually produced strategically and make a mockery of democracy. Control is always a choice and not an inevitable part of the modern world.

REFERENCES

Albert, M., Cagan, L., Chomsky, N., Hahnel, R., King, M., Sargent, L., & Sklar, H. (1986). *Liberating theory.* Boston: South End.

Apel, K. (1972). The a priori of communication and the foundation of the humanities. *Man and World, 5,* 3-37.

Apel, K. (1979). *Toward a transformation of philosophy* (G. Adey & D. Frisby, Trans.). London: Routledge & Kegan Paul.

Arrington, C., & Puxty, A. (1991). Accounting, interests, and rationality: A communicative relation. *Critical Perspectives on Accounting, 11,* 415-436.

Axley, S. (1984). Managerial and organizational communication in terms of the conduit metaphor. *Academy of Management Review, 9,* 428-437.

Barber, B. (1984). *Strong democracy.* Berkeley: University of California Press.

Barber, B. (1992). Jihad vs. McWorld: How the world is both falling apart and coming together—and what it means for democracy. *The Atlantic, 269,* 53-65.

Barlett, D., & Steele, J. (1992). *America: What went wrong?* Kansas City: Andrews and McMeel.

Baudrillard, J. (1975). *The mirror of production* (M. Poster, Trans.). St. Louis: Telos

Belay, G. (1993). Toward a paradigm shift for intercultural and international communication: New research directions. In S. Deetz (Ed.), *Communication yearbook 16* (pp. 437-459). Newbury Park, CA: Sage.

Beniger, J. (1986). *The control revolution.* Cambridge, MA: Harvard University Press.

Berger, P., Berger, B., & Kellner, H. (1973). *The homeless mind: Modernization and consciousness.* New York: Random House.

Berger, C., & Chaffee, S. (Eds.). (1987). *Handbook of communicative science.* Newbury Park, CA: Sage.

Berman, M. (1982). *All that is solid melts into air.* New York: Simon & Schuster.

Bernstein, R. (1984). *Beyond objectivism and relativism.* Philadelphia: University of Pennsylvania Press.

Bernstein, R. (1992). *The new constellation: The ethical-political horizons of modernity/postmodernity.* Philadelphia: University of Pennsylvania Press.

Blumler, J. (1983). Communication and democracy: The crises beyond and the ferment within. *Journal of Communication, 33,* 166-173.

Boland, R. (1979). Control, causality and information system requirements. *Accounting, Organizations and Society, 4,* 259-272.

Boland, R. (1987). The in-formation of information systems. In R. Boland & R. Hirschheim (Eds.), *Critical issues in information systems research* (pp. 363-379). New York: John Wiley.

Burgoon, M. (1992). PC at last! PC at last! Thank God Almighty, we are PC at last! *Journal of Communication, 42,* 95-104.

Burrell, G., & Morgan, G. (1979). *Sociological paradigms and organizational analysis.* London: Heinemann.

Carey, J. (1975). A cultural approach to communication. *Communication, 2,* 1-22.

Carey, J. (1989). *Communication as culture.* Boston: Unwin and Hyman.

Carey, J. (1992). Political studies and cultural studies. *Journal of Communication, 42,* 56-72.

Casmir, F. (1993). Third culture building. In S. Deetz (Ed.), *Communication yearbook 16* (pp. 407-428). Newbury Park, CA: Sage.

Certeau, M. de. (1984). *The practice of everyday life.* Berkeley: University of California Press.

Coleman, J. S. (1980). The structure of society and the nature of social research. *Knowledge: Creation, Diffusion, Utilization, 1*, 332-350.

Crook, S., Pakulski, J., & Waters, M. (1992). *Postmodernization: Change in advanced society.* Newbury Park, CA: Sage.

Czarniawska-Joerges, B. (1988). *Ideological control in nonideological organizations.* New York: Praeger.

Deetz, S. (1973). An understanding of science and a hermeneutic science of understanding. *Journal of Communication, 23*, 139-159.

Deetz, S. (1982). Critical-interpretive research in organizational communication. *Western Journal of Speech Communication, 46*, 131-149.

Deetz, S. (1990). Reclaiming the subject matter as a guide to mutual understanding: Effectiveness and ethics in interpersonal interaction. *Communication Quarterly, 38*, 226-243.

Deetz, S. (1992a). *Democracy in the age of corporate colonization: Developments in communication and the politics of everyday life.* Albany: State University of New York Press.

Deetz, S. (1992b). Disciplinary power in the modern corporation: Discursive practice and conflict suppression. In M. Alvesson & H. Willmott (Eds.), *Critical management studies* (pp. 21-52). London: Sage.

Epstein, C. (1988). *Deceptive distinctions.* New Haven, CT: Yale University Press.

Featherstone, M. (Ed.). (1988). *Postmodernism.* Newbury Park, CA: Sage.

Forrester, J. (1989). *Planning in the face of power.* Berkeley: University of California Press.

Foucault, M. (1980). *The history of sexuality* (R. Hurley, Trans.). New York: Vintage.

Gallie, D. (1955-1956). Essentially contested terms. *Proceedings of the Aristotelian Society, 56*, 167-198.

Geertz, C. (1983). *Local knowledge: Further essays in interpretive anthropology.* New York: Basic Books.

Gergen, K. (1978). Toward generative theory. *Journal of Personality and Social Psychology, 31*, 1344-1360.

Gergen, K. (1991). *The saturated self: Dilemmas of identity in contemporary life.* New York: Basic Books.

Gergen, K., & Davis, K. (Eds.). (1986). *The social construction of the person.* New York: Springer-Verlag.

Giddens, A. (1984). *The constitution of society.* Berkeley: University of California Press.

Gramsci, A. (1971). *Selections from the prison notebooks* (Q. Hoare & G. N. Smith, Trans.). New York: International.

Habermas, J. (1975). *Legitimation crisis* (T. McCarthy, Trans.). Boston: Beacon.

Habermas, J. (1979). *Communication and the evolution of society* (T. McCarthy, Trans.). Boston: Beacon.

Habermas, J. (1984). *The theory of communicative action: Vol. 1. Reason and the rationalization of society* (T. McCarthy, Trans.). Boston: Beacon.

Habermas, J. (1987). *The theory of communicative action: Vol. 2. Lifeworld and system* (T. McCarthy, Trans.). Boston: Beacon.

Hall, S. (1981). Notes on deconstructing "the popular." In R. Smith (Ed.), *People's history and socialist theory* (pp. 227-240). London: Routledge & Kegan Paul.

Hall, S. (1989). Ideology and communication theory. In B. Dervin, L. Grossberg, B. O'Keefe, & E. Wartella (Eds.), *Rethinking communication: Vol. 1. Paradigm issues* (pp. 40-52). Newbury Park, CA: Sage.

Hamnett, M., Porter, D., Singh, A., & Kumar, K. (1984). *Ethics, politics and international social science research.* Honolulu: East-West Center and University of Hawaii Press.

Harré, R. (1986). *The social construction of emotions.* Oxford: Basil Blackwell.

Harris, L., Alexander, A., McNamee, S., Stanback, M., & Kang, K. (1984). Forced cooperation: Violence as a communicative act. In S. Thomas (Ed.), *Communication theory and interpersonal interaction* (pp. 20-32). Norwood, NJ: Ablex.

Henriques, J., Hallway, W., Urwin, C., Venn, C., & Walkerdine, V. (Eds.). (1984). *Changing the subject*. New York: Methuen.

Hochschild, A. (1983). *The managed heart*. Berkeley: University of California Press.

Kelly, G. (1970). An introduction to personal construct theory. In D. Bannister (Ed.), *Perspectives on personal construct theory* (pp. 1-6). London: Academic Press.

Laclau, E., & Mouffe, C. (1985). *Hegemony and socialist strategy* (W. Moore & P. Cammack, Trans.). London: Verso.

Lyytinen, K. (1992). Information systems and critical theory. In M. Alvesson & H. Willmott (Eds.), *Critical management theory* (pp. 159-180). London: Sage.

McLuskie, E. (1992). The mediacentric agenda of agenda-setting research: Eclipse of the public sphere. In S. Deetz (Ed.), *Communication yearbook 15* (pp. 410-424). Newbury Park, CA: Sage.

Pearce, W. B. (1989). *Communication and the human condition*. Carbondale: Southern Illinois University Press.

Peters, J. (1986). Institutional sources of intellectual poverty in communication research. *Communication Research, 13*, 527-559.

Power, M., & Laughlin, R. (1992). Critical theory and accounting. In M. Alvesson & H. Willmott (Eds.), *Critical management theory* (pp. 113-135). London: Sage.

Ramos, A. G. (1981). *The new science of organizations*. Toronto: University of Toronto Press.

Rorty, R. (1979). *Philosophy and the mirror of nature*. Princeton, NJ: University of Princeton Press.

Rorty, R. (1989). *Contingency, irony and solidarity*. Cambridge: Cambridge University Press.

Schmookler, A. (1992). *The illusion of choice: How the market economy shapes our destiny*. Albany: State University of New York Press.

Shotter, J. (1987). Practically speaking: Whorf, the formative function of communication, and knowing of the third kind. In R. Rosnow & M. Georgoudi (Eds.), *Contextualism and understanding in behavioral science* (pp. 211-227). New York: Praeger.

Shuter, R. (1993). On third culture building. In S. Deetz (Ed.), *Communication yearbook 16* (pp. 429-436). Newbury Park, CA: Sage.

Simon, H. (Ed.). (1991). *Rhetoric of the social sciences*. Chicago: University of Chicago Press.

Smart, B. (1986). The politics of truth and the problem of hegemony. In D. Hoy (Ed.), *Foucault: A critical reader*. Oxford: Basil Blackwell.

Thompson, J. (1984). *Studies in the theory of ideology*. Berkeley: University of California Press.

Thompson, J. (1991). *Communication theory*. Cambridge: Polity.

Turow, J. (1989). Television and institutional power: The case of medicine. In B. Dervin, L. Grossberg, B. O'Keefe, & E. Wartella (Eds.), *Rethinking communication: Vol. 2. Paradigm exemplars* (pp. 454-473). Newbury Park, CA: Sage.

Watzlawick, P., Beavin, J., & Jackson, D. (1967). *Pragmatics of human communication*. New York: Norton.

Weedon, C. (1987). *Feminist practice and poststructuralist theory*. Oxford: Basil Blackwell.

Weick, K. (1987). Organizational culture and high reliability. *California Management Review, 29*, 112-127.

Whitney, C., & Wartella, E. (1992). Media coverage of the "political correctness" debate. *Journal of Communication, 42*, 83-94.

Zmud, R. (1990). Opportunities for strategic information manipulation through information technologies. In J. Fulk & C. Steinfield (Eds.), *Organizations and communication technology* (pp. 95-116). Newbury Park, CA: Sage.

AUTHOR INDEX

SUBJECT INDEX

ABOUT THE EDITOR

STANLEY A. DEETZ (Ph.D.) is Professor in the Department of Communication at Rutgers University, New Brunswick. He is author of *Democracy in an Age of Corporate Colonization: Developments in Communication and the Politics of Everyday Life* and *Managing Interpersonal Communication* as well as editor or author of five other books. He has published numerous essays in scholarly journals and books regarding decision making, human relations, and communication in corporate organizations and has lectured widely in the United States and Europe. He is past Chair of the Organizational Communication Division and a member of the Legislative Council of the Speech Communication Association and a former Chair of the Philosophy of Communication Division and Board Member-at-Large of the International Communication Association. In addition, he has been active in community health planning and served as a consultant for many organizations. Currently, he is editor of the prestigious Communication Yearbook series and continues his work on communication system design, power, and workplace democracy. He will be a Senior Fulbright Scholar lecturing and conducting research on knowledge-intensive firms in Sweden in 1994.

ABOUT THE AUTHORS

DIANE M. BADZINSKI (Ph.D., University of Wisconsin) is Assistant Professor of Speech Communication at the University of Nebraska at Lincoln. Her interests include the relationships between message behaviors and comprehension, impact of inference and metaphor on children's understanding of discourse, and the role of affect and cognition in interpersonal relationships.

DONAL CARBAUGH (Ph.D., University of Washington) is Associate Professor of Communication at the University of Massachusetts, Amherst. Recipient of Fulbright and Humanities Institute Fellowships. His special interest is to align communication studies with cultures and natural environments.

MARGARET A. CARR (Ph.D., Boston University) is a psychotherapist in private practice in Princeton, New Jersey. Her current research examines the ways that social constructions of gender influence psychoanalytic theory and technique.

GEORGE CHENEY (Ph.D., Purdue University) is Associate Professor and Director of Graduate Studies in the Department of Communication at the University of Colorado at Boulder. His teaching and research interests include issues of power and identity in the modern organization, the rhetorical criticism of public discourse, the symbolic aspects of peace and war, and the exploration of opportunities for democracy in the workplace.

LARS THØGER CHRISTENSEN (Ph.D., Odense University) is Assistant Professor in the Department of Marketing at Odense University in Odense, Denmark. His primary research interests are in the fields of organizational communication, marketing communication, public discourse, postmodernity, semiotics, and intercultural studies.

RICHARD CLÉMENT (Ph.D., University of Western Ontario) is Professor of Psychology at the University of Ottawa, Canada. His research interests include social and cross-cultural aspects of intergroup relations, communication, and second language acquisition. He has published in both French and English in education, psychology, and communication journals.

CHARLES CONRAD (Ph.D., Kansas University) is Associate Professor of Speech Communication at Texas A&M University. His primary research interests involve communication and social/organizational power relationships. He is the author of *Strategic Organizational Communication* and a number of essays on organizations, rhetoric, and society and the editor of *The Ethical Nexus*.

MARTHA COOPER (Ph.D., Pennsylvania State University) is Associate Professor of Communication Studies and Director of Graduate Studies at Northern Illinois University. An author of several books and scholarly essays, her research is centered in rhetorical theory and criticism, especially the relationship among discourse, knowledge, power, and ethics.

VERNON E. CRONEN (Ph.D., University of Illinois, Urbana) is Professor of Communication at the University of Massachusetts, Amherst. He is coauthor, with W. Barnett Pearce, of *Communication, Meaning and Action: The Creation of Social Realities* and has published numerous journal articles and book chapters in communication, psychology, and family systems. He is best known for his work with Pearce on the development of the theory of "coordinated management of meaning" (CMM). His most recent work has focused on the development of CMM theory in terms of the aesthetic dimensions of everyday life and on the intrinsic connection of communication to moral orders.

BARBARA CZARNIAWSKA-JOERGES (Ph.D., Warsaw School of Economics, Poland) holds the Chair in Business Administration at the University of Lund, Sweden. Her work focuses on control processes in complex organizations. She has published widely in the area of business administration in Polish, her native language, as well as in Swedish and English. Books in English include *Controlling Top Management in Large Organizations* (1986), *Ideological Control in Nonideological Organizations* (1988), *Exploring Complex Organizations* (1992), and *Three Dimensional Organization* (1993). Her articles have appeared in many journals including *Accounting, Organizations and Society, Scandinavian Journal of Management Studies, Management Communication, Journal of Management Studies,* and *Organization Studies.*

AIMÉE DORR (Ph.D., Stanford University) is Professor in the Graduate School of Education and member of the Committee to Administer the Undergraduate Interdepartmental Major in Communication Studies at the University of California, Los Angeles. She teaches and does research on children's and teenagers' uses of media and technology, especially television, and the cognitive, social, and emotional consequences of such use. For about 10 years, she has intermittently investigated the development of television and other literacies, and developed television literacy curricula for young children and computer literacy materials and workshops for teacher credential candidates and graduate students in education.

ERIC M. EISENBERG (Ph.D., Michigan State University) is Professor of Communication at the University of South Florida. He has twice been awarded the Speech Communication Association Award for the Outstanding Publication in Organizational Communication and most recently received the Burlington Northern Faculty Achievement Award for Excellence in Teaching. He is primarily interested in the role of language and communication in the development and evolution of organizational cultures. His textbook, *Organizational Communication: Balancing Creativity and Constraint* (with H. L. Goodall) provides his most recent attempt to promote the use of dialogue in organizations.

DONALD G. ELLIS (Ph.D., University of Utah) is Professor of Communication at the University of Hartford. His research and teaching focus on language and social interaction with particular emphasis on language codes and communication competence. He is the author of numerous research articles and is currently the editor of *Communication Theory.* He is the author of *From Language to Communication* and *Small Group Decision Making* and a coeditor of *Contemporary Issues in Language and Discourse Processes.*

KRISTINE L. FITCH (Ph.D., University of Washington) is Assistant Professor of Communication at the University of Colorado, Boulder. She was a Fulbright Doctoral Fellow in Colombia in 1987 and has published in *Communication Monographs, Research on Language and Social Interaction,* and *Journal of Multicultural and Multilingual Development,* among others. Her research concerns cultural approaches to interpersonal communication, intercultural communication, and issues of ethnic identity in the United States. Recent and current work includes culturally situated studies of directive use, methodological approaches to cultural comparison, and culturally contextualized conversation analysis.

KENNETH J. GERGEN (Ph.D., Duke University) is the Mustin Professor of Psychology at Swarthmore College. He is a central exponent of the social constructionist movement in modern psychology. He is the author of, among other works, *Toward Transformation in Social Knowledge* (Springer-Verlag, 1982) and *The Saturated Self* (Basic Books, 1991). With Sheila McNamee, he has edited *Therapy as Social Construction* (Sage, 1992).

HOWARD GILES (Ph.D., University of Bristol) is Professor of Communication at the University of California, Santa Barbara. His research interests include sociopsychological aspects of language, ethnolinguistics, intercultural communication, ethnic language attitudes, interpersonal accommodation, and intergenerational communication and the life span.

MARY M. GILL (Ph.D., University of Nebraska at Lincoln) is Assistant Professor of Communication at Buena Vista College. Her research spans topics including presidential elections, religious rhetoric, sexual harassment, and foreign accent effects on learning. Research on harassment appears in *The Basic Communication Course Annual* and *Sexual Harassment: Commu-*

nication Implications. Her major research interests focus on the interpersonal dynamics of college classrooms.

MARIA CRISTINA GONZÁLEZ (Ph.D., University of Texas, Austin) is Assistant Professor of Communication at Arizona State University. Her work focuses on how social and organizational cultures affect the ways in which people communicate face to face and how that ultimately influences well-being. She has worked largely with Mexican, Mexican American, and Native American populations in ethnographic fieldwork and applied development of culturally appropriate therapeutic communication techniques. She is currently working with psychologists in Chihuahua, Mexico, on the use of indigenous-based techniques with their clients.

WILLIAM I. GORDEN (Ph.D., Purdue University) is Professor and Coordinator of Organizational Communication Studies at Kent State University. He has been on the faculties of Purdue, Berry College, and Southwest Texas State University and taken postdoctoral work at Northwestern, Florida State, and Utah universities.

ANNE GRAVEL is a doctoral candidate in speech communication at the Pennsylvania State University. Her research centers on rhetorical and media criticism, especially as related to feminist theory and the communication practices of women.

ROM HARRÉ is a Fellow of Linacre College, Oxford, and Professor of Psychology at Georgetown University, Washington, D.C. His work includes studies in the philosophy of physical sciences, the foundations of discursive psychology, and sociolinguistics including *Pronouns and People* with P. Muhlhausler.

TERESA M. HARRISON (Ph.D., Bowling Green State University) is Associate Professor of Communication in the Department of Language, Literature & Communication at Rensselaer Polytechnic Institute. Her research interests are communication theory, organizational communication, and computer-mediated communication. She is cofounder of the Communication Institute for Online Scholarship, a nonprofit organization supporting the use of information technologies in communication scholarship and education.

RENÉE HOBBS (Ed.D., Harvard University) is Associate Professor of Communication at Babson College and Director of the Institute on Media Education at Harvard Graduate School of Education. Her main research interests concern the comprehension of film and television editing techniques by first-time viewers and the implementation and evaluation of media education curricula in secondary schools.

SUE CURRY JANSEN (Ph.D., State University of New York, Buffalo) is Associate Professor and Head of Communication Studies at Muhlenberg College in Allentown, Pennsylvania. Her areas of scholarly interest include censorship, news analysis, new information technologies, gender and ethnic studies, and representational practices in mass media. Her publications include *Censorship: The Knot That Binds Power and Knowledge* (Oxford University Press, 1988, 1991).

YOUNG YUN KIM (Ph.D., Northwestern University) is Professor of Communication at the University of Oklahoma. Her research interests include the role of communication in cross-cultural adaption and interethnic relations. She currently serves on several editorial boards including that for *Human Communication Research.* Among her recent books are *Communication and Cross-Cultural Adaption* (Multilingual Matters, 1988) and *Communication With Strangers* (Sage, 1992, with W. Gudykunst).

JOHN W. LANNAMANN (Ph.D., University of Massachusetts) is Associate Professor of Communication at the University of New Hampshire. In his recent work, he criticizes the underlying ideological assumptions of current interpersonal communication research and calls for a form of research more closely tied to social and political change. In addition to his critical work, he has focused his analysis of face-to-face communication on the study of domestic violence, family pathologies, and intercultural communication.

BARBARA LEVITT (Ph.D., Stanford University) is Assistant Professor of Management at Santa Clara University. Her primary areas of interest are organizational learning and dual-career parents in the workplace.

PAUL MESSARIS (Ph.D., University of Pennsylvania) is Associate Professor at the Annenberg School for Communication. He teaches and does research in the area of visual communication, and he has recently completed a book on visual "literacy."

HARTMUT B. MOKROS (Ph.D., University of Chicago) is Assistant Professor of Communication at Rutgers University. He is coauthor of *Interaction Structure and Strategy* and is editing volume 6 of *Information and Behavior,* which focuses on the topic of "interaction and identity."

GORDON NAKAGAWA (Ph.D., Southern Illinois University) is Associate Professor of Speech Communication at California State University, Northridge. His research interests include cultural studies with particular emphasis on racial formation. He also has teaching experience and research interests in Asian American studies, and he is a founding member and the first Chair of the Speech Communication Association's Asian-Pacific Islander Caucus.

CLIFFORD NASS (Ph.D., Princeton University) is Assistant Professor of Communication at Stanford University. His primary areas of interest are social responses to communication technologies, human-computer interaction, models of information flow in organizations, and nonparametric statistics.

MARK NEUMANN (Ph.D., University of Utah) is Assistant Professor in the Department of Communication at the University of South Florida in Tampa. His research and teaching interests include cultural studies, interpretation and criticism, and popular culture.

JOHN J. PAULY (Ph.D., University of Illinois at Urbana) is Professor and Chair of Communication at Saint Louis University. His research on mass communication has appeared in *Communication, Critical Studies in Mass Communication, Journalism Monographs, American Quarterly,* and other journals and books. Since 1989, he has been the editor of *American Journalism.*

W. BARNETT PEARCE (Ph.D., Ohio University) is Professor and Chair of the Department of Communication at Loyola University of Chicago and has taught at the Universities of North Dakota, Kentucky, and Massachusetts. He is the author (with Vernon Cronen) of *Communication, Action and Meaning: The Creation of Social Realities* and *Communication and the Human Condition* and coeditor (with Michael Weiler) of *Reagan and Public Discourse in America,* among other books and articles. His most recent project is a social constructionist textbook, *Interpersonal Communication: Making Social Worlds.*

JOHN SHOTTER (Ph.D., University of Nottingham) is Professor of Interpersonal Relations in the Department of Communication, University of New Hampshire. He is the author of, among other works, *Social Accountability and Selfhood* (Basil Blackwell, 1984), *Cultural Politics of Everyday Life: Social Constructionism, Rhetoric, and Knowing of the Third Kind* (Open University, 1993), and *Conversational Realities: The Construction of Life Through Language* (Sage, 1993). He is also the editor, with Ian Parker, of *Deconstructing Social Psychology* (Routledge, 1990).

VINCENT R. WALDRON (Ph.D., Ohio State University) is Associate Professor in the Department of Communication Studies at Arizona State University West. His research addresses the role of emotion and cognition in the production of strategic messages in both interpersonal and organizational contexts. He has published his work in *Communication Monographs, Human Communication Research, Management Communication Quarterly,* and other journals.

HUGH WILLMOTT is Reader in the Manchester School of Management, having held appointments previously at the University of Aston and the Copenhagen Business School. He has published eight books and his work has appeared in a wide range of leading management, accounting, finance, and social science journals. He is currently working on a number of conceptual and empirical projects whose common theme is the critical examination of the changing organization and management of work in modern society.

KIM WITTE (Ph.D., University of California, Irvine) is Assistant Professor of Speech Communication at Texas A&M University and Visiting Assistant Professor of Communication at Michigan State University for the 1993-1994 school year. Her work on health communication, persuasion, and organizational communication has appeared in *Communication Monographs, Communication Research, International Quarterly of Community Health Education, Social Science & Medicine,* and elsewhere.

ERIC G. ZOOK (Ph.D., Michigan State University) is Assistant Professor of Speech Communication at Pennsylvania State University. His research concentrates on the construction of illness meanings and narratives, the illness management systems of the chronically and/or terminally ill, stress and burnout associated with care providers, and issues in the philosophy of communication. Common to each of these areas is an emphasis on issues of HIV/AIDS. His work has been published in such journals as *Management Communication Quarterly* and *Communication Research.*